Mazda MX-5

Owners Workshop Manual

Martynn Randall

Models covered

(6368 - 224

MX-5 Convertible (soft top) & Roadster Coupe (folding hard top) 'Mk 3' (NC Series) with 1.8 litre (1798cc) & 2.0 litre (1999cc) engines

Does NOT cover models with automatic transmission, equipment specific to limited editions or dealer-installed modifications
Does NOT cover 'Mk 4' (ND Series) introduced August 2015

ABCDE
FGHIJ
KLMNO
PQRS

A book in the **Haynes Owners Workshop Manual Series**

ISBN **978 1 78521 368 7**

British Library Cataloguing in Publication Data
A catalogue record for this book is available from the British Library.

Printed in Malaysia

J H Haynes & Co. Ltd.
Sparkford, Yeovil, Somerset BA22 7JJ, England

Haynes North America, Inc
859 Lawrence Drive, Newbury Park, California 91320, USA

Contents

Working on your car can be dangerous. This page shows just some of the potential risks and hazards, with the aim of creating a safety-conscious attitude.

General hazards

Scalding

• Don't remove the radiator or expansion tank cap while the engine is hot.

• Engine oil, transmission fluid or power steering fluid may also be dangerously hot if the engine has recently been running.

Burning

• Beware of burns from the exhaust system and from any part of the engine. Brake discs and drums can also be extremely hot immediately after use.

Crushing

• When working under or near a raised vehicle, always supplement the jack with axle stands, or use drive-on ramps. ***Never venture under a car which is only supported by a jack.***

• Take care if loosening or tightening high-torque nuts when the vehicle is on stands. Initial loosening and final tightening should be done with the wheels on the ground.

Fire

• Fuel is highly flammable; fuel vapour is explosive.

• Don't let fuel spill onto a hot engine.

• Do not smoke or allow naked lights (including pilot lights) anywhere near a vehicle being worked on. Also beware of creating sparks (electrically or by use of tools).

• Fuel vapour is heavier than air, so don't work on the fuel system with the vehicle over an inspection pit.

• Another cause of fire is an electrical overload or short-circuit. Take care when repairing or modifying the vehicle wiring.

• Keep a fire extinguisher handy, of a type suitable for use on fuel and electrical fires.

Electric shock

• Ignition HT and Xenon headlight voltages can be dangerous, especially to people with heart problems or a pacemaker. Don't work on or near these systems with the engine running or the ignition switched on.

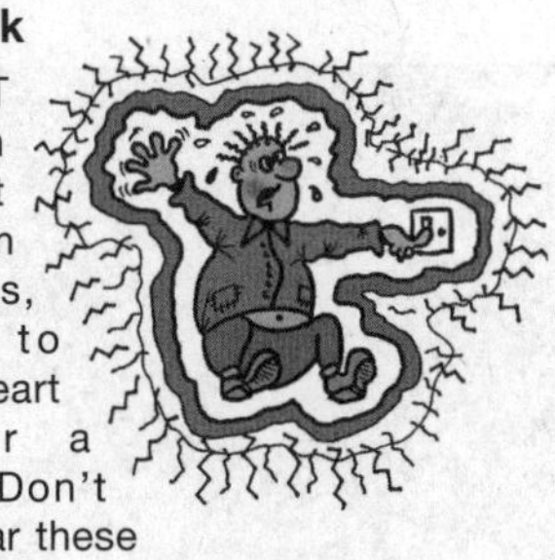

• Mains voltage is also dangerous. Make sure that any mains-operated equipment is correctly earthed. Mains power points should be protected by a residual current device (RCD) circuit breaker.

Fume or gas intoxication

• Exhaust fumes are poisonous; they can contain carbon monoxide, which is rapidly fatal if inhaled. Never run the engine in a confined space such as a garage with the doors shut.

• Fuel vapour is also poisonous, as are the vapours from some cleaning solvents and paint thinners.

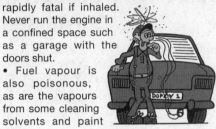

Poisonous or irritant substances

• Avoid skin contact with battery acid and with any fuel, fluid or lubricant, especially antifreeze, brake hydraulic fluid and Diesel fuel. Don't syphon them by mouth. If such a substance is swallowed or gets into the eyes, seek medical advice.

• Prolonged contact with used engine oil can cause skin cancer. Wear gloves or use a barrier cream if necessary. Change out of oil-soaked clothes and do not keep oily rags in your pocket.

• Air conditioning refrigerant forms a poisonous gas if exposed to a naked flame (including a cigarette). It can also cause skin burns on contact.

Asbestos

• Asbestos dust can cause cancer if inhaled or swallowed. Asbestos may be found in gaskets and in brake and clutch linings. When dealing with such components it is safest to assume that they contain asbestos.

Special hazards

Hydrofluoric acid

• This extremely corrosive acid is formed when certain types of synthetic rubber, found in some O-rings, oil seals, fuel hoses etc, are exposed to temperatures above 4000C. The rubber changes into a charred or sticky substance containing the acid. *Once formed, the acid remains dangerous for years. If it gets onto the skin, it may be necessary to amputate the limb concerned.*

• When dealing with a vehicle which has suffered a fire, or with components salvaged from such a vehicle, wear protective gloves and discard them after use.

The battery

• Batteries contain sulphuric acid, which attacks clothing, eyes and skin. Take care when topping-up or carrying the battery.

• The hydrogen gas given off by the battery is highly explosive. Never cause a spark or allow a naked light nearby. Be careful when connecting and disconnecting battery chargers or jump leads.

Air bags

• Air bags can cause injury if they go off accidentally. Take care when removing the steering wheel and trim panels. Special storage instructions may apply.

Diesel injection equipment

• Diesel injection pumps supply fuel at very high pressure. Take care when working on the fuel injectors and fuel pipes.

Warning: Never expose the hands, face or any other part of the body to injector spray; the fuel can penetrate the skin with potentially fatal results.

Remember...

DO

• Do use eye protection when using power tools, and when working under the vehicle.

• Do wear gloves or use barrier cream to protect your hands when necessary.

• Do get someone to check periodically that all is well when working alone on the vehicle.

• Do keep loose clothing and long hair well out of the way of moving mechanical parts.

• Do remove rings, wristwatch etc, before working on the vehicle – especially the electrical system.

• Do ensure that any lifting or jacking equipment has a safe working load rating adequate for the job.

DON'T

• Don't attempt to lift a heavy component which may be beyond your capability – get assistance.

• Don't rush to finish a job, or take unverified short cuts.

• Don't use ill-fitting tools which may slip and cause injury.

• Don't leave tools or parts lying around where someone can trip over them. Mop up oil and fuel spills at once.

• Don't allow children or pets to play in or near a vehicle being worked on.

The following pages are intended to help in dealing with common roadside emergencies and breakdowns. You will find more detailed fault finding information at the back of the manual, and repair information in the main chapters.

If your car won't start and the starter motor doesn't turn

- ☐ Open the luggage compartment and make sure that the battery terminals are clean and tight.
- ☐ Switch on the headlights and try to start the engine. If the headlights go very dim when you'r e trying to start, the battery is probably flat. Get out of trouble by jump starting using a friend's car.

If your car won't start even though the starter motor turns as normal

- ☐ Is there fuel in the tank?
- ☐ Is there moisture on electrical components under the bonnet? Switch off the ignition, then wipe off any obvious dampness with a dry cloth. Spray a water-repellent aerosol product (WD-40 or equivalent) on ignition and fuel system electrical connectors like those shown in the photos.

A Check the security of the throttle body connector.

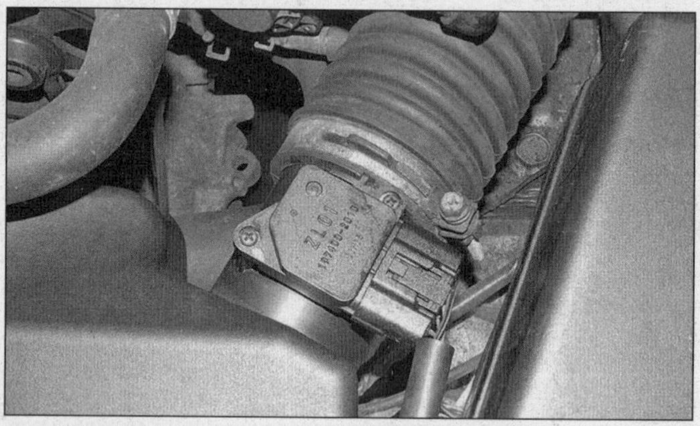

B Check the airflow meter wiring connector.

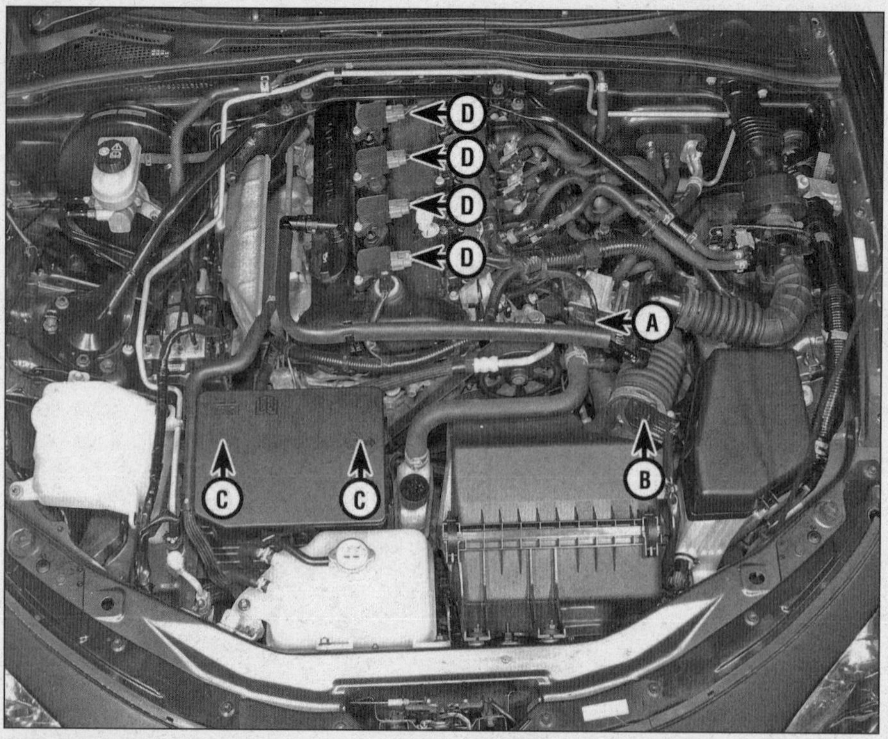

Check that electrical connections are secure (with the ignition switched off) and spray them with a water-dispersant spray like WD-40 if you suspect a problem due to damp.

C Check the security and condition of the battery terminals.

D Pull up the cover and check the ignition coil connections.

Jump starting

HAYNES HiNT ***Jump starting will get you out of trouble, but you must correct whatever made the battery go flat in the first place. There are three possibilities:***

***1** The battery has been drained by repeated attempts to start, or by leaving the lights on.*

***2** The charging system is not working properly (alternator drivebelt slack or broken, alternator wiring fault or alternator itself faulty).*

***3** The battery itself is at fault (electrolyte low, or battery worn out).*

When jump-starting a car using a booster battery, observe the following precautions:

Caution: Remove the key in case the central locking engages when the jump leads are connected

- ✓ Before connecting the booster battery, make sure that the ignition is switched off.
- ✓ Ensure that all electrical equipment (lights, heater, wipers, etc) is switched off.
- ✓ Take note of any special precautions printed on the battery case.
- ✓ Make sure that the booster battery is the same voltage as the discharged one in the vehicle.
- ✓ If the battery is being jump-started from the battery in another vehicle, the two vehicles MUST NOT TOUCH each other.
- ✓ Make sure that the transmission is in neutral (or PARK, in the case of automatic transmission).

HAYNES HiNT ***Budget jump leads can be a false economy, as they often do not pass enough current to start large capacity or diesel engines. They can also get hot.***

1 Unclip the rubber hose from the battery cover, then release the clips, open the battery cover, and connect the red jump lead to the positive (+) terminal on the battery.

2 Connect the other end of the red lead to the positive (+) terminal of the booster battery.

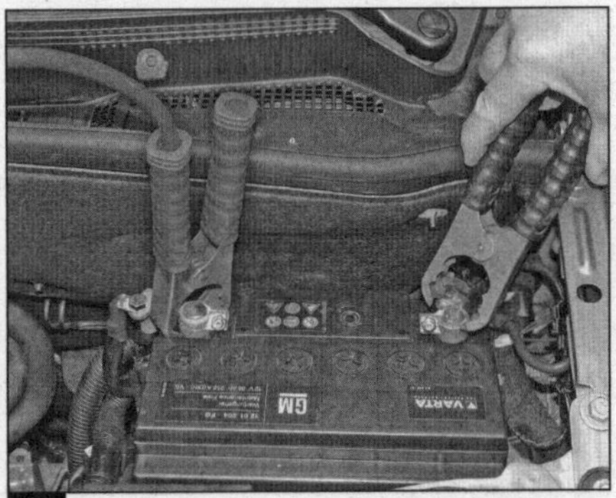

3 Connect one end of the black jump lead to the negative (-) terminal of the booster battery.

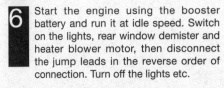

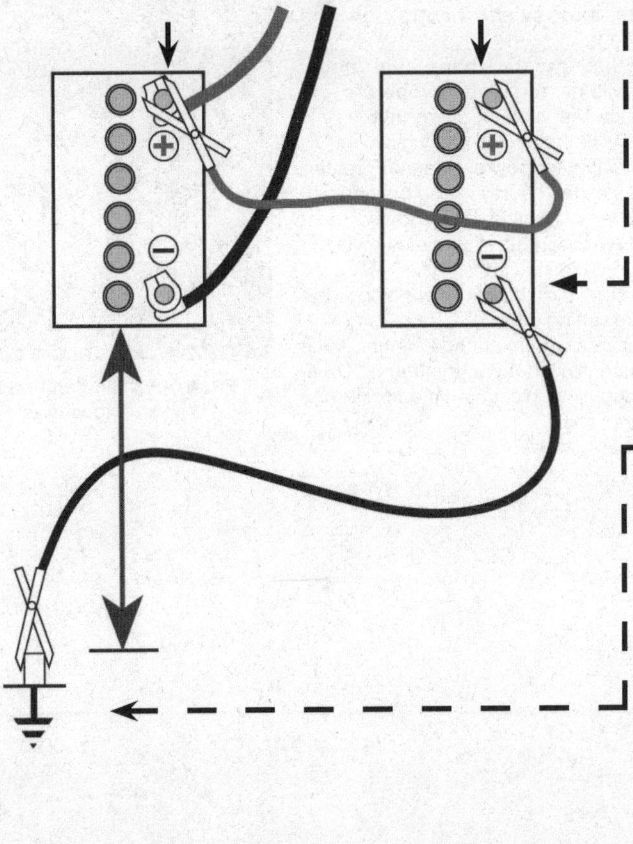

4 Connect the other end of the black jump lead to the earthing bracket behind the battery.

5 Make sure that the jump leads will not come into contact with the fan, drive-belts or other moving parts of the engine.

6 Start the engine using the booster battery and run it at idle speed. Switch on the lights, rear window demister and heater blower motor, then disconnect the jump leads in the reverse order of connection. Turn off the lights etc.

Punctures

Warning: Do not attempt to repair a punctured tyre in a situation where you risk being hit by other traffic. On busy roads, try to stop in a lay-by or a gateway. Be wary of passing traffic while sealing the puncture – it is easy to become distracted by the job in hand.

Preparation

- ☐ When a puncture occurs, stop as soon as it is safe to do so.
- ☐ Park on firm level ground, if possible, and well out of the way of other traffic.
- ☐ Use hazard warning lights if necessary.
- ☐ If you have one, use a warning triangle to alert other drivers of your presence.
- ☐ Apply the handbrake.

1 The Instant Mobility System (IMS) consists of a bottle of puncture sealant, a compressor and various associated items. Rather than change the punctured wheel, the system allows the tyre to be sealed, enabling the journey to be resumed, albeit at a reduced speed.

2 Note that the IMS should not be used in the following circumstances:

- ☐ The period of effective use has expired – check the date on label affixed to the sealant bottle.
- ☐ The tyre tear or puncture exceeds 4.0 mm.
- ☐ The damage has occured to an area other than the tyre tread.
- ☐ The vehicle has been driven with nearly no air remaining in the tyre.
- ☐ The tyre has come off the rim.
- ☐ The wheel rim is damaged.
- ☐ The tyre has more than one puncture.

3 The system is stored in a case at the front of the luggage compartment.

4 Release the restraining strap and open the case.

5 Remove the sealant bottle from the luggage compartment, and shake the contents well. Remove the cap, and screw the filler hose onto the bottle.

6 Unscrew the valve cap from the punctured wheel, and using the valve removal tool (stored with the filler hose) unscrew the core from the valve.

7 Pull the stopper from the filler hose, insert the hose into the valve, and holding the bottle upside down, squeeze the entire contents into the tyre.

8 Remove the filler hose, and screw the core back into the valve.

9 Insert the compressor plug into the vehicles accessory socket, in the centre console.

10 Connect the compressor hose to the tyre valve, and with the ignition switch turned to position I, turn the compressorw on and inflate the tyre to a pressure of 2.0 bar (29 psi). With the correct pressure achieved, disconnect the compressor and stow it in the tool kit.

11 Immediately drive the vehicle for approximately 10 minutes at a speed of between 12 and 37 mph to redistribute the sealant.

12 Stop the vehicle, connect the compressor, and check the tyre pressure. If the pressure is less than 1.3 bar (19 psi), it's not safe to continue your journey, and the vehicle must be recovered. If the pressure is above this, turn on the compressor and inflate the tyre to the normal pressure for the vehicle, as specified on the sticker in the driver's door aperture.

13 With the tyre inflated to the correct pressure, do not exceed the maximum speed of 50 mph. Have the tyre repaired or replaced at the earliest opportunity.

Towing

When all else fails, you may find yourself having to get a tow home – or of course you may be helping somebody else. Long-distance recovery should only be done by a garage or breakdown service. For shorter distances, DIY towing using another car is easy enough, but observe the following points:

- ☐ Use a proper tow-rope – they are not expensive. The vehicle being towed must display an ON TOW sign in its rear window.
- ☐ Always turn the ignition key to the 'on' position when the vehicle is being towed, so that the steering lock is released, and the direction indicator and brake lights work.
- ☐ Prise open the plastic flap in the front, or rear bumper, and screw-in the towing eye supplied in the vehicle toolkit **(see illustration)**.
- ☐ Before being towed, release the handbrake and select neutral on the transmission.
- ☐ Note that greater-than-usual pedal pressure will be required to operate the brakes, since the vacuum servo unit is only operational with the engine running.
- ☐ On models with power steering, greater-than-usual steering effort will also be required.
- ☐ The driver of the car being towed must keep the tow-rope taut at all times to avoid snatching.
- ☐ Make sure that both drivers know the route before setting off.
- ☐ Only drive at moderate speeds and keep the distance towed to a minimum. Drive smoothly and allow plenty of time for slowing down at junctions.

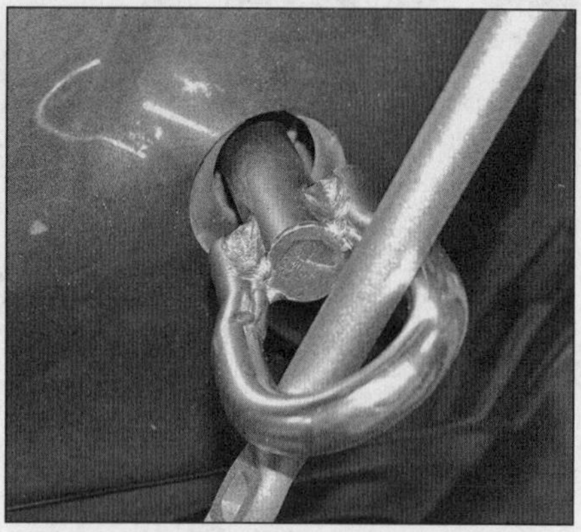

Prise open the flap and screw-in the towing eye

Identifying leaks

Puddles on the garage floor or drive, or obvious wetness under the bonnet or underneath the car, suggest a leak that needs investigating. It can sometimes be difficult to decide where the leak is coming from, especially if an engine undershield is fitted. Leaking oil or fluid can also be blown rearwards by the passage of air under the car, giving a false impression of where the problem lies.

Warning: Most automotive oils and fluids are poisonous. Wash them off skin, and change out of contaminated clothing, without delay.

HAYNES HiNT ***The smell of a fluid leaking from the car may provide a clue to what's leaking. Some fluids are distinctively coloured. It may help to remove the engine undershield, clean the car carefully and to park it over some clean paper overnight as an aid to locating the source of the leak. Remember that some leaks may only occur while the engine is running.***

Sump oil

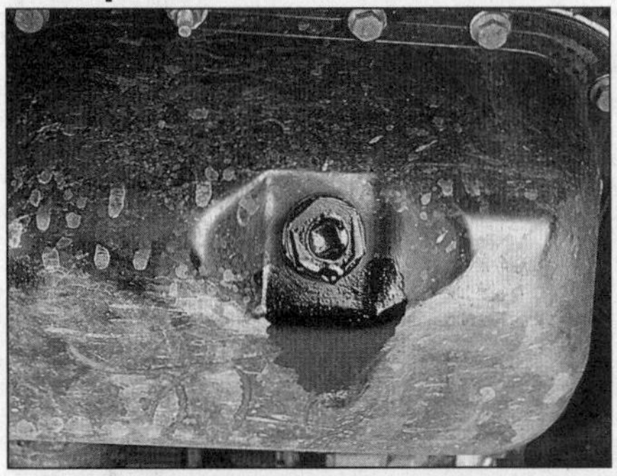

Engine oil may leak from the drain plug...

Oil from filter

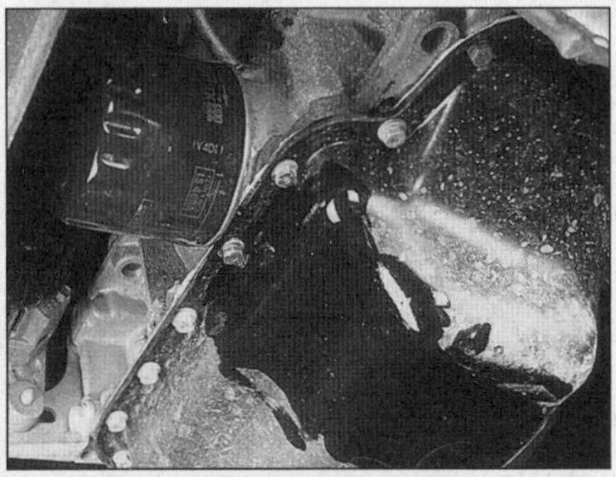

...or from the base of the oil filter.

Gearbox oil

Gearbox oil can leak from the seals at the inboard ends of the driveshafts.

Antifreeze

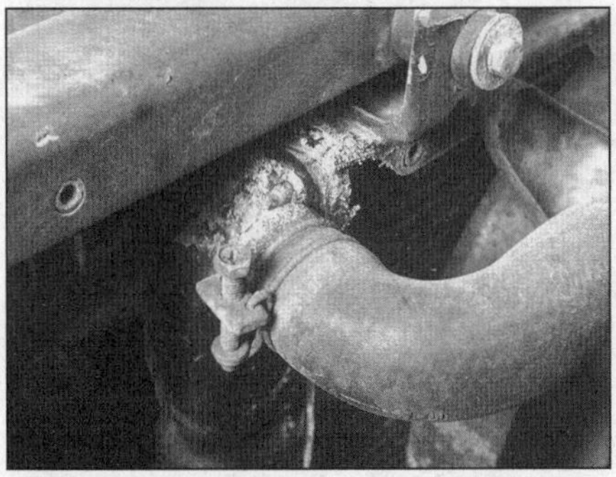

Leaking antifreeze often leaves a crystalline deposit like this.

Brake fluid

A leak occurring at a wheel is almost certainly brake fluid.

Power steering fluid

Power steering fluid may leak from the pipe connectors on the steering rack.

Introduction

There are some very simple checks which need only take a few minutes to carry out, but which could save you a lot of inconvenience and expense.

These checks require no great skill or special tools, and the small amount of time they take to perform could prove to be very well spent, for example:

☐ Keeping an eye on tyre condition and pressures, will not only help to stop them wearing out prematurely, but could also save your life.

☐ Many breakdowns are caused by electrical problems. Battery-related faults are particularly common, and a quick check on a regular basis will often prevent the majority of these.

☐ If your car develops a brake fluid leak, the first time you might know about it is when your brakes don't work properly. Checking the level regularly will give advance warning of this kind of problem.

☐ If the oil or coolant levels run low, the cost of repairing any engine damage will be far greater than fixing the leak, for example.

Underbonnet check points

▲ **2010 model shown – others similar**

1 *Engine oil level dipstick*
2 *Engine oil filler cap*
3 *Coolant expansion tank*
4 *Brake/clutch fluid reservoir*
5 *Screen washer fluid reservoir*

Engine oil level

Before you start

✔ Make sure that the car is on level ground.

✔ Check the oil level before the car is driven, or at least 10 minutes after the engine has been switched off.

> **HAYNES HiNT** *If the oil is checked immediately after driving the vehicle, some of the oil will remain in the upper engine components, resulting in an inaccurate reading on the dipstick.*

The correct oil

Modern engines place great demands on their oil. It is very important that the correct oil for your car is used (see Section 6).

Car care

- If you have to add oil frequently, you should check whether you have any oil leaks. Place some clean paper under the car overnight, and check for stains in the morning. If there are no leaks, then the engine may be burning oil.
- Always maintain the level between the upper and lower dipstick marks. If the level is too low, severe engine damage may occur. Oil seal failure may result if the engine is overfilled by adding too much oil.

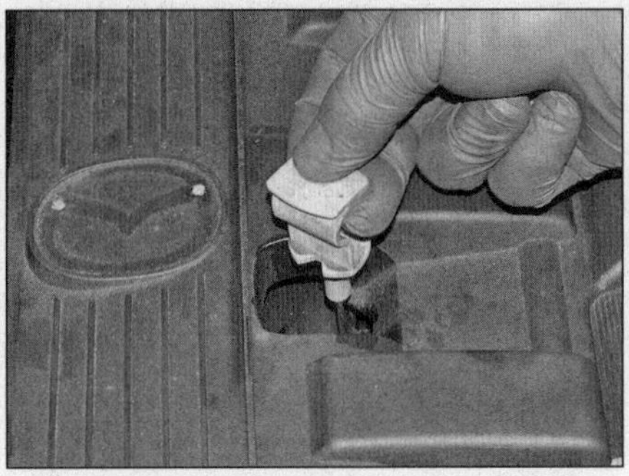

1 Withdraw the engine oil level dipstick from the top of the engine

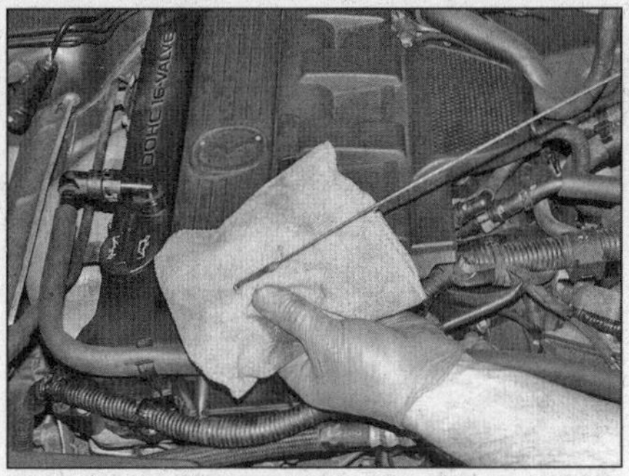

2 Using a clean rag or paper towel remove all oil from the dipstick. Insert the clean dipstick into the tube as far as it will go, then withdraw it again

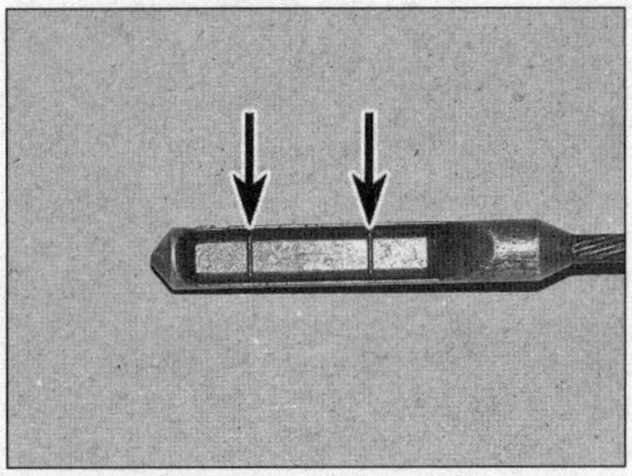

3 Note the oil level on the end of the dipstick, which should be between the upper maximum mark and lower minimum mark. Approximately 0.75 litres of oil will raise the level from the lower mark to the upper mark.

4 Oil is added through the filler cap. Unscrew the cap and top-up the level; a funnel may help to reduce spillage. Add the oil slowly, checking the level on the dipstick often. Don't overfill (see *Car care*).

Coolant level

Warning: Do not attempt to remove the expansion tank pressure cap when the engine is hot, as there is a very great risk of scalding. Do not leave open containers of coolant about, as it is poisonous.

Car care

- With a sealed-type cooling system, adding coolant should not be necessary on a regular basis. If frequent topping-up is required, it is likely there is a leak. Check the radiator, all hoses and joint faces for signs of staining or wetness, and rectify as necessary.
- It is important that antifreeze is used in the cooling system all year round, not just during the winter months. Don't top up with water alone, as the antifreeze will become diluted.

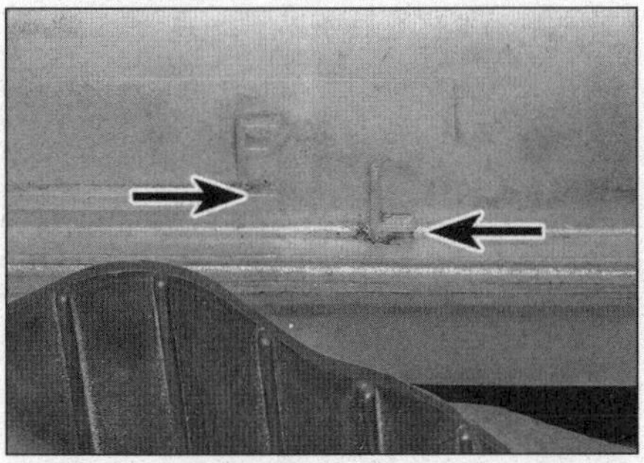

1 The coolant level must be maintained between the 'F' and 'L' marks on the coolant expansion tank.

2 If topping-up is necessary, wait until the engine is cold. Unscrew the expansion tank cap.

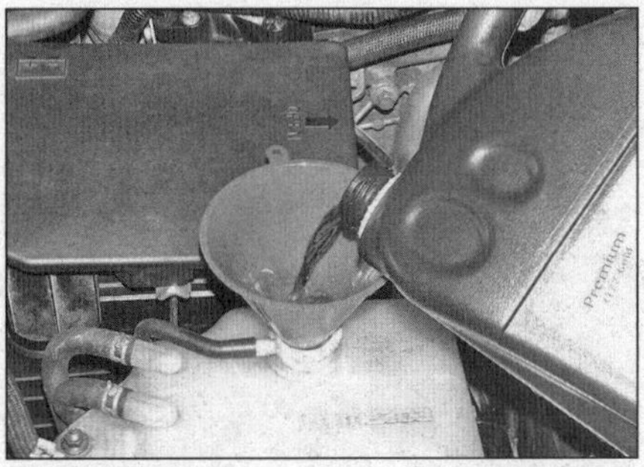

3 Add a mixture of water and antifreeze to the expansion tank until the level of the coolant is just below the 'F' mark on the expansion tank. Refit the cap and tighten it until the arrow marks align.

Brake and clutch fluid level

Warning: Brake fluid can harm your eyes and damage painted surfaces, so use extreme caution when handling and pouring it.

Warning: Do not use fluid that has been standing open for some time, as it absorbs moisture from the air, which can cause a dangerous loss of braking effectiveness.

Warning: The fluid level in the reservoir will drop slightly as the brake pads/clutch plate wear down, but the fluid level must never be allowed to drop below the MIN mark.

Before you start

✔ Make sure that your car is on level ground.

Safety first!

● If the reservoir requires repeated topping-up this is an indication of a fluid leak somewhere in the system, which should be investigated immediately.

● If a leak is suspected, the car should not be driven until the braking/clutch system has been checked. Never take any risks where brakes are concerned.

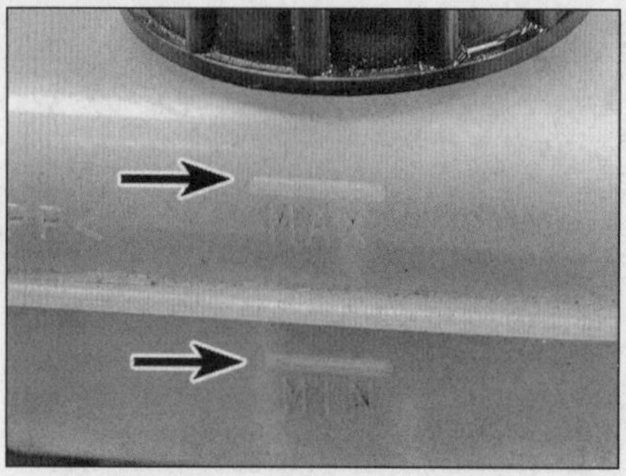

1 The MAX and MIN marks are indicated on the side of the reservoir. The fluid level must be kept between the marks at all times.

2 If topping-up is necessary, first wipe clean the area around the filler cap to prevent dirt entering the hydraulic system.

3 Unscrew the reservoir cap and carefully lift it out of position. Inspect the reservoir, if the fluid is dirty the hydraulic system should be drained and refilled (see Chapter 1, Section 18).

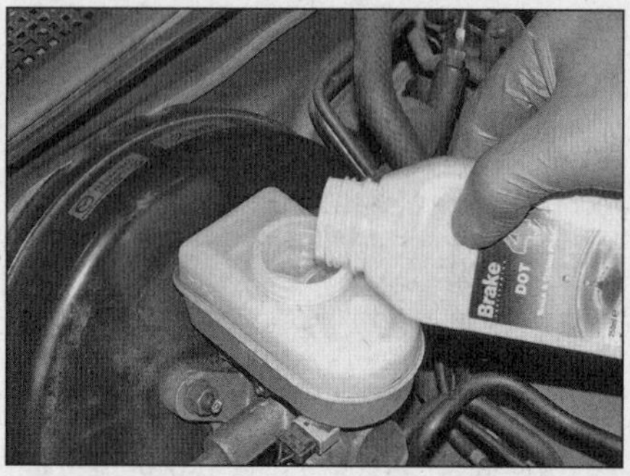

4 Carefully add fluid taking care not to spill it onto the surrounding components. Use only the specified fluid; mixing different types can cause damage to the system. After topping-up to the correct level, securely refit the cap and wipe off any spilled fluid.

Power steering fluid level

Before you start

✔ Park the vehicle on level ground.
✔ Set the steering wheel straight-ahead.
✔ The engine should be turned off and cold.

HAYNES HiNT ***For the check to be accurate, the steering must not be turned while the level is being checked.***

Safety first!

● The need for frequent topping-up indicates a leak, which should be investigated immediately.

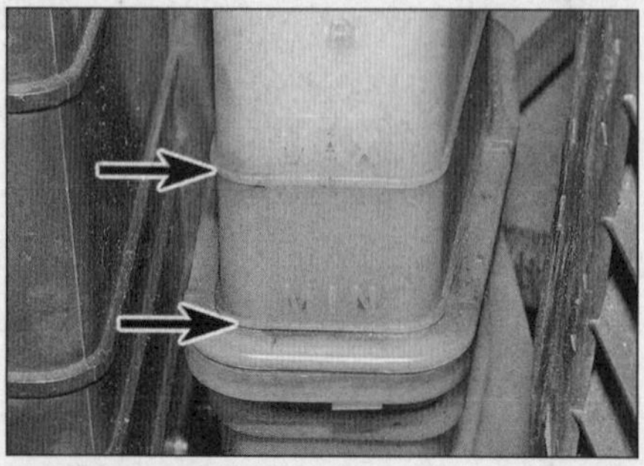

1 The reservoir is located near the front of the engine compartment. The fluid level must be kept between the Minimum and Maximum levels indicated on the side of the reservoir.

2 If topping up is necessary, unscrew the filler cap and add fluid to bring the level up to the MAX mark.

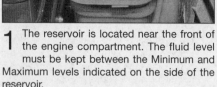

3 When topping-up, use the specified type of fluid and do not overfill the reservoir. When the level is correct, securely refit the cap.

Battery

Caution: Before carrying out any work on the vehicle battery, read the precautions given in 'Safety first!' at the start of this manual.

✔ Make sure that the battery tray is in good condition, and that the clamp is tight. Corrosion on the tray, retaining clamp and the battery itself can be removed with a solution of water and baking soda. Thoroughly rinse all cleaned areas with water. Any metal parts damaged by corrosion should be covered with a zinc-based primer, then painted.

✔ Periodically (approximately every three months), check the charge condition of the battery, as described in Chapter 5A Section 3.

✔ If the battery is flat, and you need to jump start your vehicle, see *Roadside repairs*.

1 The battery is located at the front of the engine compartment. Release the clips at the side, and lift away the battery cover.

2 Check the tightness of battery clamps to ensure good electrical connections ...

3 ... you should not be able to move them. Also check each cable for cracks and frayed conductors.

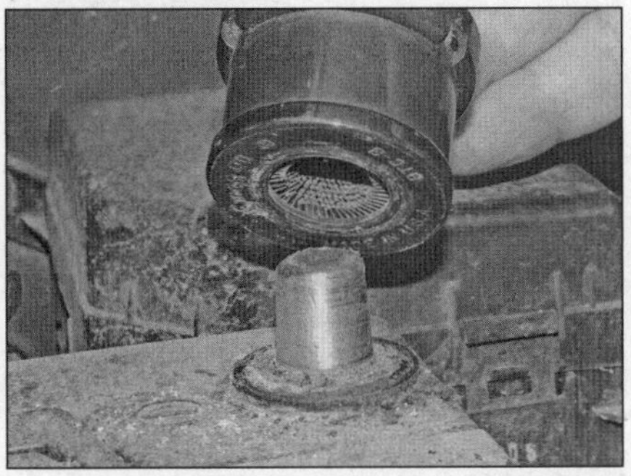

4 If corrosion (white, fluffy deposits) is evident, remove the cables from the battery terminals, clean them with a small wire brush, then refit them. Automotive stores sell a tool for cleaning the battery post ...

5 ... as well as the battery cable clamps.

Screen washer fluid level*

** On models with a headlight washer system, the screenwash is also used to clean the headlights*

● Screenwash additives not only keep the windscreen clean during bad weather, they also prevent the washer system freezing in cold weather – which is when you are likely to need it most. Don't top-up using plain water, as the screenwash will become diluted, and will freeze in cold weather.

⚠ ***Warning: On no account use engine coolant antifreeze in the screen washer system – this may damage the paintwork.***

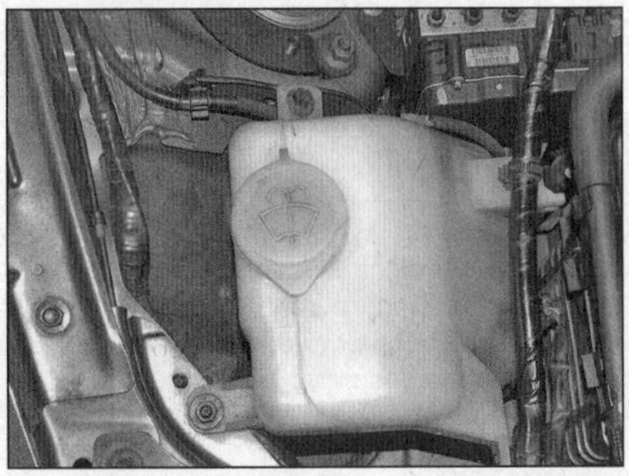

1 The screen washer fluid reservoir is located at the right-hand side of the engine compartment.

2 Unclip the cap. When topping-up, add a screenwash additive in the quantities recommended by the manufacturer.

Tyre condition and pressure

It is very important that tyres are in good condition, and at the correct pressure – having a tyre failure at any speed is highly dangerous.

Tyre wear is influenced by driving style – harsh braking and acceleration, or fast cornering, will all produce more rapid tyre wear. As a general rule, the front tyres wear out faster than the rears. Interchanging the tyres from front to rear ("rotating" the tyres) may result in more even wear. However, if this is completely effective, you may have the expense of replacing all four tyres at once!

21 Remove any nails or stones embedded in the tread before they penetrate the tyre to cause deflation. If removal of a nail does reveal that the tyre has been punctured, refit the nail so that its point of penetration is marked. Then immediately change the wheel, and have the tyre repaired by a tyre dealer.

Regularly check the tyres for damage in the form of cuts or bulges, especially in the sidewalls. Periodically remove the wheels, and clean any dirt or mud from the inside and outside surfaces. Examine the wheel rims for signs of rusting, corrosion or other damage. Light alloy wheels are easily damaged by "kerbing" whilst parking; steel wheels may also become dented or buckled. A new wheel is very often the only way to overcome severe damage.

New tyres should be balanced when they are fitted, but it may become necessary to re-balance them as they wear, or if the balance weights fitted to the wheel rim should fall off. Unbalanced tyres will wear more quickly, as will the steering and suspension components. Wheel imbalance is normally signified by vibration, particularly at a certain speed (typically around 50 mph). If this vibration is felt only through the steering, then it is likely that just the front wheels need balancing. If, however, the vibration is felt through the whole car, the rear wheels could be out of balance. Wheel balancing should be carried out by a tyre dealer or garage.

1 ***Tread Depth - visual check***

The original tyres have tread wear safety bands (B), which will appear when the tread depth reaches approximately 1.6 mm. The band positions are indicated by a triangular mark on the tyre sidewall (A).

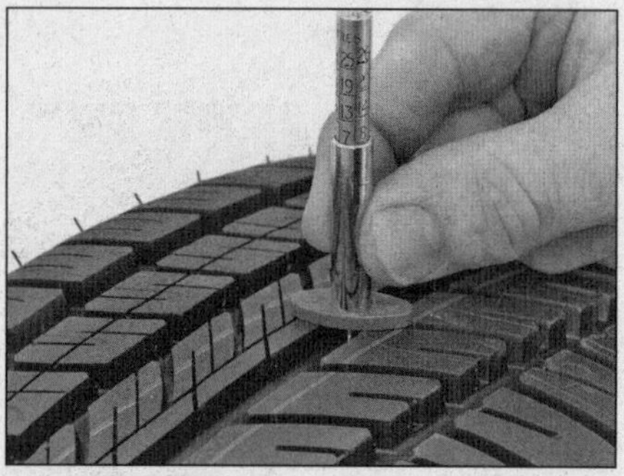

2 ***Tread Depth - manual check***

Alternatively, tread wear can be monitored with a simple, inexpensive device known as a tread depth indicator gauge.

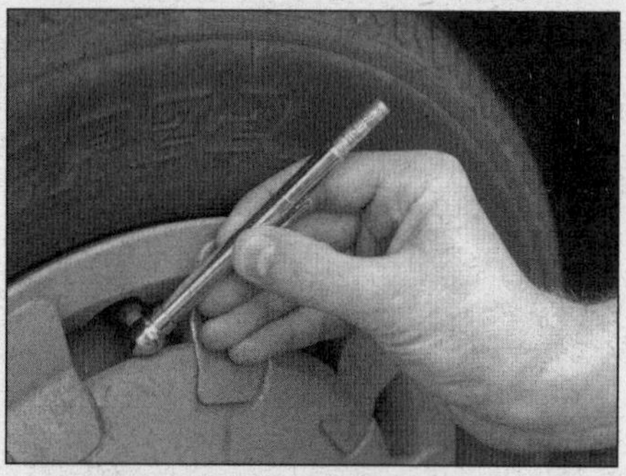

3 ***Tyre Pressure Check***

Check the tyre pressures regularly with the tyres cold. Do not adjust the tyre pressures immediately after the vehicle has been used, or an inaccurate setting will result.

Tyre tread wear patterns

Shoulder Wear

Underinflation (wear on both sides)
Under-inflation will cause overheating of the tyre, because the tyre will flex too much, and the tread will not sit correctly on the road surface. This will cause a loss of grip and excessive wear, not to mention the danger of sudden tyre failure due to heat build-up.
Check and adjust pressures
Incorrect wheel camber (wear on one side)
Repair or renew suspension parts
Hard cornering
Reduce speed!

Centre Wear

Overinflation
Over-inflation will cause rapid wear of the centre part of the tyre tread, coupled with reduced grip, harsher ride, and the danger of shock damage occurring in the tyre casing.
Check and adjust pressures

If you sometimes have to inflate your car's tyres to the higher pressures specified for maximum load or sustained high speed, don't forget to reduce the pressures to normal afterwards.

Uneven Wear

Front tyres may wear unevenly as a result of wheel misalignment. Most tyre dealers and garages can check and adjust the wheel alignment (or "tracking") for a modest charge.
Incorrect camber or castor
Repair or renew suspension parts
Malfunctioning suspension
Repair or renew suspension parts
Unbalanced wheel
Balance tyres
Incorrect toe setting
Adjust front wheel alignment
Note: *The feathered edge of the tread which typifies toe wear is best checked by feel.*

Electrical systems

✔ Check all external lights and the horn. Refer to Chapter 12 Section 2 for details if any of the circuits are found to be inoperative.

✔ Visually check all accessible wiring connectors, harnesses and retaining clips for security, and for signs of chafing or damage.

> **HAYNES HiNT** ***If you need to check your brake lights and indicators unaided, back up to a wall or garage door and operate the lights. The reflected light should show if they are working properly.***

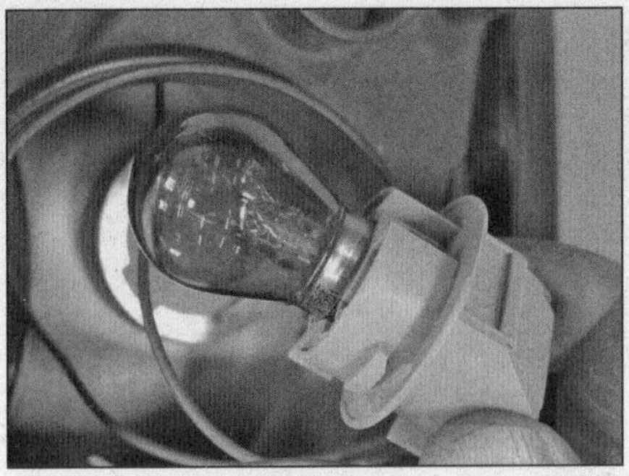

1 If a single indicator light, brake light or headlight has failed, it is likely that a bulb has blown and will need to be renewed. Refer to Chapter 12, Section 6 for details. If both brake lights have failed, it is possible that the switch has failed (see Chapter 9).

2 Of more than one indicator light or tail light has failed check that a fuse has not blown or that there is a fault in the circuit (see Chapter 12, Section 2). The fuses are located in a fusebox in the passengers side kick panel...

3 ... and in the front, left-hand corner of the engine compartment. Details of the circuits protected by the fuses are shown on the fusebox cover.

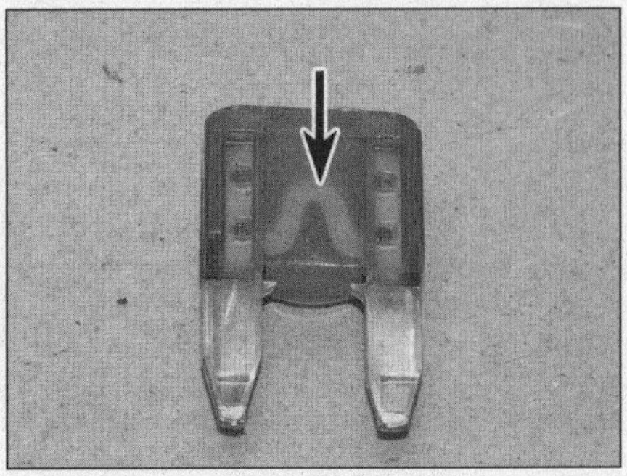

4 To renew a blown fuse, simply pull it out using the tweezers clipped to the engine compartment fusebox lid, and fit a new fuse of the correct rating (see Chapter 12, Section 4). Examine the 'bridge' between the fuse terminals. If the fuse blows again, it is important that you find out why – a complete checking procedure is given in Chapter 12, Section 2.

Wiper blades

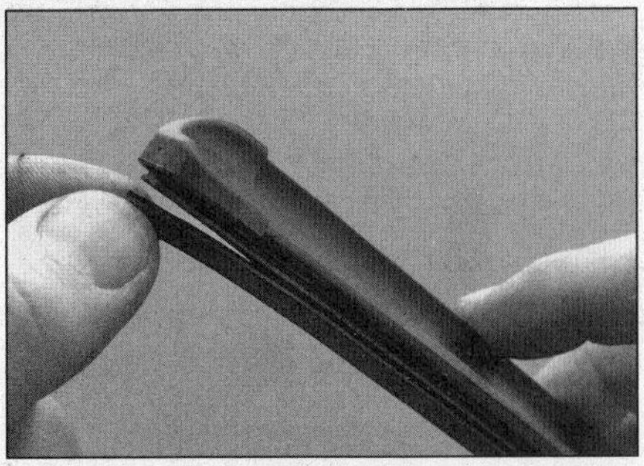

1 Check the condition of the wiper blades; if they are cracked or show any signs of deterioration, or if the glassswept area is smeared, renew them. Wiper blades should be renewed annually.

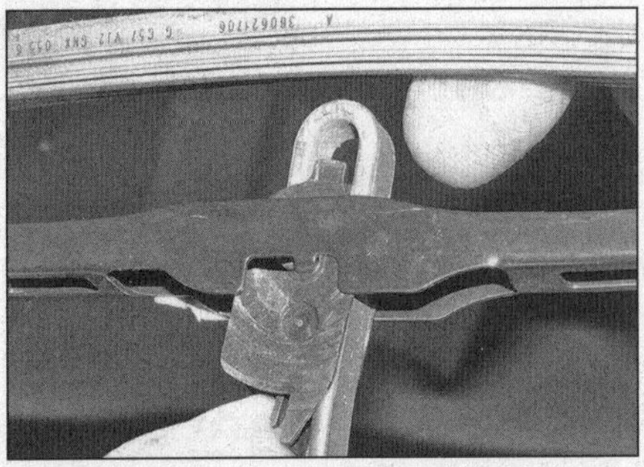

2 To remove a wiper blade, pull the arm away from the screen, then rotate the blade, compress the retaining clip ...

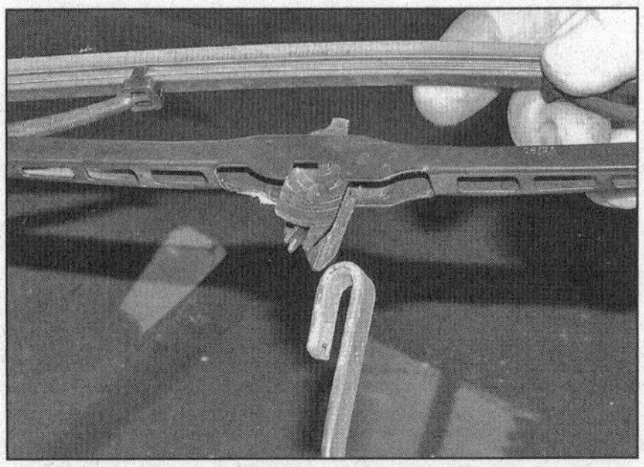

3 ... and side the blade from the arm.

Lubricants and fluids

Engine oil	
All petrol engines 2005 – 2011	5W/30 multigrade semi-synthetic or synthetic oil to specification ACEA A5. EG, Castrol Edge
All petrol engines 2011 – 2015	0W/30 multigrade semi-synthetic or synthetic oil to specification ACEA A5. EG. Castrol Edge
Coolant system	
FL22 sticker on expansion tank cap	Mazda FL22 antifreeze
Without FL22 on expansion tank cap	Silicate-free ethylene-glycol based antifreeze
Manual transmission	
5-speed transmission	75W/90 GL4 or GL5
6-speed transmission	75W/90 GL4
Final drive unit oil	SAE 90 GL5
Brake and clutch fluid	Hydraulic fluid to DOT 4
Power steering fluid	Dexron II

Tyre pressures (cold)

1 The tyre pressures are given on a label affixed to the rear edge of the driver's door **(see illustration)**.

Chapter 1
Routine maintenance and servicing

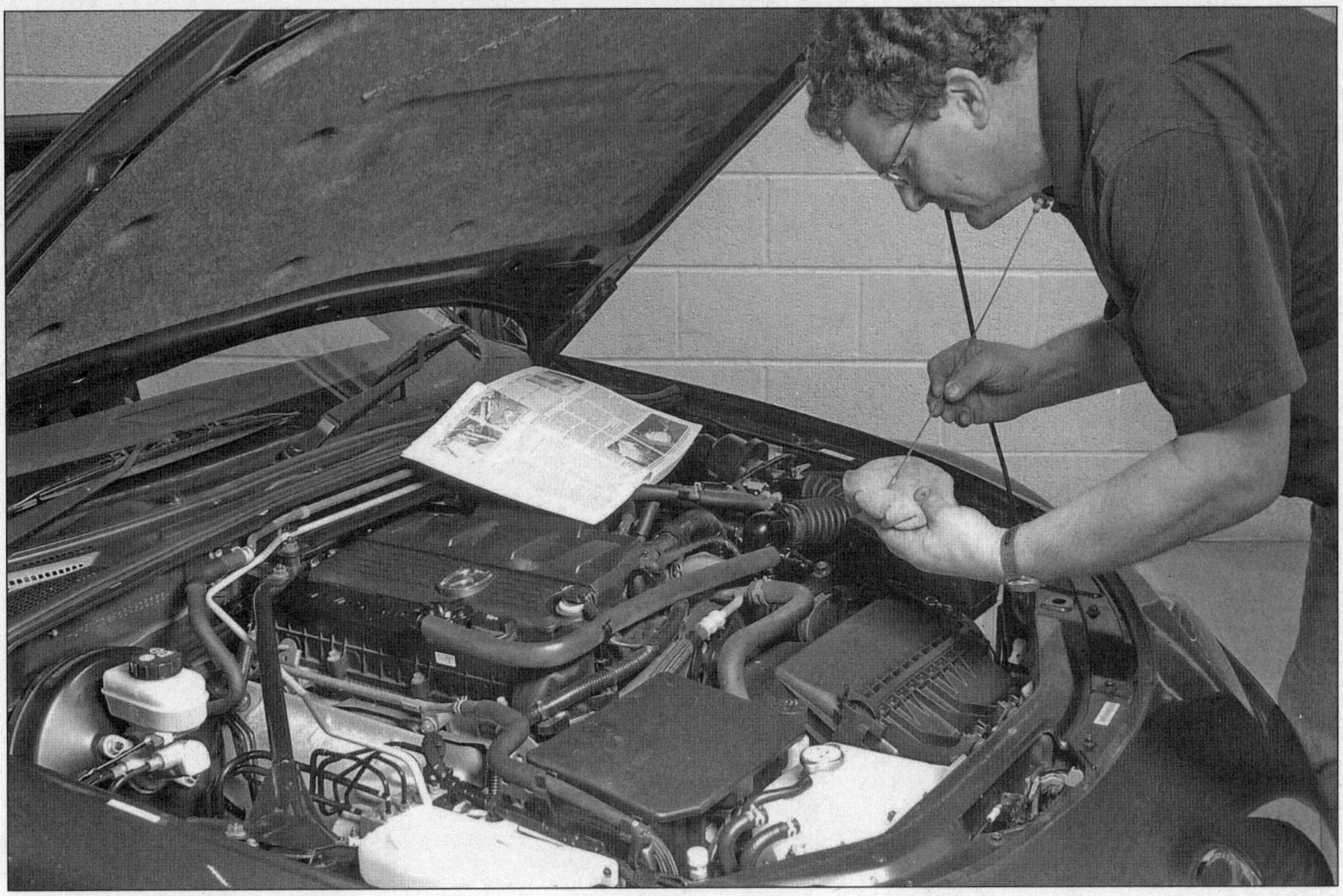

Contents

Degrees of difficulty

Easy, suitable for novice with little experience	**Fairly easy,** suitable for beginner with some experience	**Fairly difficult,** suitable for competent DIY mechanic	**Difficult,** suitable for experienced DIY mechanic	**Very difficult,** suitable for expert DIY or professional

Servicing specifications

Lubricants and fluids

Lubricants and fluids	Refer to Lubricants and fluids	
Capacities		
Engine oil (including filter)		
With oil cooler	4.55 litres	
Without oil cooler	4.45 litres	
Cooling system		
All models	7.5 litres	
Manual transmission		
5-speed	2.0 litres	
6-speed	2.1 litres	
Final drive		
All models	0.6 to 0.8 litres	
Fuel tank		
All models	50 litres	
Engine		
Valve clearances (cold):	**Inlet**	**Exhaust**
All engines	0.22 to 0.28 mm	0.27 to 0.33 mm
Cooling system		
Antifreeze mixture (50% antifreeze)	Protection down to –35°C	

Note: *Refer to antifreeze manufacturer for latest recommendations.*

Spark plugs	
Spark plugs:	
1.8 litre engines	NGK TR5AI-13
2.0 litre engines	NGK ILTR6A-13G
Spark plug gap	Preset
Remote control	
Battery type	CR1620
Brakes	
Brake pad minimum thickness:	
Rear brake pads	2.0 mm
Front brake pads	2.0 mm

Torque wrench settings

Torque wrench settings	Nm	lbf ft
Final drive:		
Filler/level plug	44	32
Drain plug	44	32
Oil filter cartridge	16	12
Roadwheel nuts	110	81
Spark plugs	12	9
Sump drain plug	35	26
Transmission oil drain plug:		
5-speed	44	32
6-speed	44	32
Transmission oil filler/level plug:		
5-speed	35	26
6-speed	44	32

1 Maintenance schedule

The maintenance intervals in this manual are provided with the assumption that you, not the dealer, will be carrying out the work. These are the minimum maintenance intervals recommended by us for vehicles driven daily. If you wish to keep your vehicle in peak condition at all times, you may wish to perform some of these procedures more often. We encourage frequent maintenance, because it enhances the efficiency, performance and resale value of your vehicle.

When the vehicle is new, it should be serviced by a dealer service department (or other workshop recognised by the vehicle manufacturer as providing the same standard of service) in order to preserve the warranty. The vehicle manufacturer may reject warranty claims if you are unable to prove that servicing has been carried out as and when specified, using only original equipment parts or parts certified to be of equivalent quality.

Every 250 miles or weekly

- ☐ Refer to Weekly checks

Every 6000 miles or 6 months – whichever comes first

- ☐ Renew the engine oil and filter (Section 5).

Note: *Oil and filter changes are good for the engine and we recommend that the oil and filter are renewed frequently, especially if the vehicle is used on a lot of short journeys*

Every 12 000 miles or 12 months – whichever comes first

In addition to the items listed above, carry out the following:

- ☐ Check the condition of the auxiliary drivebelt (Section 6).
- ☐ Hose and fluid leak check (Section 7).
- ☐ Check the brake pads for wear (Section 8).
- ☐ Check the condition of the driveshaft gaiters (Section 9).
- ☐ Check the steering and suspension components for condition and security (Section 10).
- ☐ Check the underbody and sealant for damage (Section 11).
- ☐ Check the condition of the exhaust system and its mountings (Section 12).
- ☐ Check and if necessary adjust the handbrake (Section 13).
- ☐ Lubricate all hinges and locks (Section 14).
- ☐ Carry out a road test (Section 15).
- ☐ Clean the air filter element (Section 20).

Every 24 000 miles or 2 years – whichever comes first

In addition to the items listed above, carry out the following:

- ☐ Check the engine management system (Section 17).
- ☐ Renew the brake fluid (Section 18).
- ☐ Renew the coolant – non-FL22 antifreeze only (Section 19).*

Note: **Vehicles filled with FL22 antifreeze have an identifying sticker affixed to, or adjacent to, the expansion tank filler cap.*

Every 36 000 miles or 3 years – whichever comes first

- ☐ Renew the air filter element (Section 20).
- ☐ Inspect the auxiliary drivebelt and renew if necessary (Section 6).
- ☐ Inspect the evaporative loss system (Section 21).

Every 48 000 miles or 4 years – whichever comes first

In addition to the items listed above, carry out the following:

- ☐ Renew the final drive oil (Section 23).
- ☐ Renew the remote control battery (Section 24).

Every 60 000 miles or 5 years – whichever comes first

- ☐ Renew the spark plugs (Section 16).
- ☐ Renew the manual transmission oil (Section 22).
- ☐ Renew the coolant – FL22 antifreeze only (Section 19).*

Note: **Vehicles filled with FL22 antifreeze have an identifying sticker affixed to, or adjacent to, the expansion tank filler cap.*

Every 75 000 miles

- ☐ Check, and if necessary, adjust the valve clearances (Section 25).

2 Components location

Front underbody view

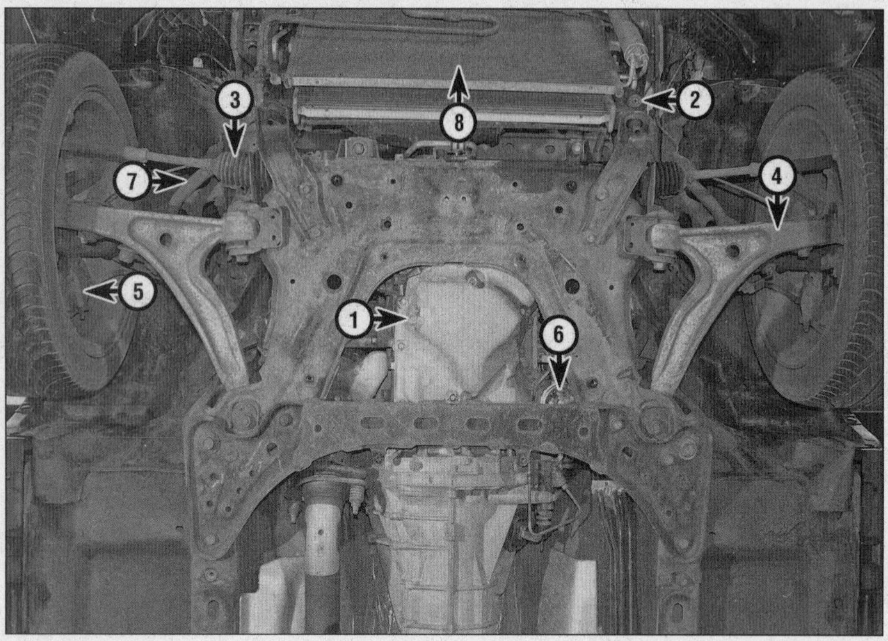

1 Engine oil drain plug
2 Radiator drain plug
3 Steering rack
4 Suspension lower arm
5 Brake caliper
6 Oil filter
7 Anti-roll bar
8 Condenser

Rear underbody view

1 Final drive fluid drain plug
2 Power plant frame
3 Driveshaft
4 Handbrake cable
5 Propeller shaft
6 Shock absorber
7 EVAP carbon canister
8 Exhaust tail box

Underbonnet view

1 Engine oil level dipstick
2 Engine oil filler cap
3 Air cleaner housing
4 Washer fluid reservoir
5 Coolant expansion tank
6 Strut brace
7 Brake/clutch fluid reservoir
8 Mass airflow sensor
9 Power steering fluid reservoir
10 Engine compartment fusebox
11 Battery cover

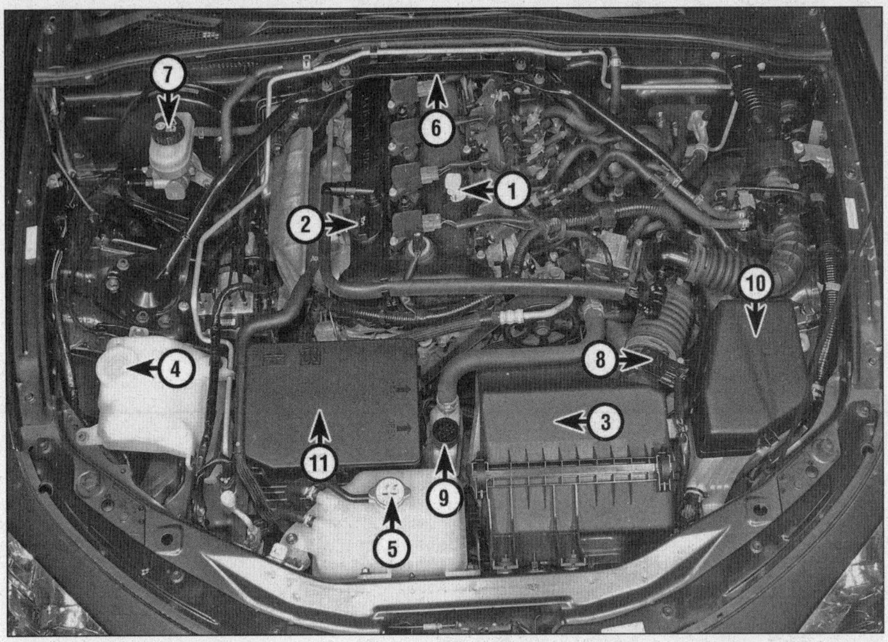

3 Introduction

1 This Chapter is designed to help the home mechanic maintain his/her vehicle for safety, economy, long life and peak performance.
2 The Chapter contains a master maintenance schedule, and Sections dealing specifically with each task in the schedule. Visual checks, adjustments, component renewal and other helpful items are included. Refer to the accompanying illustrations of the engine compartment and the underside of the vehicle for the locations of the various components.
3 Servicing your vehicle in accordance with the mileage/time maintenance schedule and the following Sections will provide a planned maintenance programme, which should result in a long and reliable service life. This is a comprehensive plan, so maintaining some items but not others at the specified service intervals, will not produce the same results.
4 As you service your vehicle, you will discover that many of the procedures can, and should, be grouped together, because of the particular procedure being performed, or because of the proximity of two otherwise unrelated components to one another. For example, if the vehicle is raised for any reason, the exhaust can be inspected at the same time as the suspension and steering components.
5 The first step in this maintenance programme is to prepare yourself before the actual work begins. Read through all the Sections relevant to the work to be carried out, then make a list and gather all the parts and tools required. If a problem is encountered, seek advice from a parts specialist, or a dealer service department.

4 Regular maintenance

1 If, from the time the vehicle is new, the routine maintenance schedule is followed closely, and frequent checks are made of fluid levels and high-wear items, as suggested throughout this manual, the engine will be kept in relatively good running condition, and the need for additional work will be minimised.
2 It is possible that there will be times when the engine is running poorly due to the lack of regular maintenance. This is even more likely if a used vehicle, which has not received regular and frequent maintenance checks, is purchased. In such cases, additional work may need to be carried out, outside of the regular maintenance intervals.
3 If engine wear is suspected, a compression test (refer to Chapter 2A, Section 2) will provide valuable information regarding the overall performance of the main internal components. Such a test can be used as a basis to decide on the extent of the work to be carried out. If, for example, a compression test indicates serious internal engine wear, conventional maintenance as described in this Chapter will not greatly improve the performance of the engine, and may prove a waste of time and money, unless extensive overhaul work is carried out first.
4 The following series of operations are those usually required to improve the performance of a generally poor-running engine:

Primary operations

- Clean, inspect and test the battery (See *Weekly checks*).
- Check all the engine-related fluids (See *Weekly checks*).
- Check the condition and tension of the auxiliary drivebelt(s) (Section 6).
- Check the condition of all hoses, and check for fluid leaks (Section 7).
- Renew the spark plugs (Section 16).
- Check the condition of the air filter, and renew if necessary (Section 20).

5 If the above operations do not prove fully effective, carry out the following secondary operations:

Secondary operations

6 All items listed under Primary operations, plus the following:

- Check the charging system (Chapter 5A, Section 5).
- Check the ignition system (Chapter 5B, Section 2).
- Check the fuel system (Chapter 4A, Section 9).

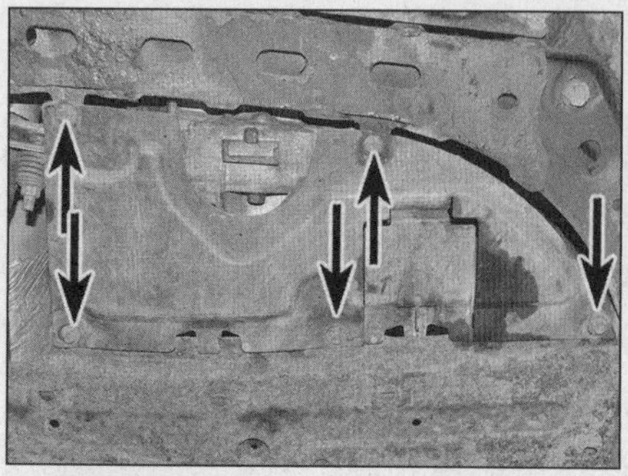
5.3 Engine under guard fasteners

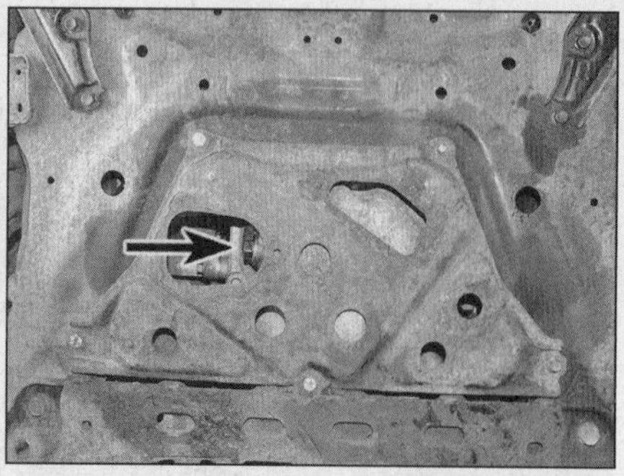
5.5a Unscrew the drain plug...

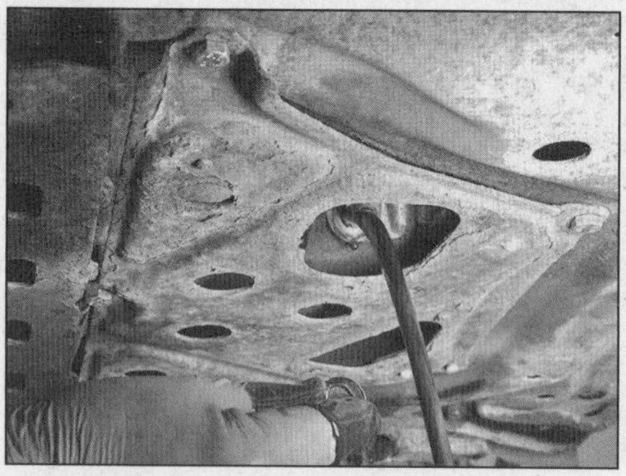
5.5b... and allow the oil to drain

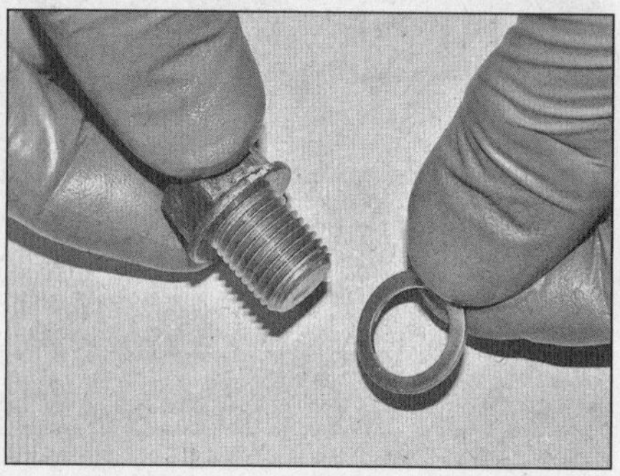
5.5c Renew the drain plug sealing washer

5 Engine oil and filter renewal

1 Frequent oil and filter changes are the most important preventative maintenance which can be undertaken by the DIY owner. As engine oil ages, it becomes diluted and contaminated, which leads to premature engine wear.

2 Before starting this procedure, gather all the necessary tools and materials. Also make sure that you have plenty of clean rags and newspapers handy to mop-up any spills. Ideally, the engine oil should be warm, as it will drain better, and any impurities suspended in the oil will be removed with it. Take care, however, not to touch the exhaust or any other hot parts of the engine when working under the vehicle. To avoid any possibility of scalding, and to protect yourself from possible skin irritants and other harmful contaminants in used engine oils, it is advisable to wear gloves when carrying out this work. Access to the underside of the vehicle will be greatly improved if it can be raised on a lift, driven onto ramps, or jacked up and supported on axle stands (see *Jacking and vehicle support*). Whichever method is chosen, make sure that the vehicle remains level, or if it is at an angle, that the drain plug is at the lowest point.

3 Undo the fasteners and remove the engine under guard (where fitted) **(see illustration)**.

4 Rotate the oil filler cap anti-clockwise and remove it.

5 Slacken the sump drain plug about half a turn **(see illustrations)**. Position the draining container under the drain plug, then remove the plug completely. Renew the sealing washer.

6 Allow some time for the old oil to drain, noting that it may be necessary to reposition the container as the oil flow slows to a trickle.

7 After all the oil has drained, wipe off the drain plug with a clean rag, then clean the area around the drain plug opening and refit the plug with a new sealing washer. Tighten the plug to the specified torque.

8 Move the container into position under the oil filter, which is located on the left-hand side of the engine **(see illustration)**.

9 Using a 76 mm oil filter removal socket or strap-wrench, slacken the filter initially, then unscrew it by hand the rest of the way **(see illustration)**. Empty the oil in the old filter into the container.

10 Use a clean rag to remove all oil, dirt and sludge from the filter sealing area on the engine. Check the old filter to make sure that the rubber sealing ring has not stuck to the engine. If it has, carefully remove it.

11 Apply a light coating of clean engine oil to the sealing ring on the new filter, then screw it into position on the engine **(see illustration)**. Tighten the filter to the specified torque.

12 Remove the old oil and all tools from under the car then lower it to the ground (if applicable).

13 Withdraw the dipstick. Fill the engine, using the correct grade and type of oil (see *Lubricants and fluids* in *Weekly checks*). An oil can spout or funnel may help to reduce spillage. Pour in half the specified quantity of oil first, then wait a few minutes for the oil to run to the sump. Continue adding oil a small quantity at a time until the level is up to the MAX mark on the dipstick. Refit the filler cap.

14 Start the engine and run it for a few minutes; check for leaks around the oil filter seal and the sump drain plug. Note that there may be a delay of a few seconds before the oil pressure warning light goes out when the engine is first started, as the oil circulates through the engine oil galleries and the new oil filter before the pressure builds-up. Where applicable, refit the engine undershield.

15 Switch off the engine, and wait a few minutes for the oil to settle in the sump once more. With the new oil circulated and the filter completely full, recheck the level on the dipstick, and add more oil as necessary.

5.8 The oil filter is located on the left-hand side of the engine

5.9 Using a filter removal socket to slacken the filter

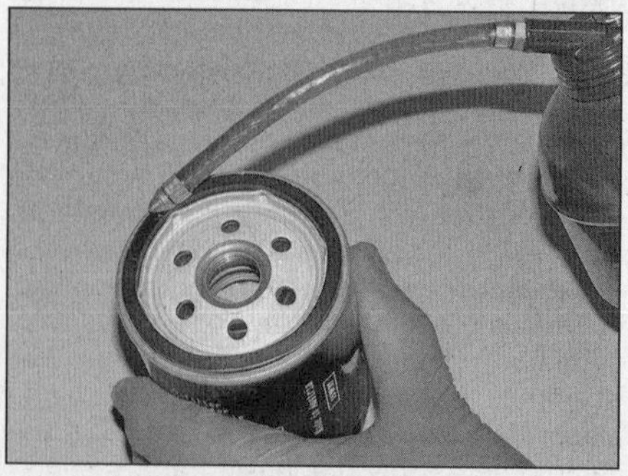
5.11 Lubricate the sealing ring with clean engine oil

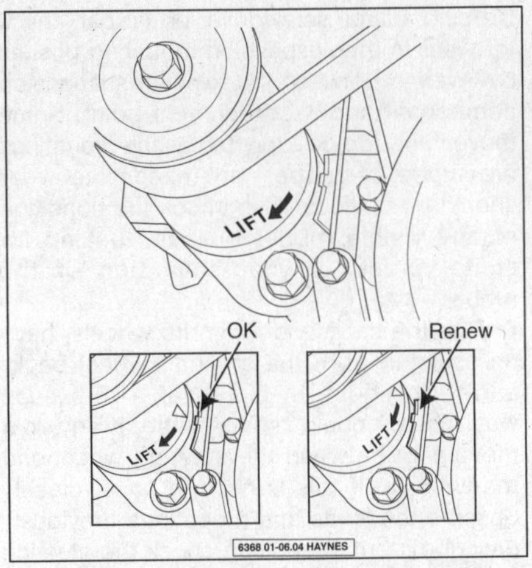

6.4 If the arrow shaped mark is beyond the edge of the bracket, renew the belt

16 Dispose of the used engine oil and filter safely, referring to *General repair procedures* in Reference. Do not discard the old filter with domestic household waste. The facility for waste oil disposal provided by many local council refuse tips generally has a filter receptacle alongside.

6 Auxiliary drivebelt – checking and renewal

Checking

1 In order to fully asses the condition of the drivebelt, remove the battery and battery tray as described in Chapter 5A Section 4.
2 Using a socket on the crankshaft pulley bolt, rotate the crankshaft so that the full length of the drivebelt can be examined. Look for cracks, splitting and fraying on the surface of the belt; check also for signs of glazing (shiny patches) and separation of the belt plies. If damage or wear is visible, the belt should be renewed.
3 If the condition of the belt is satisfactory, check the drivebelt tension as described below.
4 Using a suitable mirror, observe the position of the arrow mark on the tensioner body. If it is beyond the upper edge of the adjacent bracket, the belt has stretched excessively and should be replaced as described in this Section **(see illustration)**.

Renewal

5 Remove the battery and battery tray as described in Chapter 5A Section 4.
6 If the belt is to be reused, mark its direction of rotation so that it can be refitted the same way round.
7 Using a suitable spanner, rotate the drivebelt tensioner clockwise to relieve the tension on the belt, then slip the belt from the pulleys **(see illustration)**.

6.7 Rotate the tensioner bolt clockwise

8 Fit the new belt to the various pulleys, then rotate the tensioner clockwise and fit the belt around the tensioner pulley. Ensure the belt is routed correctly and locates fully on the various pulley grooves **(see illustration)**.
9 Slowly release the tensioner, and allow it to tension the belt.

7 Hose and fluid leak check

1 Visually inspect the engine joint faces, gaskets and seals for any signs of water or oil leaks. Pay particular attention to the areas around the camshaft cover, cylinder head, oil filter and sump joint faces. Bear in mind that, over a period of time, some very slight seepage from these areas is to be expected – what you are really looking for is any indication of a serious leak. Should a leak be found, renew the offending gasket or oil seal by referring to the appropriate Chapters in this manual.
2 Also check the security and condition of all the engine-related pipes and hoses. Ensure that all cable-ties or securing clips are in place and in good condition. Clips which are broken or missing can lead to chafing of the hoses, pipes or wiring, which could cause more serious problems in the future.

HAYNES HINT

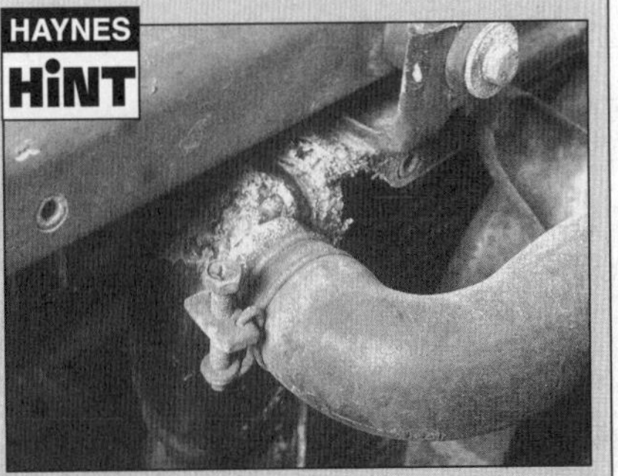

A leak in the cooling system will usually show up as white- or antifreeze coloured deposits on the area adjoining the leak.

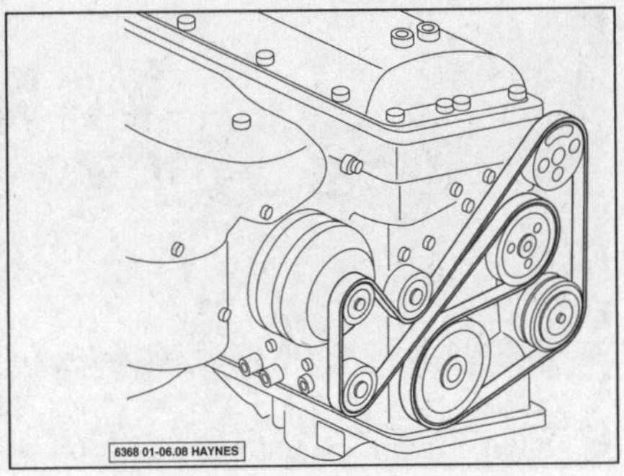

6.8 Drivebelt routing (AC model shown)

3 Carefully check the radiator hoses and heater hoses along their entire length. Renew any hose which is cracked, swollen or deteriorated. Cracks will show up better if the hose is squeezed. Pay close attention to the hose clips that secure the hoses to the cooling system components. Hose clips can pinch and puncture hoses, resulting in cooling system leaks.
4 Inspect all the cooling system components (hoses, joint faces etc.) for leaks. A leak in the cooling system will usually show up as white- or antifreeze-coloured deposits on the area adjoining the leak (see **Haynes Hint**). Where any problems of this nature are found on system components, renew the component or gasket with reference to Chapter 3.
5 With the vehicle raised, inspect the fuel tank and filler neck for punctures, cracks and other damage. The connection between the filler neck and tank is especially critical. Sometimes a rubber filler neck or connecting hose will leak due to loose retaining clamps or deteriorated rubber.
6 Carefully check all rubber hoses and metal fuel lines leading away from the fuel tank. Check for loose connections, deteriorated hoses, crimped lines, and other damage. Pay particular attention to the vent pipes and hoses, which often loop up around the filler neck and can become blocked or crimped. Follow the lines to the front of the vehicle, carefully inspecting them all the way. Renew damaged sections as necessary.
7 From within the engine compartment, check the security of all fuel hose attachments and pipe unions, and inspect the fuel hoses and vacuum hoses for kinks, chafing and deterioration.

8 Brake pad check

1 Firmly apply the handbrake, then jack up the front or rear of the car and support it securely on axle stands (see *Jacking and vehicle support*). Remove the roadwheels.
2 Using a steel rule, measure the thickness of the friction material of the brake pads on

8.2 Measure the thickness of the pad friction material (arrowed) through the aperture in the caliper body

both front brakes. Compare the measurement obtained with that given in the Specifications **(see illustration)**.

3 For a comprehensive check, the brake pads should be removed and cleaned. The operation of the caliper can then also be checked, and the condition of the brake disc itself can be fully examined on both sides. Refer to Chapter 9 for further information.

4 If any pad's friction material is worn to the specified thickness or less, all four pads must be renewed as a set. Refer to Chapter 9 Section 4 or Chapter 9, Section 5.

5 On completion refit the roadwheels and lower the car to the ground.

9 Driveshaft gaiter check

1 Raise the rear of the vehicle and support it securely on axle stands (see *Jacking and vehicle support*). Slowly rotate the roadwheel, and inspect the condition of the outer constant velocity (CV) joint rubber gaiters, squeezing the gaiters to open out the folds. Check for signs of cracking, splits or deterioration of the rubber, which may allow the grease to escape, and lead to water and grit entry into the joint. Also check the security and condition of the retaining clips. Repeat these checks on the inner CV joints **(see illustration)**. If any damage or deterioration is found, the gaiters should be renewed (see Chapter 8, Section 5).

2 At the same time, check the general condition of the CV joints themselves by first holding the driveshaft and attempting to rotate the wheel. Repeat this check by holding the inner joint and attempting to rotate the driveshaft. Any appreciable movement indicates wear in the joints, wear in the driveshaft splines, or a loose driveshaft retaining nut.

10 Steering and suspension check

Front suspension and steering

1 Firmly apply the handbrake, then jack up the front of the car and support it securely on axle stands (see *Jacking and vehicle support*).

2 Inspect the balljoint dust covers and the steering rack and pinion gaiters for splits, chafing or deterioration **(see illustration)**. Any wear of these will cause loss of lubricant, together with dirt and water entry, resulting in rapid deterioration of the balljoints or steering gear.

3 Grasp the roadwheel at the 12 o'clock and 6 o'clock positions, and try to rock it **(see illustration)**. Very slight free play may be felt, but if the movement is appreciable, further investigation is necessary to determine the source. Continue rocking the wheel while an assistant depresses the footbrake. If the movement is now eliminated or significantly reduced, it is likely that the hub bearings are at fault. If the free play is still evident with the footbrake depressed, then there is wear in the suspension joints or mountings.

4 Now grasp the wheel at the 9 o'clock and 3 o'clock positions, and try to rock it as before. Any movement felt now may again be caused by wear in the hub bearings or the steering track rod balljoints. If the inner or outer balljoint is worn, the visual movement will be obvious.

5 Using a large screwdriver or flat bar, check for wear in the suspension mounting bushes by levering between the relevant suspension component and its attachment point. Some movement is to be expected as the mountings are made of rubber, but excessive wear should be obvious. Also check the condition of any visible rubber bushes, looking for splits, cracks or contamination of the rubber.

6 With the car standing on its wheels, have an assistant turn the steering wheel back-and-forth about an eighth of a turn each way. There should be very little, if any, lost movement between the steering wheel and roadwheels. If this is not the case, closely observe the joints and mountings previously described, but in addition check the steering column universal joints for wear, and the rack and pinion steering gear itself.

Strut/shock absorber check

7 Check for any signs of fluid leakage around the suspension strut/shock absorber body, or from the rubber gaiter around the piston rod. Should any fluid be noticed, the suspension strut/shock absorber is defective internally, and should be renewed. **Note:** *Suspension struts/shock absorbers should always be renewed in pairs on the same axle.*

8 The efficiency of the suspension strut/shock absorber may be checked by bouncing the vehicle at each corner. Generally speaking, the body will return to its normal position and stop after being depressed. If it rises and returns on a rebound, the suspension strut/shock absorber is probably suspect. Examine also the suspension strut/shock absorber upper and lower mountings for any signs of wear.

11 Underbody sealant check

1 Jack up the front and rear of the car and support it securely on axle stands (see *Jacking and vehicle support*). Alternatively position the car over an inspection pit.

9.1 Check the condition of the driveshaft CV joint rubber gaiters

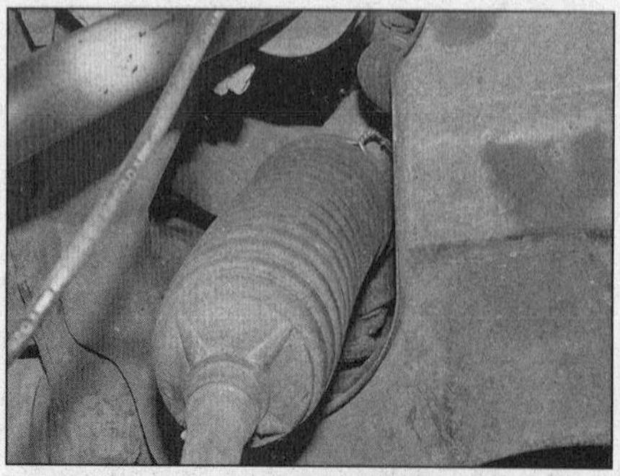

10.2 Check the condition of the steering rack rubber gaiters

10.3 Check for wear in the hub bearings by grasping the wheel and trying to rock it

2 Check the underbody, wheel housings and side sills for rust and/or damage to the underbody sealant. If evident, repair as necessary.

12 Exhaust system check

1 With the engine cold (at least an hour after the vehicle has been driven), check the complete exhaust system from the engine to the end of the tailpipe. The exhaust system is most easily checked with the car raised on a hoist, or suitably supported on axle stands (see *Jacking and vehicle support*), so that the exhaust components are readily visible and accessible.

2 Check the exhaust pipes and connections for evidence of leaks, severe corrosion and damage. Make sure that all brackets and mountings are in good condition, and that all relevant nuts and bolts are tight **(see illustration)**. Leakage at any of the joints or in other parts of the system will usually show up as a black sooty stain in the vicinity of the leak.

3 Rattles and other noises can often be traced to the exhaust system, especially the brackets and mountings. Try to move the pipes and silencers. If the components are able to come into contact with the body or suspension parts, secure the system with new mountings. Otherwise separate the joints (if possible) and twist the pipes as necessary to provide additional clearance.

13 Handbrake check and adjustment

1 Apply the handbrake two or three times, then pull the handle up through a maximum of 3 clicks of the ratchet mechanism and check that this locks the rear wheels, holding the vehicle stationary on an incline. If not, the handbrake mechanism should be adjusted as described in Chapter 9, Section 14.

14 Hinge and lock lubrication

1 Lubricate the hinges of the bonnet, doors and tailgate with a light general-purpose oil. Similarly, lubricate all latches, locks and lock strikers. At the same time, check the security and operation of all the locks, adjusting them if necessary (see Chapter 11).

2 Lightly lubricate the bonnet release mechanism and cable with suitable grease.

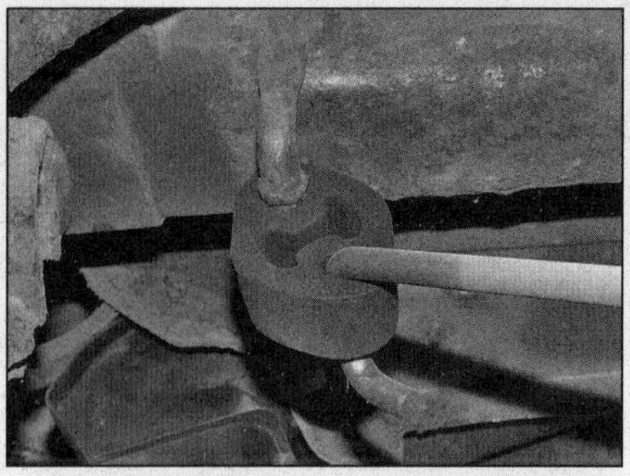

12.2 Examine the exhaust rubber mountings for signs of deterioration

15 Road test

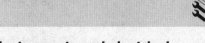

Instruments and electrical equipment

1 Check the operation of all instruments and electrical equipment.

2 Make sure that all instruments read correctly, and switch on all electrical equipment in turn, to check that it functions properly.

Steering and suspension

3 Check for any abnormalities in the steering, suspension, handling or road feel.

4 Drive the vehicle, and check that there are no unusual vibrations or noises.

5 Check that the steering feels positive, with no excessive sloppiness, or roughness, and check for any suspension noises when cornering and driving over bumps.

Drivetrain

6 Check the performance of the engine, clutch, transmission and driveshafts.

7 Listen for any unusual noises from the engine, clutch and transmission.

8 Make sure that the engine runs smoothly when idling, and that there is no hesitation when accelerating.

9 Check that, the clutch action is smooth and progressive, that the drive is taken up smoothly, and that the pedal travel is not excessive. Also listen for any noises when the clutch pedal is depressed.

10 Check that all gears can be engaged smoothly without noise, and that the gear lever action is smooth and not abnormally vague or notchy.

Braking system

11 Make sure that the vehicle does not pull to one side when braking, and that the wheels do not lock when braking hard.

12 Check that there is no vibration through the steering when braking.

13 Check that the handbrake operates correctly without excessive movement of the lever, and that it holds the vehicle stationary on a slope.

14 Test the operation of the brake servo unit as follows. With the engine off, depress the footbrake four or five times to exhaust the vacuum. Hold the brake pedal depressed, then start the engine. As the engine starts, there should be a noticeable give in the brake pedal as vacuum builds-up. Allow the engine to run for at least two minutes, and then switch it off. If the brake pedal is depressed now, it should be possible to detect a hiss from the servo as the pedal is depressed. After about four or five applications, no further hissing should be heard, and the pedal should feel considerably harder.

16.4 Use a special socket and extension to remove the spark plugs

16 Spark plug renewal

Spark plug renewal

1 The correct functioning of the spark plugs is vital for the correct running and efficiency of the engine. It is essential that the plugs fitted are appropriate for the engine. If the correct type is used and the engine is in good condition, the spark plugs should not need attention between scheduled renewal intervals. Spark plug cleaning is rarely necessary, and should not be attempted unless specialised equipment is available, as damage can easily be caused to the firing ends.

2 Remove the ignition coils as described in Chapter 5B Section 3.

3 If compressed air is available, blow any dirt or foreign material away from the spark plug area before proceeding (a common bicycle pump will also work or use a vacuum cleaner).

4 Unscrew and remove the spark plug **(see illustration)**.

5 The spark plug electrode gap is pre-set by the manufacturer and should not require adjustment.

6 Prior to installation, it's a good idea to coat the spark plug threads with a little anti-seize compound. Also, it's often difficult to insert

spark plugs into their holes without cross-threading them. To avoid this possibility, fit a short piece of 8 mm ID rubber hose over the end of the spark plug **(see illustration)**. The flexible hose acts as a universal joint to help align the plug with the plug hole. Should the plug begin to cross-thread, the hose will slip on the spark plug, preventing thread damage. Tighten the plug to the specified torque.

7 Attach the plug lead/boot to the new spark plug, again using a twisting motion on the boot until it is firmly seated on the end of the spark plug.

8 Follow the above procedure for the remaining spark plugs.

9 After fitting the spark plugs, refit the ignition coils as described in Chapter 5B Section 3.

17 Engine management system check

1 This check is part of the manufacturer's maintenance schedule, and involves testing the engine management system using special dedicated test equipment. Such testing will allow the test equipment to read any fault codes stored in the electronic control unit memory.

2 Unless a fault is suspected, this test is not essential, although it should be noted that it is recommended by the manufacturers.

3 If access to suitable test equipment is not possible, make a thorough check of all ignition, fuel and emission control system components, hoses, and wiring, for security and obvious signs of damage. Further details of the fuel system, emission control system and ignition system can be found in the relevant parts of Chapter 4A, 4B and 5B.

18 Brake fluid renewal

Warning: Brake hydraulic fluid can harm your eyes and damage painted surfaces, so use extreme caution when handling and pouring it. Do not use fluid that has been standing open for some time, as it absorbs moisture from the air. Excess moisture can cause a dangerous loss of braking effectiveness.

1 The procedure is similar to that for the bleeding of the hydraulic system as described in Chapter 9 Section 2, except that the brake fluid reservoir should be emptied by using a clean poultry baster or similar before starting, and allowance should be made for the old fluid to be expelled when bleeding a section of the circuit.

2 Working as described in Chapter 9 Section 2, open the first bleed screw in the sequence,

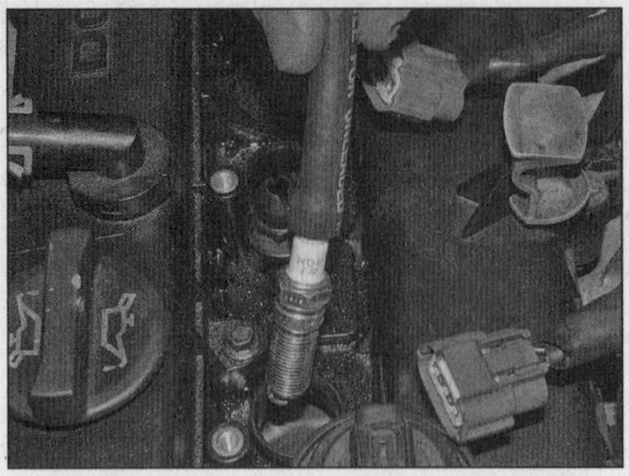

16.6 Use a length of rubber/plastic hose over the spark plug to start them in the holes, without risk of damage from cross-threading

and pump the brake pedal gently until nearly all the old fluid has been emptied from the master cylinder reservoir.

3 Top-up to the MAX level with new fluid, and continue pumping until only the new fluid remains in the reservoir, and new fluid can be seen emerging from the bleed screw. Tighten the screw, and top the reservoir level up to the MAX level line.

4 Work through all the remaining bleed screws in the sequence until new fluid can be seen at all of them. Be careful to keep the master cylinder reservoir topped-up to above the MIN level at all times, or air may enter the system and greatly increase the length of the task.

5 When the operation is complete, check that all bleed screws are securely tightened, and that their dust caps are refitted. Wash off all traces of spilt fluid, and recheck the master cylinder reservoir fluid level.

6 Check the operation of the brakes before taking the car on the road.

19 Coolant renewal

Warning: Wait until the engine is cold before starting this procedure. Do not allow antifreeze to come in contact with your skin, or with the painted surfaces of the vehicle. Rinse off spills immediately with plenty of water. Never leave antifreeze lying around in an open container, or in a puddle in the driveway or on the garage floor. Children and pets are attracted by its sweet smell, but antifreeze can be fatal if ingested.

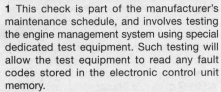

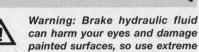

19.2 Radiator drain plug (viewed from underneath)

Cooling system draining

1 With the engine completely cold, cover the radiator cap with a wad of rag, and slowly turn the cap anti-clockwise to relieve the pressure in the cooling system (a hissing sound may be heard). Wait until any pressure remaining in the system is released, then continue to turn the cap until it can be removed.

2 Position a suitable container beneath the radiator drain plug located at the left-hand end of the radiator, then completely unscrew the drain plug and allow the coolant to drain into the container **(see illustration)**.

3 Once all the coolant has drained, tighten the drain plug securely.

Radiator flushing

4 Refer to Chapter 3 Section 3.

Cooling system filling

5 Before attempting to fill the cooling system, make sure that all hoses and clips are in good condition, and that the clips are tight. Note that an antifreeze mixture must be used all year round, to prevent corrosion of the engine components (see below).

6 Place the heater controls in the maximum heat position.

Note: *The MX-5 cooling system may be filled with two different types of antifreeze. A sticker affixed to, or adjacent to, the coolant expansion tank filler cap identifies if the system has been filled with FL22 antifreeze (Long-Life). If no sticker is present, assume that non-FL22 antifreeze has been used, and proceed under the appropriate heading as follows:*

FL22 antifreeze

7 FL22 is supplied as a pre-diluted solution – no additional water should be added.

8 Remove the filler cap, and slowly fill the system to prevent airlocks from forming. Bring the level up to the 'F' mark on the side of the reservoir.

Non-FL22 antifreeze

9 Remove the radiator cap, and fill the system by slowly pouring the coolant into the radiator to prevent airlocks from forming.

10 If the coolant is being renewed, begin by pouring in a couple of litres of water, followed by the correct quantity of antifreeze, then top-up with more water. Periodically squeeze the radiator top and bottom hoses to help expel any trapped air in the system.

Note: *Mazda recommend that demineralised water should be used.*

19.11 Fill the expansion tank to the 'F' mark

11 Fill the expansion tank to the 'F' mark **(see illustration)**.

All antifreeze

12 Refit the radiator pressure cap, then start the engine and allow it to idle until it reaches normal operating temperature.

Caution: If the temperature gauge indicates an overheating condition, stop the engine and allow it to cool completely, then recheck the coolant level.

Caution: If the coolant level falls below the 'L' mark on the reservoir during this procedure, stop the engine, allow it to cool, then add coolant up to the 'F', and continue the operation.

13 Once the engine has warmed up, increase the engine speed to 2500 rpm and hold it there for 5 minutes, then increase the engine speed to 3000 rpm for 5 seconds and allow it to return to idle.

14 Repeat the procedure in Paragraph 13 four times, then stop the engine and allow it to cool completely.

15 Top-up the expansion tank if necessary. Note that the system must be cold before an accurate level is indicated.

Antifreeze mixture

16 The antifreeze should always be renewed at the specified intervals. This is necessary not only to maintain the antifreeze properties, but also to prevent corrosion which would otherwise occur as the corrosion inhibitors become progressively less effective.

17 Always use a monoethylene-glycol based silicate-free antifreeze of the specified type (see *Lubricants and fluids* in *Weekly checks*). The quantity of antifreeze and levels of protection are indicated in the Specifications.

18 The MX-5 cooling system may be filled with two different types of antifreeze. A sticker affixed to, or adjacent to, the coolant expansion tank filler cap identifies if the system has been filled with FL22 antifreeze (Long-Life) **(see illustration)**. If no sticker is present, assume that non-FL22 antifreeze has been used.

19 Before adding antifreeze, the cooling system should be completely drained,

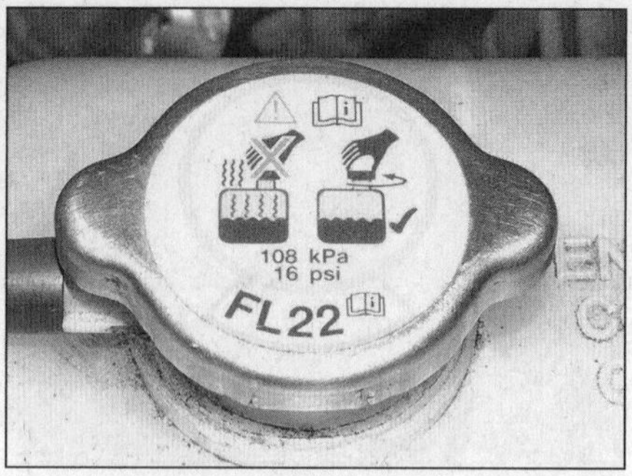

19.18 Note the FL22 sticker on the cap

preferably flushed, and all hoses checked for condition and security.

20 After filling with antifreeze, a label should be attached to the expansion tank, stating the type and concentration of antifreeze used, and the date installed. Any subsequent topping-up should be made with the same type and concentration of antifreeze.

Caution: Do not use engine antifreeze in the windscreen washer system, as it will cause damage to the vehicle paintwork. A screenwash additive should be added to the washer system in the quantities stated on the bottle.

20 Air filter cleaning and renewal

1 The air filter is located inside a housing on the left front corner of the engine compartment.

2 Release the clips attaching the air cleaner cover to the housing, then separate the housing halves and remove the air filter element **(see illustrations)**.

3 Inspect the outer surface of the filter element. If it is dirty, renew it. If it is only moderately dusty, it can be re-used by blowing it clean from the back to the front surface with compressed air. Because it is a pleated paper type filter, it cannot be washed or oiled. If it cannot be cleaned satisfactorily with compressed air, discard and renew it. While the cover is off, be careful not to drop anything down into the housing.

Caution: Never drive the vehicle with the air cleaner removed. Excessive engine wear could result and backfiring could even cause a fire under the bonnet.

4 Wipe out the inside of the air cleaner housing with a damp cloth.

5 Place the new filter into the air cleaner housing, making sure it seats properly.

6 Refitting of the cover is the reverse of removal.

21 Evaporative loss system check

1 Refer to Chapter 4B, Section 2, and check that all wiring and hoses are correctly connected to the evaporative loss system components.

22 Manual transmission oil renewal

1 At the specified time intervals, the manual transmission oil should be drained and renewed.

2 Before beginning work, purchase the specified oil and a new drain plug washer/seal.

3 The oil should be drained immediately after the vehicle has been driven. Hot oil is more effective than cold oil at removing built up sediment. Wear protective gloves.

4 After the vehicle has been driven to warm up the oil, raise the vehicle and support it securely on axle stands (see *Jacking and vehicle support*). Make sure it is safely supported and as level as possible.

5 Remove the transmission undershield **(see illustration)**.

6 Place the drain pan under the transmission

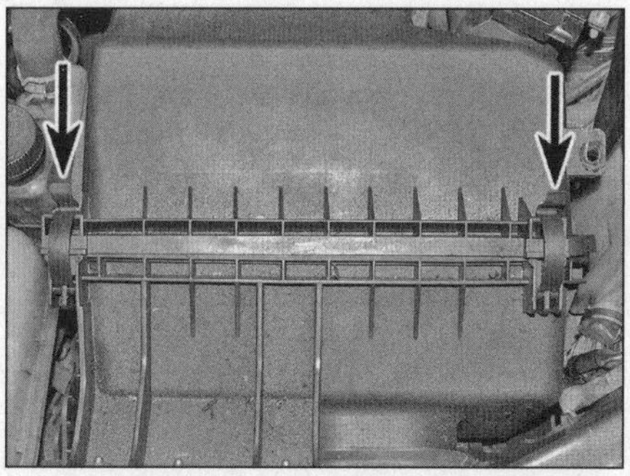

20.2a Release the clips and separate the housing halves

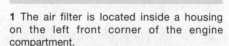

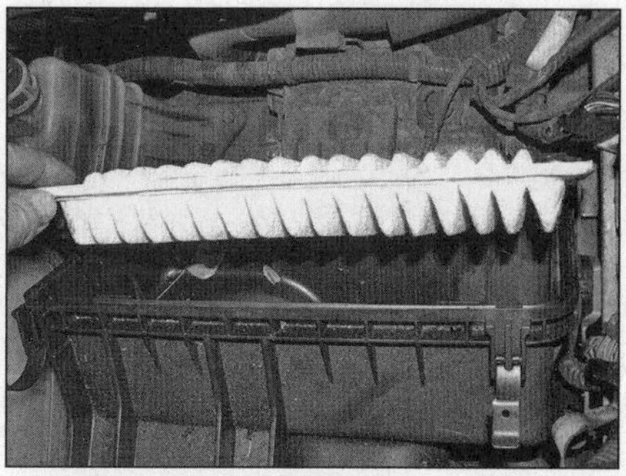

20.2b Note the orientation of the filter element

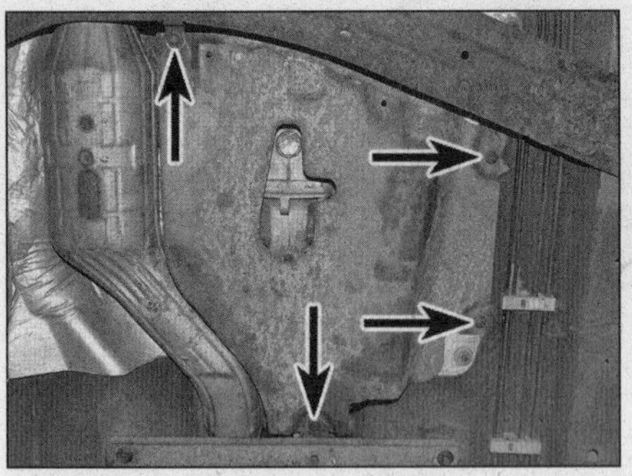

22.5 Transmission undershield fasteners

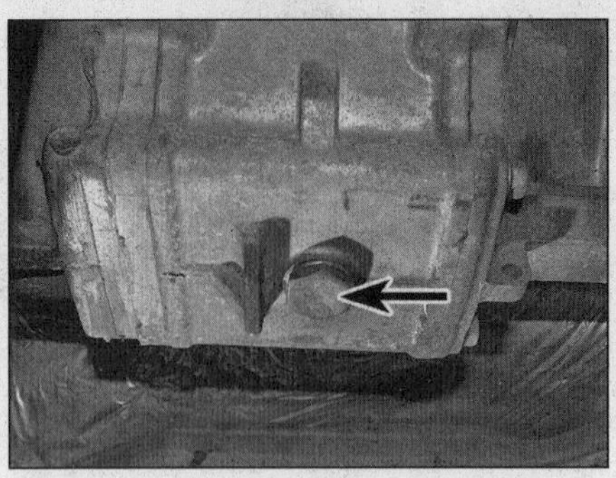

22.6a Transmission drain plug – 5-speed models

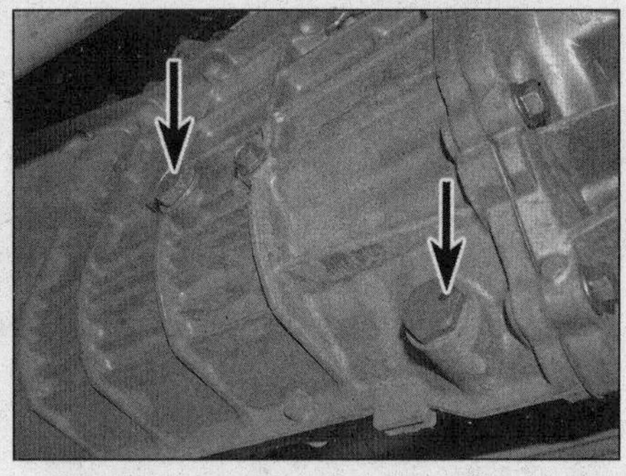

22.6b Transmission drain and filler/level plugs... 6-speed models

and slacken the drain plug **(see illustrations)**.

7 Carefully unscrew the drain plug and washer with your fingers. Be careful not to burn yourself on the oil.

8 Allow the oil to drain completely. Clean the drain plug then refit it with a new washer. Tighten the drain plug to the specified torque.

9 Unscrew the filler/level plug from the left-hand side of the transmission **(see illustration)**.

10 Add the new oil to the transmission, until it's level with the bottom of the filler/level hole. A hand pump or large syringe will be required for this. Do not overfill.

11 Refit the filler/level plug and tighten it to the specified torque.

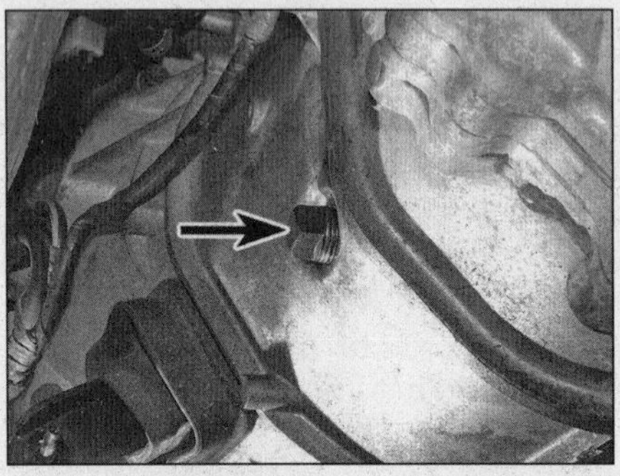

22.9 Transmission oil filler/level plug – 5-speed models

23 Final drive oil renewal

1 The oil should be drained immediately after the vehicle has been driven. Hot oil is more effective than cold oil at removing built up sediment. Wear protective gloves.

2 After the vehicle has been driven to warm up the oil, raise the vehicle and support it securely on axle stands (see *Jacking and vehicle support*). Make sure it is safely supported and as level as possible.

3 Place the drain pan under the final drive and slacken the drain plug **(see illustration)**.

4 Carefully unscrew the drain plug and washer with your fingers. Be careful not to burn yourself on the oil.

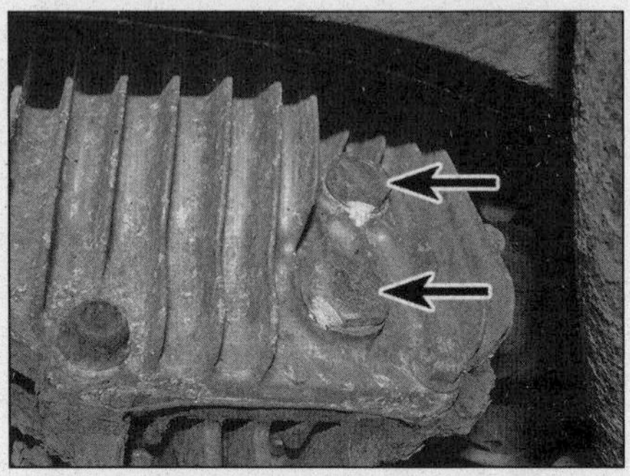

23.3 Final drive oil drain and filler/level plugs (arrowed)

5 Allow the oil to drain completely. Clean the drain plug then refit it with a new washer. Tighten the drain plug to the specified torque.

6 With the engine off, add new oil to the final drive through the filler/level plug hole.

7 Refit the filler/level plug and tighten it to the specified torque.

24 Remote control battery renewal

1 Depress the release button and unfold the key blade from the fob.

2 Insert a small flat-bladed screwdriver into the slot in the side of the key fob, depress the tab, and slid the blade-end fitting from the fob **(see illustration)**.

3 Insert the screwdriver into the slot in the now exposed end of the fob, twist slightly and separate the two halves **(see illustration)**.

4 Note the orientation of the battery, and remove it from the casing.

5 Insert the new battery into place, with the positive (+) side downwards **(see illustration)**. Avoid touching the battery or the terminals with bare fingers.

6 Snap the 2 halves of the control together, slide the end fitting back into place, and check for correct operation.

25 Valve clearance check and adjustment

1 The importance of having the valve clearances correctly adjusted cannot be overstressed, as they vitally affect the

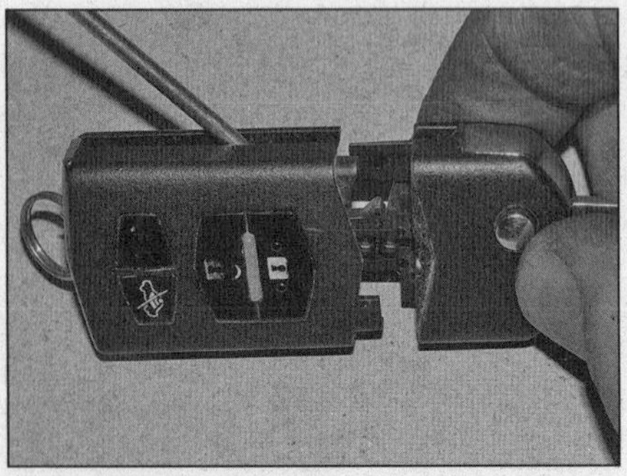

24.2 Depress the tab and detach the blade-end fitting

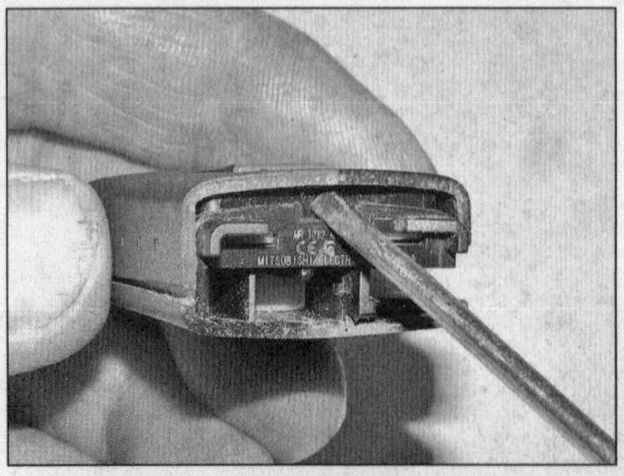

24.3 Twist the screwdriver and separate the fob halves

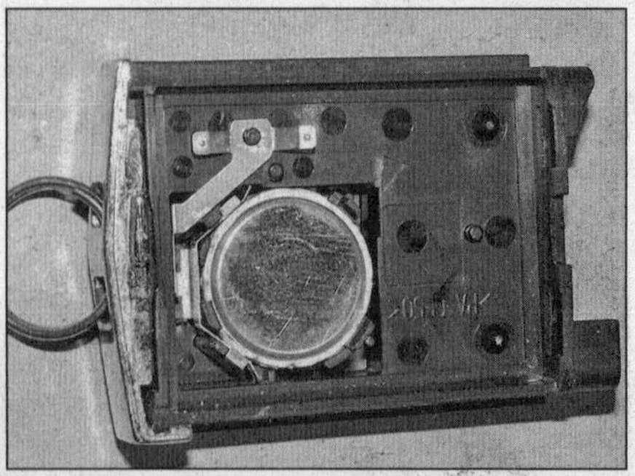

24.5 Insert the new battery with the positive (+) side down

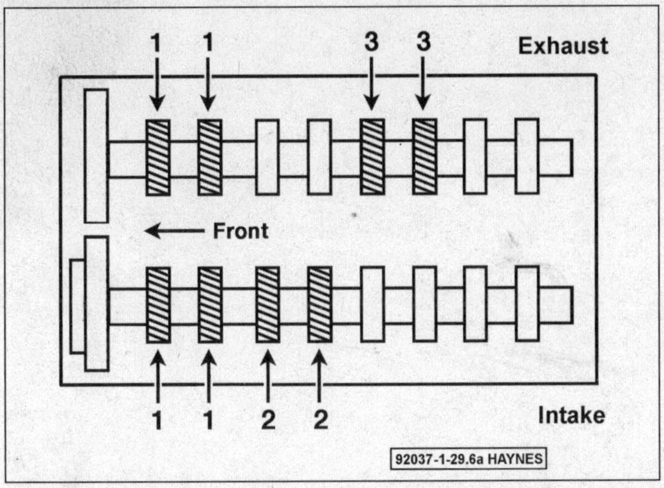

25.5a When the No.1 piston is at TDC on the compression stroke, the valve clearances for the No.1 and No.3 exhaust valves and the No.1 and No.2 inlet valves can be measured

25.5b Measure the clearance between the base of the camshaft lobe and the follower using feeler gauges

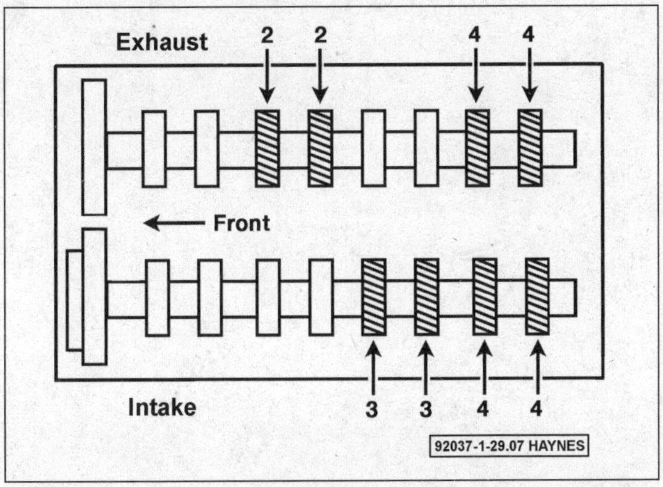

25.6 When the No.4 piston is at TDC on the compression stroke, the valve clearance for the No.2 and No.4 exhaust valves and the No.3 and No.4 inlet valves can be measured

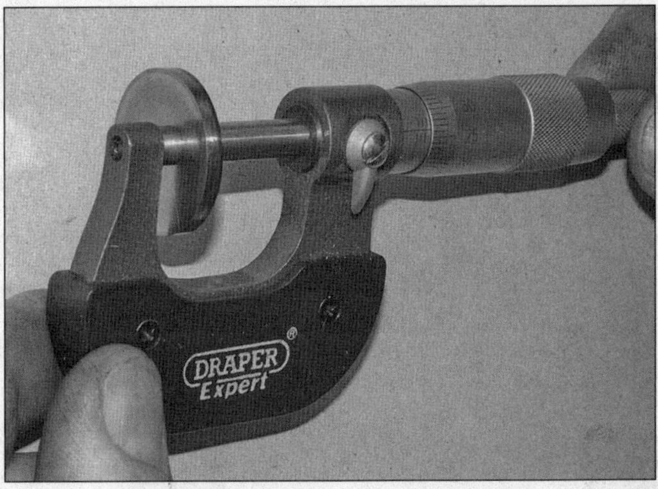

25.8 Use a micrometer to measure the shims

performance of the engine. The engine must be cold for the check to be accurate. The clearances are checked as follows.

2 Remove all spark plugs as described in Section 16.

3 Remove the cylinder head cover as described in Chapter 2A, Section 4.

4 Set the engine to TDC on the compression stroke for No. 1 piston (see Chapter 2A Section 3). Note that there is no need to lock the engine in this position at this stage.

Caution: Turn the engine only in the normal direction of rotation (clockwise) from the front of the vehicle.

5 Using feeler gauges, measure the clearance of the indicated valves **(see illustrations)** between the base of the camshaft lobe and the follower. Record all four clearances. The desired clearances are given in this Chapters Specifications. Note that clearances for inlet and exhaust valves are different.

6 Turn the crankshaft clockwise 360° to bring cylinder No.4 to TDC on the compression stroke, then measure the clearances for the indicated valves **(see illustration)**.

7 If adjustment is required, the followers must be changed by removing the camshaft(s) over the affected valve(s) as described in Chapter 2A Section 8.

8 If the valve clearance was too small, a follower with a thinner head must be fitted. If the clearance was too large, a follower with a thicker head must be fitted. The followers may have a number indicating their thickness on the inside, but if not, a micrometer will be needed to establish follower thickness **(see illustration)**.

9 To calculate the correct thickness of a replacement follower that will place the valve clearance within the specified value, use the following formula:

$N = T + (A - V)$

T = thickness of the old follower

A = valve clearance measured

N = thickness of the new follower

V = desired valve clearance

10 With the correct thickness followers installed, refit the camshafts (Chapter 2A Section 8).

11 Check that the valve clearances are now correct, as described earlier in this Section.

12 If any clearances are still not within specification, carry out the adjustment procedure again.

13 It will be helpful for future adjustment is a record is kept of the thickness of follower installed at each position.

Chapter 2 Part A
Engine in-car repair procedures

Contents

Degrees of difficulty

Easy, suitable for novice with little experience	**Fairly easy,** suitable for beginner with some experience	**Fairly difficult,** suitable for competent DIY mechanic	**Difficult,** suitable for experienced DIY mechanic	**Very difficult,** suitable for expert DIY or professional

Specifications

General

Engine code:	
1798 cc engine	L8
1999 cc engine	LF
Bore:	
1.8 litre	83.0 mm
2.0 litre	87.5 mm
Stroke:	
1.8 litre	83.1 mm
2.0 litre	83.1 mm
Direction of engine rotation	Clockwise (viewed from front of vehicle)
No 1 cylinder location	Timing chain end
Firing order	1-3-4-2
Minimum compression pressure:	
1.8 litre	12.0 bar (177.64 psi) @ 300 rpm
2.0 litre	11.8 bar (174.58 psi) @ 300 rpm
Maximum compression difference between cylinders	2.0 bar

Camshafts

Endfloat	0.24 mm max

Lubrication system

Minimum oil pressure @ 3000 rpm (100°C oil temperature):	
1.8 litre	2.3 – 5.1 bar (33.9 – 75.5 psi)
2.0 litre	3.3 – 5.8 bar (49.0 – 85.8 psi)

Cylinder head bolt shank length

New	145.2 – 145.8 mm
Maximum	146.5 mm

Torque wrench settings

Torque wrench settings	Nm	lbf ft
Auxiliary drivebelt idler pulley bolts	20	15
Camshaft bearing cap bolts:		
Stage 1	8	6
Stage 2	15	11
Camshaft sprocket bolts	72	53
Crankshaft hub/sprocket bolt: *		
Stage 1	100	74
Stage 2	Angle-tighten a further 90°	
Cylinder block lower blind plug	20	15
Cylinder head bolts: (see text)		
Stage 1	5	4
Stage 2	15	11
Stage 3	45	33
Stage 4	Angle-tighten a further 90°	
Stage 5	Angle-tighten a further 90°	
Cylinder head cover bolts	8	6
Front subframe bolts:		
Front outer bolts	100	74
Front inner bolts	110	81
Rear bolts	90	66
Engine mountings:		
Mounting-to-subframe nuts	90	66
Mounting-to-bracket nuts	90	66
Mounting brackets-to-cylinder block/sump bolts	45	33
Transmission-to-power frame nuts	140	103
Flywheel bolts*	112	82
Intake manifold bolts	18	14
Main bearing support plate bolts	20	15
Oil control valve (VVT)	10	7
Oil pick-up pipe	11	8
Oil pressure switch	15	11
Oil pump bolts:		
Stage 1	10	7
Stage 2	20	15
Oil pump sprocket bolt	25	18
Rear cross-brace bolts	23	16
Rear oil seal housing bolts	10	7
Sump-to-engine block bolts	20	15
Sump-to-transmission bolts	45	33
Sump oil drain plug	35	26
Timing chain cover bolts:		
18 shorter bolts	10	7
4 longer bolts	45	33
Timing chain guide bolts	10	7

**Do not re-use*

1 General Information

How to use this Chapter

1 This Chapter describes the repair procedures that can reasonably be carried out on the engine while it remains in the vehicle. If the engine has been removed from the vehicle and is being dismantled as described in Part B, any preliminary dismantling procedures can be ignored.

2 Part B describes the removal of the engine/transmission from the car, and the full overhaul procedures that can then be carried out.

Engine description

3 The 4-cylinder engines in this Chapter are of double overhead camshaft 16 valve design, mounted in-line, with the transmission bolted to the rear end. Engine sizes are 1.8 litre or 2.0 litre with various power/torque outputs depending on market/specification. Although different in size, the basic design of the engines is identical. These engines were equipped with variable intake camshaft timing, where the relationship of the sprocket to the camshaft is varied by hydraulic pressure, controlled by the engine management ECM. The result of this system is improved driveability, with lower emissions.

4 The two camshafts are driven by a timing chain, itself driven by a sprocket on the front end of the crankshaft. Each camshaft acts directly upon the camshaft followers, which are located directly above their respective valves. Solid followers are fitted with interchangeable shims to adjust the valve clearances.

5 The crankshaft is supported in five main bearings of the usual shell-type. Endfloat is controlled by thrustwashers fitted each side of No 2 or 5 upper main bearing.

6 The pistons are selected to be of matching weight, and incorporate fully-floating gudgeon pins retained by circlips, and are cooled by oil jets bolted to the inside of the cylinder block.

7 The rotor-type oil pump is located at the front of the engine, and is driven by a chain from a crankshaft sprocket.

Operations with engine in car

8 The following operations can be carried out without having to remove the engine from the vehicle:

- Removal and refitting of the cylinder head.
- Removal and refitting of the timing chain and sprockets.
- Removal and refitting of the camshafts.
- Removal and refitting of the sump.
- Removal and refitting of the oil pump.
- Renewal of the engine/transmission mountings.
- Removal and refitting of the flywheel.

2 Compression test – description and interpretation

1 When engine performance is down, or if misfiring occurs which cannot be attributed to the ignition or fuel systems, a compression test can provide diagnostic clues as to the engine's condition. If the test is performed regularly, it can give warning of trouble before any other symptoms become apparent.

2 The engine must be fully warmed-up to normal operating temperature, the battery must be fully charged, and all the spark plugs must be removed (Chapter 1, Section 16). The aid of an assistant will also be required.

3 Disable the fuel system by removing the fuel pump relay (see Chapter 12, Section 4).

4 Fit a compression tester to the No 1 cylinder spark plug hole – the type of tester which screws into the plug thread is to be preferred.

5 Have the assistant fully depress the throttle pedal, and crank the engine on the starter motor. After one or two revolutions, the compression pressure should build up to a maximum figure, and then stabilise. Record the highest reading obtained.

6 Repeat the test on the remaining cylinders, recording the pressure in each.

7 All cylinders should produce very similar pressures; a difference of more than 2 bars between any two cylinders indicates a fault. Note that the compression should build up quickly in a healthy engine; low compression on the first stroke, followed by gradually-increasing pressure on successive strokes, indicates worn piston rings. A low compression reading on the first stroke, which does not build up during successive strokes, indicates leaking valves or a blown head gasket (a cracked head could also be the cause). Deposits on the undersides of the valve heads can also cause low compression.

8 Mazda recommended values for compression pressures are given in the Specifications.

9 If the pressure in any cylinder is low, carry out the following test to isolate the cause. Introduce a teaspoonful of clean oil into that cylinder through its spark plug hole, and repeat the test.

10 If the addition of oil temporarily improves the compression pressure, this indicates that bore or piston wear is responsible for the pressure loss. No improvement suggests that leaking or burnt valves, or a blown head gasket, may be to blame.

11 A low reading from two adjacent cylinders is almost certainly due to the head gasket having blown between them; the presence of coolant in the engine oil will confirm this.

12 If one cylinder is about 20 percent lower than the others and the engine has a slightly rough idle, a worn camshaft lobe could be the cause.

13 If the compression reading is unusually high, the combustion chambers are probably coated with carbon deposits. If this is the case, the cylinder head should be removed and decarbonised.

14 On completion of the test, refit the spark plugs (see Chapter 1, Section 16) and refit the fuel pump relay.

3 Top Dead Center (TDC) for number 1 piston – locating

Note: *You will need two special tools for this procedure: the camshaft positioning tool, Mazda part no. 49 JE01 054, and the timing pin Mazda part no. 303-507 (1.8 litre) or part no. 49 N010 101 (2.0 litre models). Equivalent aftermarket tools are available. Try www.asttools.co.uk*

1 Remove the battery cover and disconnect the cable from the negative battery terminal (see Chapter 5A Section 4).

2 Remove the cylinder head cover (Section 4).

3 Using a spanner or socket on the crankshaft pulley bolt, rotate the crankshaft clockwise until the inlet valves for no. 1 cylinder have opened and just closed again.

4 A TDC timing hole is located near the lower right front corner of the engine block to provide a means of accurately positioning the no. 1 cylinder at TDC. When you locate this hole, remove the timing pin plug **(see illustration)**.

5 Screw in the timing pin **(see illustration)**.

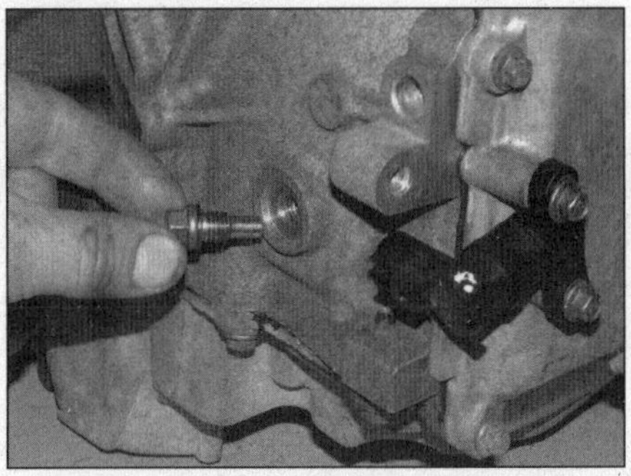

3.4 Remove the timing hole plug...

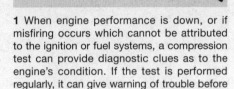

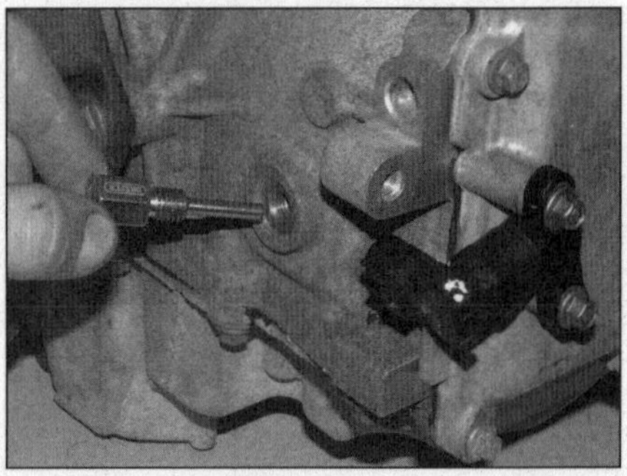

3.5... and insert the timing pin tool

3.7a Turn the engine so that the camshaft end slots are aligned...

3.7b... then insert the metal strip into the slots to locate and set the shafts to TDC

Caution: We don't recommend trying to fabricate a timing pin with a bolt because while you would be able to determine the correct bolt diameter and thread pitch, it is impossible to determine what the length of the bolt should be. These pins come in several lengths, depending on the engine family. There is no way to determine the correct pin length without comparing it to a factory or aftermarket tool designed to be used with this engine. Using a bolt of the wrong length could damage the engine. Also, never use the timing pin as a means to stop the engine from rotating – tool breakage and/or engine damage can result.

6 Turn the crankshaft slowly clockwise until the crankshaft counterweight comes into contact with the timing pin – in this position, the engine is set to TDC on no. 1 cylinder.

7 The camshafts each have a machined slot at the transmission end of the engine. Both slots will be completely horizontal, and at the same height as the cylinder head machined surface, when the engine is at TDC on the Number 1 cylinder. Manufacturer service tool 49 JE01 054 is used to check this position, and to positively locate the camshafts in position. Fortunately, a substitute tool can be made from a strip of metal 5 mm thick. While the strip's thickness is critical, its length and width are not, but should be approximately 180 to 230 mm long by 20 to 30 mm wide **(see illustrations)**.

Caution: Never use the camshaft alignment tool as a means to stop the engine from rotating – engine damage can result.

8 Before rotating the crankshaft again, make sure that the tools are removed. Do not forget to install the blanking plug and tighten it securely.

9 Once no. 1 cylinder has been positioned at TDC on the compression stroke, TDC for any of the other cylinders can then be located by rotating the crankshaft clockwise 180-degrees at a time and following the firing order.

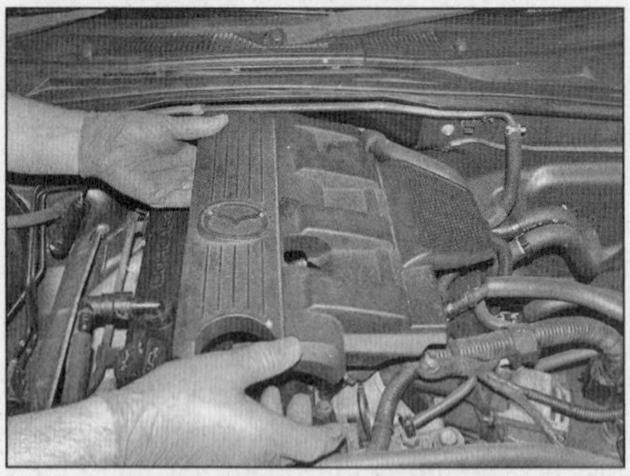

4.2 Pull the cover upwards

4.3a Press-in the clip each side...

4 Cylinder head cover – removal and refitting

Removal

1 Disconnect the battery negative lead as described in Chapter 5A Section 4.

2 Pull the engine cover upwards from its mountings **(see illustration)**.

3 Detach the PCV (Positive Crankcase Ventilation) breather hose from the cylinder head cover **(see illustrations)**.

4 Where fitted, remove the front strut brace as described in Chapter 10 Section 8.

5 Disconnect the wiring plug then undo the bolt and remove the camshaft position sensor **(see illustration)**.

6 Disconnect the wiring plug from the OCV (Oil Control Valve) at the front of the cover **(see illustration)**.

7 Remove the ignition coils as described in Chapter 5B, Section 3.

8 Remove the bracket for the wiring harness on the cylinder head cover stud at the rear of the cylinder head, unclip the harness at the front, and move them to one side.

9 Remove the bolts attaching the cylinder head cover to the cylinder head in the reverse of the sequence shown **(see illustration 4.17)**.

10 Pull out the oil level dipstick.

11 Disconnect any tubing or other connected components and move them out of the way, and remove the cylinder head cover. If the cover sticks, knock it loose with a rubber mallet or a hammer and a block of wood. Do not pry between the sealing surfaces.

12 Discard the rubber gaskets, new ones must be fitted.

Refitting

13 The mating surfaces of the housing or cylinder head and cover must be clean when the cover is installed. Carefully use a gasket scraper to remove all traces of sealant and old gasket material – be careful to not gouge the

4.3b... and disconnect the breather hose from the cover

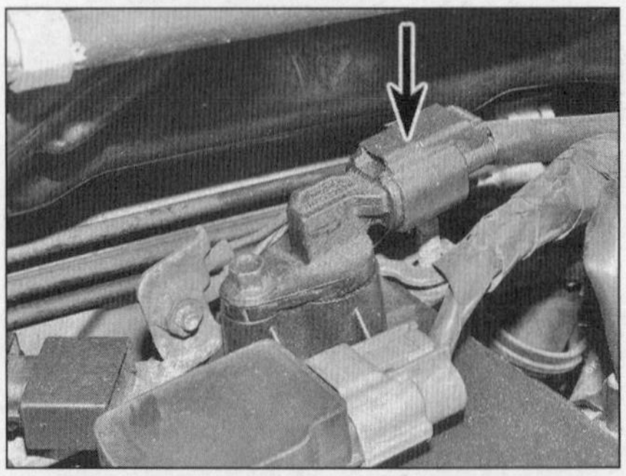

4.5 Camshaft position sensor wiring plug

4.6 Disconnect the OCV wiring plug

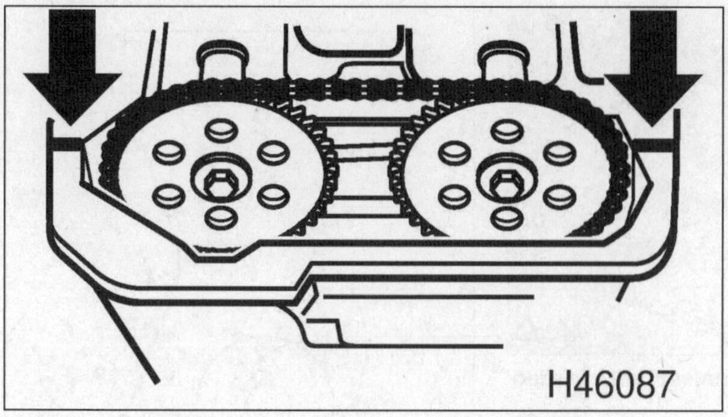

4.15 ... and rear of the cylinder head

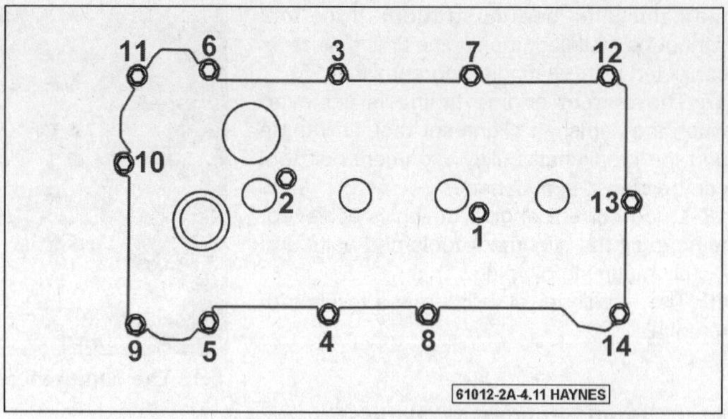

4.17 Cylinder head cover bolts TIGHTENING sequence

gasket surfaces when cleaning. Then clean the mating surfaces. If there is residue or oil on the mating surfaces when the cover is installed, oil leaks may develop.

14 Press the gaskets into the grooves of the cylinder head cover.

15 At the top of the timing chain cover, apply a thin bead of RTV sealant to the joints where the cylinder head and timing chain cover meet **(see illustration)**.

16 Position the cylinder head cover in place and insert the bolts by hand, starting the threads several turns before using a socket/spanner.

17 Following the recommended sequence **(see illustration)**, tighten the bolts to the specified torque.

18 The remainder of refitting is a reversal of removal.

19 Run the engine and check for oil leaks.

5 Crankshaft pulley – removal and installation

Removal

Caution: Once the crankshaft pulley is slackened, the crankshaft (timing) sprocket will be loose as well. The engine is considered out-of-time at this point. The installation procedure in this Section must be followed exactly to re-time the engine properly. Severe engine damage may occur otherwise.

1 Remove the auxiliary drivebelt (see Chapter 1 Section 6).

2 Set the engine to TDC using the camshaft and crankshaft positioning tools (see Section 3).

3 The crankshaft must be held to prevent its rotation while the pulley bolt is unscrewed. A special tool (205-072) to hold the crankshaft pulley is needed for this. A suitable equivalent can be fabricated from a length of strap steel, bolts, washers and nuts **(see illustration)**.

Caution: Use of a prybar or similar tool can damage the crankshaft pulley.

4 Insert the holding tool into the spaces in the front face of the pulley to hold it in place while turning the crankshaft pulley bolt with a large spanner or socket/breaker-bar combination.

Caution: Failure to hold the crankshaft pulley securely while removing the pulley bolt could result in engine damage. NEVER use the timing pin or the camshaft alignment tool as a means of locking the crankshaft – they are designed for calibration only. Engine damage could occur by using these tools for anything other than their intended purpose.

5 Unscrew the pulley bolt and remove the holding tool.

Installation

6 Lightly coat the crankshaft front seal with clean engine oil, then install the crankshaft pulley. Note: If the seal shows signs of leakage, you may want to replace it before installing the crankshaft pulley (see Section 12). Install a new crankshaft pulley bolt and washer and hand tighten only. Attempt to closely align the hole in the pulley with the threaded hole in the timing chain cover.

7 Install a crankshaft pulley alignment bolt (M6 x 18 mm) through the pulley and into the front engine cover (hand-tight only) **(see illustration)**. Rotate the pulley as necessary to do this. Note: This correctly aligns the pulley with the crankshaft.

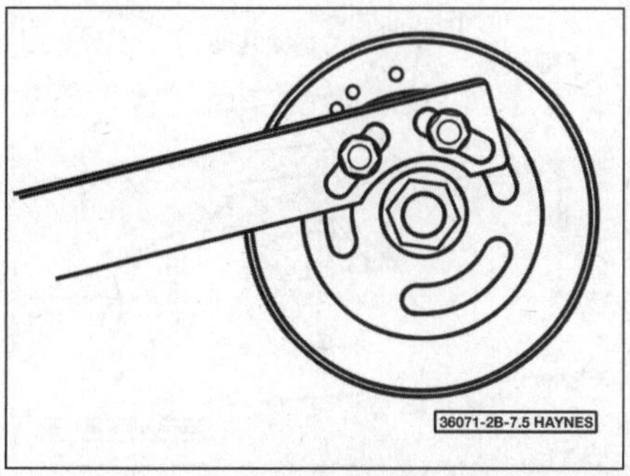

5.3 The crankshaft pulley holding tool installed

8 Insert the holding tool into the pulley and tighten the crankshaft pulley bolt to the specified torque.

9 Remove the crankshaft pulley holding tool and the threaded crankshaft alignment bolt from the pulley and front engine cover.

10 Remove the timing pin from the cylinder block.

11 Remove the camshaft alignment tool.

12 Remove the spark plugs and rotate the engine clockwise two complete revolutions by turning the crankshaft pulley bolt with a wrench or large socket.

Caution: If you feel resistance at any point, stop and find out why. If the valve timing is incorrect, the valves may be contacting the pistons.

13 Rotate the engine again to achieve TDC (see Section 3). Note: Rotate the engine in the clockwise direction only.

14 Install the timing pin into the cylinder block.

15 Install the crankshaft pulley alignment bolt (M6 x 18 mm). If it cannot be installed, the crankshaft pulley must be removed and aligned. Repeat Steps 6 through 15 until crankshaft pulley alignment is correct.

16 With the crankshaft pulley alignment bolt (M6 x 18 mm) installed, install the camshaft alignment tool and check the position of

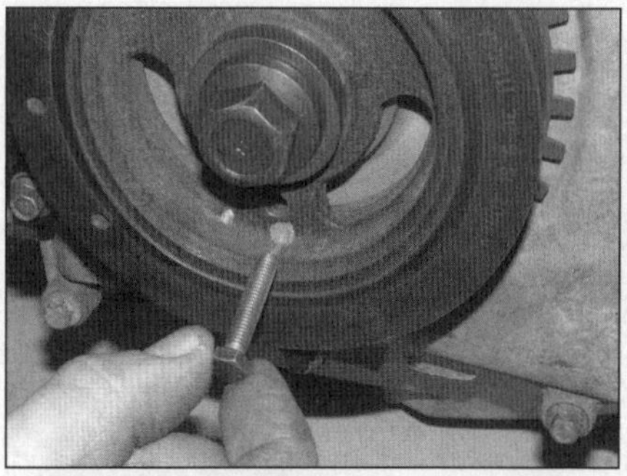

5.7 To properly align the crankshaft pulley, insert an M6 bolt through the hole in the pulley and screw it into the timing chain cover

the camshafts **(see illustration)**. If the tool cannot be installed, the engine timing must be corrected by repeating paragraphs 6 to 15.

17 The correct engine timing is achieved when the camshaft alignment tool, timing pin and the crankshaft pulley alignment bolt tool can be placed simultaneously.

18 Once correct engine timing is achieved, remove all the alignment tools and bolts and install the timing pin plug.

19 The remainder of refitting is a reversal of removal.

6 Timing chain cover, timing chain and tensioner – removal and installation

Timing chain cover

Removal

1 Remove the battery and battery tray as described in Chapter 5A Section 4.

2 Remove the air cleaner assembly as described in Chapter 4A Section 3.

3 Loosen the coolant pump pulley bolts, then remove the auxiliary drivebelt, the drivebelt idler pulley (see Chapter 1 Section 6), and the water pump pulley (see Section).

4 Remove the cylinder head cover as described in Section 4.

5 Remove the crankshaft pulley (see Section 5). After this procedure, the engine MUST remain at TDC.

6 Raise the front of the vehicle and support it securely on axle stands (see *Jacking and vehicle support*). Undo the fasteners and remove the engine undershields.

7 Remove the crankshaft position sensor as described in Chapter 4A Section 11.

8 With reference to Chapter 10 Section 18, unbolt the power steering pump and move it to one side. There's no need to disconnect the hoses.

9 Remove the crankshaft front oil seal (see Section 12).

10 Remove the bolts and the timing chain cover.

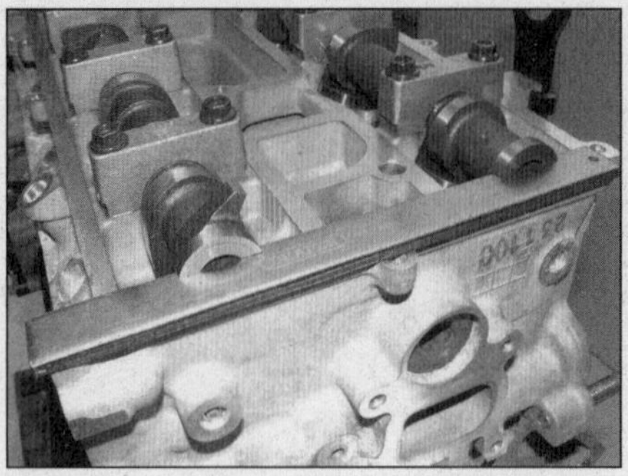

5.16 The camshaft alignment tool installed

Refitting

11 Installation is the reverse of removal, noting the following points:

a) Clean the mating surfaces of all sealant. Take care not to gouge, or use any abrasives on the mating surfaces.

*b) Tighten the timing chain cover retaining bolts a little at a time, in sequence **(see illustration)** to the specified torque.*

c) Renew the crankshaft front oil seal.

d) Be sure to re-time the engine as described in Section 5.

e) Timing chain and tensioner

Removal

12 Remove the timing chain cover as described previously in this Section.

13 If you need to remove the exhaust camshaft sprocket, slacken the sprocket bolt now, before you slacken anything else. Using a spanner on the hexagonal portion of the camshaft, hold the cam in place whilst slackening the sprocket bolt. **(see illustration 6.19)**. **Note:** *The inlet camshaft sprocket is integral with the variable valve timing actuator. The actuator can be removed, once the inlet camshaft has been removed as described in Section 8.*

Caution: Allowing the camshaft to rotate during this procedure could damage the valves.

14 Using a small screwdriver or pick, hold the chain tensioner ratchet arm away (UP) from the ratchet stem. Slowly compress the timing chain tensioner piston and place a pin

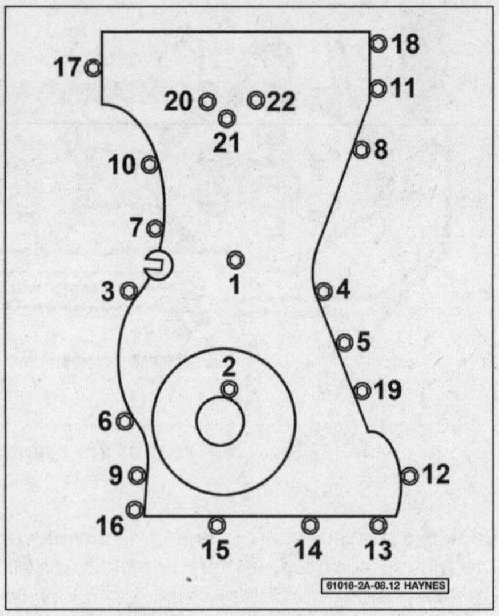

6.11 Timing chain cover bolt tightening sequence

(a drill bit or paper clip will work) into the hole to hold it in the compressed position **(see illustration)**. Note: The tensioner contacts the right-hand chain guide.Caution: Compress the round plunger and the ratchet mechanism. The ratchet is next to the plunger and has square sides. If the ratchet needs to be reset, perform the following steps**(see illustration)**:

a) Remove the tensioner and place it lightly in a vice using the plunger and tensioner housing.

b) Place a pick-type tool in the hole closest to the ratchet to relieve the tension on the ratchet mechanism.

c) While holding the pick tool in place, move the ratchet back into the tensioner, then install a pin into the other hole to keep the plunger and ratchet compressed.

d) Remove the tensioner from the vice.

15 Remove the two tensioner mounting bolts, then remove the tensioner.

16 Remove the loose timing chain guide (right-hand). Remove the timing chain.

17 The left-hand chain guide and exhaust camshaft sprocket can now be removed if necessary **(see illustration)**.

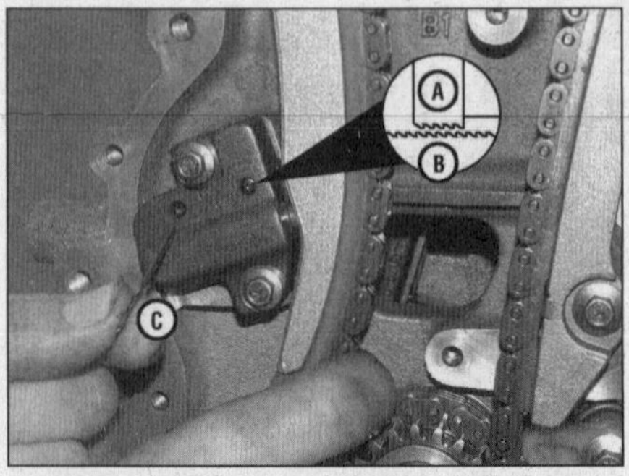

6.14a Compress the tensioner and insert the locking pin

A Ratchet arm B Ratchet stem C Locking pin

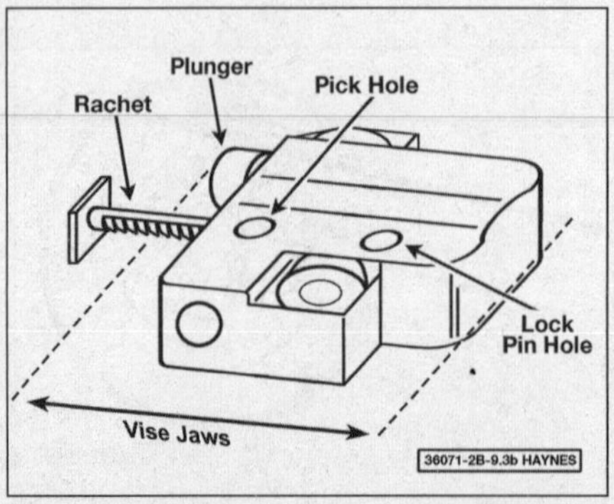

6.14b Timing chain tensioner reset details

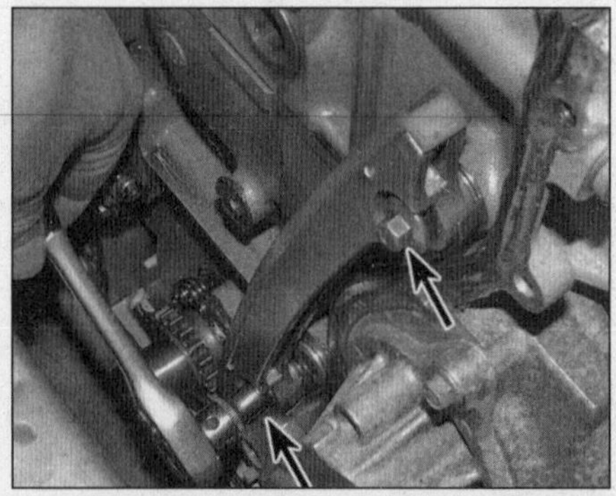

6.17 Undo the bolts and remove the left-hand timing chain guide.

6.19 Use a large spanner on the hex portion to hold the camshaft while removing/ installing the sprocket bolt (typical)

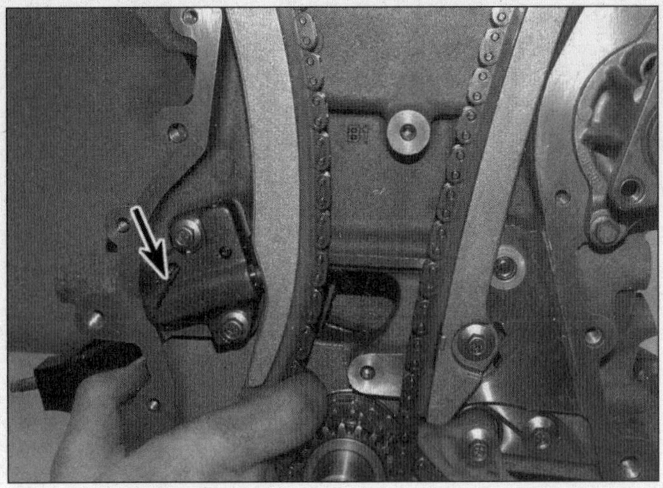

6.23 Compress the tensioner to release the lock pin

Installation

18 Remove the camshaft alignment tool (if installed).

19 Loosen, but don't remove, the exhaust camshaft sprocket bolt. Use a spanner on the hexagonal area of the camshaft to hold it while turning the camshaft sprocket bolt **(see illustration)**.

Caution: Damage to the valves or pistons may occur if the camshafts are rotated during this procedure.

20 Install the left-hand chain guide (if removed).

21 Install the timing chain.

22 Install the right-hand chain guide.

23 Install the timing chain tensioner and tighten the bolts to the specified torque. Remove the pin to release the tensioner to engage the chain guide **(see illustration)**.

24 Install the camshaft alignment tool.

25 Tighten the camshaft sprocket bolt to the specified torque while holding the camshaft in place with a wrench. **Note:** *Do not rely on the camshaft alignment tool to hold the camshafts while tightening the camshaft sprocket bolts. Tool and engine damage may occur.*

26 Refit the timing chain cover as described earlier in this Section.

7 Variable valve timing (VVT) – description and component renewal

Description

1 All engines were equipped with a mechanism which varied the relationship between the inlet camshaft and its drive sprocket. This is achieved by supplying engine oil under pressure to 'advance' or 'retard' chambers within the sprocket's variable timing actuator, bolted to the end of the camshaft. The flow of oil is controlled by an electrically operated solenoid valve, itself controlled by the engine management ECM. At low engine speed the camshaft is set in the retarded position to enhance torque output, and as the speed increases, the camshaft timing is advanced to enhance power output. The overall result is increased engine output, efficiency and driveability, with lower emissions.

Component renewal

Variable valve timing actuator

2 The actuator is integral with the inlet camshaft sprocket. In order to remove the sprocket, first remove the camshaft as described in Section 8.

3 Mark the orientation of the VVT actuator to the camshaft to ensure that the actuator in refitted in exactly the same position.

4 Secure the camshaft in a bench vice, Use plastic jaws to protect the camshaft from damage.

5 Unscrew the actuator bolt, remove the actuator and washer. Discard the washer – a new one must be fitted.

6 Using a new washer, refit the VVT actuator to the camshaft. Ensure the marks made during assembly are aligned.

7 Refit the camshaft as described in Section 8.

Oil control valve

8 The oil control valve is located on the cylinder head, between the camshafts.

9 Remove the cylinder head cover as described in Section 4.

10 Undo the retaining bolt and pull the valve from the cylinder head. Renew the O-ring seal.

11 With the valve removed, connect an ohmmeter across the valve terminals and check its resistance. The correct specification is 6.9 to 7.9 ohms. If the reading differs from this, the valve may be defective.

12 With no voltage applied to the valve, it should be in the 'fully retarded' position. Apply battery voltage to the valve and check that the spool valve within moved to the 'fully advanced' position, then returns to the original position once the voltage is removed.

13 Refitting is a reversal of removal, tightening the retaining bolt to the specified torque.

8 Camshafts and followers – removal, inspection and installation

Note: *Whenever the camshafts are to be removed for a procedure, it's a good idea to check the valve clearances before disassembly (see Chapter 1 Section 25), so any required new followers can be ordered from a dealership.*

Removal

1 Remove the timing chain (Section 6). Note: Before removing the timing chain, note the positions of the no. 1 cylinder cam lobes and the slots in the ends of the camshafts (for the alignment tool); when installing the camshafts, these must be in the same positions.

2 Remove the exhaust camshaft sprocket. When loosening the camshaft sprocket bolt, place a wrench on the hexagonal area of the camshaft to prevent it from turning **(see illustration 6.19)**.

3 All the camshaft bearing caps have a single-digit identifying number etched on them. The exhaust camshaft's bearing caps are numbered in sequence from 0 (right-hand cap) to 4 (left-hand cap); the intake's are numbered from 5 (right-hand cap) to 9 (left-hand cap). Each cap is to be installed

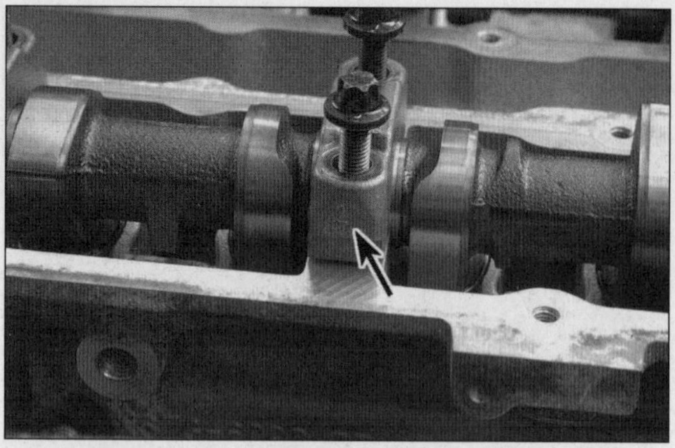

8.3 Location of the camshaft bearing cap designations

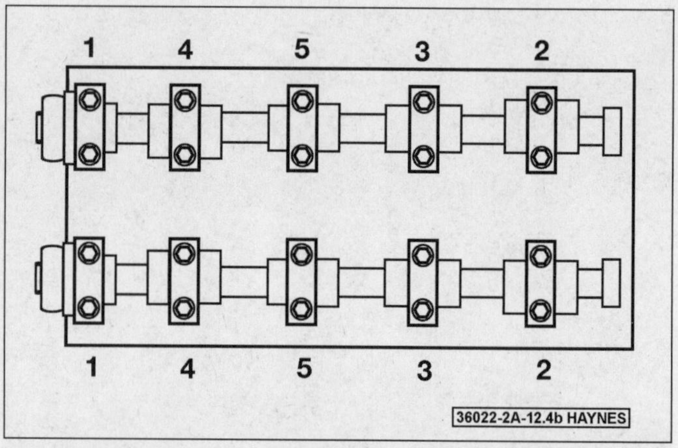

8.4 Camshaft bearing cap loosening sequence – loosen each pair of bolts on the designated bearing cap in sequence

so that its numbered side faces the same direction **(see illustration)**. If no marks are present, or they are hard to see, make your own – the bearing caps must be reinstalled in their original positions.

4 Working in the sequence shown, loosen the camshaft bearing cap bolts progressively by half a turn at a time **(see illustration)**. Work only as described, to gradually and evenly release the pressure of the valve springs on the caps.

5 Withdraw the caps, noting their markings and the presence of the locating dowels, then remove the camshafts. The intake camshaft can be identified by the reference lobe for the camshaft position sensor; therefore, there is no need to mark the camshafts.

6 Obtain sixteen small, clean containers, and number them 1 to 16. Using a rubber suction tool (such as a valve-lapping tool), withdraw each follower in turn and place them in the containers. Do not interchange the followers.

Inspection

7 With the camshafts and lifters removed, check each for signs of obvious wear (scoring, pitting, etc) and for roundness, replacing them if necessary.

8 Measure the outside diameter of each follower – take measurements at the top and bottom of each follower, then a second set at right-angles to the first; if any measurement is significantly different from the others, the follower is tapered or oval (as applicable) and must be replaced **(see illustration)**. If the necessary equipment is available, measure the inside diameter of the corresponding cylinder head bore. No manufacturer's specifications were available at the time of writing; if the followers or the cylinder head bores are excessively worn, new followers and/or a new cylinder head may be required.

9 If the engine's valve components have sounded noisy, it may be just that the valve clearances need adjusting. Although this is part of the routine maintenance schedule in Chapter 1 Section 25, the extended checking interval and the need for disassembly or special tools may result in the task being overlooked.

10 Visually examine the camshaft lobes for score marks, pitting, galling (wear due to rubbing) and evidence of overheating (blue, discolored areas). Look for flaking away of the hardened surface layer of each lobe. If any such signs are evident, replace the component concerned.

11 Examine the camshaft bearing journals and the cylinder head bearing surfaces for signs of obvious wear or pitting. If any such signs are evident, consult an automotive machine shop for advice. Also check that the bearing oilways in the cylinder head are clear **(see illustration)**.

12 Using a micrometer, measure the diameter of each journal at several points. If the diameter of any one journal is less than the specified value, replace the camshaft.

13 To check camshaft endplay, remove the followers, clean the bearing surfaces carefully and install the camshafts and bearing caps. Tighten the bearing cap bolts to the specified torque wrench setting, then measure the endplay using a dial indicator mounted on the cylinder head so that its tip bears on the camshaft right-hand end.

14 Tap the camshaft fully towards the gauge, zero the gauge, then tap the camshaft fully away from the gauge and note the gauge reading. If the endplay measured is found to be at or beyond the specified service limit, install a new camshaft and repeat the check; if the clearance is still excessive, the cylinder head must be replaced.

Refitting

15 Confirm that the crankshaft is still positioned at TDC and that the timing pin is in place.

16 Liberally oil the cylinder head lifter bores and the followers. Carefully install the followers to the cylinder head, ensuring that each follower is returned to its original bore.

17 Liberally oil the camshaft bearing surfaces in the cylinder head, taking care not to get any on the camshaft cap mating surface.

18 Ensuring that each camshaft is in its original location, install the camshafts, positioning each so that lobes for cylinder no. 1 are in the same position as noted in Step 1 and the slot in its left-hand end is parallel to, and just above, the cylinder head mating surface. Check that, as each camshaft is laid in position, the TDC setting tool will fit into the slot.

Caution: When the camshaft bearing caps are tightened, it is imperative that the camshafts do not rotate from their TDC positions.

19 Ensure that the locating dowels are pressed firmly into their recesses and check that all mating surfaces are completely clean, unmarked and free from oil.

20 Apply a little oil to the camshaft journals and lobes, then install each of the camshaft

8.8 Measure the followers outside diameter at several points

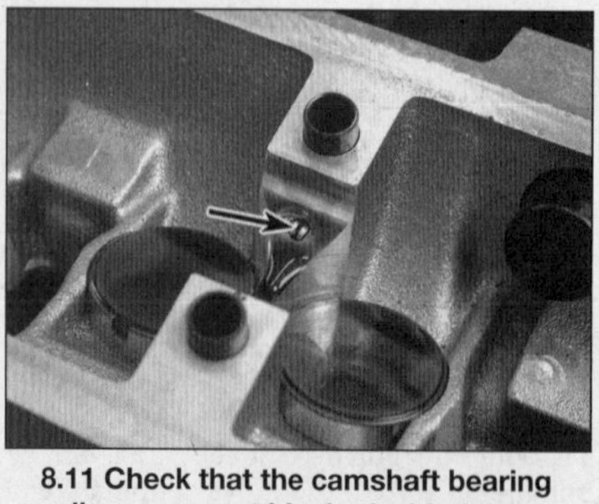

8.11 Check that the camshaft bearing oilways are not blocked with debris

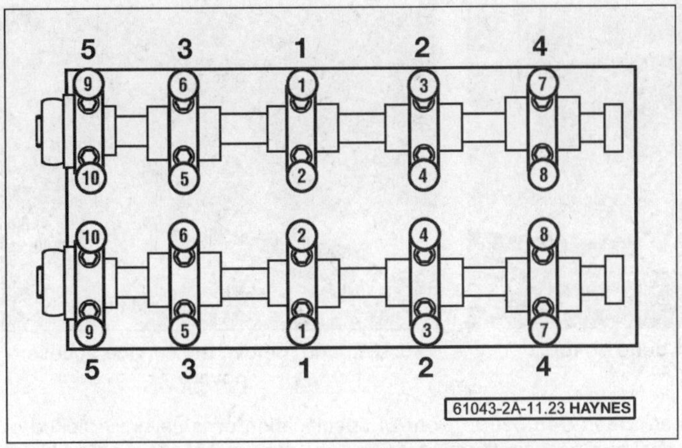

8.21 Camshaft bearing cap tightening sequence

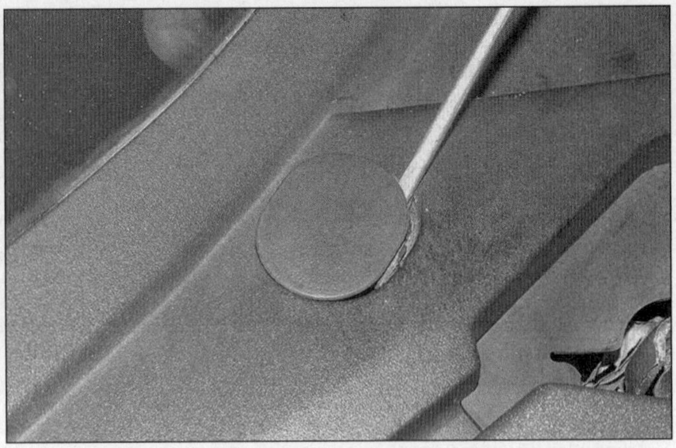

9.7 Prise up the caps, and remove the screw at each end

bearing caps to its original position, so that its numbered side faces outwards, to the front (exhaust) or to the rear (intake).

21 Ensuring that each cap is kept square to the cylinder head as it is evenly tightened down, and working in sequence **(see illustration)**, tighten the camshaft bearing cap bolts slowly and by one turn at a time, until each cap touches the cylinder head. This is the Stage 1 torque.

22 Using the same sequence, tighten the bearing cap bolts to the Stage 2 torque setting.

23 Tighten the bearing cap bolts to the Stage 3 torque setting.

24 Refit the exhaust camshaft sprocket, and finger-tighten the retaining bolt.

25 The remainder of the reassembly procedure, including replacement of the timing chain and setting the valve timing, is as described in Section 6.

26 Before installing the valve cover, check the valve clearances (see Chapter 1 Section 25).

9 Cylinder head – removal and installation

Warning: Wait until the engine is completely cool before beginning this procedure.

Removal

1 Relieve the fuel pressure (see Chapter 4A Section 7).

2 Remove the battery and battery tray as described in Chapter 5A Section 4.

3 Drain the coolant as described in Chapter 1 Section 19.

4 Remove the inlet manifold as described in Chapter 4A Section 12.

5 Remove the timing chain as described in Section 6.

6 Remove the wiper arms as described in Chapter 12 Section 14.

7 Prise up the plastic cap and remove the screw at each end of the windscreen cowl panel **(see illustration)**.

8 Unclip the washer hose from the cowl panel, and remove the rubber weatherstrip **(see illustration)**.

9 Pull up the front edge of the cowl panel, then pull it downwards from the base of the windscreen **(see illustration)**. Disconnect the washer hose as the panel is withdrawn.

10 Release the fasteners and remove the side cowl panel **(see illustrations)**.

11 Undo the nut, and unclip the heater pipe **(see illustration)**.

12 Undo the 8 bolts and remove the service

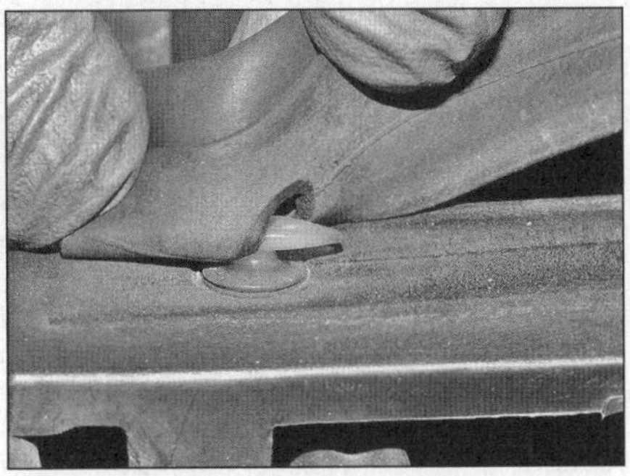

9.8 Pull the weatherstrip from the clips

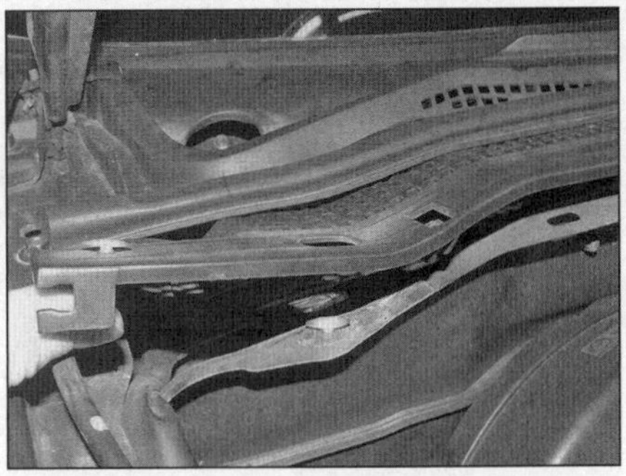

9.9 Pull up the front edge, then slide the pane down from the windscreen

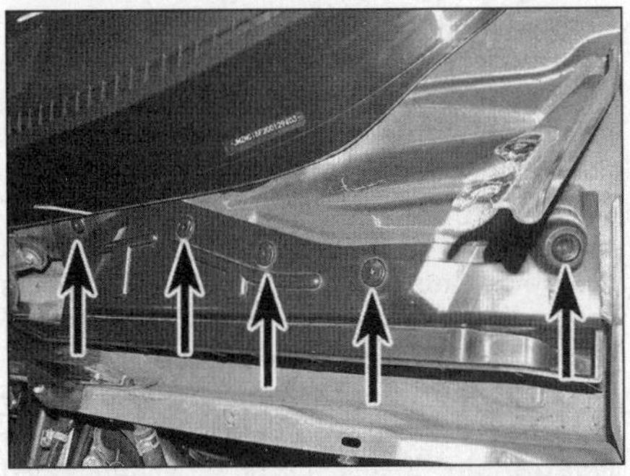

9.10a Unscrew the centre pins, lever out the expansion rivets...

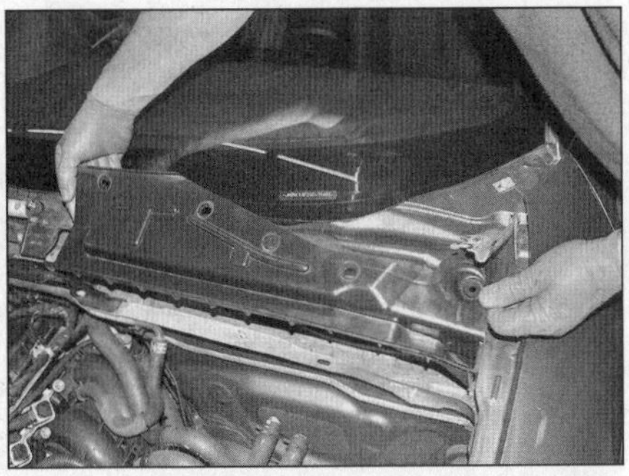

9.10b... and remove the side cowl panel

9.11 Heater pipe retaining nut

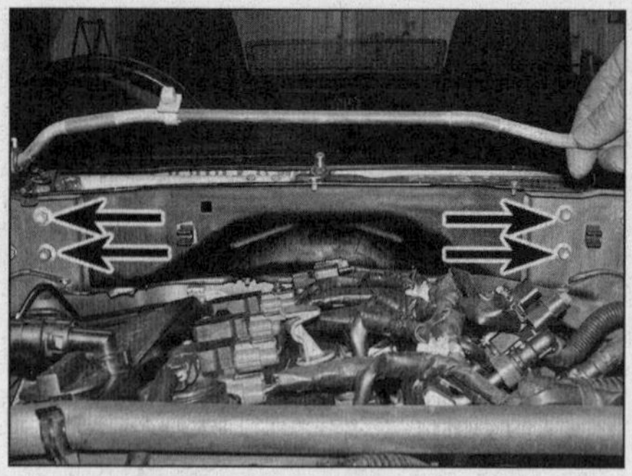

9.12a Undo the 4 bolts at the front...

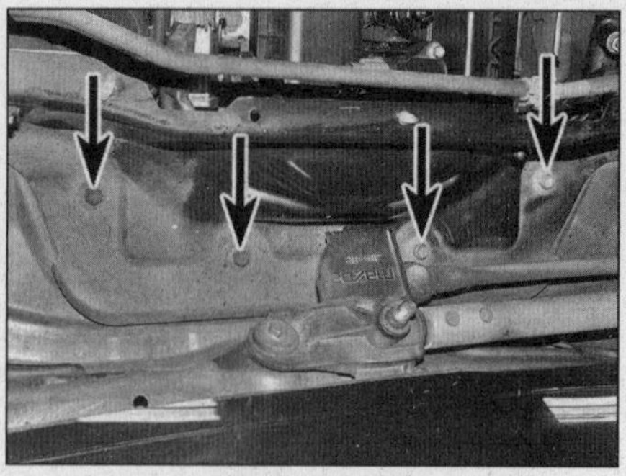

9.12b... and the 4 bolts on top...

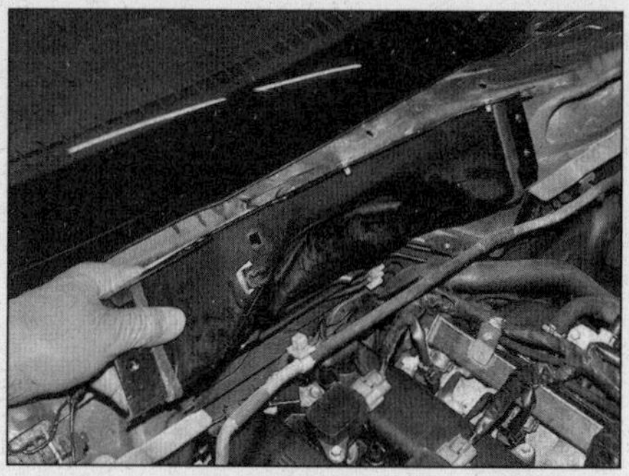

9.12c...and remove the service access cover

access cover from the engine compartment bulkhead **(see illustrations)**.

13 Undo the bolts and detach the alternator with reference to Chapter 5A Section 6. Position the alternator to one side, and secure it from falling using wire etc.

14 Remove the exhaust manifold as described in Chapter 4A Section 12.

15 Undo the bolt and pull the OCV from the cylinder head as described in Section 7.

16 Remove both camshafts as described in Section 8.

17 Loosen the ten cylinder head bolts progressively and by half a turn at a time, working in the reverse order of the tightening sequence **(see illustration 9.32a)**.

18 Lift the cylinder head from the engine compartment.

19 If the head is stuck, be careful how you choose to free it. Remember that the cylinder head is made of aluminum alloy, which is easily damaged. Striking the head with tools carries the risk of damage, and the head is located on two dowels, so its movement will be limited. Do not, under any circumstances, pry the head between the mating surfaces, as this will certainly damage the sealing surfaces for the gasket, leading to leaks. Try rocking the head free, to break the seal, taking care not to damage any of the surrounding components.

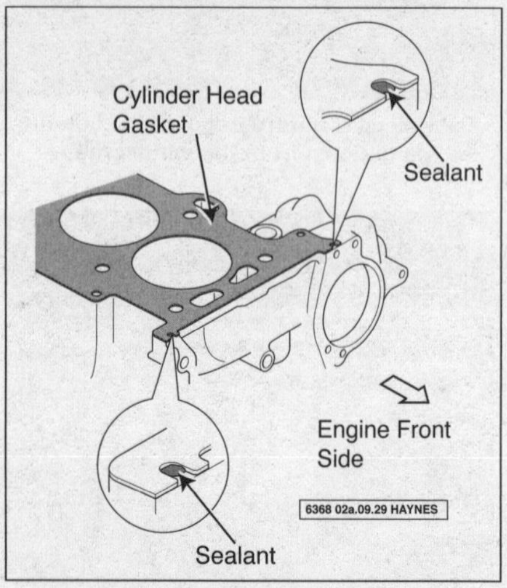

9.29 Apply a little sealant to the areas indicated

20 Once the head has been removed, remove and discard the gasket. Check for the presence of locating dowels in the cylinder block and cylinder head. If dowels are present, make sure they are returned to their original locations after cleaning the components.

Inspection

21 The mating faces of the cylinder head and cylinder block must be perfectly clean before replacing the head. Use spray-on gasket remover and a hard plastic or wood scraper to remove all traces of gasket and carbon.

22 Take particular care during the cleaning operations, as aluminum alloy is easily damaged. Also, make sure that the carbon is not allowed to enter the oil and water passages – this is particularly important for the lubrication system, as carbon could block the oil supply to the engine's components.

23 To prevent carbon entering the gap between the pistons and bores, smear a little grease in the gap. After cleaning each piston, use a small brush to remove all traces of grease and carbon from the gap, then wipe away the remainder with a clean rag.

24 Check the mating surfaces of the cylinder block and the cylinder head for nicks, deep scratches and other damage. Also check the cylinder head gasket surface and the cylinder block gasket surface with a precision straight-edge and feeler gauges. If either surface exceeds the warpage limit listed in Chapter 2B Specifications, the manufacturer states that the component out of specification must be replaced. If the gasket mating surface of your cylinder head or block is out of specification or is severely nicked or scratched, you may want to consult with an automotive machine shop for advice.

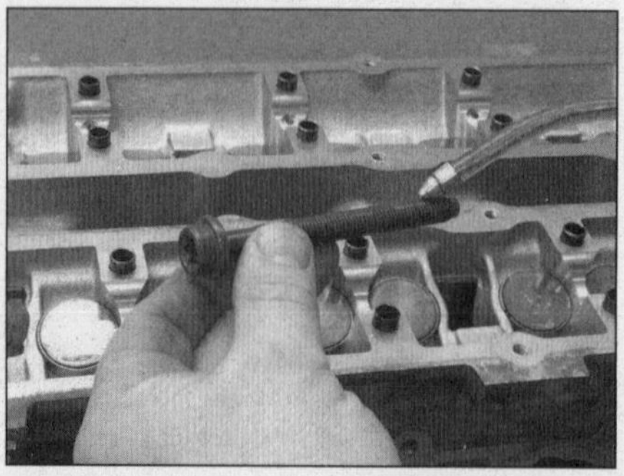

9.31 Apply a light coat of oil to the cylinder head bolt threads

Refitting

25 Wipe clean the mating surfaces of the cylinder head and cylinder block. If equipped, install the alignment dowels into their original locations.

26 The cylinder head bolt holes must be free from oil or water. This is most important, because a hydraulic lock in a cylinder head bolt hole can cause a fracture of the block casting when the bolt is tightened. Note the location of the cylinder head alignment dowels in the block.

Note: *Although Mazda state that the cylinder head bolts can be re-used providing their length (measured from under the bolt head to the end of the bolt) doesn't exceed the dimension given in the Section, we recommend that the bolts are replaced, regardless of their apparent condition.*

27 Position a new gasket on the cylinder block surface, so that the "TOP" mark is facing up.

28 As the cylinder head is such a heavy and awkward assembly to install, it is helpful to make up a pair of guide studs from two 10 mm (thread size) studs approximately 90 mm long, with a screwdriver slot cut in one end – you can use two of the old cylinder head bolts with their heads cut off. Screw these guide studs, screwdriver slot upwards to permit removal, into the bolt holes at diagonally-opposite corners of the cylinder block surface; ensure that approximately 70 mm of stud protrudes above the gasket.

29 Apply a small bead of RTV silicone sealant to the cylinder head gasket at the points shown **(see illustration)**. Note that the cylinder head must be refitted before the silicone begins to harden.

30 Refit the cylinder head, sliding it down the guide studs (if used) and locating it on the dowels. Unscrew the guide studs (if used) when the head is in place.

31 Coat the threads with engine oil – do not apply more than a light film of oil **(see illustration)**. Install the new cylinder head bolts and screw them in by hand only until finger-tight.

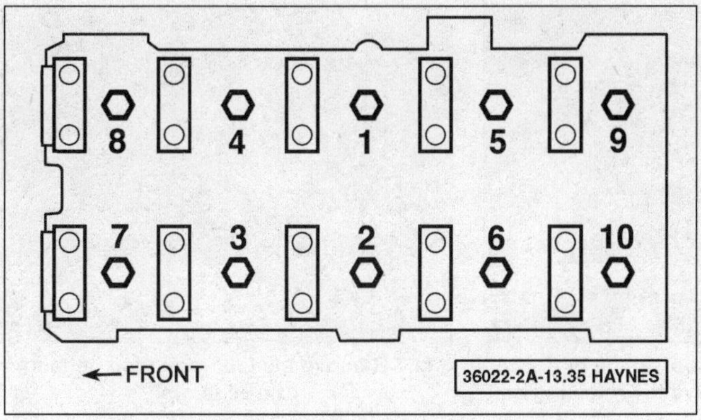

9.32a Cylinder head bolt tightening sequence

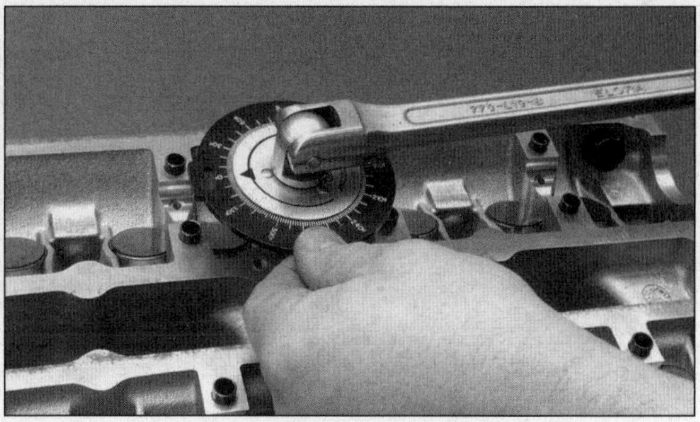

9.32b Angle-tightening gauge

32 Working progressively and in the sequence shown, first tighten all the bolts to the specified Stage 1 torque setting **(see illustration)**. Using the same sequence, gradually tighten the bolts to the subsequent Stages. Note that the final two Stages use the angle torque method **(see illustration)**.

33 The remainder of refitting is a reversal of removal.

34 Change the engine oil and filter and refill the cooling system (see Chapter 1).

10 Sump – removal and refitting

Removal

1 Remove the battery and battery tray as described in Chapter 5A Section 4.

2 Slacken the road wheel bolts, the raise the vehicle and support it securely on axle stands (see *Jacking and vehicle support*). Remove both front roadwheels.

3 Drain the engine oil and remove the oil filter as described in Chapter 1 Section 5.

4 Remove the timing chain cover as described in Section 6.

5 Undo the fasteners and remove the under cover and transverse member from beneath the sump **(see illustrations)**.

6 Remove the windscreen wiper arms as described in Chapter 12 Section 14.

7 Prise up the plastic cap and remove the screw at each end of the windscreen cowl panel **(see illustration 9.7)**.

8 Unclip the washer hose from the cowl panel, and remove the rubber weatherstrip **(see illustration 9.8)**.

9 Pull up the front edge of the cowl panel, then pull it downwards from the base of the windscreen **(see illustration 9.9)**.

10 Release the fastener and remove the side cowl panel each side **(see illustrations 9.10a and 9.10b)**.

11 Undo the 2 bolts and remove the service access cover from the engine compartment bulkhead **(see illustrations 9.11a and 9.11b)**.

12 As the engine must be lifted approximately 25 mm to provide sufficient clearance, attach an lifting hoist to the engine lifting brackets, and take the weight of the engine.

13 Undo the nuts securing the engine mountings to the crossmember and engine mounting brackets each side.

14 Raise the engine approximately 25 mm and remove the engine mountings.

15 Remove the sump-to-transmission bolts.

16 Progressively unscrew the oil sump retaining bolts in the reverse of the tightening sequence **(see illustration 10.22)**. Oil sump bolts may be of varying sizes. Mark, tag, or store each oil sump bolt/nut with the location removed from the oil sump for correct refitting later. Use a rubber mallet to loosen the oil sump seal, then lower the sump and manoeuvre it from place. Unfortunately, the use of sealant can make the sump difficult to remove. Be careful when prying between the mating surfaces, otherwise they will be damaged, resulting in leaks. With care, a putty knife can be used to cut through the sealant.

Refitting

17 Use a scraper to remove all traces of old sealant from the block and sump. Clean the mating surfaces with gasket cleaner or equivalent solvent, available at automotive parts stores. Be very careful not to scratch, bend, or otherwise damage the mating surfaces of the sump and block or oil leaks could develop.

18 Make sure the threaded bolt holes in the block are clean, and remove all traces of sealant from the sump retaining bolts.

19 Apply a 2.5 mm wide bead of silicone sealant to the oil sump flange so that the bead runs along the inside of the bolt holes. Also apply sealant to the front flange of the oil sump where it meets the timing chain cover. Note: The oil sump must be installed within 4 minutes of applying the sealant.

20 Manoeuvre the sump into position, insert the retaining bolts into their original positions, but only finger-tighten them at this stage.

21 Use a set-square or ruler to align the front edge of the sump with the cylinder block at the timing chain cover junction.

22 Working in the sequence given tighten the sump-to-cylinder block bolts to their specified torque **(see illustration)**.

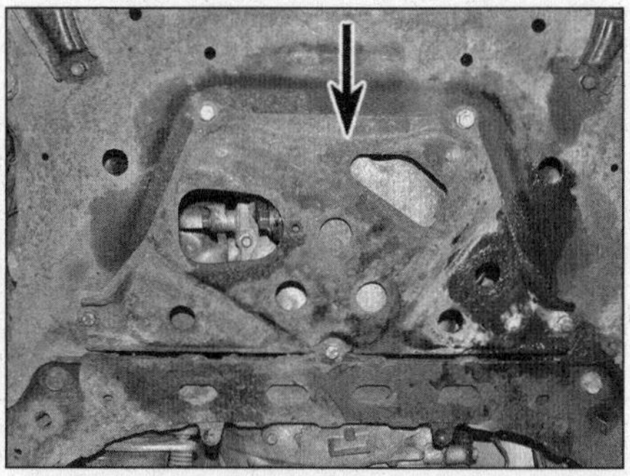

10.5a Undo the fasteners and remove the under cover...

10.5b... and the transverse member

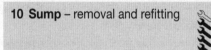

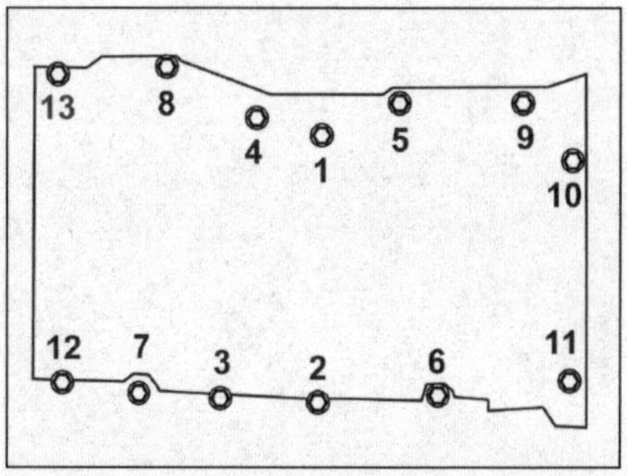

10.22 Sump bolts tightening sequence

11.4 The oil pump pick-up tube is held by two mounting bolts (typical)

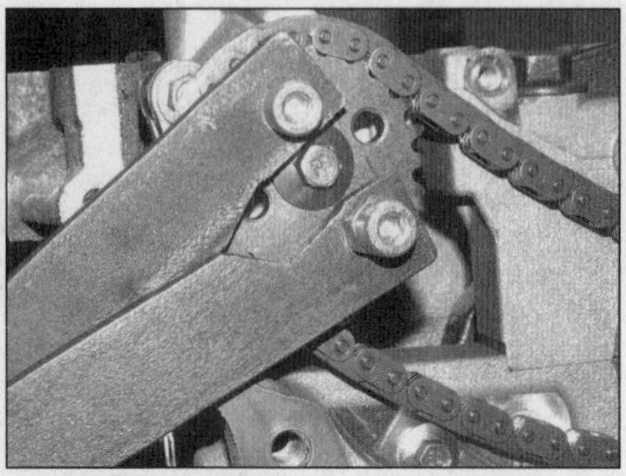

11.6 Using a holding tool on the oil pump drive sprocket to remove the retaining bolt

11.7 Remove the four mounting bolts for the oil pump

23 Now tighten the sump-to-transmission bolts to the specified torque.

24 The remainder of refitting is a reversal of removal, noting the following points:

a) Tighten all fasteners to their specified torque where given.
b) Renew the engine oil and filter as described in Chapter 1 Section 5.
c) Refit the battery and tray as described in Chapter 5A Section 4.

11 Oil pump – removal and installation

Note: *The oil pump is serviced as a complete unit without any sub-assembly or internal inspection.*

1 Drain the engine oil and remove the oil filter (see Chapter 1 Section 5).

2 Remove the timing chain cover (see Section 6).

3 Remove the oil sump (see Section 10).

4 Remove the oil pick-up tube **(see illustration)**.

5 Use a screwdriver to lever the end of the oil pump drive chain tensioner's spring from under the shouldered bolt. Remove the two bolts and the tensioner.

6 Remove the chain from the oil pump sprocket. While holding the oil pump drive sprocket with a suitable tool, remove the sprocket bolt from the oil pump, then remove the sprocket **(see illustration)**.

7 Remove the oil pump mounting bolts, then remove the pump **(see illustration)**.

8 Installation is the reverse of removal, noting the following points:

a) Replace all gaskets with new ones.
b) Tighten the oil pump mounting bolts to the specified torque in a diagonal pattern.
c) After refitting the oil sump, fit a new oil filter and refill the crankcase with oil (see Chapter 1 Section 5).
d) Be certain to check for any oil warning lights in the instrument panel after the vehicle has been started and idling.

12 Oil seals – renewal

Front oil seal

1 Remove the crankshaft pulley (see Section 5).

2 Use a screwdriver or hook tool to carefully lever out the seal. Note: Be careful not to damage the timing chain cover bore where the seal is seated, or the nose and sealing surface of the crankshaft.

3 Another procedure for removing the seal is to drill a small hole on each side of the seal and place a self-tapping screw in each hole. Use these screws as a means of pulling the seal out without having to lever on it.

4 Wipe the sealing surfaces in the engine cover and on the crankshaft. Clean and coat them with clean engine oil.

5 Start installing the new seal by pressing it into the timing chain cover **(see illustration)**.

6 Once started, use a seal driver or a suitable socket of the correct size to carefully drive the seal squarely into place **(see illustration)**.

7 The seal should be flush with the engine cover and remain square when installed.

8 Coat the lip of the seal (where it contacts the crankshaft) with clean engine oil.

9 Install the crankshaft pulley (see Section 5).

Rear oil seal

10 The one-piece rear main oil seal is pressed into the rear main oil seal carrier mounted at the rear of the block. Remove the flywheel as described in Section 13.

11 Unbolt the oil seal and carrier.

12 Clean the mating surface for the oil seal carrier on the cylinder block and the crankshaft. Carefully remove and polish any burrs or raised edges on the crankshaft that may have caused the seal to fail.

13 Apply a 4.0 mm wide bead of RTV sealant to the upper edge of the sump where it contacts the oil seal carrier **(see illustration)**.

12.5 Ensure that the oil seal is kept square as it is placed in the bore

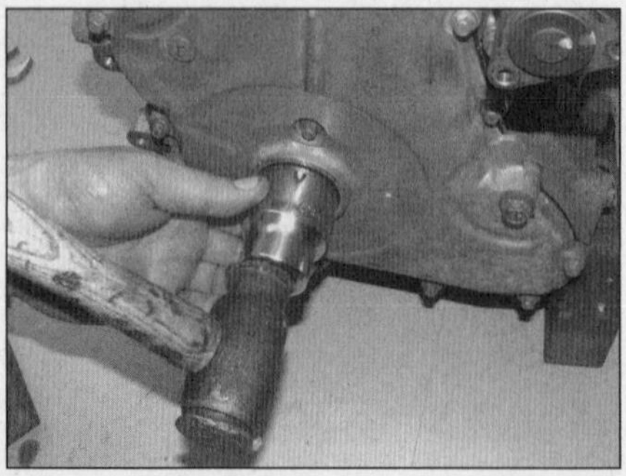

12.6 A socket of the correct size can be used to install the new seal

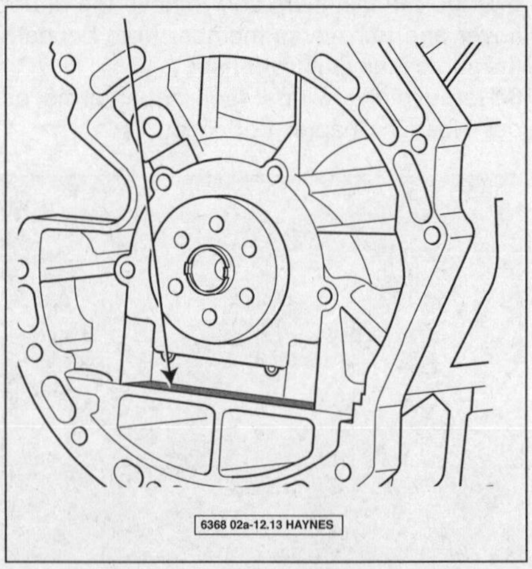

12.13 Apply a bead of silicone sealant to area arrowed

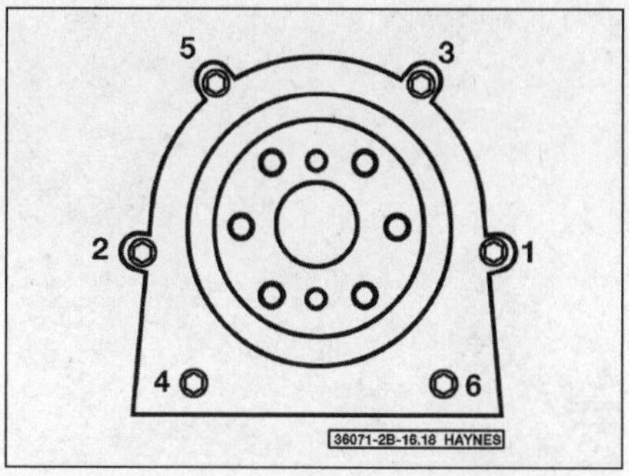

12.18 Rear oil seal carrier tightening sequence

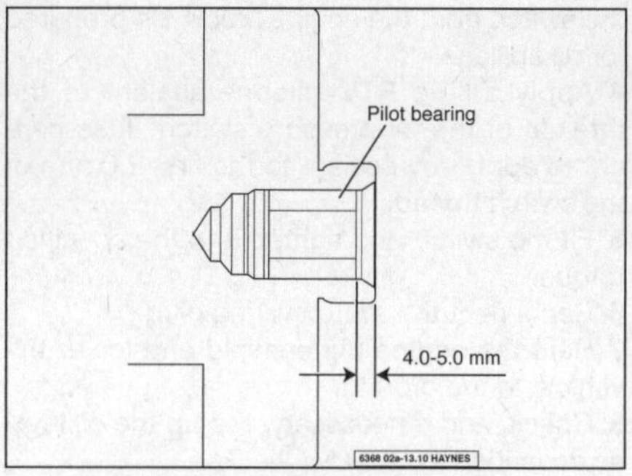

13.10 Pilot bearing fitting details

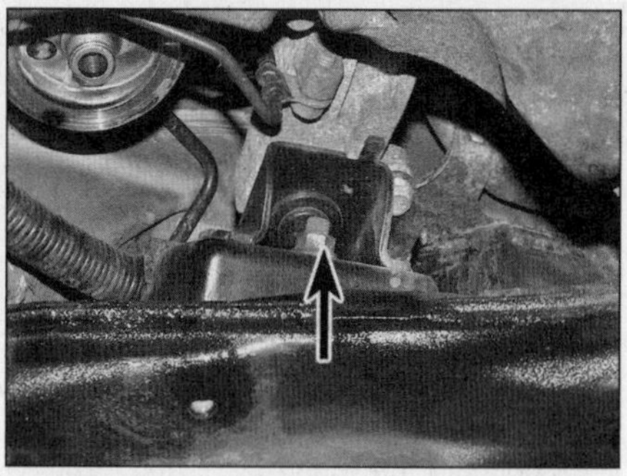

14.7 Remove the engine mounting nut

14 Lightly coat the inside lip of the new seal with clean engine oil. Use a thin (but durable) two-inch wide plastic strip (or a two-litre plastic beverage bottle cut to size) around the inside circumference of the seal to act as a liner for installation. A manufacturer tool (part no. 303-328) for this purpose also works well.
15 With the plastic seal liner or tool in place, carefully move the new carrier (with seal factory-installed) into position by sliding it onto the contact surface of the crankshaft.
16 Install the oil seal carrier bolts and finger tighten them while holding the carrier in place.
17 Carefully remove the plastic liner or tool so that the new seal contacts the crankshaft mating surface correctly.
18 Tighten the oil seal carrier to the specified torque using the proper sequence **(see illustration)**.
19 The remainder of installation is the reverse of removal.

13 Flywheel – removal, inspection and refitting

Removal

1 Remove the clutch as described in Chapter 6 Section 2. Now is a good time to check or replace the clutch components and release bearing.
2 Use a center-punch or paint to make alignment marks on the flywheel and crankshaft to make replacement easier – the bolt holes are slightly offset, and will only line up one way, but making a mark eliminates the guesswork (and the flywheel is heavy).
3 Hold the flywheel stationary and unscrew the bolts. To prevent the flywheel from turning, insert one of the transmission mounting bolts into the cylinder block and have an assistant engage a wide-bladed screwdriver with the starter ring gear teeth while the flywheel bolts are loosened.
4 Loosen and remove each bolt in turn and ensure that new bolts are obtained for reassembly. These bolts are subjected to severe stresses and so must be replaced, regardless of their apparent condition, whenever they are removed.
5 Remove the flywheel. The flywheel is very heavy – do not drop it.

Inspection

6 Clean the flywheel to remove grease and oil. Inspect the surface for cracks, rivet grooves, burned areas and score marks. Light scoring can be removed with emery cloth. Check for cracked and broken ring gear teeth. Lay the flywheel on a flat surface and use a straight-edge to check for warpage.
7 Clean and inspect the mating surfaces of the flywheel and the crankshaft. If the oil seal is leaking, replace it (see Section 12) before replacing the flywheel. If the engine has high mileage, it may be worth installing a new seal as a matter of course, given the amount of work needed to access it.
8 While the flywheel is removed, carefully clean its inboard face, particularly the recesses that serve as the reference points for the crankshaft speed/position sensor. Clean the sensor's tip and check that the sensor is securely fastened.
9 Check the condition of the pilot bearing in the end of the crankshaft. It should be smooth in operation, with virtually no play. If renewal is required, extract the bearing using a suitable internal bearing puller. Note: The bearing can be renewed with the flywheel still fitted to the end of the crankshaft.
10 Carefully drive the new pilot bearing squarely into the flywheel to a depth of 4.0 – 5.0 mm **(see illustration)**.

Refitting

11 Ensure that the engine/transmission adapter plate is in place (where necessary), then install the flywheel on the crankshaft so that all bolt holes align – it will fit only one way – check this using the marks made on removal. Install the new bolts, tightening them by hand.
12 Lock the flywheel by the method used on disassembly. Working in a diagonal sequence to tighten them evenly and increasing to the final amount in two or three stages, tighten the new bolts to the specified torque.
13 The remainder of refitting is the reverse of the removal procedure

14 Engine mountings – inspection and renewal

1 Engine mountings seldom require attention, but broken or deteriorated mountings should be renewed immediately or the added strain placed on the driveline components may cause damage or wear.

Inspection

2 During the inspection, the engine must be raised slightly to remove the weight from the mountings.
3 Raise the vehicle and support it securely on axle stands, then position a jack with a block of wood under the engine oil sump or use an engine support fixture from above. Carefully raise the engine just enough to take the weight off the mountings. Support the engine just enough to take the weight off the engine mountings but without lifting the weight of the car from the axle stands.

Warning: DO NOT place any part of your body under the engine when it's supported only by a jack!

4 Check the mountings to see if the rubber is cracked, hardened or separated from the metal portion. Occasionally, the rubber will split down the centre.
5 Check for relative movement between the mountings and the engine or chassis, using a large screwdriver or prybar to attempt to move the mountings. If movement is noted, lower the engine and tighten the mounting fasteners.

Renewal

6 Raise the vehicle and support it securely on axle stands (if not already done). Support the engine as described in Paragraph 3.
7 Renew the engine mountings as follows:
a) Remove the engine mounting nuts to detach the rubber mounting from the mounting bracket and crossmember (see illustration).
b) Reinstall the engine mountings by reversing the removal steps.
c) Tighten all bolts/nuts to the specified torque.

15 Oil pressure switch – removal and refitting

1 The oil pressure switch is located on the left-hand side of the engine, on the rear of the oil filter housing **(see illustration)**.

2 Raise the front of the vehicle and support it securely on axle stands (see *Jacking and vehicle support*). Undo the fasteners and remove the engine undershield.

3 Disconnect the wiring plug, and unscrew the switch from the engine block. Be prepared for oil spillage.

4 Apply a little RTV silicone sealant to the threads of the oil pressure switch. Take care not to apply any sealant to the first 2.0 mm of the switch threads.

5 Fit the switch and tighten it to the specified torque.

6 Reconnect the switch wiring plug.

7 Refit the engine undershield and lower the vehicle to the ground.

8 Check, and if necessary, top up the oil level as described in *Weekly Checks*.

15.1 Oil pressure switch location

Chapter 2 Part B
Engine removal and overhaul procedures

Contents

Degrees of difficulty

Easy, suitable for novice with little experience	**Fairly easy,** suitable for beginner with some experience	**Fairly difficult,** suitable for competent DIY mechanic	**Difficult,** suitable for experienced DIY mechanic	**Very difficult,** suitable for expert DIY or professional

Specifications

Cylinder head

Maximum gasket face distortion:	
All engines	0.10 mm

Torque wrench settings

1 Refer to Chapter 2A, Specifications

1 General Information

1 Included in this Chapter are details of removing the engine from the car and general overhaul procedures for the cylinder head, cylinder block/crankcase and all other engine internal components.

2 The information given ranges from advice concerning preparation for an overhaul and the purchase of parts, to detailed step-by-step procedures covering removal, inspection, renovation and refitting of engine internal components.

3 After Section 5, all instructions are based on the assumption that the engine has been removed from the car. For information concerning in-car engine repair, as well as the removal and refitting of those external components necessary for full overhaul, refer to Part A of this Chapter and to Section 5. Ignore any preliminary dismantling operations described in Part A that are no longer relevant once the engine has been removed from the car.

4 Apart from torque wrench settings, which are given at the beginning of Part A, all specifications relating to engine overhaul are at the beginning of this Chapter.

2 Engine overhaul – general information

1 It is not always easy to determine when, or if, an engine should be completely overhauled, as a number of factors must be considered.

2 High mileage is not necessarily an indication that an overhaul is needed, while low mileage does not preclude the need for an overhaul. Frequency of servicing is probably the most important consideration. An engine which has had regular and frequent oil and filter changes, as well as other required maintenance, should give many thousands of miles of reliable service. Conversely, a neglected engine may require an overhaul very early in its life.

3 Excessive oil consumption is an indication that piston rings, valve seals and/or valve guides are in need of attention. Make sure that oil leaks are not responsible before deciding that the rings and/or guides are worn. Perform a compression test, as described in Chapter 2A, Section 2, to determine the likely cause of the problem.

4 Check the oil pressure with a gauge fitted in place of the oil pressure switch, and compare it with that specified. If it is extremely low, the main and big-end bearings, and/or the oil pump, are probably worn out.

5 Loss of power, rough running, knocking or metallic engine noises, excessive valve gear noise, and high fuel consumption may also point to the need for an overhaul, especially if they are all present at the same time. If a complete service does not cure the situation, major mechanical work is the only solution.

6 A full engine overhaul involves restoring

all internal parts to the specification of a new engine. During a complete overhaul, the pistons and the piston rings are renewed, and the cylinder bores are reconditioned. New main and big-end bearings are generally fitted; if necessary, the crankshaft may be reground, to compensate for wear in the journals. The valves are also serviced as well, since they are usually in less-than-perfect condition at this point. Always pay careful attention to the condition of the oil pump when overhauling the engine, and renew it if there is any doubt as to its serviceability. The end result should be an as-new engine that will give many trouble-free miles.

7 Critical cooling system components such as the hoses, thermostat and coolant pump should be renewed when an engine is overhauled. The radiator should also be checked carefully, to ensure that it is not clogged or leaking.

8 Before beginning the engine overhaul, read through the entire procedure, to familiarise yourself with the scope and requirements of the job. Check on the availability of parts and make sure that any necessary special tools and equipment are obtained in advance. Most work can be done with typical hand tools, although a number of precision measuring tools are required for inspecting parts to determine if they must be renewed.

9 The services provided by an engineering machine shop or engine reconditioning specialist will almost certainly be required, particularly if major repairs such as crankshaft regrinding or cylinder reboring are necessary. Apart from carrying out machining operations, these establishments will normally handle the inspection of parts, offer advice concerning reconditioning or renewal and supply new components such as pistons, piston rings and bearing shells. It is recommended that the establishment used is a member of the Federation of Engine Re-Manufacturers, or a similar society.

10 Always wait until the engine has been completely dismantled, and until all components (especially the cylinder block/crankcase and the crankshaft) have been inspected, before deciding what service and repair operations must be performed by an engineering works. The condition of these components will be the major factor to consider when determining whether to overhaul the original engine, or to buy a reconditioned unit. Do not, therefore, purchase parts or have overhaul work done on other components until they have been thoroughly inspected. As a general rule, time is the primary cost of an overhaul, so it does not pay to fit worn or sub-standard parts.

11 As a final note, to ensure maximum life and minimum trouble from a reconditioned engine, everything must be assembled with care, in a spotlessly-clean environment.

Note: *No information concerning the crankshaft, connecting rods or pistons is provided by the manufacturer. Consequently, should a fault develop with these components, consult a Mazda dealer or engine overhaul specialist.*

3 Engine removal – methods and precautions

Caution: The engine is removed from the bottom of the engine compartment, along with the transmission and crossmember, by raising the vehicle sufficiently to slide the assembly out ; this procedure requires the use of a vehicle hoist. Only begin this procedure if all of the necessary equipment is at hand. With only a trolley and and axlestands, the vehicle can't safely be raised high enough for the engine/transmission/crossmember to slide out from underneath.

1 If you have decided that the engine must be removed for overhaul or major repair work, several preliminary steps should be taken.

2 Locating a suitable place to work is extremely important. Adequate work space, along with storage space for the car, will be needed. If a workshop or garage is not available, at the very least, a flat, level, clean work surface is required.

3 Cleaning the engine compartment and engine before beginning the removal procedure will help keep tools clean and organised.

4 The help of an assistant is essential. Apart from the safety aspects involved, there are many instances when one person cannot simultaneously perform all of the operations required during engine removal.

5 Plan the operation ahead of time. Before starting work, arrange for the hire of or obtain all of the tools and equipment you will need. Some of the equipment necessary to perform engine removal and installation safely (in addition to an engine hoist) is as follows: a heavy duty trolley jack, complete sets of spanners and sockets as described in the rear of this manual, wooden blocks, and plenty of rags and cleaning solvent for mopping-up spilled oil, coolant and fuel. If the hoist must be hired, make sure that you arrange for it in advance, and perform all of the operations possible without it beforehand. This will save you money and time.

6 Plan for the car to be out of use for quite a while. An engineering machine shop or engine reconditioning specialist will be required to perform some of the work which cannot be accomplished without special equipment. These places often have a busy schedule, so it would be a good idea to consult them before removing the engine, in order to accurately estimate the amount of time required to rebuild or repair components that may need work.

7 During the engine removal procedure, it is advisable to make notes of the locations of all brackets, cable-ties, earthing points, etc, as well as how the wiring harnesses, hoses and electrical connections are attached and routed around the engine and engine compartment. An effective way of doing this is to take a series of photographs of the various components before they are disconnected or removed; the resulting photographs will prove invaluable when the engine is refitted.

8 Always be extremely careful when removing and refitting the engine. Serious injury can result from careless actions. Plan ahead and take your time, and a job of this nature, although major, can be accomplished successfully.

4 Engine – removal and refitting

Note: *Such is the complexity of the power unit arrangement on these vehicles, and the variations that may be encountered according to model and optional equipment fitted, that the following should be regarded as a guide to the work involved, rather than a step-by-step procedure. Where differences are encountered, or additional component disconnection or removal is necessary, make notes of the work involved as an aid to refitting.*

Removal

Note: *Engine removal on these models is a difficult job, especially for the do-it-yourself mechanic working at home. Because of the vehicle's design, the manufacturer states that the engine/transmission and subframe have to be removed as a unit from the bottom of the vehicle, not the top. With a trolley jack and axlestands, the vehicle can't be raised high enough and supported safely enough for the engine/transmission/subframe assembly to slide out from underneath. The manufacturer recommends that removal of the engine/transmission/subframe assembly only be performed on a chassis-contact type vehicle hoist. The procedure is complicated and is not recommended for the home mechanic.*

Note: *Read through the entire Section before beginning this procedure. The engine and transmission are removed as a unit from below and then separated outside the vehicle.*

Note: *Keep in mind that during this procedure you'll have to adjust the height of the vehicle to perform certain operations.*

1 Park the vehicle on a chassis-contact type vehicle hoist, then engage the arms of the hoist with the jacking points of the vehicle. Raise the hoist arms until they contact the vehicle, but not so much that the wheels come off the ground.

2 Place protective covers on the front wings.

3 Remove the battery and battery tray as described in Chapter 5A Section 4.

4 Loosen the front wheel nuts, then raise the vehicle and remove the front wheels.

5 Remove the engine/transmission undershields, and the wheelarch liners.

6 Drain the engine coolant, engine oil and transmission oil as described in Chapter 1.

7 Remove the air cleaner housing assembly (Chapter 4A Section 3).

8 Remove the throttle body (Chapter 4A Section 10).

9 Remove the PCM (see Chapter 4A Section 11), the cooling duct and the air filter housing insulator.

10 Remove the radiator and coolant reservoir (see Chapter 3).

11 Remove the auxiliary drivebelt (Chapter 1 Section 6).

12 Remove the alternator air duct.

13 Disconnect the servo vacuum hose.

14 Disconnect the hoses from the power steering pump and drain the fluid into a container.

15 Disconnect the fuel pipe from the fuel rail (see Chapter 4A Section 11).

16 Disconnect the heater hoses from the heater matrix tubes at the engine compartment bulkhead (see Chapter 3 Section 8).

17 Remove the air conditioning compressor and support it out of the way with a length of rope from above (Chapter 3 Section 10). Note: Do not disconnect the refrigerant lines.

18 Mark and disconnect any remaining wires or hoses between the engine and the vehicle body.

19 Remove the centre console as described in Chapter. 11 Section 27

20 Remove the clutch release cylinder and support it out of the way (Chapter 6). Don't disconnect the hydraulic hose.

Caution: Do not depress the clutch pedal with the release cylinder removed.

21 Remove the brake calipers (Chapter 9 Section 8) and hang them from above with rope or wire. Don't disconnect the hoses and don't let the calipers hang by the hoses.

22 Remove the tunnel member (the cross-brace under the propeller shaft).

23 Remove the exhaust pipe (Chapter 4A Section 13).

24 Remove the cross-brace under the transmission.

25 Disconnect the steering intermediate shaft from the steering gear (Chapter 10 Section 15).

26 Remove the propeller shaft as described in Chapter 8 Section 6.

27 Raise the vehicle on the hoist, then move a large, sturdy workbench under the vehicle. Slowly and carefully lower the vehicle onto axlestands or blocks placed on the workbench, which must contact the rear of the transmission and the subframe.

28 Remove the power plant frame (Chapter 7 Section 5).

29 With the transmission and engine/subframe supported by the axlestands, remove the subframe-to-body bolts. Make sure nothing is still connected between the engine/transmission/subframe and the body, then slowly raise the vehicle on the hoist until it clears the engine/transmission assembly.

30 The transmission and engine can now be separated. An engine hoist can then be attached to the engine for transferring to an engine stand.

Refitting

31 Refitting is the reverse of removal, noting the following points:

a) Check the engine and transmission mountings. If they're worn, replace them.

b) When positioning the subframe beneath the vehicle, make a plumb bob from a piece of string and a nut. Hold the string at each subframe bolt hole on the body and verify that its corresponding subframe bolt hole is directly below it. This will eliminate trying to adjust the subframe as the vehicle is lowered over it.

c) Tighten all fasteners to their specified torque where given.

d) Refill the cooling system with the proper mixture of coolant. Refill the engine with the recommended oil, the transmission with the recommended lubricant and the power steering system with the recommended fluid (Chapter 1).

e) Have the wheel alignment checked and, if necessary, adjusted.

5 Engine overhaul – dismantling sequence

Note: *On all petrol engines covered by this manual, it is not possible to remove the intermediate/main bearing section or to remove the crankshaft or pistons. No separate parts are available, and replacement/exchange units are supplied with crankshaft, pistons, connecting rods, etc, already fitted. Consult a Mazda dealer or parts specialist for further information.*

1 It is much easier to dismantle and work on the engine if it is mounted on a portable engine stand. These stands can often be hired from a tool hire shop. Before the engine is mounted on a stand, the flywheel should be removed, so that the stand bolts can be tightened into the end of the cylinder block/crankcase.

2 If a stand is not available, it is possible to dismantle the engine with it blocked up on a sturdy workbench, or on the floor. Be extra careful not to tip or drop the engine when working without a stand.

3 If you are going to obtain a reconditioned engine, all the external components must be removed first, to be transferred to the new engine (just as they will if you are doing a complete engine overhaul yourself). These components include the following:

- Engine wiring harness and supports.
- Alternator and air conditioning compressor mounting brackets (as applicable).
- Coolant pump (where applicable) and inlet/outlet housings.
- Dipstick tube.
- Fuel system components.
- All electrical switches and sensors.
- Intake and exhaust manifolds.
- Flywheel.

Note: *When removing the external components from the engine, pay close attention to details that may be helpful or important during refitting. Note the fitted position of gaskets, seals, spacers, pins, washers, bolts, and other small items.*

4 If you are obtaining a 'short' engine (which consists of the engine cylinder block/crankcase, crankshaft, pistons and connecting rods all assembled), then the cylinder head, sump, oil pump, and timing belt will have to be removed also.

5 Before beginning the dismantling and overhaul procedures, make sure that you have all of the correct tools necessary. See *Tools and working facilities* in Reference for further information.

6 Cylinder head – dismantling

Note: *New and reconditioned cylinder heads maybe available from the manufacturer, and from engine overhaul specialists. Due to the fact that some specialist tools are required for the dismantling and inspection procedures, and that new components may not be readily available, it may be more practical and economical for the home mechanic to purchase a reconditioned head rather than to dismantle, inspect and recondition the original head. A valve spring compressor tool will be required for this operation.*

1 With the cylinder head removed as described in Chapter 2A Section 9, clean away all external dirt.

2 To remove a valve, fit a valve spring compressor tool. Ensure that the arms of the compressor tool are securely positioned on the head of the valve and the spring cap **(see illustration)**.

3 Compress the valve spring to relieve the pressure of the spring cap acting on the collets.

4 Extract the two split collets by hooking them out using a small screwdriver, then

6.2 Ensure the valve spring compressor is securely positioned

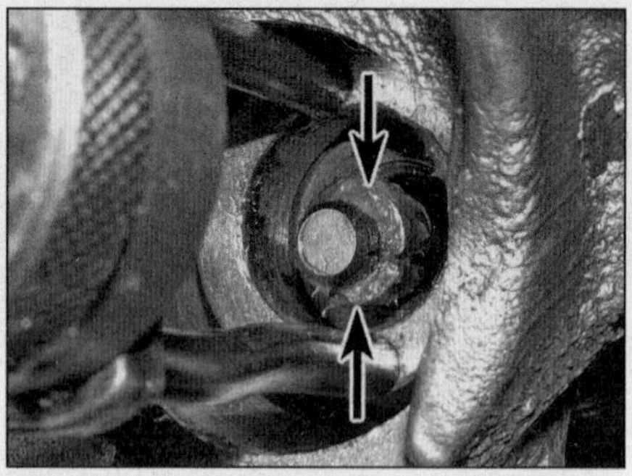

6.4 Extract the 2 collets (arrowed)

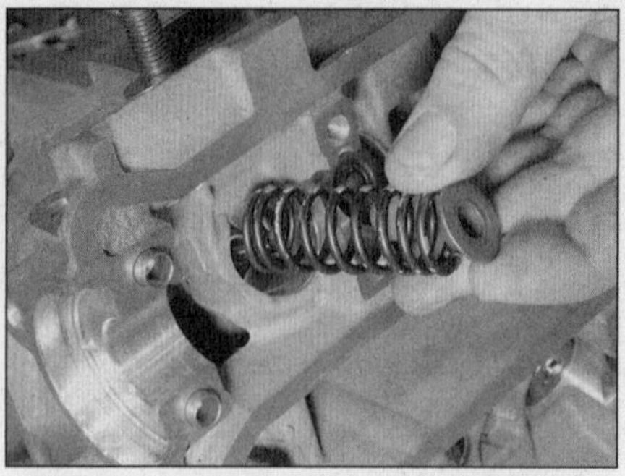

6.5a Remove the valve spring and cap

6.5b Use long-nosed pliers to extract the valve stem oil seal

slowly release the compressor tool **(see illustration)**.

5 Remove the valve cap, and spring then withdraw the valve through the combustion chamber. Remove the valve stem oil seal (using long-nosed pliers if necessary) **(see illustrations)**.

6 Repeat the procedure for the remaining valves, keeping all components in strict order so that they can be refitted in their original positions, unless all the components are to be renewed. If the components are to be kept and used again, place each valve assembly in a labelled polythene bag or a similar small container **(see illustration)**. Note that, as with cylinder numbering, the valves are normally numbered from the timing chain end of the engine. Make sure that the valve components are identified as intake and exhaust, as well as numbered.

7 Cylinder head and valve components – cleaning and inspection

Note: *Thorough cleaning of the cylinder head and valve components, followed by a detailed inspection, will enable a decision to be made on whether further work is necessary before reassembling the components.*

Cleaning

1 Scrape away all traces of old gasket material and sealing compound from the cylinder head surfaces. Take care not to damage the cylinder head surfaces, as the head is made of light alloy.

2 Scrape away the carbon from the combustion chambers and ports, then wash the cylinder head thoroughly with paraffin or a suitable solvent.

3 Scrape off any heavy carbon deposits that may have formed on the valves, then use a power-operated wire brush to remove deposits from the valve heads and stems.

Inspection

Note: *Be sure to perform all the following inspection procedures before concluding that the services of a machine shop or engine overhaul specialist are required. Make a list of all items that require attention.*

Cylinder head

4 Inspect the head very carefully for cracks, evidence of coolant leakage, and other damage. If cracks are found, a new cylinder head should be obtained.

5 Use a straight-edge and feeler blades to check that the cylinder head surface is not distorted **(see illustration)**. If the specified distortion limit is exceeded, it may be possible to have the cylinder head resurfaced.

6 Examine the valve seats in each of the combustion chambers. If the seats are severely pitted, cracked or burned, then they will need to be examined by an engine overhaul specialist. If only slight pitting is evident, this can be removed by grinding the valve heads and seats together with coarse, then fine, grinding paste, as described later in this Section.

7 If the valve guides are worn, indicated by a side-to-side motion of the valve, oversize valve guides maybe available, and valves with oversize stems can be fitted. This work is best carried out by an engine overhaul specialist. A dial gauge may be used to determine whether the amount of side play of a valve exceeds the specified maximum.

8 Check the follower bores in the cylinder head for wear. If excessive wear is evident, the cylinder head must be renewed. Also check the follower oil holes in the cylinder head for obstructions.

Valves

9 Examine the head of each valve for pitting, burning, cracks and general wear, and check the valve stem for scoring and wear ridges. Rotate the valve, and check for any obvious indication that it is bent. Look for pitting and excessive wear on the end of each valve stem. If the valve appears satisfactory at this stage, measure the valve stem diameter at several points using a micrometer **(see illustration)**. Any significant difference in the readings obtained indicates wear of the valve stem. Should any of these conditions be apparent, the valve(s) must be renewed. If the valves are in satisfactory condition, they should be ground (lapped) onto their respective seats to ensure a smooth gas-tight seal.

10 Valve grinding is carried out as follows. Place the cylinder head upside-down on a bench, with a block of wood at each end to give clearance for the valve stems.

6.6 Place the components in a labelled bag

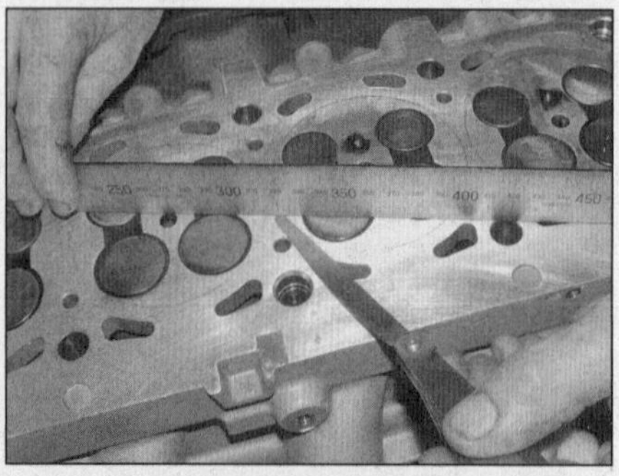

7.5 Use a straight-edge to check for surface distortion

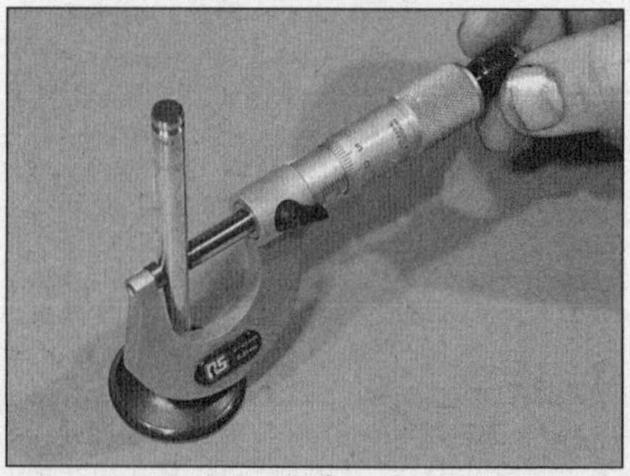

7.9 Measure the valve stem diameter at several points

8.2a Locate the valve stem oil seal on the valve guide...

8.2b... and press the seal firmly onto the guide using a suitable socket

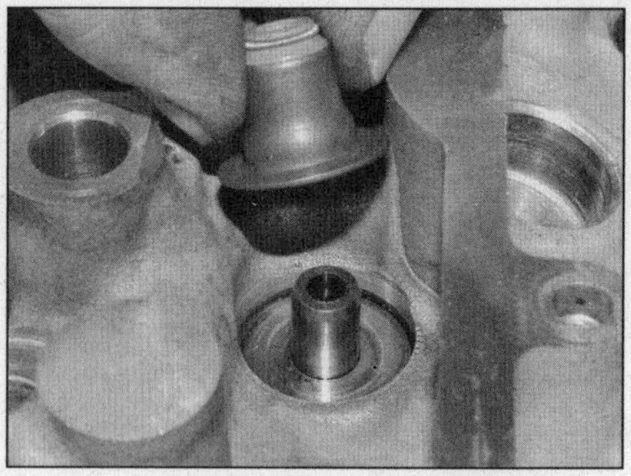

8.2c On some engines, the valve stem oil seal is integral with the spring seat

11 Smear a trace of coarse carborundum paste on the seat face in the cylinder head, and press a suction grinding tool onto the relevant valve head. With a semi-rotary action, grind the valve head to its seat, lifting the valve occasionally to redistribute the grinding paste. When a dull, matt, even surface is produced on the faces of both the valve seat and the valve, wipe off the paste and repeat the process with fine carborundum paste. When a smooth unbroken ring of light grey matt finish is produced on both the valve and seat faces, the grinding operation is complete. Carefully clean away every trace of grinding paste, taking great care to leave none in the ports or in the valve guides. Clean the valves and valve seats with a paraffin-soaked rag, then with a clean rag, and finally, if an airline is available, blow the valves, valve guides and cylinder head ports clean.

Valve springs

12 Check that all the valve springs are intact. If any one is broken, all should be renewed.

13 If possible, check the free height of the springs against new ones, then stand each spring on a flat surface and check it for squareness. If a spring is found to be too short, or damaged in any way, renew all the springs as a set. Springs suffer from fatigue, and it is a good idea to renew them even if they look serviceable.

8 Cylinder head – reassembly

Note: *New valve stem oil seals should be used on reassembly. A valve spring compressor tool will be required for this operation.*

1 With all the components cleaned, starting at one end of the cylinder head, fit the valve components as follows.

2 Working on the first valve assembly, refit the spring seat then dip the new valve stem oil seal in fresh engine oil. Locate the seal on the valve guide and press the seal firmly onto the guide using a suitable socket **(see illustrations)**.

3 New valve stem oil seals may be supplied with a fitting sleeve, which fits over the collet groove in the valve stem, to prevent damage to the oil seal as it is slid down the valve stem. If no sleeve is supplied, wind a short length of tape round the top of the valve stem to cover the collet groove.

4 Insert the appropriate valve into its guide (if new valves are being fitted, insert each valve into the location to which it has been ground), ensuring that the valve stem is well-lubricated with clean engine oil. If the original components are being refitted, all components must be refitted in their original positions.

5 Fit the valve spring and the spring cap.

6 Fit the spring compressor tool, and compress the valve spring until the spring cap passes beyond the collet groove in the valve stem.

7 Refit the split collets to the groove in the valve stem, with the narrow ends nearest the spring.

HAYNES HiNT ***Use a little dab of grease to hold the collets in position on the valve stem while the spring compressor is released.***

8 Slowly release the compressor tool, ensuring that the collets are not dislodged from the groove. When the compressor is fully released, give the top of the valve assembly a tap with a soft-faced mallet to settle the components.

9 Repeat the procedure for the remaining valves, ensuring that if the original components are being used, they are all refitted in their original positions.

9 Engine – initial start-up after overhaul

1 With the engine refitted in the vehicle, double-check the engine oil and coolant levels. Make a final check that everything has been reconnected, and that there are no tools or rags left in the engine compartment.

2 Start the engine, noting that this may take a little longer than usual. Make sure that the oil pressure warning light goes out.

3 While the engine is idling, check for fuel, water and oil leaks. Don't be alarmed if there are some odd smells and smoke from parts getting hot and burning off oil deposits.

4 Assuming all is well, keep the engine idling until hot water is felt circulating through the top hose, then switch off the engine.

5 After a few minutes, recheck the oil and coolant levels as described in *Weekly checks*, and top-up as necessary.

6 Note that there is no need to retighten the cylinder head bolts once the engine has first run after reassembly.

Chapter 3
Cooling, heating and ventilation systems

Contents

Degrees of difficulty

Easy, suitable for novice with little experience	**Fairly easy,** suitable for beginner with some experience	**Fairly difficult,** suitable for competent DIY mechanic	**Difficult,** suitable for experienced DIY mechanic	**Very difficult,** suitable for expert DIY or professional

Specifications

General

Radiator cap	0.93 to 1.23 bar

Coolant temperature sensor

Resistance:	
20°C	35.48 to 39.20 kΩ
80°C	3.65 to 4.02 kΩ

Thermostat

Opening temperature	80 to 84°C
Fully open	97°C

Air conditioning system

Refrigerant:	
Type	R-134a
Quantity	450g
Compressor oil:	
Type	DH-PR
Quantity	130 cc

Torque wrench settings

Torque wrench settings	Nm	lbf ft
Coolant pump bolts	10	7
Coolant temperature sensor	10	7
Thermostat housing cover bolts	10	7

1 General information and precautions

1 The cooling system is of pressurised type, comprising a pump driven by the auxiliary drivebelt, an aluminium crossflow radiator, electric cooling fan, and a thermostat. The system functions as follows. Cold coolant from the radiator passes through the hose to the coolant pump, where it is pumped around the cylinder block and head passages. After cooling the cylinder bores, combustion surfaces and valve seats, the coolant reaches the underside of the thermostat, which is initially closed. The coolant passes through the heater, and is returned to the coolant pump.

2 When the engine is cold, the coolant circulates only through the cylinder block, cylinder head and heater. When the coolant reaches a predetermined temperature, the thermostat opens and the coolant passes through to the radiator. As the coolant circulates through the radiator, it is cooled by the inrush of air when the car is in forward motion. Airflow is supplemented by the action of the electric cooling fan when necessary. Once the coolant has passed through the radiator, and has cooled, the cycle is repeated.

3 The electric cooling fan, mounted on the rear of the radiator, is controlled by the ECT (Engine Coolant Temperature) sensor. At a predetermined coolant temperature, the fan is actuated.

4 An expansion tank is fitted into the engine compartment to accommodate expansion of the coolant when it gets hot. The expansion tank is connected to the top of the radiator by a small bore rubber hose.

Warning: Do not attempt to remove the expansion tank filler cap, or disturb any part of the cooling system, while the engine is hot; there is a high risk of scalding. If the expansion tank filler cap must be removed before the engine and radiator have fully cooled (even though this is not recommended) the pressure in the cooling system must first be relieved. Cover the cap with a thick layer of cloth, to avoid scalding, and slowly unscrew the filler cap until a hissing sound can be heard. When the hissing has stopped, indicating that the pressure has reduced, slowly unscrew the filler cap until it can be removed; if more hissing sounds are heard, wait until they have stopped before unscrewing the cap completely. At all times, keep well away from the filler cap opening.

Warning: Do not allow antifreeze to come into contact with skin, or with the painted surfaces of the vehicle. Rinse off spills immediately, with plenty of water. Never leave antifreeze lying around in an open container, or in a puddle on the driveway or garage floor. Children and pets are attracted by its sweet smell, but antifreeze can be fatal if ingested.

Warning: If the engine is hot, the electric cooling fan may start rotating even if the engine is not running; be careful to keep hands, hair and loose clothing well clear when working in the engine compartment.

Warning: Refer to Section 9 for precautions to be observed when working on models equipped with air conditioning.

2 Cooling system hoses – disconnection and renewal

Note: *Refer to the warnings given in Section 1 of this Chapter before proceeding. Do not attempt to disconnect any hose while the system is still hot.*

1 If the checks described in Chapter 1, Section 7 reveal a faulty hose, it must be renewed as follows.

2 First drain the cooling system (see Chapter 1, Section 19). If the coolant is not due for renewal, it may be re-used if it is collected in a clean container.

3 Before disconnecting a hose, first note its routing in the engine compartment, and whether it is secured by any additional retaining clips or cable-ties. Use a pair of pliers to release the clamp-type clips, or a screwdriver to slacken the screw-type clips, then move the clips along the hose, clear of the relevant inlet/outlet union. Carefully work the hose free.

4 Note that the radiator inlet and outlet unions are fragile; do not use excessive force when attempting to remove the hoses. If a hose proves to be difficult to remove, try to release it by rotating the hose ends before attempting to free it.

5 When fitting a hose, first slide the clips onto the hose, then work the hose into position. If clamp-type clips were originally fitted, it is a good idea to use screw-type clips when refitting the hose. If the hose is stiff, use a little soapy water (washing-up liquid is ideal) as a lubricant, or soften the hose by soaking it in hot water.

6 Work the hose into position, checking that it is correctly routed and secured. Slide each clip along the hose until it passes over the flared end of the relevant inlet/outlet union, before tightening the clips securely.

7 Refill the cooling system with reference to Chapter 1, Section 19.

8 Check thoroughly for leaks as soon as possible after disturbing any part of the cooling system.

3 Radiator – removal, inspection and refitting

Removal

1 Raise the front of the vehicle and support it securely on axle stands (see *Jacking and vehicle support*). Undo the fasteners and remove the engine undershield **(see illustrations)**. Release the wheel speed

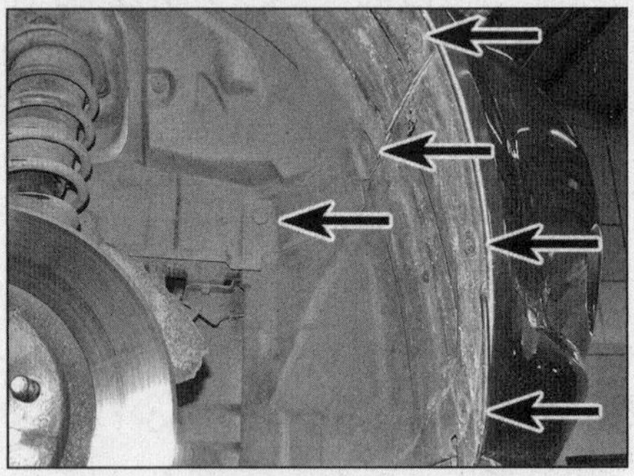

3.1a Remove the fasteners and release the front lower section of the wheel arch liner each side...

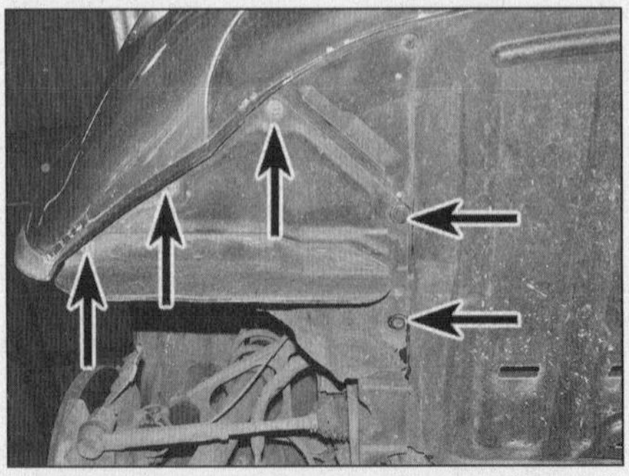

3.1b... and the fasteners underneath

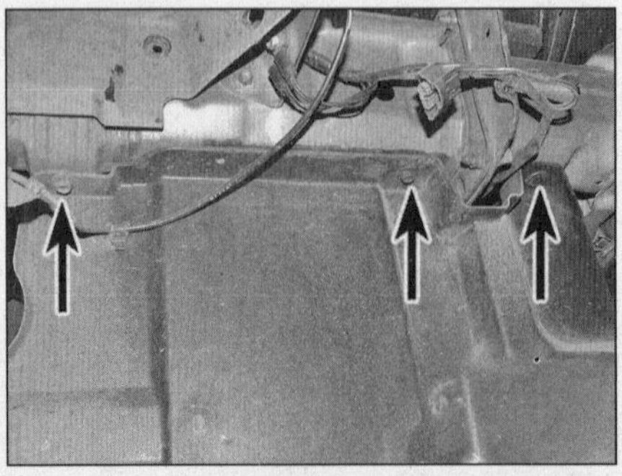

3.1c Release the fastener/screws each side...

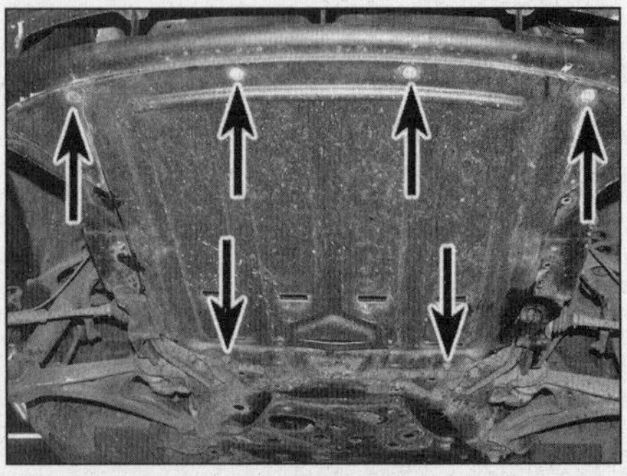

3.1d Then undo the screws and remove the engine undershield

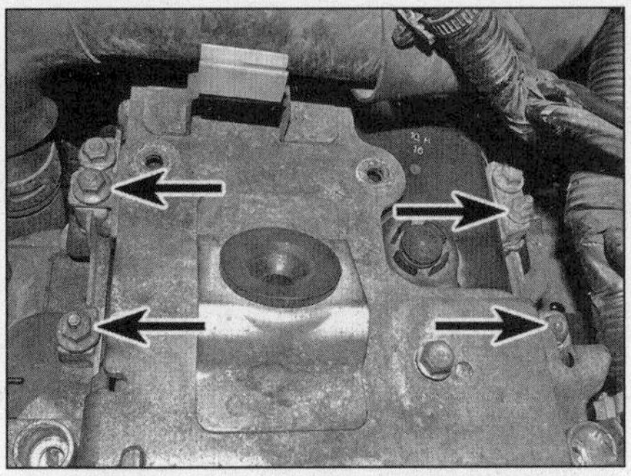

3.5a Undo the PCM retaining nuts...

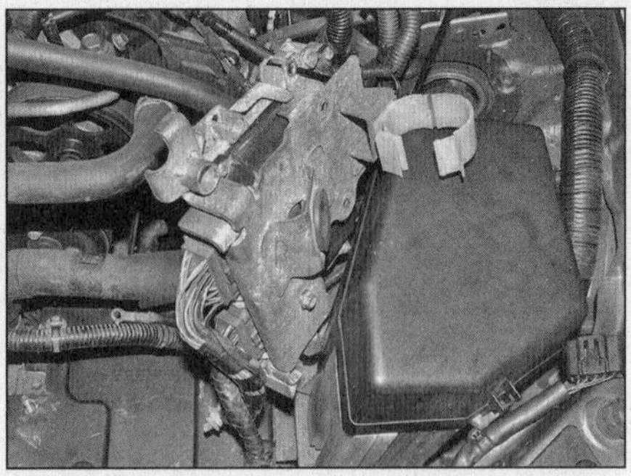

3.5b... and move the assembly to one side

3.6 Undo the nut and remove the cooling duct beneath the PCM

sensor wiring from the clips each side of the central undershield.

2 Drain the engine coolant as described in Chapter 1, Section 19.

3 Remove the battery and battery tray as described in Chapter 5A Section 4.

4 Remove the air cleaner assembly (see Chapter 4A Section 3).

5 Unclip the coolant hose, undo the 4 retaining nuts, release the wiring harness clips and lift the PCM from place **(see illustrations)**. Move the PCM assembly to one side, and secure it with a cable tie.

6 Undo the plastic nut and remove the PCM cooling duct **(see illustration)**.

7 Undo the nuts, lift the coolant expansion tank from place, then release the clips and disconnect the various hoses **(see illustration)**.

8 Disconnect the cooling fan wiring plug, then unclip the wiring harness.

9 Unclip the power steering pipe clamp from the cooling fan frame.

10 Undo the centre pin, prise up the plastic expansion rivet, and remove the plastic cooling duct each side of the radiator **(see illustration)**.

11 Release the clamps then disconnect the coolant hoses from the radiator **(see illustrations)**.

12 Release the power steering cooler pipe and the air conditioning condenser (where applicable) from the radiator (see Section 10). Note: Do not disconnect the hoses from either the power steering coolant pipe or the condenser.

13 Release any hoses from the clips attached to the cooling fan shroud/frame.

14 Remove the upper and lower radiator insulator mounting brackets each side **(see illustrations)**.

15 Lower the radiator and cooling fan assembly from place.

16 If required, detach the cooling fan assembly from the radiator as described in Section 5.

Inspection

17 With the radiator removed, it can be inspected for leaks, damage and internal blockage. If in need of repairs, have a professional radiator repairer perform the work as special techniques are required.

18 Insects and dirt can be cleaned from the radiator with compressed air and a soft brush. Don't bend the cooling fins as this is done.

3.7 Coolant expansion tank retaining nuts and hoses

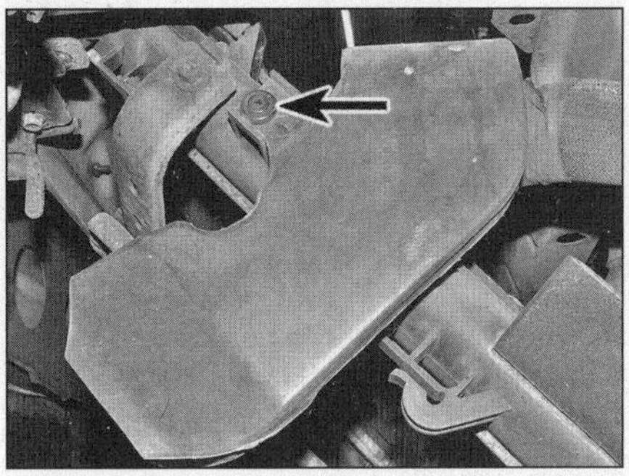

3.10 Remove the plastic expansion rivet to release the cooling ducts

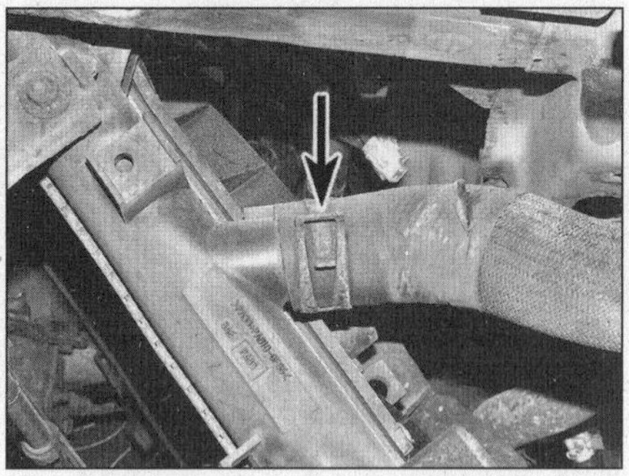

3.11a Release the clamps and disconnect the coolant hoses from the left-...

3.11b... and right-hand sides

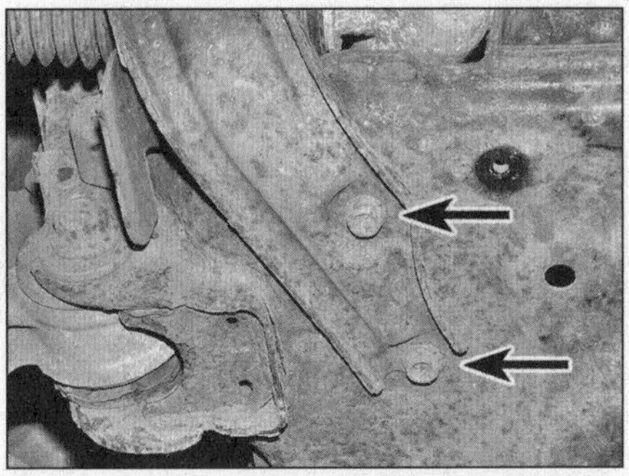

3.14a Lower insulator mounting bracket bolts

3.14b Upper insulator mounting bracket bolts

Warning: Wear eye protection when using compressed air.

Radiator flushing

19 Disconnect the top and bottom hoses and any other relevant hoses from the radiator.

20 Insert a garden hose into the radiator top inlet. Direct a flow of clean water through the radiator, and continue flushing until clean water emerges from the radiator bottom outlet.

21 If after a reasonable period, the water still does not run clear, the radiator can be flushed with a good proprietary cleaning agent. It is important that their manufacturer's instructions are followed carefully. If the contamination is particularly bad, insert the hose in the radiator bottom outlet, and reverse-flush the radiator.

Refitting

22 Refitting is a reversal of removal, bearing in mind the following points:

a) *Ensure that all hoses are correctly reconnected, and their retaining clips securely tightened.*

b) *On completion, refill the cooling system as described in Chapter 1, Section 19.*

4 Thermostat – testing, removal and refitting

Testing

1 Before assuming the thermostat is responsible for a cooling system problem, check the coolant level (*Weekly checks*), drivebelt tension (Chapter 1, Section 6) and temperature gauge (or light) operation.

2 If the engine takes a long time to warm up (as indicated by the temperature gauge or heater operation), the thermostat is probably stuck open. Renew the thermostat.

3 If the engine runs hot, use your hand to check the temperature of the upper radiator hose. If the hose is not hot, but the engine is, the thermostat is probably stuck in the closed position, preventing the coolant inside the engine from traveling through the radiator. Renew the thermostat.

4 If the lower radiator hose is hot, it means that the coolant is flowing and the thermostat is open. Consult the *Fault finding* in Reference at the end of this manual for further diagnosis.

Removal

5 Disconnect the negative cable from the battery as described in Chapter 5A, Section 4.

6 Drain the coolant from the radiator (see Chapter 1, Section 19).

7 Remove the throttle body as described in Chapter 4A Section 10.

8 Release the clamps and disconnect the coolant hoses from the thermostat cover **(see illustration)**.

9 Undo the retaining bolts and remove the thermostat cover. Be prepared for fluid spillage.

10 Remove and discard the thermostat cover gasket. Note that the thermostat is integral with the cover.

11 Thoroughly clean the sealing surfaces.

Refitting

12 Using a new gasket, fit the new thermostat and cover, then tighten the retaining bolts to the specified torque.

13 The remainder of refitting is a reversal of removal, remembering to refill the cooling system (Chapter 1 Section 19).

5 Electric cooling fan – removal and refitting

Warning: If the engine is hot, the cooling fan may start up at any time. Take extra precautions when working in the vicinity of the fan.

Removal

1 Remove the radiator and cooling fan assembly as described in Section 3.

2 Unclip the coolant hose from the fan shroud.

3 Release the upper clips and detach the cooling fan shroud from the radiator **(see illustration)**.

4 If required, undo the nut and pull the fan blade from the motor **(see illustration)**.

5 Undo the bolts and detach the fan motor from the shroud.

Refitting

6 Refitting is a reversal of removal, bearing in mind the following points:

a) *Ensure that the shroud is correctly located on the radiator.*

b) *Use new cable-ties to secure all disturbed wiring harnesses.*

c) *On completion, start the engine and run it until it reaches normal operating temperature; continue to run the engine, and check that the cooling fan cuts in and functions correctly.*

6 Engine coolant temperature sensor (ECT) – testing, removal and refitting

Testing

1 Remove the ECT sensor as described later in this Section.

2 If the temperature gauge indicates excessive temperature after running a while, see the Fault finding Section at the end of the manual.

3 Connect a multimeter to the sensor terminals, then place the sensor is a pan of water at 20°C. Measure the resistance between the sensor terminals and compare the reading obtained with that specified at the beginning of this Chapter.

4 Now bring the water temperature up to 80°C, and measure the resistance again. Compare the reading with that given in the Specifications. If the readings obtained differ greatly from those specified, the sensor is most likely to be faulty.

Removal

5 Drain the coolant (see Chapter 1, Section 19).

6 Remove the wiper arms as described in Chapter 12 Section 14.

7 Prise up the plastic cap and remove the

4.8 Slacken the clamps and disconnect the hoses from the thermostat cover

5.3 Release the clip each side securing the shroud to the radiator

5.4 Undo the nut and pull the blade from the motor

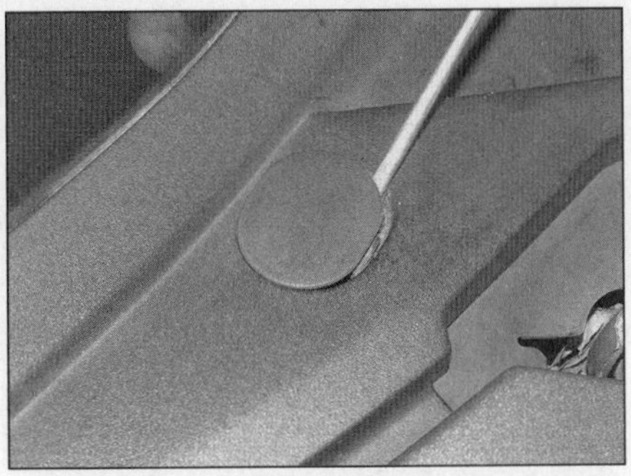
6.7 Prise up the caps and undo the screws

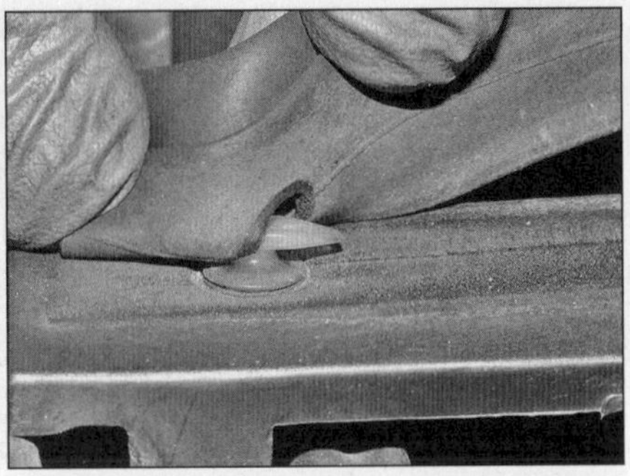
6.8 Remove the rubber weatherstrip

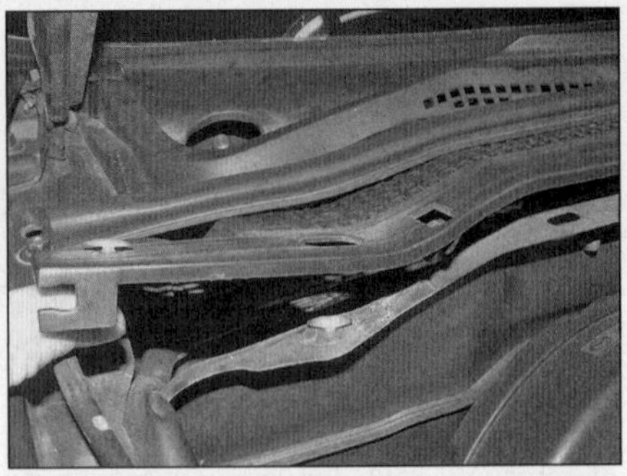
6.9 Pull up the front edge of the cowl panel

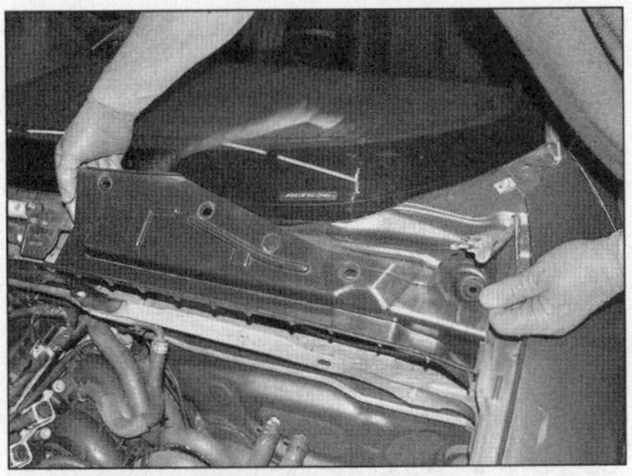
6.10 Remove the side cowl panel each side

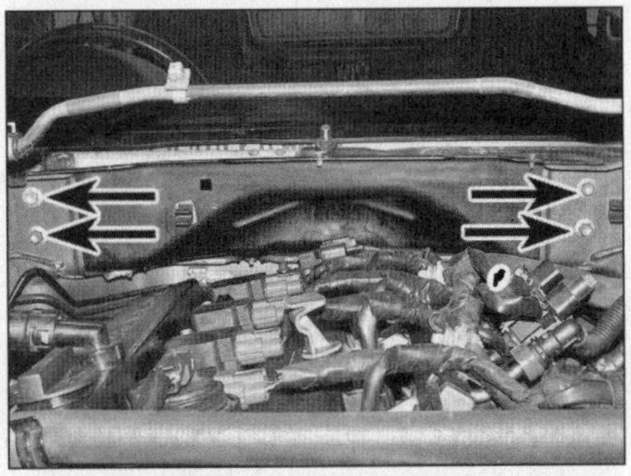
6.12a The service access cover is secured by 4 bolts at the front...

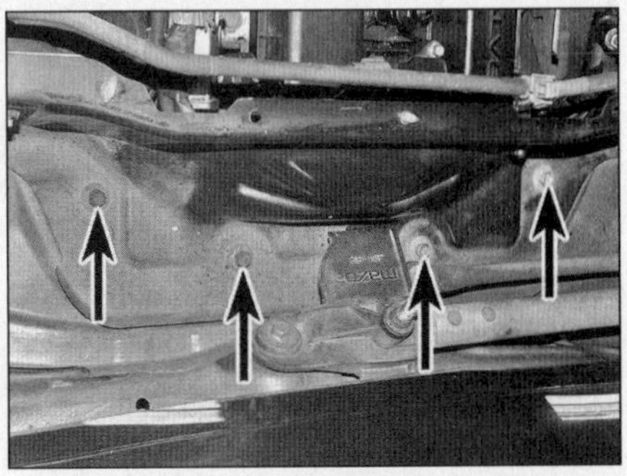
6.12b... and 4 bolts at the top

screw at each end of the windscreen cowl panel **(see illustration)**.

8 Unclip the washer hose from the cowl panel, and remove the rubber weatherstrip **(see illustration)**.

9 Pull up the front edge of the cowl panel, the pull it downwards from the base of the windscreen **(see illustration)**.

10 Release the fasteners and remove the side cowl panel each side **(see illustration)**.

11 Unclip the heater hose/pipe and move it to one side.

12 Undo the bolts and remove the service access cover from the engine compartment bulkhead **(see illustrations)**.

13 Disconnect the wiring connector from the sensor **(see illustration)**.

14 Using a deep socket or a spaner, remove the sensor.

Refitting

15 Install the new sensor, and tighten it to the specified torque. Do not use thread sealer as it may electrically insulate the sending unit. Connect the electrical connector.

16 Refitting is a reversal of removal. Refill the cooling system and check for coolant leakage and proper gauge operation.

7 Coolant pump – removal and refitting

⚠ ***Warning: Wait until the engine is completely cool before beginning this procedure.***

Removal

1 Remove the battery cover and disconnect the cable from the negative battery terminal (see Chapter 5A Section 4).

2 Drain the cooling system (see Chapter 1 Section 19).

3 Remove the air cleaner assembly as described in Chapter 4A Section 3.

4 Loosen the coolant pump pulley bolts, then remove the auxiliary drivebelt (see Chapter 1 Section 6).

5 Remove the coolant pump pulley **(see illustration)**.

6 Remove the bolts attaching the coolant pump to the engine block and remove the pump from the engine **(see illustration)**. If the pump is stuck, gently tap it with a soft-faced hammer to break the seal.

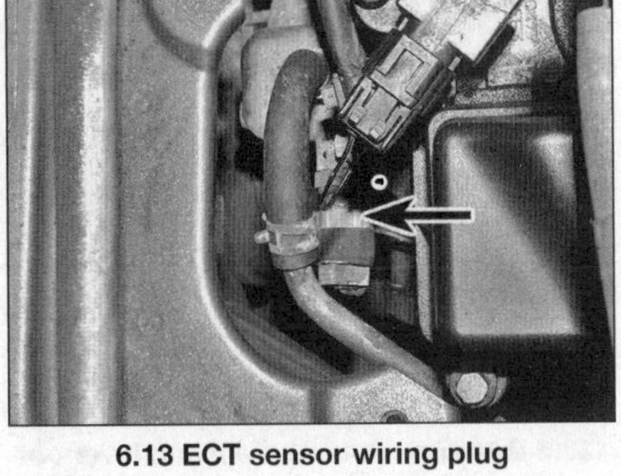
6.13 ECT sensor wiring plug

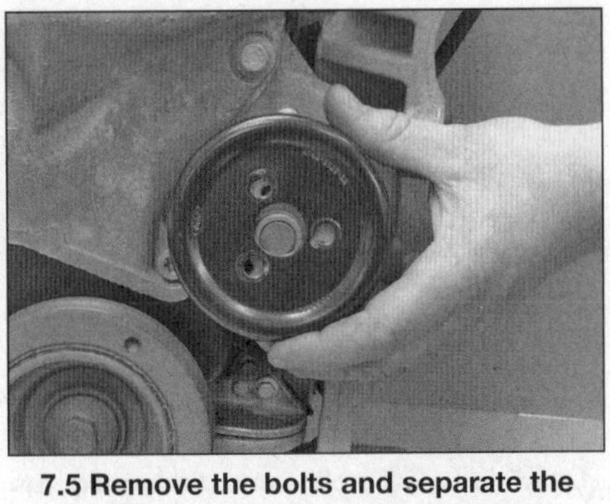
7.5 Remove the bolts and separate the coolant pump pulley from the pump

7.6 Remove the water pump bolts

7 Clean the bolt threads and the threaded holes in the engine and remove all corrosion and sealant. Discard the O-ring seal.

Installation

8 Apply a thin film of clean engine oil to the new O-ring seal, then fit the seal to the pump and carefully mate the pump to the housing.

9 Install the coolant pump bolts and tighten them to the specified torque.

10 The remainder of installation is the reverse of removal. Refill the cooling system as described in Chatper 1 Section 19.

11 Operate the engine to check for leaks.

8 Heater/ventilation system components – removal and refitting

Heater/air conditioning controls – removal and refitting

1 Disconnect the battery negative terminal as described in Chapter 5A Section 4.

2 Remove the centre console as described in Chapter 11 Section 27.

3 Remove the facia centre panel as described in Chapter 11 Section 28.

4 Undo the 4 retaining screws, and detach the control unit from the centre panel **(see illustration)**.

5 Refitting is a reversal of removal.

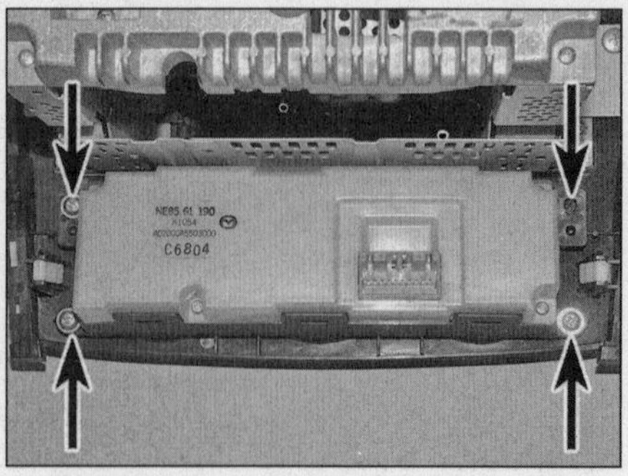

8.4 Heater control panel retaining screws

Heater matrix

Removal

6 Remove the air conditioning/heater/air distribution housing as described later in this Section.

7 Carefully peel back the foam seal, then undo the screws and remove the pipe connection flange **(see illustration)**. Recover the rubber grommets around the pipes.

8 Undo the two screws, release the clips around the edge, disconnect the wiring plug and remove the central demister flap housing **(see illustrations)**.

9 Undo the two screws, disconnect the wiring plug, and remove the servo motor from the matrix housing **(see illustration)**.

10 Lift the heater matrix from place **(see illustration)**.

11 If required, prise off the clips and detach the pipes from the matrix **(see illustration)**. Note the new seals and clips will be required.

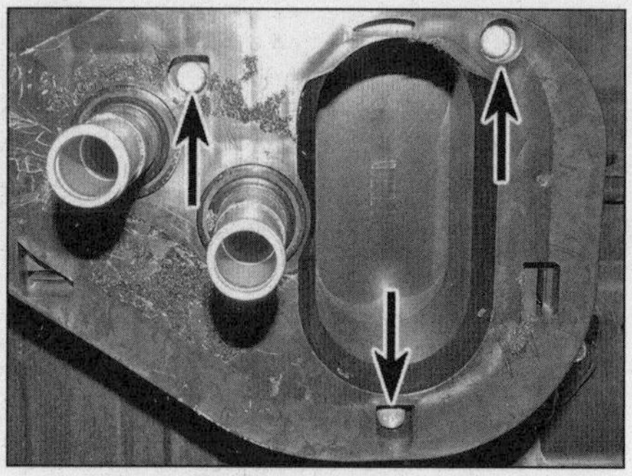

8.7 Undo the screws and remove the pipe connection flange

Refitting

12 Refitting is a reversal of the removal procedure.

Heater blower motor

Removal

13 Disconnect the battery negative terminal as described in Chapter 5A Section 4.

14 Pull up and remove the passengers side door sill trim panel as described in Chapter 11 Section 26.

15 Pull the rubber weatherstrip from the passengers side A-pillar, then undo the fastener and pull the kick panel into the cabin to release the retaining clips **(see illustration)**.

16 Reach under the passenger's side of the

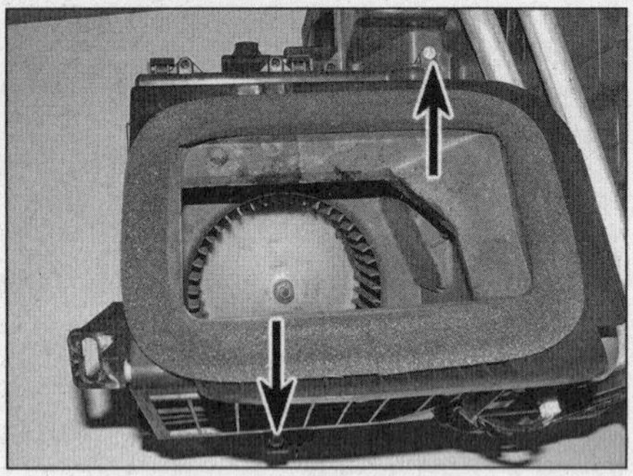

8.8a Undo the screws...

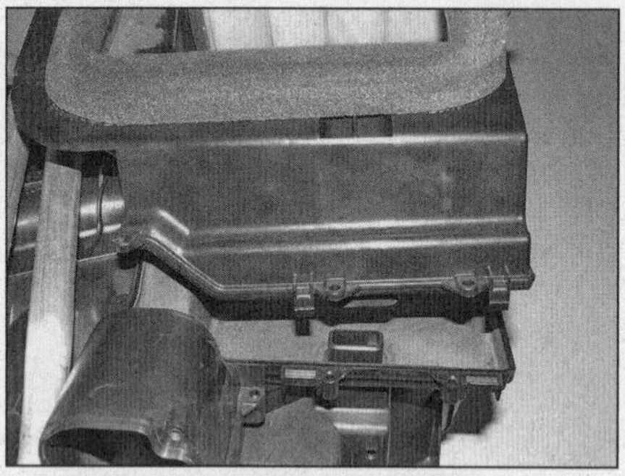

8.8b... release the clips and lift the flap housing

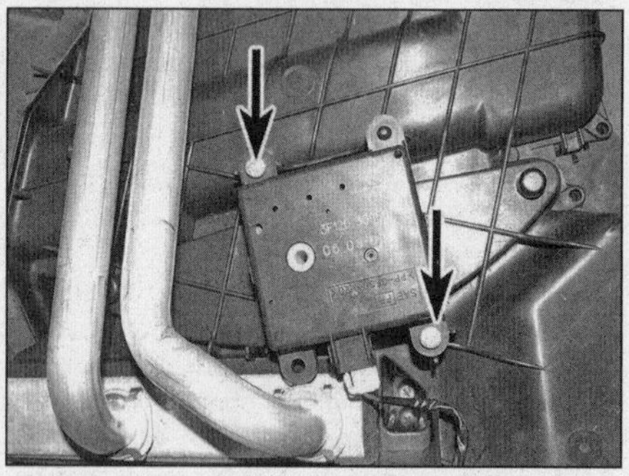

8.9 Undo the screws and remove the servo motor

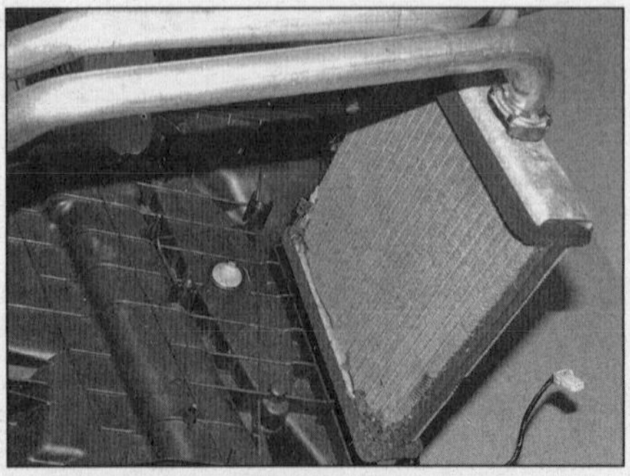

8.10 Slide the matrix upwards from the housing

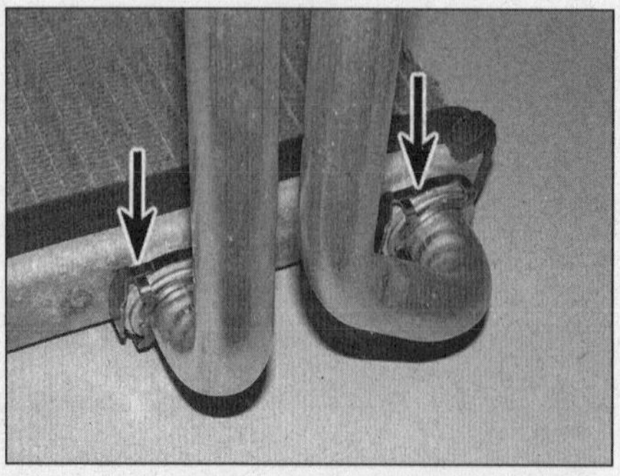

8.11 Prise off the clips and disconnect the pipes

8.15 Prise up the centre pin and lever out the plastic expansion rivet

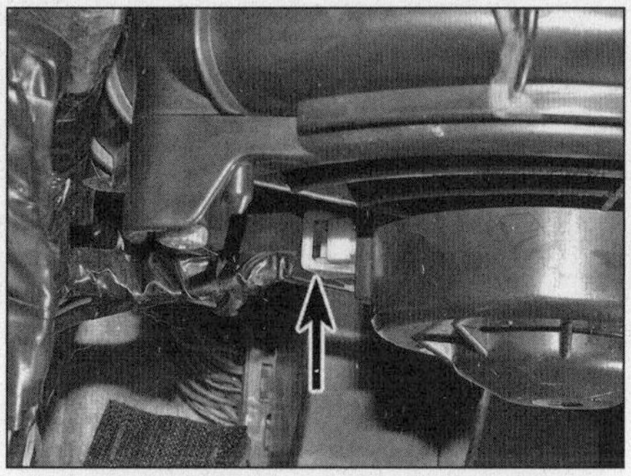

8.16 Blower motor wiring plug

facia, disconnect the blower motor wiring plug **(see illustration)**.

17 Undo the retaining screws, and lower the blower motor from the air distribution housing **(see illustration)**.

Refitting

18 Refitting is a reversal of the removal procedure.

Power MOS FET

Removal

19 The Power Metal Oxide Semiconductor Field Effect Transistor (MOS FET) controls the blower motor speed, and is located on the side of the air distribution housing.

20 Disconnect the battery negative terminal as described in Chapter 5A Section 4.

21 Remove the passengers side kick panel (Chapter 11 Section 28) then peel back the carpet.

8.26a The housing is secured by a nut at the right-hand end...

8.26c... to the right of the blower motor...

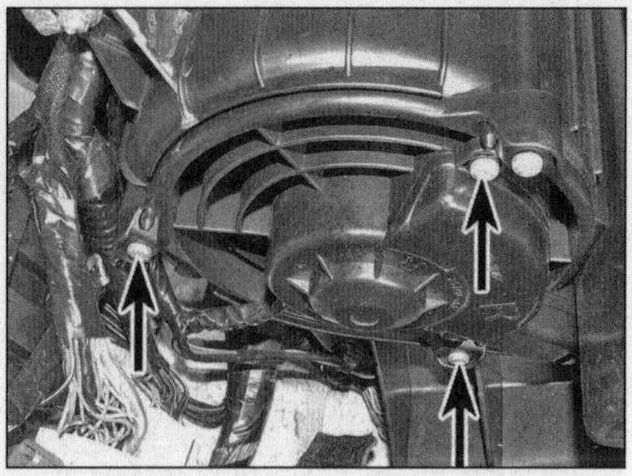

8.17 Blower motor retaining screws

22 The MOS FET is located on the front of the air distribution housing, and access is extremely limited. Disconnect the MOS FET wiring plug.

23 Using a short cross-head screwdriver, undo the two retaining screws then pull the MOS FET forwards, and manoeuvre it from the housing **(see illustration)**.

Refitting

24 Refitting is the reverse of removal.

Air conditioning/heating/air distribution housing

Note: *On models with air conditioning, it is not possible to remove the air distribution housing without opening the refrigerant circuit. Have the refrigerant discharged at a dealer service department or an automotive air conditioning repair facility before proceeding.*

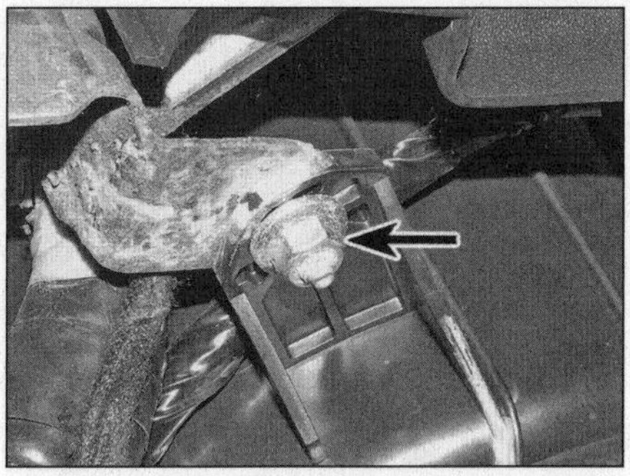

8.26b... a nut to the left of the blower motor...

8.26d... and one on the front face of the housing

8.23 Power MOS FET retaining screws (heater housing removed for clarity)

Removal

25 Remove the complete facia assembly as described in Chapter 11 Section 28.

26 Undo the retaining nuts, disconnect any wiring plugs from the housing, then with the help of an assistant, detach the facia and crossmember from the housing **(see illustrations)**.

Refitting

27 Refitting is the reverse of removal, noting the following points:

a) *Renew the refrigerant pipe O-ring seals, and apply a little refrigerant oil to them prior to fitting.*
b) *Renew the coolant as described in Chatper 1 Section 19.*
c) *Have the refrigerant circuit tested and recharged upon completion.*

9 Air conditioning system – general information and precautions

General information

1 Air conditioning is available on most models. It enables the temperature of incoming air to be lowered, and also dehumidifies the air, which makes for rapid demisting and increased comfort.

2 The cooling side of the system works in the same way as a domestic refrigerator. Refrigerant gas is drawn into a belt-driven compressor, and passes into a condenser mounted in front of the radiator, where it loses heat and becomes liquid. The liquid passes through an expansion valve to an evaporator, where it changes from liquid under high pressure to gas under low pressure. This change is accompanied by a drop in temperature, which cools the evaporator. The refrigerant returns to the compressor, and the cycle begins again.

3 Air blown through the evaporator passes to the air distribution unit, where it is mixed with hot air blown through the heater matrix, to achieve the desired temperature in the passenger compartment.

4 The heating side of the system works in the same way as on models without air conditioning.

9.6a Air conditioning refrigerant circuit service ports are located at the front of the engine compartment...

9.6b... and at the rear

5 The operation of the system is controlled electronically. Any problems with the system should be referred to a Mazda dealer or air conditioning specialist.

Air conditioning service ports

6 The low-pressure and high-pressure service ports are located within the engine compartment **(see illustrations)**.

Precautions

7 It is necessary to observe special precautions whenever dealing with any part of the system, its associated components, and any items which necessitate disconnection of the system.

Warning: The refrigeration circuit contains a liquid refrigerant. This refrigerant is potentially dangerous, and should only be handled by qualified persons. If it is splashed onto the skin, it can cause frostbite. It is not itself poisonous, but in the presence of a naked flame it forms a poisonous gas; inhalation of the vapour through a lighted cigarette could prove fatal. Uncontrolled discharging of the refrigerant is dangerous, and potentially damaging to the environment. It is therefore dangerous to disconnect any part of the system without specialised knowledge and equipment. If for any reason the system must be disconnected, entrust this task to your Mazda dealer or air conditioning specialist.

Caution: Do not operate the air conditioning system if it is known to be short of refrigerant, as this may damage the compressor.

10 Air conditioning system components – removal and refitting

Warning: The air conditioning system is under high pressure. Do not loosen any fittings or remove any components until after the system has been discharged. Air conditioning refrigerant should be properly discharged into an approved type of container at a dealer service department or an automotive air conditioning repair facility capable of handling R134a refrigerant. Cap or plug the pipe lines as soon as they are disconnected, to prevent the entry of moisture. Always wear eye protection when disconnecting air conditioning system fittings.

Note: *This Section refers to the components of the air conditioning system itself – refer to Section 8 for details of components common to the heating/ventilation system.*

Condenser

1 Raise the front of the vehicle and support it securely on axle stands (see *Jacking and vehicle support*). Undo the fasteners and remove the undershield beneath the radiator.

2 Detach the power steering cooling pipe from the condenser **(see illustrations)**. There's no need to disconnect the pipe.

3 Undo the bolts and disconnect the refrigerant pipes from each end of the condenser **(see illustration)**. Plug the openings immediately to prevent contamination and oil loss.

4 Undo the mounting bolts and lift the condenser out from under the vehicle and store it upright, to prevent fluid loss **(see illustration)**. Take care not to damage the condenser or radiator fins.

5 Refitting is the reverse of removal. Renew the O-rings and lubricate with refrigerant oil.

6 If a new condenser has been fitted, add 20 ml of refrigerant oil to the system during recharge.

7 Have the system evacuated, charged and leak-tested by the specialist who discharged it.

10.2a The power steering cooling pipe is secured by a bolt on the left-hand side...

10.2b... and one on the right-hand side

10.3a Disconnect the refrigerant pipe on the right-hand side...

10.3b... and on the left-hand side

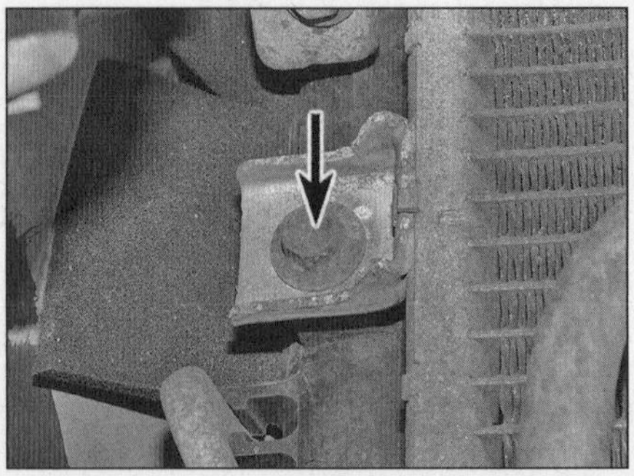

10.4 Undo the condenser mounting bolt each side

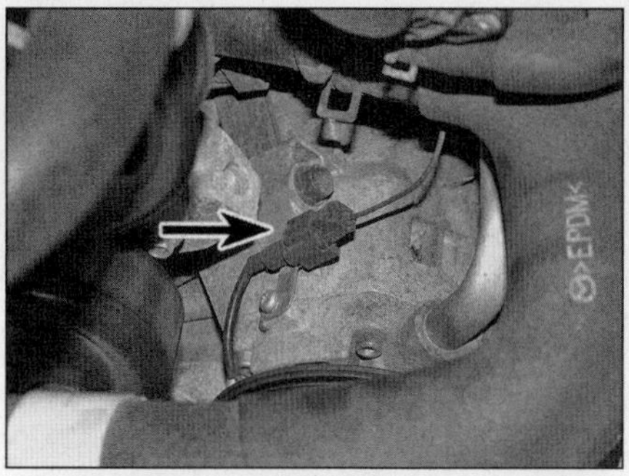

10.20 Disconnect the compressor wiring plug

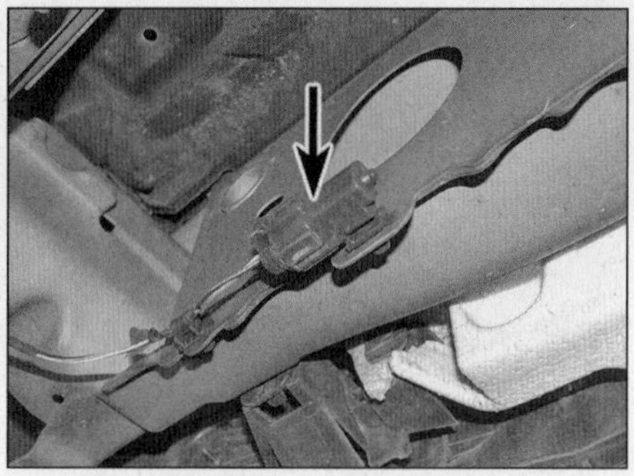

10.27 Ambient temperature sensor

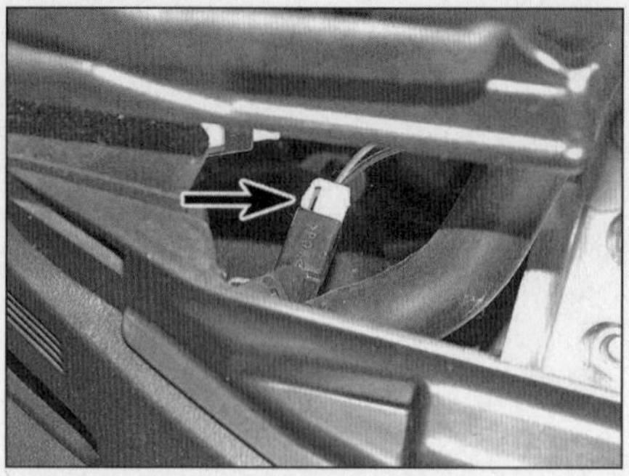

10.31 Cabin temperature sensor wiring plug

Evaporator and expansion valve

8 Have the refrigerant discharged at a dealer service department or a suitably-equipped repairer.

9 Remove the heater matrix as described in Section 8.

10 Remove the evaporator along with the pipes and expansion valve.

11 Disconnect the expansion valve fittings and remove the expansion valve from the evaporator. Immediately plug/cover the open fittings to keep moisture and contamination out of the system.

12 Check the evaporator core and fittings for cracks or any other damage. Renew the evaporator if necessary.

13 Evaporator housing refitting is the reverse of removal. Renew any O-rings with new ones and lubricate them with refrigerant oil prior to installation.

14 Have the system evacuated, charged and leak-tested by the specialist who discharged it.

Compressor

15 Have the refrigerant discharged at a dealer service department or a suitably-equipped repairer.

16 Disconnect the battery negative terminal as described in Chapter 5A, Section 4.

17 Remove the air cleaner assembly as described in Chapter 4A Section 3.

18 Remove the PCM as described in Chapter 4A Section 11.

19 Remove the auxiliary drivebelt as described in Chapter 1, Section 6.

20 Disconnect the refrigerant pipes and compressor electrical connector **(see illustration)**. Plug the pipes and openings to prevent contamination and oil loss.

21 Remove the upper and lower mounting bolts, then manoeuvre the compressor from place.

22 If a new or rebuilt compressor is being fitted, follow the directions supplied with the compressor regarding the proper level of refrigerant oil prior to installation.

23 Refit the compressor in the reverse order of removal; renew all seals disturbed.

24 Have the system evacuated, charged and leak-tested by the specialist that discharged it.

Ambient temperature sensor

25 Raise the front of the vehicle and support it securely on axle stands (see *Jacking and vehicle support*). Undo the fasteners and remove the undershield beneath the radiator.

26 Disconnect the battery negative lead as described in Chapter 5A Section 4.

27 Disconnect the wiring plug then unclip and remove the sensor **(see illustration)**.

28 Refitting is a reversal of removal.

Cabin temperature sensor

29 Disconnect the battery negative lead as described in Chapter 5A Section 4.

30 Unclip and remove the trim panel beneath the steering column.

31 Disconnect the wiring plug, then unclip and remove the sensor **(see illustration)**. The sensor is located to the left of the steering column.

32 Refitting is a reversal of removal.

Solar sensor

33 Disconnect the battery negative lead as described in Chapter 5A Section 4.

34 Carefully prise the solar sensor from the facia.

35 Disconnect the sensor wiring plug.

36 Refitting is a reversal of removal.

Chapter 4 Part A
Fuel and exhaust systems

Contents

Degrees of difficulty

Easy, suitable for novice with little experience	**Fairly easy,** suitable for beginner with some experience	**Fairly difficult,** suitable for competent DIY mechanic	**Difficult,** suitable for experienced DIY mechanic	**Very difficult,** suitable for expert DIY or professional

Specifications

System type

All models	Indirect sequential multi-point injection with electronic engine management

Fuel system data

Fuel pump type	Electric, immersed in tank
Fuel pump output pressure	3.7 to 4.5 bar
Fuel hold pressure	at least 2.0 bar
Injector resistance	12 to 16 Ω
Idle air control valve resistance	11.4 to 12.6 Ω

Torque wrench settings

Torque wrench settings	Nm	lbf ft
Camshaft position sensor bolt	6	4
Crankshaft position sensor bolt	6	4
Exhaust manifold nuts	50	37
Fuel rail	22	16
Intake manifold	20	15
Throttle body	10	7

1 General information and precautions

1 The fuel supply system consists of a fuel tank (which is mounted under the rear of the vehicle, with an electric fuel pump immersed in it), a fuel filter, and fuel supply pipe. The fuel pump supplies fuel to the fuel rail, which acts as a reservoir for the fuel injectors which inject fuel into the intake tracts. A fuel filter and pressure regulator are incorporated into the fuel supply circuit.

Warning: Many of the procedures in this Chapter required the disconnection of fuel lines and connections, which may result in some fuel spillage. Before carrying out any operation on the fuel system, refer to the precautions given in 'Safety first!', and follow then implicitly. Petrol is a highly dangerous and volatile liquid, and the precautions necessary when handling it cannot be overstressed.

Warning: Residual pressure will remain in the fuel lines long after the vehicle was last used. When disconnecting any fuel line, first depressurise the fuel system as described in Section 7.

2 Fuel pipes and fittings – general information and disconnection

1 Disconnect the cable from the negative battery terminal (see Chapter 5A Section 4) before proceeding.
2 The fuel supply pipe connects the fuel pump in the fuel tank to the fuel rail on the engine.
3 Whenever you're working under the vehicle, be sure to inspect all fuel and evaporative emission pipes for leaks, kinks, dents and other damage. Always replace a damaged fuel pipe immediately.
4 If you find signs of dirt in the pipes during disassembly, disconnect all pipes and blow them out with compressed air. Inspect the fuel strainer on the fuel pump pick-up unit for damage and deterioration.

Steel tubing

5 It is critical that the fuel pipes be replaced with pipes of equivalent type and specification.
6 Some steel fuel pipes have threaded fittings. When loosening these fittings, hold the stationary fitting with a spanner while turning the union nut.

Plastic tubing

Warning: When removing or installing plastic fuel tubing, be careful not to bend or twist it too much, which can damage it. Also, plastic fuel tubing is NOT heat resistant, so keep it away from excessive heat.

7 When replacing fuel system plastic tubing, use only original equipment replacement plastic tubing.

Flexible hoses

8 When replacing fuel system flexible hoses, use original equipment replacements, or hose to the same specification.
9 Don't route fuel hoses (or metal pipes) within 100 mm of the exhaust system or within 280 mm of the catalytic converter. Make sure that no rubber hoses are installed directly against the vehicle, particularly in places where there is any vibration. If allowed to touch some vibrating part of the vehicle, a hose can easily become chafed and it might start leaking. A good rule of thumb is to maintain a minimum of 8.0 mm clearance around a hose (or metal pipe) to prevent contact with the vehicle underbody.

Disconnecting Fuel pipe Fittings

10 Typical fuel pipe fittings:

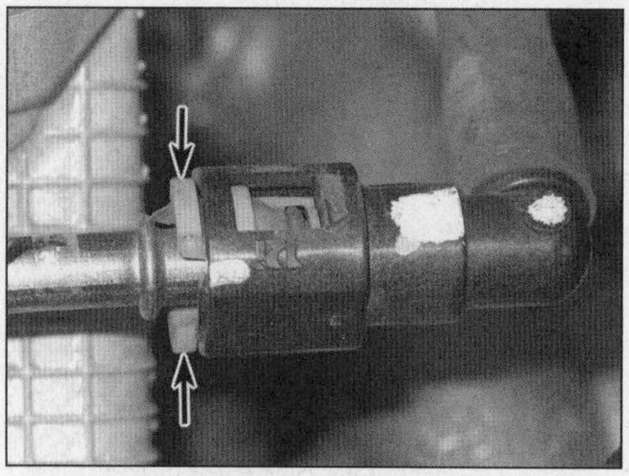

2.10a Two-tab type fitting; depress both tabs with your fingers, then pull the fuel pipe and the fitting apart

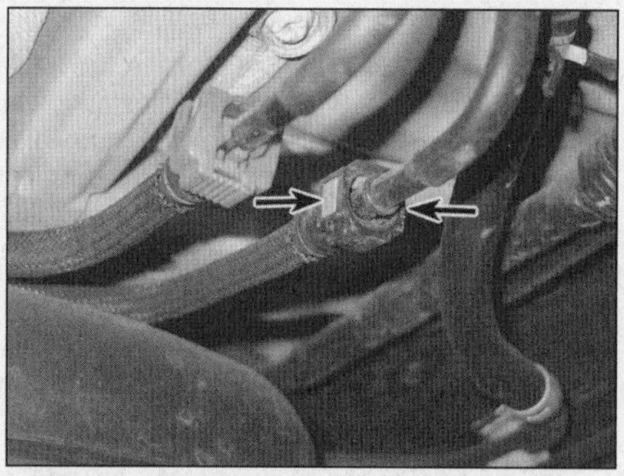

2.10b On this type of fitting, depress the two buttons on opposite sides of the fitting, then pull it off the fuel pipe

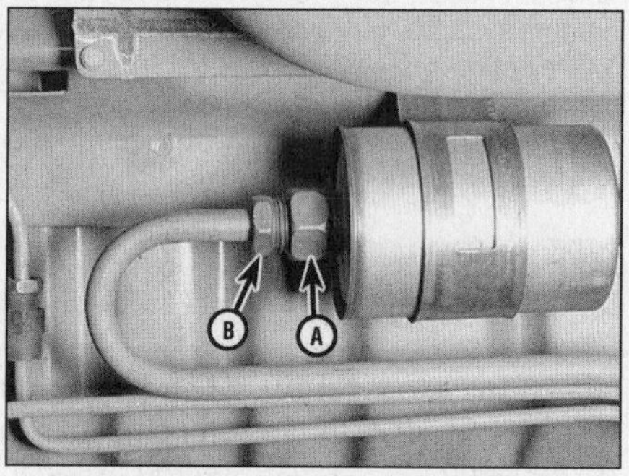

2.10c Threaded fuel pipe fitting; hold the stationary portion of the pipe or component (A) while loosening the union nut (B) with a flare-nut spanner

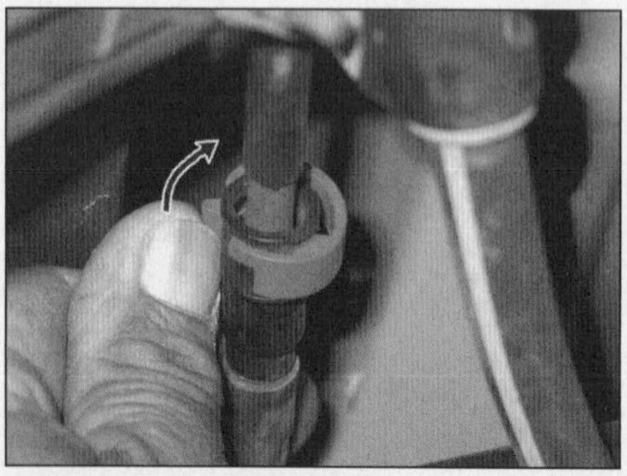

2.10d Plastic collar-type fitting; rotate the outer part of the fitting

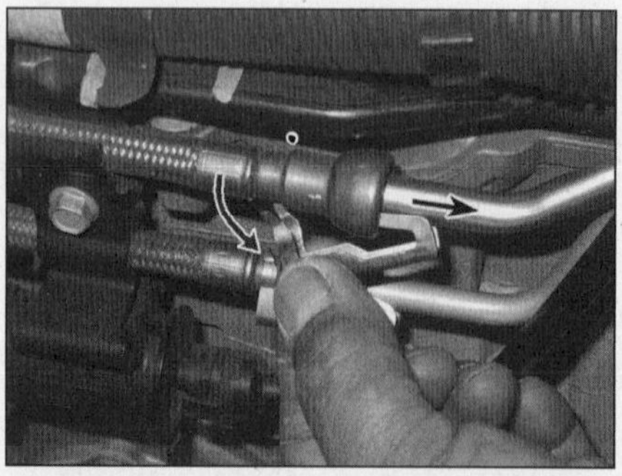

2.10e Metal collar quick-connect fitting; pull the end of the retainer off the fuel pipe and disengage the other end from the female side of the fitting...

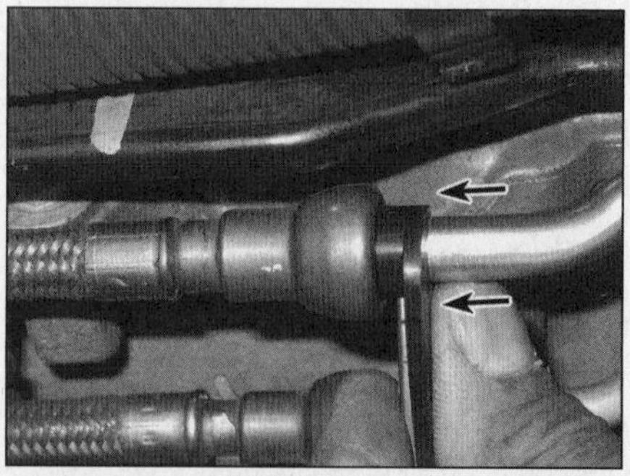

2.10f... insert a fuel pipe separator tool into the female side of the fitting, push it into the fitting and pull the fuel pipe off the pipe

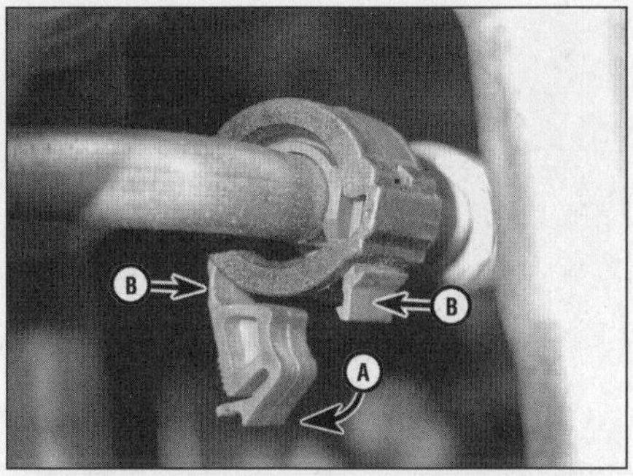

2.10g Some fittings are secured by lock tabs. Release the lock tab (A) and rotate it to the fully-opened position, squeeze the two smaller lock tabs (B)...

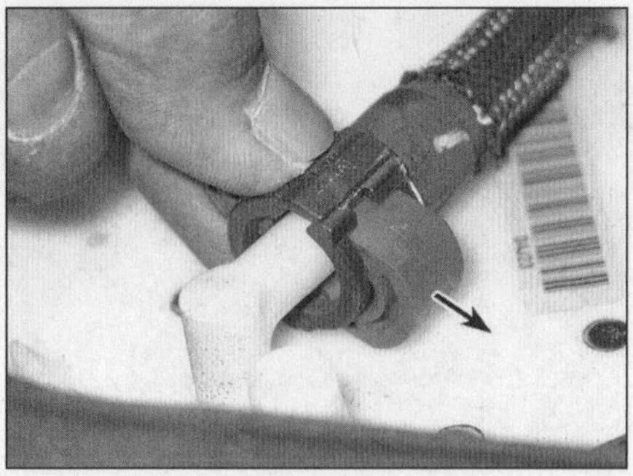

2.10h... then push the retainer out and pull the fuel pipe off the pipe

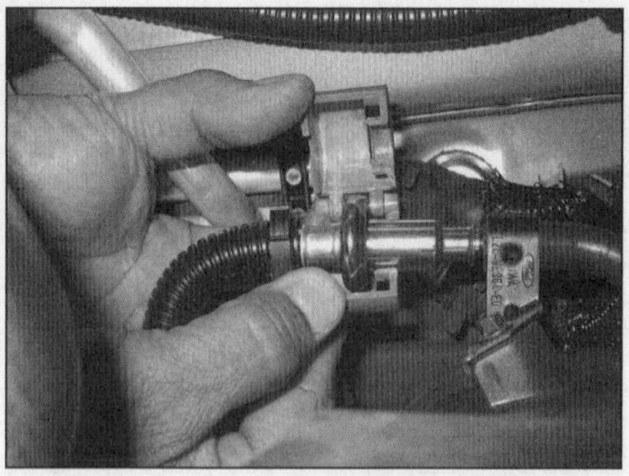

2.10i Spring-lock coupling; remove the safety cover, install a coupling release tool and close the tool around the coupling...

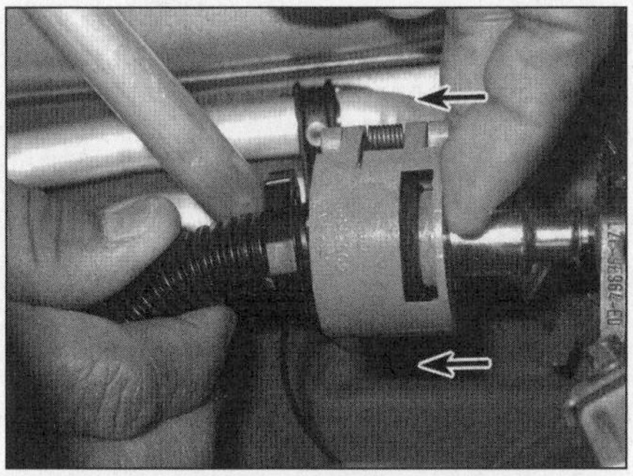

2.10j... push the tool into the fitting, then pull the two pipes apart

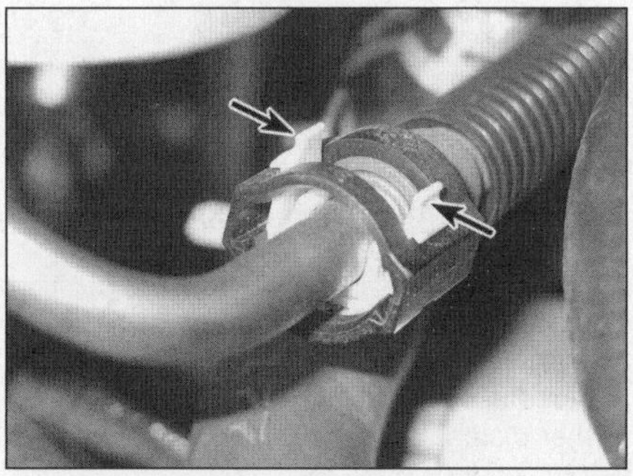

2.10k Hairpin clip type fitting: push the legs of the retainer clip together, then push the clip down all the way until it stops and pull the fuel pipe off the pipe

3 Air cleaner assembly – removal and refitting

1 Loosen the hose clamp and disengage the air intake duct from the air filter housing cover **(see illustration)**.

2 Disconnect the mass airflow sensor wiring plug and release the wiring harness.

3 Unclamp the air filter housing cover, remove the cover and lift out the filter element **(see illustrations)**.

4 Remove the two filter housing mounting nuts **(see illustrations)**, then pull the locator

3.1 Slacken the intake duct clamp

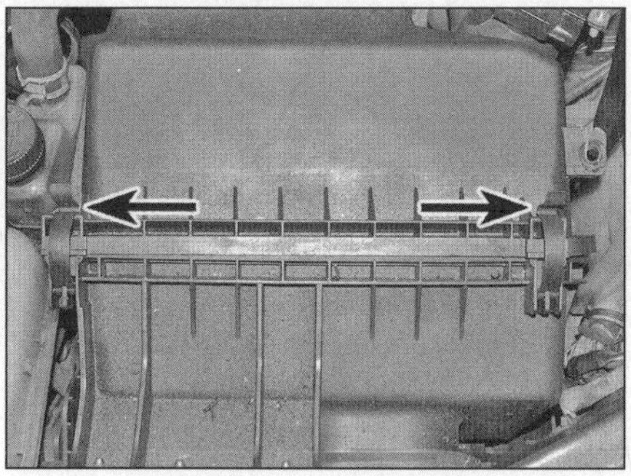

3.3a Release the clamps...

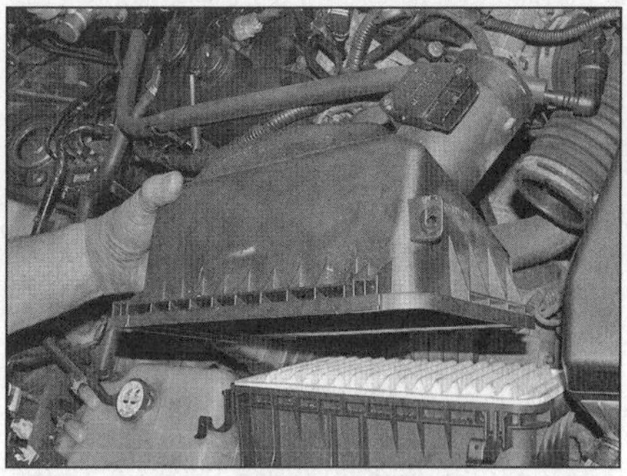

3.3b... remove the cover...

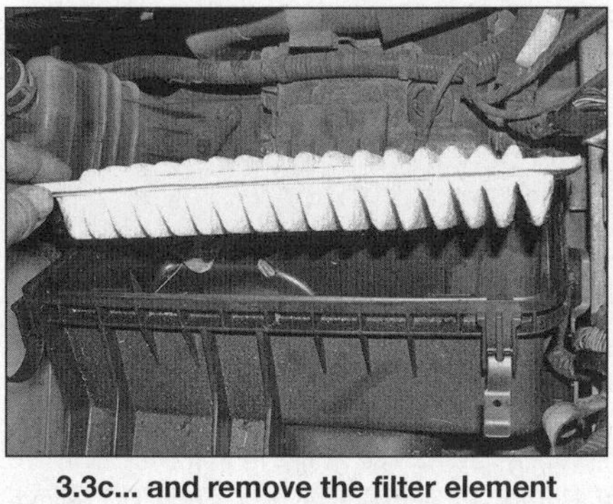

3.3c... and remove the filter element

3.4a Undo the mounting nuts...

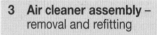

3.4b... and pull the locator pin from the grommet

4.6 Undo the bolts and remove the access panel

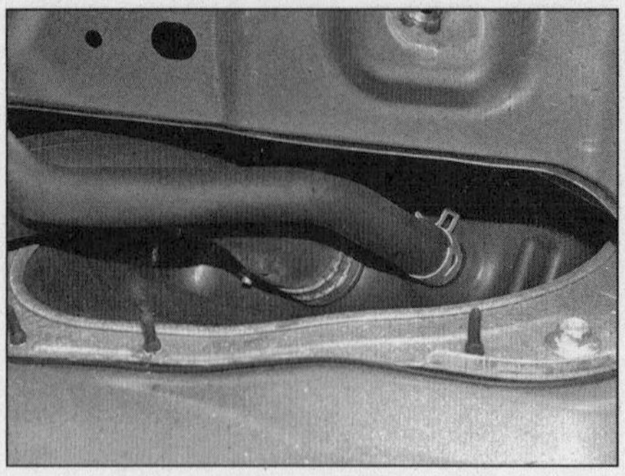

4.7 Release the clamps and disconnect the hoses

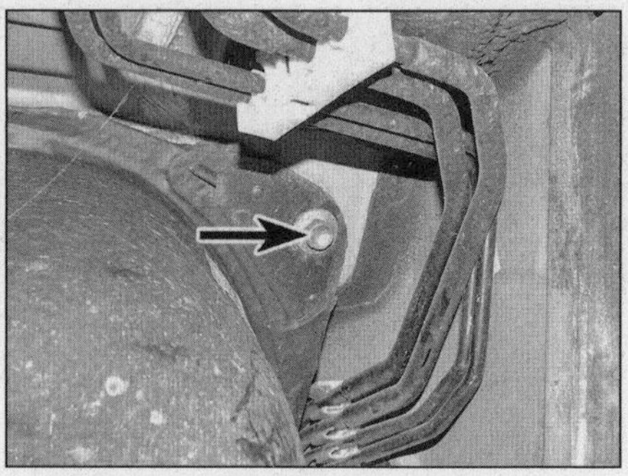

4.8 Remove the bolts from the brackets

pin out of its insulator grommet and remove the filter housing.

5 Inspect the condition of the insulator grommet. If it's cracked, torn or otherwise deteriorated, replace it.

6 Refitting is a reversal of removal.

4 Fuel tank – removal and refitting

Removal

1 Before removing the fuel tank, all fuel should be drained from the tank. Since a fuel tank drain plug is not provided, it is preferable to carry out the removal operation when the tank is nearly empty.

2 Raise the vehicle and support it securely on axle stands (see *Jacking and vehicle support*).

3 Familiarise yourself with the layout of the fuel tank assembly before proceeding. Refer to Section and disconnect the fuel pump hoses and electrical connectors.

4 Remove the power plant frame (see Chapter 7 Section 5), and the propeller shaft, driveshaftand differential (see Chapter 8). At this point, the entire rear suspension/crossmember assembly must be supported with a transmission jack, unbolted from the body and removed from under the vehicle. This will also necessitate disconnecting thebrake hoses at the crossmember and detaching the parking brake cables from the calipers (see Chapter 9).

5 Remove the tank protector. Support the fuel tank with a floor jack. Place a sturdy plank between the jack head and the fuel tank to protect the tank.

6 Inside the boot, unclip the trim panels, then remove the access panel **(see illustration)**.

7 Detach the hoses at the tank **(see illustration)**. Note: Plug the openings to prevent leakage and contamination.

8 Remove the bolts from the fuel tank retaining brackets **(see illustration)**.

9 Remove the tank from the vehicle.

Refitting

10 Refitting is the reverse of removal. Bleed the brakes as described in Chapter 9 Section 2.

5 Accelerator pedal assembly – removal and refitting

Removal

1 Disconnect the battery negative lead as described in Chapter 5A Section 4.

2 Disconnect the wiring plug from the position sensor at the top of the pedal assembly.

3 Undo the two retaining bolts and remove the pedal assembly **(see illustration)**. No further dismantling of the pedal assembly is recommended.

Refitting

4 Refitting is the reverse of removal.

6 Fuel injection system – general information

1 The fuel system consists of a fuel tank, an electric fuel pump (located in the fuel tank), an EFI/fuel pump relay, fuel injectors, a fuel pressure regulator, an air cleaner assembly and a throttle body unit. All models covered by this manual are equipped with a multi point fuel injection (MPFI) system.

Fuel injection system

2 Multi-point fuel injection (MPFI) uses timed impulses to sequentially inject the fuel directly into the intake port of each cylinder. The injectors are controlled by the Powertrain Control Module (PCM). The PCM monitors various engine parameters and delivers the exact amount of fuel, in the correct sequence, into the intake ports. The throttle body serves only to control the amount of air passing into the system. Because each cylinder is equipped with an injector mounted immediately adjacent to the intake valve, much better control of the fuel/air mixture ratio is possible.

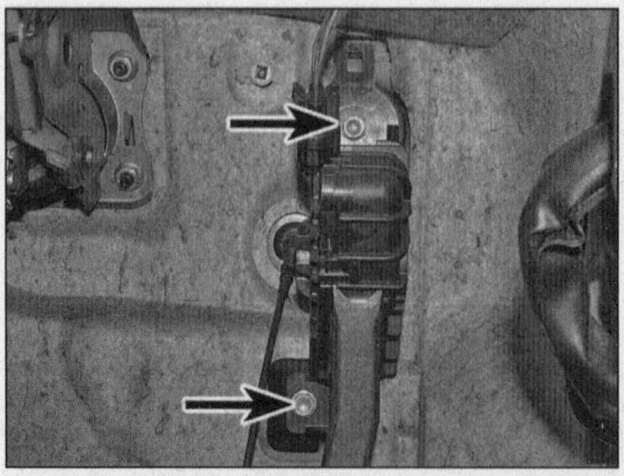

5.3 Accelerator pedal assembly retaining bolts

Fuel pump and pipes

3 Fuel is supplied from the fuel tank to the fuel injection system through a metal pipe running along the underside of the vehicle. An electric fuel pump is attached to the fuel level sending unit inside the fuel tank. A 'return-less' system is used, whereby a pressure regulator incorporated into the pump assembly returns excess fuel straight back into the reservoir of fuel.

4 The fuel pump will operate as long as the engine is cranking or running, and the PCM is receiving ignition reference pulses from the electronic ignition system (see Chapter 5B, Section 1). If there are no reference pulses, the fuel pump will shut off after 2 or 3 seconds.

Exhaust system

5 The exhaust system includes an exhaust manifold, a catalytic converter, an exhaust pipe, and a silencer.

6 The catalytic converter is an emission control device added to the exhaust system to reduce pollutants. A single-bed converter is used in combination with a three-way (reduction) catalyst.

7 Fuel injection system depressurisation

Depressurisation

1 Before servicing any fuel system component, you must relieve the fuel pressure to minimise the risk of fire or injury.

2 Remove the fuel filler cap – this will relieve any pressure built up in the tank.

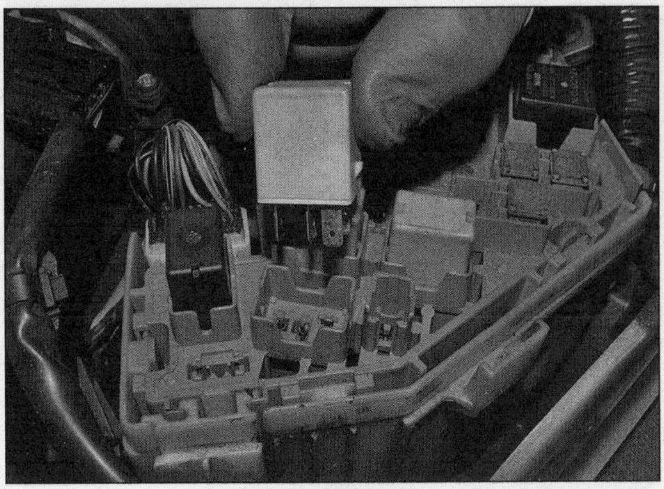

7.3 Fuel pump relay

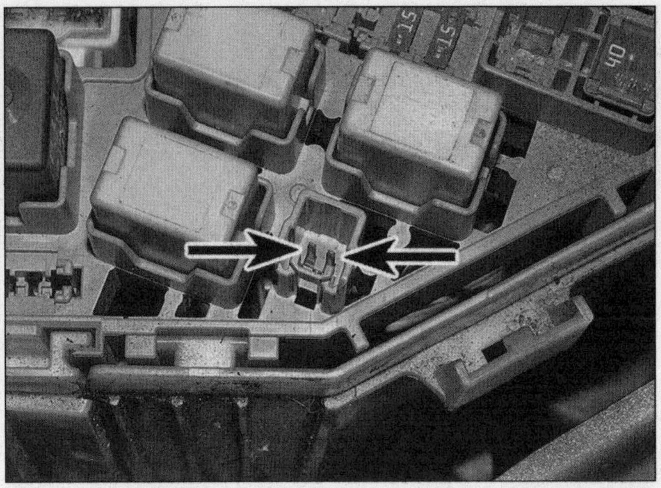

7.8 Connect the earth and fuel pump terminals (arrowed) together

3 Locate the fuel pump relay in the engine compartment fusebox **(see illustration)**.
4 Pull the relay from the socket.
5 Start the engine and wait for it to stall (it might not even start).
6 After the engine stalls, crank the engine several times. The system is now depressurised.
7 Turn the ignition off, and refit the relay.

Priming

8 Whenever fuel system pressure has been relieved, the fuel system should be primed before the vehicle is placed back in operation to prevent excessive cranking of the starter, as follows:

a) Locate the diagnostic connector in the engine compartment fusebox.
b) Connect the earth and fuel pump terminals together with a short jumper wire ***(see illustration)***
c) Turn the key to On for approximately 10 seconds (but don't operate the starter), then turn the key off. Remove the jumper wire from the diagnostic connector.
d) Check for any fuel leaks before operating the vehicle.

8 Fuel pump, level sensor and pressure regulator – removal and refitting

1 Depressurise the fuel system as described in Section 7.
2 Disconnect the battery negative lead as described in Chapter 5A, Section 4.
3 Remove the centre console, quarter trims, door sill trim, tyre house trim, Aeroboard, seat back bar trim and back trim as described in Chapter 11.
4 Undo the 3 screws and lift the fuel pump access cover **(see illustration)**.
5 Disconnect the wiring plug from the top of the fuel pump.
6 Disconnect the fuel supply hose from the pump **(see illustrations)**. Plug the openings to prevent contamination
7 Remove the 8 fuel pump retainer plate screws, then remove the retainer plate **(see illustration)**.
8 Manoeuvre the fuel pump/level sender assembly from the tank **(see illustration)**.
9 Release the clip, slide the fuel level sensor

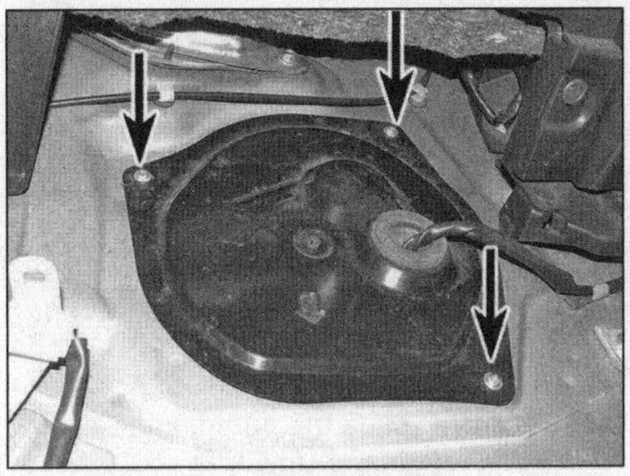

8.4 Access cover retaining screws

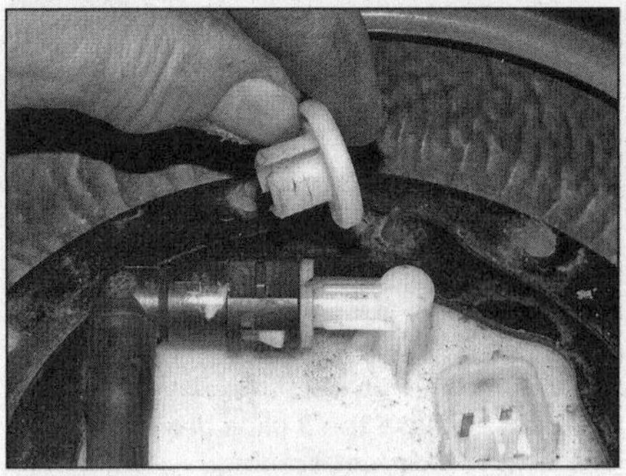

8.6a Slide a sleeve-type tool into the end of the hose...

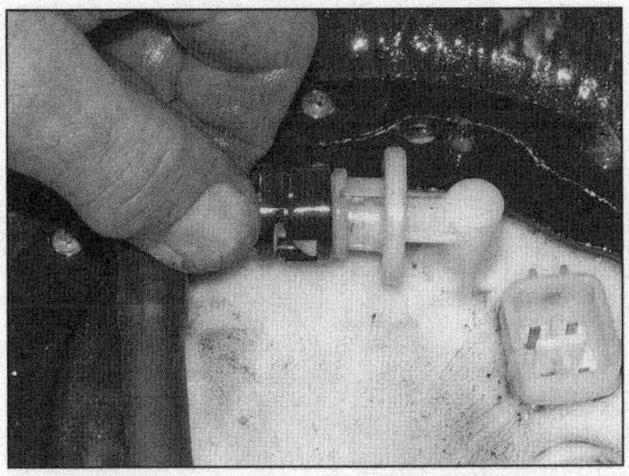

8.6b... to spread the clip and disconnect the hose

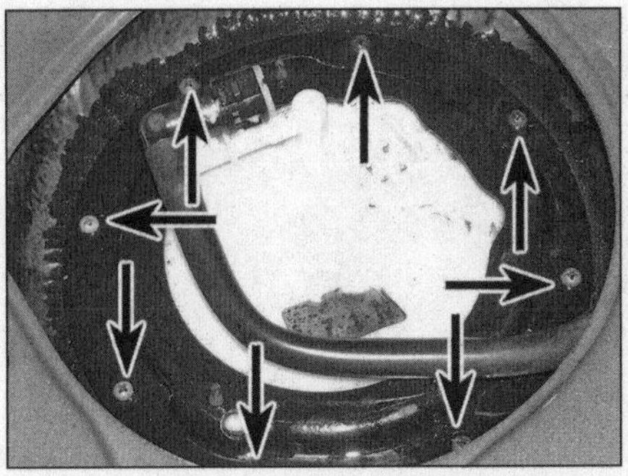

8.7 Retainer plate screws

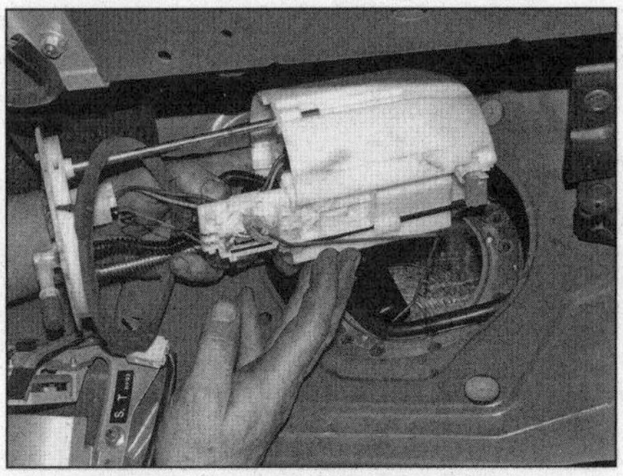

8.8 Take care not to damage the sensor float arm

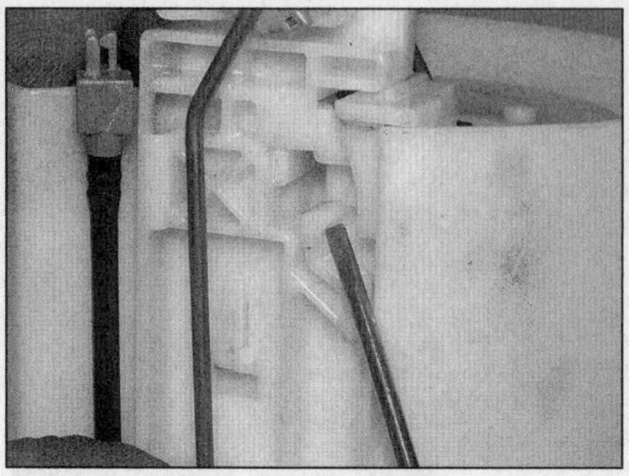
8.9a Release the clip...

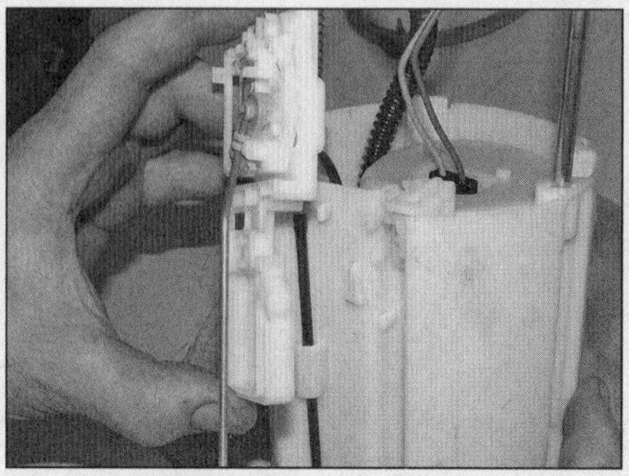
8.9b... slide the fuel level sensor upwards...

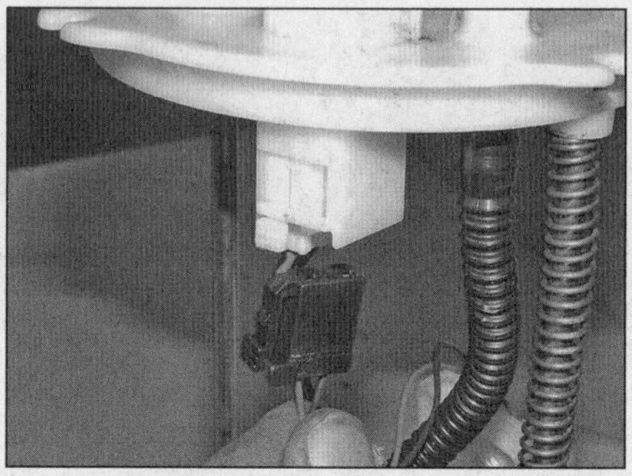
8.9c... and disconnect the wiring plug

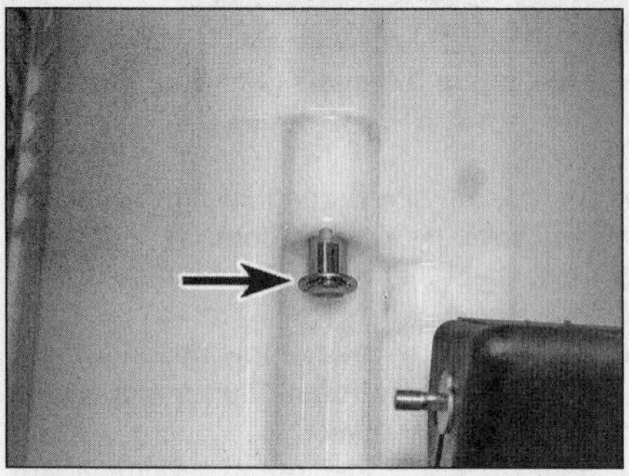
8.10 Carefully prise off the 'E' clip

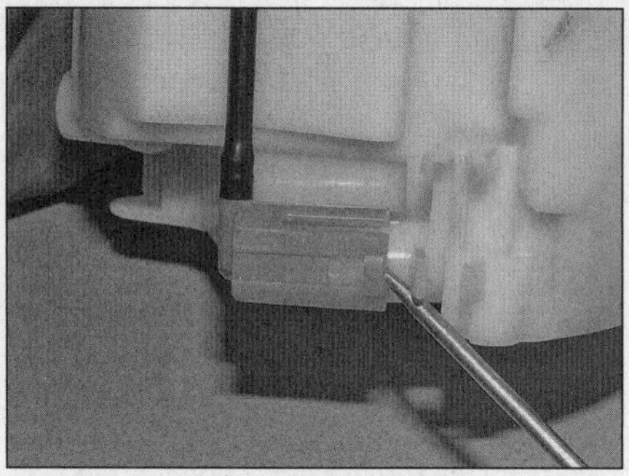
8.11 Disconnect the return pipe from the housing

upwards, then disconnect the wiring plug **(see illustrations)**.

10 Prise off the retaining clip securing the top plate to the housing **(see illustration)**.

11 Release the clip and disconnect the return pipe from the base of the housing **(see illustration)**.

12 Release the 3 clips and remove the pump, filter and regulator assembly **(see illustrations)**,

13 Unclip the filter assembly from the base of the pump **(see illustration)**.

14 If required, pull out the fuel pressure regulator. Renew the O-ring seals **(see illustration)**.

15 To test the fuel level sensor, move the float arm to the maximum deflection (full position) and measure the resistance across the plug terminals A and C (nearest the plug catch). Now fully lower the arm (empty position) and measure the resistance again **(see illustration)**. Compare the measurement obtained with those specified below.

Maximum deflection (full position)	9.0 to 11.0 ohms
Minimum deflection (empty position)	200.5 to 205.5 ohms

16 If the readings obtained differ greatly from those specified, the sensor may be faulty.

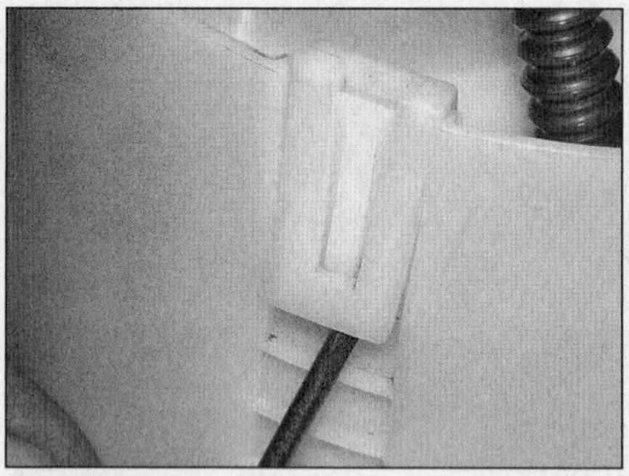
8.12a Release the 3 clips around the circumference...

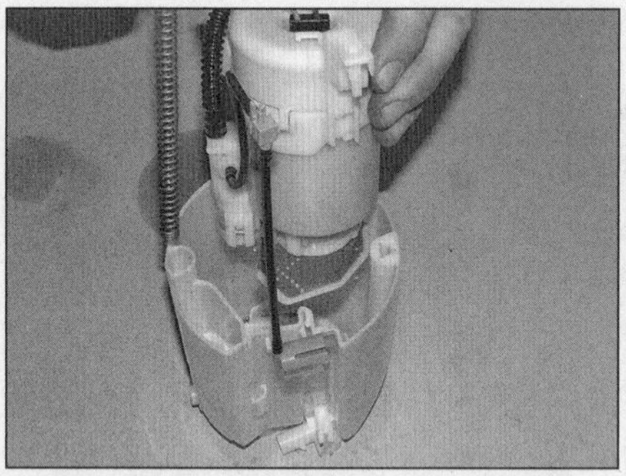
8.12b... then slide the pump, filter and regulator upwards

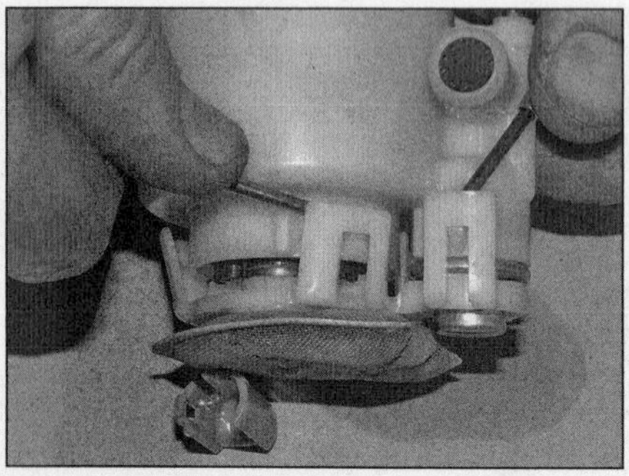
8.13 Unclip the filter assembly

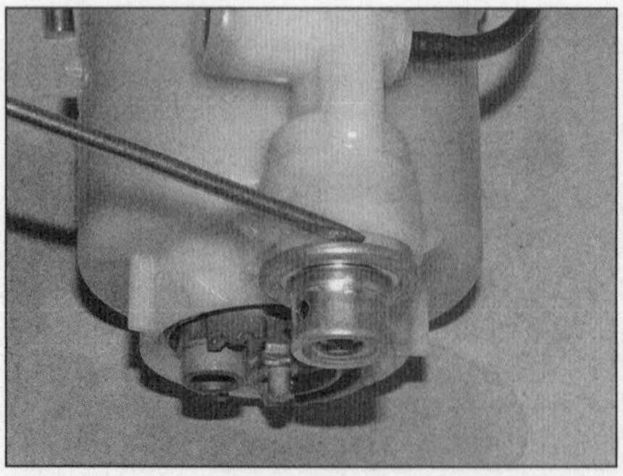
8.14 Prise out the fuel pressure regulator

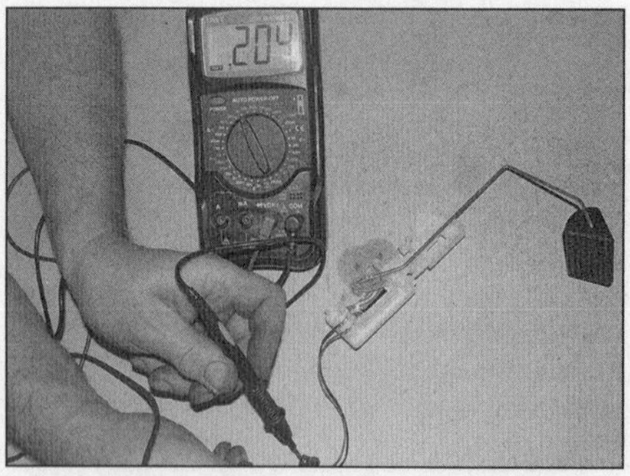
8.15 Measure the resistance across the level sensor wiring plug terminals

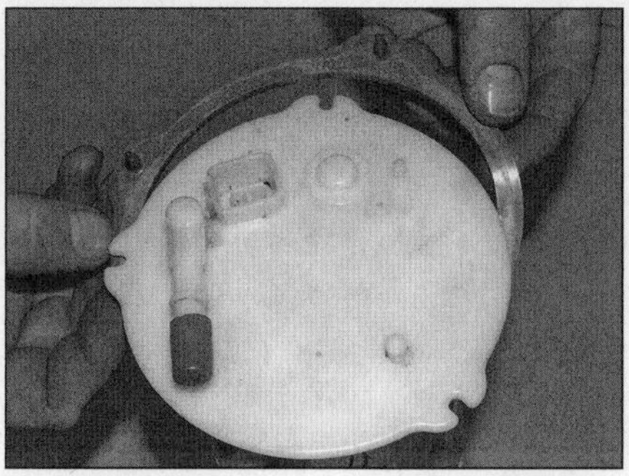

8.17 Examine the retaining plate seal

9.9 The service diagnostic connector is located under the drivers side of the facia

10.1 Slacken the air intake duct clamps

17 Refitting is the reverse of removal. Examine the retaining plate seal and renew if necessary **(see illustration)**.

9 Fuel injection system – testing and adjustment

Testing

1 Check the earth wire connections for tightness. Check all wiring and electrical connectors that are related to the system. Loose electrical connectors and poor earths can cause many problems that resemble more serious malfunctions.

2 Check to see that the battery is fully charged, as the control unit and sensors depend on an accurate supply voltage in order to properly meter the fuel.

3 Check the air filter element – a dirty or partially blocked filter will severely impede performance and economy (see Chapter 1, Section 20).

4 If a blown fuse is found, renew it and see if it blows again. If it does, search for an earthed wire in the harness related to the system.

5 Check the air intake duct from the air cleaner housing to the intake manifold for leaks, which will result in an excessively lean mixture. Also check the condition of the vacuum hoses connected to the intake manifold.

6 Remove the air intake duct from the throttle body and check for carbon and residue build-up. If it's dirty, clean it with aerosol carburettor cleaner (make sure the can says it's safe for use with oxygen sensors and catalytic converters) and a toothbrush.

Caution: Be sure not to remove the thin sealing film from the edge of the throttle plate and the area where it seats inside the throttle body.

7 With the engine running, place a stethoscope against each injector, one at a time, and listen for a clicking sound, indicating operation. If you don't have an automotive stethoscope you can use a long screwdriver; just place the tip of the screwdriver against the injector body and press your ear against the handle.

8 With the engine Off and the fuel injector electrical connectors disconnected, measure the resistance of each injector. Compare the measured resistance to the values listed (see Specifications). Out of range injectors are probably faulty.

9 The remainder of the system checks should be left to a dealer service department or other qualified repairer, as there is a chance that the control unit may be damaged if not performed properly. For information, the service diagnostic connector is located under the drivers side of the facia **(see illustration)**.

Adjustment

10 Experienced home mechanics with a considerable amount of skill and equipment (including a tachometer and an accurately calibrated exhaust gas analyser) may be able to check the exhaust CO level and the idle speed. However, if these are found to be in need of adjustment, the car should be taken to a Mazda dealer or suitably-equipped specialist for further testing.

10 Throttle body – removal and refitting

Removal

1 Slacken the clamps, disconnect the air intake duct from the throttle body and air filter, then move it to one side **(see illustration)**.

2 Disconnect the wiring plug from the throttle body **(see illustration)**.

3 Release the clamps and disconnect the coolant hoses from the throttle body **(see illustration)**. Quickly plug the hoses to prevent excessive coolant loss.

4 Remove the 4 throttle body mounting bolts **(see illustration)**.

10.2 Depress the clip and disconnect the wiring plug

10.3 Coolant hose clamps

10.4 Throttle body bolts

5 Detach the throttle body and gasket from the intake manifold **(see illustration)**.

6 Using a soft brush and carburettor cleaner, thoroughly clean the throttle body casting, then blow out all passages with compressed air.

Refitting

7 Refitting of the throttle body is the reverse of removal, using a new gasket. Tighten all fasteners to their specified torque where given.

11 Fuel injection system components – removal and refitting

Powertrain Control Module (PCM)

1 Disconnect the battery negative lead, as described in Chapter 5A, Section 4. **Note:** *It is recommended that the fault code memory of the module is interrogated using special test equipment prior to battery disconnection. Entrust this task to a Mazda dealer or suitably-equipped specialist.*

2 Remove the air cleaner assembly as described in Section 3.

3 Unclip the coolant hose and wiring harness from the PCM cover and move them to one side **(see illustration)**.

4 Undo the security bolts securing the PCM cover. This can be achieved by cutting a slot

10.5 Renew the throttle body gasket

in the top the bolts, then using a screwdriver, or drilling out the head of the bolts **(see illustrations)**. New security bolts will be required.

5 Undo the retaining nuts and lift away the PCM cover **(see illustration)**.

6 Open the levers, and disconnect the wiring plugs from the PCM **(see illustration)**.

7 Manoeuvre the PCM from place.

8 Refitting is a reversal of removal, noting the following points:

a) *When refitting the PCM cover, install the new security bolts, then tighten them until they shear.*

b) *If a new PCM has been fitted, it must be programmed using Mazda diagnostic equipment.*

c) *Reconnect the battery as described in Chapter 5A Section 4.*

11.3 Unclip the coolant hose, and wiring harness

Fuel rail and injectors

Warning: Refer to the warning notes in Section 1 before proceeding.

9 Relieve the fuel pressure as described in Section 7.

10 Disconnect the battery negative lead as described in Chapter 5A, Section 4.

11 Pull the engine cover upwards from its mountings.

12 Disconnect the fuel supply pipe quick-connect fitting from the fuel rail **(see illustration)**. Plug the openings to prevent contamination.

13 Disconnect the electrical connectors from the ignition coils and from the fuel injectors, detach the harness clips and set the harness aside **(see illustration)**.

14 Unscrew the fuel rail mounting bolts, and

11.4a Use a drill to remove the heads of the shear bolts...

11.4b... securing the PCM cover

11.5 PCM cover retaining nuts

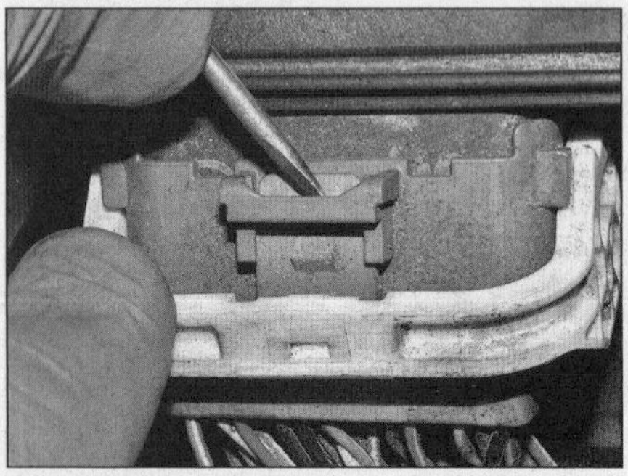

11.6 Depress the clip, fold down the lever and disconnect the wiring plug

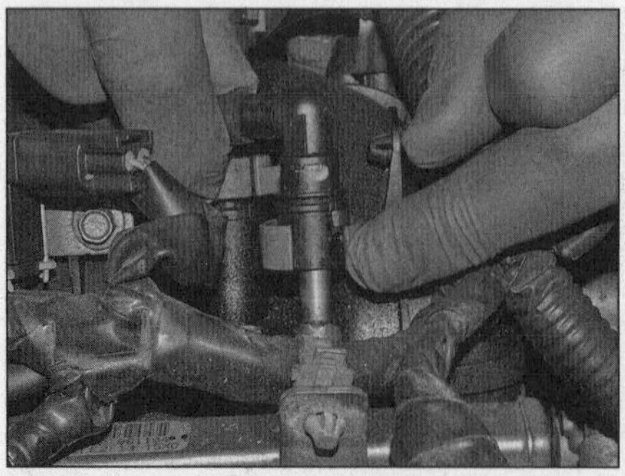

11.12 Rotate the collar and disconnect the fuel supply pipe

11.13 Depress the clip and disconnect the wiring plug

11.14a Undo the fuel rail mounting bolts...

11.14b... and pull the rail, with injectors, upwards

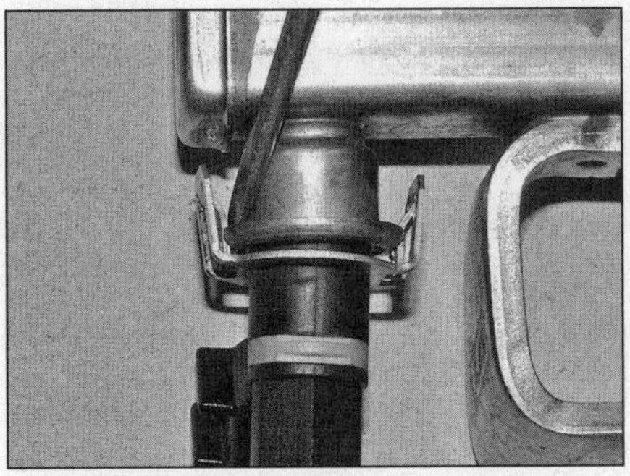

11.15 Spread the tab each side of the clip, and pull the injector from the rail

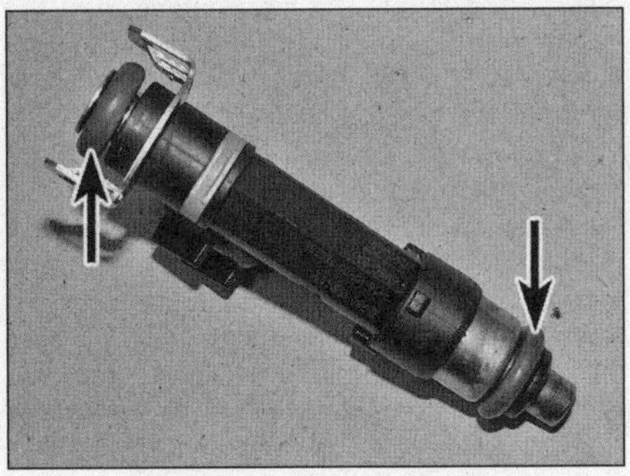

11.17 Renew the O-rings

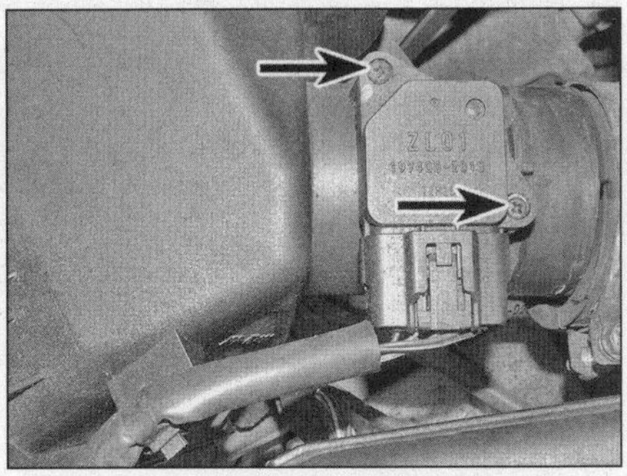

11.21 Sensor retaining screws

pull rail and injectors assembly upwards from place **(see illustrations)**.

15 Remove the clip and pull out each injector **(see illustration)**.

16 Set the fuel injectors aside in a clearly-labelled storage container so they can be returned to the same bores if reused.

17 If you intend to re-use the same injectors, renew the O-rings **(see illustration)**.

18 Refitting of the fuel injectors is the reverse of removal. Apply a thin coating of clean engine oil to the injector O-ring prior to fitting. Tighten the fuel rail mounting bolts to the specified torque.

Mass airflow/ intake air temperature sensor

19 Disconnect the battery negative lead as described in Chapter 5A Section 4.

20 Disconnect the wiring plug from the sensor, located in the air outlet duct from the air filter housing.

21 Undo the screws and remove the sensor **(see illustration)**.

22 Refitting is a reversal of removal.

Manifold Absolute Pressure (MAP) sensor

23 Disconnect the battery negative lead as described in Chapter 5A Section 4.

24 The sensor is located on the underside of the manifold. Remove the intake manifold as described in Section 12.

25 Undo the screw and pull the sensor from the manifold.

26 Refitting is a reversal of removal.

Coolant temperature sensor

27 Removal of the sensor is described in Chapter 3, Section 6.

Crankshaft position sensor

28 Remove the battery and battery tray as described in Chapter 5A Section 4.

29 Remove the air cleaner assembly as described in Section 3.

30 Remove the auxiliary drivebelt as described in Chapter 1 Section 6.

31 Raise the front of the vehicle and support it securely on axle stands (see *Jacking and vehicle support*). Undo the fasteners and remove the engine undershield.

32 Disconnect the sensor wiring plug, then undo the two retaining bolts and remove the sensor **(see illustration)**.

33 Bring the No.1 piston to TDC as described in Chapter 2A Section 3.

34 Look at the CKP sensor's signal wheel, or timing plate, that's mounted on the backside of the crankshaft pulley. Note the small teeth that stick out from the circumference of the timing plate. At about ten o'clock there is a blank spot on the edge on the timing plate, where there are no teeth. From this blank area, count five teeth in a anti-clockwise

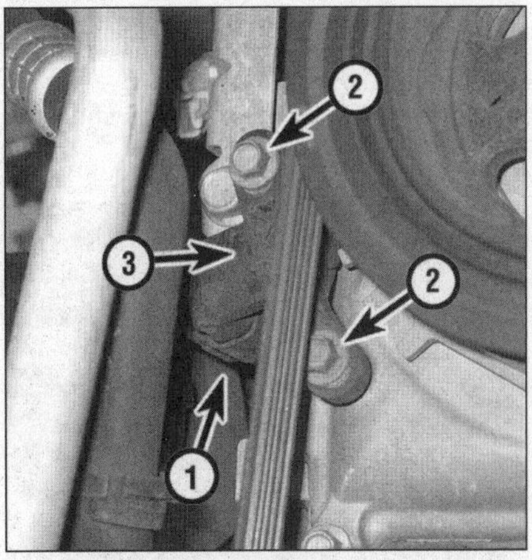

11.32 Crankshaft position sensor

1 Wiring plug
2 Mounting bolts
3 Crankshaft position sensor

direction, then, using a straight-edge, draw a straight line from the centre of this fifth tooth through the centre of the crankshaft pulley **(see illustration)**.

35 Place the CKP sensor in position, align the centre of the sensor with the line that you made in the previous paragraph, then tighten the sensor bolts to the specified torque.

36 The remainder of refitting is a reversal of removal.

Camshaft position sensor

37 Disconnect the battery negative lead as described in Chapter 5A Section 4.

38 Pull up the plastic cover from the top of the engine.

39 The sensor is located at the rear of the cylinder head. Disconnect the sensor wiring plug.

40 Undo the retaining bolt and pull the sensor from place **(see illustration)**.

41 Refitting is a reversal of removal.

Oxygen sensor

42 Refer to Chapter 4B, Section 2.

12 Manifolds – removal and refitting

Intake manifold

Note: *The plenum/intake manifold assembly has a lot of components, hoses and wiring attached or connected to it. Clearly label things as you disconnect and/or remove them to avoid confusion when installing the plenum/intake manifold.*

Removal

1 Depressurise the fuel system as described in Section 7.

2 Disconnect the battery negative lead as described in Chapter 5A Section 4.

3 Drain the cooling system as described in Chapter 1 Section 19.

4 Remove the air cleaner assembly as described in Section 3.

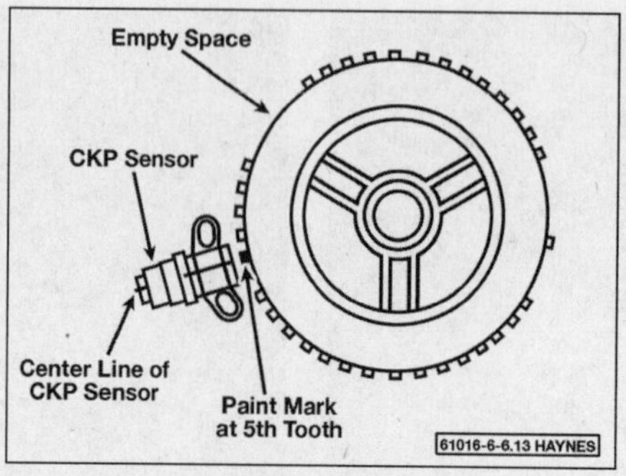

11.34 Crankshaft position sensor alignment details

5 Pull the engine cover upwards from its mountings.

6 Where fitted, remove the left-hand part of the strut brace (see Chapter 10 Section 8).

7 Detach the cooler and heater pipes from the bulkhead. Slide back the heater hose clamp, disconnect the heater hose from the heater pipe and set the hose and pipe aside.

8 Remove the throttle body as described in Section 10.

9 Remove the fuel rail and injectors as described in Section 11.

10 Raise the front of the vehicle and support it securely on axle stands (see *Jacking and vehicle support*). Undo the fasteners and remove the engine undershield.

11 Disconnect the electrical connector from the EGR valve and disconnect the connectors from all other electrical components attached to the underside of the plenum/intake manifold assembly. Detach all electrical harnesses from the plenum/intake manifold and set them aside **(see illustration)**.

12 Disconnect all coolant and heater hoses connected to the EGR valve, the thermostat and the underside of the plenum/intake manifold and set them aside **(see illustration)**.

13 Disconnect the electrical connectors from the air conditioning compressor and from the knock sensor.

14 Remove the upper and lower plenum fasteners. Remove the plenum and the plenum gasket.

15 Remove the intake manifold, then remove the intake manifold gasket.

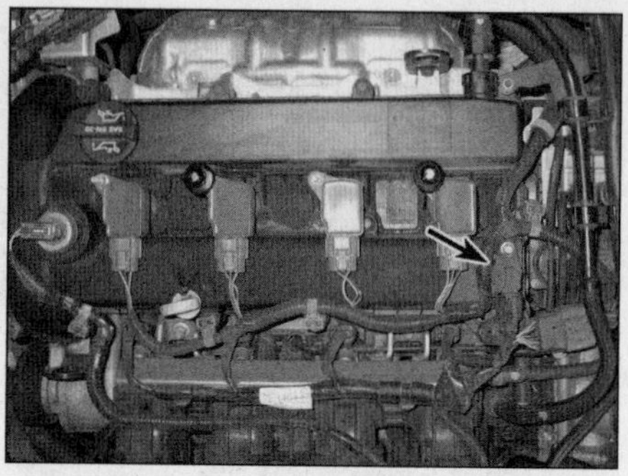

11.40 Camshaft position sensor location

Refitting

16 If you're replacing the plenum/intake manifold, remove all components from the old plenum and install them on the new one.

17 Installation is the reverse of removal. Be sure to use a new gasket and tighten all fasteners to the specified torque.

18 Refill the coolant system (see Chapter 1 Section 19), reconnect the battery, start the engine and check for leaks.

Exhaust manifold

Removal

19 Remove the battery and battery tray as described in Chapter 5A, Section 4.

20 Remove the auxiliary drivebelt as described in Chapter 1 Section 6.

21 Raise the front of the vehicle and support it securely on axle stands (see *Jacking and vehicle support*). Undo the fasteners and remove the engine undershield.

22 Remove the right-hand side of the strut brace (where fitted) as described in Chapter 10 Section 8.

23 Remove the alternator as described in Chapter 5A Section 6.

24 Remove the insulator **(see illustration)**.

25 Remove the bolts, then remove the upper shield.

26 Remove the bolts and remove the lower heat shield from the exhaust manifold.

27 Undo the nuts/bolt and remove the manifold lower bracket **(see illustration)**.

12.11 Disconnect the wiring plugs from the variable tumble solenoid, and the variable air intake solenoid

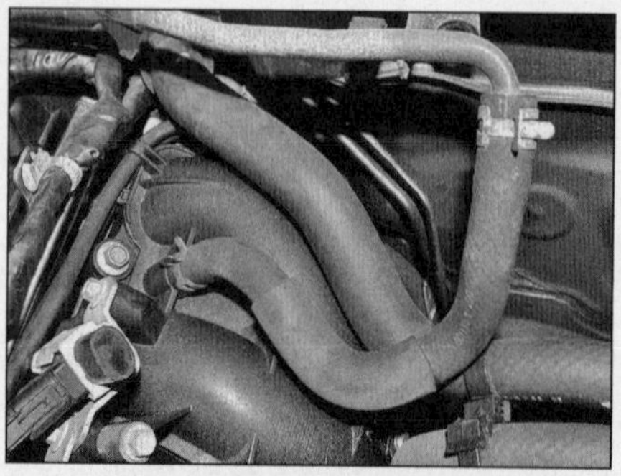

12.12 Disconnect all hoses from the plenum chamber

12.24 Remove the insulator

12.27 Remove the manifold lower bracket

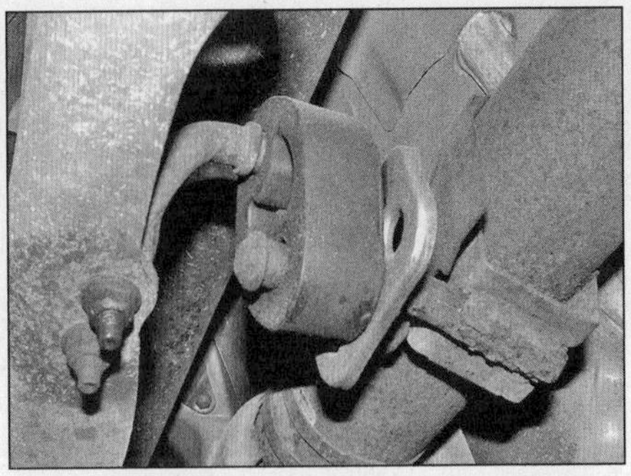

13.1 Check the condition of the exhaust rubber hangers

13.2 Check the condition of the exhaust components

28 Disconnect the electrical connectors from the upstream and downstream oxygen sensors

29 Trace the oxygen sensor (located on the exhaust manifold) wiring harness back to the wiring plug and disconnect it. If the manifold is being renewed, remove the sensor as described in Chapter 4B, Section 2.

30 Move the coolant pipe and heater hose aside.

31 Disconnect the crankcase ventilation hose from the cylinder head and move it aside.

32 Remove the nuts from the exhaust manifold flange and pull off the exhaust pipe.

33 Remove the fasteners and remove the exhaust manifold from the cylinder head.

34 Replace the exhaust manifold gasket and the sealing ring that fits inside the exhaust pipe flange. You might have to free the sealing ring from the flange with a small screwdriver; make sure that you don't damage the exhaust pipe flange.Installation

Refitting

35 Use a scraper to remove all traces of old gasket material and carbon deposits from the manifold and cylinder head mating surfaces.

Caution: When scraping, be very careful not to gouge or scratch the delicate aluminium cylinder head manifold mounting surface.

36 Position a new exhaust manifold gasket over the studs on the cylinder head.

37 Refit the manifold, then evenly tighten the nuts/bolts to the specified torque.

38 The remainder of refitting is a reversal of removal.

13 Exhaust system – removal and refitting

Caution: Inspection and repair of exhaust system components should be done only after the system components have cooled completely.

1 The exhaust system consists of the exhaust manifold, catalytic converter, the silencer, the tailpipe and all connecting pipes, brackets, hangers and clamps. The exhaust system is attached to the body with mounting brackets and rubber hangers **(see illustration)**. If any of these parts are damaged or deteriorated, excessive noise and vibration will be transmitted to the body.

2 Conducting regular inspections of the exhaust system will keep it safe and quiet. Look for any damaged or bent parts, open seams, holes, loose connections, excessive corrosion or other defects which could allow exhaust fumes to enter the vehicle **(see illustration)**. Deteriorated exhaust system components should not be repaired – they should be renewed.

3 If the exhaust system components are extremely corroded or rusted together, they will probably have to be cut from the exhaust system. The convenient way to accomplish this is to have an exhaust specialist remove the corroded sections with a cutting torch. If, however, you want to save money by doing it yourself and you don't have an oxygen/acetylene welding outfit with a cutting torch, simply cut off the old components with a hacksaw. If you have compressed air, special pneumatic cutting chisels can also be used. If you do decide to tackle the job at home, be sure to wear eye protection to guard your eyes from metal chips and work gloves to protect your hands.

4 Here are some simple guidelines to apply when repairing the exhaust system:

a) Work from the back to the front when removing exhaust system components.

b) Apply penetrating oil to the exhaust system component fasteners to make them easier to remove.

c) Use new gaskets, hangers and clamps when installing exhaust system components.

d) Apply anti-seize compound to the threads of all exhaust system fasteners during reassembly.

5 Be sure to allow sufficient clearance between newly installed parts and all points on the underbody to avoid overheating the floor pan and possibly damaging the interior carpet and insulation. Pay particularly close attention to the catalytic converter and its heat shield.

Warning: The catalytic converter operates at very high temperatures and takes a long time to cool. Wait until it's completely cool before attempting to remove the converter. Failure to do so could result in serious burns.

Chapter 4 Part B
Emission control systems

Contents

Degrees of difficulty

Easy, suitable for novice with little experience	**Fairly easy,** suitable for beginner with some experience	**Fairly difficult,** suitable for competent DIY mechanic	**Difficult,** suitable for experienced DIY mechanic	**Very difficult,** suitable for expert DIY or professional

Specifications

Torque wrench settings	Nm	lbf ft
Exhaust gas recirculation (EGR) valve bolts	20	15
Oxygen sensors	45	33

1 General Information

1 All models use unleaded petrol and also have various other features built into the fuel system to help minimise harmful emissions. All models are equipped with a crankcase emission control system, a catalytic converter, an exhaust gas recirculation (EGR) system and an evaporative emission control system to keep fuel vapour/exhaust gas emissions down to a minimum.

2 The emission control systems function as follows.

Crankcase emission control

3 To reduce the emission of unburned hydrocarbons from the crankcase into the atmosphere, the engine is sealed and the blow-by gases and oil vapour are drawn from inside the crankcase, through a wire mesh oil separator, into the intake tract to be burned by the engine during normal combustion.

4 Under conditions of high manifold depression (idling, deceleration) the gases will be sucked positively out of the crankcase through a small diameter pipe and into the intake tract 'downstream' of the throttle valve. A larger diameter pipe, 'upstream' of the throttle valve, allows fresh air to be drawn back into the crankcase, and mix with the crankcase gases. Under conditions of low manifold depression (acceleration, full-throttle running) the gases are forced out of the crankcase by the (relatively) higher crankcase pressure; and drawn through both pipes 'upstream and downstream' of the throttle valve.

Exhaust emission control

5 To minimise the amount of pollutants which escape into the atmosphere, all models are fitted with a catalytic converter in the exhaust system. The system is of the closed-loop type, in which an oxygen sensor(s) in the exhaust system supplies a voltage signal to the engine management system PCM, enabling the PCM to adjust the mixture to provide the best possible conditions for the converter to operate. Two oxygen sensors are fitted. One fitted to the exhaust manifold or front exhaust pipe (pre-catalyst sensor), and the 2nd one is fitted 'downstream' of the catalytic converter (post-catalyst sensor). Some oxygen sensor(s) have a built-in heating element which is controlled by the PCM; the heating element is used to warm the sensor when the engine is cold to bring it quickly up to an efficient operating temperature.

6 The oxygen sensor's tip is sensitive to oxygen and sends the PCM a varying voltage depending on the amount of oxygen in the exhaust gases; the leaner the air/fuel mixture, the higher the oxygen content, and the lower the voltage from the sensor(s). If the intake air/fuel mixture is too rich, the exhaust gases are low in oxygen so the sensor sends a higher-voltage signal. Peak conversion efficiency of all major pollutants occurs if the intake air/fuel mixture is maintained at the chemically-correct ratio for the complete combustion of petrol of 14.7 parts (by weight) of air to 1 part of fuel (the 'stoichiometric' ratio). The sensor output voltage alters in a large step at this point, the PCM using the signal change as a reference point and correcting the intake air/fuel mixture accordingly by altering the fuel injector pulse width.

Evaporative emission control

7 To minimise the escape into the atmosphere of unburned hydrocarbons, an evaporative emissions control system is also fitted to all models. The fuel tank filler cap is sealed and a charcoal canister is mounted in the engine compartment. The canister collects the petrol vapours generated in the tank when the car is parked and stores them until they can be cleared from the canister (under the control of the engine management system PCM) via the purge valve into the intake tract to be burned by the engine during normal combustion.

8 To ensure that the engine runs correctly when it is cold and/or idling and to protect the catalytic converter from the effects of an over-rich mixture, the purge control valve is not opened by the PCM until the engine has warmed up, and the engine is under load; the valve solenoid is then modulated on and off to allow the stored vapour to pass into the intake tract.

Exhaust gas recirculation (EGR)

9 This system is designed to recirculate small quantities of exhaust gas into the intake tract, and therefore into the combustion process. This process reduces the level of unburnt hydrocarbons present in the exhaust gas before it reaches the catalytic converter. The system is controlled by the engine management system PCM, using the information from its various sensors, via the EGR valve connecting the intake and exhaust manifolds.

2 Engine emission control systems – testing and component renewal

Crankcase emission control

General information

1 The positive crankcase ventilation (PCV) system reduces hydrocarbon emissions by scavenging crankcase vapours. It does this by circulating fresh air from the air cleaner through the crankcase, where it mixes with blow-by gases and is then rerouted through a PCV valve to the intake manifold.

2 The main components of the PCV system are the PCV valve, a fresh air intake and the vacuum hoses connecting these components to the engine.

3 To maintain idle quality, the PCV valve restricts the flow when the intake manifold vacuum is high. If abnormal operating conditions (such as piston ring problems) arise, the system is designed to allow excessive amounts of blow-by gases to flow back through the crankcase vent tube into the air cleaner to be consumed by normal combustion.

4 This system directs the blow-by into the throttle body which, over time, can cause an oily residue build up in the area near the throttle plate. Consequently, it is a good idea to periodically clean this residue from the throttle body. Refer to Chapter 4A, Section 10 for this cleaning procedure.

Check

5 To check the valve, first pull it out of the grommet in the valve cover and shake the valve. It should rattle, indicating that it's not clogged with deposits. If the valve does not rattle, renew it.

6 Start the engine and allow it to idle, then place your finger over the valve opening. If vacuum is felt, the PCV valve is working properly. If no vacuum is felt, the PCV valve may be bad or the hose may be plugged. Also, check for vacuum leaks at the valve, engine oil filler cap and all the hoses.

Renewal

7 Remove the intake manifold as described in Chapter 4A Section 12.

8 Slacken the hose clamp and disconnect the hose from the PCV valve.

9 Using a small screwdriver, carefully push the PCV valve retaining ring up over the locking tab.

10 Pull the PCV valve out of the crankcase oil separator.

11 Refitting is a reversal of removal.

Evaporative emission control

Testing

12 If the system is thought to be faulty, disconnect the hoses from the charcoal canister and purge control valve and check that they are clear by blowing through them. Full testing of the system can only be carried out using specialist electronic equipment which is connected to the engine management system diagnostic wiring connector (see Chapter 4A, Section 9). If the purge control valve or charcoal canister is thought to be faulty, they must be renewed.

Charcoal canister renewal

13 The canister is located under the rear of the vehicle, adjacent to the fuel tank **(see illustration)**. Raise the rear of the vehicle and support it securely on axle stands (see *Jacking and vehicle support*).

14 Note the fitted locations of the pipes. Disconnect the tank air and purge pipes from the canister **(see illustration)**.

15 Undo the mounting nut/bolt, and remove the canister.

16 Refitting is a reverse of the removal procedure, ensuring the hoses are correctly and securely reconnected.

Purge valve renewal

17 The valve is located on a bracket on the left-hand side of the engine compartment **(see illustration)**.

18 Ensure the ignition is switched off, and disconnect the wiring plug from the valve.

19 Note their fitted locations and disconnect the hoses from the valve.

20 Undo the retaining nut and detach the valve from the bracket.

21 Refitting is a reversal of removal. Ensure the hoses are securely held by the retaining clips.

Exhaust emission control

Testing

22 To reduce hydrocarbon, carbon monoxide and oxides of nitrogen emissions, all vehicles are equipped with a three-way catalyst system which oxidizes and reduces these chemicals, converting them into harmless nitrogen, carbon dioxide and water.

23 The performance of the catalytic converter can be checked only by measuring the exhaust gases using a good-quality, carefully-calibrated exhaust gas analyser.

24 If the CO level at the tailpipe is too high, the vehicle should be taken to a Mazda dealer or specialist so that the complete fuel injection and ignition systems, including the oxygen sensor, can be thoroughly checked using the special diagnostic equipment. Once these have been checked and are known to be free from faults, the fault must be in the catalytic converter, which may need to be renewed.

Catalytic converter renewal

25 The catalytic converter is an integral component of the exhaust manifold, and is therefore covered in Chapter 4A Section 12.

Oxygen sensor(s) renewal

Note: *The oxygen sensor is delicate and will not work if it is dropped or knocked, if its power supply is disrupted, or if any cleaning materials are used on it.*

26 Ensure the ignition is switched off then trace the wiring back from the oxygen sensor(s). Free the connector(s) from its retaining clip and disconnect the two halves of the connector.

27 Unscrew the sensor and remove it from the manifold or exhaust pipe as applicable. Note that because of the restricted access, the use of a special deep, split socket is not possible – use an open-ended spanner **(see illustration)**.

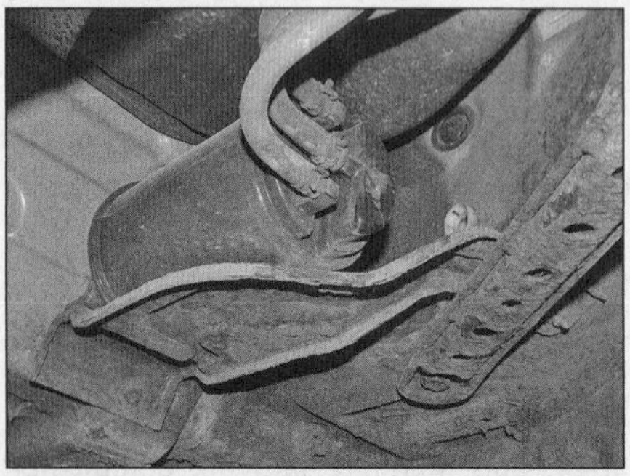

2.13 The charcoal canister is located under the rear, right-hand side of the vehicle

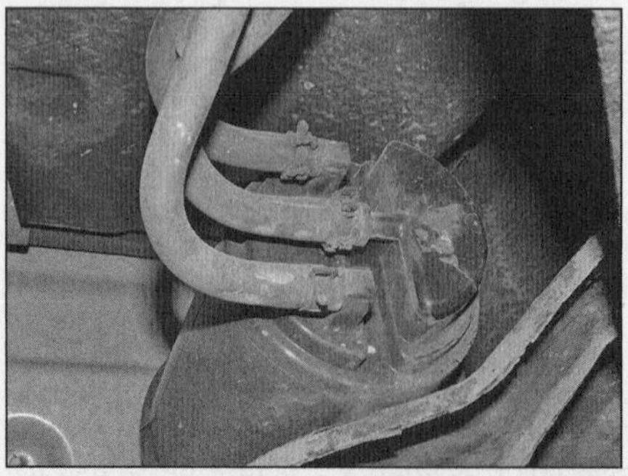

2.14 Label and disconnect the hoses from the charcoal canister

2.17 The purge valve is located on the left-hand side of the engine compartment

2.27 Unscrew the oxygen sensor using a special deep socket slotted to accommodate the wiring lead

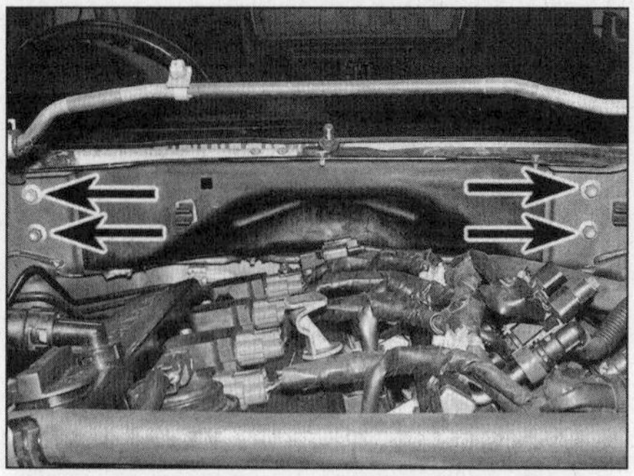

2.35a Undo the 4 bolts at the front...

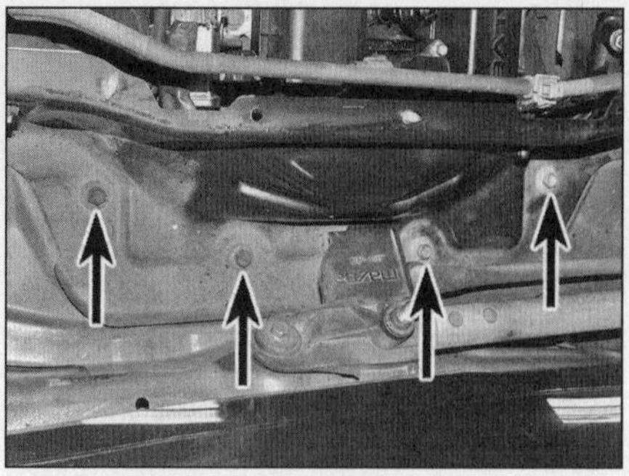

2.35b... 4 bolts on the top...

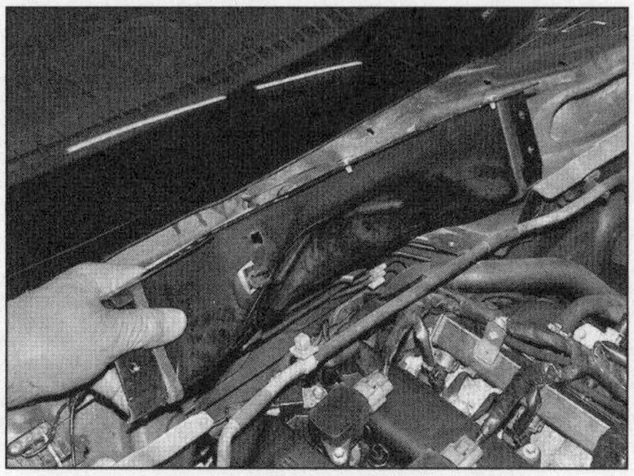

2.35c... and remove the cover

2.37 Depress the clip and disconnect the EGR valve wiring plug

28 Refitting is a reverse of the removal procedure. Apply a little high-temperature anti-seize compound (Copperslip) to the threads, then tighten the sensor to the specified torque and ensure that the wiring is correctly routed and in no danger of contacting either the exhaust manifold or the engine.

Exhaust gas recirculation (EGR)

Testing

29 Comprehensive testing of the system can only be carried out using specialist electronic equipment which is connected to the injection system diagnostic wiring connector (see Chapter 4A, Section 9). If the EGR valve or solenoid valve are thought to be faulty, they must be renewed as follows.

EGR valve renewal

Note: *The EGR valve is located behind the cylinder head. It's extremely difficult to access. The EGR valve mounting bolts are particularly difficult to reach. Unless you have the right combination of tools, these two bolts are extremely difficult to remove and install. Mazda offers a special tool (SST 49 N013 001) for this job. We recommend that you obtain this tool before trying to replace the EGR valve yourself on these models.*

30 Pull the engine cover upwards from its mountings.

31 Disconnect the battery negative lead as described in Chapter 5A Section 4.

32 Drain the engine coolant as described in Chapter 1 Section 19.

33 Remove the strut brace (where fitted) (see Chapter 10 Section 8), the cowl grille and windshield wiper motor and linkage assembly (see Chapter 12 Section 15) and the strut reinforcement brace.

34 Disconnect the heater hose and move the heater pipe out of the way.

35 Undo the bolts and remove the service hole cover from the engine compartment bulkhead **(see illustrations)**.

36 Undo the bolts/nuts and move the harness bracket to one side at the back of the cylinder head.

37 Disconnect the EGR valve wiring plug **(see illustration)**.

38 Using a torch and a mirror, locate the EGR mounting bolts, which are located near the lower end of the EGR valve and face toward the bulkhead. Using the special Mazda tool, or a suitable equivalent tool, remove the EGR valve mounting bolts.

39 Tap the EGR valve, if necessary, with a small rubber mallet to knock it loose from the cylinder head, then pull the valve up so that you can disconnect the coolant hose from the valve. Remove the EGR valve.

40 Discard the EGR valve gasket.

41 Make sure that the gasket surfaces of both the cylinder head and the EGR valve are clean before installing the new gasket. Tighten the EGR valve bolts securely. Refitting is otherwise the reverse of removal.

3 Catalytic converter – general information and precautions

1 The catalytic converter is a reliable and simple device which needs no maintenance in itself, but there are some facts which an owner should be aware if the converter is to function properly for its full service life.

- DO NOT use leaded petrol in a car equipped with a catalytic converter – the lead will coat the precious metals, reducing their converting efficiency and will eventually destroy the converter.
- Always keep the ignition and fuel systems well-maintained in accordance with the manufacturer's schedule.
- If the engine develops a misfire, do not drive the car at all (or at least as little as possible) until the fault is cured.
- DO NOT push- or tow-start the car – this will soak the catalytic converter in unburned fuel, causing it to overheat when the engine does start.
- DO NOT switch off the ignition at high engine speeds.
- DO NOT use fuel or engine oil additives – these may contain substances harmful to the catalytic converter.
- DO NOT continue to use the car if the engine burns oil to the extent of leaving a visible trail of blue smoke.
- Remember that the catalytic converter operates at very high temperatures. DO NOT, therefore, park the car in dry undergrowth, over long grass or piles of dead leaves after a long run.
- Remember that the catalytic converter is FRAGILE – do not strike it with tools during servicing work.
- In some cases a sulphurous smell (like that of rotten eggs) may be noticed from the exhaust. This is common to many catalytic converter-equipped cars and once the car has covered a few thousand miles the problem should disappear
- The catalytic converter, used on a well-maintained and well-driven car, should last for between 50 000 and 100 000 miles – if the converter is no longer effective it must be renewed

Notes

Chapter 5 Part A
Starting and charging systems

Contents

Degrees of difficulty

Easy, suitable for novice with little experience	**Fairly easy,** suitable for beginner with some experience	**Fairly difficult,** suitable for competent DIY mechanic	**Difficult,** suitable for experienced DIY mechanic	**Very difficult,** suitable for expert DIY or professional

Specifications

System type	12 volt negative earth	
Alternator		
Regulated voltage	13.0 to 15.0 volts	
Output	100 A	
Brush length:		
New	22.5 mm	
Minimum	5.0 mm	
Starter		
Brush length:		
New	12.3 mm	
Minimum	5.5 mm	
Torque wrench settings	**Nm**	**lbf ft**
Alternator	45	33
Oil filter housing bolts	25	17
Starter motor mounting bolts	45	33

1 General information and precautions

1 The engine electrical system consists mainly of the charging and starting systems. Because of their engine-related functions, these components are covered separately from the body electrical devices such as the lights, instruments, etc (which are covered in Chapter 12). For information on the ignition system refer to Chapter 5B.
2 The electrical system is of the 12 volt negative earth type.
3 The battery is charged by the alternator, which is belt-driven from the crankshaft pulley.
4 The starter motor is of the pre-engaged type incorporating an integral solenoid. On starting, the solenoid moves the drive pinion into engagement with the flywheel ring gear before the starter motor is energised. Once the engine has started, a one-way clutch prevents the motor armature being driven by the engine until the pinion disengages from the flywheel.

Precautions

5 Further details of the various systems are given in the relevant Sections of this Chapter. While some repair procedures are given, the usual course of action is to renew the component concerned. The owner whose interest extends beyond mere component renewal should obtain a copy of the Automobile Electrical and Electronic Systems Manual, available from the publishers of this manual.
6 It is necessary to take extra care when working on the electrical system to avoid damage to semi-conductor devices (diodes and transistors), and to avoid the risk of personal injury. In addition to the precautions given in *Safety first!* at the beginning of this manual, observe the following when working on the system:

- Always remove rings, watches, etc, before working on the electrical system. Even with the battery disconnected, capacitive discharge could occur if a component's live terminal is earthed through a metal object. This could cause a shock or nasty burn.
- Do not reverse the battery connections. Components such as the alternator, electronic control modules/units, or any other components having semi-conductor circuitry could be irreparably damaged.
- Never disconnect the battery terminals, the alternator, any electrical wiring or any test instruments when the engine is running.
- Do not allow the engine to turn the alternator when the alternator is not connected.
- Never 'test' for alternator output by 'flashing' the output lead to earth.
- Never use an ohmmeter of the type incorporating a hand-cranked generator for circuit or continuity testing.
- Always ensure that the battery negative lead is disconnected when working on the electrical system.
- Before using electric-arc welding equipment on the car, disconnect the battery, alternator and components such as the fuel injection/ignition electronic control unit to protect them from the risk of damage.

7 If an audio unit with a built-in security code is fitted, note the following precautions. If the power source to the unit is cut, the anti-theft system will activate. Even if the power source is immediately reconnected, the audio unit will not function until the correct security code has been entered. Therefore, if you do not know the correct security code for the audio unit do not disconnect the battery negative terminal of the battery or remove the audio unit from the vehicle.

2 Electrical fault finding – general information

1 Refer to Chapter 12, Section 2.

3 Battery – testing and charging

Note: *The following is intended as a guide only. Always refer to the manufacturer's recommendations (often printed on a label attached to the battery) before charging a battery.*
1 All models may be fitted with a maintenance-free battery in production, which should require no maintenance under normal operating conditions.
2 If the condition of the battery is suspect, remove the battery as described in Section 4, and check that the electrolyte level in each cell is up to the MAX mark on the outside of the battery case (about 5.0 mm above the tops of the plates in the cells). If necessary, the electrolyte level can be topped-up by removing the cell plugs from the top of the battery and adding distilled water (not acid).
3 An approximate check on battery condition can be made by checking the specific gravity of the electrolyte, using the following as a guide.
4 Use a hydrometer to make the check and compare the results with the following table. The temperatures quoted are ambient (air) temperatures. Note that the specific gravity readings assume an electrolyte temperature of 15°C; for every 10°C below 15°C subtract 0.007. For every 10°C above 15°C add 0.007.

	Above 25°C	Below 25°C
Fully-charged	1.210 to 1.230	1.270 to 1.290
70% charged	1.170 to 1.190	1.230 to 1.250
Discharged	1.050 to 1.070	1.110 to 1.130

5 If the battery condition is suspect, first check the specific gravity of electrolyte in each cell. A variation of 0.040 or more between any cells indicates loss of electrolyte or deterioration of the internal plates.
6 If the specific gravity variation is 0.040 or more, the battery should be renewed. If the cell variation is satisfactory but the battery is discharged, it should be charged in accordance with the manufacturer's instructions.
7 In cases where a 'sealed for life' maintenance-free battery is fitted, topping-up and testing of the electrolyte in each cell is not possible. The condition of the battery can therefore only be tested using a battery condition indicator or a voltmeter.
8 Models may be fitted with a battery with a built-in charge condition indicator. The indicator is located in the top of the battery casing, and indicates the condition of the battery from its colour. If the indicator shows green, then the battery is in a good state of charge. If the indicator turns darker, eventually to black, then the battery requires charging. If the indicator shows clear/yellow, then the electrolyte level in the battery is too low to allow further use, and the battery should be renewed. Do not attempt to charge, load or jump start a battery when the indicator shows clear/yellow.
9 If testing the battery using a voltmeter, connect the voltmeter across the battery. A fully-charged battery should give a reading of 12.5 volts or higher. The test is only accurate if the battery has not been subjected to any kind of charge for the previous six hours. If this is not the case, switch on the headlights for 30 seconds, then wait four to five minutes before testing the battery after switching off the headlights. All other electrical circuits must be switched off, so check that the doors and boot lid are fully shut when making the test.
10 Generally speaking, if the voltage reading is less than 12.2 volts, then the battery is discharged, whilst a reading of 12.2 to 12.4 volts indicates a partially-discharged condition.

4 Battery and battery tray – disconnection, removal and refitting

Note: *When the battery is disconnected, any fault codes stored in the engine management ECM memory will be erased. If any faults are suspected, do not disconnect the battery until the fault codes have been read by a Mazda dealer or specialist. If the vehicle is fitted with a code-protected audio unit, refer to the Owners handbook before Disconnecting the battery.*
Caution: For vehicles with Dynamic Stability Control (DSC), if the negative battery lead is disconnected, the stored initial position of the steering angle sensor will be cleared and the DSC will not operate properly, making the vehicle unsafe to drive. Perform the steering angle sensor initialisation procedure after connecting the negative battery cable.

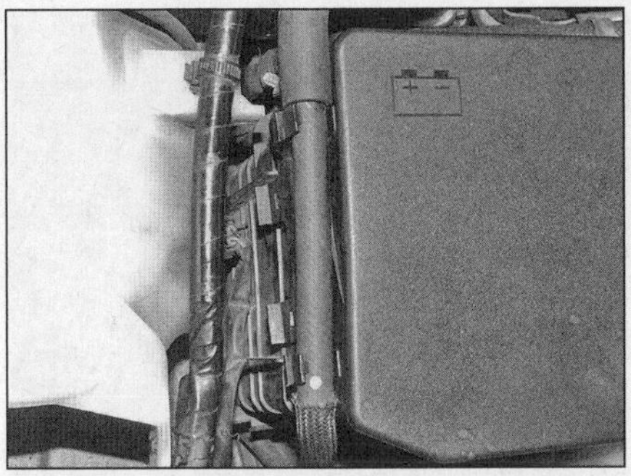

4.2a Lift the rubber hose from the clips

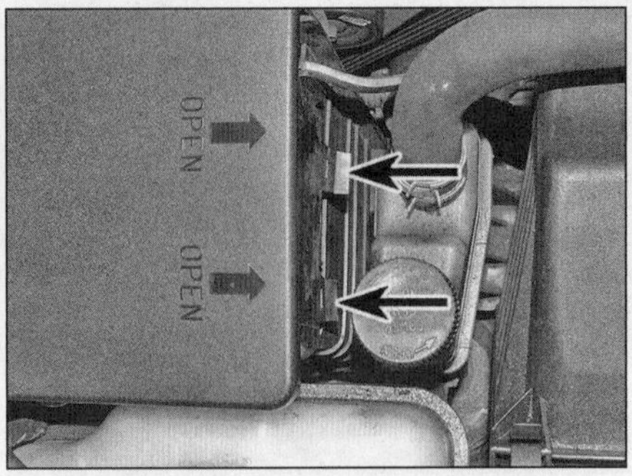

4.2b Then release the clips...

4.2c... and remove the battery cover

4.3 Disconnect the battery negative lead

4.6 Lift the plastic cover and slacken the positive clamp nut

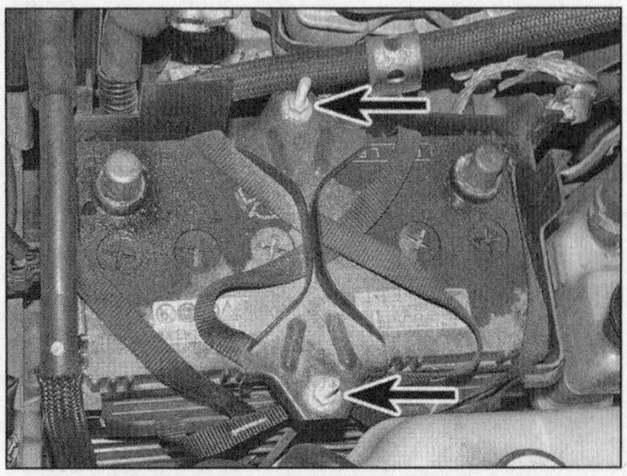

4.7 Battery hold-down clamp nuts

Battery

Disconnection

1 The battery is located in the engine compartment.

2 Unclip the rubber hose, then release the clips and remove the battery cover **(see illustrations)**.

3 Slacken the nut and disconnect the battery negative lead **(see illustration)**.

4 Upon reconnection, ensure the battery terminal and lead clamp are clean, then reconnect the negative lead and tighten the retaining nut securely.

Removal

5 Disconnect the battery negative lead as described previously.

6 Prise up the plastic cover (where fitted), slacken the retaining nut and pull the positive lead from the battery terminal **(see illustration)**.

7 Undo the nuts and remove the battery hold-down clamp **(see illustration)**.

8 Disconnect the vent hose (where fitted) and lift the battery from place. Take care as the battery is heavy!

9 Release the clips and remove the battery case **(see illustration)**.

10 Unclip the wiring harness, undo the four bolts and lift the battery tray from place **(see illustration)**.

Refitting and reconnection

11 Refitting is a reversal of removal. Always reconnect the positive lead first, and the negative lead last. Tighten the clamp bolts securely.

Steering angle sensor initialisation

12 For vehicles with Dynamic Stability Control (DSC), if the negative battery lead is disconnected, the stored initial position of the steering angle sensor will be cleared and the DSC will not operate properly, making the vehicle unsafe to drive. Consequently this procedure must be carried out after connecting the negative battery cable.

13 Turn the ignition on, and confirm that the DSC indicator light illuminates, and that the DSC OFF light flashes.

14 Turn the steering wheel to full right-hand lock, then to the left-hand full lock.

4.9 Depress the clips and remove the battery case

4.10 Battery tray retaining bolts

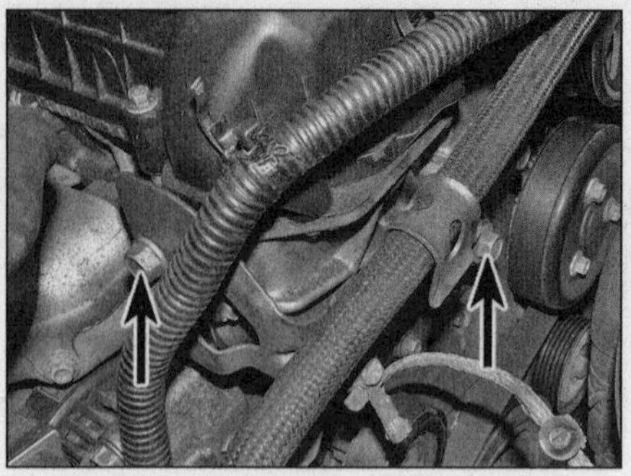

7.3 Undo the bolts and remove the hose bracket

7.4 Remove the wiring harness bracket bolt

7.5 Air scoop retaining bolt

15 Confirm that the DSC light extinguishes.
16 Turn the ignition off.
17 Turn the ignition on, and confirm that the DSC light extinguishes. If it doesn't, repeat the procedure again.
18 Drive the vehicle for approximately 10 minutes, and confirm that the ABS and DSC lights do not illuminate.

5 Charging system – testing

Note: *Refer to the warnings given in 'Safety first!' and in Section 1 of this Chapter before starting work.*

1 If the ignition warning light fails to illuminate when the ignition is switched on, first check the alternator wiring connections for security. If satisfactory, check that the warning light bulb has not blown, and that the bulbholder is secure in its location in the instrument panel. If the light still fails to illuminate, check the continuity of the warning light feed wire from the alternator to the bulbholder. If all is satisfactory, the alternator is at fault and should be renewed or taken to an auto-electrician for testing and repair.

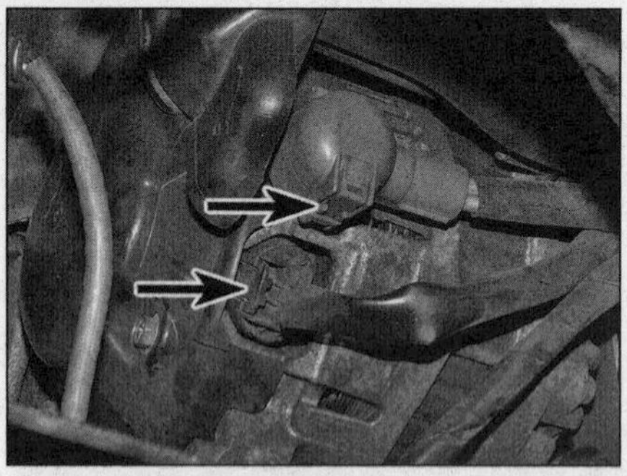

7.6 Release the catches, then undo the nut and disconnect the main battery cable and wiring plug

2 If the ignition warning light illuminates when the engine is running, stop the engine and check that the drivebelt is correctly tensioned (see Chapter 1, Section 6) and that the alternator connections are secure. If all is so far satisfactory, have the alternator checked by an auto-electrician for testing and repair. See the note in the previous paragraph.
3 If the alternator output is suspect even though the warning light functions correctly, the regulated voltage may be checked as follows.
4 Connect a voltmeter across the battery terminals and start the engine.
5 Increase the engine speed until the voltmeter reading remains steady; the reading should be approximately 12 to 13 volts, and no more than 15.0 volts.
6 Switch on as many electrical accessories (eg, the headlights, heated rear window and heater blower) as possible, and check that the alternator maintains the regulated voltage at around 13 to 14 volts.
7 If the regulated voltage is not as stated, the fault may be due to worn alternator brushes, weak brush springs, a faulty voltage regulator, a faulty diode, a severed phase winding or worn or damaged slip-rings. The alternator should be renewed or taken to an auto-electrician for testing and repair.

6 Alternator drivebelt – removal, refitting and tensioning

1 Refer to the procedure given for the auxiliary drivebelt(s) in Chapter 1, Section 6.

7 Alternator – removal and refitting

Removal

1 Disconnect the battery negative lead (see Section 4).
2 Remove the alternator drivebelt as described in Chapter 1, Section 6.
3 Unclip the power steering hose, then undo the bolts and remove the hose bracket **(see illustration)**.
4 Undo the bolt securing the wiring harness bracket at the front of the alternator **(see illustration)**.
5 Undo the bolt, then unclip the alternator air scoop **(see illustration)**.
6 Open the plastic cap, undo the nut and disconnect the main battery cable from the alternator, then disconnect the wiring plug beneath it **(see illustration)**.
7 Undo the three alternator mounting bolts and manoeuvre it from position **(see illustrations)**.

Refitting

8 Refitting is a reversal of removal, tightening all fasteners to the specified torque where given.

7.7a Alternator upper mounting bolt...

7.7b... lower front mounting bolt...

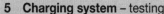

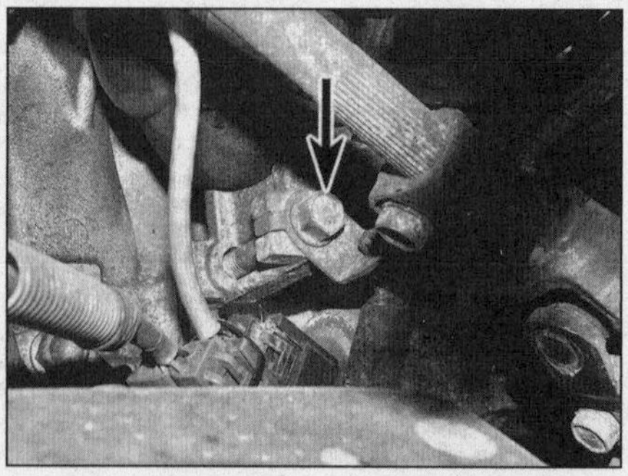

7.7c... and lower rear mounting bolt

8 Alternator – testing and overhaul

1 If the alternator is thought to be suspect, it should be removed from the vehicle and taken to an auto-electrician for testing. Most auto-electricians will be able to supply and fit brushes at a reasonable cost. However, check on the cost of repairs before proceeding as it may prove more economical to obtain a new or exchange alternator.

9 Starting system – testing

Note: *Refer to the precautions given in 'Safety first!' and in Section 1 of this Chapter before starting work.*

1 If the starter motor fails to operate when the ignition key is turned to the appropriate position, the following possible causes may be to blame.

a) The battery is faulty.

b) The electrical connections between the switch, solenoid, battery and starter motor are somewhere failing to pass the necessary current from the battery through the starter to earth.

c) The solenoid is faulty.

d) The starter motor is mechanically or electrically defective.

2 To check the battery, switch on the headlights. If they dim after a few seconds, this indicates that the battery is discharged – recharge or renew the battery. If the headlights glow brightly, operate the ignition switch and observe the lights. If they dim, then this indicates that current is reaching the starter motor, therefore the fault must lie in the starter motor. If the lights continue to glow brightly (and no clicking sound can be heard from the starter motor solenoid), this indicates that there is a fault in the circuit or solenoid – see following paragraphs. If the starter motor turns slowly when operated, but the battery is in good condition, then this indicates that either the starter motor is faulty, or there is considerable resistance somewhere in the circuit.

3 If a fault in the circuit is suspected, disconnect the battery leads (including the earth connection to the body), the starter/solenoid wiring and the engine/transmission earth strap. Thoroughly clean the connections, and reconnect the leads and wiring, then use a voltmeter or test lamp to check that full battery voltage is available at the battery positive lead connection to the solenoid, and that the earth is sound. Smear petroleum jelly around the battery terminals to prevent corrosion – corroded connections are amongst the most frequent causes of electrical system faults.

10.3 Remove the transverse member

4 If the battery and all connections are in good condition, check the circuit by disconnecting the wire from the solenoid blade terminal. Connect a voltmeter or test lamp between the wire end and a good earth (such as the battery negative terminal), and check that the wire is live when the ignition switch is turned to the 'start' position. If it is, then the circuit is sound – if not the circuit wiring can be checked as described in Chapter 12, Section 2.

5 The solenoid contacts can be checked by connecting a voltmeter or test lamp between the battery positive feed connection on the starter side of the solenoid, and earth. When the ignition switch is turned to the 'start' position, there should be a reading or lighted bulb, as applicable. If there is no reading or lighted bulb, the solenoid is faulty and should be renewed.

6 If the circuit and solenoid are proved sound, the fault must lie in the starter motor. In this event, it may be possible to have the starter motor overhauled by a specialist, but check on the cost of spares before proceeding, as it may prove more economical to obtain a new or exchange motor.

10 Starter motor – removal and refitting

Removal

1 Disconnect the battery negative lead as described in Section 4.

2 Slacken the left-hand front road wheel nuts, raise the front of the vehicle and support it securely on axle stands (see *Jacking and vehicle support*). Remove the road wheel.

3 Undo the fasteners and remove the undershield beneath the transmission, including the transverse member **(see illustration)**. Note that the fasteners are likely to be corroded. Liberally apply releasing fluid to the fasteners prior to removal.

4 Leaving the pipe attached, unbolt the clutch slave cylinder and move it to one side.

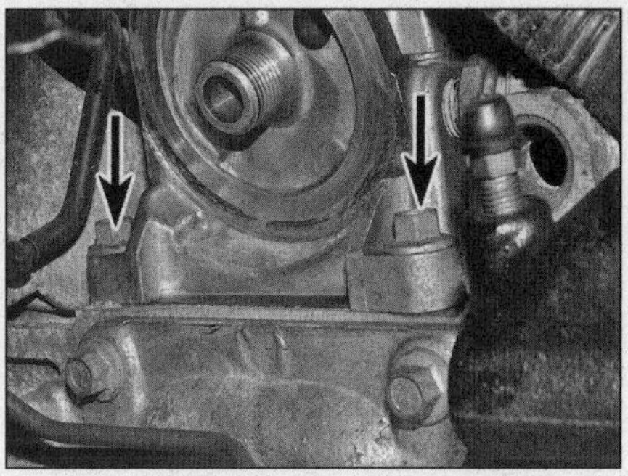

10.5 Oil filter housing/cooler lower mounting bolts

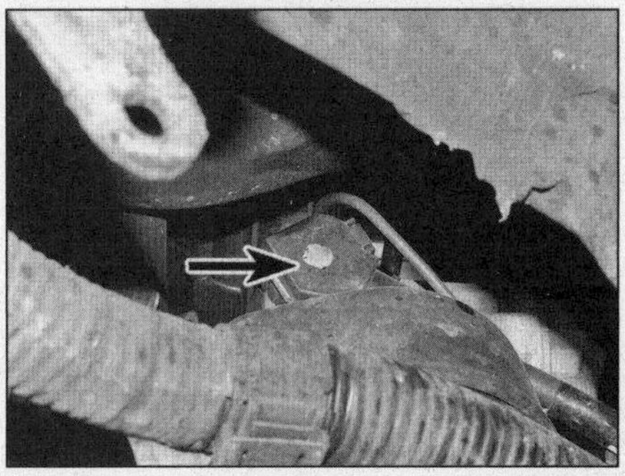

10.6 Open the plastic cover and disconnect the lead

5 Unscrew the oil filter cartridge, then leaving the pipes attached, undo the four bolts and move the oil filter housing/cooler to one side **(see illustration)**. Disconnect the oil pressure warning switch wiring plug.

6 Open the weatherproof plastic cover and disconnect the battery lead from the stud, and the wiring plug **(see illustration)**.

7 Remove the nut from the starter motor stud, and remove the starter mounting bolt. Note that the starter harness bracket is secured by the starter mounting nut.

8 Manoeuvre the starter motor through the wheel arch.

Refitting

9 Refitting is a reversal of removal. Tighten the starter motor mounting bolts to the specified torque.

11 Starter motor – testing and overhaul

1 If the starter motor is thought to be suspect, it should be removed from the vehicle and taken to an auto-electrician for testing. Most auto-electricians will be able to supply and fit brushes at a reasonable cost. However, check on the cost of repairs before proceeding, as it may prove more economical to obtain a new or exchange motor.

Chapter 5 Part B
Ignition system

Contents

Degrees of difficulty

Easy, suitable for novice with little experience	**Fairly easy,** suitable for beginner with some experience	**Fairly difficult,** suitable for competent DIY mechanic	**Difficult,** suitable for experienced DIY mechanic	**Very difficult,** suitable for expert DIY or professional

Specifications

General

System type	Electronic distributorless ignition system controlled by engine management system (electronic control module), 1 coil per cylinder
Firing order	1-3-4-2
Location of No 1 cylinder	Timing chain end

Ignition system data

Ignition timing (see text)	Approximately 8° BTDC – not adjustable

Torque wrench settings

	Nm	lbf ft
Ignition coil bolt	8	6
Knock sensor	20	15

1 Ignition system – general information and precautions

1 The electronic ignition system includes the ignition switch, the battery, the ignition coils and the spark plugs. Each spark plug is equipped with its own coil, mounted directly above the spark plug. The ignition system is controlled by the engine management Powertrain Control Module (PCM). Using data provided by information sensors which monitor various engine functions (such as rpm, intake air volume, engine temperature, etc), the PCM ensures a perfectly timed spark under all conditions.

2 When diagnosing the electronic ignition system, be sure to make all the necessary ignition system checks before renewing any components.

3 The information contained in this Chapter concentrates on the ignition-related components of the engine management system. Information covering the fuel, exhaust and emission control components can be found in Chapter 4A and 4B.

Precautions

4 When working on the ignition system, take the following precautions:

a) *Do not keep the ignition switch on for more than 10 seconds if the engine will not start.*

b) *Always connect a tachometer in accordance with the manufacturer's instructions. Some tachometers may be incompatible with this ignition system.*

c) *Never allow the ignition coil terminals to touch earth. Earthing the coil could result in damage to the igniter and/or the ignition coil.*

d) *Do not disconnect the battery when the engine is running.*

Warning: Voltages produced by an electronic ignition system are considerably higher than those produced by conventional ignition systems. Extreme care must be taken when working on the system with the ignition switched on. Persons with surgically-implanted cardiac pacemaker devices should keep well clear of the ignition circuits, components and test equipment.

2 Ignition system – testing

General

1 The components of the ignition system are normally very reliable; most faults are far more likely to be due to loose or dirty connections, or to dampness or damaged insulation, than to the failure of any of the system's components.

Always check all wiring thoroughly before condemning an electrical component, and work methodically to eliminate all other possibilities before deciding that a particular component is faulty.

2 The following tests should be carried out when an obvious fault such as non-starting or a clearly detectable misfire exists. Some faults, however, are more obscure and are often disguised by the fact that the PCM will adopt an emergency program (limp-home) mode to maintain as much driveability as possible. Faults of this nature usually appear in the form of excessive fuel consumption, poor idling characteristics, lack of performance, knocking or pinking noises from the engine under certain conditions, or a combination of these conditions. Where problems such as this are experienced, the best course is to refer the car to a suitably-equipped garage for diagnostic testing using dedicated test equipment.

Engine will not start

Note: *Remember that a fault with the anti-theft alarm or immobiliser will give rise to apparent starting problems. Make sure that the alarm or immobiliser has been deactivated, referring to the vehicle handbook for details.*

3 If the engine either will not turn over at all, or only turns very slowly, check the battery and starter motor. Connect a voltmeter across the battery terminals (meter positive probe to battery positive terminal) then note the voltage reading obtained while turning the engine over on the starter for (no more than) ten seconds. If the reading obtained is less than approximately 9.5 volts, first check the battery, starter motor and charging system as described in Chapter 5A.

Engine misfires

4 An irregular misfire is probably due to a loose connection to one of the ignition coils or system sensors.

5 With the ignition switched off, check carefully through the system, ensuring that all connections are clean and securely fastened.

6 Regular misfiring indicates a problem with one of the ignition coils or spark plugs. As no resistance values are available, testing the coils is best left to a Mazda dealer or suitable-equipped specialist.

7 Any further checking of the system components should be carried out after first checking the ECM for fault codes.

3.6 Pull the cover upwards from the engine

3.8 Depress the clip and disconnect the wiring plug

3.9a Undo the screw...

3.9b... and pull the coil upwards from each plug

3 Electronic ignition HT coil(s) – testing and renewal

Testing

1 Perform the ignition system checks as described in Section 2.

2 The only method of testing the coils available to the DIY'er, is substitution. If a misfire is suspected, remove the spark plugs as described in Chapter 1 Section 16, then remove the fuel pump relay (see Chapter 12 Section 4).

3 Reconnect the wiring plugs to the coils, then reconnect the spark plugs to the coils.

4 Earth the spark plug outer electrodes to a suitable metal part of the engine, and have an assistant crank the engine. A strong, blue spark should be visible at each plug.

5 If the spark isn't visible or is weak, swap around the coils/plugs to identify if a coil or plug is at fault.

Renewal

6 Disconnect the battery negative lead as described in Chapter 5A, Section 4, then pull the plastic cover on the top of the engine upwards from its mountings **(see illustration).**

7 Where fitted, remove the centre section of the strut brace as described in Chapter 10 Section 8.

8 Depress the clip and disconnect the wiring plug from each coil **(see illustration).**

9 Undo the retaining screws, grasp the coils firmly and pull them from the top of the spark plugs **(see illustrations).**

10 Refitting is a reversal of removal. Tighten the coils retaining screws to the specified torque.

4 Knock sensor – removal and refitting

1 Disconnect the battery negative lead as described in Chapter 5A, Section 4.

2 The knock sensor(s) is located on the right-hand side of the cylinder block under the intake manifold. Remove the intake manifold as described in Chapter 4A, Section 12.

3 Trace the wiring back from the sensor to the connector, then disconnect the wiring plug.

4 Note its fitted position, then unscrew the sensor from the cylinder block.

5 Refitting is a reversal of removal. Note that tightening the knock sensor to the specified torque is absolutely essential. Failure to do so could impair the performance of the sensor, causing engine damage.

Chapter 6
Clutch

Contents

Degrees of difficulty

Easy, suitable for novice with little experience	**Fairly easy,** suitable for beginner with some experience	**Fairly difficult,** suitable for competent DIY mechanic	**Difficult,** suitable for experienced DIY mechanic	**Very difficult,** suitable for expert DIY or professional

Specifications

Type	Single dry plate with diaphragm spring, hydraulically-operated	
Friction disc		
Minimum lining thickness above rivet head	0.3 mm	
Torque wrench setting	**Nm**	**lbf ft**
Clutch cover-to-flywheel bolts	30	22
Clutch slave cylinder bolts	22	16
Master cylinder nuts	22	16

1 General Information

1 All models are fitted with a single dry plate clutch, which consists of five main components; friction disc, pressure plate, diaphragm spring, cover and release bearing.
2 The friction disc is free to slide along the splines of the gearbox input shaft, and is held in position between the flywheel and the pressure plate by the pressure exerted on the pressure plate by the diaphragm spring. Friction lining material is riveted to both sides of the friction disc.
3 The diaphragm spring is mounted on pins, and is held in place in the cover by annular fulcrum rings.
4 The release bearing is located on a guide sleeve at the front of the gearbox, and the bearing is free to slide on the sleeve, under the action of the release arm which pivots inside the clutch bellhousing.
5 The release mechanism is operated by the clutch pedal, using hydraulic pressure. The pedal acts on the hydraulic master cylinder pushrod, and a slave cylinder, mounted on the gearbox bellhousing, operates the clutch release lever via a pushrod.
6 When the clutch pedal is depressed, the release arm pushes the release bearing forwards, to bear against the centre of the diaphragm spring, thus pushing the centre of the diaphragm spring inwards. The diaphragm spring acts against the fulcrum rings in the cover, and so as the centre of the spring is pushed in, the outside of the spring is pushed out, so allowing the pressure plate to move backwards away from the friction disc.
7 When the clutch pedal is released, the diaphragm spring forces the pressure plate into contact with the friction linings on the friction disc, and simultaneously pushes the friction disc forwards on its splines, forcing it against the flywheel. The friction disc is now firmly sandwiched between the pressure plate and the flywheel, and drive is taken up.

2 Clutch assembly – removal, inspection and refitting

Warning: Dust created by clutch wear and deposited on the clutch components may contain asbestos, which is a health hazard. DO NOT blow it out with compressed air, or inhale any of it. DO NOT use petrol (or petroleum-based solvents) to clean off the dust. Brake system cleaner or methylated spirit should be used to flush the dust into a suitable receptacle. After the clutch components are wiped clean with rags, dispose of the contaminated rags and cleaner in a sealed, marked container.

Removal

1 Remove the gearbox, as described in Chapter 7 Section 6.
2 If the original clutch is to be refitted,

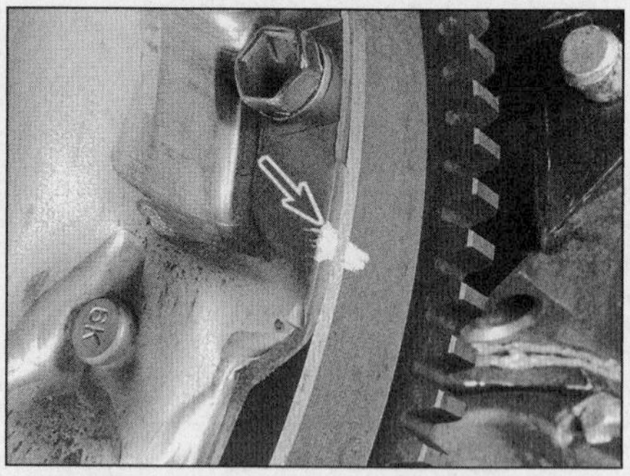

2.2 Make alignment marks between the clutch cover and flywheel

make alignment marks between the clutch cover and the flywheel, so that the clutch can be refitted in its original position **(see illustration)**.

3 Progressively unscrew the bolts securing the clutch cover/pressure plate assembly to the flywheel, and where applicable recover the washers.

4 Withdraw the clutch cover from the flywheel. Be prepared to catch the clutch friction disc, which may drop out of the cover as it is withdrawn, and note which way round the friction disc is fitted – the two sides of the disc are often marked 'Engine side' and 'Transmission side'. The greater projecting side of the hub faces away from the flywheel.

Inspection

5 With the clutch assembly removed,

2.7a Inspect the pressure plate surface for excessive score marks, cracks and signs of overheating

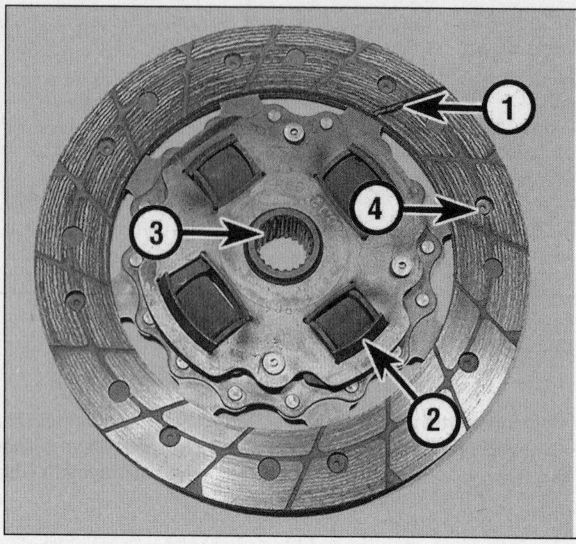

2.6 The clutch friction disc

1 *Lining – this will wear down in use*
2 *Springs or dampers – check for cracking and deformation*
3 *Splined hub – the splines must not be worn and should slide smoothly on the transmission input shaft splines*
4 *Rivets – these secure the lining and will damage the flywheel if allowed to contact the surfaces*

clean off all traces of dust using a dry cloth. Although most friction discs now have asbestos-free linings, some do not, and it is wise to take suitable precautions; asbestos dust is harmful, and must not be inhaled.

6 Examine the linings of the friction disc for wear and loose rivets, and the disc for distortion, cracks, and worn splines. The surface of the friction linings may be highly glazed, but, as long as the friction material pattern can be clearly seen, this is satisfactory **(see illustration)**. If there is any sign of oil contamination, indicated by a continuous, or patchy, shiny black discolouration, the disc must be renewed. The source of the contamination must be traced and rectified before fitting new clutch components; typically, a leaking crankshaft rear oil seal or gearbox input shaft oil seal – or both – will be to blame. The disc must also be renewed if the lining thickness has worn down to, or just above, the level of the rivet heads. Note that Mazda specify a minimum friction material thickness above the heads of the rivets (see Specifications).

7 Check the machined faces of the flywheel and pressure plate. If either is grooved, or heavily scored, renewal is necessary. The pressure plate must also be renewed if any cracks are apparent, or if the diaphragm spring is damaged or its pressure suspect **(see illustrations)**.

8 With the clutch removed, it is advisable to check the condition of the release bearing, as described in Section 3.

9 Check the pilot bearing in the flywheel. Make sure that it turns smoothly and quietly. If the gearbox input shaft contact face on the bearing is worn or damaged, fit a new bearing, as described in Chapter 2A Section 13.

Refitting

10 If new clutch components are to be fitted, where applicable, ensure that all anti-corrosion preservative is cleaned from the friction material on the disc, and the contact surfaces of the pressure plate.

11 It is important to ensure that no oil or grease gets onto the friction disc linings, or the pressure plate and flywheel faces. It is advisable to refit the clutch assembly with clean hands, and to wipe down the pressure plate and flywheel faces with a clean rag before assembly begins.

12 Offer the disc to the flywheel, with the greater projecting side of the hub facing away from the flywheel (most friction discs will have an 'Engine side' or Transmission side' marking which should face the flywheel or gearbox as applicable). Using a suitable Mazda tool or a suitable alternative manufactured by an

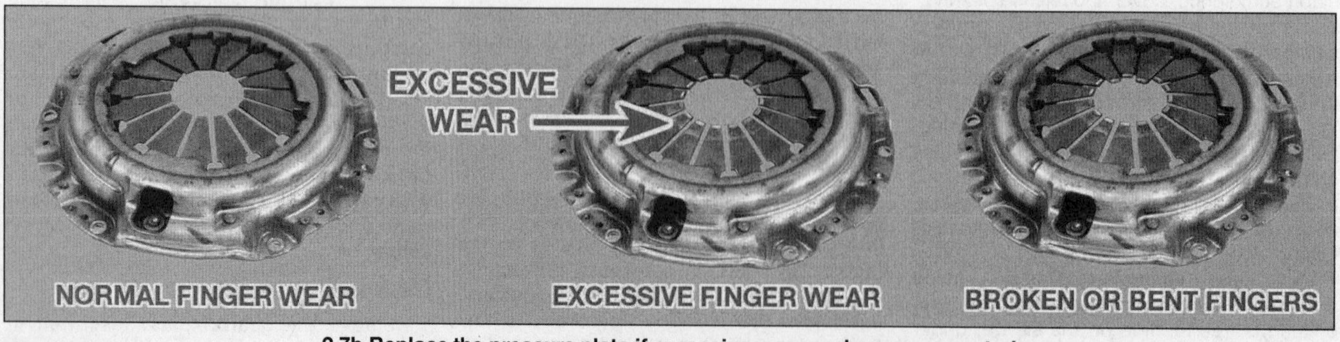

2.7b Replace the pressure plate if excessive wear or damage are noted

automotive tool specialist, centre the friction disc in the flywheel **(see illustration)**.

13 Fit the clutch cover assembly, where applicable aligning the marks on the flywheel and clutch cover. Ensure that the clutch cover locates over the dowels on the flywheel. Insert the securing bolts and washers, and tighten them to the specified torque.

14 Using high-temperature grease, lubricate the inner groove of the release bearing (see Section 3). Also place grease on the release lever contact areas and the transmission input shaft bearing retainer.

Caution: Only use a thin smear of grease – excessive amounts may contaminate the friction surfaces.

15 Refit the gearbox as described in Chapter 7 Section 6.

3 Clutch release bearing and lever – removal, inspection and refitting

Warning: Dust created by clutch wear and deposited on the clutch components may contain asbestos, which is a health hazard. DO NOT blow it out with compressed air, or inhale any of it. DO NOT use petrol (or petroleum-based solvents) to clean off the dust. Brake system cleaner or methylated spirit should be used to flush the dust into a suitable receptacle. After the clutch components are wiped clean with rags, dispose of the contaminated rags and cleaner in a sealed, marked container.

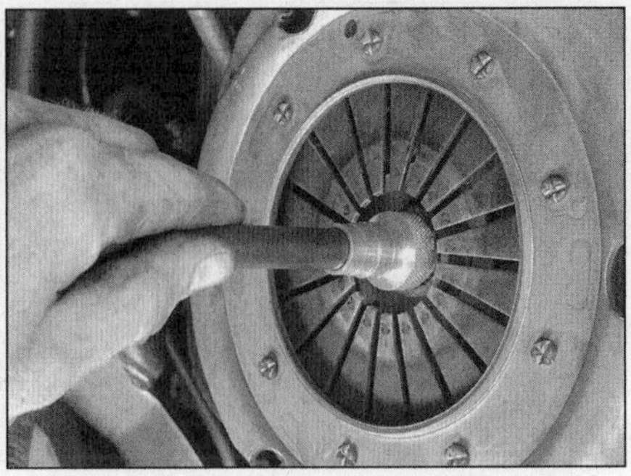

2.12 Using an aligning tool, centre the friction disc on the flywheel

Removal

1 Remove the gearbox as described in Chapter 7, Section 6.

2 Remove the clutch release lever from the ball stud, then remove the bearing from the lever **(see illustration)**.

Inspection

3 Hold the bearing by the outer race and rotate the inner race while applying pressure. If the bearing doesn't turn smoothly or if it's noisy, renew the bearing/hub assembly. Wipe the bearing with a clean rag and inspect it for damage, wear and cracks. Don't immerse the bearing in solvent – it's sealed for life and soaking or dipping in solvent would ruin it. Also check the release lever for cracks and bends.

4 Check the release lever boot for cracks or deterioration. If there are problems, pull it out of the hole and renew it.

3.2 Pull the lever from the ball stud and slide out the bearing

Installation

5 Fill the inner groove of the release bearing with high-temperature molybdenum grease. Also apply a light coat of the same grease to the transmission input shaft splines and the ball stud **(see illustrations)**.

6 Lubricate the release lever ball socket and lever ends with high-temperature molybdenum grease **(see illustrations)**.

7 Attach the release bearing to the release lever.

8 Slide the release bearing onto the transmission input shaft front bearing retainer while passing the end of the release lever through the opening in the clutch housing. Push the clutch release lever onto the ball stud until it's firmly seated **(see illustration)**.

9 The remainder of refitting is the reverse of the removal procedure.

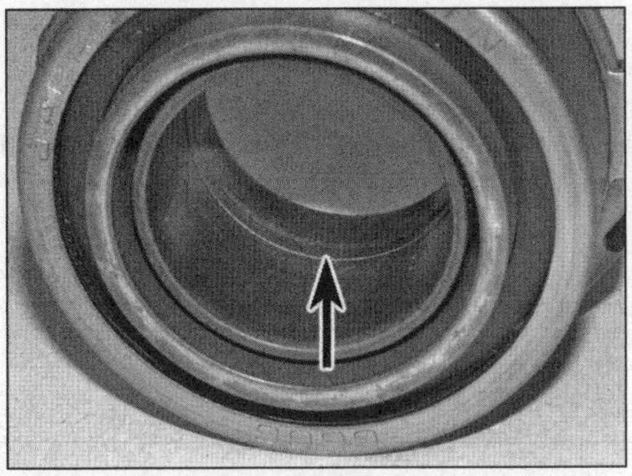

3.5a Apply a thin layer of high-temperature moly grease to release bearing inner groove ...

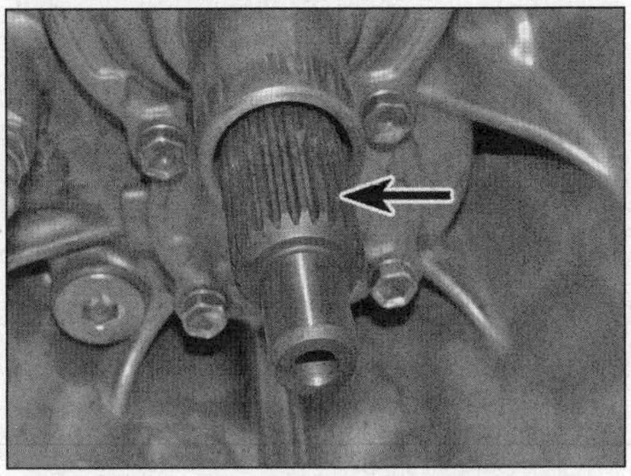

3.5b ... the input shaft splines ...

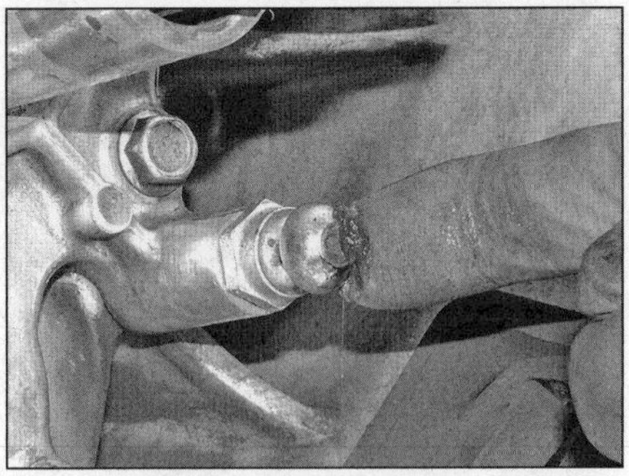

3.5c ... the ball stud ...

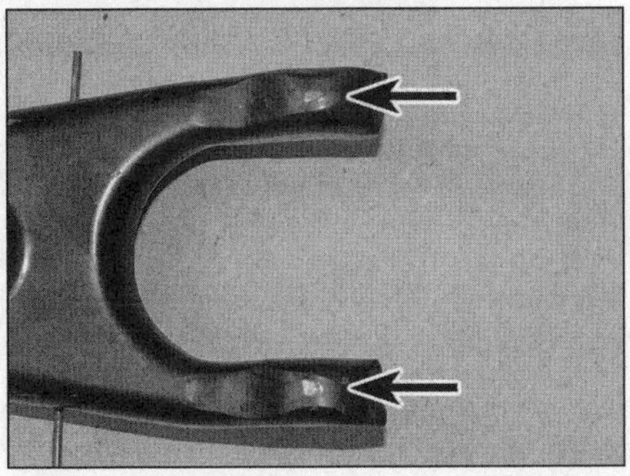

3.6a ... the release lever ends (arrowed) ...

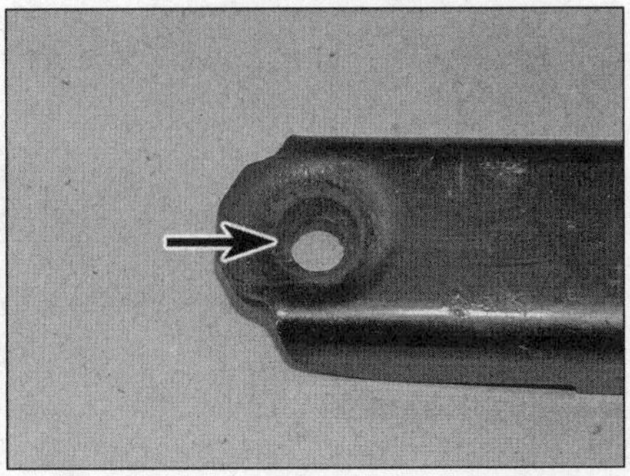

3.6b ... and the lever ball socket (arrowed)

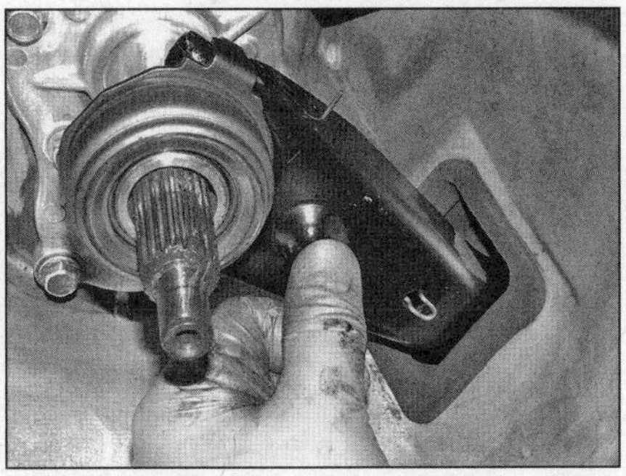

3.8 Firmly press the release lever onto the ball stud

4.2 Slave cylinder pipe union and mounting bolts

4.4 Remove the pushrod and rubber boot

4.5 Use low-pressure air to force the piston out – note the block of wood to 'catch' the piston

4 Hydraulic slave cylinder – removal, inspection and refitting

Warning: Hydraulic fluid is poisonous; wash off immediately and thoroughly in the case of skin contact, and seek immediate medical advice if any fluid is swallowed or gets into the eyes. Certain types of hydraulic fluid are inflammable, and may ignite when allowed into contact with hot components; when servicing any hydraulic system, it is safest to assume that the fluid is inflammable, and to take precautions against the risk of fire as though it is petrol that is being handled. Hydraulic fluid is also an effective paint stripper, and will attack plastics; if any is spilt, it should be washed off immediately, using copious quantities of fresh water. Finally, it is hygroscopic (it absorbs moisture from the air) – old fluid may be contaminated and unfit for further use. When topping-up or renewing the fluid, always use the recommended type, and ensure that it comes from a freshly-opened sealed container.

Note: *Before beginning this procedure, contact local parts stores and dealer service departments concerning the purchase of a rebuild kit or a new slave cylinder. Availability and cost of the necessary parts may dictate whether the cylinder is rebuilt or renewed. If it's decided to rebuild the cylinder, inspect the bore as described in paragraph 7 before purchasing parts.*

Removal

1 Raise the vehicle and support it securely on axle stands (see *Jacking and vehicle support*). Remove the transmission undershield.

2 The slave (release) cylinder is located on the left-hand side of the transmission. Disconnect the hydraulic pipe at the slave cylinder **(see illustration)**. If available, use a flare-nut spanner on the fitting, which will prevent the fitting from being rounded off. Have a container and rags handy, as some fluid will be spilled as the pipe is disconnected. Plug the pipe to prevent contamination.

3 Remove the slave cylinder mounting bolts and remove it **(see illustration 4.2)**.

Overhaul

4 Remove the pushrod and the boot **(see illustration)**.

5 Tap the cylinder on a block of wood to eject the piston and seal. If the piston won't come out easily, blow low-pressure air into the fluid pipe fitting **(see illustration)**.

Warning: The piston can shoot out forcefully enough to cause injury. Don't use any more air pressure than necessary. Be sure to point the open end of the cylinder at a block of wood. Keep your fingers out of the way.

6 Remove the spring from inside the cylinder **(see illustration)**.

7 Carefully inspect the bore of the cylinder. Check for deep scratches, score marks and ridges. The bore must be smooth to the touch. If any imperfections are found, the slave cylinder must be renewed.

8 Using the new parts in the rebuild kit, assemble the components using plenty of fresh brake fluid for lubrication **(see illustration)**. Note the installed direction of the spring and the seal.

Refitting

9 Refit the slave cylinder on the clutch housing. Make sure the pushrod is seated in the release fork pocket.

10 Connect the hydraulic pipe to the slave cylinder. Tighten the connection.

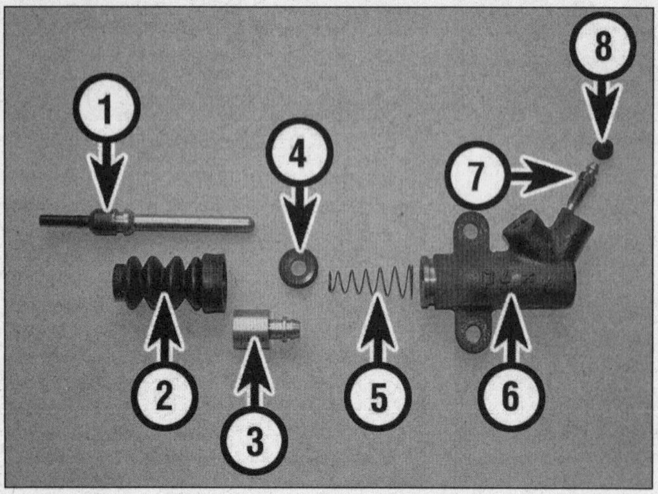

4.6 Slave cylinder components

1 Pushrod
2 Rubber boot
3 Piston
4 Seal
5 Spring
6 Cylinder body
7 Bleed screw
8 Dust cap

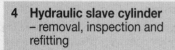

4.8 Ensure the seal is fitted correctly to the piston

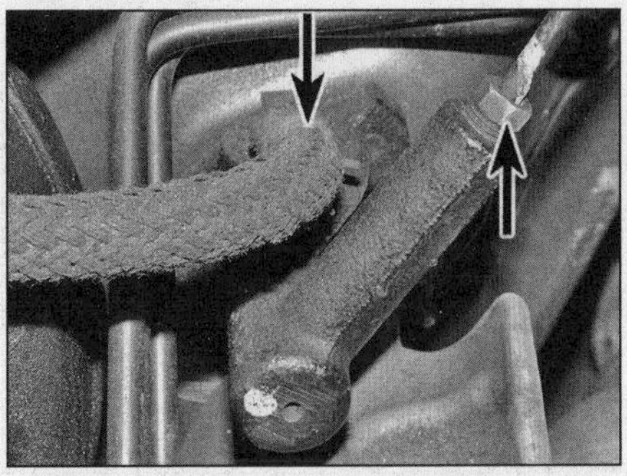

5.2 Disconnect the fluid supply hose and pressure pipe

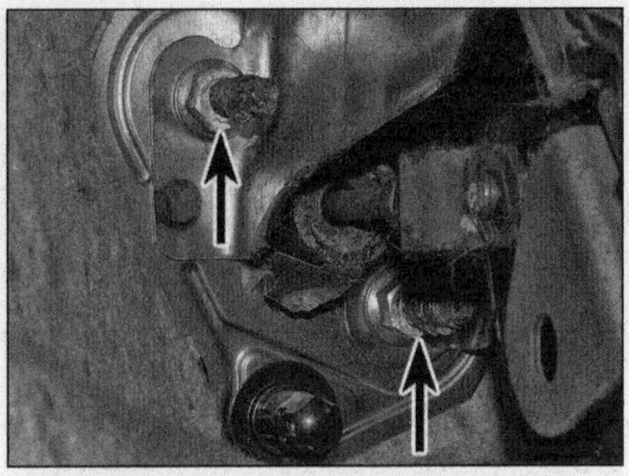

5.4 Master cylinder retaining nuts

5.6 Remove the circlip to release the piston

11 Fill the clutch master cylinder with brake fluid.
12 Bleed the system (see Section 6).
13 Lower the vehicle.

5 Hydraulic master cylinder – removal, inspection and refitting

Warning: Hydraulic fluid is poisonous; wash off immediately and thoroughly in the case of skin contact, and seek immediate medical advice if any fluid is swallowed or gets into the eyes. Certain types of hydraulic fluid are inflammable, and may ignite when allowed into contact with hot components; when servicing any hydraulic system, it is safest to assume that the fluid is inflammable, and to take precautions against the risk of fire as though it is petrol that is being handled. Hydraulic fluid is also an effective paint stripper, and will attack plastics; if any is spilt, it should be washed off immediately, using copious quantities of fresh water. Finally, it is hygroscopic (it absorbs moisture from the air) – old fluid may be contaminated and unfit for further use. When topping-up or renewing the fluid, always use the recommended type, and ensure that it comes from a freshly-opened sealed container.

Note: *Before beginning this procedure, contact local parts stores and dealer service departments concerning the purchase of a rebuild kit or a new master cylinder. Availability and cost of the necessary parts may dictate whether the cylinder is rebuilt or renewed. If you decide to rebuild the cylinder, inspect the bore as described in paragraph 8 before purchasing parts.*

Removal

1 Open the bonnet and place rags beneath the clutch master cylinder.
2 Disconnect the hose from the brake reservoir and the clutch hydraulic pipe fitting **(see illustration)**.
3 Working inside the vehicle, remove the facia lower panel above the pedals as described in Chapter 11 Section 28.
4 Undo the retaining nuts and remove the master cylinder from the engine compartment bulkhead, again being careful not to spill fluid from the master cylinder **(see illustration)**.

Overhaul

5 Turn the master cylinder over and allow the trapped fluid to drain from the fluid pipe opening into a container.
6 Place the cylinder in a vice with the piston end up. Push the piston down with a screwdriver and remove the circlip with circlip pliers **(see illustration)**. **Note:** *Do not damage the pushrod contact surface of the piston.*
7 Tap the master cylinder on a block of wood to eject the piston, spacer, primary cup and spring from inside the bore **(see illustration)**. **Note:** *If the rebuild kit supplies a complete piston assembly, ignore the paragraphs which don't apply.*
8 Carefully remove the seal from the piston.
9 Inspect the bore of the master cylinder for deep scratches, score marks and ridges. The surface must be smooth to the touch. If the bore isn't perfectly smooth, the master cylinder must be renewed or a reconditioned unit used.
10 If the cylinder will be rebuilt, use the new parts contained in the rebuild kit and follow any specific instructions which may have accompanied the rebuild kit. Wash all parts to be re-used with brake cleaner, denatured alcohol or clean brake fluid. DO NOT use petroleum-based solvents.
11 Attach a new seal to the piston. The seal lips must face away from the pushrod end of the piston **(see illustration)**.

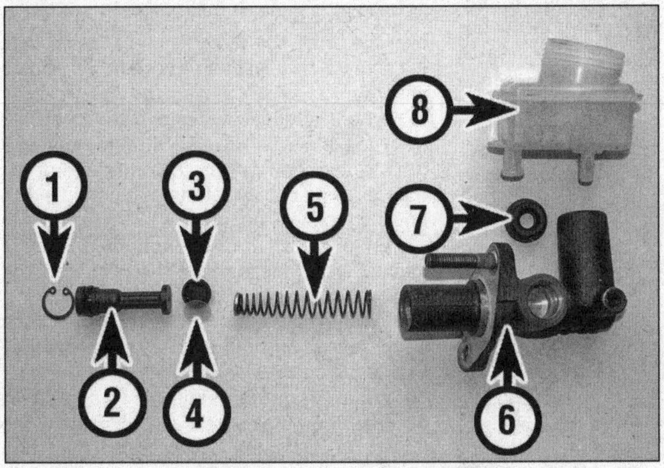

5.7 Master cylinder components

1 Circlip
2 Piston and seal
3 Primary cup
4 Spacer
5 Spring
6 Cylinder body
7 Sealing grommet
8 Reservoir

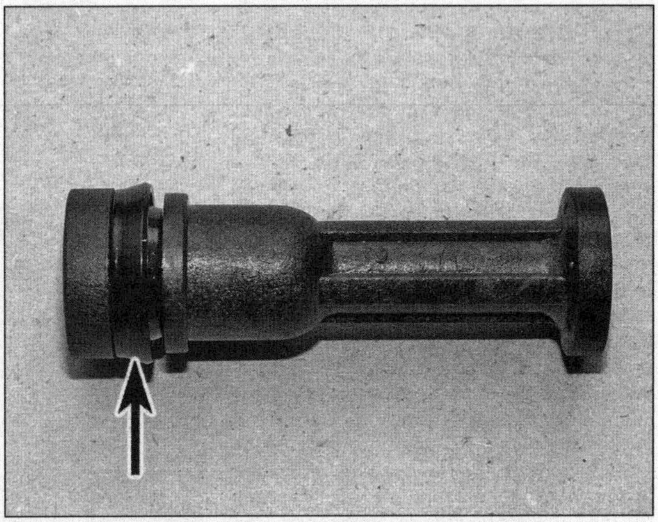

5.11 Ensure the seal (arrowed) is fitted correctly

5.13a Fit the primary cup ...

5.13b ... spacer ...

5.13c ... and piston

12 Lubricate the bore of the cylinder, the spring, primary cup, spacer and piston with plenty of fresh brake fluid.

13 Carefully guide the spring, primary cup, spacer and piston into the cylinder bore **(see illustrations)**.

14 Again place the cylinder in a vice with the piston end up. Push the piston down with a screwdriver and fit a new circlip.

Refitting

15 Apply a small amount of grease on the end of the pushrod. Position the master cylinder on the pushrod and against the bulkhead, the refit the retaining nuts finger-tight.

16 Connect the hydraulic pipe to the master cylinder, moving the cylinder slightly as necessary to thread the fitting properly into the bore. Don't cross-thread the fitting as it's fitted.

17 Tighten the retaining nuts and the hydraulic pipe fitting securely.

18 Fill the clutch fluid reservoir with brake fluid and bleed the clutch system (see Section 6).

6 Hydraulic system – bleeding

Warning: Hydraulic fluid is poisonous; wash off immediately and thoroughly in the case of skin contact, and seek immediate medical advice if any fluid is swallowed or gets into the eyes. Certain types of hydraulic fluid are inflammable, and may ignite when allowed into contact with hot components; when servicing any hydraulic system, it is safest to assume that the fluid is inflammable, and to take precautions against the risk of fire as though it is petrol that is being handled. Hydraulic fluid is also an effective paint stripper, and will attack plastics; if any is spilt, it should be washed off immediately, using copious quantities of fresh water. Finally, it is hygroscopic (it absorbs moisture from the air) – old fluid may be contaminated and unfit for further use. When topping-up or renewing the fluid, always use the recommended type, and ensure that it comes from a freshly-opened sealed container.

General

1 The correct operation of any hydraulic system is only possible after removing all air from the components and circuit; this is achieved by bleeding the system.

2 During the bleeding procedure, add only clean, unused hydraulic fluid of the recommended type; never re-use fluid that has already been bled from the system. Ensure that sufficient fluid is available before starting work.

3 If there is any possibility of incorrect fluid being already in the system, the clutch components and circuit must be flushed completely with uncontaminated, correct fluid, and new seals should be fitted to the various components.

4 If hydraulic fluid has been lost from the system, or air has entered because of a leak, ensure that the fault is cured before proceeding further.

5 To improve access, apply the handbrake, then jack up the front of the vehicle, and support it securely on axle stands (see *Jacking and vehicle support*). Remove the transmission undershield.

6 Check that the clutch hydraulic pipe(s) and hose(s) are secure, that the unions are tight, and that the bleed screw on the rear of the clutch slave cylinder (mounted under the vehicle on the lower left-hand side of the gearbox bellhousing) is closed. Clean any dirt from around the bleed screw **(see illustration)**.

7 Unscrew the brake/clutch fluid reservoir cap, and top the fluid up to the MAX level line; refit the cap loosely, and remember to maintain the fluid level at least above the MIN level line throughout the procedure, or there is a risk of further air entering the system.

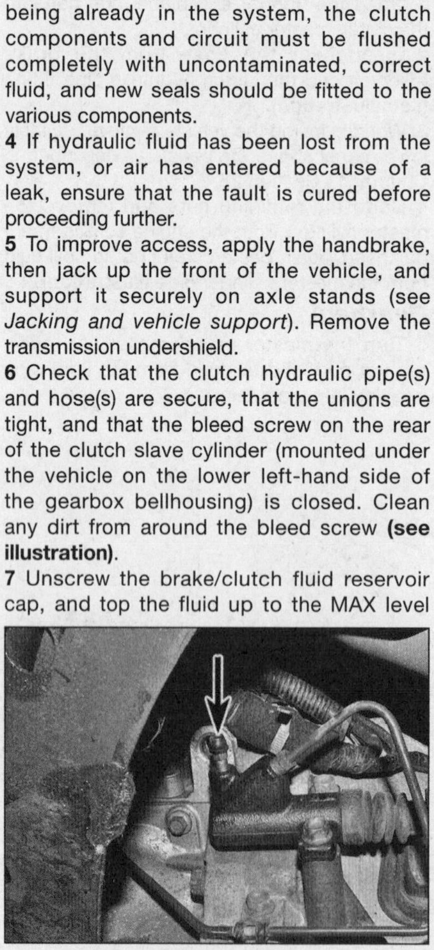

6.6 Slave cylinder bleed screw

8 It is recommended that pressure-bleeding equipment is used to bleed the system. Alternatively, there are a number of one-man, do-it-yourself brake bleeding kits currently available from motor accessory shops. These kits greatly simplify the bleeding operation, and also reduce the risk of expelled air and fluid being drawn back into the system. If such a kit is not available, the basic (two-man) method must be used, which is described in detail below.

9 If pressure-bleeding equipment or a one-man kit is to be used, prepare the vehicle as described previously, and follow the equipment/kit manufacturer's instructions, as the procedure may vary slightly according to the type being used; generally, they are as outlined below in the relevant sub-section.

10 Whichever method is used, the same basic process must be followed to ensure that the removal of all air from the system.

Bleeding

Basic (two-man) method

11 Collect a clean glass jar, a suitable length of plastic or rubber tubing which is a tight fit over the bleed screw, and a ring spanner to fit the screw. The help of an assistant will also be required.

12 Where applicable, remove the dust cap from the bleed screw. Fit the spanner and tube to the screw, place the other end of the tube in the jar, and pour in sufficient fluid to cover the end of the tube.

13 Ensure that the reservoir fluid level is maintained at least above the MIN level line throughout the procedure.

14 Have the assistant fully depress the clutch pedal several times to build-up pressure, then maintain it on the final downstroke.

15 While pedal pressure is maintained, unscrew the bleed screw (approximately one turn) and allow the compressed fluid and air to flow into the jar. The assistant should maintain pedal pressure, following it down to the floor if necessary, and should not release it until instructed to do so. When the flow stops, tighten the bleed screw again, have the assistant release the pedal slowly, and recheck the reservoir fluid level.

16 Repeat the steps given in paragraphs 14 and 15 until the fluid emerging from the bleed screw is free from air bubbles.

17 When no more air bubbles appear, tighten the bleed screw securely. Do not overtighten the bleed screw.

18 Remove the tube and spanner, and refit the dust cap to the bleed screw.

19 Refit the slave cylinder to the bellhousing, and tighten the securing nuts securely.

Using a one-way valve kit

20 As their name implies, these kits consist of a length of tubing with a one-way valve fitted, to prevent expelled air and fluid being drawn back into the system; some kits include a translucent container, which can be positioned so that the air bubbles can be more easily seen flowing from the end of the tube.

21 The kit is connected to the bleed screw, which is then opened. The user returns to the driver's seat, depresses the clutch pedal with a smooth, steady stroke, and slowly releases it; this is repeated until the expelled fluid is clear of air bubbles.

22 Note that these kits simplify work so much that it is easy to forget the reservoir fluid level; ensure that this is maintained at least above the MIN level line at all times.

Using a pressure-bleeding kit

23 These kits are usually operated by the reservoir of pressurised air contained in the spare tyre. However, note that it will probably be necessary to reduce the pressure to a lower level than normal; refer to the instructions supplied with the kit.

24 By connecting a pressurised, fluid-filled container to the fluid reservoir, bleeding can be carried out simply by opening the bleed screw, and allowing the fluid to flow out until no more air bubbles can be seen in the expelled fluid.

7.3 Clutch pedal switch and wiring plug

25 This method has the advantage that the large reservoir of fluid provides an additional safeguard against air being drawn into the system during bleeding.

All methods

26 If after following the instructions given, it is suspected that air is still present in hydraulic system, remove the slave cylinder (Section 4) without disconnecting the hydraulic pipes, push the cylinder piston all the way in, and holding the cylinder with the bleed screw uppermost, bleed the system again. Note: Steps must be taken to ensure that the slave cylinder piston is prevented from extending during the bleeding procedure. If necessary, use a metal strip and two threaded bars to fabricate a tool to hold the piston in.

27 When bleeding is complete, and firm pedal feel is restored, wash off any spilt fluid, check that the bleed screw is tightened securely, and refit the dust cap.

28 Check the hydraulic fluid level in the reservoir, and top-up if necessary (see *Weekly checks*).

29 Discard any hydraulic fluid that has been bled from the system; it will not be fit for re-use.

30 Check the feel of the clutch pedal. If it feels at all spongy, air must still be present in the system, and further bleeding is required. Failure to bleed satisfactorily after a reasonable repetition of the bleeding procedure may be due to worn master or slave cylinder seals.

31 On completion, lower the vehicle to the ground.

7 Clutch switch – testing and renewal

Testing

1 Verify that the engine will not start when the clutch pedal is released. Verify that the engine will start when the clutch pedal is depressed all the way.

2 If the clutch switch doesn't perform as described, renew it. Begin by removing the panel beneath the steering column as described in Chapter 11 Section 28.

3 Locate the switch on the clutch pedal assembly and unplug the electrical connector **(see illustration)**.

4 Connect an ohmmeter between the terminals of the switch. Verify that there is continuity between the switch terminals when the switch is On (pedal depressed).

5 Verify that no continuity exists between the switch terminals when the switch is Off (pedal released).

6 If the switch fails either of the tests, renew it.

Renewal

7 Disconnect the switch wiring plug.

8 Rotate the switch anti-clockwise and pull it from place.

9 Refitting is the reverse of removal.

Notes

Chapter 7
Manual gearbox

Contents

Degrees of difficulty

Easy, suitable for novice with little experience	**Fairly easy,** suitable for beginner with some experience	**Fairly difficult,** suitable for competent DIY mechanic	**Difficult,** suitable for experienced DIY mechanic	**Very difficult,** suitable for expert DIY or professional

Specifications

Type

5-speed	M15M-D
6-speed	P66M-D

Torque wrench settings

	Nm	lbf ft
Gearbox-to-engine bolts/nuts	44	32
Gear lever retaining bolts	10	7
Member bracket bolts	20	15
Power plant frame:		
Frame-to-transmission nuts	135	100
Frame-to-final drive nuts	135	100
Reversing light switch	30	22
Tunnel crossmember bolts	20	15

1 General Information

1 The gearbox is a 5- or 6-speed unit, and is contained in a cast-alloy casing bolted to the rear of the engine.

2 Drive is transmitted from the crankshaft via the clutch to the input shaft, which has a splined extension to accept the clutch friction disc. The output shaft transmits the drive via the propeller shaft to the rear differential.

3 The input shaft runs in line with the output shaft. The input shaft and output shaft gears are in constant mesh with the layshaft gear cluster. Selection of gears is by sliding synchromesh hubs, which lock the appropriate output shaft gears to the output shaft.

4 Gear selection is via a floor-mounted lever and selector. The selector mechanism causes the appropriate selector fork to move its respective synchro-sleeve along the shaft, to lock the gear pinion to the synchro-hub. Since the synchro-hubs are splined to the output shaft, this locks the pinion to the shaft, so that drive can be transmitted.

5 To ensure that gearchanging can be made quickly and quietly, a synchromesh system is fitted to all forward gears, consisting of baulk rings and spring-loaded fingers, as well as the gear pinions and synchro-hubs. The synchromesh cones are formed on the mating faces of the baulk rings and gear pinions.

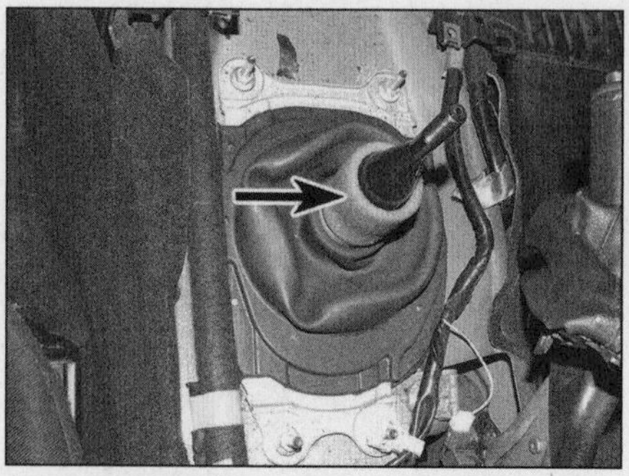

2.2a Remove the insulator...

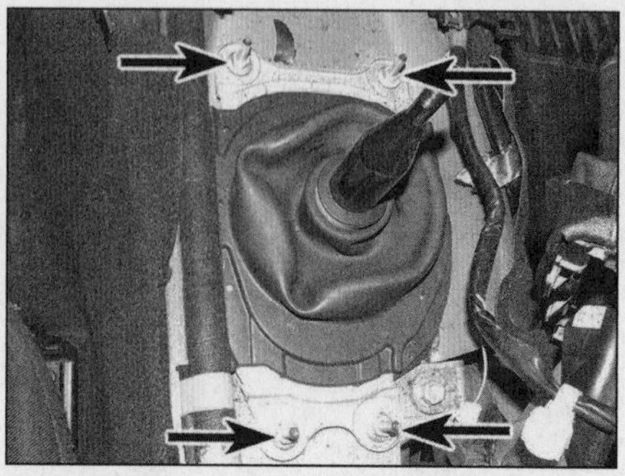

2.2b... then undo the nuts and remove the rubber gaiter

2.3a Undo the bolts...

2.3b... and remove the gearchange lever

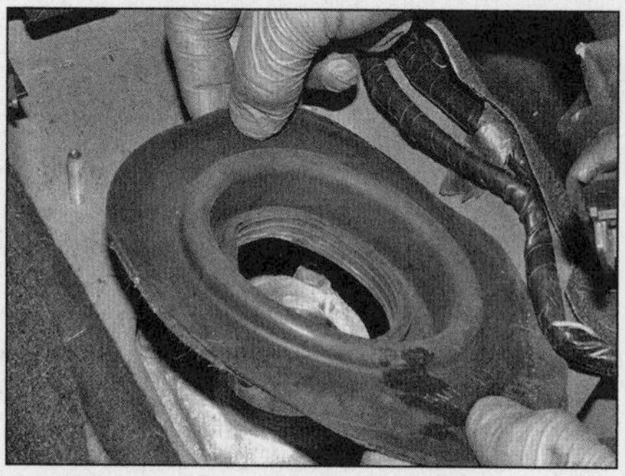

2.3c If required, remove the gaiter around the extension housing aperture

2.4 Add 300 cc of transmission oil to the extension housing

2 Gearchange lever – removal and refitting

1 Remove the centre console as described in Chapter 11, Section 27.

2 Place the gearchange lever in Neutral, remove the insulatorm undo the four nuts and remove the rubber gaiter **(see illustrations)**.

3 Remove the three retaining bolts and lift the gearchange lever straight up and out of the transmission **(see illustrations)**.

4 If the extension housing has been removed, or the gearbox rebuilt, refill it with 80 to 230 cc of 75W/90 API GL-4 before refitting the gearchange lever **(see illustration)**.

5 Coat both sides of a new gasket with sealant, place it in position, lubricate the gearchange lever base and lower it into the transmission.

6 Refit the retaining bolts and tighten them to the specified torque.

7 Refit the centre console as described in Chapter 11, Section 27.

3.4 Carefully prise the oil seal from the extension housing

3 Extension housing oil seal – renewal

1 Oil leaks frequently occur due to wear of the extension housing oil seal. Renewal of the seal is relatively easy, since the repairs can usually be performed without removing the transmission from the vehicle.

2 The extension housing oil seal is located at the extreme rear of the transmission, where the propeller is attached. If leakage at the seal is suspected, raise the vehicle and support it securely on axle stands (see *Jacking and vehicle support*). If the seal is leaking, transmission lubricant will be built up on the front of the propeller shaft and may be dripping from the rear of the transmission.

3 Refer to Chapter 8, Section 6 and remove the propeller shaft.

4 Using a screwdriver or pry bar, carefully pry the oil seal out of the rear of the transmission **(see illustration)**. Do not damage the splines on the transmission output shaft.

5 If the oil seal cannot be removed with a screwdriver or pry bar, a special oil seal removal tool (available at automotive parts retailers/tool specialists) will be required.

6 Using a large section of pipe or a very large deep socket as a drift, fit the new oil seal. Drive it into the bore squarely and make sure it's completely seated.

7 Lubricate the splines of the transmission output shaft and the outside of the driveshaft sleeve yoke with lightweight grease, then refit the propeller shaft as described in Chapter 8, Section 6. Be careful not to damage the lip of the new seal.

4 Reversing light and neutral switches – testing, removal and refitting

Testing

1 The reversing light circuit is controlled by a plunger-type switch screwed into the left-hand side (5-speed transmission) or top (6-speed) of the gearbox casing. If a fault develops in the circuit, first ensure that the circuit fuse has not blown.

2 To test the switch, disconnect the wiring connector, and use a multimeter (set to the resistance function) or a battery-and-bulb test circuit to check that there is continuity between the switch terminals only when reverse gear is selected. If this is not the case, and there are no obvious breaks or other damage to the wires, the switch is faulty, and must be renewed.

4.4 Reversing light switch – 5-speed transmissions

4.5 Neutral light switch

4.7 Reversing light switch

Removal

3 Jack up the vehicle and support securely on axle stands (see *Jacking and vehicle support*).

5-speed transmission

4 Disconnect the wiring connector, then unscrew the switch from the gearbox casing **(see illustration)**. Renew the sealing washer.

6-speed transmission

Neutral switch

5 Disconnect the wiring plug, then unscrew the switch from the gearbox casing **(see illustration)**.

Reversing light switch

6 Remove the transmission as described in Section 6.

7 Disconnect the wiring plug and unscrew the switch from the transmission **(see illustration)**.

Refitting

8 Using a new sealing washer, refit the switch back into position in the gearbox housing and tighten it to the specified torque.

9 The remainder of refitting is a reversal of removal.

5 Power plant frame – removal and refitting

Removal

1 The power plant frame is a brace installed along the left side of the transmission. It connects the transmission to the final drive.

2 Raise the vehicle and support it securely on axle stands (see *Jacking and vehicle support*).

3 Where fitted, undo the bolts and remove the undershield from beneath the transmission.

4 Remove the four tunnel member mounting bolts **(see illustration 6.6)** and remove the tunnel member.

5 Support the transmission with a jack, and wedge a piece of wood between the rear of the final drive housing and the rear axle to prevent the housing dropping when the frame is removed **(see illustration)**.

6 Remove the eight power plant frame nuts – four at the transmission and four at the final drive – and unbolt the power plant frame **(see illustrations)**. Note: Failure to support the transmission before removing the power plant frame could damage cables and/or electrical wiring connected to the transmission.

Refitting

7 Manoeuvre the power plant frame into position, then refit the retaining nuts, and lightly tighten nuts no. 1, 2 and 3 in the order shown **(see illustration)**.

8 Now tighten nut no. 2 to the specified torque until the power plant frame is seating in the final drive.

9 Lightly tighten nuts no. 4 and 5.

10 Refit the tunnel member, and tighten the retaining bolts to the specified torque.

11 Using a jack, raise the front end of the power plant frame until the gap between the lower edge of the frame and the upper edge of the tunnel member is 26.7 to 34.7 mm **(see illustration)**.

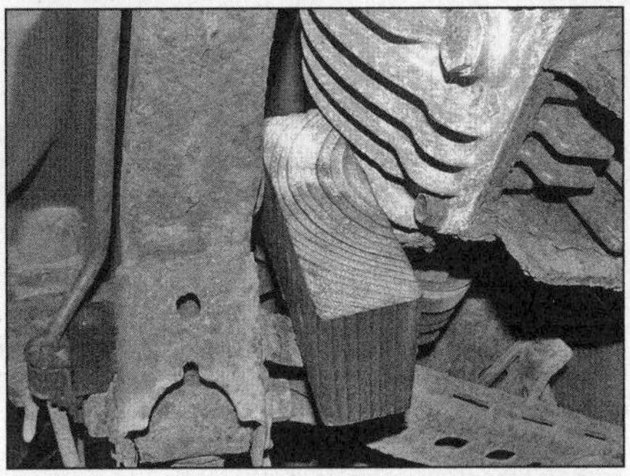

5.5 Jam a piece of wood between the axle and housing to prevent it from dropping

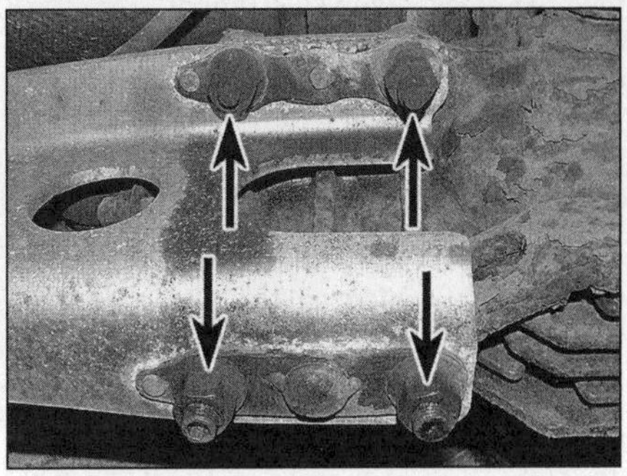

5.6a Undo the nuts securing the power plant frame to the final drive...

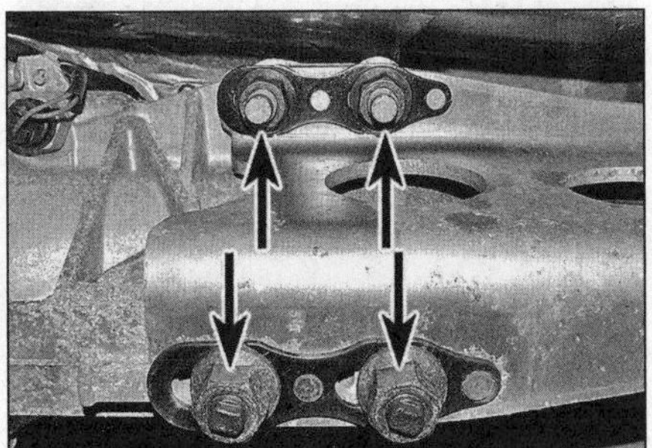

5.6b... and the transmission

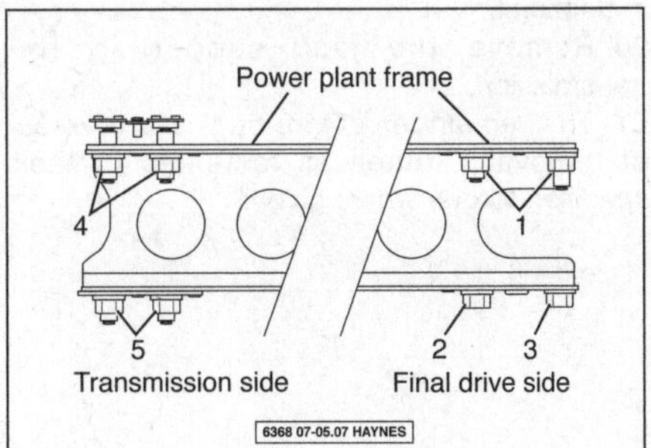

5.7 Power plant frame nuts tightening sequence

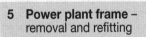

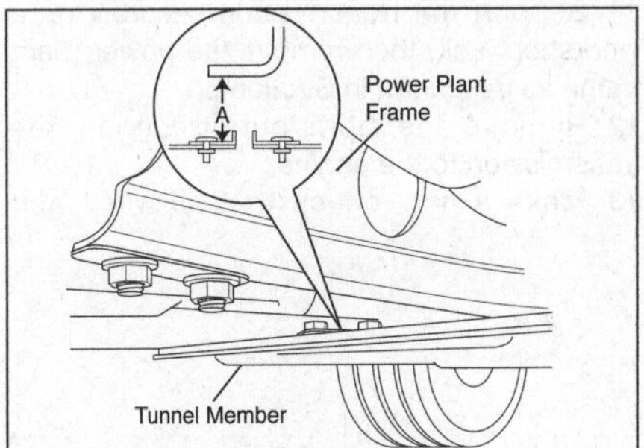

5.11 The gap (A) between the power plant frame and the tunnel member should be set at 26.7 to 34.7 mm

Note: *If there is a possibility of age-related bending/deterioration of the mounting, adjust the gap dimension to approximately 15 mm higher than the adjustment value to obtain the correct dimension.*

12 Tighten the power plant frame nuts to the specified torque.

13 Check the gap between the power plant frame and the tunnel member again. If the gap is not as specified, adjust it again.

14 The remainder of refitting is a reversal of removal.

6 Manual gearbox – removal and refitting

Note: *This is an involved operation. Read through the procedure thoroughly before starting work, and ensure that adequate lifting tackle and/or jacking/support equipment is available.*

Removal

1 Disconnect the battery negative lead as described in Chapter 5A, Section 4.

2 Remove the gearchange lever as described in Section 2.

3 Raise the vehicle and support it securely on axle stands (see *Jacking and vehicle support*).

4 Working as described in Chapter 5A Section 10, slacken the starter motor bolts.

5 Undo the fasteners and remove the transmission undershields (where fitted), and member bracket **(see illustration)**.

6 Undo the fasteners and remove the tunnel member **(see illustration)**.

7 Remove the complete exhaust system as described in Chapter 4A Section 13.

8 Remove the propeller shaft as described in Chapter 8 Section 6. Use a plastic bag to cover the end of the transmission to prevent fluid loss and contamination.

9 Remove the clutch slave cylinder as described in Chapter 6 Section 4. Note that it's not necessary to disconnect the fluid pipe from the slave cylinder.

10 Make note of their fitted locations, then disconnect the various wiring plug and unclip the wiring harness from the transmission.

11 Support the transmission securely on a workshop jack, then remove the power plant frame as described in Section 5.

12 Remove the bolts/nuts securing the transmission to the engine.

13 Make a final check that all wires and hoses have been disconnected from the transmission and then move the transmission and jack toward the rear of the vehicle until the transmission input shaft is clear of the clutch friction disc. Keep the transmission level as this is done. Take care, the transmission is heavy!

Caution: Don't shake the transmission up and down or from side to side in an effort to make it slide out. This may damage the camshaft position sensor on rear of the engine.

14 Once the input shaft is clear, lower the transmission and remove it from under the vehicle.

15 The clutch components can be inspected at this time (see Chapter 6 Section 2). In most cases, new clutch components should be routinely fitted if the transmission is removed.

Refitting

16 If removed, fit the clutch components as described in Chapter 6 Section 2.

17 With the transmission securely supported, raise it into position behind the engine and then carefully slide it forward, engaging the input shaft with the clutch plate hub. Do not use excessive force to install the transmission – if the input shaft does not slide into place, readjust the angle of the transmission so it's level and/or turn the input shaft so the splines engage properly with the clutch.

18 Refit the transmission-to-engine bolts/nuts. Tighten the bolts/nuts to the specified torque.

19 Refit the power plant frame as described in Section 5.

20 Remove the jack supporting the transmission.

21 The remainder of refitting is a reversal of removal. Tighten all fasteners to their specified torque where given.

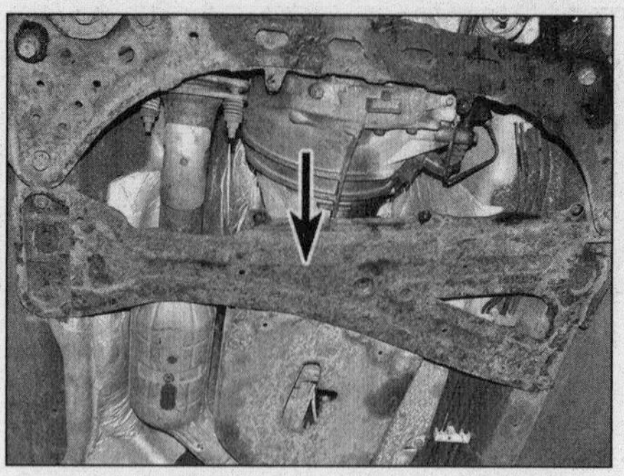

6.5 Remove the member bracket

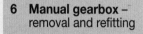

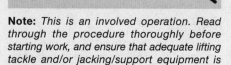

6.6 Remove the tunnel member

7 Manual gearbox overhaul – general information

1 Overhauling a manual gearbox is a difficult and involved job for the DIY home mechanic. In addition to dismantling and reassembling many small parts, clearances must be precisely measured and, if necessary, changed by selecting shims and spacers. Internal gearbox components are also often difficult to obtain, and in many instances, extremely expensive. Because of this, if the gearbox develops a fault or becomes noisy, the best course of action is to have the unit overhauled by a specialist repairer, or to obtain an exchange reconditioned unit. Be aware that some gearbox repairs can be carried out with the gearbox in the car.

2 Nevertheless, it is not impossible for the more experienced mechanic to overhaul the gearbox, provided the special tools are available, and the job is done in a deliberate step-by-step manner, so that nothing is overlooked.

3 The tools necessary for an overhaul include internal and external circlip pliers, bearing pullers, a slide hammer, a set of pin punches, a dial test indicator, and possibly a hydraulic press. In addition, a large, sturdy workbench and a vice will be required.

4 During dismantling of the gearbox, make careful notes of how each component is fitted, to make reassembly easier and more accurate.

5 Before dismantling the gearbox, it will help if you have some idea what area is malfunctioning. Certain problems can be closely related to specific areas in the gearbox, which can make component examination and renewal easier. Refer to the Fault finding Section at the end of this manual for more information.

Chapter 8
Final drive, driveshafts and propeller shaft

Contents

Degrees of difficulty

Easy, suitable for novice with little experience	**Fairly easy,** suitable for beginner with some experience	**Fairly difficult,** suitable for competent DIY mechanic	**Difficult,** suitable for experienced DIY mechanic	**Very difficult,** suitable for expert DIY or professional

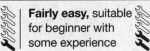

Specifications

Final drive

Type	Unsprung, attached to rear suspension crossmember
Capacity	Refer to Chapter 1 Specifications

Driveshaft

Type	Steel shafts with ball-and-cage type constant velocity joints at the outer ends, and tripod type sliding joints at the inner ends
Constant velocity joint grease capacity:	
Outer joint:	
Tripod joint housing	135 – 155g in each joint
Gaiter	90 – 110g in each gaiter
Inner joint	Use the grease provided in the repair kit
Standard length:	
Left-hand side	778.5 to 788.5 mm
Right-hand side	818.5 to 828.5 mm

Propeller shaft

Type	One-piece with front and rear universal joints

Torque wrench settings

Torque wrench settings	Nm	lbf ft
Final drive unit		
Mounting nuts	90	66
Pinion nut (see text): *		
Minimum	155	115
Maximum	380	280
**Do not re-use*		
Driveshaft		
Driveshaft nut*	255	188
**Do not re-use*		
Propeller shaft		
Shaft to final drive	55	41
Roadwheels		
Wheel nuts	110	81

1 General Information

1 Power is transmitted from the transmission to the rear axle by a one-piece propeller shaft. On all models, the rear end of the shaft is attached to the final drive pinion by bolts and nuts, whilst the front end is a sliding fit on the transmission output shaft. Universal joints are fitted to the front and rear of the shaft.

2 The final drive assembly includes the drive pinion, the ring gear, and the differential. The drive pinion, which drives the ring gear, is also known as the differential input shaft and is connected to the propeller shaft via an input flange. The differential is bolted to the ring gear and drives the rear wheels through a pair of driveshafts. The differential allows the wheels to turn at different speeds when cornering. Note that some models are equipped with a Limited Slip Differential (LSD).

3 The driveshafts deliver power from the final drive unit to the rear wheels. The inner ends of the driveshafts are equipped with sliding constant velocity joints, which are capable of both angular and axial motion. Each inner joint assembly consists of a tripod bearing and a joint housing (outer race) in which the joint is free to slide in and out as the driveshaft moves up and down with the wheel. The joints can be disassembled and cleaned in the event of a boot failure, but if any parts are damaged, the joints must be replaced as a unit.

4 The outer CV joints are the “ball joint” type which have ball bearings running between an inner race and an outer cage, allowing angular but not axial movement. The outer joints should be cleaned, inspected and repacked, but they cannot be disassembled. If an outer joint is damaged, it must be replaced along with the driveshaft (the outer joint and driveshaft are sold as a single component).

5 Major repair work on the differential assembly components (drive pinion, ring-and-pinion, and differential) requires many special tools and a high degree of expertise, and therefore should not be attempted by the home mechanic. If major repairs become necessary, we recommend that they be performed by a Mazda service department or other suitably-equipped automotive engineer.

2 Final drive unit – removal and refitting

Removal

1 Slacken the rear roadwheel nuts, jack up the rear end of the vehicle and support it securely on axle stands (see *Jacking and vehicle support*). Remove the rear wheels.

2 Remove the exhaust system (see Chapter 4A, Section 13).

3 Remove the propeller shaft (see Section 6).

4 Remove the power plant frame (see Chapter 7, Section 5).

Caution: Once the power plant frame has been removed, the transmission must be supported by a jack at all times, otherwise the transmission will drop down.

5 Remove the driveshafts as described in Section 4.

6 Support the final drive with a jack. Remove the mounting nuts from the upper mount on each side of the final drive. Move the final drive forward and lower it clear of the vehicle.

Refitting

7 Refitting is the reverse of the removal steps. Tighten all fasteners to their specified torques where given.

8 Check the final oil level and top it up if necessary as described in Chapter 1, Section 23.

9 We recommend the rear wheel alignment is checked at the earliest opportunity.

3 Final drive unit oil seals – renewal

Propeller shaft flange oil seal

Note: *A new flange nut retaining plate will be required.*

1 Raise the rear of the vehicle and place it securely on axle stands (see *Jacking and vehicle support*). Remove the rear wheels and brake calipers as described in Chapter 9, Section 9. There is no need to disconnect the fluid pipes from the calipers.

2 Remove the rear section of the exhaust system (see Chapter 4A, Section 13).

3 Mark the propeller shaft and pinion flange for ease of realignment during assembly, then remove the propeller shaft as described in Section 6.

4 Remove the drain plug from the differential housing and allow the differential lubricant to drain into a container as described in Chapter 1, Section 23. When the draining is complete, refit the drain plug.

5 Using a suitable torque wrench, slowly turn the pinion shaft nut and measure the amount of torque necessary to start the pinion shaft turning **(see illustration)**. Write down this figure.

6 Mark the relationship of the pinion nut and flange **(see illustration)**. Using a suitable tool, counterhold the flange and remove the pinion nut **(see illustration)**. Remove the flange, using a puller if necessary.

3.5 Use a deflection-type torque wrench to measure the pinion turning torque

7 After noting the orientation of the oil seal, carefully prise it out of the differential with a screwdriver or lever bar. Be careful not to damage the splines on the pinion shaft or disturb the position of the shaft.

8 Clean the oil seal mounting surface, then tap the new seal into place, taking care to insert it squarely.

9 Inspect the splines on the pinion shaft for burrs and nicks. Remove any rough areas with a crocus cloth. Wipe the splines clean.

10 Install the companion flange, aligning it with the marks made during removal. Gently tap the flange on with a soft-faced hammer until you can start the pinion nut on the pinion shaft.

11 Using a suitable tool, hold the companion flange while tightening the pinion nut to the minimum torque listed (see Specifications). Continue tightening, taking frequent rotational torque measurements, using the torque wrench, until the measurement recorded in paragraph 5 is reached. Increase the nut torque in small increments and check the preload after each increase.

Caution: Under no circumstances should the pinion nut be backed off to reduce pinion bearing preload.

12 Refit the propeller shaft, brake calipers and wheels.

13 Refill the final drive as described in Chapter 1, Section 23.

3.6a Make alignment marks between the pinion, nut and flange (arrowed)

3.6b Counterhold the pinion flange, and undo the nut

3.16 Carefully prise the driveshaft oil seal from the housing

3.17 Drive the new oil seal squarely into place using a suitably-sized socket

4.2 Use a small punch to 'unstake' the driveshaft nut

14 Lower the vehicle and test drive it to check for leaks.

Driveshaft oil seal

15 Remove the driveshafts as described in Section 4.

16 Prise out the seal with a removal tool or screwdriver **(see illustration)**.

17 Use a hammer and a seal driver, large socket or section of pipe to install the new seal **(see illustration)**.

18 Fit a new circlip on the splined end of the output shaft or driveshaft.

19 Apply a film of clean oil to the lips of the seal, then refit the driveshaft.

20 Fill the differential with oil (see Chapter 1, Section 23).

4 Driveshaft – removal and refitting

Note: *A new driveshaft retaining nut will be required on refitting.*

Removal

1 If the design of the vehicle's wheels allows access to the driveshaft nuts without removing the wheels, loosen the rear wheel nuts 1/4 turn. Using a hammer and punch, unstake the driveshaft nut and loosen it 1/4 turn. Raise the vehicle and support it securely on axle stands. Remove the wheels.

2 If the wheels must be removed for access to the nut, loosen the rear wheel nuts 1/4 turn. Raise the vehicle and support it securely on axle stands (see *Jacking and vehicle support*). Remove the wheels, then unstake the nut **(see illustration)**.

3 Remove the driveshaft nut. To prevent the hub from turning, attach two lengths of steel to two of the wheel studs and allow the bar to rest against the ground **(see illustration)**.

4 Remove the ABS sensor and the rear brake caliper (see Chapter 9) and secure them out of the way. Disconnect the anti-roll bar bar link from the rear trailing link and disconnect all links from the rear hub carrier (see Chapter 10).

5 Loosen the driveshaft from the hub splines with a puller that will attach to the wheel studs **(see illustration)**. If the driveshaft is reluctant to release (quite likely), remove the hub carrier (see Chapter 10 Section 11) complete with the driveshaft, and use a press to release the driveshaft.

Caution: Applying force to the end of the driveshaft, beyond just breaking it loose from the hub, can damage the driveshaft or differential.

6 After withdrawing the outer end of the driveshaft from the hub carrier, support the carrier by reattaching it to the rear upper lateral link (see Chapter 10 Section 11). Don't let the driveshaft hang by the inner CV joint after the outer end has been detached from the hub carrier, as the inner joint could become damaged. Support the outer end of the driveshaft with a piece of wire, if necessary.

7 Place a container underneath the differential to catch any lubricant that may spill out when the driveshafts are removed.

4.3 Attach two lengths of steel to counterhold the hub flange whilst slackening the driveshaft nut

8 Mark the relationship of the inner CV joint and differential. Gently prise the inner CV joint out of the differential, being careful not to damage the dust cover or oil seal **(see illustration)**.

9 Refer to Section 3 for the driveshaft oil seal renewal procedure.

Refitting

10 Refitting is the reverse of the removal procedure, but note the following additional points:

Caution: The sharp edges of the driveshaft circlip can slice or puncture the oil seal.

*a) Install a new circlip on the end of the driveshaft inner CV joint **(see illustration)**, apply molybdenum based grease to the*

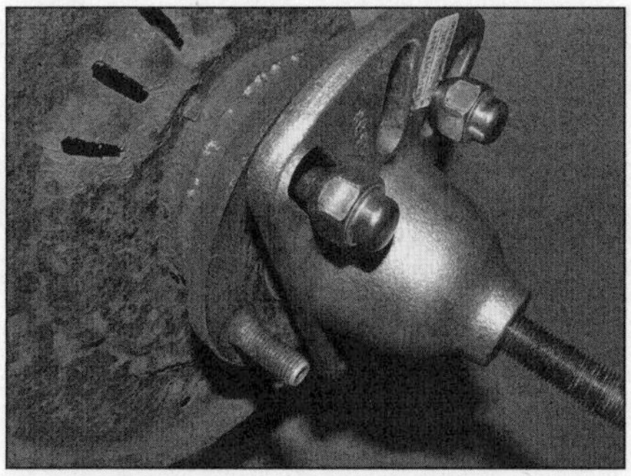

4.5 Use a suitable puller to release the driveshaft from the hub splines

4.8 Use a lever to carefully prise the inner CV joint from the differential

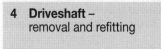

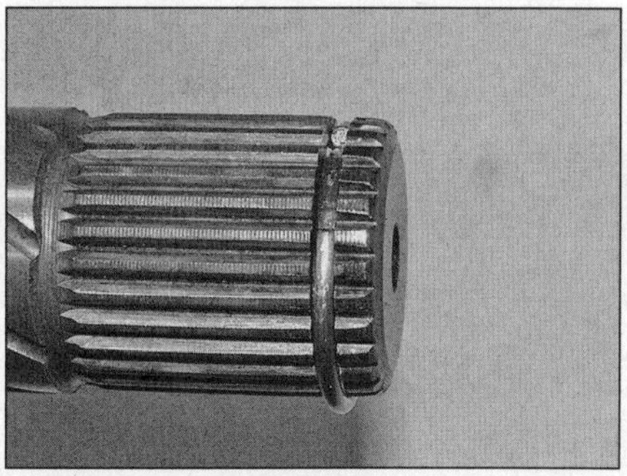

4.10 Fit a new circlip to the end of the shaft

splines and wipe the differential oil seal with differential oil. With the end gap of the circlip facing up, push the driveshaft sharply in to seat the clip on the inner CV joint in the groove of the differential side gear.
b) Install a new driveshaft nut, tighten it to the specified torque and stake the nut with a punch
c) Install the wheel and nuts, lower the vehicle and tighten the nuts to the specified torque.
d) Check the final drive fluid level, and if necessary, top it up as described in Chapter 1, Section 23.

5 Driveshaft gaiters renewal and CV joint inspection

1 Remove the driveshaft as described in Section 4.

Inner CV joint and gaiter

Disassembly

2 Check the CV joint for excessive play in the radial direction, which indicates worn parts. Check for smooth operation throughout the full range of motion for each CV joint. If a gaiter is torn or damaged, disassemble the joint, clean the components and inspect for damage due to loss of lubrication and possible contamination by foreign matter.

3 Prise the gaiter clamp retaining tabs up with a small screwdriver and slide the clamps off the gaiter **(see illustration)**. If necessary, cut the clamp from the gaiter with a hacksaw.

5.3 Prise up the tabs and release the gaiter clamps

5.4 Make alignment marks between the housing and shaft.

4 Mark the relationship of the driveshaft and joint housing, then slide the housing from the tripod joint **(see illustration)**. Note that the tripod joint bearings may fall out as the housing is removed.

5 Clean the grease away, then make alignment marks between the end of the shaft and the tripod. Remove the circlip and pull the joint from the shaft **(see illustrations)**. Note that a new circlip will be needed for reassembly.

6 Remove the old gaiter and clamps from the shaft.

7 No further dismantling is recommended

Inspection

8 Clean the components with solvent to remove all traces of grease. Inspect the housing and tripod joint for pitting, score marks, cracks and other signs of wear and damage. Shiny, polished spots are normal and will not adversely affect joint performance.

9 Check the bearings rotate freely with no signs of excess play or roughness.

Reassembly

10 Wrap the end of the shaft with plastic insulating tape to prevent any damage, then slide the new gaiter over the tape, onto the shaft, and remove the tape **(see illustration)**.

11 Fill the inside of the gaiter with 90 – 110 g of grease (normally supplied with the gaiter kit).

12 Align the mark on the end of the shaft with the mark on the tripod joint. Gently tap the joint onto the shaft using a brass drift (or similar) **(see illustrations)**. Note that the side of the tripod with with the chamfered hole, must be fitted towards the driveshaft.

13 With the tripod joint fully installed on the shaft, fit the new circlip into the groove **(see illustration)**.

5.5a Make further alignment marks between the tripod joint and the shaft

5.5b Remove the circlip from the end of the shaft...

5.5c... and slide the tripod joint from the shaft

5.12a Slide the new gaiter and clamp onto the shaft

5.12b Install the tripod with the chamfered edge facing the shaft

5.13 Secure the tripod with a new circlip

5.14 Align the marks and slide the housing onto the tripod

5.17a Install the gaiter clamps...

5.17b... fold over the 'ears'...

14 Fill the joint and housing with 135 – 155 g of grease (normally supplied with the gaiter kit), and slide it onto the tripod, aligning the previously made marks **(see illustration)**.

15 Wipe any excess grease from the driveshaft gaiter groove on the housing. Seat the small diameter of the gaiter in the recessed area on the driveshaft. Push the other end of the boot onto the housing and move the housing in or out to adjust the driveshaft to the length listed in this Chapter's Specifications.

16 Release any trapped air from the gaiter by carefully lifting the inner end with a blunt screwdriver (or similar).

17 Install the gaiter clamps **(see illustrations)**.

18 Refit the driveshaft as described in Section 4.

Outer CV joint and gaiter

Disassembly

19 Following paragraphs 1 to 6, remove the inner tripod joint from the driveshaft and disassemble it.

20 Remove the outer CV joint gaiter clamps, using the technique described in paragraph 3. Slide the gaiter off the driveshaft.

Inspection

21 Thoroughly wash the inner and outer CV joints in clean solvent and blow them dry with compressed air, if available. **Note:** *Because the outer CV joint cannot be disassembled, it's difficult to wash away all the old grease and rid the bearing of solvent once it's clean.*

22 Bend the outer CV joint housing at an angle to the driveshaft to expose the bearings, inner race and cage **(see illustration)**. Inspect the bearing surfaces for signs of wear. If the bearings are damaged or worn, renew the driveshaft.

Reassembly

23 Slide the new outer gaiter onto the driveshaft. It's a good idea to wrap vinyl tape around the splines of the shaft to prevent damage to the gaiter. When the gaiter is in position, add the grease supplied with the gaiter kit to the outer joint and the gaiter (pack the joint with as much grease as it will hold and squeeze the rest into the gaiter). Slide the gaiter on the rest of the way and install the new clamps **(see illustrations)**.

24 Clean and reassemble the inner tripod joint by following paragraphs 10 to 17, then refit the driveshaft as described in Section 4.

5.17c... and secure them with the tabs

5.22 Inspect the outer CV joint through its full range of motion

5.23a Pack the joint with the grease supplied

5.23b Locate the inner end of the gaiter into the groove in the shaft

5.23c Install the new clamps and crimp them with special pliers

5.23d Ensure both clamps are correctly fitted

6.4 Make alignment marks between the propeller shaft and the pinion flange

6 Propeller shaft – removal and refitting

1 Chock the front wheels. Jack up the rear of the vehicle and support it on axle stands (see *Jacking and vehicle support*).
2 Remove the tunnel member as described in Chapter 7 Section 5.
3 Remove the exhaust system as described in Chapter 4A Section 13.
4 Mark the relationship of the propeller shaft to the differential input pinion flange **(see illustration)**.
5 Remove the bolts and separate the propeller from the pinion flange. Pull the propeller shaft toward the rear to remove it.
6 Wrap a plastic bag tightly around the extension housing of the transmission to prevent fluid loss.
7 Refitting is the reverse of removal. Be sure to align the reference marks made during removal.

7 Propeller shaft universal joints – check and renewal

Check

1 Wear in the universal joints is characterised by vibration in the transmission, noise during acceleration, and metallic squeaking and grating sounds as the bearings disintegrate. The joints can be checked with the propeller shaft still fitted.
2 Check for any oil leakage at the front and rear of the propeller shaft. Leakage where the propeller shaft enters the transmission indicates a defective transmission rear seal. Leakage where the propeller shaft enters the differential indicates a defective pinion seal.
3 While under the vehicle, have an assistant turn the rear wheel so the driveshaft will rotate. As it does, make sure the universal joints are operating properly without binding, noise or looseness.
4 The universal joints can also be checked with the propeller motionless, by gripping your hands on either side of the joint and attempting to twist the joint. Any movement at all in the joint is a sign of considerable wear. Lifting up on the propeller shaft will also indicate movement in the universal joints.
5 Finally, check the propeller mounting bolts at the ends to make sure they are tight.

Renewal

6 At the time of writing, no spare parts were available to enable renewal of the universal joints to be carried out. Therefore, if any joint shows signs of damage or wear the complete propeller shaft assembly must be renewed. Consult your Mazda dealer for latest information on parts availability.
7 If renewal of the propeller shaft is necessary, it may be worthwhile seeking the advice of an automotive engineering specialist. They may be able to repair the original assembly or supply a reconditioned shaft on an exchange basis.

Chapter 9
Braking system

Contents

Degrees of difficulty

Easy, suitable for novice with little experience	**Fairly easy,** suitable for beginner with some experience	**Fairly difficult,** suitable for competent DIY mechanic	**Difficult,** suitable for experienced DIY mechanic	**Very difficult,** suitable for expert DIY or professional

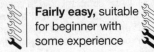

Specifications

General

Brake pedal height	167 mm
Brake pedal freeplay	2.0 to 5.0 mm

Front brakes

Disc minimum thickness	20.0 mm
Maximum disc run-out	0.05 mm
Brake pad friction material minimum thickness	2.0 mm

Rear disc brakes

Disc minimum thickness	8.0 mm
Maximum disc run-out	0.05 mm
Brake pad friction material minimum thickness	2.0 mm

Torque wrench settings

	Nm	lbf ft
ABS wheel sensor retaining bolts	10	7
Brake hose banjo bolt-to-caliper	26	19
Combines sensor nuts	10	7
Front brake caliper:		
Guide pin bolts	26	19
Mounting bracket bolts	90	66
Master cylinder mounting nuts	15	11
Rear brake caliper:		
Guide pin bolts	22	16
Mounting bracket bolts	60	44
Roadwheel nuts	110	81
Servo mounting nuts	22	16

1 General Information

1 The braking system is of the servo-assisted, dual-circuit hydraulic type. Under normal circumstances, both circuits operate in unison. However, if there is hydraulic failure in one circuit, full braking force will still be available at two wheels.
2 All models are fitted with front and rear disc brakes. ABS is fitted as standard to all models (refer to Section 17 for further information on ABS operation).
3 The front disc brakes are actuated by single-piston sliding type calipers, which ensure that equal pressure is applied to each disc pad.
4 All models are fitted with rear disc brakes, actuated by single-piston sliding calipers, incorporating the handbrake actuation mechanism.
Note: *When servicing any part of the system, work carefully and methodically; also observe scrupulous cleanliness when overhauling any part of the hydraulic system. Always renew components (in axle sets, where applicable) if in doubt about their condition, and use only genuine Mazda parts, or at least those of known good quality. Note the warnings given in 'Safety first!' and at relevant points in this Chapter concerning the dangers of asbestos dust and hydraulic fluid.*

2 Hydraulic system – bleeding

Warning: Hydraulic fluid is poisonous; wash off immediately and thoroughly in the case of skin contact, and seek immediate medical advice if any fluid is swallowed or gets into the eyes. Certain types of hydraulic fluid are flammable, and may ignite when allowed into contact with hot components; when servicing any hydraulic system, it is safest to assume that the fluid is flammable, and to take precautions against the risk of fire as though it is petrol that is being handled. Hydraulic fluid is also an effective paint stripper, and will attack plastics; if any is spilt, it should be washed off immediately, using copious quantities of fresh water. Finally, it is hygroscopic (it absorbs moisture from the air) – old fluid may be contaminated and unfit for further use. When topping-up or renewing the fluid, always use the recommended type, and ensure that it comes from a freshly-opened sealed container.

Warning: Under no circumstances should the hydraulic pipes/hoses linking the master cylinder, hydraulic unit and the accumulator be disturbed. If these unions are disturbed and air enters the high-pressure hydraulic system, bleeding of the system can only be safely carried out by a Mazda dealer or suitably-equipped specialist using the special service tester.

General

1 The correct operation of any hydraulic system is only possible after removing all air from the components and circuit; this is achieved by bleeding the system.
2 During the bleeding procedure, add only clean, unused hydraulic fluid of the recommended type; never re-use fluid that has already been bled from the system. Ensure that sufficient fluid is available before starting work.
3 If there is any possibility of incorrect fluid being already in the system, the brake components and circuit must be flushed completely with uncontaminated, correct fluid, and new seals should be fitted to the various components.
4 If hydraulic fluid has been lost from the system, or air has entered because of a leak, ensure that the fault is cured before continuing further.
5 Park the vehicle on level ground, switch off the engine and select first or reverse gear, then chock the wheels and release the handbrake.
6 Check that all pipes and hoses are secure, unions tight and bleed screws closed. Clean any dirt from around the bleed screws.
7 Unscrew the master cylinder reservoir cap, and top the master cylinder reservoir up to the MAX level line; refit the cap loosely, and remember to maintain the fluid level at least above the MIN level line throughout the procedure, or there is a risk of further air entering the system.
8 There are a number of one-man, do-it-yourself brake bleeding kits currently available from motor accessory shops. It is recommended that one of these kits is used whenever possible, as they greatly simplify the bleeding operation, and reduce the risk of expelled air and fluid being drawn back into the system. If such a kit is not available, the basic (two-man) method must be used, which is described in detail below.
9 If a kit is to be used, prepare the vehicle as described previously, and follow the kit manufacturer's instructions, as the procedure may vary slightly according to the type being used; generally, they are as outlined below in the relevant sub-section.
10 Whichever method is used, the same sequence must be followed (paragraphs 11 and 12) to ensure the removal of all air from the system.

Bleeding

Sequence

11 If the system has been only partially disconnected, and suitable precautions were taken to minimise fluid loss, it should be necessary only to bleed that part of the system.
12 If the complete system is to be bled, then it should be done working on the caliper furthest from the master cylinder first.

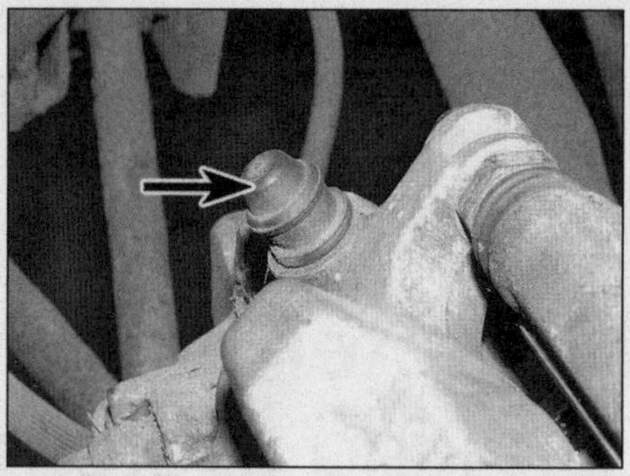

2.14 Pull up the dust cap

Basic (two-man) method

13 Collect a clean glass jar, a suitable length of plastic or rubber tubing which is a tight fit over the bleed screw, and a ring spanner to fit the screw. The help of an assistant will also be required.
14 Remove the dust cap from the first screw in the sequence **(see illustration)**. Fit the spanner and tube to the screw, place the other end of the tube in the jar, and pour in sufficient fluid to cover the end of the tube.
15 Ensure that the master cylinder reservoir fluid level is maintained at least above the MIN level line throughout the procedure.
16 Have the assistant fully depress the brake pedal several times to build-up pressure, then maintain it on the final downstroke.
17 While pedal pressure is maintained, unscrew the bleed screw (approximately one turn) and allow the compressed fluid and air to flow into the jar. The assistant should maintain pedal pressure, following it down to the floor if necessary, and should not release it until instructed to do so. When the flow stops, tighten the bleed screw again, have the assistant release the pedal slowly, and recheck the reservoir fluid level.
18 Repeat the steps in paragraphs 16 and 17 until the fluid emerging from the bleed screw is free from air bubbles. If the master cylinder has been drained and refilled, and air is being bled from the first screw in the sequence, allow about 5 seconds between cycles for the master cylinder passages to refill.
19 When no more air bubbles appear, tighten the bleed screw securely, remove the tube and spanner, and refit the dust cap. Do not overtighten the bleed screw.
20 Repeat the procedure on the remaining screws in the sequence, until all air is removed from the system and the brake pedal feels firm again.

Using a one-way valve kit

21 As their name implies, these kits consist of a length of tubing with a one-way valve

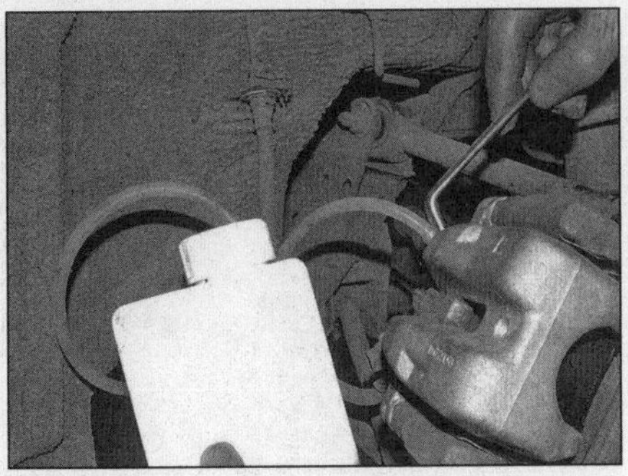

2.21 Attach the kit to the bleed screw on the caliper

fitted, to prevent expelled air and fluid being drawn back into the system; some kits include a translucent container, which can be positioned so that the air bubbles can be more easily seen flowing from the end of the tube **(see illustration)**.

22 The kit is connected to the bleed screw, which is then opened. The user returns to the driver's seat, depresses the brake pedal with a smooth, steady stroke, and slowly releases it; this is repeated until the expelled fluid is clear of air bubbles.

23 Note that these kits simplify work so much that it is easy to forget the master cylinder reservoir fluid level; ensure that this is maintained at least above the MIN level line at all times.

Using a pressure-bleeding kit

24 These kits are usually operated by the reservoir of pressurised air contained in the spare tyre. However, note that it will probably be necessary to reduce the pressure to a lower level than normal; refer to the instructions supplied with the kit. **Note:** *Mazda specify that a pressure of 2 bar (29 psi) should not be exceeded.*

25 By connecting a pressurised, fluid-filled container to the master cylinder reservoir, bleeding can be carried out simply by opening each screw in turn (in the specified sequence), and allowing the fluid to flow out until no more air bubbles can be seen in the expelled fluid.

26 This method has the advantage that the large reservoir of fluid provides an additional safeguard against air being drawn into the system during bleeding.

27 Pressure-bleeding is particularly effective when bleeding 'difficult' systems, or when bleeding the complete system at the time of routine fluid renewal.

All methods

28 When bleeding is complete, and firm pedal feel is restored, wash off any spilt fluid, tighten the bleed screws securely, and refit their dust caps.

29 Check the hydraulic fluid level in the master cylinder reservoir, and top-up if necessary (*see Weekly checks*).

30 Discard any hydraulic fluid that has been bled from the system; it will not be fit for re-use.

31 Check the feel of the brake pedal. If it feels at all spongy, air must still be present in the system, and further bleeding is required. Failure to bleed satisfactorily after a reasonable repetition of the bleeding procedure may be due to worn master cylinder seals.

3 Hydraulic pipes and hoses – renewal

Note: *Before starting work, refer to the warnings at the beginning of Section 2.*

1 If any pipe or hose is to be renewed, minimise fluid loss by first removing the master cylinder reservoir cap, then tightening it down onto a piece of polythene to obtain an airtight seal. Alternatively, flexible hoses can be sealed, if required, using a proprietary brake hose clamp; metal brake pipe unions can be plugged (if care is taken not to allow dirt into the system) or capped immediately they are disconnected. Place a wad of rag under any union that is to be disconnected, to catch any spilt fluid.

2 If a flexible hose is to be disconnected, unscrew the brake pipe union nut before removing the spring clip which secures the hose to its mounting bracket.

3 To unscrew the union nuts, it is preferable to obtain a brake pipe spanner of the correct size; these are available from most large motor accessory shops. Failing this, a close-fitting open-ended spanner will be required, though if the nuts are tight or corroded, their flats may be rounded-off if the spanner slips. In such a case, using self-locking pliers is often the only way to unscrew a stubborn union, but it follows that the pipe and the damaged nuts must be renewed on reassembly. Always clean a union and surrounding area before disconnecting it. If disconnecting a component with more than one union, make a careful note of the connections before disturbing any of them.

4 If a brake pipe is to be renewed, it can be obtained, cut to length and with the union nuts and end flares in place, from Mazda dealers. All that is then necessary is to bend it to shape, following the line of the original, before fitting it to the car. Alternatively, most motor accessory shops can make up brake pipes from kits, but this requires very careful measurement of the original, to ensure that the new one is of the correct length. The safest answer is usually to take the original to the shop as a pattern.

5 On refitting, do not overtighten the union nuts. It is not necessary to exercise brute force to obtain a sound joint.

6 Ensure that the pipes and hoses are correctly routed, with no kinks, and that they are secured in the clips or brackets provided. After fitting, remove the polythene from the reservoir, and bleed the hydraulic system as described in Section 2. Wash off any spilt fluid, and check carefully for fluid leaks.

4 Front brake pads – renewal

Warning: Renew both sets of front brake pads at the same time – never renew the pads on only one wheel, as uneven braking may result. Note that the dust created by wear of the pads may contain asbestos, which is a health hazard. Never blow it out with compressed air, and do not inhale any of it. An approved filtering mask should be worn when working on the brakes. DO NOT use petrol or petroleum-based solvents to clean brake parts; use brake cleaner or methylated spirit only.

1 Apply the handbrake, then loosen the front roadwheel nuts. Jack up the front of the vehicle and support it securely on axle stands (see *Jacking and vehicle support*). Remove both front roadwheels.

2 Follow the accompanying photos **(illustrations 4.2a to 4.2t)** for the pad renewal procedure. Be sure to stay in order and read the caption under each illustration.

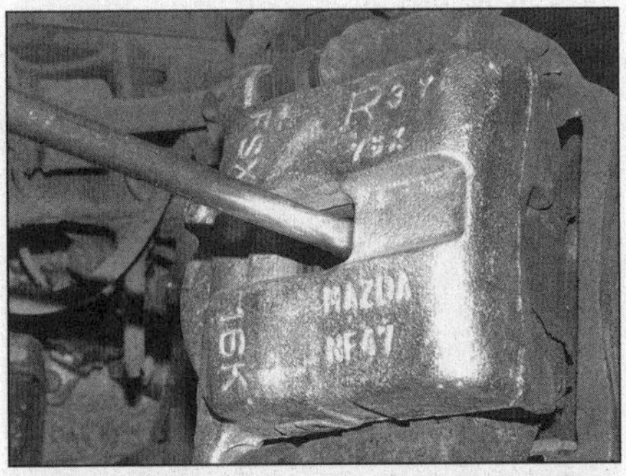

4.2a If there's a wear lip on the edge of the disc, you may need to lever between the disc and caliper body to force the piston back into the caliper a little

4.2b Using a spanner to hold the guide pin, undo the lower guide pin bolt ...

4.2c ... pivot the caliper upwards and slide the upper guide pin from the bracket

4.2d Secure the caliper to the spring to prevent straining the fluid hose

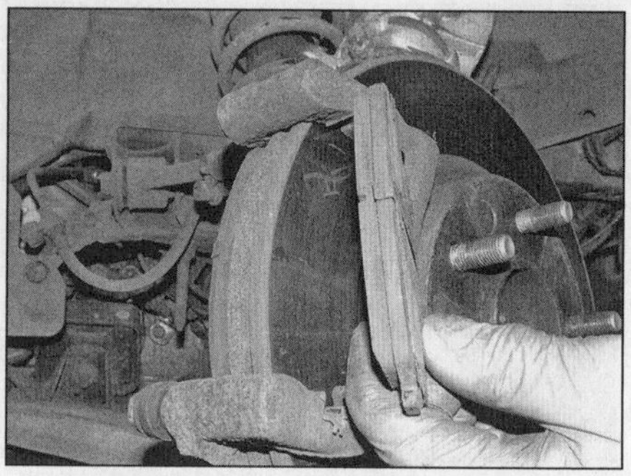

4.2e Remove the outer pad ...

4.2f ... followed by the inner pad

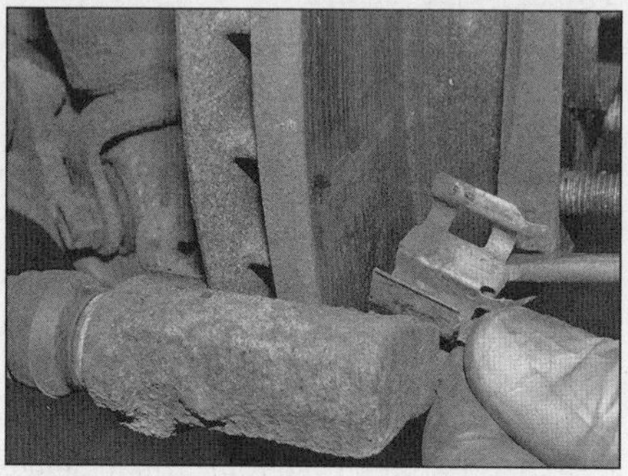

4.2g Remove the lower shims ...

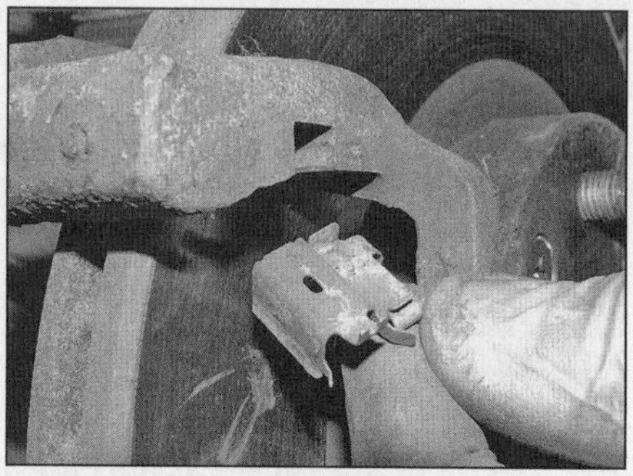

4.2h ... and the upper shims

4.2i Clean the pad mounting surfaces using aerosol brake cleaner and a soft brush

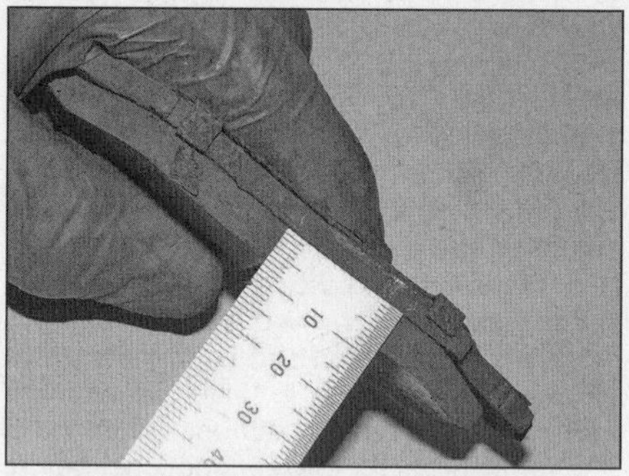

4.2j Measure the thickness of the pad friction material – renew all 4 pads if it's less than the dimension given in Specifications at the start of the Chapter

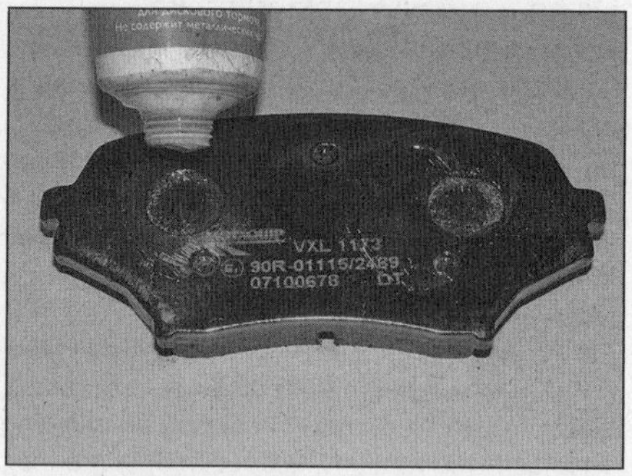

4.2k Apply a thin smear of high-temperature anti-seize grease to the pad backplate where it contact the caliper mounting bracket

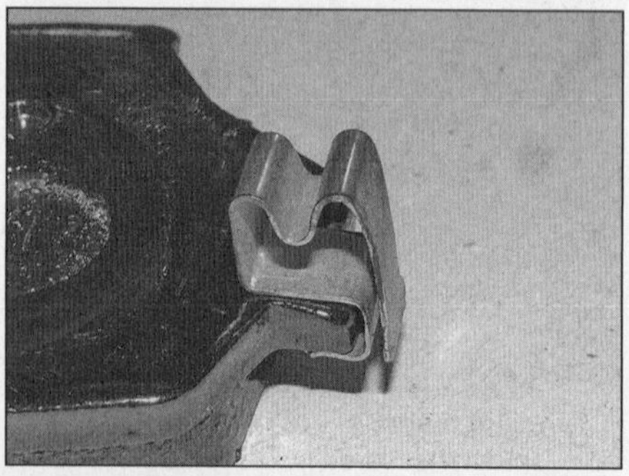

4.2l Where applicable, fit the audible wear indicators to the outer pad each side

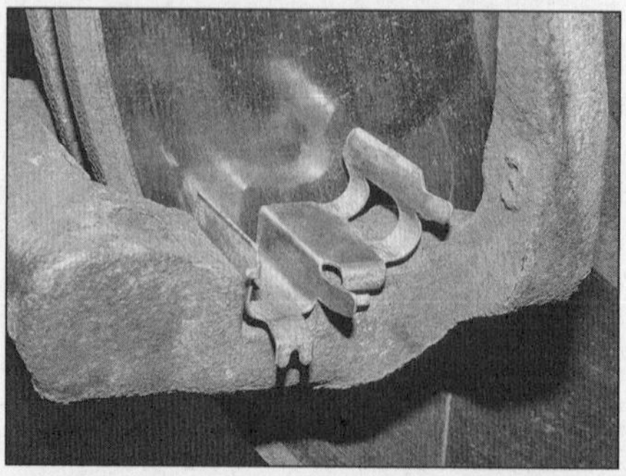

4.2m Refit the lower shims each side ...

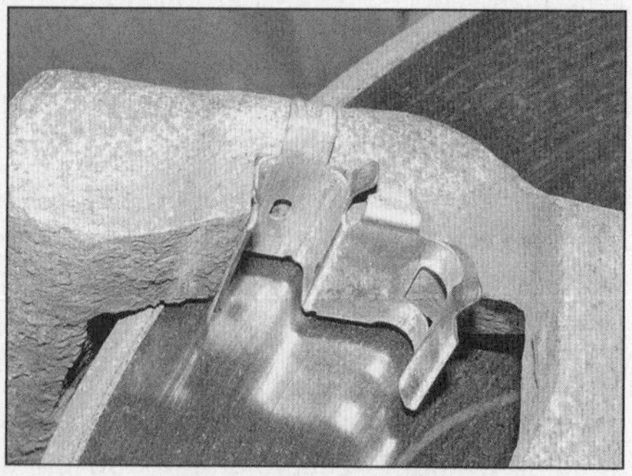

4.2n ... and upper shims

4.2o Fit the outer pad – ensure the friction material is against the disc...

4.2p ... followed by the inner pad

4.2q If new pads have been fitted, push the piston back into the caliper using a retraction tool. Keep an eye on the fluid level in the reservoir

4.2r Slide the upper guide pin into the hole in the mounting bracket

4.2s Lower the caliper into place and refit the lower guide pin bolt ...

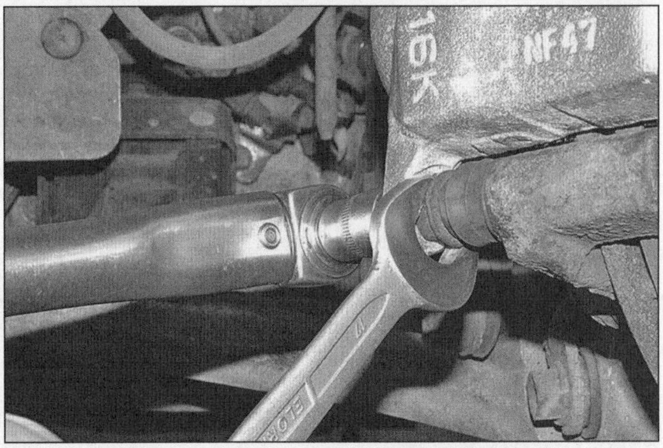

4.2t ... and tighten it to the specified torque

3 Depress the brake pedal repeatedly, until the pads are pressed into firm contact with the brake disc, and normal (non-assisted) pedal pressure is restored.

4 Repeat the above procedure on the remaining front brake caliper.

5 Refit the roadwheels, then lower the vehicle to the ground and tighten the roadwheel nuts to the specified torque.

6 Check the hydraulic fluid level as described in *Weekly checks*.

Caution: New pads will not give full braking efficiency until they have bedded-in. Be prepared for this, and avoid hard braking as far as possible for the first hundred miles or so after pad renewal.

5 Rear brake pads – renewal

Caution: Renew BOTH sets of rear brake pads at the same time – NEVER renew the pads on only one wheel, as uneven braking may result. Note that the dust created by wear of the pads may contain asbestos, which is a health hazard. Never blow it out with compressed air, and don't inhale any of it. An approved filtering mask should be worn when working on the brakes. DO NOT use petroleum-based solvents to clean brake parts – use brake cleaner or methylated spirit only.

1 Chock the front wheels, fully release the handbrake, then loosen the rear roadwheel nuts. Jack up the rear of the vehicle and support it securely on axle stands (see *Jacking and vehicle support*). Remove both rear roadwheels.

2 Follow the accompanying photos **(illustrations 5.2a to 5.2t)** for the pad renewal procedure. Be sure to stay in order and read the caption under each illustration.

3 Depress the brake pedal repeatedly, until the pads are pressed into firm contact with the brake disc, and normal (non-assisted) pedal pressure is restored.

4 Repeat the above procedure on the remaining rear brake caliper.

5 Refit the roadwheels, then lower the vehicle to the ground and tighten the roadwheel nuts to the specified torque.

6 Check the hydraulic fluid level as described in *Weekly checks*.

7 Check and if necessary, adjust the handbrake as described in Section 14.

Caution: New pads will not give full braking efficiency until they have bedded-in. Be prepared for this, and avoid hard braking as far as possible for the first hundred miles or so after pad renewal.

5.2a Using an open-ended spanner to hold the guide pin, remove the upper...

5.2b... and lower guide pin bolts

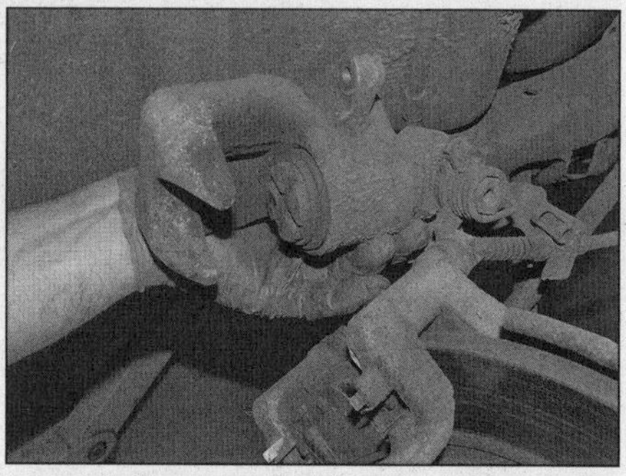

5.2c Remove the caliper and suspend it from the shock absorber coil spring with a piece of wire to protect the brake hydraulic hose and the parking brake cable.

5.2d Remove the outer brake pad and shim...

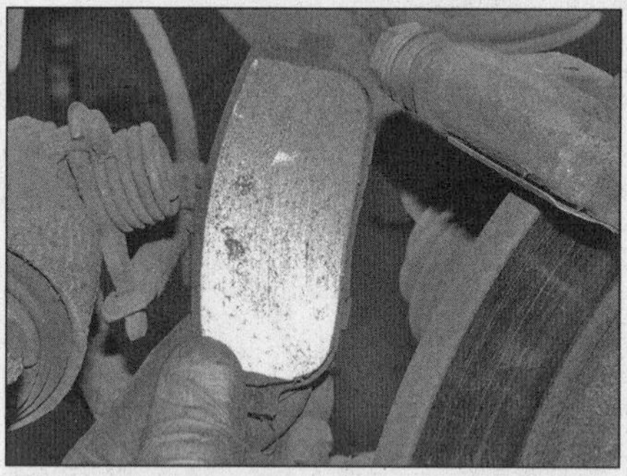

5.2e ... followed by the inner brake pad and shim

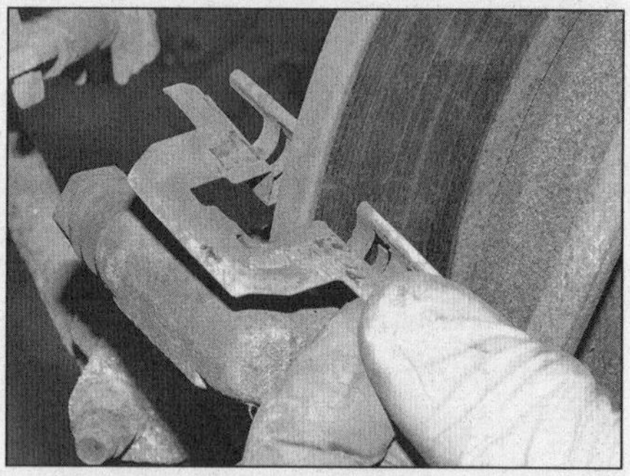

5.2f Remove the lower shim from the caliper mounting bracket...

5.2g... and the upper shim

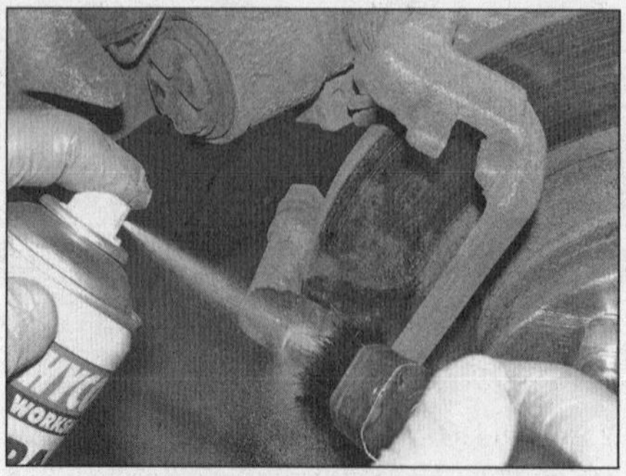

5.2h Clean the pad contact surfaces on the mounting bracket using aerosol brake cleaner and a soft brush

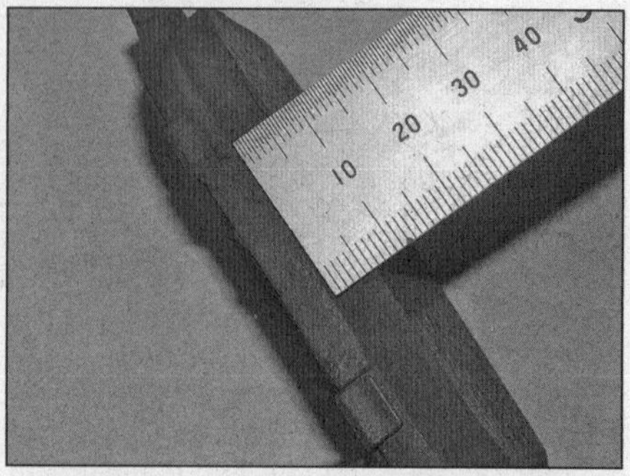

5.2i Measure the thickness of the pad friction material – renew all 4 pads if it's less than the dimension given in Specifications at the start of the Chapter

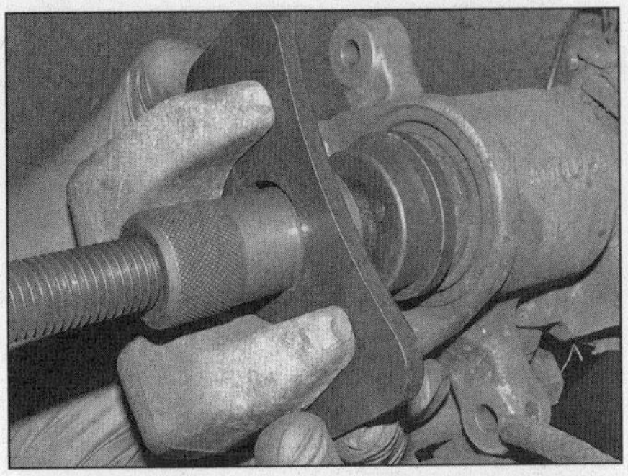

5.2j If new pads are to be fitted, The piston must be fully retracted into the caliper body. This is best achieved using a piston retraction tool that rotates the piston clockwise at the same time as pushing the piston into the body. In the absence of this tool, it is possible to achieved the same result with a pair of thin-nosed pliers. Keep an eye on the brake fluid level in the reservoir as the piston is retracted. If necessary, remove excess fluid with a syringe

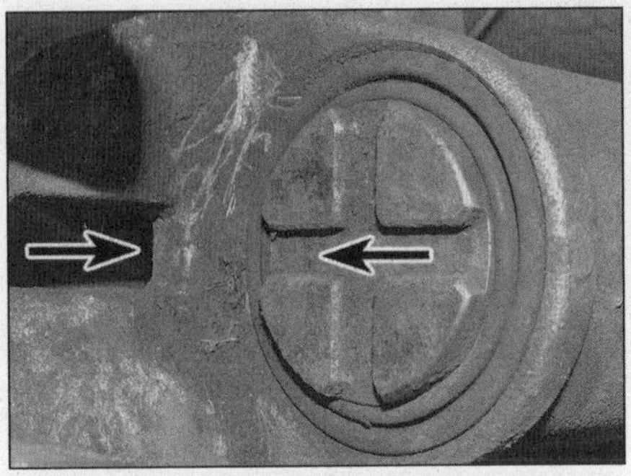

5.2k When the piston if fully retracted, rotate it anti-clockwise a little until a groove in the piston face aligns with the centre of the caliper body

5.2l Fit the lower shim to the caliper mounting bracket...

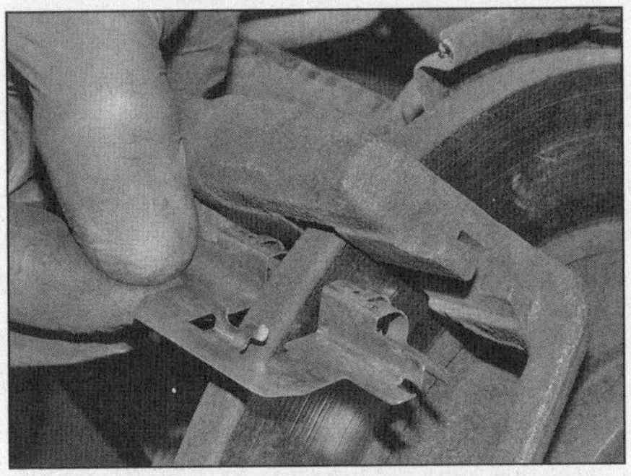

5.2m... and the upper shim

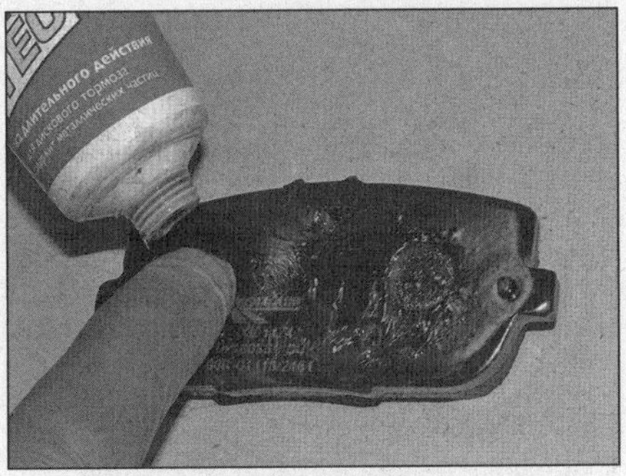

5.2n Apply a thin smear of high-temperature anti-seize grease to the pads backplates...

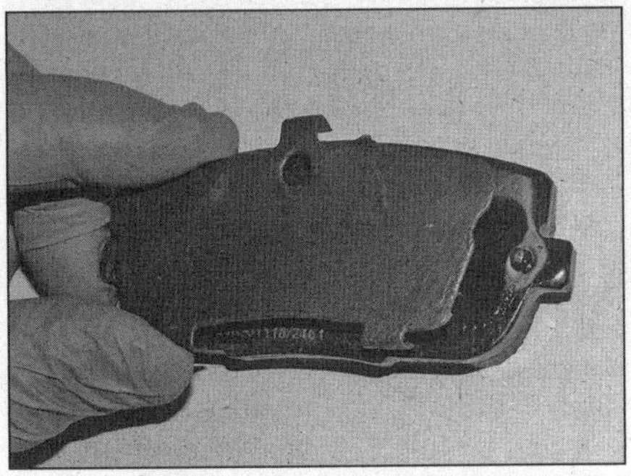

5.2o... and refit the shims

5.2p Fit the outer pad – ensure the friction material is against the disc. Note that the pad with the audible wear indicator should be fitted to the outer location on the right-hand brake

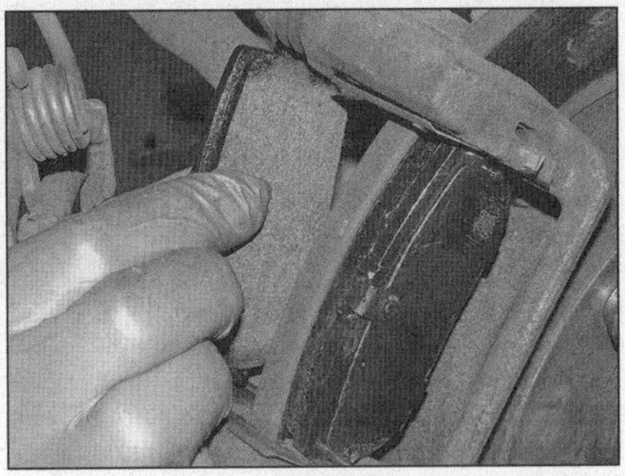

5.2q Locate the inner pad in the mounting bracket

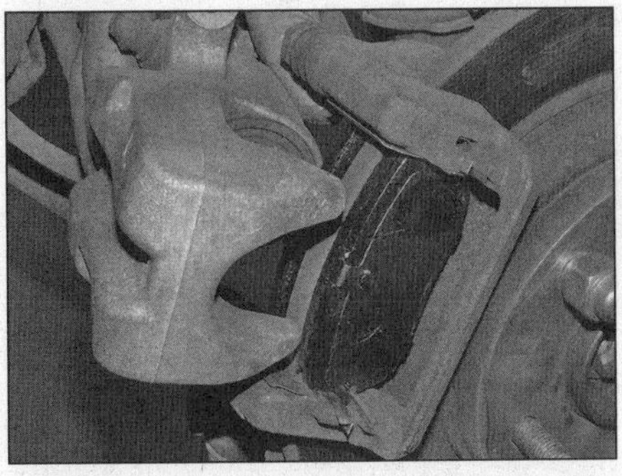

5.2r Slide the caliper into position over the pads ...

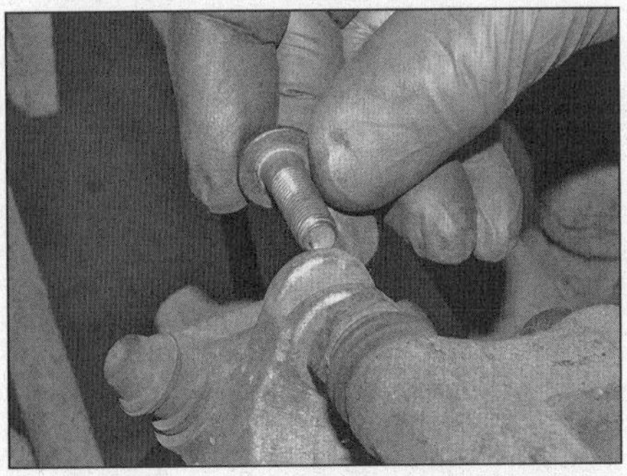

5.2s ... refit the guide pins ...

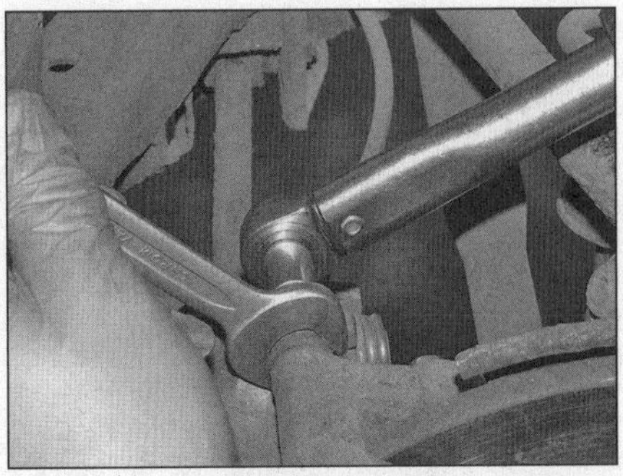

5.2t... and tighten them to the specified torque

6.3 Measure the thickness of the disc using a micrometer

6.4 Checking for disc run-out using a Dial Test Indicator gauge (DTI)

6.7 Brake disc retaining screw

6 Front brake disc – inspection, removal and refitting

Note: *Before starting work, refer to the note at the beginning of Section 4 concerning the dangers of asbestos dust.*

Note: *If either disc requires renewal, BOTH should be renewed at the same time, to ensure even and consistent braking. New brake pads should also be fitted.*

Inspection

1 Apply the handbrake, then jack up the front of the car and support it on axle stands (see *Jacking and vehicle support*. Remove the appropriate front roadwheel.

2 Slowly rotate the brake disc so that the full area of both sides can be checked; remove the brake pads if better access is required to the inboard surface (see Section 4). Light scoring is normal in the area swept by the brake pads, but if heavy scoring or cracks are found, the disc must be renewed.

3 It is normal to find a lip of rust and brake dust around the disc's perimeter; this can be scraped off if required. If, however, a lip has formed due to excessive wear of the brake pad swept area, then the disc's thickness must be measured using a micrometer **(see illustration)**. Take measurements at several places around the disc, at the inside and outside of the pad swept area; if the disc has worn at any point to the specified minimum thickness or less, the disc must be renewed.

4 If the disc is thought to be warped, it can be checked for run-out. Either use a dial gauge mounted on any convenient fixed point, while the disc is slowly rotated, or use feeler blades to measure (at several points all around the disc) the clearance between the disc and a fixed point, such as the caliper mounting bracket **(see illustration)**. If the measurements obtained are at the specified maximum or beyond, the disc is excessively warped, and must be renewed; however, it is worth checking first that the hub bearing is in good condition (Chapter 10, Section 3). If the run-out is excessive, the disc must be renewed.

5 Check the disc for cracks, especially around the wheel bolt holes, and any other wear or damage, and renew if necessary.

Removal

6 Unscrew the two bolts securing the brake caliper mounting bracket to the hub carrier, then slide the caliper assembly off the disc. Using a piece of wire or string, tie the caliper to the front suspension coil spring, to avoid placing any strain on the hydraulic brake hose.

7 Use chalk or paint to mark the relationship of the disc to the hub, then undo the retaining screw and remove the disc **(see illustration)**. If the disc is tight, lightly tap its rear face with a hide or plastic mallet.

Refitting

8 Refitting is the reverse of the removal procedure, noting the following points:

a) *Ensure that the mating surfaces of the disc and hub are clean and flat.*
b) *Align (if applicable) the marks made on removal.*
c) *If a new disc has been fitted, use a suitable solvent to wipe any preservative coating from the disc, before refitting the caliper*
d) *Slide the caliper and bracket into position over the disc, making sure the pads pass either side of the disc. Tighten the caliper mounting bracket bolts to the specified torque setting.*
e) *Refit the roadwheel, then lower the vehicle to the ground and tighten the roadwheel nuts to the specified torque. On completion, repeatedly depress the brake pedal until normal (non-assisted) pedal pressure returns.*

7 Rear brake disc – inspection, removal and refitting

Note: *Before starting work, refer to the note at the beginning of Section 5 concerning the dangers of asbestos dust.*

Note: *If either disc requires renewal, BOTH should be renewed at the same time, to ensure even and consistent braking. New brake pads should also be fitted.*

Inspection

1 Firmly chock the front wheels, then jack up the rear of the car and support it on axle stands (see *Jacking and vehicle support*). Remove the appropriate rear roadwheel. Release the handbrake.

2 Inspect the disc as described in Section 6.

Removal

3 Remove the rear brake pads as described in Section 5.

4 Unscrew the two bolts securing the brake caliper mounting bracket in position, then slide the caliper assembly off the disc. Using a piece of wire or string, tie the caliper to the rear suspension coil spring, to avoid placing any strain on the hydraulic brake hose. If necessary unclip the rubber brake hose from the lower mounting bracket to provide enough slack to manoeuvre the caliper and bracket.

5 It should now be possible to withdraw the brake disc from the hub by hand. If it is tight, lightly tap its rear face with a hide or plastic mallet.

Refitting

6 If a new disc is been fitted, use a suitable solvent to wipe any preservative coating from the disc.

7 Refit the caliper mounting bracket and tighten the retaining bolts to the specified torque.

8 Fit the rear brake pads as described in Section 5.

9 Refit the roadwheel, then lower the car to the ground, and tighten the roadwheel nuts to the specified torque. On completion, repeatedly depress the brake pedal until normal (non-assisted) pedal pressure returns. Check the handbrake adjustment.

8 Front brake caliper – removal, overhaul and refitting

Note: *Before starting work, refer to the note at the beginning of Section 2 concerning the dangers of hydraulic fluid, and to the warning at the beginning of Section 4 concerning the dangers of asbestos dust.*

8.3 Recover the copper sealing washers

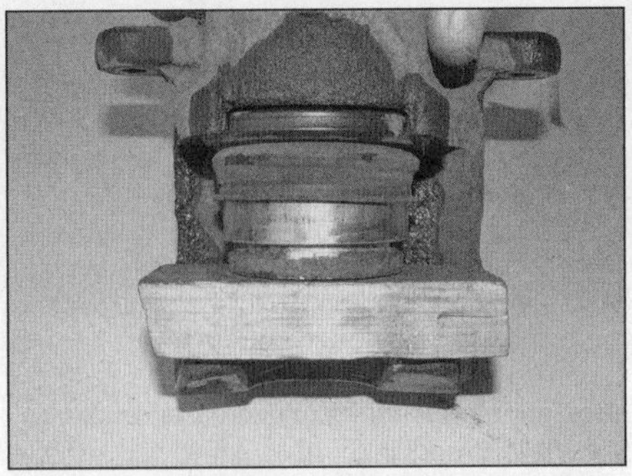

8.7 Place a wooden block to 'catch' the piston if it's ejected using compressed air

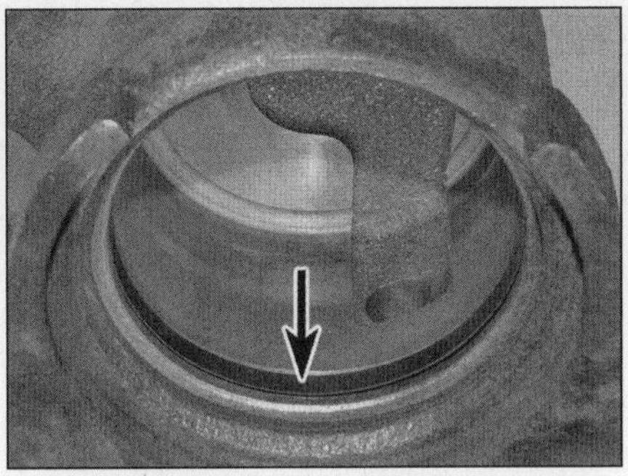

8.8 Carefully extract the hydraulic seal from the caliper bore

Removal

1 Apply the handbrake, then jack up the front of the vehicle and support it on axle stands (see *Jacking and vehicle support*). Remove the appropriate roadwheel.

2 Minimise fluid loss by using a brake hose clamp, a G-clamp or a similar tool to clamp the flexible hose.

3 Clean the area around the union, then undo the brake hose union bolt. Recover the copper sealing washers **(see illustration)**. Note: Don't disconnect the hose if you are only removing the caliper for access to other components.

4 Remove the brake pads (see Section 4).

5 Unscrew the remaining caliper guide pin bolt, remove it from the vehicle.

Overhaul

6 With the caliper on the bench, wipe away all traces of dust and dirt, but avoid inhaling the dust, as it is a health hazard.

7 Withdraw the partially-ejected piston from the caliper body, and remove the dust seal **(see illustration)**. Note: If the piston cannot be withdrawn by hand, it can be pushed out by applying compressed air to the brake hose union hole. Only low pressure should be required, such as is generated by a foot pump. As the piston is expelled, take great care not to trap your fingers between the piston and caliper.

8 Using a small screwdriver, extract the piston hydraulic seal, taking great care not to damage the caliper bore **(see illustration)**.

9 Thoroughly clean all components, using only methylated spirit, isopropyl alcohol or clean hydraulic fluid as a cleaning medium. Never use mineral-based solvents such as petrol or paraffin, as they will attack the hydraulic system's rubber components. Dry the components immediately, using compressed air or a clean, lint-free cloth. Use compressed air to blow clear the fluid passages.

10 Check all components, and renew any that are worn or damaged. Check particularly the cylinder bore and piston; these should be renewed (note that this means the renewal of the complete body assembly) if they are scratched, worn or corroded in any way. Similarly check the condition of the guide pins and their bushes; both pins should be undamaged and (when cleaned) a reasonably tight sliding fit in the bushes **(see illustration)**. If there is any doubt about the condition of any component, renew it.

11 If the assembly is fit for further use, obtain the appropriate repair kit; the components are available from Mazda dealers in various combinations. All rubber seals should be renewed as a matter of course; these should never be re-used.

12 On reassembly, ensure that all components are clean and dry.

13 Soak the piston and the new piston (fluid) seal in clean hydraulic fluid. Smear clean fluid on the cylinder bore surface.

14 Fit the new piston (fluid) seal, using only your fingers (no tools) to manipulate it into the cylinder bore groove.

15 Fit the new dust seal to the piston. Locate the rear of the seal in the recess in the caliper body, and refit the piston to the cylinder bore using a twisting motion. Ensure that the piston enters squarely into the bore, and press it fully home **(see illustrations)**.

8.10 Check the condition of the guide pin and rubber sleeve

8.15a Fit the new seal to the inner end of the piston ...

8.15b ... locate the lip of the seal into the recess in the caliper body ...

8.15c ... then push/twist the piston into the caliper body ...

8.15d ... ensuring the inner lip of the seal locates in the piston recess

Refitting

16 Refit the brake pads (see Section 4).
17 Reconnect the brake pipe using new copper sealing washers, and tighten the union bolt securely.
18 Remove the brake hose clamp or polythene, as applicable, and bleed the hydraulic system as described in Section 2. Note that, providing the precautions described were taken to minimise brake fluid loss, it should only be necessary to bleed the relevant front brake.
19 Refit the roadwheel, then lower the vehicle to the ground and tighten the roadwheel nuts to the specified torque. On completion, check the hydraulic fluid level as described in *Weekly checks*.

9 Rear brake caliper – removal and refitting

Note: *Before starting work, refer to the note at the beginning of Section 2 concerning the dangers of hydraulic fluid, and to the warning at the beginning of Section 5 concerning the dangers of asbestos dust.*

Note: *Due to the complexity of the rear calipers on these models, we do not recommend overhauling them. Replacing them as a pair with rebuilt units will provide better service for less cost.*

Removal

1 Chock the front wheels, then jack up the rear of the vehicle and support on axle stands (see *Jacking and vehicle support*). Remove the relevant rear wheel.
2 Minimise fluid loss by using a brake hose clamp, a G-clamp or a similar tool to clamp the flexible hose.
3 Clean the area around the union, undo the hose union banjo bolt.
4 Remove the brake pads as described in Section 5.

Overhaul

5 Due to the complexity of the rear calipers, we do not recommend dismantling them. Renewing them will provide better service for less cost.

Refitting

6 Refit the brake pads (refer to Section 5).
7 Using new copper sealing washers, reconnect the hose to the caliper, and tighten the banjo bolt to the specified torque.
8 Remove the brake hose clamp or polythene, as applicable, and bleed the hydraulic system as described in Section 2. Note that, providing the precautions described were taken to minimise brake fluid loss, it should only be necessary to bleed the relevant rear brake.
9 Refit the roadwheel, then lower the vehicle to the ground and tighten the roadwheel nuts to the specified torque. On completion, check the hydraulic fluid level as described in *Weekly checks*.

10 Master cylinder – removal, overhaul and refitting

Removal

1 Follow the wiring harness from the master cylinder to the electrical connector for the fluid level warning switch **(see illustration)**. Unplug the connector. Check continuity with an ohmmeter at the level sensor terminals; no continuity should be measured when the fluid level is above MIN.
2 Carefully remove the brake fluid reservoir cap and remove as much fluid as possible from the reservoir with a syringe. Check continuity of the level sensor; continuity should be measured when fluid level is below the MIN level.
3 Place rags under the fittings and prepare caps or plastic bags to cover the ends of the pipes once they are disconnected. Loosen the fittings at the ends of the brake pipes where they enter the master cylinder **(see illustration)**. To prevent rounding off the flats, use a flare-nut spanner, which wraps around the fitting union.
4 Remove the nuts attaching the master cylinder to the brake servo unit **(see illustration)**.
5 Pull the brake pipes away from the master cylinder and plug the ends to prevent contamination. Slide the proportioning valve mounting bracket off the studs.
6 Pull the master cylinder off the studs to remove it. Again, be careful not to spill the fluid as this is done.

Overhaul

7 It would appear that master cylinder overhaul kits are no longer available. Consequently, should a fault develop, renewal of the complete assembly may be the only option.

Refitting

8 Refit the master cylinder and proportioning valve bracket over the studs on the servo unit, and tighten the nuts only finger-tight at this time.
9 Thread the brake pipe union nuts into the master cylinder. Since the master cylinder is still loose, it can be moved slightly so the union nuts thread in easily by hand. Be careful not to strip the threads as the fittings are tightened.
10 Connect the remaining brake pipe to the master cylinder with the union bolt, using a new sealing washer on each side of the fitting.
11 Tighten the master cylinder mounting nuts and union bolt to the specified torque. Tighten the brake pipe union nuts securely using a flare-nut spanner.
12 Fill the master cylinder reservoir with fluid, then bleed the master cylinder and the brake system (see Section 2). Check the operation of the brake system carefully before driving the vehicle.

11 Brake pedal – check and adjustment

Pedal height

1 Measure the pedal height **(see illustration)** and compare your measurement to the pedal height listed (see Specifications).
2 If the pedal height is incorrect, adjust it as follows:
3 Unplug the electrical connector from the brake light switch.
4 Mazda insist that if the pedal height needs to be adjusted, a new brake light switch must be fitted. Remove the switch as described in Section 16.
5 Loosen the pushrod locknut.

10.1 Disconnect the fluid level warning switch wiring plug

10.3 Slacken the brake pipe unions where they enter the master cylinder

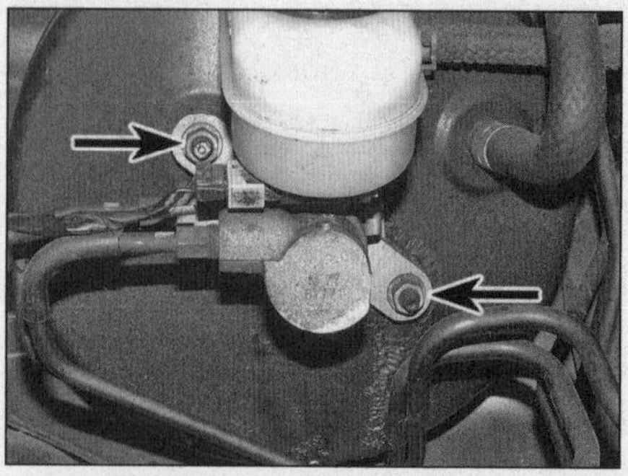

10.4 Master cylinder retaining nuts

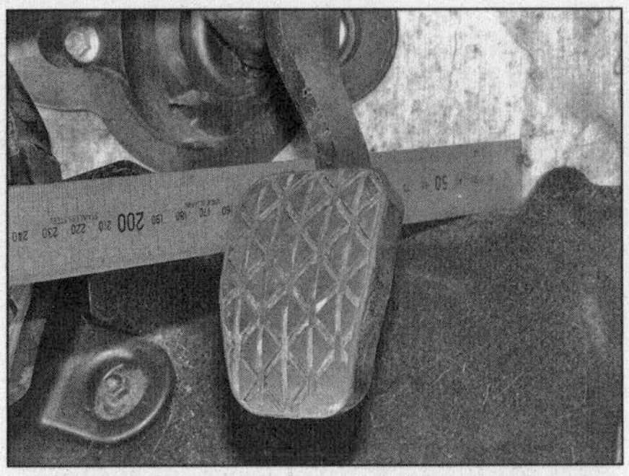

11.1 Measure from the bulkhead insulation material to the centre of the pedal

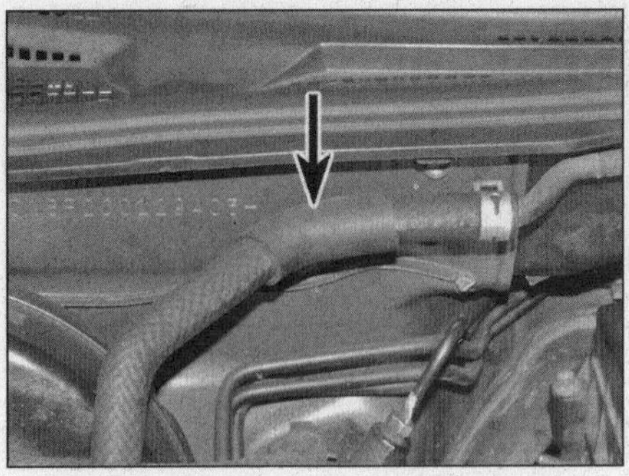

12.5 The check valve is integral with the servo vacuum hose

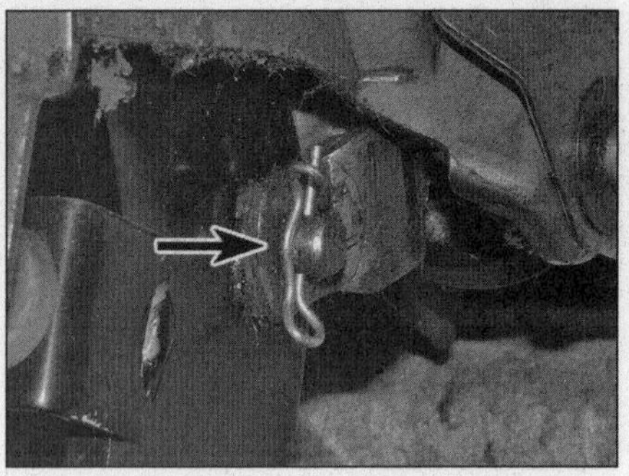

12.8 Remove the clip and pull out the servo pushrod clevis pin

6 Adjust the pedal height by turning the pedal pushrod.
7 Tighten the pushrod locknut.
8 Fit the new brake light switch as described in Section 16.
9 Check that brake lights come on when the brake pedal is depressed, and go off when the brake pedal is released.

12 Vacuum servo unit – testing, removal and refitting

Testing

1 To test the operation of the servo unit, depress the footbrake several times to exhaust the vacuum, then start the engine whilst keeping the pedal firmly depressed. As the engine starts, there should be a noticeable 'give' in the brake pedal as the vacuum builds-up. Allow the engine to run for at least two minutes, then switch it off. If the brake pedal is now depressed it should feel normal, but further applications should result in the pedal feeling firmer, with the pedal stroke decreasing with each application.
2 If the servo does not operate as described, first inspect the servo unit check valve as described in Section 13.
3 If the servo unit still fails to operate satisfactorily, the fault lies within the unit itself. Repairs to the unit are not possible – if faulty, the servo unit must be renewed.

Removal

4 Servo units shouldn't be disassembled. They require special tools not normally found in most automotive repair workshops. Because of its critical relationship to brake performance, the servo should be replaced with a new or rebuilt one.
5 Disconnect the vacuum hose/check valve leading from the engine to the servo **(see illustration)**. Be careful not to damage the hose when removing it from the servo fitting.
6 Remove the brake master cylinder (see Section 10).
7 Undo the screws and remove the trim panel beneath the steering column.
8 Locate the pushrod clevis connecting the servo to the brake pedal **(see illustration)**. Remove the R-clip from the clevis pin with pliers and pull out the clevis pin.
9 Remove the four nuts holding the brake servo to the bulkhead **(see illustration)**.
10 Slide the servo straight out from the bulkhead until the studs clear the holes. Be careful not to tear or damage the brake servo gasket between the bulkhead and the servo.

Refitting

11 Refitting is basically the reverse of removal. Tighten the servo mounting nuts to the specified torque. Be sure to use a new clevis retaining clip if the old clip is loose.
12 When refitting the servo unit vacuum hose/check valve, be sure to fit the vacuum hose/check valve with the arrows on the vacuum hose toward the engine.
13 After the final installation of the master cylinder and brake hoses and pipes, the brake system must be bled.

13 Vacuum servo unit check valve – removal, testing and refitting

Removal

1 Before starting, depress the brake pedal several times, to collapse any vacuum in the servo.
2 Working in the engine compartment, release the clamps and disconnect the hose from the intake manifold to the servo unit **(see illustration 12.5)**. The check valve is integral with the hose.

12.9 Servo retaining nuts

Testing

3 Examine the check valve for signs of damage, and renew if necessary.
4 The valve may be tested by blowing through it in both directions; air should flow through the valve in one direction only – when blown through from the servo unit end of the hose. Renew the valve and hose assembly if this is not the case.

Refitting

5 Reconnect the hose securely to the servo unit and intake manifold.

14 Handbrake – adjustment

1 The handbrake lever, when properly adjusted, should travel 3 clicks when a moderrate pulling force (90 N, 22 lbft) is applied. If it travels less than the specified minimum number of clicks, the handbrake may not be releasing completely and could cause the rear brakes to drag. If the lever can be pulled up more than the specified maximum number of clicks, the handbrake may not hold adequately on an incline, allowing the car to roll.
2 To gain access to the handbrake cable adjuster, carefully prise up the lever gaiter **(see illustration)**.
3 Securely block the front wheels so the vehicle won't roll. Jack up the rear end just until the tyres are off the ground, then place

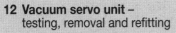

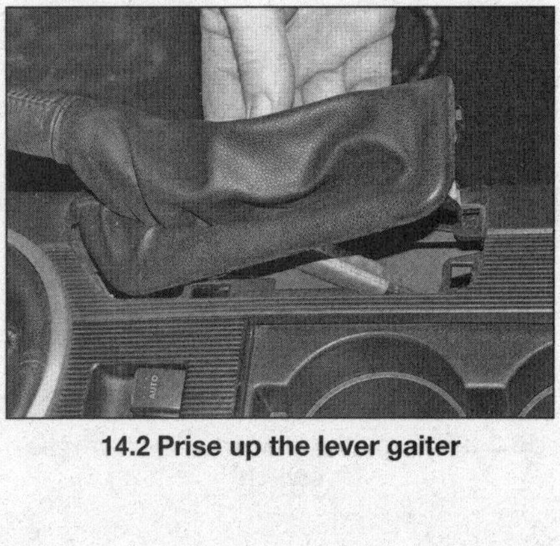

14.2 Prise up the lever gaiter

14.4 Handbrake adjuster nut (console removed for clarity)

it securely on axle stands (see *Jacking and vehicle support*). Place the transmission in Neutral and release the handbrake completely.
4 Turn the adjusting nut until the desired travel is attained **(see illustration)**.

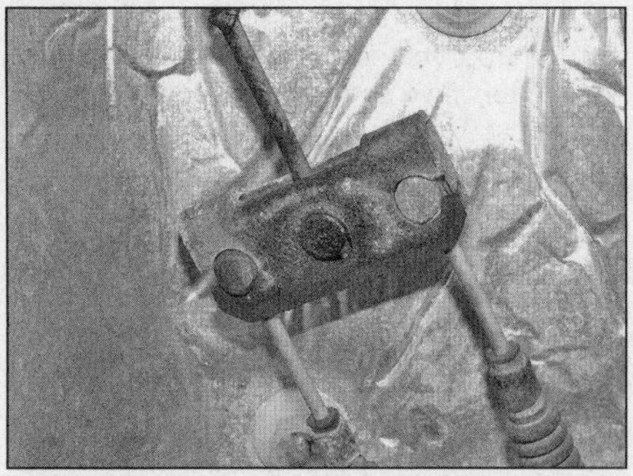

15.5 Disengage the rear cables from the equaliser

15.9 Prise up the clip, slide out the cable from the bracket and disconnect the end fitting

16.2 Disconnect the wiring plug from the switch

15.4 Undo the bolts securing the cable outer fitting

5 Pull the handbrake lever one click. The handbrake warning light should come on. Release the lever and make sure the rear wheels turn freely.
6 Refit the cover and lower the vehicle.

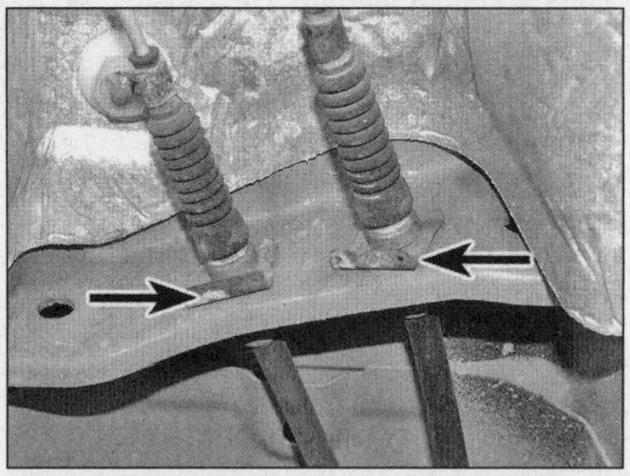

15.8 Slide down the cable retaining clips

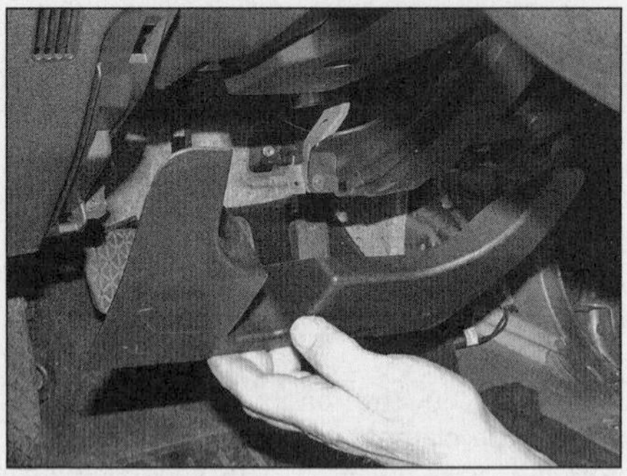

16.1 Pull the trim panel beneath the column rearwards

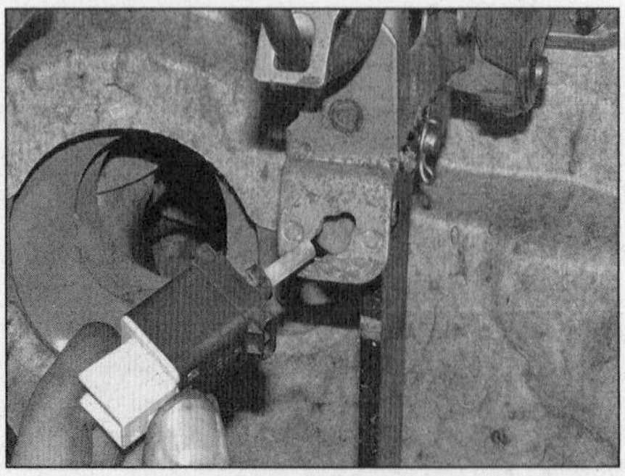

16.4 Insert the new switch, then rotate it 45° anti-clockwise

15 Handbrake cables – removal and refitting

1 Slacken the rear roadwheel nuts, raise the rear of the vehicle and support it securely on axle stands (see *Jacking and vehicle support*). Remove the rear roadwheel.

Equaliser-to-brake lever cable

2 Make sure the handbrake is completely released, then carefully prise up the lever gaiter **(see illustration 14.2)**.
3 Remove the handbrake lever adjusting nut.
4 Under the vehicle,undo the bolts securing the front cable outer fitting to the vehicle body **(see illustration)**.
5 Disengage the rear cables from the equaliser, and pull the front cable from place **(see illustration)**.
6 Refitting is the reverse of removal. Apply a light coat of grease to the portion of the cables that engage with the equaliser. Also coat the sealing edge of the rubber grommet with silicone to ensure that it remains watertight.

Equaliser-to-caliper cables

7 Remove the handbrake cable mounting bolts located along the vehicle chassis.
8 Remove the handbrake cable retaining clips at the equaliser **(see illustration)**.
9 Detach the handbrake cable from the caliper **(see illustration)**. Free the cable ends from the equaliser and pull the cable out from under the vehicle.
10 Refitting is the reverse of removal. Apply a light coat of grease to the portion of the cable end that engages with the equaliser.
11 Adjust the handbrake as described in Section 14.

16 Brake light switch – removal and refitting

Note: *Mazda insist that once removed, the brake light switch must not be refitted – a new switch will be required.*

Removal

1 Remove the trim panel from beneath the steering column **(see illustration)**.
2 Disconnect the wiring plug from the switch **(see illustration)**.
3 Rotate the switch 45° clockwise and remove it.

Refitting

4 Depress the brake pedal slightly, then insert the new switch into the bracket and rotate it 45° anti-clockwise **(see illustration)**. Gently release the brake pedal.
5 Reconnect the switch wiring plug.
6 Check the operation of the brake lights, then refit the trim panel.

17 Anti-lock braking system (ABS) – general information

1 ABS is fitted to all models. The system comprises a hydraulic block which contains the hydraulic solenoid valves and the electrically-driven pump, the four roadwheel sensors (one fitted to each wheel), and the electronic control unit (ECU). The purpose of the system is to prevent the wheel(s) locking during heavy braking. This is achieved by automatic release of the brake on the relevant wheel, followed by re-application of the brake.

2 The solenoids are controlled by the ECU, which itself receives signals from the four wheel sensors (one fitted on each hub), which monitor the speed of rotation of each wheel. By comparing these signals, the ECU can determine the speed at which the vehicle is travelling. It can then use this speed to determine when a wheel is decelerating at an abnormal rate, compared to the speed of the vehicle, and therefore predicts when a wheel is about to lock. During normal operation, the system functions in the same way as a non-ABS braking system.

3 If the ECU senses that a wheel is about to lock, it operates the relevant solenoid valve in the hydraulic unit, which then isolates the brake caliper on the wheel which is about to lock from the master cylinder, effectively sealing-in the hydraulic pressure.

4 If the speed of rotation of the wheel continues to decrease at an abnormal rate, the ECU switches on the electrically-driven pump operates, and pumps the hydraulic fluid back into the master cylinder, releasing pressure on the brake caliper so that the brake is released. Once the speed of rotation of the wheel returns to an acceptable rate, the pump stops; the solenoid valve opens, allowing the hydraulic master cylinder pressure to return to the caliper, which then re-applies the brake. This cycle can be carried out at up to 10 times a second.

5 The action of the solenoid valves and return pump creates pulses in the hydraulic circuit. When the ABS system is functioning, these pulses can be felt through the brake pedal.

6 The operation of the ABS system is entirely dependent on electrical signals. To prevent the system responding to any inaccurate signals, a built-in safety circuit monitors all signals received by the ECU. If an inaccurate signal or low battery voltage is detected, the ABS system is automatically shut down, and the warning light on the instrument panel is illuminated, to inform the driver that the ABS system is not operational. Normal braking should still be available, however.

7 If a fault does develop in the ABS system, the vehicle must be taken to a Mazda dealer or suitably-equipped specialist for fault diagnosis and repair.

18 Anti-lock braking system (ABS)/Dynamic stabiity control (DSC) components – removal and refitting

Hydraulic/electronic control unit

1 Although it is possible for the home mechanic to remove the hydraulic unit, the unit's self-diagnosis system must be interrogated by dedicated test equipment before and after removal. Consequently, we recommend that removal and refitting the hydraulic unit should be entrusted to a Mazda dealer or suitably-equipped specialist.

Front wheel sensor

2 Chock the rear wheels, then firmly apply the handbrake, jack up the front of the vehicle and support on axle stands (see *Jacking and vehicle support*). Remove the appropriate front roadwheel.

3 Release the various fasteners and remove the wheel arch liner.

4 Trace the wiring back from the sensor, and disconnect the wiring plug.

5 Undo the screws/clip and release the wiring harness/guide.

6 Slacken and remove the bolt securing the sensor to the hub carrier, and remove the sensor and lead assembly from the vehicle **(see illustration)**.

7 Ensure that the sensor and hub carrier sealing faces are clean, then fit the sensor to the hub. Refit the retaining bolt and tighten it to the specified torque.

8 Ensure that the sensor wiring is correctly routed and retained by all the necessary clips, and reconnect it to its wiring connector. Refit the sensor wiring harness guide.

9 Manoeuvre the wheel arch liner back into place and secure it with the fasteners.

10 Refit the roadwheel, then lower the vehicle to the ground and tighten the roadwheel nuts to the specified torque.

Rear wheel sensor

11 Chock the front wheels, then jack up the rear of the vehicle and support it on axle stands (see *Jacking and vehicle support*). Remove the appropriate roadwheel.

12 If removing the left-hand sensor, remove the fuel filler pipe protector.

13 Trace the wiring back from the sensor and disconnect the wiring plug. Release the wiring harness from any retaining clips/brackets.

14 Slacken and remove the bolt securing the sensor to the hub carrier, and remove the sensor and lead assembly from the vehicle **(see illustration)**.

15 Refitting is a reversal of removal.

Steering angle sensor

16 The steering angle sensor is integral with the steering column combination switch (see Chapter 12 Section 5).

17 Note that every time the battery is disconnect, the steering angle sensor must be initialised as described in Chapter 5A Section 4.

Combined sensor (lateral acceleration and yaw rate)

18 The combines sensor informs the ABS/DSC control unit of yaw rate and lateral acceleration of the vehicle. Note that it the sensor is renewed, it will not function until it has been initialised using Mazda diagnostic equipment. Entrust this to a Mazda dealer or suitably equipped repairer.

19 Remove the centre console as described in Chapter 11 Section 27.

20 Disconnect the sensor wiring plug **(see illustration)**.

21 Undo the retaining nuts and remove the sensor.

Caution: Handle the sensor with care. It's extremely delicate and easily damaged.

22 Refitting is a reversal of removal, tightening the retaining nuts to the specified torque. Note that the arrow on the sensor points to the rear of the vehicle.

18.6 Front wheel speed sensor retaining bolt

18.14 Rear wheel speed sensor bolt

18.20 Combined sensor

Chapter 10
Suspension and steering

Contents

Degrees of difficulty

Easy, suitable for novice with little experience	**Fairly easy,** suitable for beginner with some experience	**Fairly difficult,** suitable for competent DIY mechanic	**Difficult,** suitable for experienced DIY mechanic	**Very difficult,** suitable for expert DIY or professional

Specifications

Front suspension

Type . . . . . . Independent, with MacPherson struts incorporating coil springs and telescopic shock absorbers. Anti-roll bar fitted to all models

Rear suspension

Type . . . . . . Independent, with MacPherson struts incorporating coil springs and telescopic shock absorbers. Anti-roll bar fitted to all models

Steering

Type . . . . . . Rack and pinion. Power assistance on all models

Wheel alignment and steering angles

Note: *Vehicle must be unladen but have a full fuel tank*

Front wheels:		
Camber angle:		
Vehicle ride height: *	Upto serial no. 200000	From serial no. 200001
16" wheels:		
356-365 mm	-0°41' ± 1°	-0°34' ± 1°
366-375 mm	-0°22' ± 1°	-0°19' ± 1°
376-385 mm	-0°06' ± 1°	-0°07' ± 1°
386-395 mm	0°09' ± 1°	0°04' ± 1°
396-405 mm	0°21' ± 1°	0°12' ± 1°
17" wheels:		
351-360 mm	-0°51' ± 1°	-0°42' ± 1°
361-370 mm	-0°31' ± 1°	-0°26' ± 1°
371-380 mm	-0°14' ± 1°	-0°13' ± 1°
381-390 mm	0°02' ± 1°	-0°01' ± 1°
391-400 mm	0°15' ± 1°	0°08' ± 1°
Castor angle:		
Vehicle ride height: *		
16" wheels:		
354-363 mm	6°27' ± 1°	6°24' ± 1°
364-373 mm	6°13' ± 1°	6°10' ± 1°
374-383 mm	5°59' ± 1°	5°56' ± 1°
384-393 mm	5°45' ± 1°	5°43' ± 1°
394-403 mm	5°31' ± 1°	5°29' ± 1°
17" wheels:		
349-358 mm	6°34' ± 1°	6°32' ± 1°
359-368 mm	6°20' ± 1°	6°18' ± 1°
369-378 mm	6°06' ± 1°	6°04' ± 1°
379-388 mm	5°53' ± 1°	5°50' ± 1°
389-398 mm	5°39' ± 1°	5°36' ± 1°
Maximum difference between sides	1°	
Toe setting (total):		
16" wheels:		
Tyre	2.0 ± 4.0 mm (0°11' ± 22)	16 ± 4.0 mm (0°09' ± 22')
Rim inner	1.2 ± 2.4 mm (0°11' ± 22')	1.1 ± 2.6 mm (0°09' ± 22')
17" wheels:		
Tyre	2.0 ± 4.0 mm (0°11' ± 22')	1.6 ± 4.0 mm (0°09' ± 22')
Rim inner	1.4 ± 2.8 mm (0°11' ± 22')	1.1 ± 2.8 mm (0°09' 1 22')
Rear wheels:		
Camber angle:		
Vehicle ride height: *		
16" wheels:		
354-363 mm	-1°33' ± 1°	
364-373 mm	-1°18' ± 1°	
374-383 mm	-1°04' ± 1°	
384-393 mm	-0°54' ± 1°	
394-403 mm	-0°45' ± 1°	
17" wheels:		
349-358 mm	-1°42' ± 1°	
359-368 mm	-1°25' ± 1°	
369-378 mm	-1°11' ± 1°	
379-388 mm	-0°59' ± 1°	
389-398 mm	-0°49' ± 1°	
Maximum difference between sides	1°	
Toe setting (total):		
16" wheels:		
Tyre	3.0 ± 4.0 mm (0°17' ± 22')	
Rim inner	1.8 ± 2.4 mm (0°17' ± 22')	
17" wheels:		
Tyre	3.0 ± 4.0 mm (0°17' ± 22')	
Rim inner	2.2 ± 2.8 mm (0°17' ± 22')	

**Measured from the edge of the wheelarch to the wheel centre*

Torque wrench settings

	Nm	lbf ft
Front suspension		
Anti-roll bar mounting clamp nuts	45	33
Anti-roll bar-to-link rod nuts	50	37
Hub-to-carrier bolts	57	42
Lower balljoint nut	125	92
Lower wishbone/arm nuts	130	96
Strut brace nuts	22	16
Strut damper/piston rod nut*	40	30
Strut mounting-to-body nuts	50	37
Strut to wishbone/arm	90	66
Upper balljoint nut	64	47
Upper wishbone/arm bolt	90	66
**Do not re-use*		
Rear suspension		
Anti-roll bar clamps	22	16
Anti-roll bar link nuts	50	37
Lateral link nuts:		
Lower*	120	88
Upper:		
Inner	88	65
Outer*	117	86
Strut damper/piston rod nut*	42	31
Strut lower mounting bolt	105	77
Strut mounting to body	48	35
Toe control link:		
Inner	80	60
Outer pinch bolt/nut	35	26
Trailing arm link:		
Upper*	80	60
Lower	80	60
**Do not re-use*		
Steering		
Power steering pipe union nuts	40	30
Power steering pump bolts	22	16
Steering column bolts/nuts	20	15
Steering column universal joint clamp/pinch-bolt	22	16
Steering rack mounting bolts	90	66
Steering wheel*	45	33
Track rod end balljoint retaining nut: *		
Upto serial no. 200000	45	33
From serial no. 200001	50	37
**Do not re-use*		
Roadwheels		
Roadwheel nuts	110	81

1 General Information

1 The independent front and rear suspension is of the MacPherson strut type, incorporating coil springs and integral telescopic shock absorbers. The front MacPherson struts are located by a lower wishbone/arm suspension arms, which use rubber inner mounting bushes, and incorporate a balljoint at the outer ends. The upper wishbone/arm suspension arms also use rubber inner mounting bushes and incorporate a balljoint at the outer ends. The hub carriers, which carry the brake calipers and the hub/disc assemblies, are connected to the upper and lower wishbone/arms through the balljoints. The rear struts are bolted directly to the hub carriers, which in turn are located to the axle assembly by link rods. Front and rear anti-roll bars are fitted to all models. The front anti-roll bar is rubber-mounted and is connected to both suspension lower wishbone/arms by connecting links, whilst the rear connects the axle to the rear lateral lower link.

2 The steering column is connected to the steering rack by an intermediate shaft, which incorporates a universal joint.

3 The steering rack is mounted onto the front subframe, and is connected by two track rods, with balljoints at their outer ends, to the steering arms projecting forwards from the hub carriers. The track rod ends are threaded, to facilitate adjustment.

4 Power-assisted steering is fitted to all models. The hydraulic steering system is powered by a belt-driven pump, which is driven off the crankshaft pulley.

2 Front hub assembly – removal and refitting

Removal

1 Remove the hub carrier as described in Section 3.

2 Undo the four retaining bolts and detach

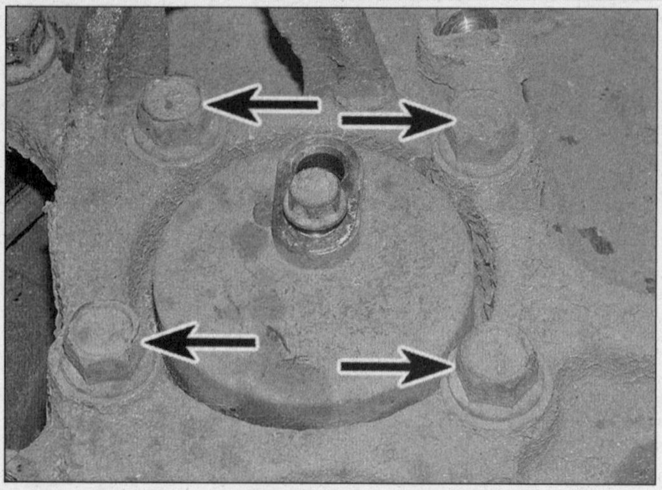
2.2 Hub retaining bolts

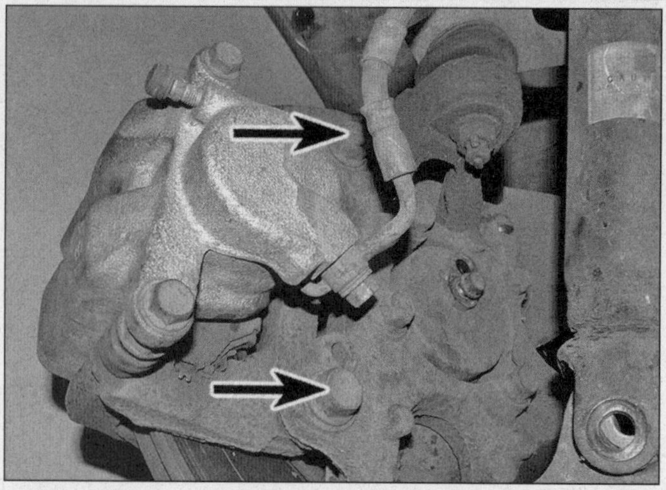
3.3 Undo the bolts and slide the caliper and bracket from the disc

the hub and backplate from the hub carrier **(see illustration)**.

Refitting

3 Refitting is the reverse of removal. Tighten the hub-to-carrier bolts to the specified torque.

3 Front hub carrier – removal and refitting

Removal

1 Slacken the front roadwheel nuts, raise the front of the vehicle and support it securely on axle stands (see *Jacking and vehicle support*). Remove the wheel.

2 Remove the ABS wheel speed sensor as described in Chapter 9.

3 Undo the brake caliper mounting bracket bolts and slide the caliper, pads and bracket from the disc **(see illustration)**. Suspend the assembly from the suspension strut to prevent straining the rubber hose.

4 Undo the retaining screws and remove the brake disc.

5 Disconnect the track rod end from the hub carrier as described in Section 21.

6 Remove the split-pins (where fitted), undo the nuts and disconnect the balljoints from the hub carrier using a balljoint separator tool **(see illustrations)**, then remove the hub carrier from the vehicle.

7 If required, detach the hub and backplate from carrier as described in Section 2.

Refitting

8 Refitting is the reverse of removal. Tighten all fasteners to their specified torque.

4 Front strut – removal, overhaul and refitting

Removal

1 Chock the rear wheels, apply the handbrake, then jack up the front of the car and support on axle stands (see *Jacking and vehicle support*). Remove the appropriate roadwheel.

2 Remove the strut brace assembly (where fitted) as described in Section 8.

3 Undo the bolt securing the brake hose bracket to the upper arm **(see illustration)**.

4 Remove the strut mounting plate nuts and the strut mounting plate **(see illustration)**. Note: The nuts that secure the mounting plate also secure the upper end of the shock absorber to the shock tower.

5 Remove the nut and bolt that secures the lower end of the shock absorber to the lower control arm **(see illustration)**.

6 Disconnect the upper control arm **(see**

3.6a Disconnect the lower balljoint...

3.6b... and upper balljoint

4.3 Brake hose bracket retaining bolt

4.4 Undo the nuts and remove the strut mounting plate

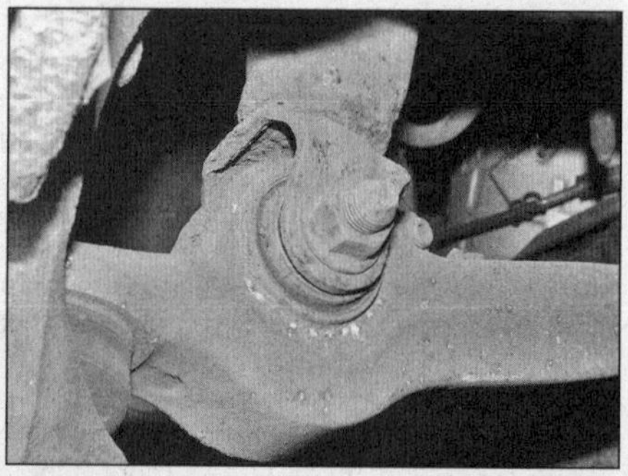
4.5 Shock absorber lower mounting bolt/nut

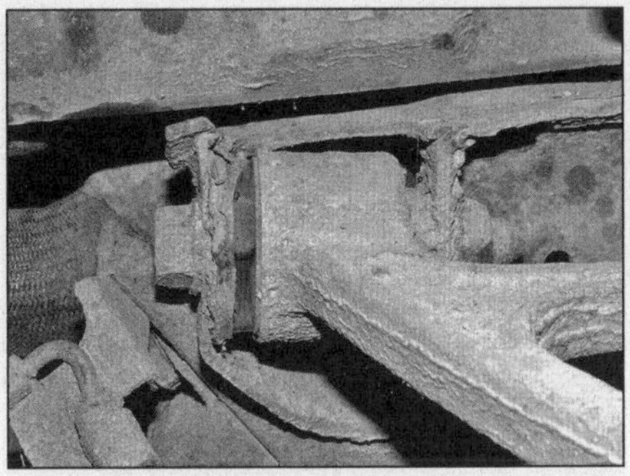

4.6a Upper control arm front mounting bolt...

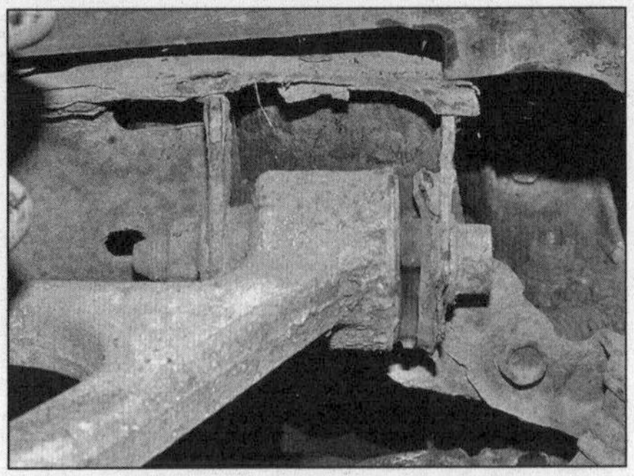

4.6b... and rear mounting bolt

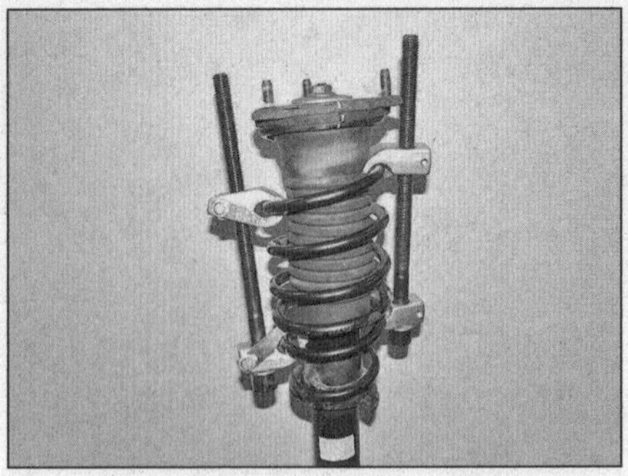

4.12 Use spring compressors

4.13 Stop the shaft from turning with an Allen key/bit

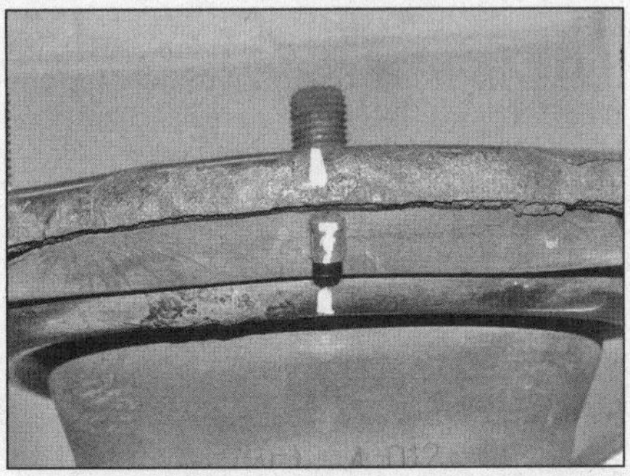

4.14a Make alignment marks between the spring, seat and mounting plate

4.14b Remove the nut ...

illustrations), then remove the upper control arm and shock absorber. **Note:** *The shock absorber cannot be removed unless you remove the upper control arm with it.*

7 Check the shock absorber body for leaking fluid, dents, cracks and other obvious damage which would warrant renewal.

8 Check the coil spring for chips or cracks in the spring coating (this will cause premature spring failure due to corrosion). Inspect the spring seat for cuts and general deterioration.

9 If any undesirable conditions exist, renew the unit using the information in this Section.

Overhaul

Warning: Before attempting to dismantle the front suspension strut, a suitable tool to hold the coil spring in compression must be obtained. Adjustable coil spring compressors are readily available, and are recommended for this operation. Any attempt to dismantle the strut without such a tool is likely to result in damage or personal injury.

10 With the strut removed from the car, clean away all external dirt, then mount it upright in a vice.

11 Prise the cap (where fitted) from the top centre of the shock/coil spring assembly. Slacken the damper shaft nut(s) beneath the cap, but DO NOT remove it/them yet. Use an Allen key to counterhold the damper rod whilst slackening the nuts.

12 Following the tool manufacturer's instructions, fit the spring compressor on the spring and compress it sufficiently to relieve all pressure from the upper spring seat **(see illustration)**. This can be verified by wiggling the spring.

13 Slacken the damper shaft nut. Prevent the shaft from turning with an Allen key/bit while slackening the nut. Note that a new nut will be required upon reassembly **(see illustration)**.

4.14c ... retainer...

4.14e... spacer...

14 Mark the outer side of the spring and mounting plates so they can be refitted in the same orientation to the spring. Remove the bushing, spacer, and upper spring seat **(see illustrations)**. Check the mounting plate for cracking and general deterioration. If there is any doubt about its condition, renew it.

4.14d ... bushing ...

4.14f ... and upper mounting, complete with the gaiter

4.15a Lift off the bushing ...

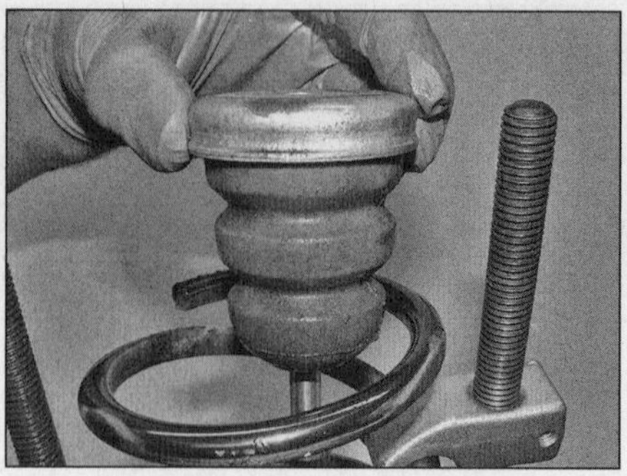

4.15b...and bump stop

4.19 Ensure the end of the spring locates in the step of the seat

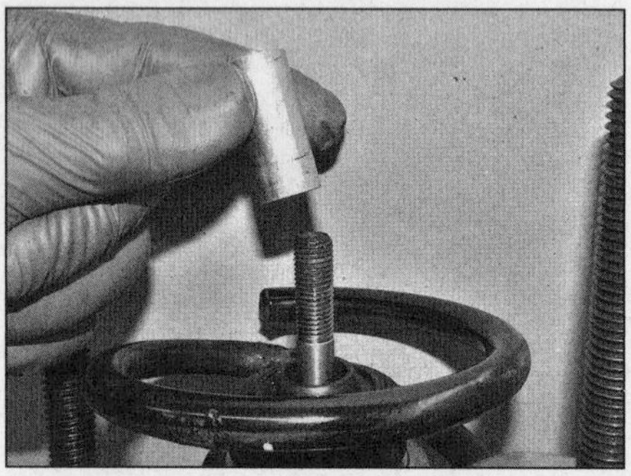

4.20 Refit the spacer before fitting the gaiter and upper mounting

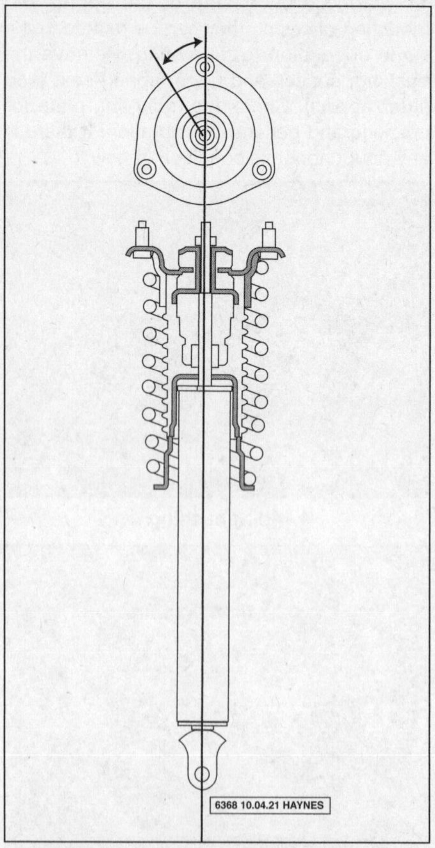

4.21 The mounting studs must be at an angle of 27° – 33° to the shock absorber mounting bracket

15 Lift the bushing and bump stop (as applicable) from the damper shaft **(see illustrations)**. Check the rubber for cracking and hardness, renewing it if necessary.

16 Carefully lift the compressed spring from the assembly and set it in a safe place.

Warning: Keep the ends of the spring pointed away from your body.

17 With the strut assembly now completely dismantled, examine all the components for wear, damage or deformation, and check the upper mounting bearing for smoothness of operation. Renew any of the components as necessary.

18 Examine the strut for signs of fluid leakage. Check the strut piston for signs of pitting along its entire length, and check the strut body for signs of damage.

Reassembly

19 Place the coil spring onto the lower spring seat, with the end of the spring resting in the step (lowest part of the seat) **(see illustration)**.

20 Extend the damper rod to its full length and refit the bump stop, bushing, spacer and gaiter **(see illustration)**.

21 Refit the upper mounting, aligning the mounting plate with the marks made on removal. If a new spring is being fitted, install the mounting so the the mounting stud is at a 27° – 33° angle to the shock absorber mounting bracket **(see illustration)**.

22 Refit the bushing, retainer and damper shaft nut then partially tighten it.

23 Remove the spring compressor tool.

5.4 Insert an Allen key into the balljoint shank to counterhold the anti-roll bar link

24 Tighten the damper shaft nut to the specified torque.

Refitting

25 Refitting is a reversal of removal, noting the following points:

a) Tighten all fasteners to their specified torque where given.

b) We recommend the front wheel alignment is checked at the earliest opportunity.

5 Front wishbones/arms – removal, overhaul and refitting

Note: *New lower arm front balljoint nuts will be required on refitting.*

Lower wishbone/arm

Removal

1 Chock the rear wheels, firmly apply the handbrake, then jack up the front of the car and support on axle stands (see *Jacking and vehicle support*). Remove the appropriate front roadwheel.

2 On models with Xenon gas discharge headlights, undo the bolts and detach the height sensor link arm bracket from the lower arm.

3 Remove the hub carrier as described in Section 3.

4 Disconnect the anti-roll bar link rod from the lower wishbone/arm **(see illustration)**.

5 Undo the nut, and withdraw the shock absorber lower mounting bolt.

6 Mark the position of the caster adjusting

5.6a Mark the position of the rear cam beneath the arm...

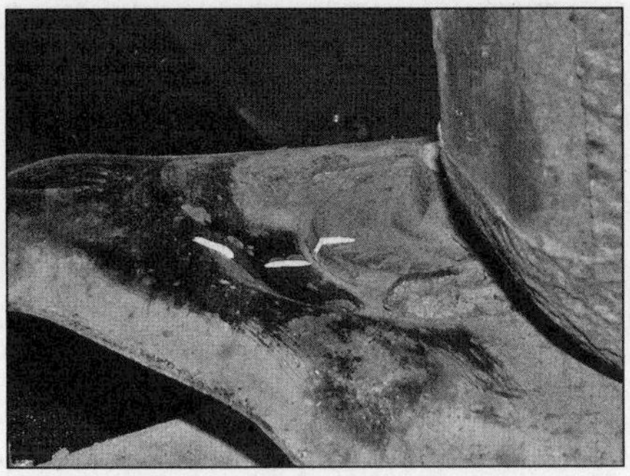

5.6b... and above the arm

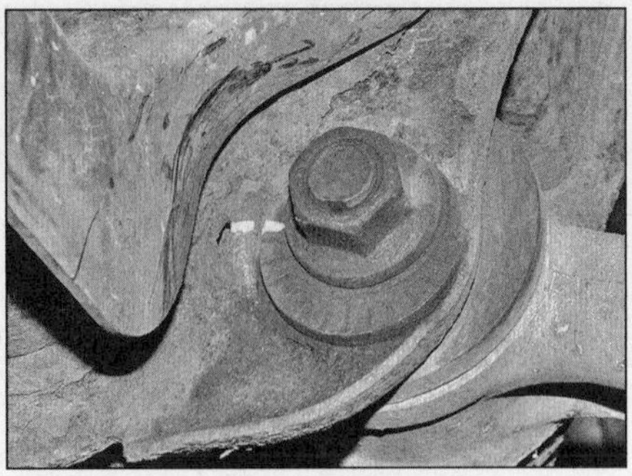

5.7a Mark the position of the adjusting cam each side...

5.7b... of the front pivot bolt

cams, then remove the lower control arm rear pivot bolt/nut **(see illustrations)**.
7 Mark the position of the camber adjusting cam, then remove the lower control arm front pivot bolt/nut and remove the lower control arm **(see illustrations)**.

Overhaul

8 Inspect the front and rear bushings in the lower control arm. If either bushing is torn or cracked, take the control arm to an automotive workshop and have the old bushings pressed out and new ones pressed in.

Refitting

9 Refitting is the reverse of the removal procedure. Tighten the balljoint bolts to the specified torque while the vehicle is still raised. Tighten the remaining fasteners (lower arm pivots, anti-roll bar link rod, shock absorber lower bolt) loosely at first, then refit the wheels and lower the vehicle. Tighten the fasteners to the specified torque with the vehicle's weight resting on the wheels.
10 Have front end alignment checked at the earliest opportunity.

Upper wishbone/arm

Removal

11 Remove the shock absorber as described in Section 4. **Note:** *It's not possible to remove the upper arm without removing the shock absorber.*

Overhaul

12 Mazda insist that no overhaul of the upper wishbone/arm is possible. If there is any sign of damage or deterioration in the ball joint or bushes, renew the arm.

Refitting

13 Installation is the reverse of removal. Be sure to tighten all fasteners to the torque listed in this Chapter's Specifications. **Note:** *Before tightening any fastener that runs through a rubber bushing, raise the outer end of the lower control arm with a floor jack to simulate normal ride height.*
14 Have front end alignment checked at the earliest opportunity.

6 Front arm balljoints – renewal

1 It is not possible to renew the ball joints independently of the wishbones/arms. If the ball joints show any sign of damage or deterioration, renew the complete wishbone/arm assembly.

7 Front anti-roll bar – removal and refitting

Removal

1 Chock the rear wheels, firmly apply the handbrake, then jack up the front of the car and support on axle stands (see *Jacking and vehicle support*). Remove the appropriate front roadwheel. Undo the fasteners and engine undershields (where fitted).
2 Undo the bolts and remove the radiator mounting brackets **(see illustration)**.
3 Disconnect the anti-roll bar link rod from the lower wishbone/arm **(see illustration 5.4)**. Use an Allen key to counterhold the link rod balljoint shank.
4 Undo the retaining nuts and remove the anti-roll bar clamps **(see illustration)**.

7.4 Undo the nuts and remove the clamps

5 Withdrawn the anti-roll bar from under the vehicle and remove the rubber bushings.
6 Check the rubber bushings and link rod grommets for cracks and tears. Renew all damaged bushings; renew the links if the grommets are damaged.

Refitting

7 Install the rubber bushings against the flanges on the anti-roll bar, then position the anti-roll bar, refit the clamps and tighten the retaining bolts to the specified torque. Note that the marking on the anti-roll bar should be on the right-hand side of the vehicle **(see illustration)**.
8 The remainder of refitting is a reversal of removal.

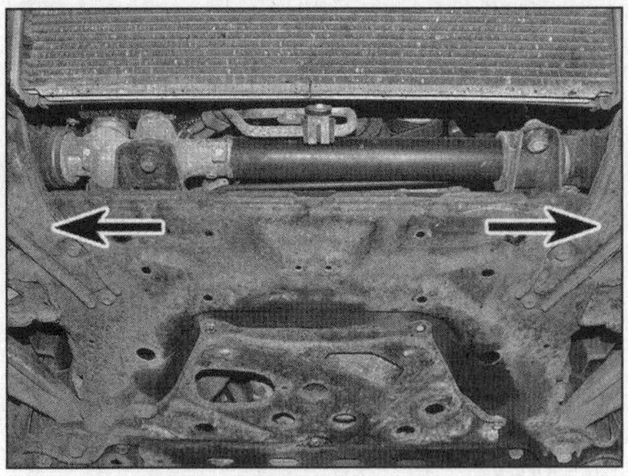

7.2 Remove the radiator mounting brackets

7.7 The right-hand side of the anti-roll bar has a paint-spray mark for identification

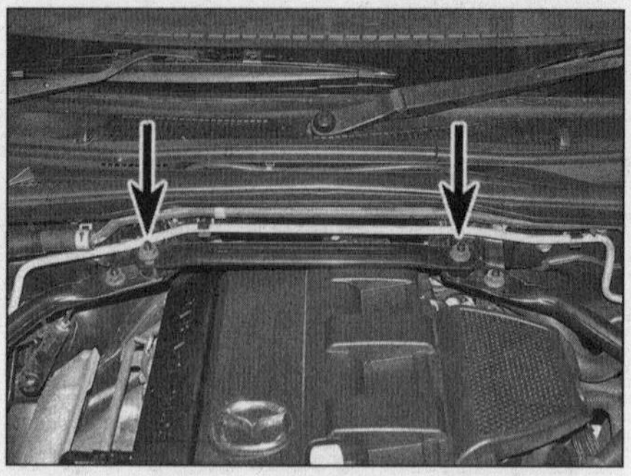

8.1 Strut brace centre joint retaining nuts

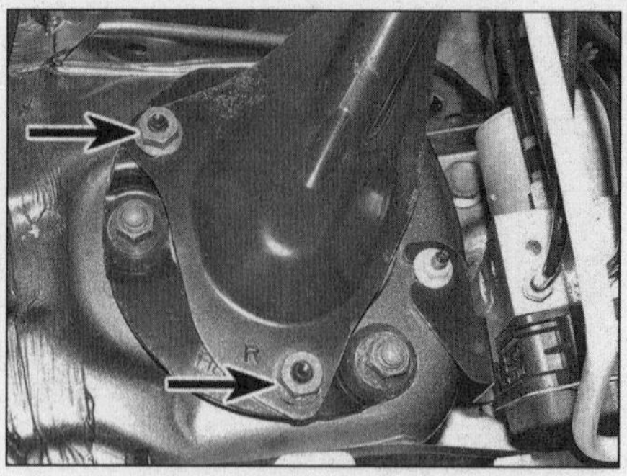

8.2 Undo the nuts at each end of the strut brace

9.2 Press the hub from the centre of the wheel bearing

8 Front strut brace – removal and refitting

1 Remove the nut from each end of the strut brace centre joint **(see illustration)** and remove the centre joint.

2 Undo the nuts at each end of the strut braces and manoeuvre them from position **(see illustration)**.

3 If required, undo the nuts and remove the mounting brackets.

4 Refitting is a reversal of removal. Tighten the fasteners to their specified torque where given.

9 Rear hub and bearing – removal and refitting

Note: *The hub assembly should not be removed unless it, or the hub bearing, is to be renewed. The hub is a press-fit in the bearing inner race, and removal of the hub will damage the bearings. If the hub is to be removed, be prepared to renew the hub bearing at the same time.*

Removal

1 Remove the hub carrier assembly as described in Section 11.

2 Use a hydraulic press and suitable sized spacers to force the hub from the centre of the bearing **(see illustration)**.

3 Remove the circlip, then press the bearing from the hub carrier **(see illustration)**. Do not remove the disc shield unless absolutely necessary.

4 If the hub is to be re-used, remove the bearing inner race using a chisel, or bearing remover **(see illustration)**.

Refitting

5 Thoroughly clean the hub carrier bore, removing all traces of dirt and grease, and polish away any burrs or raised edges which might hinder reassembly. Renew the circlip if there is any doubt about its condition.

6 On reassembly, apply a light film of clean engine oil to the bearing outer race to aid installation.

7 Locate the bearing in the hub carrier and press it into position, ensuring that it enters the carrier squarely, using a suitable tubular spacer which bears only on the bearing outer race.

8 Secure the bearing in position with the new circlip, making sure it is correctly located in the hub carrier groove.

9 Apply a smear of oil to the hub surface, and locate it in the bearing inner race.

10 Press the hub into place supporting the bearing with a spacer that bears only on the bearing inner race. **Note:** *Do not be tempted to knock the hub into position with a hammer and drift, as this will almost certainly damage the bearing.*

11 Refit the hub carrier as described in Section 11.

10 Rear strut – removal, overhaul and refitting

Removal

1 Chock the front wheels, then jack up the rear of the car and support on axle stands (see *Jacking and vehicle support*). Remove the rear roadwheels.

2 Undo the nut and detach the lower end of the drop link from the anti-roll bar, then working as described in Chapter 9 Section 5, slide the brake caliper from place, and suspend it from a suitable point to prevent straining the rubber hose.

3 Undo the nut and detach the outer end of the lower rear lateral link as described in Section 12.

4 Undo the bolt and detach the inner end of the upper rear lateral link as described in Section 12.

5 Remove the shock absorber lower mounting bolt and washer **(see illustration)**.

9.3 Remove the circlip and press the bearing from the hub carrier

9.4 Ideally, remove the bearing inner race using a bearing remover

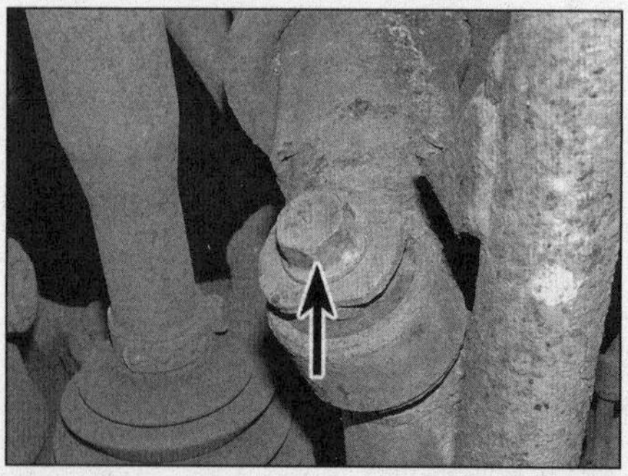

10.5 Shock absorber lower mounting bolt

6 With reference to Chapter 11 Section 26, remove the carpet and trim from the sides of the boot.

7 Where applicable, undo the bolts and remove the fuel filler pipe protection panel **(see illustration)**.

8 Remove the upper mounting nuts and bolt **(see illustrations)**. Lower the shock absorber from place and manoeuvre it from under the wheel arch.

Overhaul

9 Inspection and renewal of the damper unit or coil spring are the same as for front shock absorber/coil spring assemblies (Section 4).

Refitting

10 Refitting is the reverse of removal. Tighten all fasteners to their specified torque.

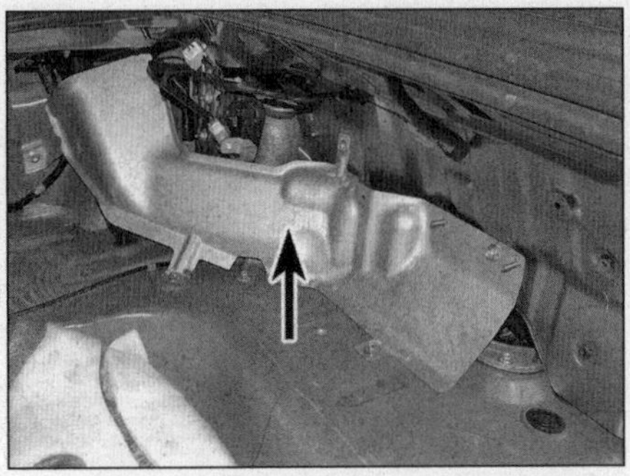

10.7 Fuel filler pipe protection panel

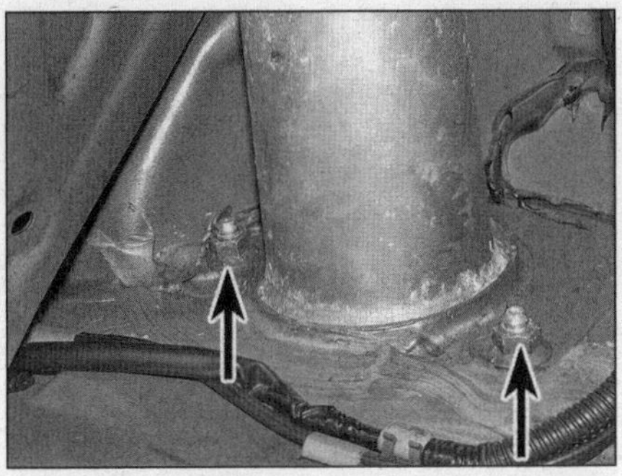

10.8a Remove the upper mounting nuts...

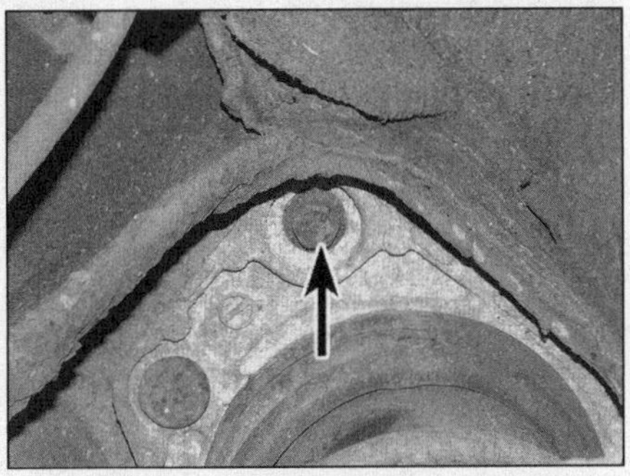

10.8b... and the mounting bolt from underside

10.8c Manoeuvre the shock absorber from under the wheel arch

11 Rear hub carrier – removal, overhaul and refitting

Removal

1 Chock the front wheels, then jack up the rear of the car and support it on axle stands (see *Jacking and vehicle support*). Remove the relevant roadwheel.

2 Remove the brake disc and ABS wheel speed sensor as described Chapter 9.

3 Remove the driveshaft/hub nut, and release the driveshaft from the hub splines, as described in Chapter 8, Section 4.

4 Undo the bolt securing the lower end of the shock absorber to the hub carrier.

5 Disconnect the toe-control link, the upper and lower trailing links and the upper and lower lateral links from the hub carrier (see Section 12).

6 Pull the hub carrier off the driveshaft. Support the driveshaft assembly to protect the outer CV joint boot while the hub carrier is disconnected and removed from the multi-link suspension. **Note:** *Only remove the disc shield if it is absolutely necessary.*

Overhaul

7 Examine the rubber bush for cracks, damage and deterioration. If necessary, remove the bush using an hydraulic press. In the absence of a press, a combination of spacers, threaded rod, washers and nuts will suffice.

8 Ensure the bore of the hub carrier is clean and free from burrs/rust.

9 Coat the new bush liberally with soapy water, then draw it into position in the hub carrier, again using suitable spacers, threaded rod, etc.

Refitting

10 Refitting is a reversal of removal, noting the following points:

a) Tighten all fasteners to their specified torque.

b) Apply lithium grease to the driveshaft contact area on the wheel bearing inner race prior to refitting.

c) Before tightening any fastener that runs through a rubber bushing, raise the hub carrier with a trolley jack to simulate normal ride height.

d) Have the rear wheel alignment checked at the earliest opportunity.

12 Rear links/arms – removal, overhaul and refitting

1 Slacken the rear roadwheel nuts, chock the front wheels, raise the rear of the vehicle and support it securely on axle stands (see *Jacking and vehicle support*). Remove the rear roadwheels.

Rear trailing link – upper

Removal

2 Loosen, but don't remove, the nut from the upper trailing link ball joint stud **(see illustration)**, install a ball joint separator tool, and push the ball joint stud out of the rear hub carrier. Remove the nut and separate the ball joint stud from the hub carrier.

3 Unscrew the inner retaining bolt **(see illustration)** and remove the upper trailing link.

12.2 Slacken the rear upper trailing link nut

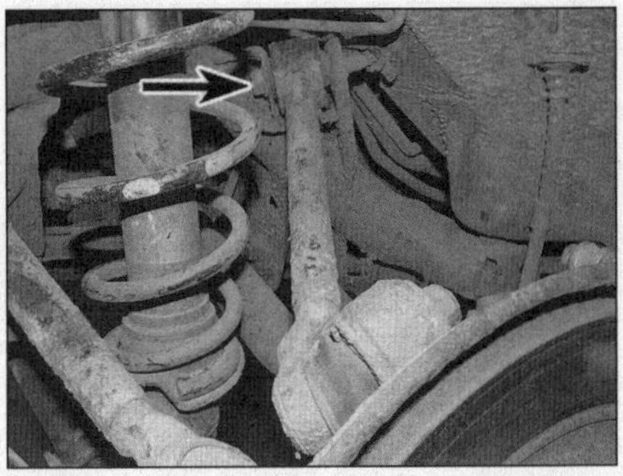

12.3 Rear upper trailing link inner retaining bolt

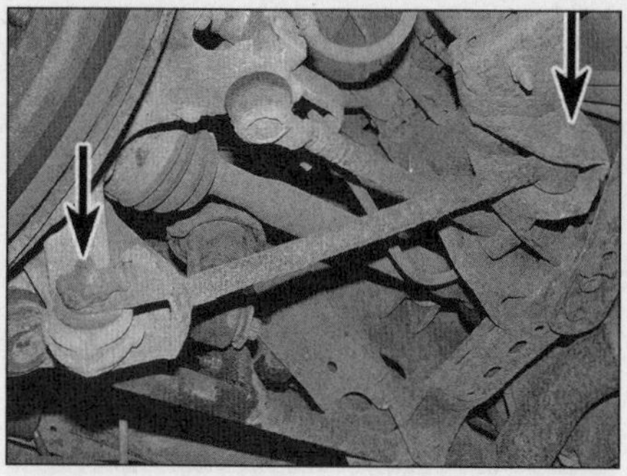

12.7 Rear lower trailing link inner and outer bolts

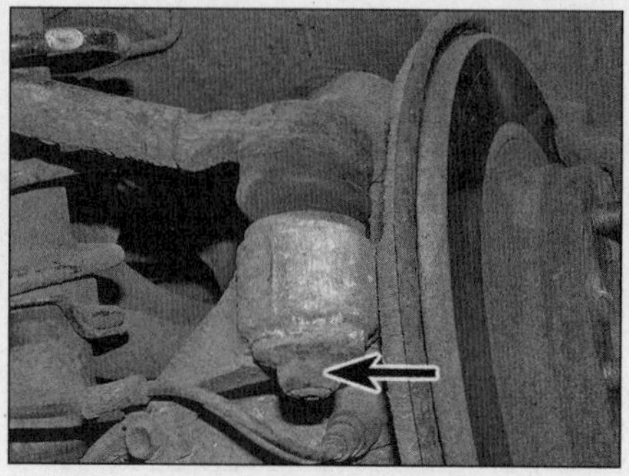

12.12a Undo the nut...

12.12b... then detach the ball joint from the hub carrier with a separator tool

Overhaul

4 The inner bush and outer balljoint are integral with the link arm. If the bush or balljoint show signs of damage or deterioration, the complete link arm should be renewed.

Refitting

5 Refitting is the reverse of removal. Be sure to tighten all fasteners to their specified torque. **Note:** *Before tightening any fastener that runs through a rubber bushing, raise the rear hub carrier with a workshop jack to simulate normal ride height.*

6 Have rear wheel alignment checked and adjusted if necessary at the earliest opportunity.

Rear trailing link – lower

Removal

7 Remove the lower trailing link-to-rear hub carrier bolt **(see illustration)**.

8 Undo the inner retaining bolt and remove the rear lower trailing link.

Overhaul

9 If the link arm shows any signs of damage or deterioration, it should be renewed.

Refitting

10 Refitting is the reverse of removal. Tighten the fasteners to their specified torque. Note: Before tightening any fastener that runs through a rubber bushing, raise the rear hub carrier with a workshop jack to simulate normal ride height.

11 Have the rear wheel alignment checked at the earliest opportunity.

Rear lateral link – upper

Removal

12 Loosen, but don't remove, the nut from the upper lateral link ball joint stud, install a ball joint separator tool, and push the ball joint stud out of the rear hub carrier **(see illustrations)**. Remove the nut and separate the ball joint stud from the hub carrier. Note that a new nut will be required for refitting.

13 Unscrew the inner retaining nut and bolt, then remove the lateral link **(see illustration)**.

Overhaul

14 The inner bush and outer balljoint are integral with the link arm. If the bush or balljoint show signs of damage or deterioration, the complete link arm should be renewed.

Refitting

15 Refitting is the reverse of removal. Tighten the fasteners to their specified torque. **Note:** *Before tightening any fastener that runs through a rubber bushing, raise the rear hub carrier with a workshop jack to simulate normal ride height.*

16 Have the rear wheel alignment checked at the earliest opportunity.

Rear lateral link – lower

Removal

17 Undo the nut and disconnect the anti-roll bar drop link from the lower lateral link.

18 Loosen, but don't remove, the nut **(see illustrations)** from the lower lateral link ball joint stud, install a ball joint separator tool, and push the ball joint stud out of the rear hub carrier. Remove the nut and separate the ball joint stud from the hub carrier. Note that a new nut will be required for refitting.

19 Mark the position of the lower lateral link cam. Remove the lower lateral link pivot bolt and remove the lower lateral link **(see illustrations)**.

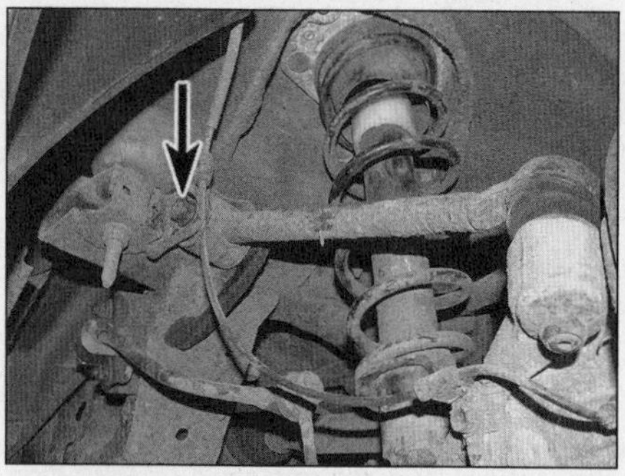

12.13 Rear upper lateral link inner bolt

12.18a Insert an Allen key to prevent the ball joint shank rotating

12.18b Detach the ball joint stud from the hub carrier using a separator tool

12.19a Mark the position of the cam each side of the mounting

12.19b Lower rear lateral link pivot bolt

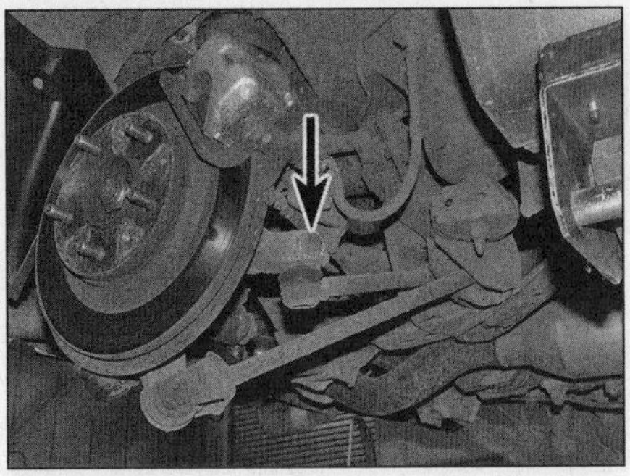

12.22 Undo the nut and remove the pinch bolt

12.23 Gently spread the clamp gap

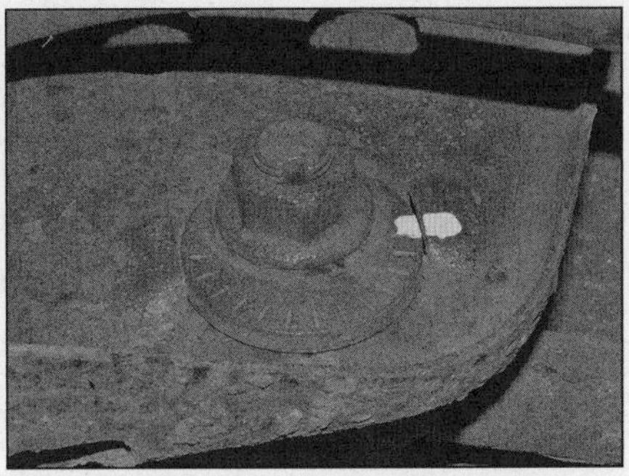

12.24 Mark the position of the cam each side of the mounting

Overhaul

20 The inner bush and outer balljoint are integral with the link arm. If the bush or balljoint show signs of damage or deterioration, the complete link arm should be renewed.

Refitting

21 Refitting is a reversal of removal, noting the following points:

a) Align the inner bolt cam with the mark made on removal.

b) Renew the balljoint nut.

c) Tighten the fasteners to their specified torque. **Note:** Before tightening any fastener that runs through a rubber bushing, raise the rear hub carrier with a workshop jack to simulate normal ride height.

d) Have the rear wheel alignment checked at the earliest opportunity.

Toe control link

Removal

22 Undo the nut and remove the pinch bolt from the hub carrier **(see illustration)**.

23 Using a chisel or similar wedge tool, gently spread the clamp gap at the outer ball joint a little, and pull the ball joint from the hub carrier **(see illustration)**.

24 Mark the position of the toe control link cam **(see illustration)**. Remove the toe control link pivot bolt/nut and remove the link.

Overhaul

25 The inner bush and outer balljoint are integral with the link arm. If the bush or balljoint show signs of damage or deterioration, the complete link arm should be renewed.

Refitting

26 Refitting is a reversal of removal, noting the following points:

a) Align the inner bolt cam with the mark made on removal.

b) Tighten the fasteners to their specified torque. **Note:** Before tightening any fastener that runs through a rubber bushing, raise the rear hub carrier with a workshop jack to simulate normal ride height.

c) Have the rear wheel alignment checked at the earliest opportunity.

13 Rear anti-roll bar – removal and refitting

Removal

1 Slacken the rear roadwheel nut, chock the front wheels, then jack up the rear of the car and support on axle stands (see *Jacking and vehicle support*). Remove the rear roadwheels.

2 Unbolt the anti-roll bar bushing clamps from the body **(see illustration)**.

3 Unbolt the anti-roll bar from the upper ends of the link rods **(see illustration)**. The anti-roll bar can now be removed from the vehicle. Pull the bushings off the anti-roll bar using a rocking motion.

4 Unbolt the lower ends of the anti-roll link rod on each side of the vehicle and remove the rods.

5 Check the bushings for wear, hardness, distortion, cracking and other signs of deterioration, renewing them if necessary. Also check the anti-roll bar link rod bushings for the same conditions, and renew if necessary.

6 Using a wire brush, clean the areas of the bar where the bushings ride.

Refitting

7 Refitting is the reverse of the removal procedure. Apply rubber lubricant to the bushings prior to installation.

13.2 Anti-roll bar clamp nuts

Caution: Do not use petroleum-based products or brake fluid, as these will damage the rubber.

8 Install the bushings at the anti-roll bar clamps with the bushing flat bottom/split facing the crossmember, and with the bushing located on the installation position line painted on the anti-roll bar.

9 The painted identification mark on the anti-roll bar must be on the right-hand side when refitting.

10 Refit and tighten the anti-roll bar clamp bolts and link rod bolts. Tighten them loosely at first. Refit the road wheel and retaining nuts then tighten them loosely.

11 Lower the vehicle. Tighten the anti-roll bar fasteners and roadwheel nuts to the specified torque.

14 Steering wheel – removal and refitting

Removal

1 Set the front wheels in the straight-ahead position.

2 Remove the airbag unit from the centre of the steering wheel, referring to Chapter 12, Section 22.

3 Slacken and remove the steering wheel retaining nut. Disconnect the steering

13.3 Insert an Allen key into the end of the ball joint shank then undo the nut

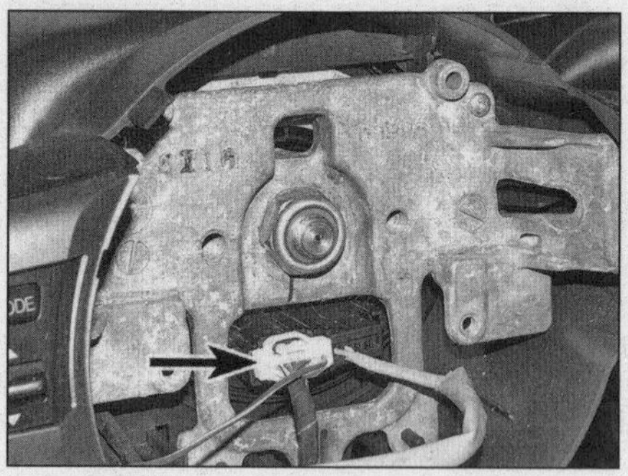

14.3 Disconnect the wiring plug and slacken the wheel retaining nut

14.5a If necessary, use a puller to release the steering wheel

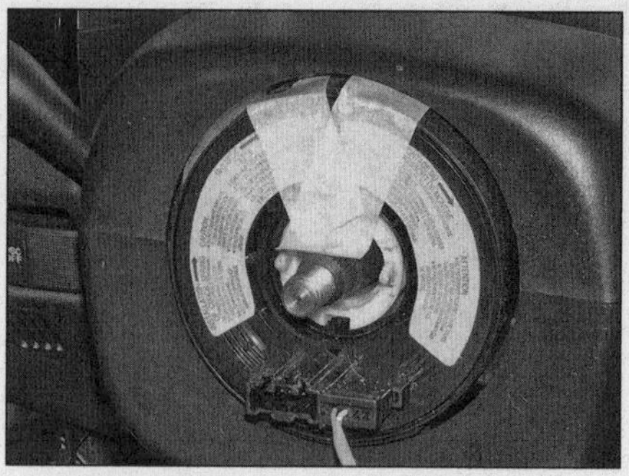

14.5b Use tape to prevent the rotary contact unit from moving

wheel wiring plug(s) where fitted **(see illustration)**.

4 Make alignment marks between the steering wheel and the column shaft to aid refitting.

5 Lift the steering wheel off the column splines. If it is tight, tap it up near the centre, using the palm of your hand, or twist it from side to side, whilst pulling upwards to release it from the shaft splines. If the steering wheel is still reluctant to release, bolt a length of steel strip across the end of the column (using the holes provided in the steering wheel centre) **(see illustrations)**. Use adhesive tape to secure the airbag rotary contact unit; do not attempt to rotate it whilst the wheel is removed.

Caution: Under no circumstances should the end of the column shaft be hit with a hammer. This could cause the shaft to collapse.

Refitting

6 Refitting is the reverse of removal, noting the following points.

a) *If the contact unit has been rotated with the wheel removed, centralise it by rotating its centre fully clockwise. From this position, rotate the centre back through 2.75 complete rotations in a anti-clockwise direction.*
b) *Engage the wheel with the column splines, aligning the previously-made marks*
c) *Where applicable, ensure the lugs on the indicator cancelling sleeve locate correctly with the holes on the front of the steering wheel boss.*
d) *Tighten the steering wheel retaining nut to the specified torque.*
e) *Refit the airbag unit (see Chapter 12, Section 22).*

15.4 Undo the nuts securing the bulkhead grommet assembly

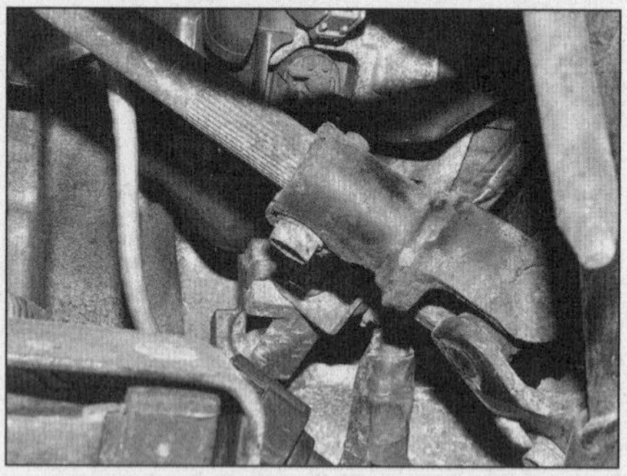

15.5 Undo the column pinch bolt

15.6a Remove the column mounting nuts at the rear...

15.6b... and at the front

15 Steering column – removal, inspection and refitting

Removal

1 Remove the steering column combination switch assembly as described in Chapter 12, Section 5.

2 Disconnect any remaining wiring plugs and release any wiring harnesses from the column assembly.

3 Remove the lower facia panel as described in Chapter 11 Section 28.

4 Undo the nuts and slide the bulkhead grommet assembly up the column shaft **(see illustration)**.

5 Slacken and remove the clamp bolt, make alignment marks and disengage the universal joint from the steering column shaft **(see illustration)**.

6 Undo the mounting nuts and pull the column to the rear **(see illustrations)**. Note that it's only necessary to slacken the front nuts.

Inspection

7 The steering column incorporates a telescopic safety feature. In the event of a front-end crash, the shaft collapses and prevents the steering wheel injuring the driver. Before refitting the steering column, examine the column and mountings for damage and deformation, and renew as necessary.

8 Check the steering shaft for signs of free play in the column bushes. If any damage or wear is found on the steering column bushes, the column should be overhauled. Overhaul of the column is a complex task requiring several special tools, and should be entrusted to a Mazda dealer.

Refitting

9 Manoeuvre the column into position and engage it with the steering rack pinion splines, aligning the marks made prior to removal.

10 Locate the column in position and refit the mounting nuts. Tighten them to the specified torque.

11 The remainder of refitting is a reversal of removal.

16.2 The steering column lock is secured by 2 shear bolts

17.6 Steering rack mounting bolts

18.3 Fluid return hose clamp

16 Steering column lock – removal and refitting

1 Remove the steering column as described in Section 15.
2 The steering column lock is secured by shear bolts. Use a sharp chisel on the bolt heads to undo them **(see illustration)**.
3 Remove the lock assembly.
4 Position the steering lock assembly on the column, then fit the new shear bolts and tighten them until the heads shear off.
5 Refit the steering column as described in Section 15.

17 Steering rack assembly – removal and refitting

Removal

1 Chock the rear wheels, firmly apply the handbrake, then jack up the front of the car and support on axle stands (see *Jacking and vehicle support*). Remove both front roadwheels, undo the fasteners and remove the engine undershields.
2 Set the steering in the 'straight-ahead' position and engage the steering lock. Disconnect the battery negative lead as described in Chapter 5A, Section 4.
3 Place a container under the steering rack, then disconnect the power steering pressure and return pipes. Cap or cover the ends to prevent excessive fluid loss and contamination.
4 Mark the relationship of the steering column universal joint at the steering rack pinion. Remove the steering column universal joint pinch-bolt **(see illustration 15.4)**.
5 Separate the track rod ends from the hub carrier as described in Section 21.
6 Support the steering rack and remove the steering rack mounting bolts **(see illustration)**. Separate the steering column shaft from the steering rack pinion and remove the rack assembly.

Warning: Do NOT turn the steering wheel while the steering rack is removed. If the steering wheel is inadvertently turned, check the airbag rotary connector for damage and adjust as necessary (see Chapter 12, Section 22).

7 Check the steering rack mounting grommets for excessive wear or deterioration, renewing them if necessary.

Refitting

8 Raise the steering rack into position and connect the pinion to the universal joint, aligning the marks.
9 Install the steering rack mounting brackets and bolts and tighten them to the specified torque.
10 Connect the track rod ends to the hub carriers and tighten them to the specified torque as described in Section 21.
11 Fit the universal joint pinch-bolt and tighten it to the specified torque.
12 Connect the power steering pressure and return hoses to the steering rack and fill the power steering pump reservoir with the recommended fluid (see *Lubricants and fluids* in Reference).
13 Lower the vehicle and bleed the steering system (see Section 19).
14 We recommend having the front wheel alignment checked at the earliest opportunity.

18 Power steering pump – removal and refitting

Removal

1 Remove the auxiliary drivebelt as described in Chapter 1, Section 6.
2 Using a large syringe or old poultry baster, remove as much fluid out of the power steering fluid reservoir as possible. Place a container under the vehicle to catch any fluid that spills out when the hoses are disconnected. Cap or cover the hoses to prevent entry of dirt or other contaminants.
3 Slacken the clamp and disconnect the fluid return hose from the pump **(see illustration)**. Detach the electrical connector from the pressure sensor on the pump, if applicable.
4 Disconnect the pressure pipe from the pump.
5 Disconnect the wiring plug, undo the mounting bolts, then remove the pump from the vehicle.
6 If access to engine components is required, remove the pump mounting bracket mounting bolts and remove the mounting bracket.

Refitting

7 Refitting is the reverse of removal. Be sure to tighten the pressure pipe fitting to the specified torque.
8 Refit the auxiliary drivebelt as described in Chapter 1, Section 6.
9 Top off the fluid level in the reservoir (see *Weekly checks*) and bleed the system (see Section 19).

19 Power steering system – bleeding

1 Following any operation in which the power steering fluid lines have been disconnected, the power steering system must be bled to remove all air and obtain proper steering performance.
2 Before starting the engine and with the front wheels in the straight-ahead position, check the power steering fluid level and, if low, add fluid until it reaches the L (Low) mark on the dipstick.
3 Without starting the engine, turn the steering wheel from lock to lock several times, then recheck the fluid level. To reduce the amount of effort required to turn the steering wheel, raise the front of the vehicle and support it securely on axle stands (see *Jacking and vehicle support*).
4 Start the engine and allow it to run at a fast idle. Turn the steering wheel from lock to lock several times, then recheck the fluid level and add more power steering fluid if necessary to reach the L mark on the dipstick.
5 Bleed the system by turning the wheels from side to side, without hitting the stops. This will remove the air from the system. Continuously check the reservoir and keep the reservoir full of fluid as this is done.
6 When the air is removed from the system, return the wheels to the straight-ahead position and keep the engine running for several more minutes before turning it off, or road test as follows before turning the engine off.

20.2 Steering rack gaiter clamps

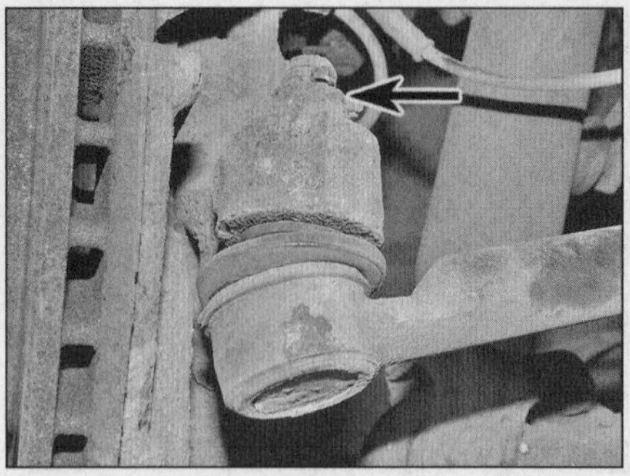
21.2 Remove the split pin from the balljoint shank

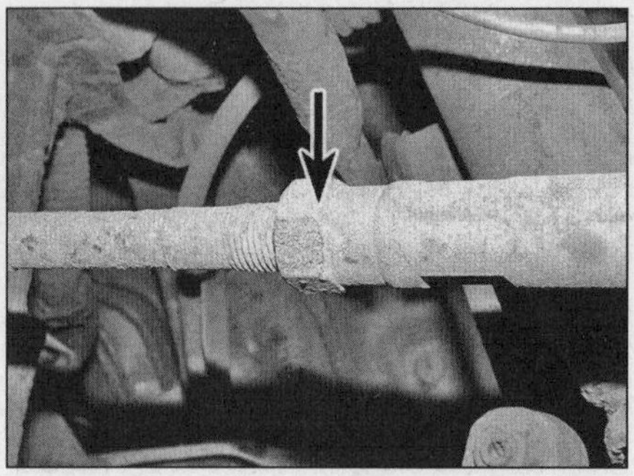
21.3 Slacken the track rod end locknut

7 Road test the vehicle to ensure the steering system is functioning normally and is noise-free.
8 Recheck and top-up the power steering fluid level to the F (Full) mark on the dipstick while the engine is at normal operating temperature. Add fluid if necessary (see *Weekly checks*).

20 Steering rack rubber gaiters – renewal

1 Remove the track rod end from the steering rack as described in Section 21.
2 Release the clamps securing the gaiter to the steering rack, and pull the gaiter over the track rod **(see illustration)**.
3 Thoroughly clean the track rod and the steering rack housing, using fine abrasive paper to polish off any corrosion, burrs or sharp edges, which might damage the new gaiter's sealing lips on installation. Scrape off all the grease from the old gaiter, and apply it to the track rod inner balljoint. (This assumes that grease has not been lost or contaminated as a result of damage to the old gaiter. Use fresh grease if in doubt – consult a Mazda dealer or parts specialist.)
4 Apply a little grease to the track rod so the gaiter will slide, then carefully fit the new gaiter (with the retaining clips in place) over the track rod, and locate it on the steering rack housing. Position the outer edge of the gaiter on the track rod.
5 Secure the gaiter to the rack and track rod with the retaining clamps.
6 Refit the track rod end as described in Section 21.

21 Track rod end – removal and refitting

Removal

1 Apply the handbrake, then jack up the front of the car and support it on axle stands (see *Jacking and vehicle support*). Remove the appropriate front roadwheel.
2 Remove the split pin **(see illustration)** and slacken the nut on the track rod end stud.
3 Hold the track rod end with a pair of locking pliers or spanner and slacken the locknut enough to mark the position of the track rod end end in relation to the threads **(see illustration)**.
4 Use a balljoint separator to detach the track rod end from the hub carrier **(see illustration)**.
5 Unscrew the track rod end from the track rod.

Refitting

6 Thread the track rod end to the marked position on the track rod and insert the track rod end stud into the hub carrier. Tighten the locknut securely.
7 Fit the castellated nut on the stud and tighten it to the specified torque. Install a new split pin. If the hole for the split pin does not line up with one of the slots in the nut, tighten the nut an additional amount until it slides through easily; do not slacken the nut.
8 Have the wheel alignment checked at the earliest opportunity.

22 Wheel alignment and steering angles – general information

Definitions

1 A car's steering and suspension geometry is defined in four basic settings **(see illustration)** – all angles are usually expressed

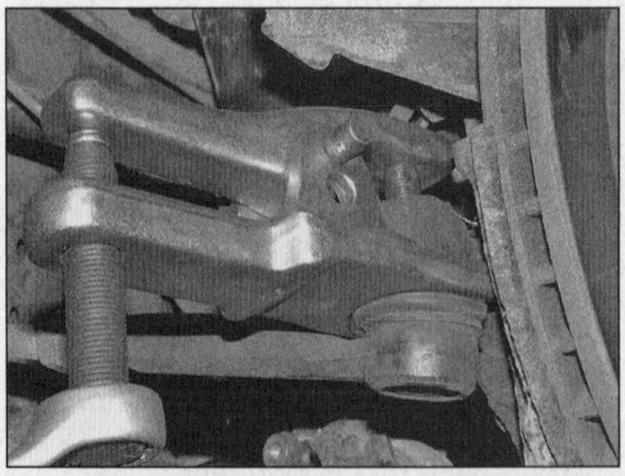
21.4 Use a balljoint separator tool to detach the track rod end from the hub carrier

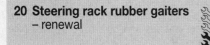

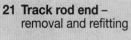

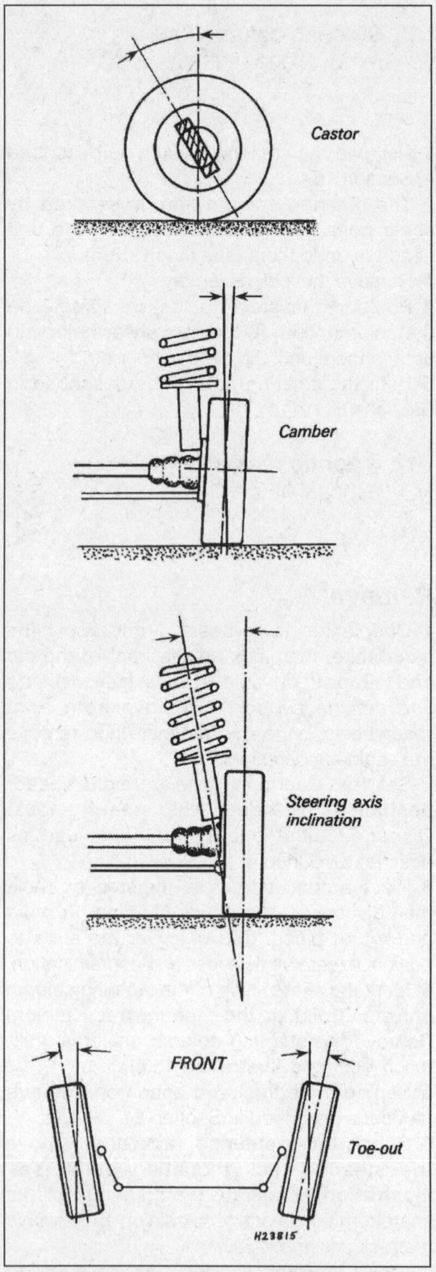

22.1 Steering geometry details

in degrees (toe settings are also expressed as a measurement); the steering axis is defined as an imaginary line drawn through the axis of the suspension strut, extended where necessary to contact the ground.

2 Camber is the angle between each roadwheel and a vertical line drawn through its centre and tyre contact patch, when viewed from the front or rear of the car. Positive camber is when the roadwheels are tilted outwards from the vertical at the top; negative camber is when they are tilted inwards.

3 The front camber angle is not adjustable, and is given for reference only. The rear camber angle is adjustable and can be adjusted using a camber angle gauge.

4 Castor is the angle between the steering axis and a vertical line drawn through each roadwheel's centre and tyre contact patch, when viewed from the side of the car. Positive castor is when the steering axis is tilted so that it contacts the ground ahead of the vertical; negative castor is when it contacts the ground behind the vertical.

5 Castor is not adjustable, and is given for reference only; while it can be checked using a castor checking gauge, if the figure obtained is significantly different from that specified, the car must be taken for careful checking by a professional, as the fault can only be caused by wear or damage to the body or suspension components.

6 Toe is the difference, viewed from above, between lines drawn through the roadwheel centres and the car's centre-line. 'Toe-in' is when the roadwheels point inwards, towards each other at the front, while 'toe-out' is when they splay outwards from each other at the front.

7 The front wheel toe setting is adjusted by screwing the track rod in or out of the tack rod end, to alter the effective length of the track rod assembly.

8 Rear wheel toe/camber setting is adjusted by means of eccentric washers integral with the inner pivot bolts of the lower later links and toe control links.

Checking and adjustment

Front wheel toe setting

9 Due to the special measuring equipment necessary to check the wheel alignment, and the skill required to use it properly, the checking and adjustment of these settings is best left to a Mazda dealer or similar expert. Note that most tyre-fitting shops now possess sophisticated checking equipment.

10 To check the toe setting, a tracking gauge must first be obtained. Two types of gauge are available, and can be obtained from motor accessory shops. The first type measures the distance between the front and rear inside edges of the roadwheels, as previously described, with the car stationary. The second type, known as a 'scuff plate', measures the actual position of the contact surface of the tyre, in relation to the road surface, with the car in motion. This is achieved by pushing or driving the front tyre over a plate, which then moves slightly according to the scuff of the tyre, and shows this movement on a scale. Both types have their advantages and disadvantages, but either can give satisfactory results if used correctly and carefully.

11 Make sure that the steering is in the straight-ahead position when making measurements.

12 If adjustment is necessary, apply the handbrake then jack up the front of the car and support it securely on axle stands.

13 First clean the track rod threads; if they are corroded, apply penetrating fluid before starting adjustment. Release the rubber gaiter outer clips, peel back the gaiters and apply a smear of grease so that both are free and will not be twisted or strained as their respective track rods are rotated.

14 Retain the track rod with a suitable spanner and slacken the balljoint locknut. Alter the length of the track rod, by screwing them into or out of track rod ends, rotating the track rod using an open-ended spanner fitted to the track rod flats provided; shortening the track rods (screwing them onto their balljoints) will reduce toe-in/increase toe-out.

15 When the setting is correct, hold the track rod and tighten the balljoint locknut to the specified torque setting. If after adjustment, the steering wheel spokes are no longer horizontal when the wheels are in the straight-ahead position, remove the steering wheel and reposition it (see Section 14).

16 Check that the toe setting has been correctly adjusted by lowering the car to the ground and rechecking the toe setting; re-adjust if necessary. Ensure that the rubber gaiters are seated correctly and are not twisted or strained, and secure them in position with the retaining clips; where necessary fit a new retaining clip (see Section 20).

Wheel camber angle

17 Checking and adjusting of the camber angle should be entrusted to a Mazda dealer or other suitably-equipped specialist. Note that most tyre-fitting shops now possess sophisticated checking equipment. For reference, adjustments are made by slackening the lower wishbone/arm pivot bolts, and rotating the eccentric washer. Once adjustment is correct, tighten the bolts to the specified torque.

Chapter 11
Bodywork and fittings

Contents

Degrees of difficulty

Easy, suitable for novice with little experience	**Fairly easy,** suitable for beginner with some experience	**Fairly difficult,** suitable for competent DIY mechanic	**Difficult,** suitable for experienced DIY mechanic	**Very difficult,** suitable for expert DIY or professional

Specifications

Torque wrench settings	Nm	lbf ft
Retractable hardtop link bracket bolts	22	16
Retractable hardtop retaining bolts	22	16
Seat back crossmember bolts/nuts	25	18
Seat belt mounting bolts M10	60	44
Seat belt mounting bolts M6	10	7
Seat belt stalk mounting bolt	44	32
Seat mounting bolts	44	32

1 General Information

1 The bodyshell is made of pressed-steel and aluminium, with high-tensile steel used in structural areas. Most components are welded together, but some use is made of structural adhesives. Certain components that are venerable to crash damage can be unbolted, and repaired or replaced.

2 The door and some other vulnerable panels are made of zinc-coated metal, and are further protected by being coated with an anti-chip primer before being sprayed.

3 Extensive use is made of plastic materials, mainly in the interior, but also in exterior components. The front and rear bumpers are injection-moulded from a synthetic material that is very strong and yet light.

2 Maintenance – bodywork and underframe

1 The condition of a vehicle's bodywork is the one thing that significantly affects its value. Maintenance is easy, but needs to be regular. Neglect, particularly after minor damage, can lead quickly to further deterioration and costly repair bills. It is important also to keep watch on those parts of the vehicle not immediately visible, for instance the underside, inside all the wheel arches, and the lower part of the engine compartment.

2 The basic maintenance routine for the bodywork is washing – preferably with a lot of water, from a hose. This will remove all the loose solids which may have stuck to the vehicle. It is important to flush these off in such a way as to prevent grit from scratching the finish. The wheel arches and underframe need washing in the same way, to remove any accumulated mud which will retain moisture and tend to encourage rust. Oddly enough, the best time to clean the underframe and wheel arches is in wet weather, when the mud is thoroughly wet and soft. In very wet weather, the underframe is usually cleaned of large accumulations automatically, and this is a good time for inspection.

3 Periodically, except on vehicles with a wax-based underbody protective coating, it is a good idea to have the whole of the underframe of the vehicle steam-cleaned, engine compartment included, so that a thorough inspection can be carried out to see what minor repairs and renovations are necessary. Steam cleaning is available at many garages, and is necessary for the removal of the accumulation of oily grime, which sometimes is allowed to become thick in certain areas. If steam-cleaning facilities are not available, there are some excellent grease solvents available which can be brush-applied; the dirt can then be simply hosed off. Note that these methods should not be used on vehicles with wax-based underbody protective coating, or the coating will be removed. Such vehicles should be inspected annually, preferably just before Winter, when the underbody should be washed down, and repair any damage to the wax coating. Ideally, a completely fresh coat should be applied. It would also be worth considering the use of such wax-based protection for injection into door panels, sills, box sections, etc, as an additional safeguard against rust damage, where such protection is not provided by the vehicle manufacturer.

4 After washing paintwork, wipe off with a chamois leather to give an unspotted clear finish. A coat of clear protective wax polish will give added protection against chemical pollutants in the air. If the paintwork sheen has dulled or oxidised, use a cleaner/polisher combination to restore the brilliance of the shine. This requires a little effort, but such dulling is usually caused because regular washing has been neglected. Care needs to be taken with metallic paintwork, as special non-abrasive cleaner/polisher is required to avoid damage to the finish. Always check that the door and ventilator opening drain holes and pipes are completely clear, so that water can be drained out. Brightwork should be treated in the same way as paintwork. Windscreens and windows can be kept clear of the smeary film which often appears, by proprietary glass cleaner. Never use any form of wax or other body or chromium polish on glass.

3 Maintenance – upholstery and carpets

1 Mats and carpets should be brushed or vacuum-cleaned regularly, to keep them free of grit. If they are badly stained, remove them from the vehicle for scrubbing or sponging, and make quite sure they are dry before refitting. Seats and interior trim panels can be kept clean by wiping with a damp cloth and a proprietary brand of cleaner. If they do become stained (which can be more apparent on light-coloured upholstery), use a little liquid detergent and a soft nail brush to scour the grime out of the grain of the material. Do not forget to keep the headlining clean in the same way as the upholstery. When using liquid cleaners inside the vehicle, do not over-wet the surfaces being cleaned. Excessive damp could get into the seams and padded interior, causing stains, offensive odours or even rot. If the inside of the vehicle gets wet accidentally, it is worthwhile taking some trouble to dry it out properly, particularly where carpets are involved. Do not leave oil or electric heaters inside the vehicle for this purpose.

4 Minor body damage – repair

Minor scratches

1 If the scratch is very superficial, and does not penetrate to the metal of the bodywork, repair is very simple. Lightly rub the area of the scratch with a paintwork renovator or a very fine cutting paste to remove loose paint from the scratch, and to clear the surrounding bodywork of wax polish. Rinse the area with clean water.

2 Apply touch-up paint to the scratch using a fine paint brush; continue to apply fine layers of paint until the surface of the paint in the scratch is level with the surrounding paintwork. Allow the new paint at least two weeks to harden, then blend it into the surrounding paintwork by rubbing the scratch area with a paintwork renovator or a very fine cutting paste. Finally, apply wax polish.

3 Where the scratch has penetrated right through to the metal of the bodywork, causing the metal to rust, a different repair technique is required. Remove any loose rust from the bottom of the scratch with a penknife, then apply rust-inhibiting paint to prevent the formation of rust in the future. Using a rubber or nylon applicator, fill the scratch with bodystopper paste. If required, this paste can be mixed with cellulose thinners to provide a very thin paste which is ideal for filling narrow scratches. Before the stopper-paste in the scratch hardens, wrap a piece of smooth cotton rag around the top of a finger. Dip the finger in cellulose thinners, and quickly sweep it across the surface of the stopper-paste in the scratch; this will ensure that the surface of the stopper-paste is slightly hollowed. The scratch can now be painted over as described earlier in this Section.

Dents

4 When deep denting of the vehicle's bodywork has taken place, the first task is to pull the dent out, until the affected bodywork almost attains its original shape. There is little point in trying to restore the original shape completely, as the metal in the damaged area will have stretched on impact, and cannot be reshaped fully to its original contour. It is better to bring the level of the dent up to a point which is about 3 mm below the level of the surrounding bodywork. In cases where the dent is very shallow anyway, it is not worth trying to pull it out at all. If the underside of the dent is accessible, it can be hammered out gently from behind, using a mallet with a wooden or plastic head. Whilst doing this, hold a suitable block of wood firmly against the outside of the panel, to absorb the impact from the hammer blows and thus prevent a large area of the bodywork from being 'belled-out'.

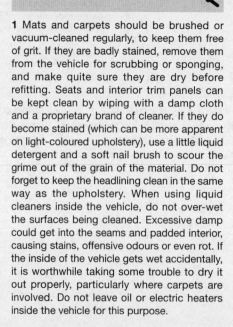

5 Should the dent be in a section of the bodywork which has a double skin, or some other factor making it inaccessible from behind, a different technique is called for. Drill several small holes through the metal inside the area – particularly in the deeper section. Then screw long self-tapping screws into the holes, just sufficiently for them to gain a good purchase in the metal. Now the dent can be pulled out by pulling on the protruding heads of the screws with a pair of pliers.

6 The next stage of the repair is the removal of the paint from the damaged area, and from an inch or so of the surrounding 'sound' bodywork. This is accomplished most easily by using a wire brush or abrasive pad on a power drill, although it can be done just as effectively by hand, using sheets of abrasive paper. To complete the preparation for filling, score the surface of the bare metal with a screwdriver or the tang of a file, or alternatively, drill small holes in the affected area. This will provide a good 'key' for the filler paste.

7 To complete the repair, see the Section on filling and respraying.

Rust holes or gashes

8 Remove all paint from the affected area, and from an inch or so of the surrounding 'sound' bodywork, using an abrasive pad or a wire brush on a power drill. If these are not available, a few sheets of abrasive paper will do the job most effectively. With the paint removed, you will be able to judge the severity of the corrosion, and therefore decide whether to renew the whole panel (if this is possible) or to repair the affected area. New body panels are not as expensive as most people think, and it is often quicker and more satisfactory to fit a new panel than to attempt to repair large areas of corrosion.

9 Remove all fittings from the affected area, except those which will act as a guide to the original shape of the damaged bodywork (eg, headlamp shells, etc). Then, using tin snips or a hacksaw blade, remove all loose metal and any other metal badly affected by corrosion. Hammer the edges of the hole inwards, to create a slight depression for the filler paste.

10 Wire-brush the affected area to remove the powdery rust from the surface of the remaining metal. Paint the affected area with rust-inhibiting paint; if the back of the rusted area is accessible, treat this also.

11 Before filling can take place, it will be necessary to block the hole in some way. This can be achieved with aluminium or plastic mesh, or aluminium tape.

12 Aluminium or plastic mesh, or glass-fibre matting, is probably the best material to use for a large hole. Cut a piece to the approximate size and shape of the hole to be filled, then position it in the hole so that its edges are below the level of the surrounding bodywork. It can be retained in position by several blobs of filler paste around its periphery.

13 Aluminium tape should be used for small or very narrow holes. Pull a piece off the roll, trim it to the approximate size and shape required, then pull off the backing paper (if used) and stick the tape over the hole; it can be overlapped if the thickness of one piece is insufficient. Burnish down the edges of the tape with the handle of a screwdriver or similar, to ensure that the tape is securely attached to the metal underneath.

Filling and respraying

14 Before using this Section, see the Sections on dent, deep scratch, rust holes and gash repairs.

15 Many types of bodyfiller are available, but generally speaking, those proprietary kits which contain a tin of filler paste and a tube of resin hardener are best for this type of repair which can be used directly from the tube. A wide, flexible plastic or nylon applicator will be found invaluable for imparting a smooth and well-contoured finish to the surface of the filler.

16 Mix up a little filler on a clean piece of card or board – measure the hardener carefully (follow the maker's instructions on the pack), otherwise the filler will set too rapidly or too slowly. Using the applicator, apply the filler paste to the prepared area; draw the applicator across the surface of the filler to achieve the correct contour and to level the surface. When a contour that approximates to the correct one is achieved, stop working the paste – if you carry on too long, the paste will become sticky and begin to 'pick-up' on the applicator. Continue to add thin layers of filler paste at 20-minute intervals, until the level of the filler is just proud of the surrounding bodywork.

17 Once the filler has hardened, the excess can be removed using a metal plane or file. From then on, progressively-finer grades of abrasive paper should be used, starting with a 40-grade production paper, and finishing with a 400-grade wet-and-dry paper. Always wrap the abrasive paper around a flat rubber, cork, or wooden block – otherwise the surface of the filler will not be completely flat. During the smoothing of the filler surface, the wet-and-dry paper should be periodically rinsed in water. This will ensure that a very smooth finish is imparted to the filler at the final stage.

18 At this stage, the 'dent' should be surrounded by a ring of bare metal, which in turn should be encircled by the finely 'feathered' edge of the good paintwork. Rinse the repair area with clean water, until all the dust produced by the rubbing-down operation has gone.

19 Spray the whole area with a light coat of primer – this will show up any imperfections in the surface of the filler. Repair these imperfections with fresh filler paste or bodystopper, and again smooth the surface with abrasive paper. If bodystopper is used, it can be mixed with cellulose thinners, to form a thin paste which is ideal for filling small holes. Repeat this spray-and-repair procedure until you are satisfied that the surface of the filler, and the feathered edge of the paintwork, are perfect. Clean the repair area with clean water, and allow to dry fully.

20 The repair area is now ready for final spraying. Paint spraying must be carried out in a warm, dry, windless and dust-free atmosphere. This condition can be created artificially if you have access to a large indoor working area, but if you are forced to work in the open, you will have to pick your day very carefully. If you are working indoors, dousing the floor in the work area with water will help to settle the dust which would otherwise be in the atmosphere. If the repair area is confined to one body panel, mask off the surrounding panels; this will help to minimise the effects of a slight mis-match in paint colours. Bodywork fittings (eg chrome strips, door handles etc) will also need to be masked off. Use genuine masking tape, and several thickness of newspaper, for the masking operations.

21 Before starting to spray, agitate the aerosol can thoroughly, then spray a test area (an old tin, or similar) until the technique is mastered. Cover the repair area with a thick coat of primer; the thickness should be built up using several thin layers of paint, rather than one thick one. Using 400 grade wet-and-dry paper, rub down the surface of the primer until it is smooth. While doing this, the work area should be thoroughly doused with water, and the wet-and-dry paper periodically rinsed in water. Allow to dry before spraying on more paint.

22 Spray on the top coat, again building up the thickness by using several thin layers of paint. Start spraying at the top of the repair area, and then, using a side to side motion, work downwards until the whole repair area and about 2 inches of the surrounding original paintwork is covered. Remove all masking material 10 to 15 minutes after spraying on the final coat of paint.

23 Allow the new paint at least two weeks to harden, then, using a paintwork renovator or a very fine cutting paste, blend the edges of the paint into the existing paintwork. Finally, apply wax polish.

Plastic components

24 With the use of more and more plastic body components by the vehicle manufacturers (eg, bumpers. spoilers, and in some cases major body panels), rectification of more serious damage to such items has become a matter of either entrusting repair work to a specialist in this field, or renewing complete components. Repair of such damage by the DIY owner is not feasible, owing to the cost of the equipment and materials required for effecting such repairs. The basic technique involves making a groove along the line of the crack in the plastic, using a rotary burr in a power drill. The damaged part is then welded back together, using a hot air gun to heat up and fuse a plastic filler rod into the groove. Any excess plastic is then removed, and the area rubbed down to a smooth finish. It is important that a filler rod of the correct plastic is used, as body components can be made of different types (eg, polycarbonate, ABS, polypropylene).

25 Damage of a less serious nature (abrasions, minor cracks etc) can be repaired by the DIY owner using a two-part epoxy filler repair material which can be used directly from the tube. Once mixed in equal proportions, this is used in similar fashion to the bodywork filler used on metal panels. The filler is usually cured in twenty to thirty minutes, ready for sanding and painting.

26 If the owner is renewing a complete component himself, or if he has repaired it with epoxy filler, he will be left with the problem of finding a suitable paint for finishing which is compatible with the type of plastic used. At one time, the use of a universal paint was not possible, owing to the complex range of plastics met with in body component applications. Standard paints, generally speaking, will not bond to plastic or rubber satisfactorily, but professional matched paints, to match any plastic or rubber finish, can be obtained from some dealers. However, it is now possible to obtain a plastic body parts finishing kit which consists of a pre-primer treatment, a primer and coloured top coat. Full instructions are normally supplied with a kit, but basically the method of use is to first apply the pre-primer to the component concerned, and allow it to dry for up to 30 minutes. Then the primer is applied, and left to dry for about an hour before finally applying the special-coloured top coat. The result is a correctly coloured component, where the paint will flex with the plastic or rubber, a property that standard paint does not normally possess.

5 Major body damage – repair

1 Where serious damage has occurred, or large areas need renewal due to neglect, it means that complete new panels will need welding-in, and this is best left to professionals. If the damage is due to impact, it will also be necessary to check completely the alignment of the bodyshell, and this can only be carried out accurately by a Mazda dealer or specialist using jigs. If the body is left misaligned, it is primarily dangerous, as the car will not handle properly, and secondly, uneven stresses will be imposed on the steering, suspension and possibly transmission, causing abnormal wear, or complete failure, particularly to such items as the tyres.

6 Front bumper – removal and refitting

Removal

1 Slacken the front roadwheel nuts, then raise the front of the vehicle and support it securely on axle stands (see *Jacking and vehicle support*). Remove the front roadwheels.

2 Open the bonnet and remove the eight bolts that secure the upper trailing edge of the bumper **(see illustration)**.

3 Remove the ten screws securing the lower trailing edge of the bumper.

4 Pull out the trim covers, and undo the screw each side in the grille area **(see illustrations)**.

5 Release the fasteners securing the front section of the wheel arch liners to the bumper, and pull the liners rearwards a little to access the remaining bumper fasteners **(see illustration)**.

6 Disconnect the electrical connectors from the front fog lights (where fitted).

7 Undo the two nuts and bolt each side securing the bumper in the wheel arch area **(see illustration)**.

8 With the help of an assistant, manoeuvre the bumper forwards.

Refitting

9 Refitting is a reversal of removal.

7 Rear bumper – removal and refitting

Removal

1 Chock the front wheels, slacken the rear roadwheel nuts, then raise the rear of the vehicle and support it securely on axle stands (see *Jacking and vehicle support*). Remove the roadwheels.

2 Remove the rear lights as described in Chapter 12 Section 8.

3 Undo the three bolts and remove the rear section of the wheel arch liner each side **(see illustration)**.

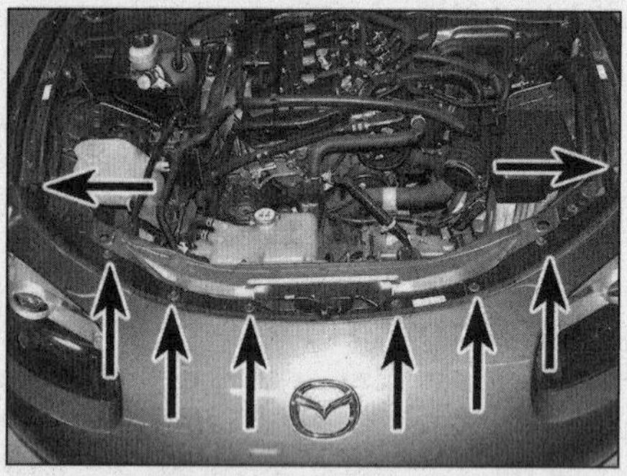

6.2 Remove the eight bolts along the upper edge of the bumper

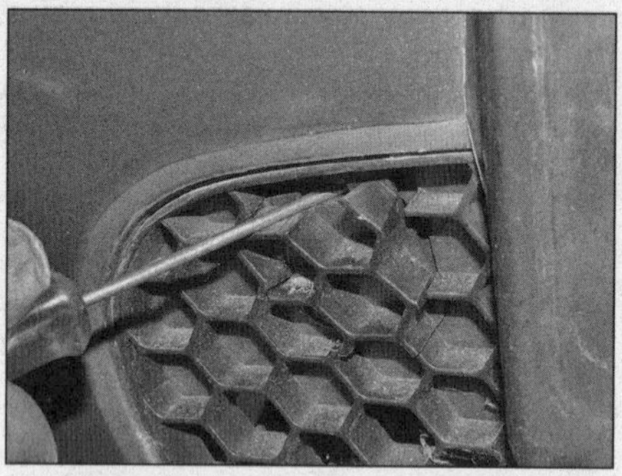

6.4a Depress the clip and pull out the trim covers

6.4b On some models the the cover and screws are within the grille area, whilst on others, they are just above

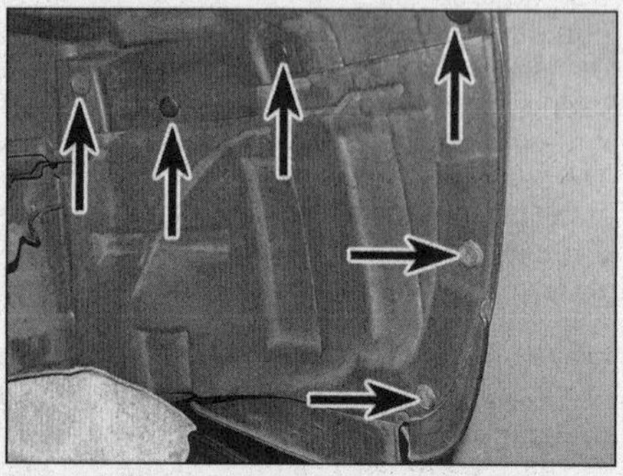

6.5 Remove the fasteners and pull back the wheelarch liner

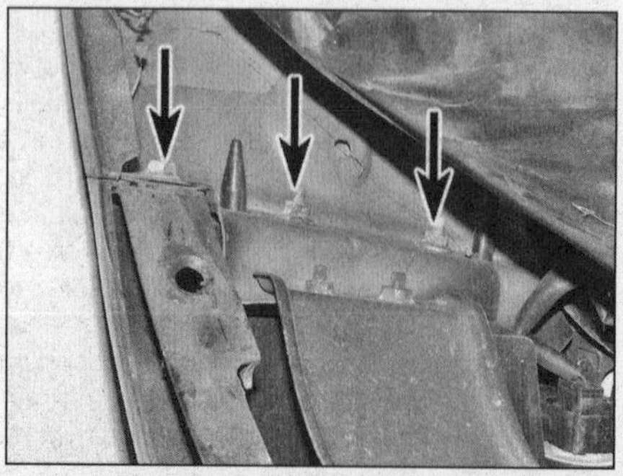

6.7 Undo the nuts/bolt each side securing the bumper

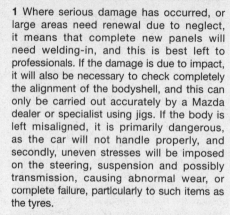

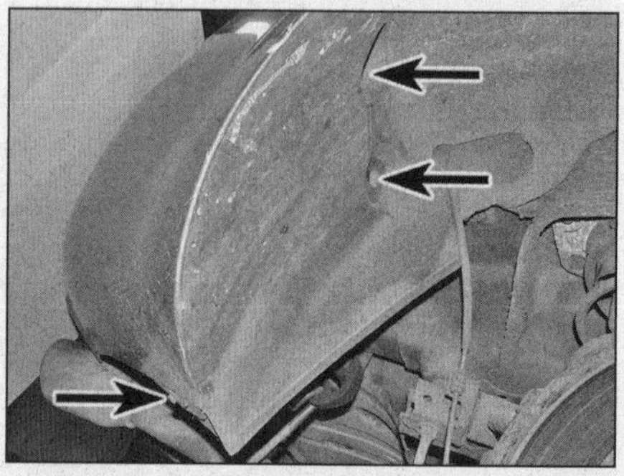

7.3 Undo the bolts and remove the wheel arch liner section

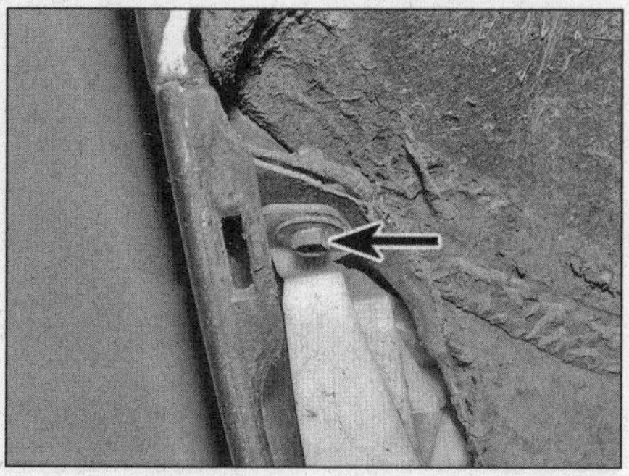

7.4 Undo the bolt at the upper edge of the bumper

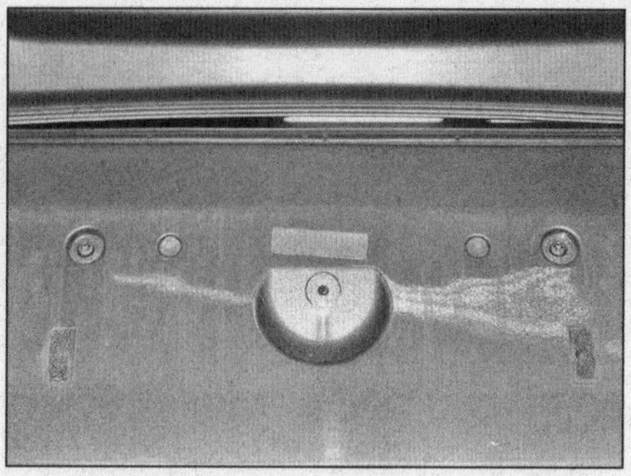

7.5 Undo the Torx screws behind the number plate

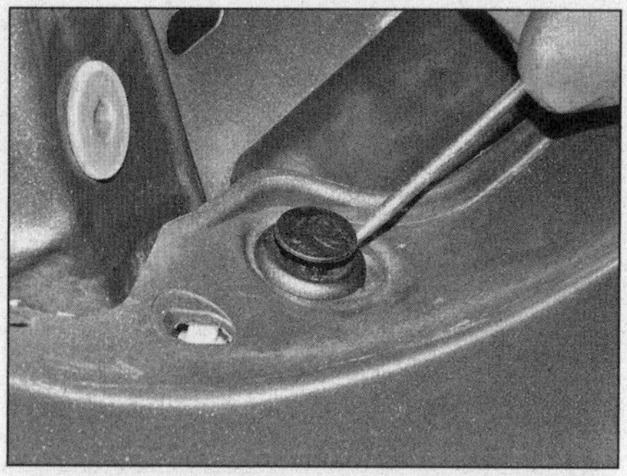

7.6 Remove the expansion rivets in the light apertures

4 Remove the bolt each side securing the front, upper edge of the bumper to the rear wing **(see illustration)**.

5 Remove the number plate, then undo the two Torx screws now exposed **(see illustration)**.

6 Prise up the centre pins and lever out the plastic expansion rivet each side in the rear light apertures **(see illustration)**.

7 Undo the two screws at the upper edge of the bumper, then with the help of an assistant, pull out the front edges slightly and manoeuvre the bumper rearwards **(see illustrations)**.

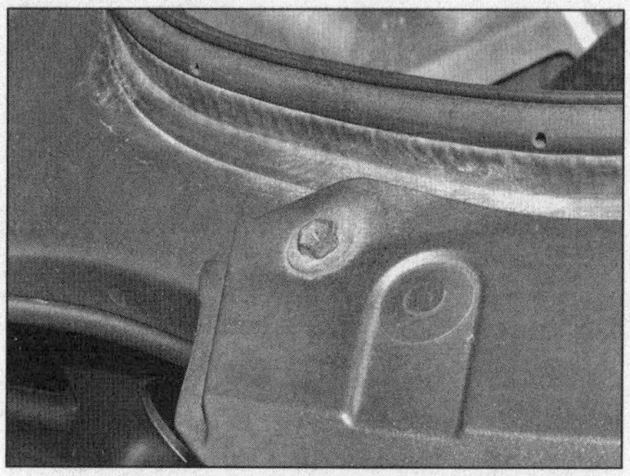

7.7a Undo the screw each side at the upper edge of the bumper

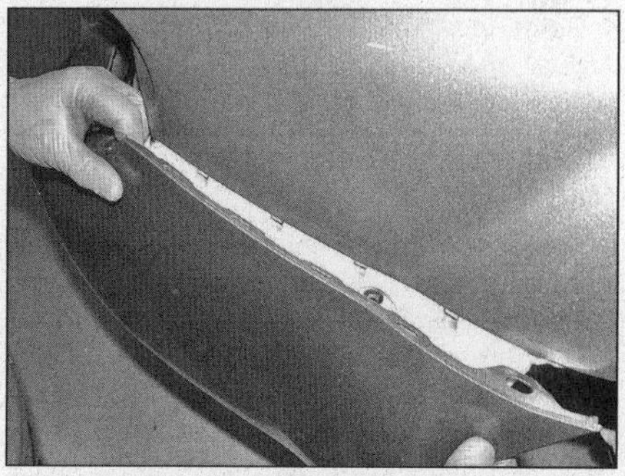

7.7b Pull out the front edges slightly and remove the bumper

Refitting

8 Refitting is a reverse of the removal procedure ensuring that the bumper ends are correctly positioned.

8 Bonnet – removal, refitting and adjustment

Removal and refitting

1 Disconnect the battery negative lead as described in Chapter. 5A Section 4

2 Make alignment marks around the hinges to ensure proper alignment during refitting.

3 Use blankets or pads to cover the cowl area of the body and wings. This will protect the body and paint as the wing is removed.

4 Have an assistant support the bonnet, then undo the hinge-to-bonnet bolts and remove it from the vehicle **(see illustration)**.

5 Refitting is the reverse of removal.

Adjustment

6 Fore-and-aft and side-to-side adjustment of the bonnet is achieved by moving the hinge after slackening the bolts where it attaches to the inner wing. Access to the bolts is only possible once the wings have been removed. This is beyond the scope of this manual. Consequently, we recommend that bonnet alignment should be entrusted to a body repair workshop.

9 Bonnet lock and release cable – removal and refitting

Lock

1 Trace the electrical lead from the lock to the wiring plug and disconnect it.

2 Pull the bonnet release cable out of its retaining bracket **(see illustration)**, then disengage the cable end from the slot in the lock mechanism.

3 Make a mark around the lock to aid alignment when refitting, then remove the bonnet lock mounting bolts **(see illustration)**. Remove the lock.

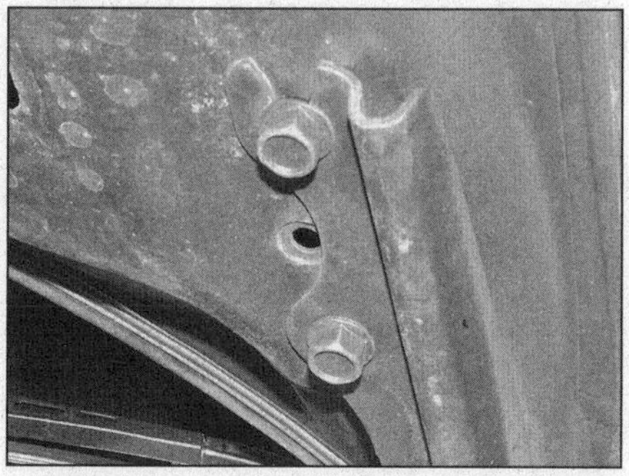

8.4 Slacken the upper bolt, and remove the lower

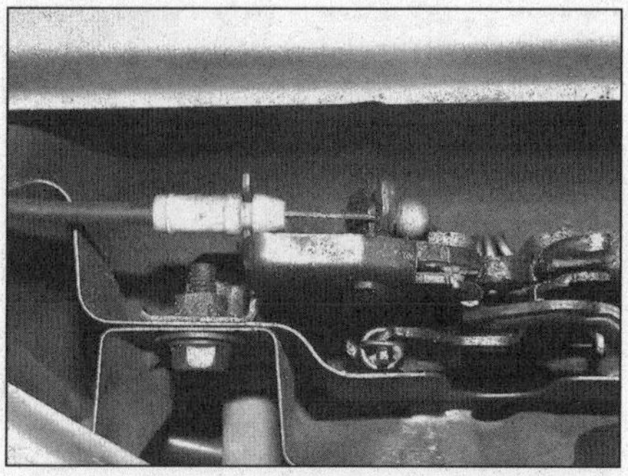

9.2 Slide the cable from the bracket, and disengage the end

9.3 Bonnet lock mounting bolts

9.7 Insert a screwdriver into the slot, and pull it rearwards to release the tab (lever removed for clarity)

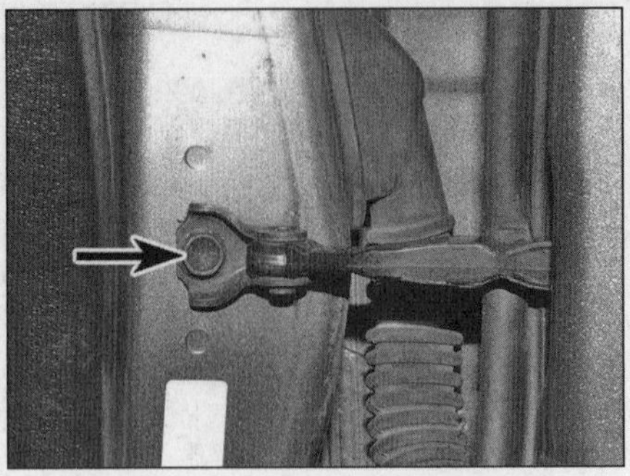

10.4 Check strap retaining bolt

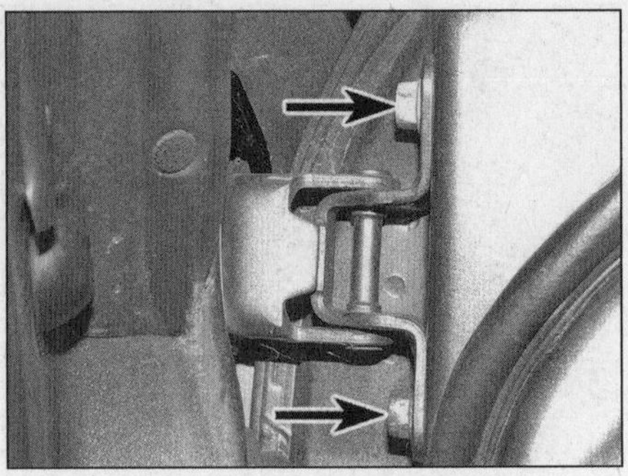

10.5 Door hinge bolts

4 Refitting is the reverse of removal. **Note:** *Adjust the lock so the bonnet engages securely when closed and the bonnet buffers are slightly compressed.*

Cable

5 Disconnect the bonnet release cable from the lock as described previously.

6 Attach a piece of thin wire or string to the end of the cable and unfasten all remaining cable retaining clips.

7 The connet release lever is secured to the trim panel at the lower right-hand corner of the instrument panel by three small mounting tabs and a single larger mounting tab. To remove it, pull the release lever as if you were releasing the bonnet latch and insert a screwdriver into the slot **(see illustration)**. Pry the tab loose by pulling the screwdriver handle toward you so that the screwdriver tip forces then tab down and disengages it from the trim panel. Pull the release lever assembly down and toward you to disengage the large mounting tab at the front end of the release lever assembly.

8 Pull the cable and grommet rearward into the passenger compartment until you can see the wire or string. Ensure that the new cable has a grommet attached, then remove the old cable from the wire or string and replace it with the new cable.

9 Working in the engine compartment, pull the wire or string back through the bulkhead, pulling the cable with it.

10 The remainder of refitting is a reversal of removal. **Note:** *Push the cable grommet with your fingers from inside the passenger compartment to seat the grommet into the bulkhead correctly.*

10 Door – removal, refitting and adjustment

Removal and refitting

1 Lower the window completely then disconnect the battery negative lead as described in Chapter 5A, Section 4.

2 Open the door all the way and support it on jacks or blocks covered with rags to prevent damaging the paint.

3 Pull the wiring conduit from the pillar, then fold down the lever and disconnect the wiring plug.

4 Undo the bolt securing the check strap to the pillar **(see illustration)**.

5 Mark around the door hinges and hinge bolts to aid alignment when refitting **(see illustration)**.

6 Remove the hinge-to-door bolts and carefully withdraw the door.

7 Refitting is the reverse of removal. Adjust and securely tighten the door hinge bolts and striker bolts, if removed, as described below.

Adjustment

8 Following refitting, locate the alignment marks made during door removal. Make sure the door is aligned properly and adjust it if necessary as follows:

a) Adjustments are made by loosening the hinge-to-body bolts and moving the door, as necessary. A special offset tool may be required to reach some of the bolts.

b) The door lock striker can also be adjusted both up-and-down and sideways to provide a positive engagement with the locking mechanism. This is done by loosening the screws and moving the striker by hand or by lightly tapping with a soft-faced hammer, as necessary.

c) Check the alignment of the wedge attached to the lower part of the doorjamb with the dovetail in the door. Adjust if necessary by loosening the wedge screws and moving the wedge up or down.

11 Door inner trim panel – removal and refitting

Removal

1 Remove the trim cover from the inside door handle and remove the trim panel retaining screw **(see illustration)**.

Early models

2 Remove the trim cap from the upper end of the door pull **(see illustration)**.

Later models

3 Using a blunt, flat-bladed screwdriver, carefully prise the door pull handle cover away from the door **(see illustration)**.

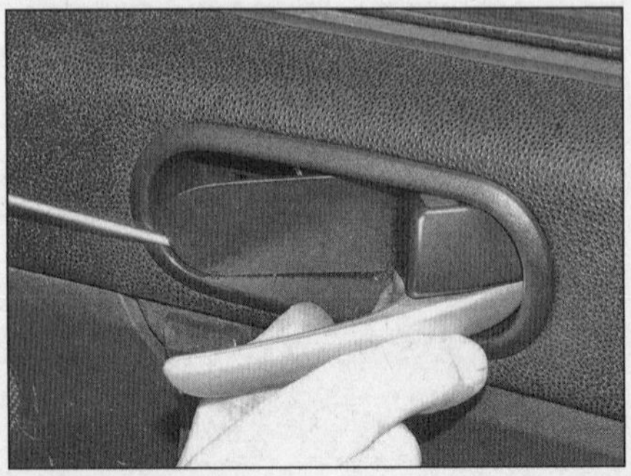

11.1 Prise out the trim cover and undo the screw exposed

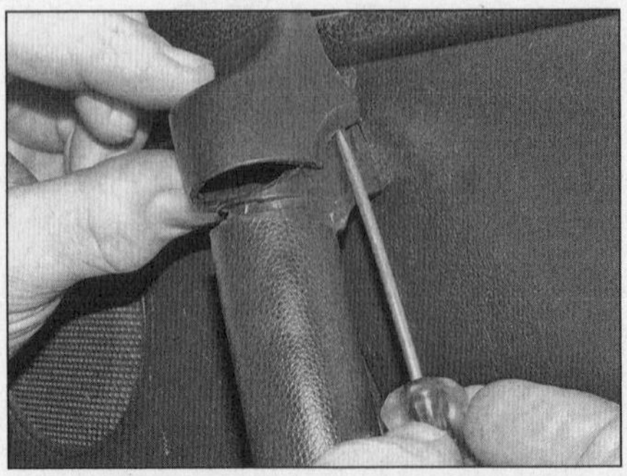

11.2 Release the clip each side and slide up the cap

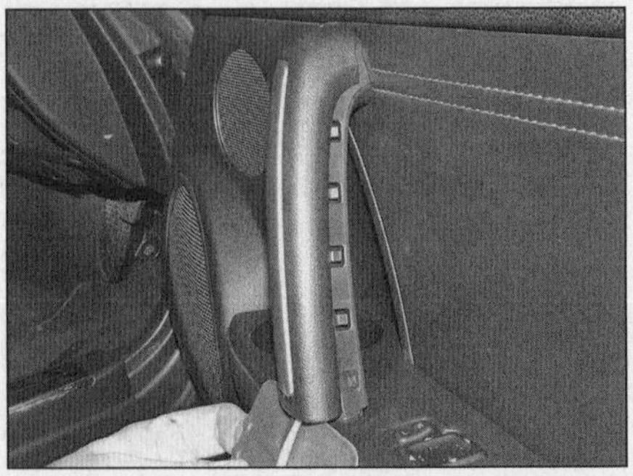

11.3 Prise the handle cover inwards from the door

All models

4 Remove the retaining screw from the upper end of the door pull, and inside the cup holder **(see illustration)**.

5 Remove the door trim panel **(see illustration)**. Use a trim panel removal tool to prise loose the clips. Start from the bottom of the trim panel and work around the perimeter until all the fasteners have been released from the door.

6 Pull the trim panel away from the door slightly and disengage the cable ends from the inside door handle. To disengage each cable end, align the foot on the lower end of the connecting pin with the elongated hole in the handle lever, then lift the pin straight up **(see illustration)**.

7 Disconnect all electrical connectors from the inside of the and manoeuvre it from place.

8 When refitting the door trim panel, start with the upper edge. Align the three clips along the upper edge and pull down on the trim panel to engage the clips, then pop all the other clips into place.

9 The remainder of refitting is a reversal of removal.

Refitting

10 To refit the door trim panel, first press the weatherproof membrane back into place. If necessary, add more sealant to hold it in place. Refit the interior release handle and polystyrene block if it was removed.

11 Prior to refitting the door trim panel, be sure to refit any clips which may have come out of the door trim panel during removal.

12 Place the door trim panel in position, making sure that any door panel electrical connectors are connected or routed through the panel as necessary. Press the door trim panel into place until the clips are seated.

13 The remainder of refitting is the reverse of the removal steps. If the vehicle has manual

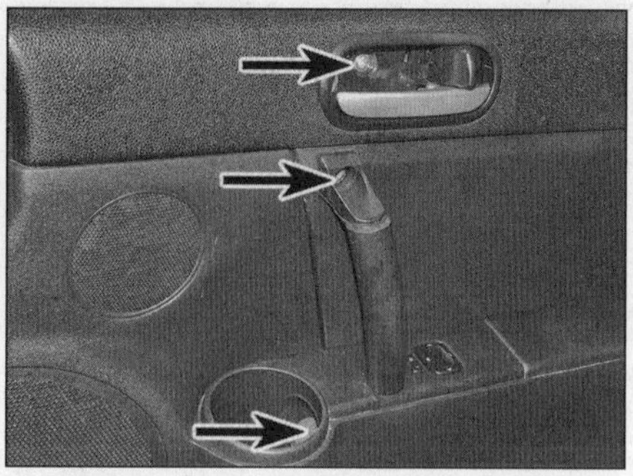

11.4 Door inner trim panel retraining screws

windows, place the clip on the window winder handle, then push the handle onto the shaft until the clip engages.

12 Door handle and lock components – removal and refitting

Door unit

Note: *The door unit is the metal inner door panel that protects the trim panel from moisture, just like the plastic watershield used on earlier models. The door unit must be removed to remove the door latch and actuator, the outside door handle, the window glass, the window glass regulator and the outside power mirror.*

1 Remove the door trim panel as described in Section 11.

2 Remove the door speaker as described in Chapter 12 Section 18.

3 Disconnect the electrical connectors for the power mirror, the door lock actuator and the electric window motor, remove all door

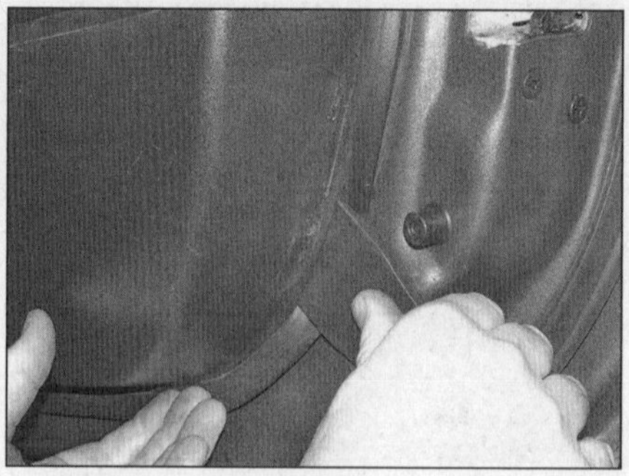

11.5 Carefully prise the trim panel from the door

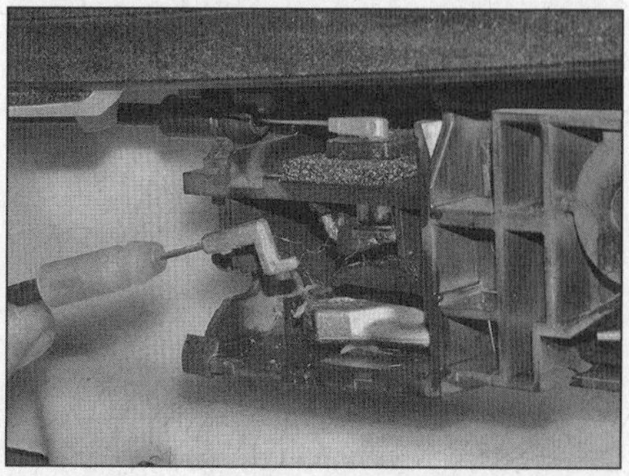

11.6 Disconnect the cable from the interior release handle

unit fasteners and remove the door unit **(see illustrations)**.

4 Unclip the wiring harness from the door panel as it's withdrawn.

5 Refitting is a reversal of removal.

Door lock and actuator

6 Remove the door unit as described previously in this Section.

7 Prise out the grommet, undo the retaining

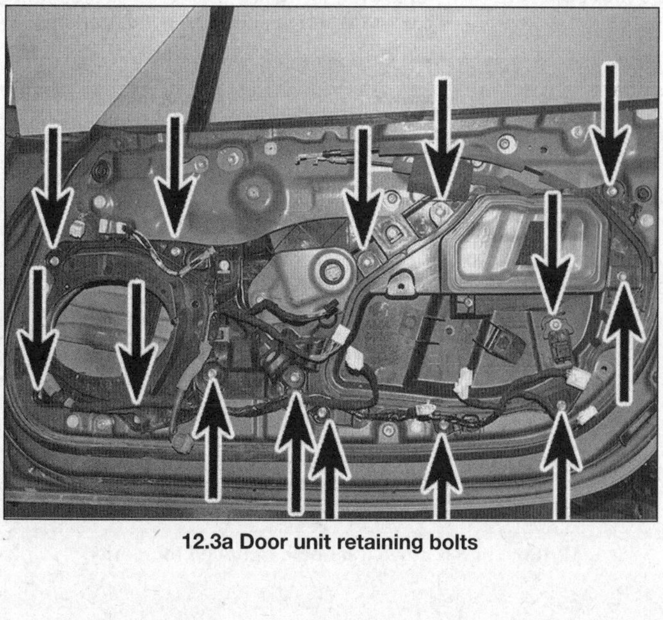

12.3a Door unit retaining bolts

12.3b Remove the door unit

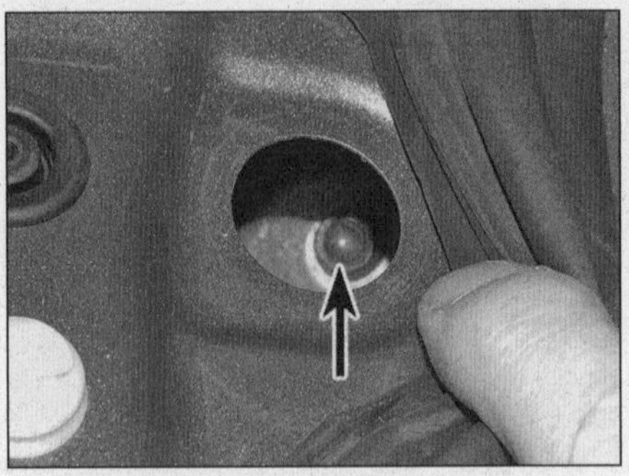
12.7a Prise out the grommet, undo the bolt...

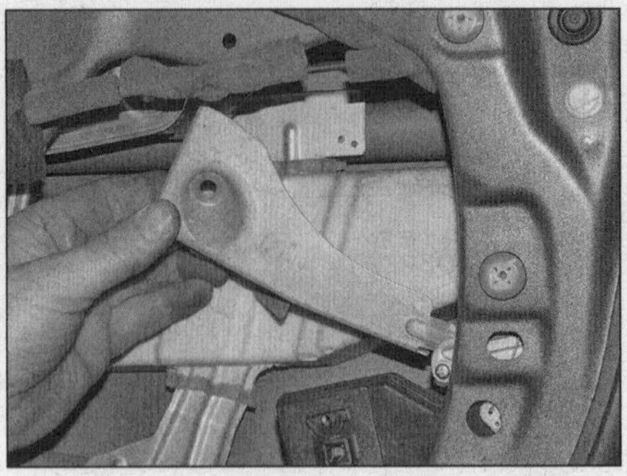
12.7b... and remove the lock shield

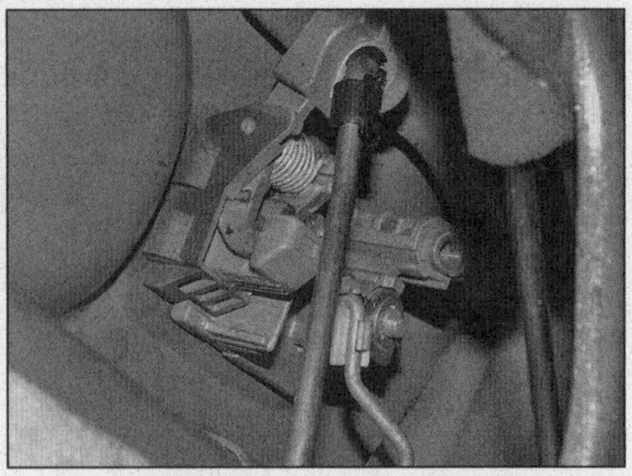
12.8 Unclip and disconnect the rods from the lock cylinder (where applicable) and the exterior door handle

12.10 Door lock retaining screws

12.11 Door lock operating cables

12.17a Remove the handle front bolt...

12.17b... and the rear bolt

bolt and remove the lock shield **(see illustrations)**.

8 Disengage the rods from the key lock cylinder and the exterior door handle **(see illustration)**.

9 Unclip the cable from the door.

10 Remove the 3 door lock retaining screws **(see illustration)** and remove the lock and actuator.

11 If required, disconnect the operating cables from the lock assembly **(see illustration)**.

12 Refitting is a reversal of removal.

Exterior handle

13 Remove the door unit as described earlier in this Section.

14 Disengage the rod from the outside door handle **(see illustration 12.8)**.

15 Prise out the rubber grommet, undo the bolt and remove the lock shield **(see illustrations 12.7a and 12.7b)**.

16 Disengage the rod from the exterior door handle **(see illustration 12.8)**.

17 Undo the handle retaining bolts **(see illustrations)**.

18 Working from inside the door, grasp the lock cylinder assembly, rotate it 45° anti-clockwise and remove it **(see illustrations)**.

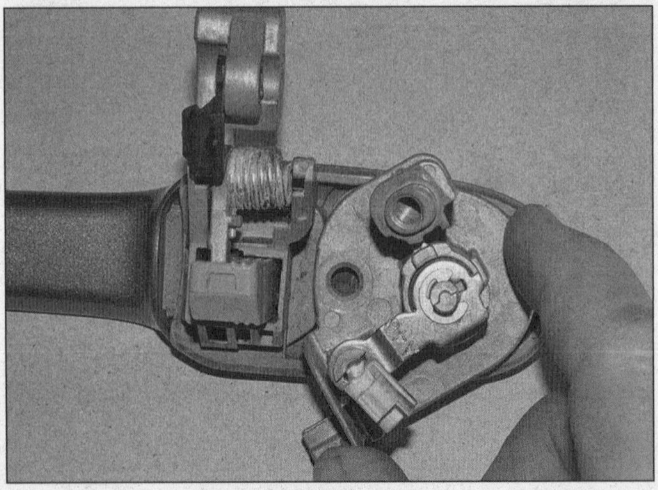
12.18a Rotate the cylinder assembly 45° anti-clockwise...

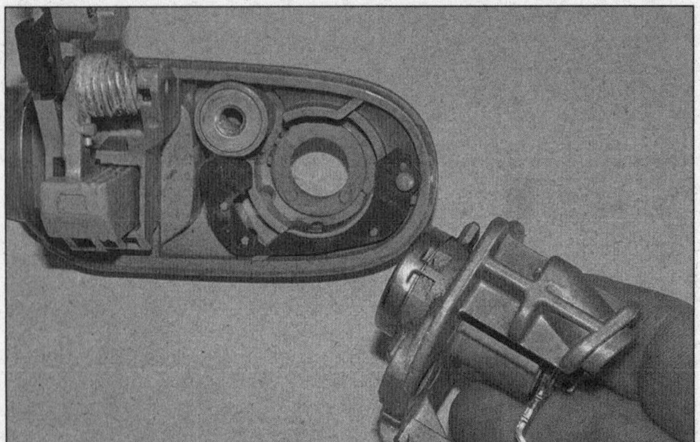
12.18b... and remove it (handle removed for clarity)

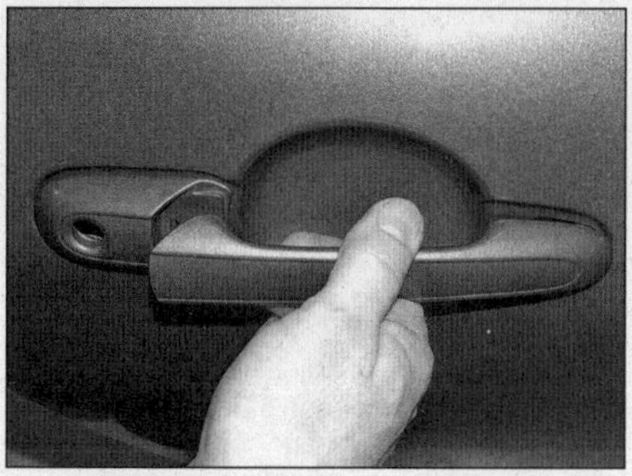

12.19a Pull out the door handle...

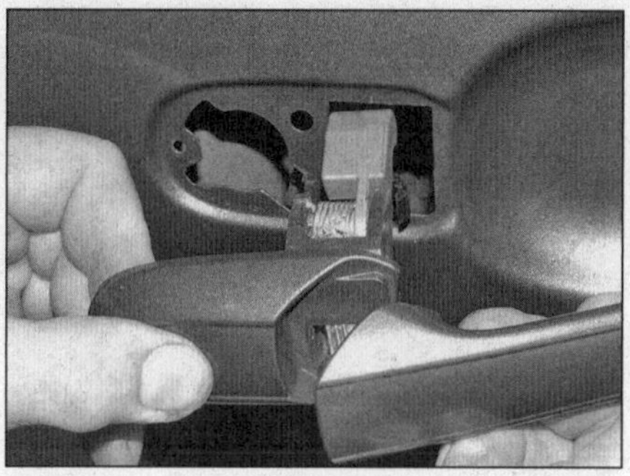

12.19b... and manoeuvre the rear part from the door

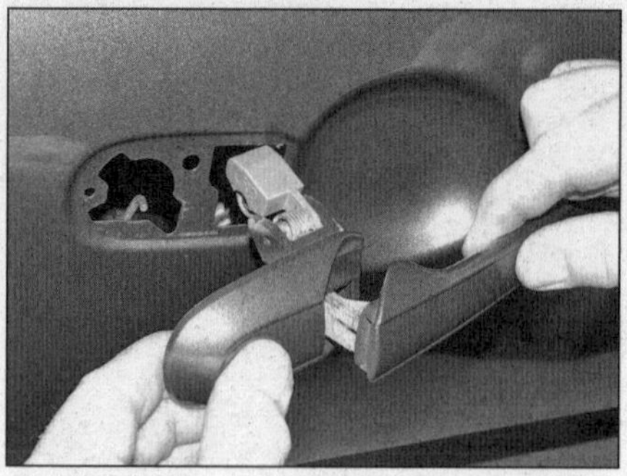

12.20 Engage the handle with the lock cylinder assembly, and manoeuvre it into place

19 Pull the door handle lever out (as if you were opening the door) and manoeuvre the rear part of the outside handle from the door **(see illustrations)**. Be careful not to scratch the paint.

20 Refitting is a reversal of removal **(see illustration)**.

Lock cylinder

21 Lock cylinder removal is part of the exterior handle removal procedure, described previously in this Section.

13 Door window glass – removal, refitting and adjustment

Door sliding glass

Removal and refitting

1 Lower the door window glass so that the top of the glass is approximately 110 mm above the beltline moulding **(see illustration)**.

2 Remove the door unit as described in Section 12.

3 Undo the retaining bolts **(see illustration)** and remove the glass stoppers.

4 Remove the nuts that secure the door window glass to the regulator **(see illustration)**.

5 Pull up the window glass and manoeuvre it out of the door, tilting the upper edge of the glass inward (toward the vehicle).

6 Refitting is a reversal of removal.

Adjustment

7 With the glass refitted, slacken the glass stopper retaining bolts, the window regulator nuts, and the glass retaining nuts, then temporarily reconnect the regulator motor wiring plug. Fully close the window.

8 Align the rear edge of the glass with the rear edge of the beltline moulding lip **(see illustration)**. Note: The standard position for the rear edge of the moulding cap is 1.0 mm from the rear edge of the door panel.

9 Lightly tighten the window regulator and glass retaining nuts.

10 Align the upper edge of the glass with the 1/4 light pillar. The edge of the glass should be 0.0 – 1.5 mm below the top of the pillar **(see illustration)**.

11 Check and if necessary, adjust the position of the glass so its height is 347 – 349 mm above the beltline, measured 210 mm from the rear edge of the glass **(see illustration)**.

12 With the glass correctly aligned, fully

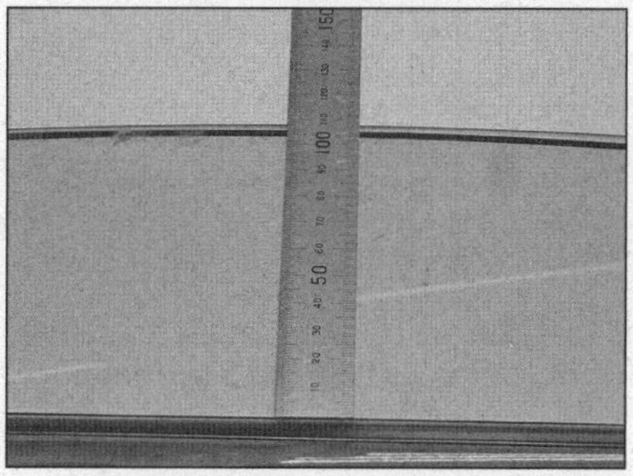

13.1 Set the glass 110 mm above the moulding

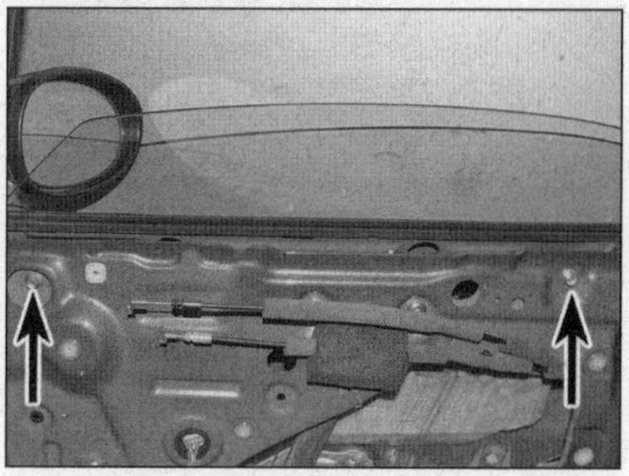

13.3 Undo the glass stoppers retaining bolts

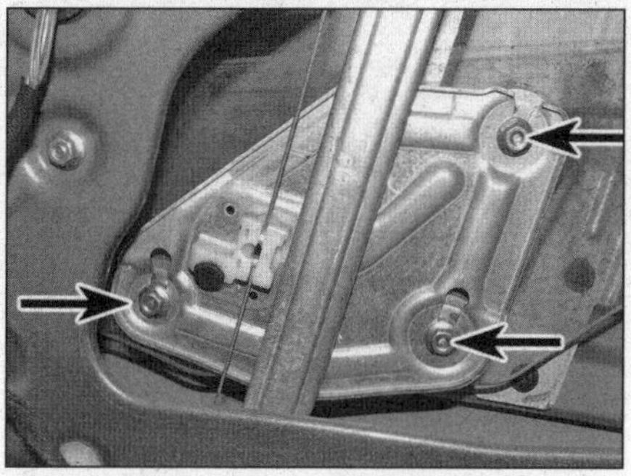

13.4 Undo the nuts securing the glass to the regulator

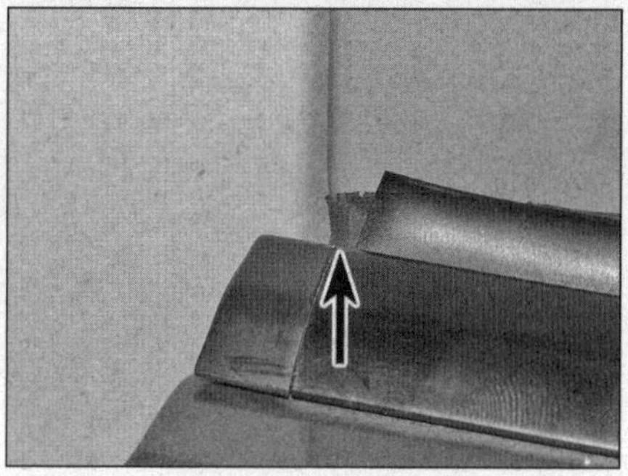

13.8 Align the glass with the rear edge of the moulding

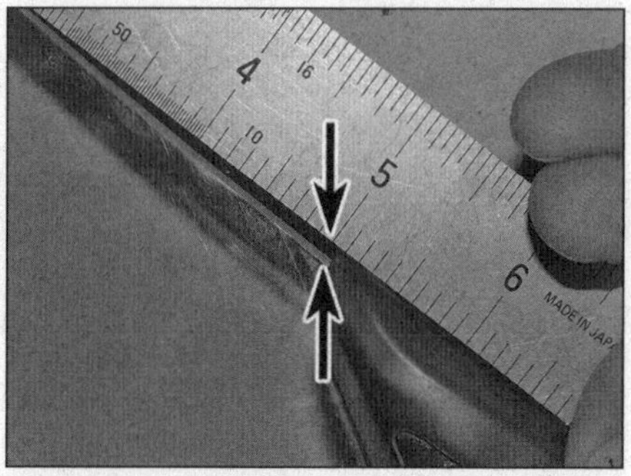

13.10 The edge of the glass should be 0.0 – 1.5 mm below the top of the pillar

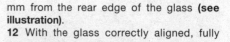

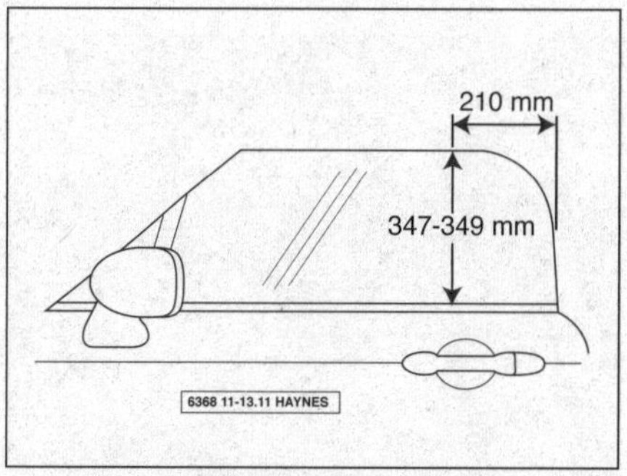

13.11 Set the glass so the top edge is 347 – 349 mm above the beltline, 210 mm from the rear edge

tighten the window regulator and glass retaining nuts, then press-down slightly on the glass stoppers and tighten their retaining bolts.

13 Check that the window opens and closes smoothly, then refit the door unit.

Quarter glass

Removal and refitting

14 Remove the door window glass as previously described in this Section.

15 Remove the nut and bolts **(see illustrations)**, then remove the door glass guide.

16 Remove the bolts and detach the quarter glass from the guide **(see illustration)**.

17 When refitting position the adjustment nut on the guide as shown **(see illustration)**. The remainder of refitting is a reversal of removal.

14 Door window regulator – removal and refitting

1 Remove the door window glass as described in Section 13.

2 Remove the window regulator retaining nuts **(see illustrations)**, then manoeuvre the regulator from the door.

3 Refitting is a reversal of removal

15 Boot lid – removal, refitting and adjustment

Caution: The boot lid is heavy and somewhat awkward to remove and refit – at least two people should perform this procedure.

Removal and refitting

1 Open the boot, then disconnect the battery negative lead as described in Chapter 5A Section 4.

2 Disconnect the boot lid wiring harness connector, remove the clips that secure the boot lid harness and set the harness safely aside where it won't be damaged during boot lid removal.

3 Make alignment marks around the hinges with a marking pen or paint **(see illustration)**.

4 Pry off the protective clips from each end of the two boot lid struts **(see illustration)**. With an assistant holding up the trunk lid, pry loose the spherical bearings at each end of the two trunk lid struts and remove both struts.

5 While an assistant supports the boot lid, remove the lid-to-hinge nuts on both sides and remove it.

6 Refitting is the reverse of removal. Note: When refitting the boot lid, align the hinges with the marks made during removal.

Adjustment

7 Fore-and-aft and side-to-side adjustment of the boot lid is accomplished by moving the

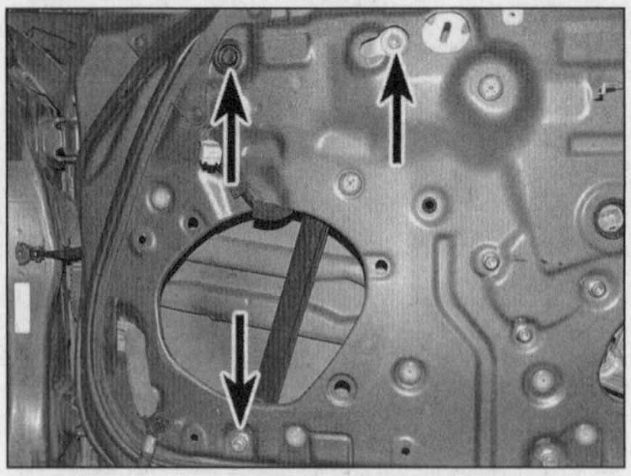

13.15a Prise out the grommet, undo the bolts/nut...

13.15b... and slide the quarter glass and guide upwards from the door

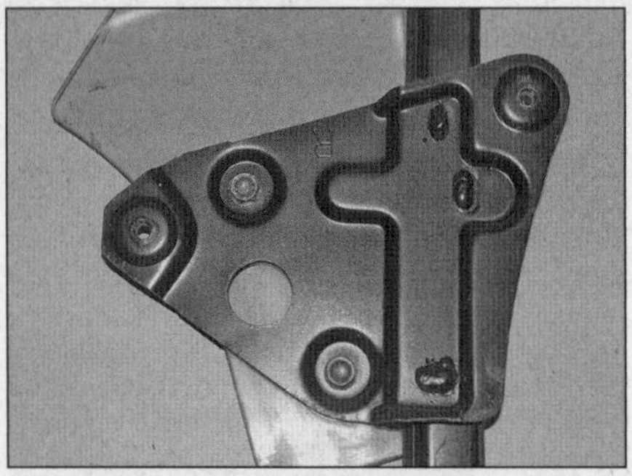

13.16 Undo the bolts and separate the glass from the guide

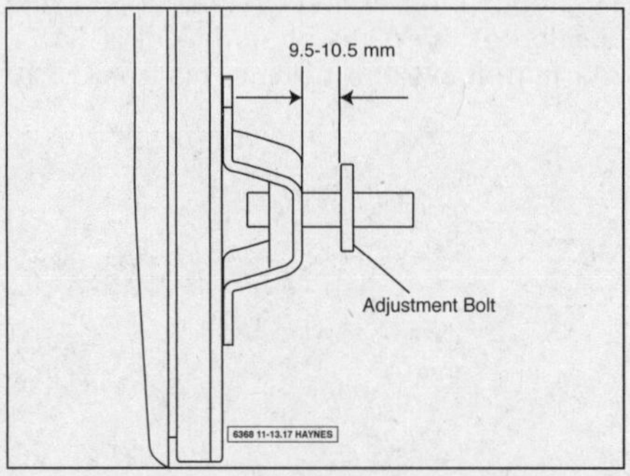

13.17 Position the adjustment bolt as shown

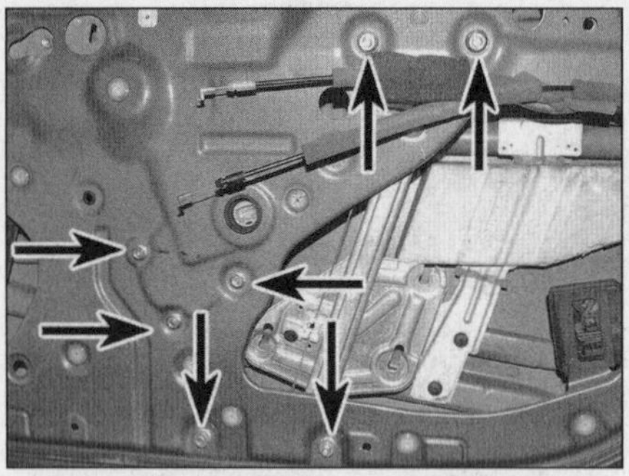

14.2a Undo the window regulator nuts...

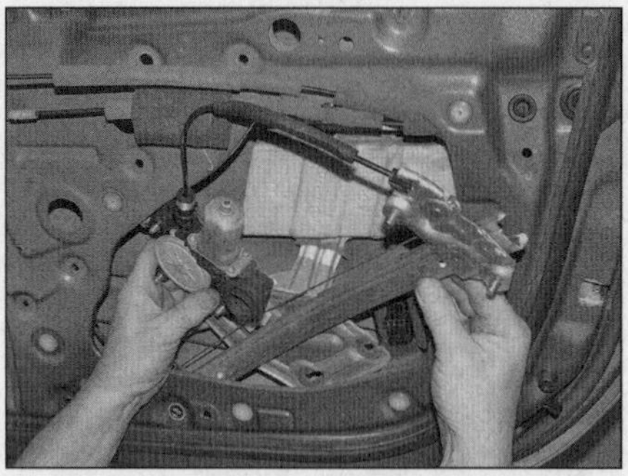

14.2b... and manoeuvre the regulator assembly from the door

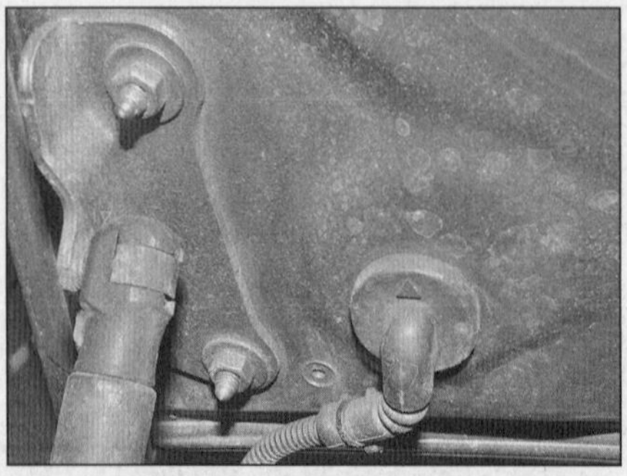

15.3 Make alignment marks around the hinges

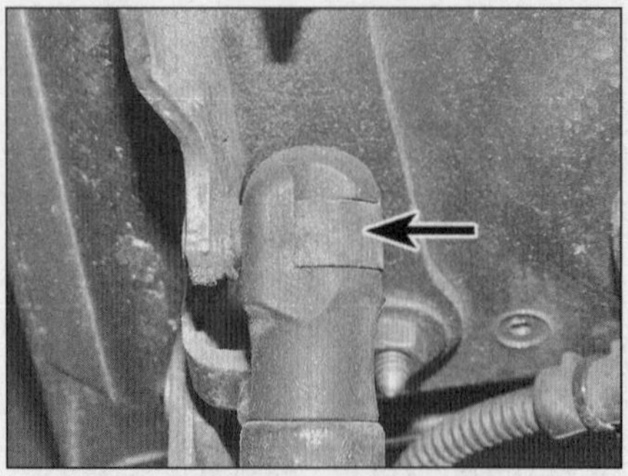

15.4 Prise off the clips from the struts

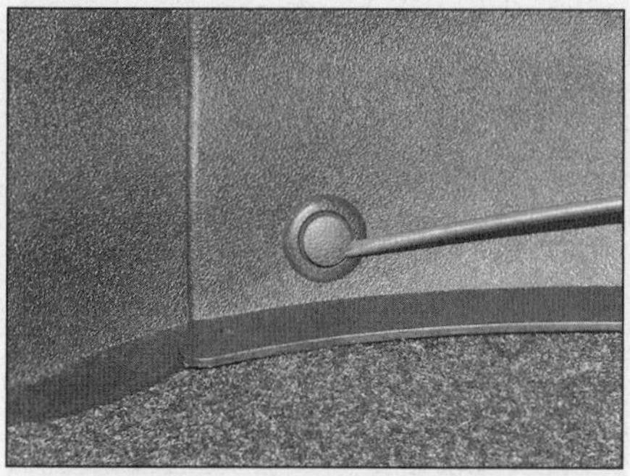

16.1 Prise up the centre pins and lever out the plastic expansion rivets

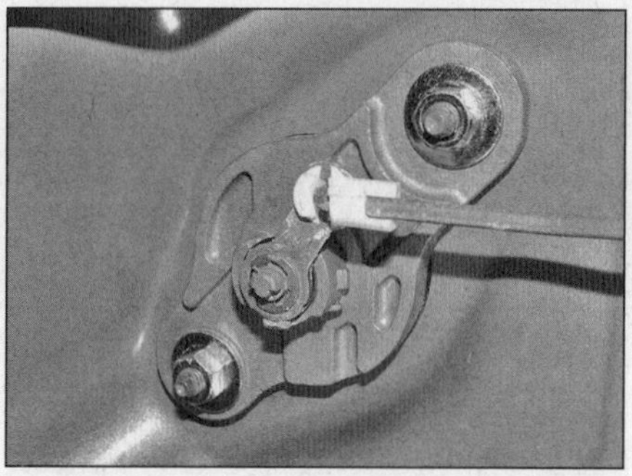

16.2 Disconnect the actuator rod from the lock cylinder

16.3 Boot lock retaining bolts

lid in relation to the hinge after loosening the bolts or nuts.

8 Scribe a line around the entire hinge plate as described earlier in this Section so you can determine the amount of movement.

9 Loosen the nuts and move the boot lid into correct alignment. Move it only a little at a time. Tighten the hinge nuts and carefully lower the boot lid to check the alignment.

16 Boot lid lock components – removal and refitting

Boot lid lock

1 Open the boot, prise up the centre pins, lever out the plastic expansion rivets and pull the rear trim panel forwards to remove it **(see illustration)**.

2 Disengage the boot lid lock actuator rod **(see illustration)**.

3 Make alignment marks between the lock and the panel, then undo the retaining bolts and remove the lock **(see illustration)**. Disconnect any wiring plugs as the lock is withdrawn.

4 Refitting is the reverse of removal.

Boot lock cylinder

5 Open the boot, prise up the centre pins, lever out the plastic expansion rivets, then pull the rear trim panel forwards to remove it **(see illustration 16.1)**.

6 Prise the retaining clip loose from the actuator rod, and separate the actuator rod from the lock cylinder **(see illustration 16.2)**.

7 Trace the electrical lead to its wiring plug and disconnect it.

8 Undo the retaining nuts and take the lock cylinder out of the rear body panel **(see illustration 16.2)**.

9 Refitting is the reverse of removal.

17 Central locking components – removal and refitting

Door/boot lock actuators

1 The actuators are integral with the door/boot locks. Refer to Section 12.

Keyless control module

2 Unlock the doors, then disconnect the battery negative lead as described in Chapter 5A, Section 4.

3 Remove the side panel from the passengers side footwell, as described in Section 28.

4 Undo the nut and bolt, them manoeuvre the keyless control module from place **(see illustration)**. Disconnect the wiring plugs as the module is withdrawn.

5 Refitting is the reverse of removal. Note that if a new module is fitted, is must be programmed using Mazda diagnostic equipment.

Keyless receiver unit

6 Disconnect the battery negative lead as described in Chapter 5A Section 4.

7 Remove the drivers side lower facia panel as described in Section 28.

8 Undo the retaining nut and manoeuvre the keyless receiver from place **(see illustration)**. Disconnect the wiring plug as the receiver is withdrawn.

9 Refitting is a reversal of removal.

Remote transmitter battery

10 Battery renewal is described in Chapter 1, Section 24.

18 Exterior mirrors – removal and refitting

Complete assembly

1 Remove the door unit as described in Section 12.

2 Disconnect the mirror wiring plug and unclip the wiring harness.

3 Rotate the mirror to expose the mounting screws **(see illustration)**. Undo the screws and remove the mirror.

4 Refitting is the reverse of removal.

Mirror glass

5 Push in the inner edge of the mirror, then using a forked, flat-bladed tool, carefully prise

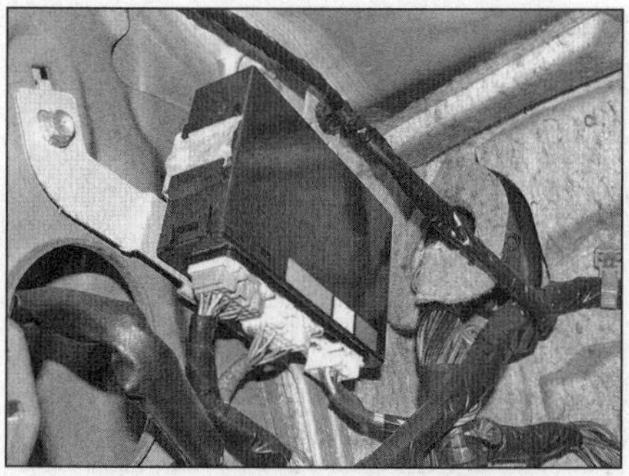

17.4 Keyless control module

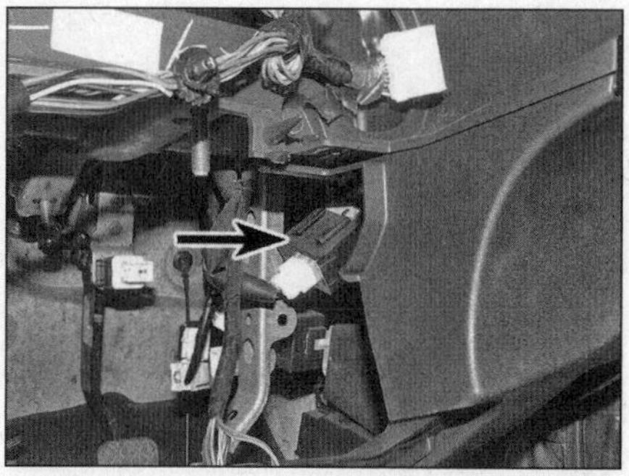

17.8 Keyless receiver unit (steering column removed for clarity)

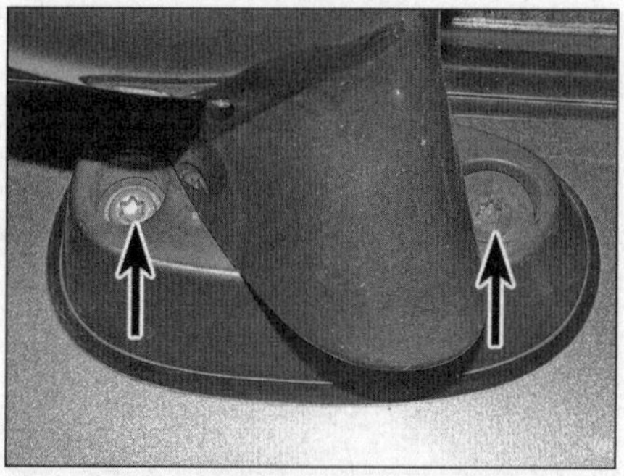

18.3 Twist the mirror to expose the mounting Torx screws

the outer adjustment ball joint from the socket on the mirror base **(see illustration)**.

6 Push in the upper edge of the mirror, then release the lower balljoint in the same manner.

7 Carefully prise the mirror rearwards to release the central clip. Disconnect the wiring plugs as the mirror is withdrawn **(see illustration)**.

8 To refit, reconnect any wiring plugs, insert the inner edge of the mirror glass holder (with the mirror) into the frame, then press the mirror centre forwards to engage the retaining clips. Check that the balljoints engage correctly.

19 Windscreen and rear screen – removal and refitting

1 These areas of glass are secured by the tight fit of the weatherstrip in the body aperture, and are either bonded in position with a special adhesive, or required complete dismantling of the retractable hard top. Renewal of such fixed glass is a difficult, messy and time-consuming task, which is beyond the scope of the home mechanic. It is difficult, unless one has plenty of practice, to obtain a secure, waterproof fit. Furthermore, the task carries a high risk of breakage; this applies especially to the laminated glass windscreen. In view of this, owners are strongly advised to have this sort of work carried out by one of the many specialist windscreen fitters or a Mazda dealer.

18.5 Carefully prise the ball joint from the socket on the mirror base

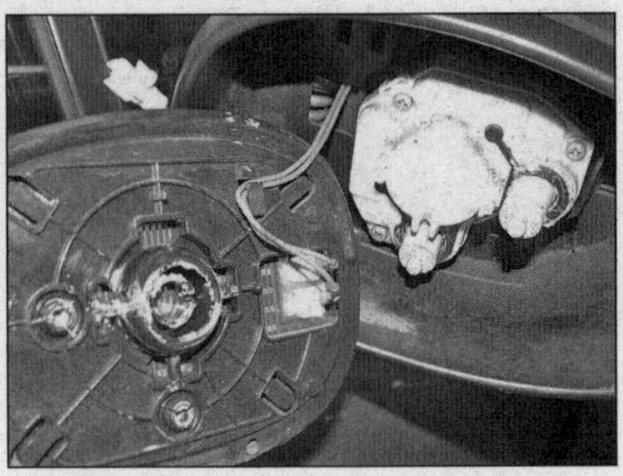

18.7 Disconnect the mirror wiring plug

20 Convertible soft-top roof – removal, refitting and adjustment

Removal and refitting

1 Pad the rear window on both sides with towels to protect it from scratches.

2 Unlock the latch at the front of the roof.

3 Disconnect the battery negative lead as described in Chapter 5A Section 4.

4 Remove the centre console as described in Section 27.

5 Remove the quarter trim, sill trim, tyre house trim, aeroboard, seat back bar garnish, seat back crossmember, rear side trim, rear package trim and side shelf as described in Section 26.

6 Disconnect the rear window defroster wiring plug.

7 The soft-top assembly is now secured by 2 bolts and nut each side in the hinge area, and 13 nuts securing the band around its circumference. Undo these fasteners, remove the band, and with the help of an assistant, carefully lift the roof assembly from place **(see illustrations)**.

8 Refitting is the reverse of the removal steps. Ensure the rain rail and moulding lip engages correctly, and the link bracket sits on its mounting studs with no gaps before tightening the mounting bolts/nut securely **(see illustrations)**.

9 Prior to refitting the trim panels, take the opportunity to clean out the water drain tray, and ensure the drain holes are clear **(see illustrations)**.

20.7a The soft-top assembly is secured by 2 bolts and a nut each side...

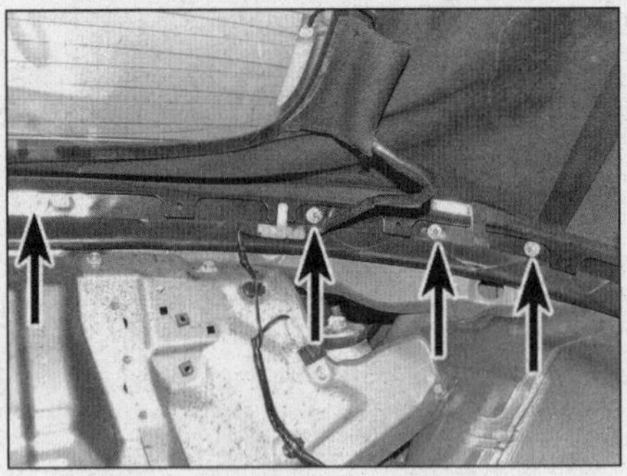

20.7b... and 13 nuts around its circumference

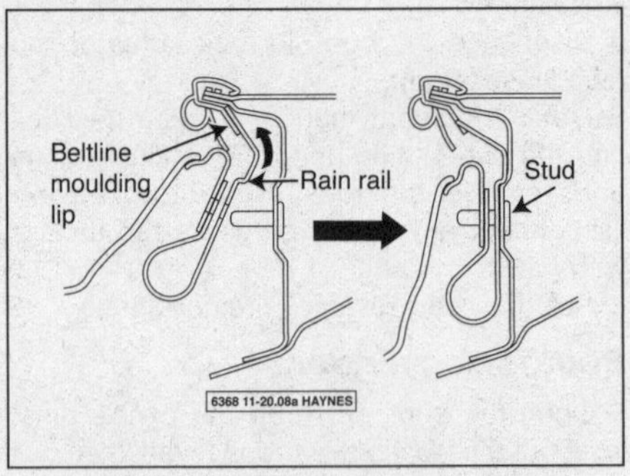

20.8a Insert the rain rail into the moulding lip, then press it over the studs

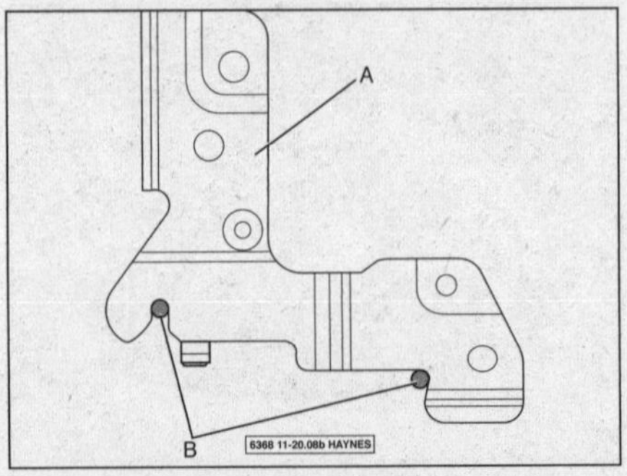

20.8b Ensure the link bracket (A) sits on the mounting studs (B) with no gaps

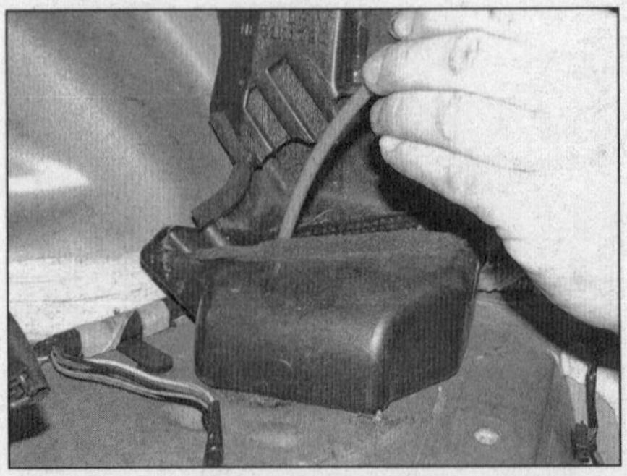

20.9a Insert a length of flexible hose into the drain holes...

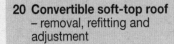

20.9b... and push any debris through the exit holes

20.10a Disconnect the return spring...

20.10b... then remove the circlip by sliding it along the pin

20.11a Slide out the pin

20.11b Undo the screws and remove the cover

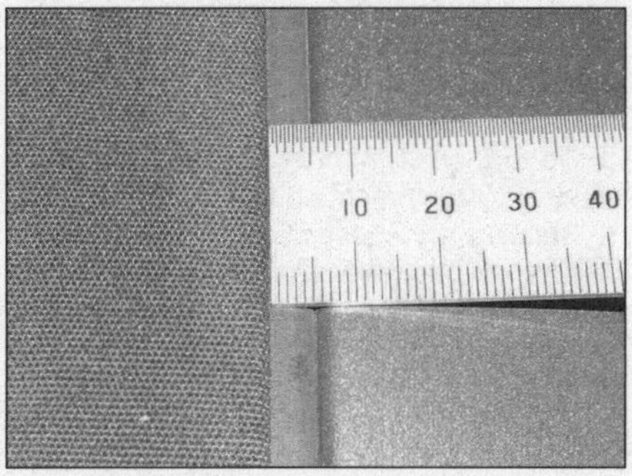

20.12a Measure the gap between the end of the soft-top and the windscreen header

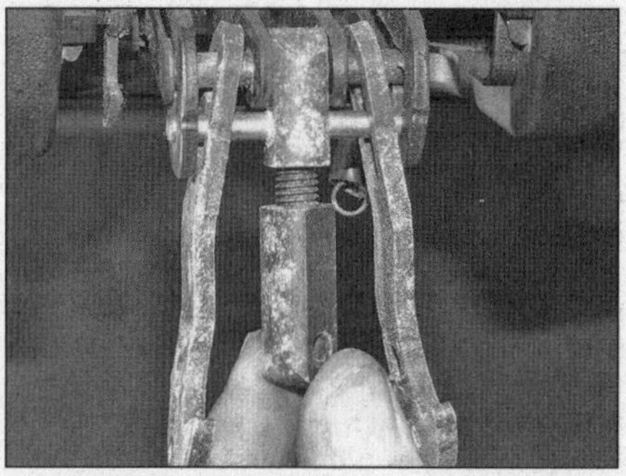

20.12b Adjust the gap by rotating the adjustment nut

Adjustment

10 Detach the top latch return spring, and carefully slide the circlip along the pin **(see illustrations)**.

11 Slide out the pin, undo the two screws and remove the latch cover **(see illustrations)**.

12 The gap between the front edge of the soft-top and the windscreen header should be 4 – 8 mm. Adjustment of this gap is achieved by rotating the adjustment nut clockwise to decrease the gap, or anti-clockwise to increase it **(see illustrations)**.

13 Refitting is a reversal of removal.

21 Retractable hard top – removal and refitting

Note: *The hard top is heavy and somewhat awkward to remove and refit – enlist the help of an assistant.*

Complete hard top

1 Unlock the roof top latch.

2 Operate the roof controls and fully open the deck panel.

3 Pad the rear window on both sides with towels to protect it from scratches.

4 Disconnect the battery negative lead as described in Chapter 5A Section 4.

5 Remove both front seats as described in Section 23.

6 Remove the centre console as described in Section 27.

7 With reference to Section 26, remove the following parts:

a) Quarter trim
b) Sill trim
c) Tyre house trim
d) Aeroboard
e) Seat back bar garnish
f) Back trim

8 Remove the seat belt upper anchorage bolt as described in Section 25.

9 Undo the 7 bolts securing the the link bracket each side **(see illustration)**.

10 Remove the seat back crossmember as described in Section 26.

11 Release the clips, rotate the link brackets upwards and manoeuvre them from place.

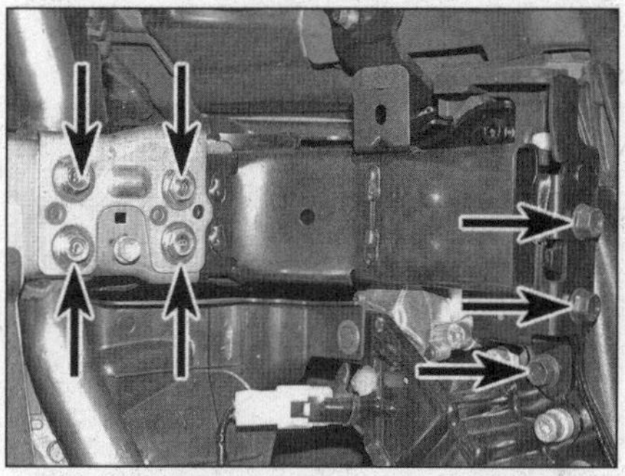

21.9 Link bracket retaining bolts

12 Prise out the clips and remove the cab-side weatherstrip each side **(see illustrations)**.

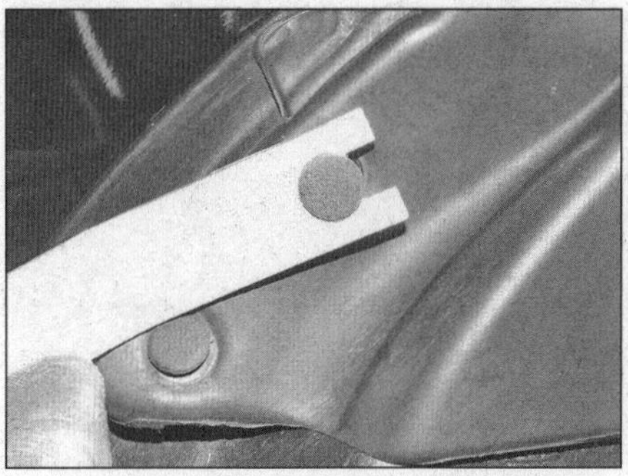

21.12a Prise out the two clips on the outside...

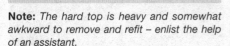

21.12b... and the single clip on the inside of the weatherstrip

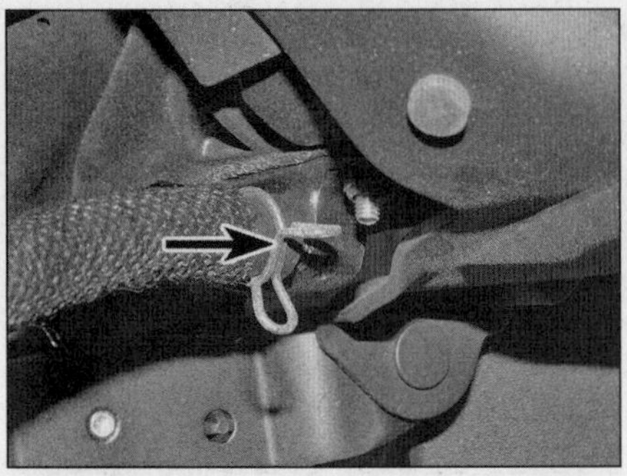

21.13 Release the clip and disconnect the drain hose

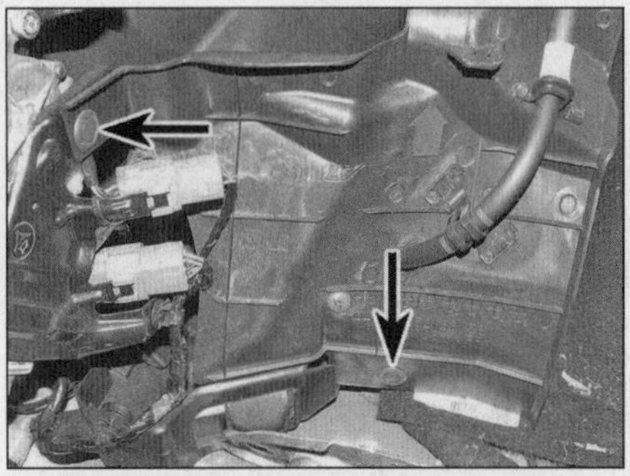

21.14 Prise up the centre pins and lever out the plastic expansion rivets

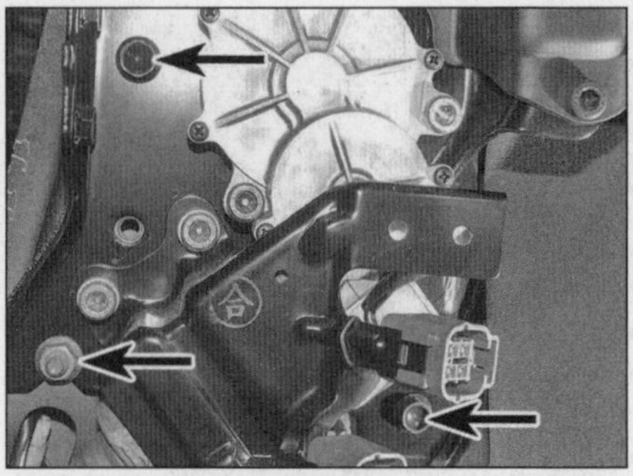

21.16 The roof is secured by two bolts and one nut each side

13 Release the clip and disconnect the drain hose each side **(see illustration)**.

14 Prise out the centre pins, lever out the plastic expansion rivets and remove the plastic panel each side **(see illustration)**.

15 Disconnect the wiring plugs from the roof motors, rear window defroster and roof motor limit switch.

16 The roof is now secured by one nut and two bolts each side **(see illustration)**. Remove the bolts/nuts. Note that the rearmost bolt is easily accessible from the deck aperture.

17 Hold the forward part of the top with one hand and have an assistant do the same on the other side. Carefully lift the hard top straight up and off the vehicle.

18 No further dismantling of the retractable hard top is recommended.

19 Refitting is the reverse of removal. Ensure there is no gap between the main bracket each side and their mounting studs **(see illustration)**.

Hard top motor

20 Carry out the procedures described in Paragraphs 1 to 10 of this Section.

21 Disconnect the roof motor wiring plug.

22 Undo the retaining bolts and move the roof motor bracket to one side **(see illustration)**. There's no need to unclip the wiring plugs.

23 Undo the retaining bolts and remove the motor **(see illustration)**.

24 Refitting is a reversal of removal.

Retractable hard top control module

25 Disconnect the battery negative lead as described in Chapter 5A Section 4.

26 Remove the service hole cover from the back trim, and partially peel back the cover **(see illustrations)**.

27 Undo the nut and detach the roof hook cable case **(see illustration)**.

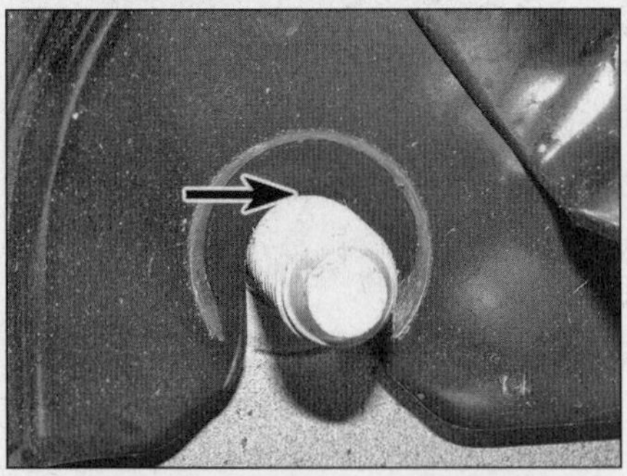

21.19 There should be no gap between the main bracket and the mounting stud

21.22 Roof motor bracket retaining bolts

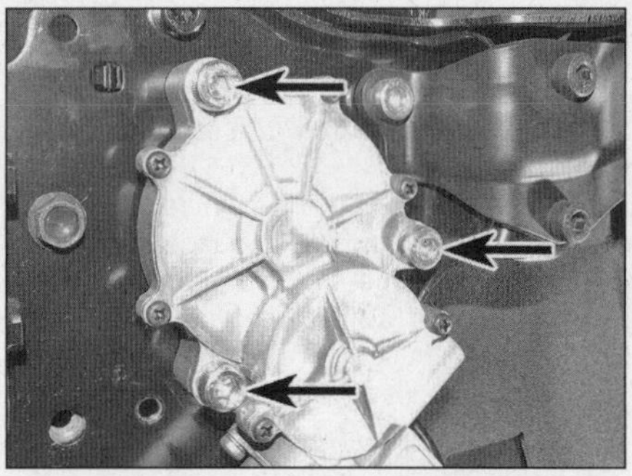

21.23 Roof motor retaining bolts

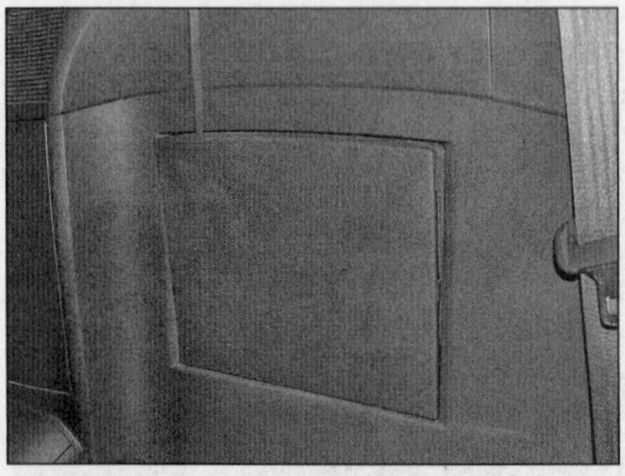

21.26a Starting at the top, prise open the service hole cover behind the passengers seat

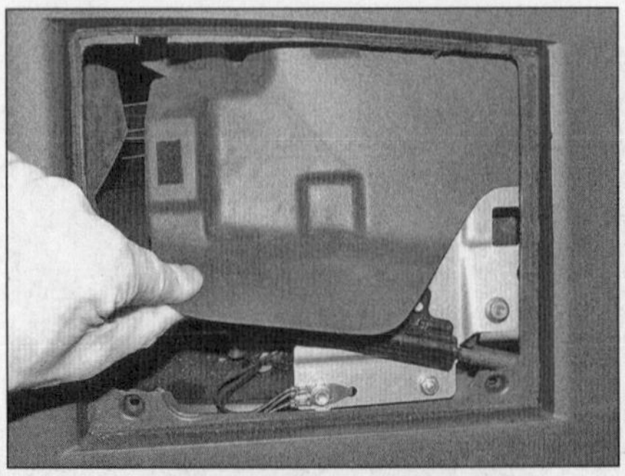

21.26b Peel back the cover

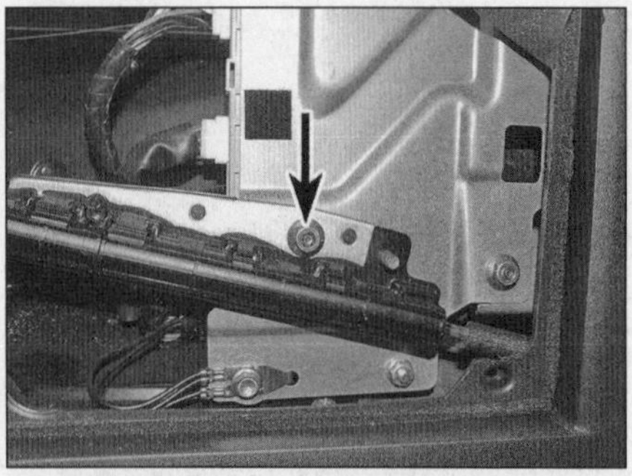

21.27 Undo the nut and move the cable case to one side

28 Undo the two retaining nuts, disconnect the wiring plugs and remove the control module **(see illustration)**.
29 Refitting is a reversal of removal.

22 Body exterior fittings – removal and refitting

Wheel arch liners and body under-panels

1 The various plastic covers fitted to the underside of the vehicle are secured in position by a mixture of screws, nuts and retaining clips and removal will be fairly obvious on inspection. Work methodically around, removing its retaining screws and releasing its retaining clips until the panel is free and can be removed from the underside of the vehicle. Most clips used on the vehicle are simply prised out of position. Other clips can be released by unscrewing/prising out the centre pins and then removing the clip.
2 Where fitted, disconnect the tyre pressure transmitter wiring plug as the wheel arch liner is withdrawn.
3 On refitting, renew any retaining clips that may have been broken on removal, and ensure that the panel is securely retained by all the relevant clips and screws.

Body trim strips and badges

4 The various body trim strips and badges are held in position with a special adhesive tape. Removal requires the trim/badge to be heated, to soften the adhesive, and then cut away from the surface. Due to the high risk of damage to the vehicle's paintwork during this operation, it is recommended that this task should be entrusted to a Mazda dealer or suitably-equipped specialist.

23 Seats – removal and refitting

Warning: Read Section 24 before proceeding.

1 Disconnect the battery negative lead as described in Chapter 5A, Section 4, then wait at least 1 minute for any residual electrical energy to dissipate.

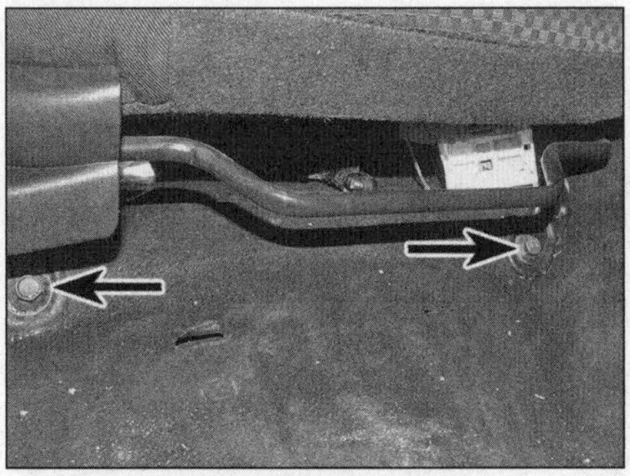

23.3a Undo the front...

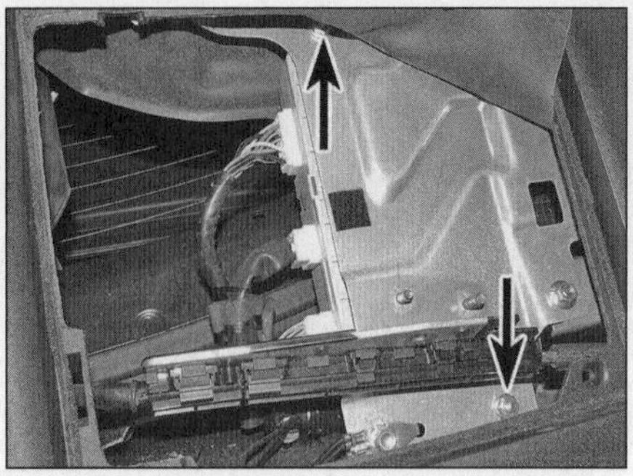

21.28 Roof module retaining nuts

2 Working underneath the seat, release the locking lever and disconnect the wiring plug **(see illustration)**.
3 Remove the seat rail retaining bolts at the floor, and lift the seat from the vehicle **(see illustrations)**.
4 Refitting is the reverse of removal. Tighten the bolts to the specified torque.

24 Seat belt tensioning mechanism – general information

1 All models are fitted with a front seat belt tensioner system. The system is designed to instantaneously take up any slack in the seat belt in the case of a sudden frontal impact, therefore reducing the possibility of injury to the seat occupants. The pretensioner function is integral with the inertia reel seat belt retractors.
2 The seat belt tensioner is triggered by a frontal impact above a predetermined force. Lesser impacts, including impacts from behind, will not trigger the system.
3 When the system is triggered, a pyrotechnic device is detonated which acts on the inertia reel mechanism, and keeps the occupant in position in the seat. Once the tensioner has been triggered, the seat belt will be permanently locked and the assembly must be renewed.
4 There is a risk of injury if the system is triggered inadvertently when working on the vehicle. If any work is to be carried out on the seat/seat belt, disable the tensioner by disconnecting the battery negative lead (see Chapter 5A Section 4), and waiting at least 1 minute before proceeding.

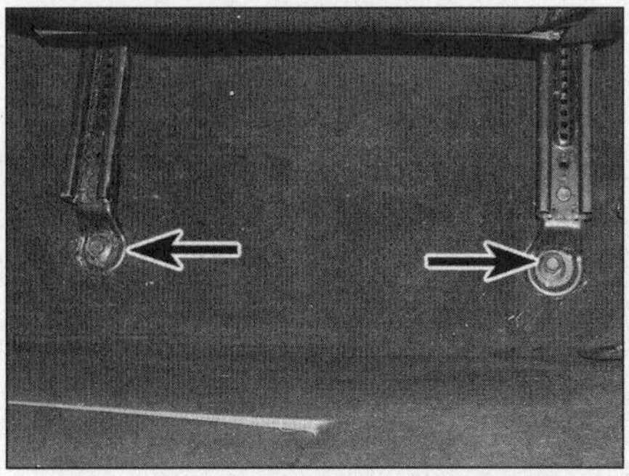

23.3b ... and rear seat retaining bolts

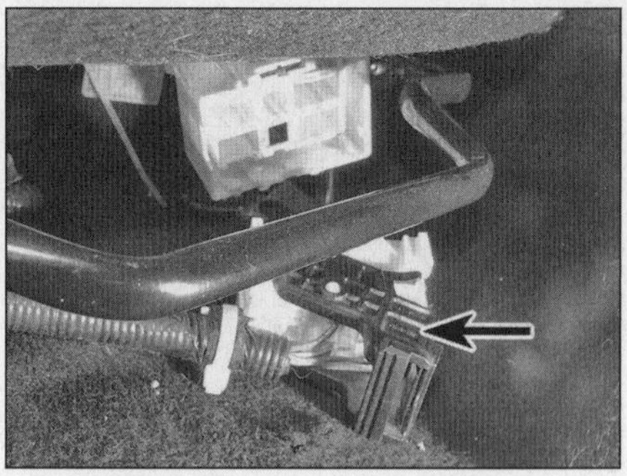

23.2 Fold over the locking lever and disconnect the wiring plug

5 Also note the following warnings before contemplating any work on a seat.

Warning: If the tensioner mechanism is dropped, it must be renewed, even it has suffered no apparent damage.

Warning: Do not allow any solvents to come into contact with the tensioner mechanism.

Warning: Do not subject the seat to any form of shock as this could accidentally trigger the seat belt tensioner.

25 Seat belt components – removal and refitting

Warning: Read Section 24 before proceeding.

Removal

Seat belt/inertia reel

1 Remove the centre console as described in Section 27.
2 With reference to Section 26, remove the following parts:
a) Quarter trim
b) Sill trim
c) Tyre housing trim
d) Aeroboard
e) Seat back bar garnish
f) Back trim
3 Prise out the locking clip a little and disconnect the seat belt inertia reel wiring plug **(see illustration)**.

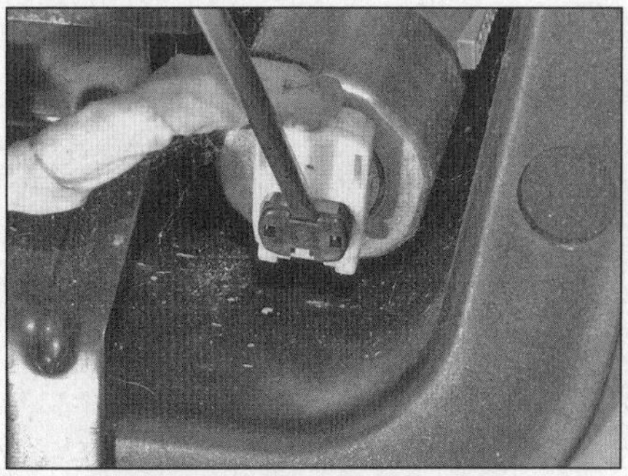

25.3 Prise out the locking clip and disconnect the wiring plug

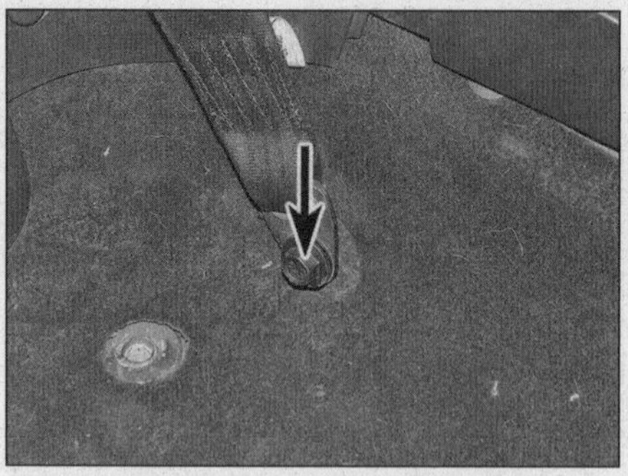

25.4 Lower anchorage bolt

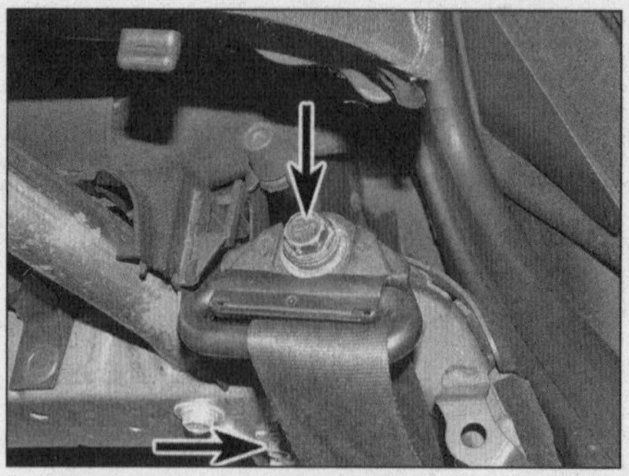

25.5 Upper anchorage and belt guide bolts

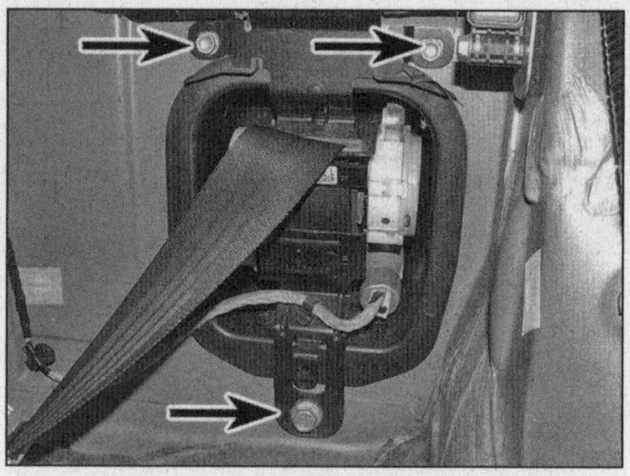

25.6 Inertia reel retaining bolts

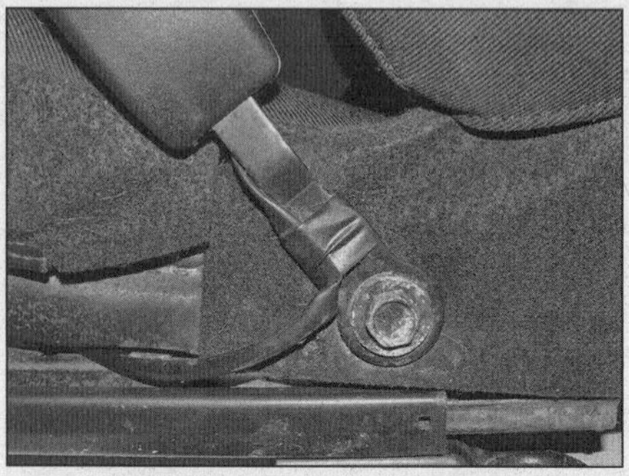

25.9 Seat belt stalk retaining bolt

4 Remove the lower anchorage bolt **(see illustration)**. Note the fitted location of any spacers/washers to aid refitting.
5 Remove the upper anchorage bolt and belt guide bolt **(see illustration)**.
6 Undo the inertia reel retaining bolts **(see illustration)**.

Seat belt stalk

7 Remove the seat as described in Section 23.
8 Unclip the seat belt stalk wiring plug from the main connector.
9 Undo the retaining bolt and detach the stalk from the seat base. Note the positions of the washers/spacers to aid refitting **(see illustration)**.

Refitting

10 Refitting is a reversal of the removal procedure, ensuring that all fasteners are tightened to their specified torque where given. Apply a little thread-locking compound to the mounting bolts.

26.6 Hood locating cup screws

26 Interior trim – removal and refitting

Interior trim panels

1 The interior trim panels are secured using either screws or various types of trim fasteners, usually studs or clips.
2 Check that there are no other panels overlapping the one to be removed; usually there is a sequence that has to be followed that will become obvious on close inspection.
3 Remove all obvious fasteners, such as screws. If the panel will not come free, it is held by hidden clips or fasteners. These are usually situated around the edge of the panel and can be prised up to release them; note, however that they can break quite easily so renewals should be available. The best way of releasing such clips without the correct type of tool, is to use a large flat-bladed screwdriver. Note that some panels are secured by plastic expanding rivets, where the centre pin must be prised up before the rivet can be removed. Note in many cases that the adjacent sealing strip must be prised back to release a panel.
4 When removing a panel, never use excessive force or the panel may be damaged; always check carefully that all fasteners have been removed or released before attempting to withdraw a panel.
5 Refitting is the reverse of the removal procedure; secure the fasteners by pressing them firmly into place and ensure that all disturbed components are correctly secured to prevent rattles.

Front header trim

6 Make alignment marks around the hood locating cups, then undo the Torx screws and remove them **(see illustration)**.
7 Remove the A-pillar trim each side as described later in this Section.
8 Undo the two Torx retaining screws, then carefully pull the trim away from the windscreen surround to release the retaining clips **(see illustration)**. Disconnect the wiring plug as the trim is withdrawn.
9 Refitting is a reversal of removal.

A-pillar trim

10 Make alignment marks around the hood locating cups, then undo the screws and remove them **(see illustration 26.6)**.
11 Pull the trim to the centre of the vehicle, starting at the top. Note the lugs at the base of the trim panel **(see illustrations)**.

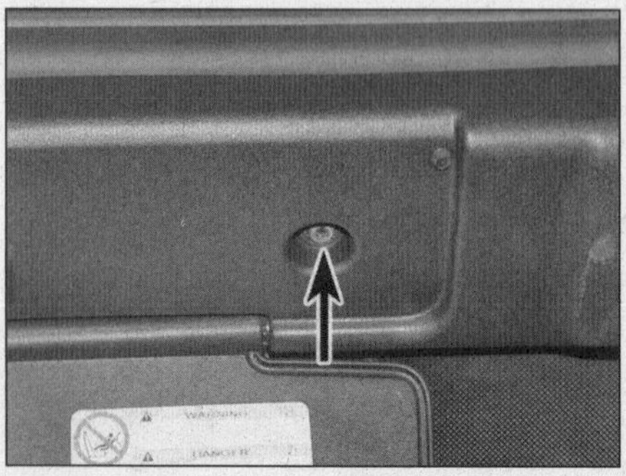

26.8 Undo the Torx screw each side and pull the header trim away

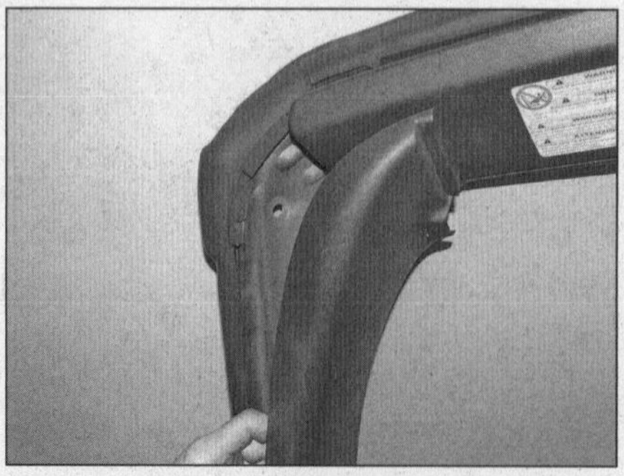

26.11a Pull the A-pillar trim inwards to release the clips

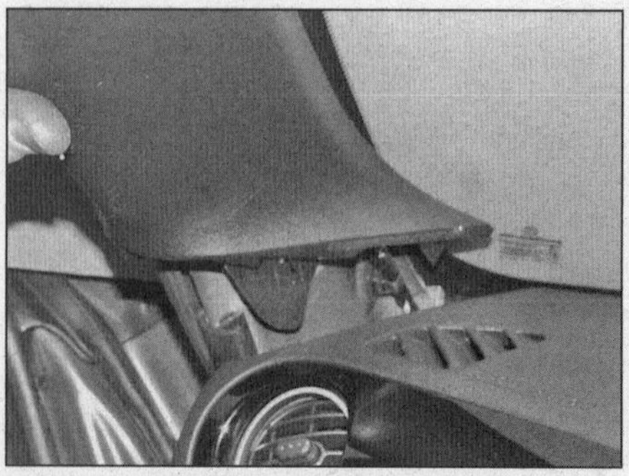

26.11b Note the lugs at the base of the pillar trim

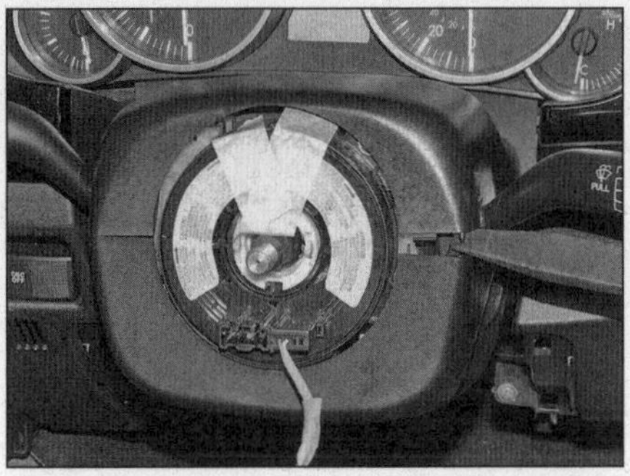

26.13 Carefully prise the shroud upwards to release the catches

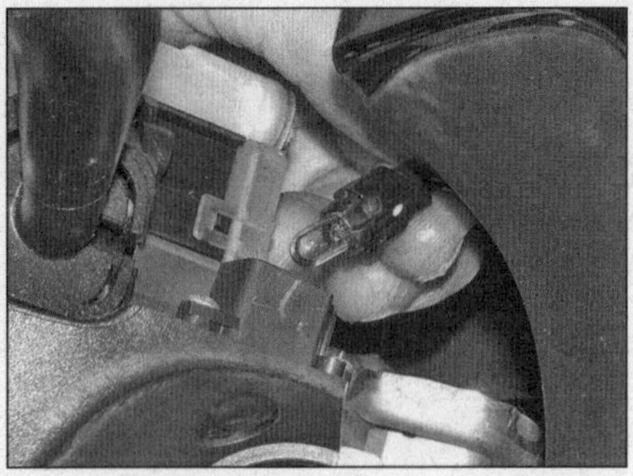

26.14 Rotate the bulbholder anti-clockwise and pull it from the shroud

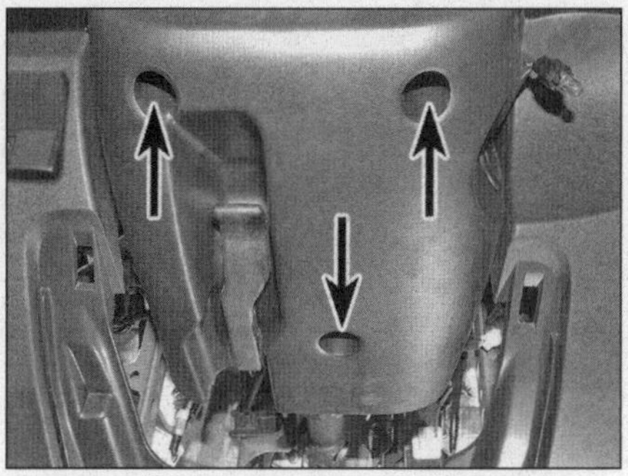

26.15 Lower shroud retaining screws

12 Refitting is the reverse of the removal procedure; secure the fasteners by pressing them firmly into place and ensure that all disturbed components are correctly secured to prevent rattles.

Steering column shrouds

13 Release the catches and remove the upper column shroud **(see illustration)**.

14 Remove the ignition key illumination bulb **(see illustration)**.

15 Undo the screws and remove the steering column lower shroud **(see illustration)**.

16 Refitting is a reversal of removal.

Front side trim

17 Remove the sill trim as described later in this Section.

18 Pull away the rubber weatherstrip from the door aperture adjacent to the side trim panel.

19 Remove the fastener at the lower edge of the side trim **(see illustration)**.

20 Pull the side trim inwards to release the retaining clips.

21 Refitting is the reverse of the removal procedure; secure the fasteners by pressing them firmly into place and ensure that all disturbed components are correctly secured to prevent rattles.

Glovebox

22 Open the glovebox.

23 Release the damper cord, then bend the stoppers inwards a little, and fully open the glovebox **(see illustrations)**.

24 Manoeuvre the glovebox from place **(see illustration)**.

25 Refitting is a reversal of removal.

Carpets

26 The passenger compartment floor carpet is in one piece, secured at its edges by screws or clips, usually the same fasteners used to secure the various adjoining trim panels.

27 Carpet removal and refitting is reasonably straightforward but very time-consuming because all adjoining trim panels must be removed first, as must components such as the seats, the centre console and seat belt lower anchorages.

Quarter trim

28 Remove the seat(s) as described in Section 23, then undo the fastener at the front edge of the quarter trim **(see illustration)**.

29 Carefully release the two clips at the inner edge of the trim, then pull the rear edge upwards to release the rear clip **(see illustration)**. Feed the seat belt through the slot in the trim as it's withdrawn.

30 Refitting is a reversal of removal.

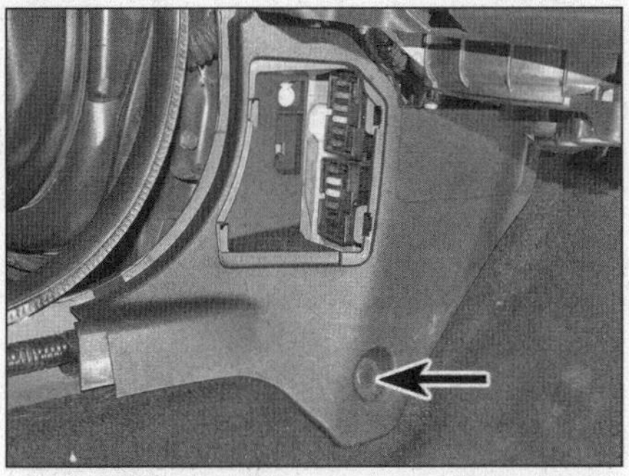

26.19 Prise up the centre pin and lever out the plastic expansion rivet

26.23a Detach the damper end fitting from the glovebox

26.23b Squeeze in the sides to release the stoppers

26.24 Lift the glovebox from the facia

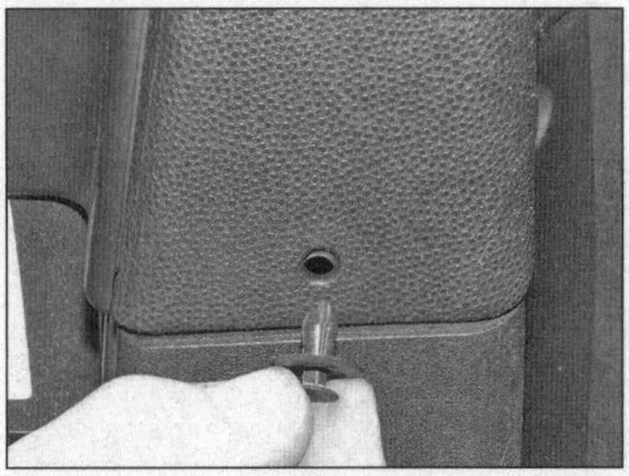

26.28 Prise up the centre pin and lever out the plastic expansion rivet

26.29 Pull the quarter trim upwards to release the clip

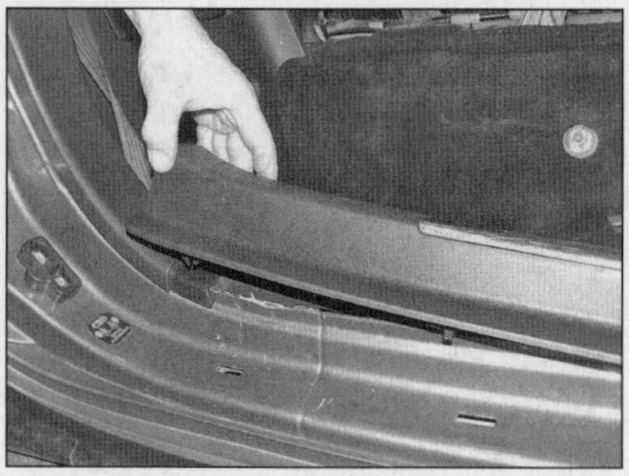

26.31 Pull the sill trim upwards, starting at the rear

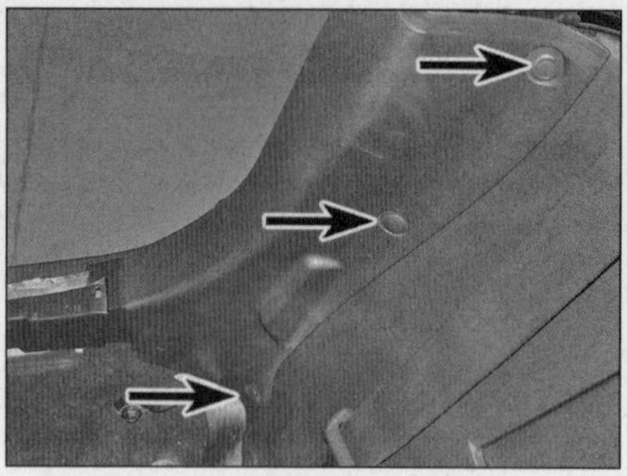

26.34a Remove the clips...

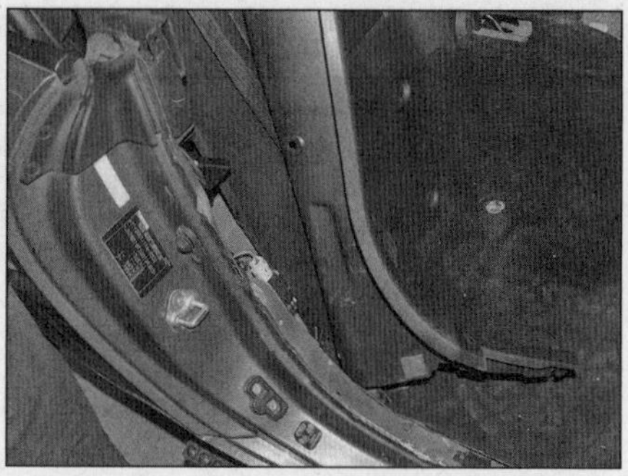

26.34b... and pull the tyre house trim forwards

Sill trim

31 Starting at the rear, carefully pull the sill trim upwards from place to release the retaining clips **(see illustration)**.

32 Refitting is a reversal of removal.

Tyre house trim

33 Remove the Quarter trim and Sill trim as described previously in this Section.

34 Prise up the centre pins, lever out the three plastic rivets, then pull the tyre house trim forwards to release the retaining clips **(see illustrations)**.

35 Refitting is a reversal of removal.

Aeroboard

36 Insert a blunt, flat-bladed screwdriver into the service hole at the lower edge of the Aeroboard, then release the retaining clips **(see illustrations)**. Lift the Aeroboard from place.

37 Refitting is a reversal of removal.

Seat back bar garnish

38 Carefully prise the front section of the seat back bar garnish forwards to release the retaining clips **(see illustration)**.

39 Undo the two retaining screws, then pull the rear section upwards from place **(see illustration)**.

40 Refitting is a reversal of removal.

Back trim

41 Remove the centre console as described in Section 27.

42 As described previously in this Section, remove the following:

a) Quarter trim
b) Sill trim
c) Tyre house trim
d) Aeroboard
e) Seat back bar garnish

43 On soft-top models, pull the open hook lever outwards and remove it whilst squeezing together the tabs **(see illustration)**.

44 Remove the fasteners, then pull the Back trim forwards to release the various retaining clips **(see illustrations)**.

45 Manoeuvre the back trim from place.

46 Refitting is a reversal of removal.

Seat back crossmember

47 Remove the centre console as described in Section 27.

48 Remove the following as described elsewhere in this Section.

a) Quarter trim
b) Sill trim
c) Tyre house trim
d) Aeroboard
e) Seat back bar garnish
f) Back trim

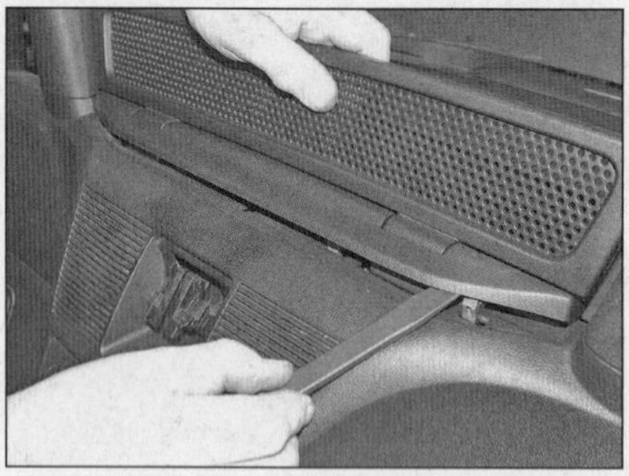

26.36 Prise the Aeroboard upwards to release the clips

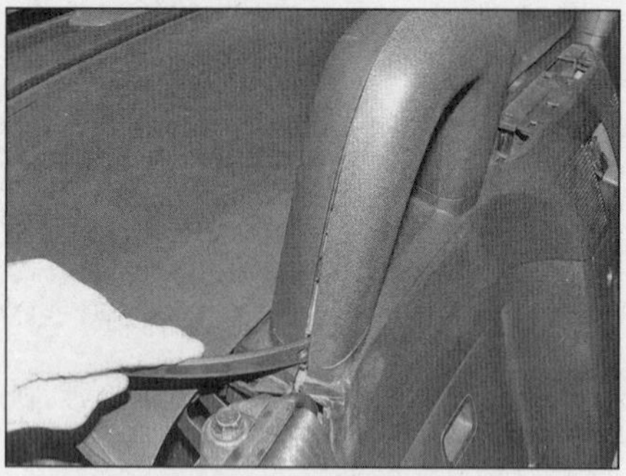

26.38 Prise the front section of the seat back bar garnish forwards

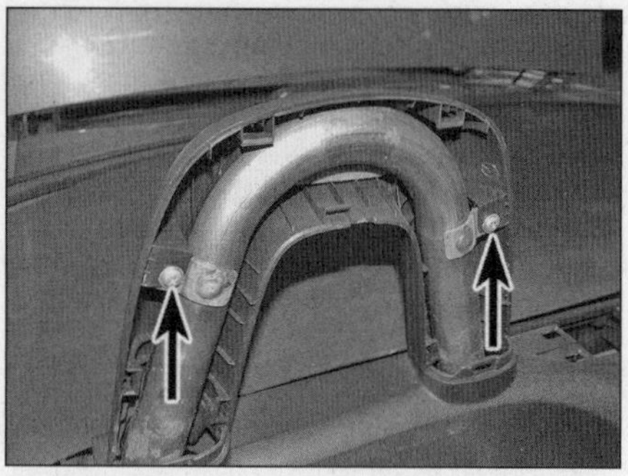

26.39 Undo the screws and remove the rear section

26.43 Squeeze together the tabs

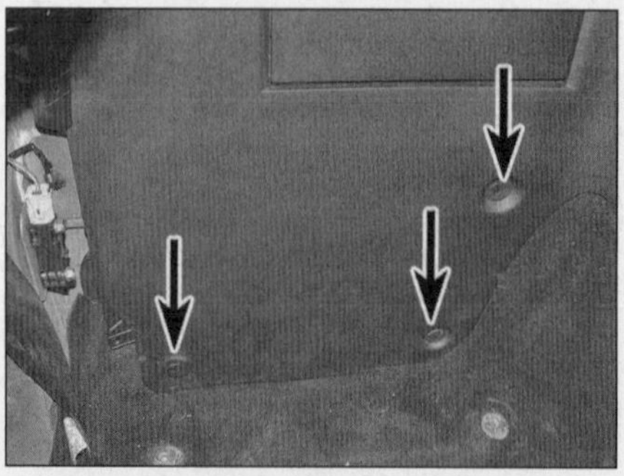

26.44a Remove the Back trim fasteners (right-hand fasteners arrowed)

26.44b Pull the Back trim forwards to release the clips

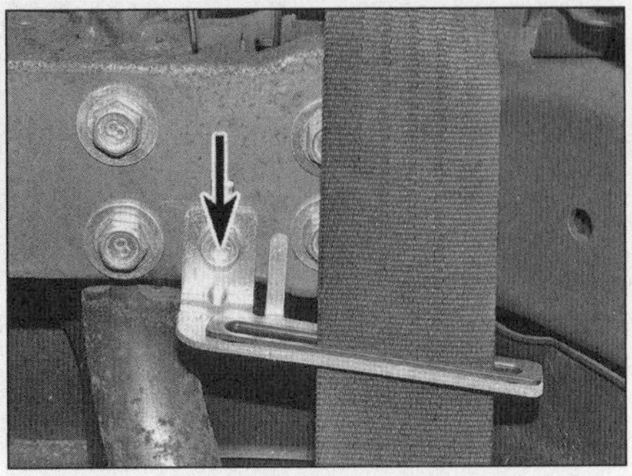

26.50 Seat belt guide bolt

26.51 Remove the junction bracket each side

26.54a Remove the crossmember upper bolts...

49 Remove the rear speaker as described in Chapter 12 Section 18.

50 Remove the seat belt upper anchorage bolt as described in Section 25, then undo the bolt and release the seat belt guide **(see illustration)**.

51 Undo the two bolts and remove the 'junction' bracket each side **(see illustration)**.

52 On models with a retractable hard-top, temporarily reconnect the battery negative lead and half-open the roof. If the crossmember is removed with the roof fully open, it may contact and damage the middle roof panel.

53 Unclip the speaker wiring harness, then note their fitted positions and disconnect any necessary wiring plugs from the crossmember.

54 Undo the various bolts/nut and manoeuvre the crossmember from place **(see illustrations)**.

55 Refitting is a reversal of removal.

Rear side trim

Soft-top convertible models

56 Remove the seat back crossmember as described in this Section.

Retractable hard-top models

57 Remove the Back trim as described previously in this Section.

58 Release the clip and disconnect the roof drain hose **(see illustration 21.13)**.

All models

59 Undo the fasteners, then pull the rear side trim inwards to release the retaining clips **(see illustration)**.

60 Refitting is a reversal of removal.

Rear package trim

61 Remove the Rear side trims as described previously in this Section.

62 Prise up the centre pins, lever out the plastic expansion rivets (three each side), and lift the Rear package trim from place **(see illustrations)**.

63 Refitting is a reversal of removal.

Side shelf

Soft-top convertible models

64 Remove the Rear package trim as described previously in this Section.

Retractable hard-top models

65 Remove the Rear side trim as described previously in this Section.

All models

66 Prise up the centre pins, lever out the plastic expansion rivets (three each side) then pull the shelf outwards to release the retaining clip **(see illustration)**.

67 Refitting is a reversal of removal.

26.54b... and lower bolts/nut

26.59 Prise up the centre pins and lever out the rear side trim fasteners

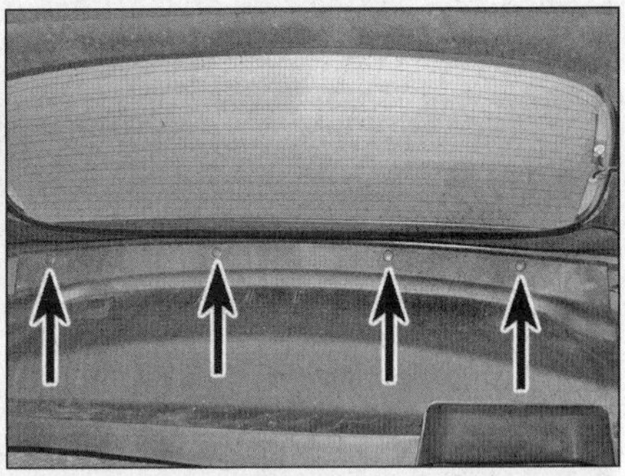

26.62a Remove the plastic expansion rivets at the rear...

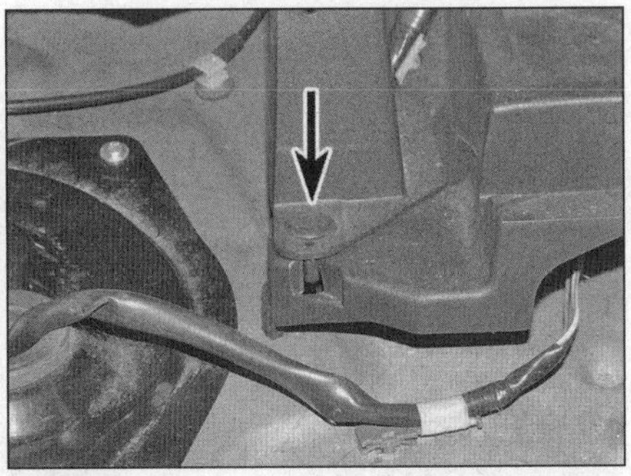

26.62b... and one each side at the front...

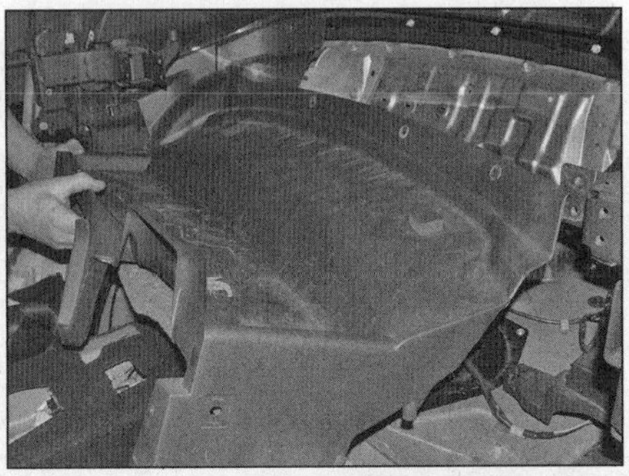

26.62c... then release any wiring plugs and remove the package trim

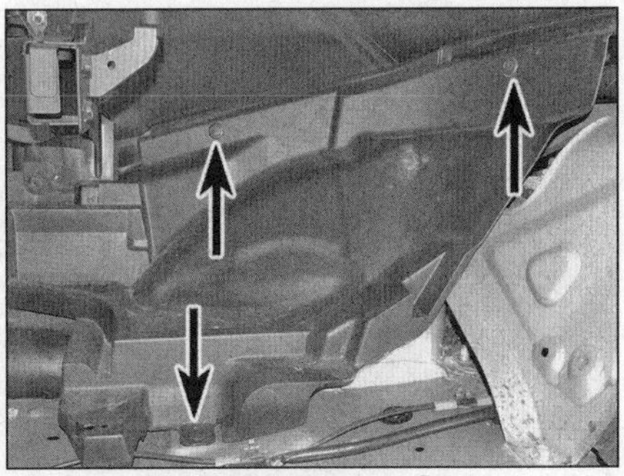

26.66 Side shelf fasteners

27.2 Rotate the gearchange lever knob anti-clockwise to remove it

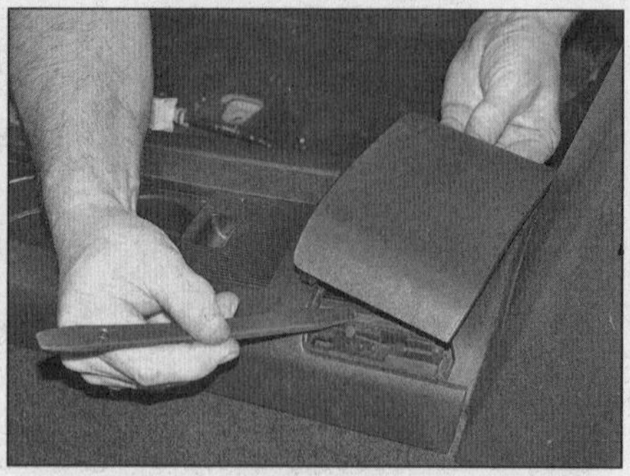

27.3a Prise up the rear...

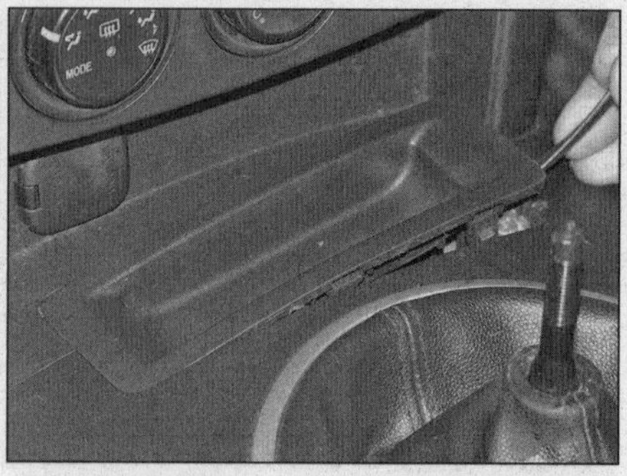

27.3b.. and front covers from the console

27 Centre console – removal and refitting

Removal

1 Disconnect the negative battery lead as described in Chapter 5A, Section 4.

2 Unscrew the gearchange lever knob **(see illustration)**.

Early models

3 Using a trim removal tool, prise up and remove the front and rear covers from the console **(see illustrations)**.

4 Prise up the cover in the base of the cupholder, and undo the screw exposed **(see illustration)**.

5 Carefully prise up the handbrake lever gaiter **(see illustration)**.

6 Undo the two screws at the front of

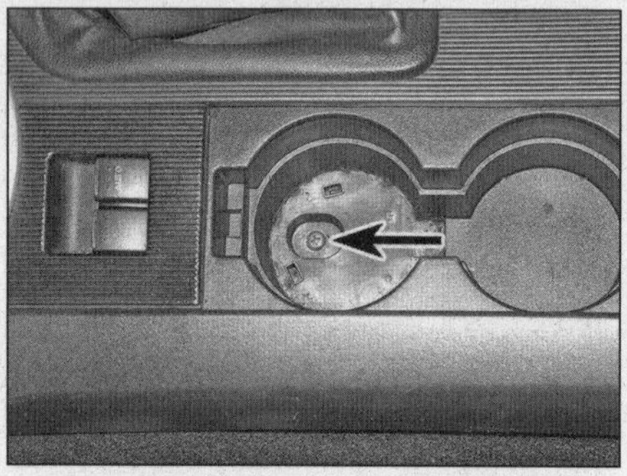

27.4 Undo the screw in the base of the cupholder

the console, and the two at the rear **(see illustrations)**.

Later models

7 Remove the rubber mat at the front of the console, and prise up the cover at the rear **(see illustrations)**.

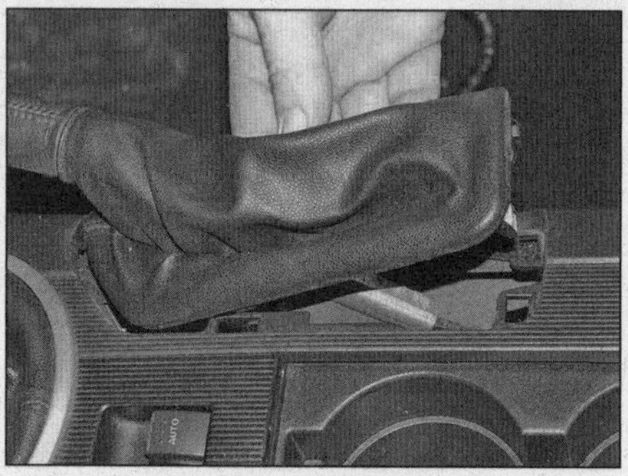

27.5 Prise the handbrake gaiter from the console

8 Starting at the rear, carefully prise up the handbrake lever gaiter and slide it over the lever handle **(see illustration 27.5)**.

9 Lift out the cupholder guide, then remove the mat in the base of the cupholder and remove the screw **(see illustrations)**.

10 Undo the two screws at the rear of the

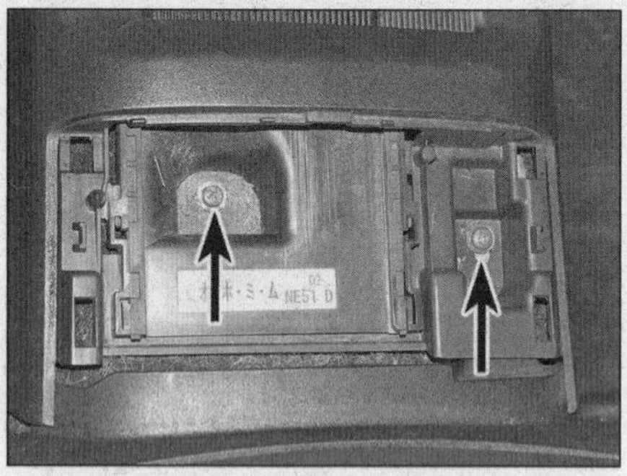

27.6a The console is secured by two screws at the rear...

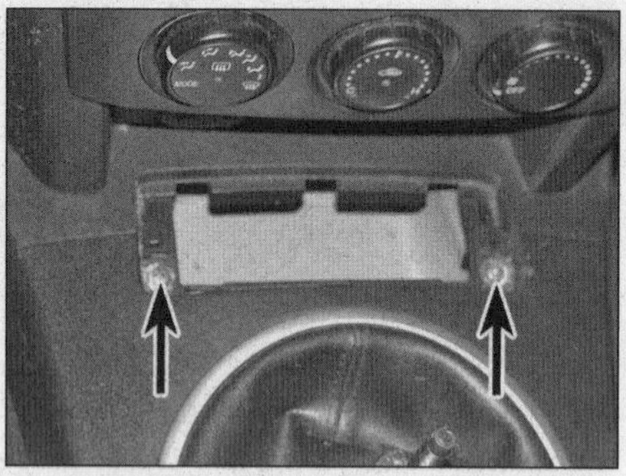

27.6b... and two screws at the front

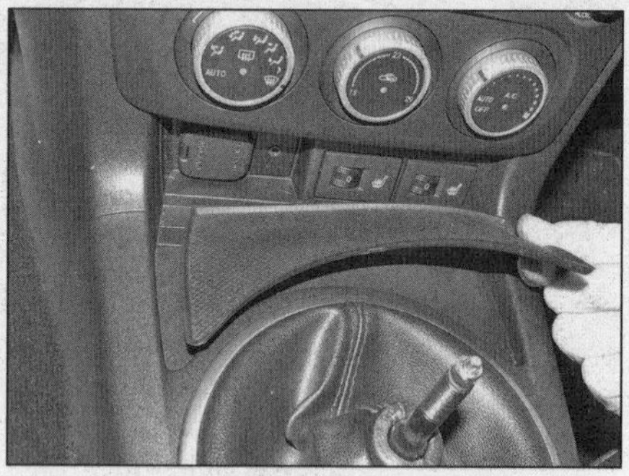

27.7a Remove the rubber mat

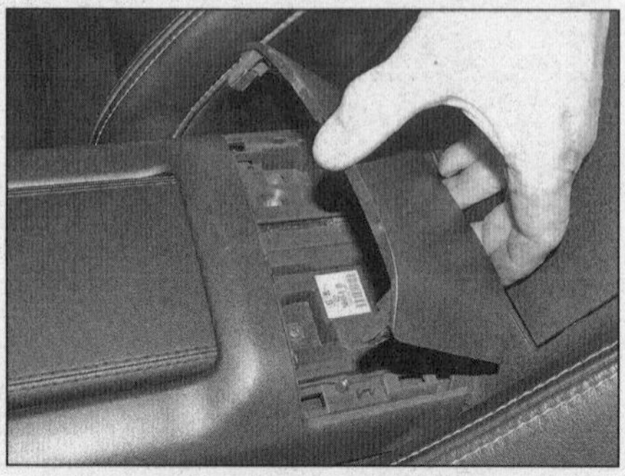

27.7b Prise up the cover at the rear

27.9a Slide up the cupholder guide

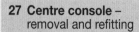

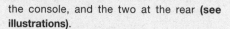

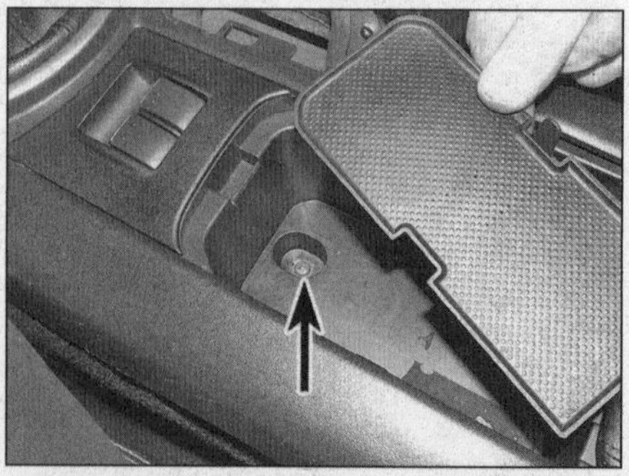

27.9b Lift out the mat and remove the screw

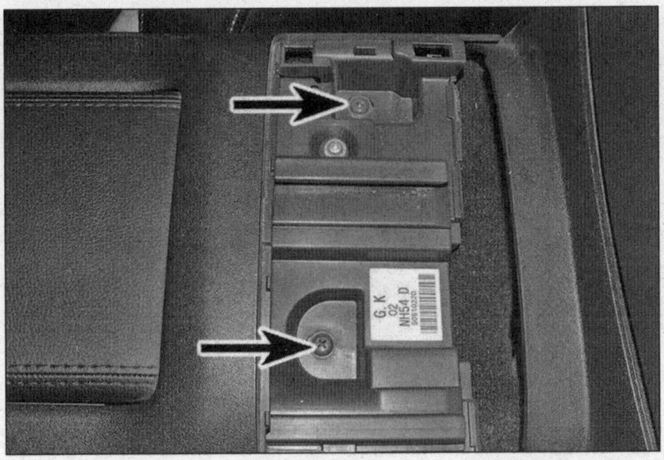

27.10 Undo the screws at the rear of the console

28.2 Carefully prise the instrument cluster trim panel upwards to release the clips

console, and the screw in cupholder aperture **(see illustration)**.

All models

11 Lift the console slightly, and disconnect the wiring plugs from its underside.

12 Manoeuvre the console from place.

Refitting

13 Manoeuvre the centre console over the gearchange and handbrake levers. The remainder of refitting is the reverse of removal making sure all fasteners are securely tightened.

28 Facia panels – removal and refitting

Removal

HAYNES HiNT ***Label each wiring connector as it is disconnected from its relevant component. The labels will prove useful on refitting, when routing the wiring and feeding the wiring through the facia apertures.***

1 Disconnect the battery negative lead as described in Chapter 5A Section 4.

Instrument cluster trim panel

2 Using a trim removal tool, carefully pry loose the four instrument cluster trim panel retaining clips from the instrument panel **(see illustration)** and remove it.

Console panel

3 Remove the centre console as described in Section 27, and the two side panels as described later in this Section.

4 Remove the console panel retaining screws **(see illustration)**.

5 Pull the console panel to the rear to disengage the locator pin and mounting tab from each side **(see illustration)**.

6 Disconnect the wiring plugs and remove the panel.

Side panels

7 Remove the centre console as described in Section 27, then on early models, using a trim removal tool or a taped screwdriver, carefully prise the side panel rewards from the facia. On later models, undo the screw at the rear edge and prise the panel rearwards **(see illustrations)**.

Facia end panels

8 Using a trim removal tool, carefully prise the end panel out from the end of the facia to disengage the mounting clips **(see illustration)**. Pull the panel rearward to

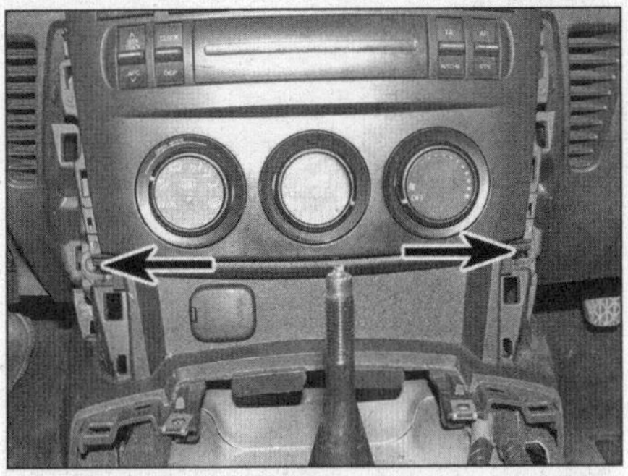

28.4 Undo the panel retaining screws

28.5 Pull the console panel rearwards

28.7a Carefully prise the side panel rearwards

28.7b On later models, undo the screws at the rear edges of the side panels

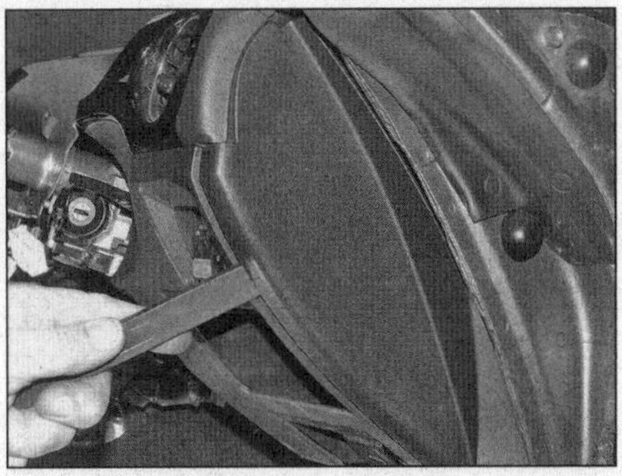

28.8 Prise the panel from the end of the facia

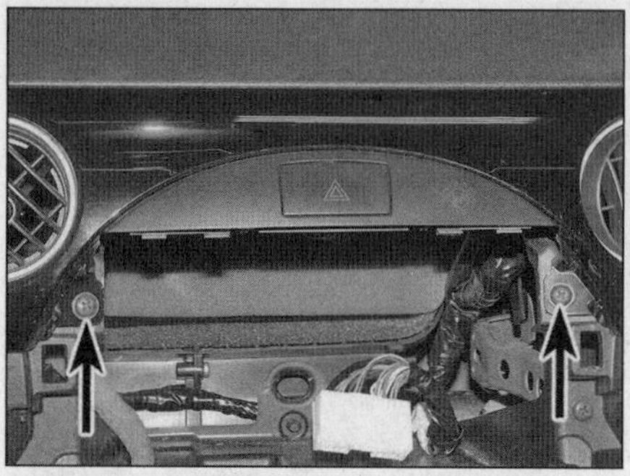

28.11a Undo the screws in the centre...

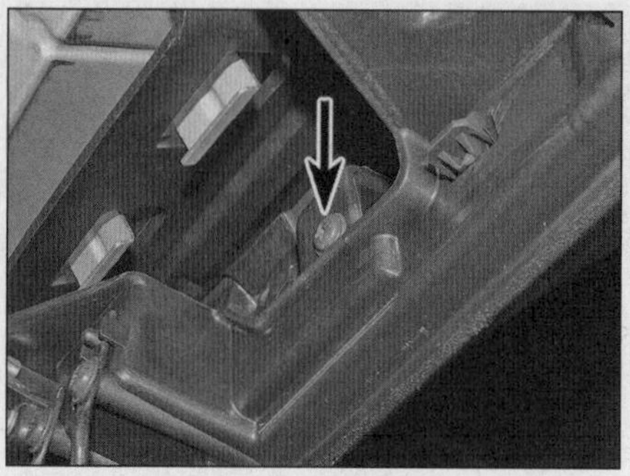

28.11b... and the screw above the glovebox latch

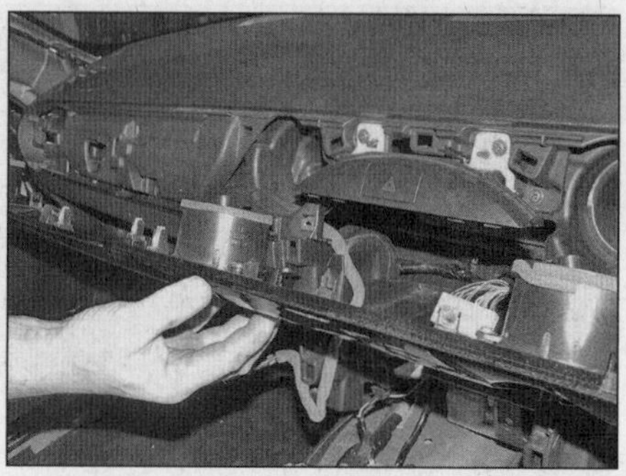

28.12 Pull the vent trim panel rearwards to release the clips

28.14 Pull the drivers side lower facia panel rearwards

28.18 Undo the panel retaining screw each side

disengage the mounting tab at the lower end of the panel and remove the panel.

Vent trim panels

Left-hand panel

9 Remove the side panel, and centre panel as described in this Section.

10 Remove the glovebox as described in Section 26.

11 Remove the three vent trim panel retaining screws **(see illustrations)**. Two of the screws are located in the upper part of the cavity for the center panel unit; the third screw is located in the roof of the cavity for the glove box, above the glovebox latch.

12 Grasp the vent trim panel firmly and carefully pull it straight back to disengage the mounting clips **(see illustration)**.

Right-hand panel

13 Using a trim removal tool, carefully prise the vent panel rearwards to release the retaining clips.

Drivers side lower facia panel

14 Pull the upper edge of the panel rearwards to release the clips, then lift it from place **(see illustration)**.

Centre panel

15 Disconnect the battery negative lead as described in Chapter 5A Section 4.

16 Remove the centre console as described in Section 27.

17 Remove the drivers side lower facia panel, and both side panels as described in this Section.

18 Remove the centre panel retaining screws **(see illustration)**.

19 Pull out the centre panel unit and disconnect the antenna lead from the radio **(see illustration)**. Disconnect the electrical connectors from the radio and the heater and air conditioning control assembly. Disconnecting the antenna lead and the electrical connector from the radio is extremely difficult on these models because the space behind the radio and the heater and air conditioning control assembly is extremely tight. Before disconnecting them, disengage the harness clip to put enough slack in the harness to disconnect the connectors. Access the harness clip and connectors from the right side of the glove box receptacle.

Caution: When installing the centre panel unit, make sure that the wiring harness and antenna lead are not trapped between the unit, the facia and/or the bulkhead. If the wiring harness or the antenna lead is pinched or kinked, it might cause the radio and/or the heater and air conditioning control assembly to malfunction.

Facia

20 On models with air conditioning, have the refrigerant circuit evacuated by a suitable equipped specialist, then disconnect the refrigerant pipes at the engine compartment bulkhead **(see illustration)**. Plug the openings to prevent contamination.

21 Drain the coolant as described in Chapter 1 Section 19, then release the clamps and disconnect the heater hoses at the bulkhead **(see illustration)**.

22 Disconnect the battery negative lead as described in Chapter 5A Section 4.

23 Remove the centre console as described in Section 27.

28.19 Pull the unit rearwards and disconnect the wiring plugs

28.20 Undo the bolt and disconnect the refrigerant pipes

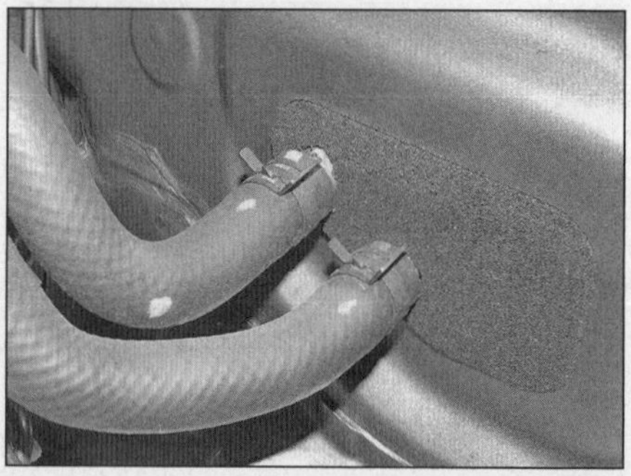

28.21 Release the clamps and disconnect the heater hoses

28.29 Slide the fuse boxes rearwards

28.31a Remove the two bolts each side at the A-pillars...

24 Remove the glovebox, A-pillar trims and front side trims as described in Section 26.

25 With reference to this Section, remove the following:

a) Side panels

b) Console panel

c) Centre panel

d) Instrument cluster trim panel

e) Facia end panels

26 Remove the steering column as described in Chapter 10 Section 15.

27 Remove the instrument cluster as described in Chapter 12 Section 12.

28 Remove the bonnet release lever as described in Section 9.

29 Slide the interior fuse boxes rearwards from the mounting bracket **(see illustration)**.

30 Disconnect all facia wiring harness plugs.

31 Remove the facia mounting nuts and bolts **(see illustration)**:

a) Two bolts each end at the A-pillars

b) Two bolts (under covers) at the drivers end of the facia, and one at the passengers end

c) Three bolts in the centre section

d) One nut at the base the air distribution housing

32 Ensure all fasteners and wiring harnesses/plugs are released, then with the help of an assistant, manoeuvre the facia, crossmeber and heater assembly from the vehicle.

Refitting

33 Refitting is a reversal of the removal procedure, noting the following points:

a) Manoeuvre the facia into position and ensure that the wiring is correctly routed and securely retained by its facia clips.

b) Clip the facia back into position, making sure all the wiring connectors are fed through their respective apertures, then refit all the facia fasteners, and tighten them securely.

c) On completion, reconnect the battery and check that all the electrical components and switches function correctly.

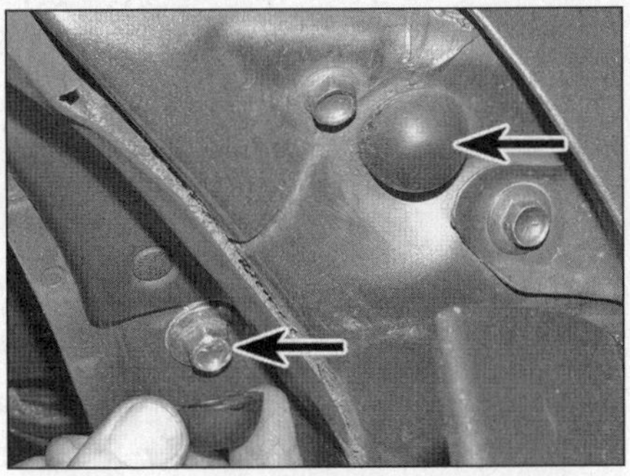

28.31b... two bolts (under covers) at the drivers end of the facia...

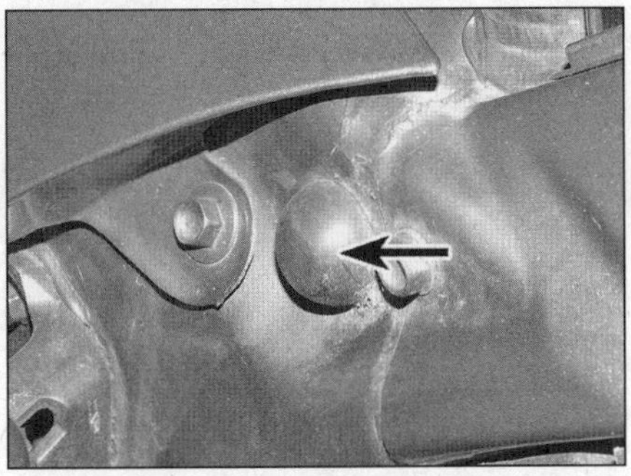

28.31c... one bolt (under the cover) at the passengers end of the facia...

29 Fuel filler flap cable – removal and refitting

1 Open the boot, prise out the centre pins, lever out the two expansion rivets, then pull

28.31d... two bolts at the base of the central support bracket...

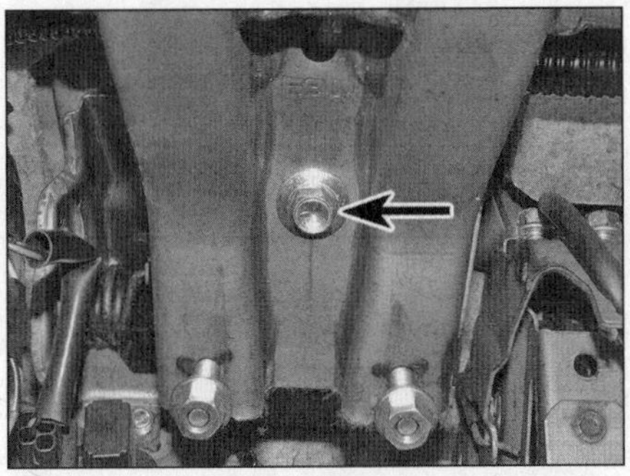

28.31e... one bolt in the steering column area...

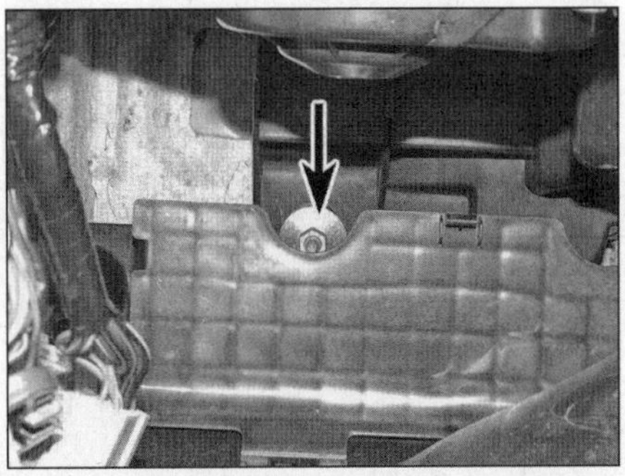

28.31f... and one nut at the base of the heater housing on the passengers side

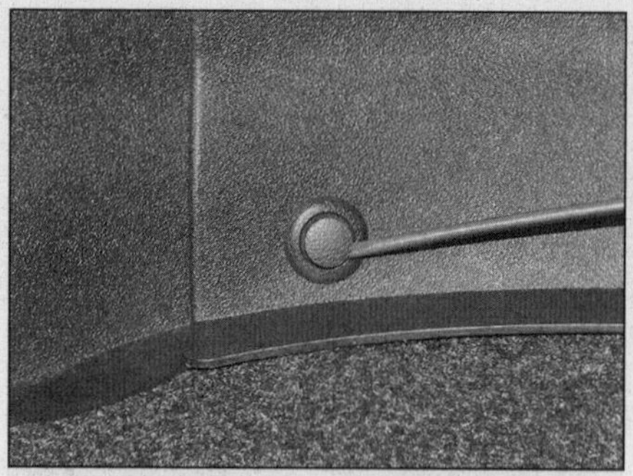

29.1a Prise up the centre pins, lever out the plastic expansion rivets...

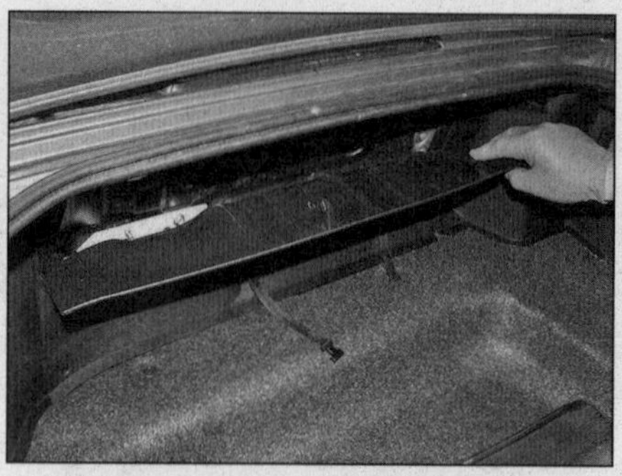

29.1b... and remove the rear trim, front trim...

29.2... and left-hand side trim

29.4 Undo the nut and detach the cable

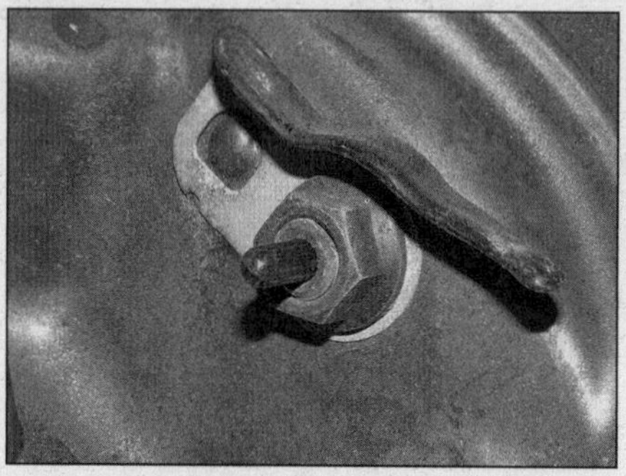

29.5 Undo the nut and remove the opener

the boot rear trim forwards to release the retaining clips **(see illustrations)**. Disconnect any wiring plugs as the trim is withdrawn.

2 Undo the fasteners and remove the left-hand side boot side trim **(see illustration)**.

3 Remove the Back trim as described in Section 26.

4 Undo the nut and detach the opener from the support bracket **(see illustrations)**.

5 Undo the nut and remove the opener cable along with the release lever **(see illustration)**.

6 Unclip the cable from the various clips on the boot floor.

7 Refitting is a reversal of removal. Check for correct operation before closing the fuel filler flap.

Chapter 12
Body electrical systems

Contents

Degrees of difficulty

Easy, suitable for novice with little experience	**Fairly easy,** suitable for beginner with some experience	**Fairly difficult,** suitable for competent DIY mechanic	**Difficult,** suitable for experienced DIY mechanic	**Very difficult,** suitable for expert DIY or professional

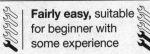

Specifications

System type	12 volt negative earth	
Fuses	See fusebox lid	
Exterior lights	**Wattage**	
Direction indicator side repeater	5 capless	
Direction indicator	21 capless	
Front foglight	55 H11	
Headlight:		
Main beam	60 HB3	
Halogen	55 H7	
Xenon (Gas discharge)	35 DS2	
Sidelight	5 capless	
High-level brake light	LED	
Number plate light	5 capless	
Rear foglight	21 capless	
Reversing light	16 capless	
Brake/tail light	21/5 capless	
Interior lights		
Interior lights	10 festoon	
Luggage compartment light	8 festoon	
Torque wrench settings	**Nm**	**lbf ft**
Airbag system fixings:		
Control unit bolts	10	7
Driver's airbag	10	7
Front impact sensor bolts	10	7
Passenger's airbag retaining nuts	10	7

1 General information and precautions

Warning: Before carrying out any work on the electrical system, read through the precautions given in 'Safety first!' at the beginning of this manual and Chapter 5A, Section 1.

1 The electrical system is of the 12 volt negative earth type. Power for the lights and all electrical accessories is supplied by a lead-acid type battery which is charged by the alternator.

2 This Chapter covers repair and service procedures for the various electrical components not associated with engine. Information on the battery, alternator and starter motor can be found in Chapter 5A.

3 It should be noted that prior to working on any component in the electrical system, the battery negative terminal should first be disconnected to prevent the possibility of electrical short circuits and/or fires (see Chapter 5A, Section 4).

2 Electrical fault finding – general information

Note: *Refer to the precautions given in 'Safety first!' and in Section 1 of this Chapter before starting work. The following tests relate to testing of the main electrical circuits, and should not be used to test delicate electronic circuits (such as anti-lock braking systems), particularly where an electronic control module/unit (ECM/ECU) is used.*

General

1 A typical electrical circuit consists of an electrical component, any switches, relays, motors, fuses, fusible links or circuit breakers related to that component, and the wiring and connectors which link the component to both the battery and the chassis. To help to pin-point a problem in an electrical circuit, wiring diagrams are included at the end of this Chapter.

2 Before attempting to diagnose an electrical fault, first study the appropriate wiring diagram to obtain a complete understanding of the components included in the particular circuit concerned. The possible sources of a fault can be narrowed down by noting if other components related to the circuit are operating properly. If several components or circuits fail at one time, the problem is likely to be related to a shared fuse or earth connection.

3 Electrical problems usually stem from simple causes, such as loose or corroded connections, a faulty earth connection, a blown fuse, a melted fusible link, or a faulty relay. Visually inspect the condition of all fuses, wires and connections in a problem circuit before testing the components. Use the wiring diagrams to determine which terminal connections will need to be checked in order to pin-point the trouble spot.

4 The basic tools required for electrical fault finding include a circuit tester or voltmeter (a 12 volt bulb with a set of test leads can also be used for certain tests); a self-powered test light (sometimes known as a continuity tester); an ohmmeter (to measure resistance); a battery and set of test leads; and a jumper wire, preferably with a circuit breaker or fuse incorporated, which can be used to bypass suspect wires or electrical components. Before attempting to locate a problem with test instruments, use the wiring diagram to determine where to make the connections.

5 To find the source of an intermittent wiring fault (usually due to a poor or dirty connection, or damaged wiring insulation), a 'wiggle' test can be performed on the wiring. This involves wiggling the wiring by hand to see if the fault occurs as the wiring is moved. It should be possible to narrow down the source of the fault to a particular section of wiring. This method of testing can be used in conjunction with any of the tests described in the following sub-Sections.

6 Apart from problems due to poor connections, two basic types of fault can occur in an electrical circuit – open circuit, or short circuit.

7 Open circuit faults are caused by a break somewhere in the circuit, which prevents current from flowing. An open circuit fault will prevent a component from working, but will not cause the relevant circuit fuse to blow.

8 Short circuit faults are caused by a 'short' somewhere in the circuit, which allows the current flowing in the circuit to 'escape' along an alternative route, usually to earth. Short circuit faults are normally caused by a breakdown in wiring insulation, which allows a feed wire to touch either another wire, or an earthed component such as the bodyshell. A short circuit fault will normally cause the relevant circuit fuse to blow.

Finding an open circuit

9 To check for an open circuit, connect one lead of a circuit tester or voltmeter to either the negative battery terminal or a known good earth.

10 Connect the other lead to a connector in the circuit being tested, preferably nearest to the battery or fuse.

11 Switch on the circuit, bearing in mind that some circuits are live only when the ignition switch is moved to a particular position.

12 If voltage is present (indicated either by the tester bulb lighting or a voltmeter reading, as applicable), this means that the section of the circuit between the relevant connector and the battery is problem-free.

13 Continue to check the remainder of the circuit in the same fashion.

14 When a point is reached at which no voltage is present, the problem must lie between that point and the previous test point with voltage. Most problems can be traced to a broken, corroded or loose connection.

Finding a short circuit

15 To check for a short circuit, first disconnect the load(s) from the circuit (loads are the components which draw current from a circuit, such as bulbs, motors, heating elements, etc).

16 Remove the relevant fuse from the circuit, and connect a circuit tester or voltmeter to the fuse connections.

17 Switch on the circuit, bearing in mind that some circuits are live only when the ignition switch is moved to a particular position.

18 If voltage is present (indicated either by the tester bulb lighting or a voltmeter reading, as applicable), this means that there is a short circuit.

19 If no voltage is present, but the fuse still blows with the load(s) connected, this indicates an internal fault in the load(s).

Finding an earth fault

20 The battery negative terminal is connected to 'earth' – the metal of the engine/transmission and the car body – and most systems are wired so that they only receive a positive feed, the current returning through the metal of the car body. This means that the component mounting and the body form part of that circuit. Loose or corroded mountings can therefore cause a range of electrical faults, ranging from total failure of a circuit, to a puzzling partial fault. In particular, lights may shine dimly (especially when another circuit sharing the same earth point is in operation), motors (eg, wiper motors or the radiator cooling fan motor) may run slowly, and the operation of one circuit may have an apparently unrelated effect on another. Note that on many vehicles, earth straps are used between certain components, such as the engine/transmission and the body, usually where there is no metal-to-metal contact between components due to flexible rubber mountings, etc **(see illustrations)**.

21 To check whether a component is properly earthed, disconnect the battery and connect one lead of an ohmmeter to a known good earth point. Connect the other lead to the wire or earth connection being tested. The resistance reading should be zero; if not, check the connection as follows.

22 If an earth connection is thought to be faulty, dismantle the connection and clean back to bare metal both the bodyshell and the wire terminal or the component earth connection mating surface. Be careful to remove all traces of dirt and corrosion, then use a knife to trim away any paint, so that a clean metal-to-metal joint is made. On reassembly, tighten the joint fasteners securely; if a wire terminal is being refitted, use serrated washers between the terminal and the bodyshell to ensure a clean and secure connection. When the connection is remade, prevent the onset of corrosion in the future by applying a coat of petroleum jelly or silicone-based grease or by spraying on (at regular intervals) a proprietary ignition sealer or a water dispersant lubricant.

2.20a The main earth strap is from the battery negative lead to a bracket on the engine

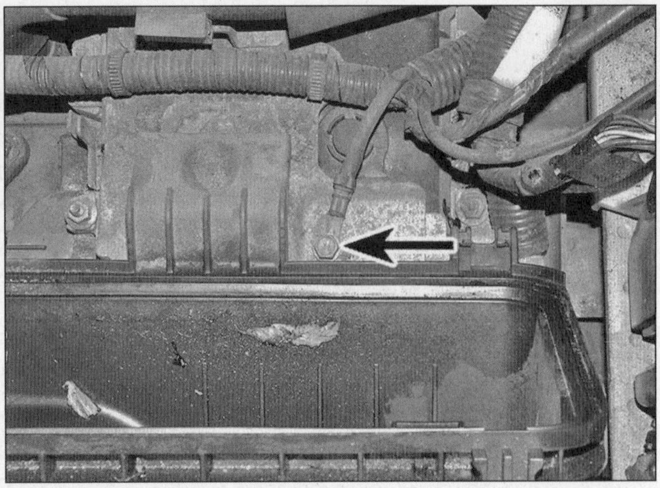

2.20b Other earth points include beneath the air cleaner housing...

2.20c... behind each front wheel arch liner...

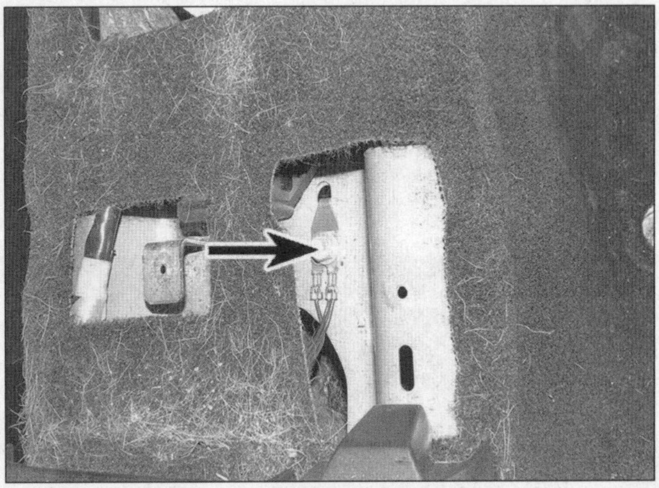

2.20d... under the centre console...

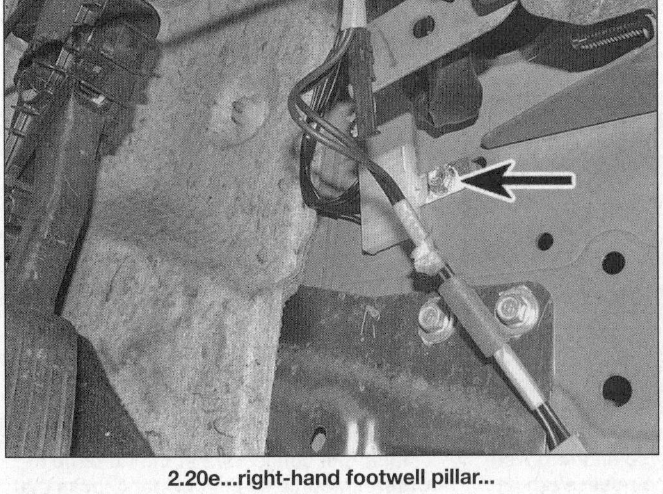

2.20e...right-hand footwell pillar...

2.20f...and the inner wing in the engine compartment

3 Electrical connectors – general information

1 Most electrical connections on these vehicles are made with multiwire plastic connectors. The mating halves of many connectors are secured with locking clips molded into the plastic connector shells. The mating halves of some large connectors, such as some of those under the instrument panel, are held together by a bolt through the center of the connector.

2 To separate a connector with locking clips, use a small screwdriver to pry the clips apart carefully, then separate the connector halves. Pull only on the shell, never pull on the wiring harness, as you may damage the individual wires and terminals inside the connectors. Look at the connector closely before trying to separate the halves. Often the locking clips are engaged in a way that is not immediately clear. Additionally, many connectors have more than one set of clips.

3 Each pair of connector terminals has a male half and a female half. When you look at the end view of a connector in a diagram, be sure to understand whether the view shows the harness side or the component side of the connector. Connector halves are mirror images of each other, and a terminal shown on the right side end-view of one half will be on the left side end-view of the other half.

4 It is often necessary to take circuit voltage measurements with a connector connected. Whenever possible, carefully insert a small straight pin (not your meter probe) into the rear of the connector shell to contact the terminal inside, then clip your meter lead to the pin. This kind of connection is called "backprobing." When inserting a test probe into a terminal, be careful not to distort the terminal opening. Doing so can lead to a poor connection and corrosion at that terminal later. Using the small straight pin instead of a meter probe results in less chance of deforming the terminal connector. "T" pins are a good choice as temporary meter connections. They allow for a larger surface area to attach the meter leads too.

Electrical connectors

5 Typical electrical connectors:

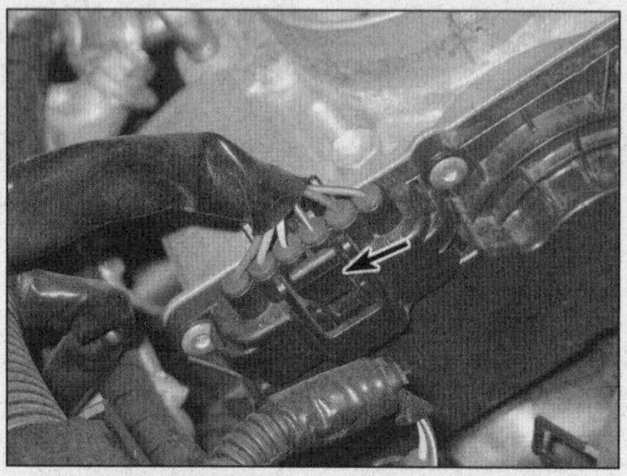

3.5a Most electrical connectors have a single release tab that you depress to release the connector

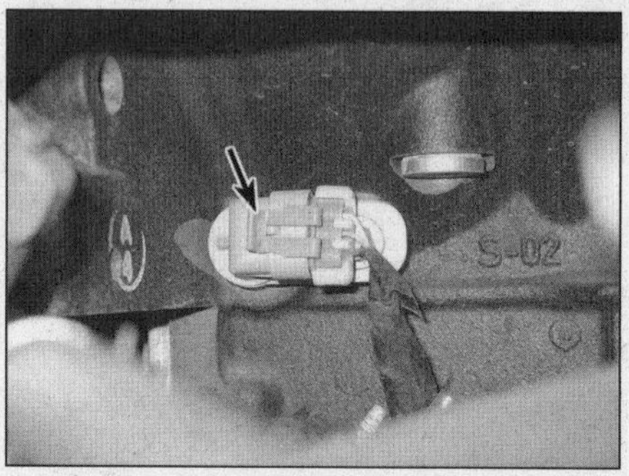

3.5b Some electrical connectors have a retaining tab which must be pried up to free the connector

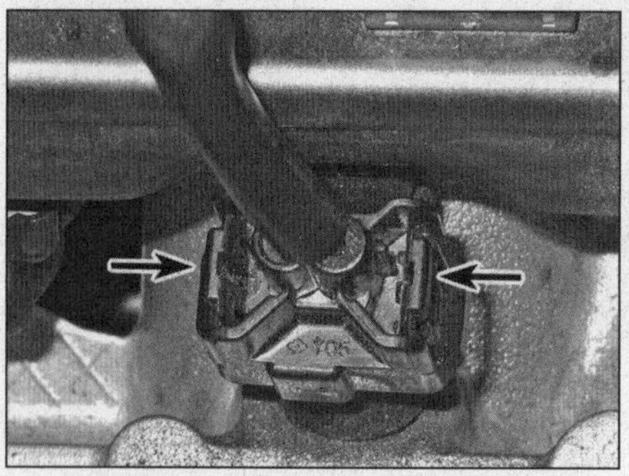

3.5c Some connectors have two release tabs that you must squeeze to release the connector

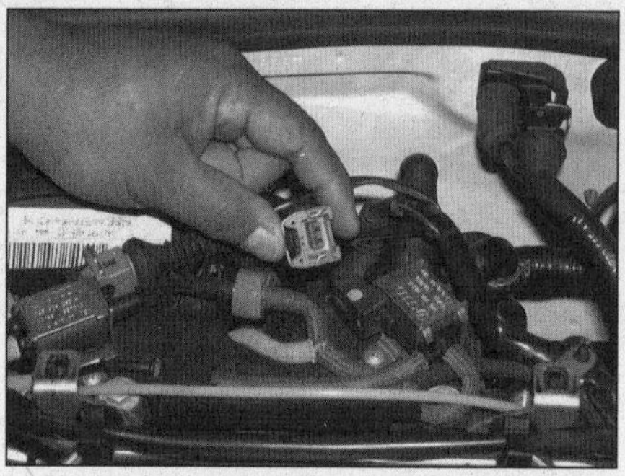

3.5d Some connectors use wire retainers that you squeeze to release the connector

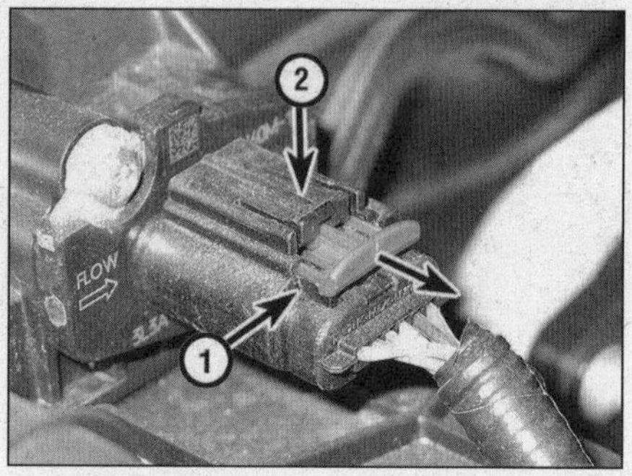

3.5e Critical connectors often employ a sliding lock (1) that you must pull out before you can depress the release tab (2)

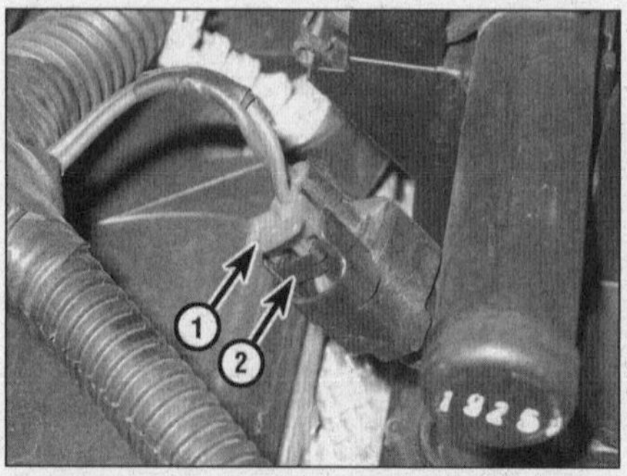

3.5f Here's another sliding-lock style connector, with the lock (1) and the release tab (2) on the side of the connector

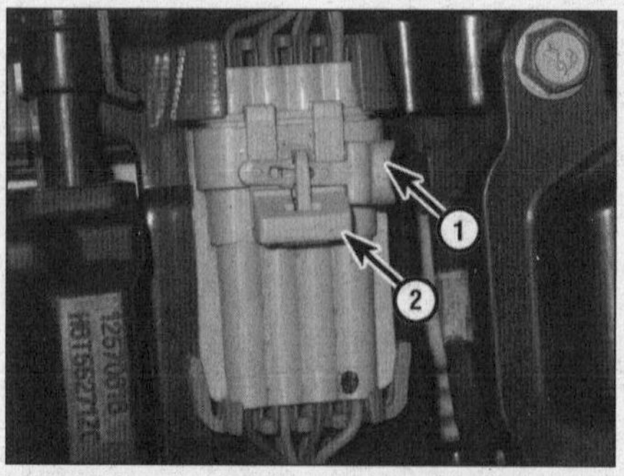

3.5g On some connectors the lock (1) must be pulled out to the side and removed before you can lift the release tab (2)

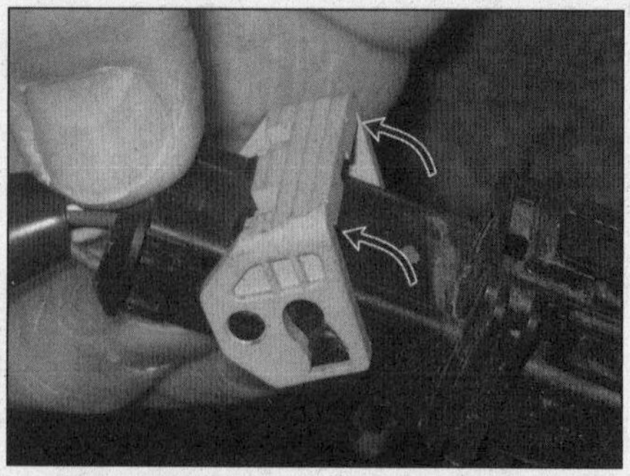

3.5h Some critical connectors, like the multi-pin connectors at the Electronic Control Module employ pivoting locks that must be flipped open

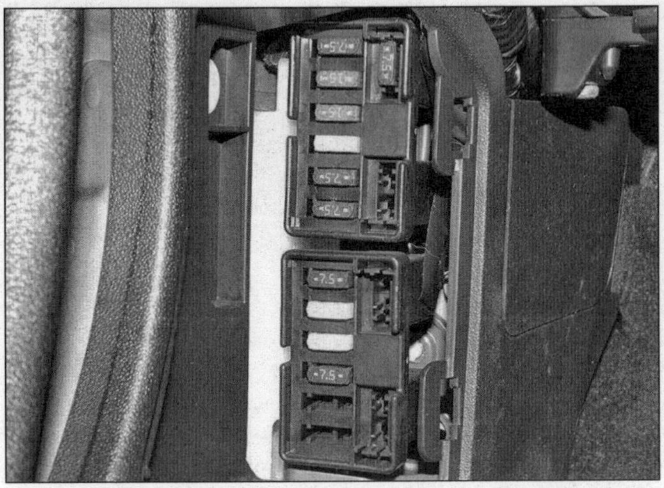

4.1a Main fusebox under the left-hand side of the facia

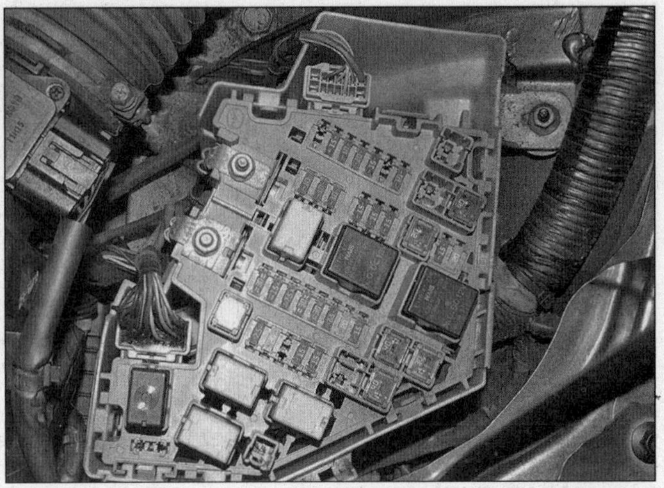

4.1b The engine compartment fusebox is located on the left-hand side

4 Fuses and relays – general information

Main fuses

1 The fuses are located in the engine compartment on the left-hand side, whilst some others are located underneath the facia **(see illustrations).**

2 A list of the circuits each fuse protects is given on fusebox cover. A pair of tweezers for removing the fuses is also clipped to the fusebox lid. High amperage fuses are located in the main fusebox in the engine compartment.

3 To remove a fuse, first switch off the circuit concerned (or the ignition), then pull the fuse out of its terminals **(see illustration).** The wire within the fuse should be visible; if the fuse is blown it will be broken or melted.

4 Always renew a fuse with one of an identical rating; never use a fuse with a different rating from the original or substitute anything else. Never renew a fuse more than once without tracing the source of the trouble. The fuse rating is stamped on top of the fuse; note that the fuses are also colour-coded for easy recognition.

5 If a new fuse blows immediately, find the cause before renewing it again; a short to earth as a result of faulty insulation is most likely. Where a fuse protects more than one circuit, try to isolate the defect by switching on each circuit in turn (if possible) until the fuse blows again. Always carry a supply of spare fuses of each relevant rating on the vehicle, a spare of each rating should be clipped into the base of the fusebox.

Relays

6 Many electrical accessories in the vehicle use relays to switch the electrical supply to the component. If the relay is defective, that component will not operate properly. Relay locations vary by model year.

7 The main relays are located on the left-hand side of the engine compartment **(see illustrations).**

8 If a circuit or system controlled by a relay develops a fault and the relay is suspect, operate the system; if the relay is functioning it should be possible to hear it click as it is energised. If this is the case the fault lies with the components or wiring of the system. If the relay is not being energised then either the relay is not receiving a main supply or a switching voltage or the relay itself is faulty. Testing is by the substitution of a known good unit but be careful; while some relays are identical in appearance and in operation, others look similar but perform different functions.

9 To renew a relay first ensure that the ignition switch is off. The relay can then simply be pulled out from the socket and the new relay pressed in.

5 Switches – removal and refitting

Note: *Disconnect the battery negative lead before removing any switch, and reconnect the lead after refitting the switch (see Chapter 5A Section 4).*

Ignition switch

1 Remove the steering column upper and lower shrouds as described in Chapter 11 Section 26.

2 Disconnect the electrical connector from the switch.

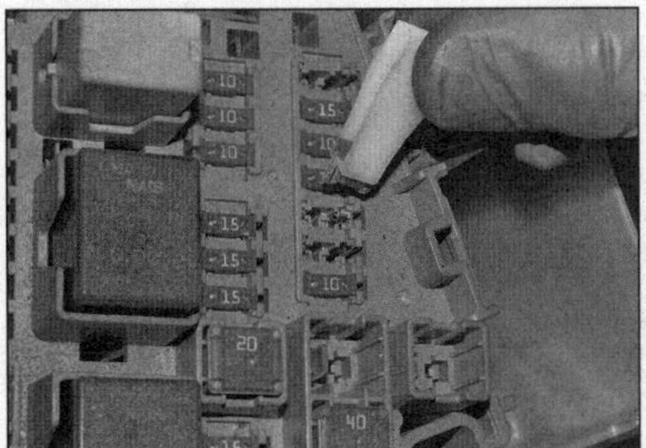

4.3 Use the tweezers provided to remove a fuse

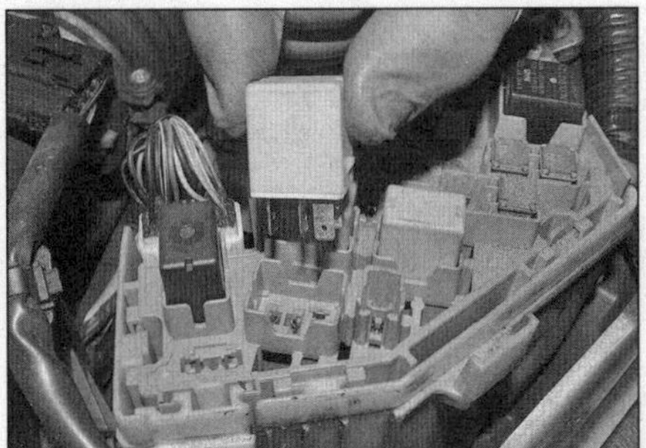

4.7a The main relays are in the engine compartment fuse box

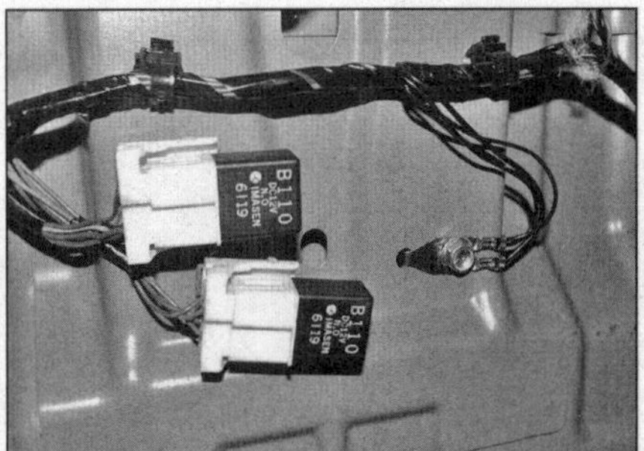

4.7b The boot lid opener and fog light relays are located on the rear panel in the luggage compartment

5.3 Ignition switch retaining screw

5.7a The combination switch is secured by one screw underneath...

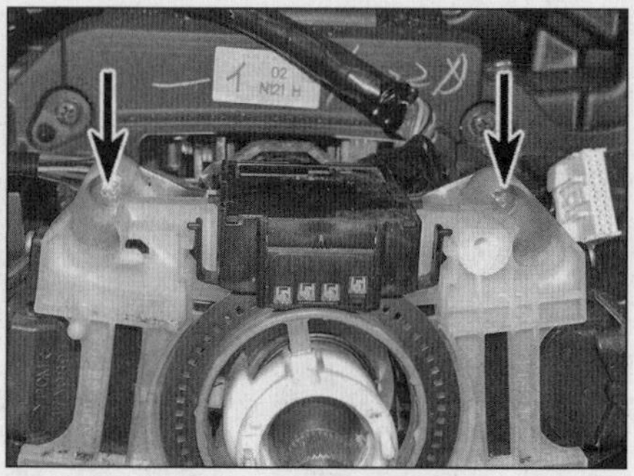
5.7b... and two above

3 Remove the screw and separate the switch from the steering lock assembly **(see illustration)**.
4 Refitting is the reverse of removal.

Steering column combination switch

5 Remove the drivers airbag rotary contact unit (clockspring) as described in Section 22.
6 Note their fitted positions, then disconnect the wiring plugs from the combination switch.
7 Remove the combination switch retaining screws **(see illustrations)**.
8 Remove the combination switch assembly.
9 If required, undo the screw each side and separate the washer/wiper and light switches from the combination switch body **(see illustration 5.13)**.
10 Refitting is a reversal of removal.
Note: *On models with Dynamic Stability Control (DSC), whenever the battery is reconnected, it's imperative that the steering angle sensor be re-initialised as described in Chapter 5A Section 4.*

Washer/wiper and light switches

11 Remove the steering column shrouds as described in Chapter 11 Section 26.
12 Disconnect the wiring plug from the relevant switch.
13 Undo the retaining screws and gently pull the relevant switch from the combination switch body **(see illustration)**.
14 Refitting is a reversal of removal.

Hazard warning/roof switches

15 Remove the left-hand side vent trim panel as described in Chapter 11 Section 28.
16 Undo the two retaining screws at the upper edge, pull the switch assembly rearwards a little, and disconnect the wiring plug **(see illustration)**.
17 Refitting is a reversal of removal.

Electric window switches

18 Remove the centre console as described in Chapter 11 Section 27.
19 Depress the tabs each side and detach the switch assembly **(see illustration)**.
20 Refitting is a reversal of removal.

Exterior mirror switches

21 Remove the door trim panel as described in Chapter 11 Section 11.
22 Undo the three retaining screws and remove the switch **(see illustration)**. Disconnect the wiring plug as the switch is withdrawn.
23 Refitting is a reversal of removal.

Clutch pedal switch

24 Refer to Chapter 6 Section 7.

Brake light switch

25 Refer to Chapter 9 Section 16.

Courtesy light switches

26 Undo the retaining screw, and pull the light switch from the door aperture **(see illustration)**. Disconnect the wiring plug as the switch is withdrawn.
27 Refitting is a reversal of removal.

Handbrake warning light switch

28 Remove the centre console as described in Chapter 11 Section 27.

5.13 Switch retaining screws

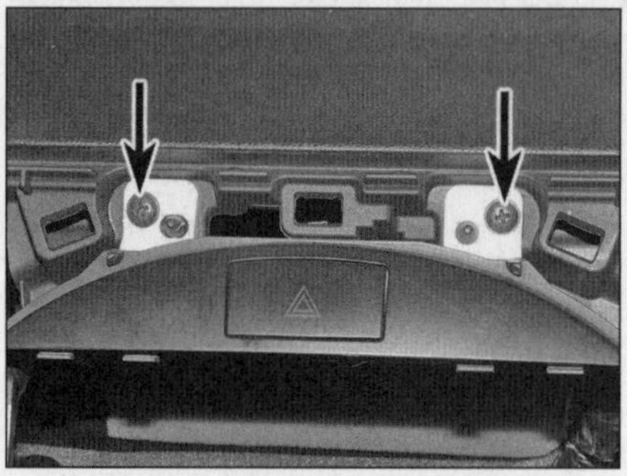
5.16 Hazard warning switch retaining screws

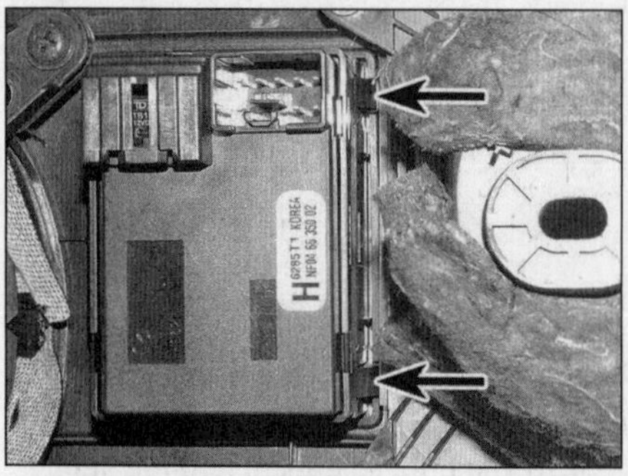
5.19 Depress the tab each side of the switch

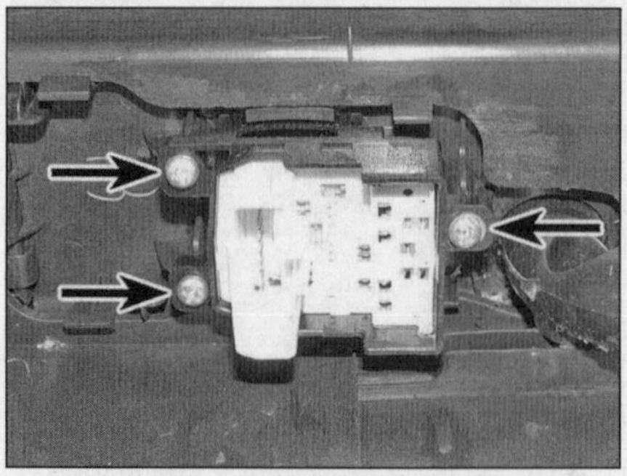
5.22 Electric mirror switch retaining screws

5.26 Undo the screw and withdraw the courtesy light switch

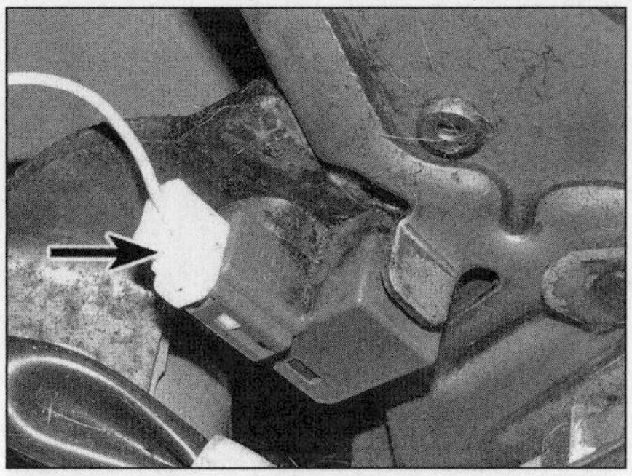

5.29 Handbrake warning light switch wiring plug

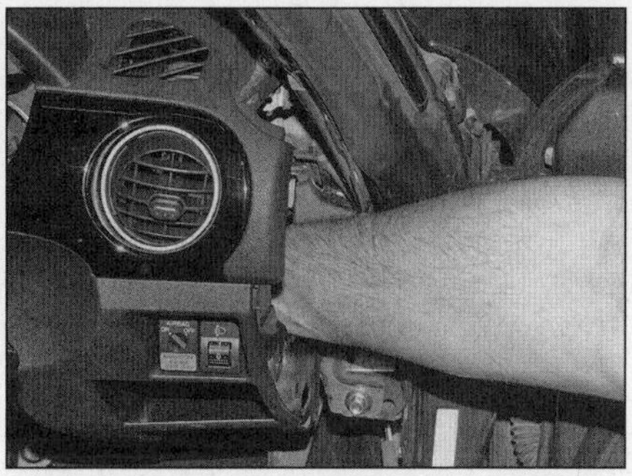

5.33 Push the headlight levelling switch from the facia

5.35 Reach behind and push the switch from place

29 Disconnect the switch wiring plug **(see illustration)**.
30 Undo the retaining screw and remove the switch.
31 Refitting is a reversal of removal.

Headlight levelling switch

32 Carefully prise the end panel from the facia.
33 Reach behind the facia and push/pull the levelling switch from place **(see illustration)**.
34 Disconnect the wiring plug as the switch is withdrawn.

Boot lid release switch

35 Reach up under the facia and push the switch from place **(see illustration)**.
36 Disconnect the switch wiring plug.
37 Refitting is a reversal of removal.

Heated seat switches

38 Remove the console panel as described in Chapter 11 Section 28.
39 Depress the clips each side and detach the switches from the panel **(see illustration)**.
40 Refitting is a reversal of removal.

6 Bulbs (exterior lights) – renewal

General

1 Whenever a bulb is renewed, note the following points.

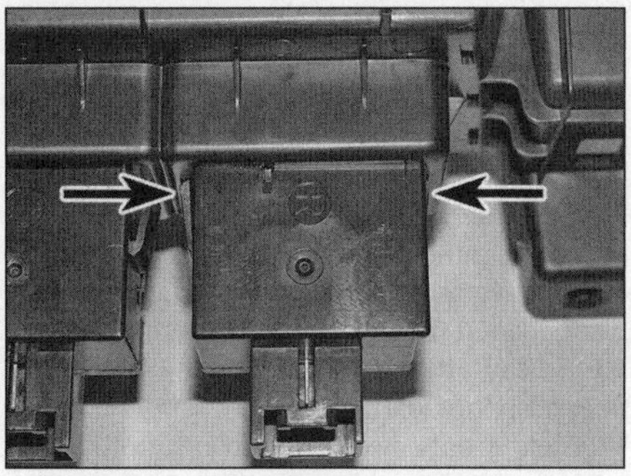

5.39 Depress the clips each side of the switch

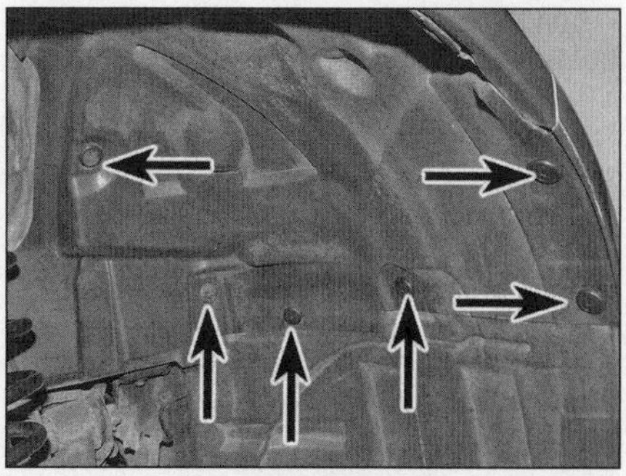

6.3 Remove the fasteners and pull back the wheelarch liner

a) Remember that if the light has just been in use the bulb may be extremely hot.
b) Always check the bulb contacts and holder, ensuring that there is clean metal-to-metal contact between the bulb and its live(s) and earth. Clean off any corrosion or dirt before fitting a new bulb.
c) Wherever bayonet-type bulbs are fitted ensure that the live contact(s) bear firmly against the bulb contact.
d) Always ensure that the new bulb is of the correct rating and that it is completely clean before fitting it; this applies particularly to headlight/foglight bulbs (see below).
e) When handling the new bulb, use a tissue or clean cloth to avoid touching the glass with the fingers; moisture and grease from the skin can cause blackening and rapid failure of the bulb. If the glass is accidentally touched, wipe it clean using methylated spirit.

Headlight

Dipped beam

2 The dipped beam bulbs are accessed by bending back the front section of the wheelarch liner. In order to access the liner fasteners, turn the steering wheel to the full lock position, on the right-, or left-hand side as applicable.
3 Unscrew the centre pin, prise out the plastic expansion rivets, and pull back the front section of the wheelarch liner **(see illustration)**.

Halogen bulb

4 Depress the tab and disconnect the bulb wiring plug, then remove the cover from the rear of the headlight **(see illustration)**.
5 Press the end of the bulb retaining clip forwards, then downwards and fold it rearwards **(see illustration)**.
6 Gently extract the bulb and socket from the headlight **(see illustration)**.

6.4 Pull the cover from the rear of the headlight

6.5 Release the clip and fold it rearwards

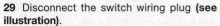

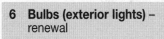

6.6 Extract the bulb and socket

6.7 Pull the bulb from the socket

6.8 Align the tab with the slot in the reflector

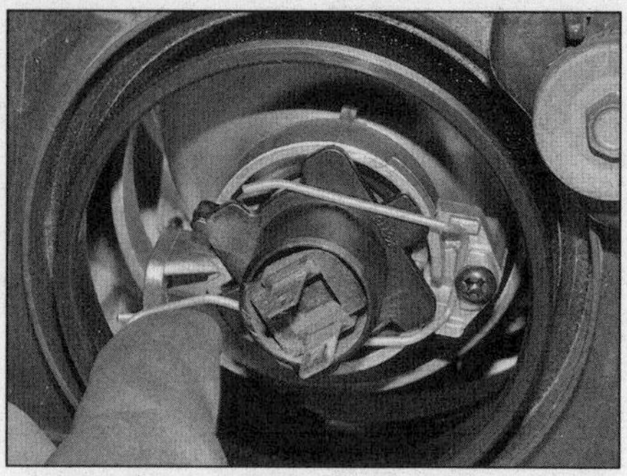

6.9 Engage the end of the clip with the hook

7 Pull the bulb from the socket **(see illustration)**.

8 Taking care not to touch the bulb glass with bare skin, firmly press the new bulb into the socket, then manoeuvre the bulb into the headlamp. Align the tab on the socket flange with the slot in the headlight reflector **(see illustration)**.

9 Fold the retaining clip forwards, and engage the end with the hook **(see illustration)**.

10 Refit the headlight cover, and reconnect the wiring plug.

Gas discharge (Xenon) bulbs

Warning: These bulbs operate at high-voltage. It's imperative that the battery is disconnected (see Chapter 5A Section 4), then allow at least 5 minutes for any residual electrical energy to dissipate.

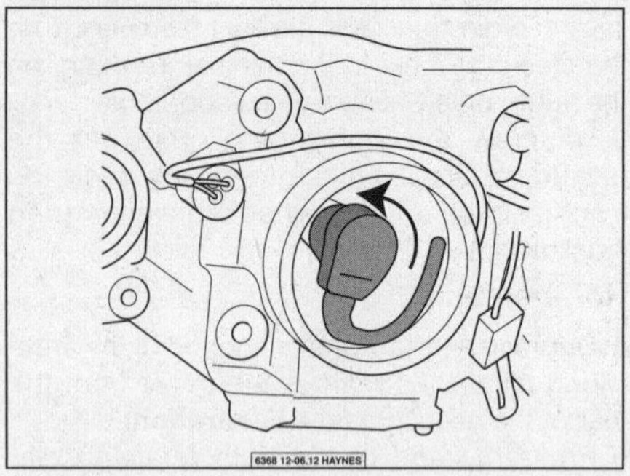

6.12 Rotate the wiring plug anti-clockwise

Warning: Gas discharge (Xenon) bulbs are highly pressurised. We strongly recommend that protective glasses and gloves are worn during this procedure.

11 Rotate the cover on the rear of the headlight anti-clockwise and remove it.

12 Rotate the wiring plug anti-clockwise and disconnect it **(see illustration)**.

13 Release the spring clips and remove the bulb from the headlight.

14 Taking care not to touch the bulb glass with bare skin, insert the bulb into the headlight reflector and secure it with the spring clip.

15 Reconnect the wiring plug and refit the cover to the rear of the headlight.

All dipped bulbs

16 Press the wheelarch liner back into place, insert the plastic expansion rivets, then press-in the centre pins to secure them.

6.17 Disconnect the main beam bulb wiring plug

Main beam bulbs

17 Working in the engine compartment, depress the locking tab and disconnect the wiring plug from the main beam bulb **(see illustration)**.

18 Rotate the bulb and socket assembly anti-clockwise and withdraw it from the headlight **(see illustration)**.

19 Taking care not to touch the bulb glass with bare skin, insert the bulb and socket assembly into the headlight, then rotate it clockwise to the stop.

20 Securely reconnect the wiring plug.

Front sidelight

21 Open the bonnet.

Left-hand side bulb

22 Release the clip and move the wiring harness at the rear of the headlight to one side.

23 Rotate the bulbholder anti-clockwise and pull it from the headlight.

24 Pull the capless bulb from the holder.

Right-hand side bulb

25 Unclip and remove the battery cover **(see illustration)**.

26 Undo the retaining nuts and move the coolant reservoir to one side **(see illustration)**. There's no need to disconnect any hoses.

6.18 Rotate the bulb/socket anti-clockwise and remove it

6.25 Remove the battery cover

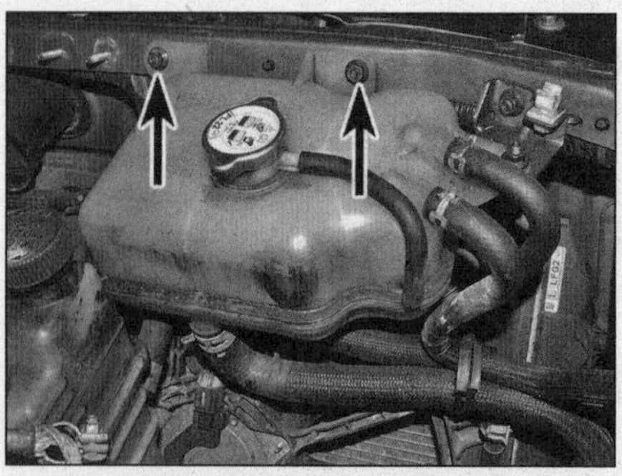

6.26 Coolant reservoir retaining nuts

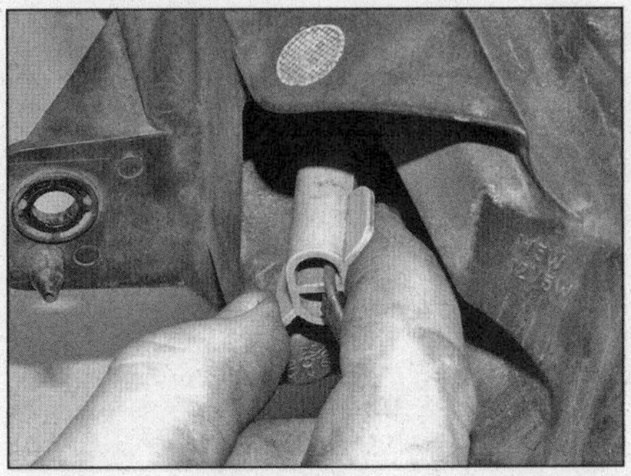
6.27 Rotate the bulbholder anti-clockwise

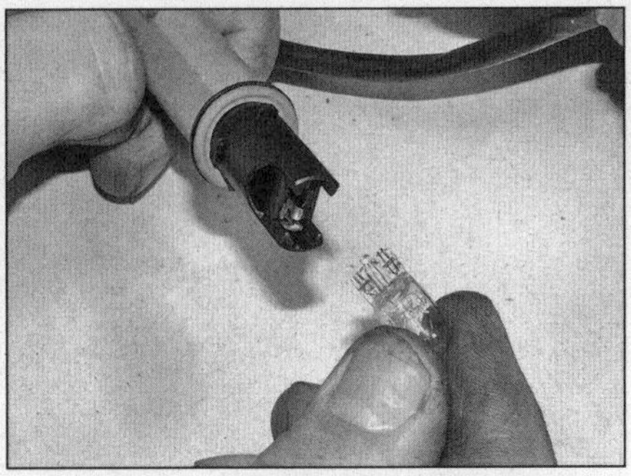
6.28 Pull the bulb from the holder

6.32 Rotate the bulbholder anti-clockwise

27 Rotate the bulbholder anti-clockwise and pull it from the headlight **(see illustration)**.

28 Pull the capless bulb from the holder **(see illustration)**.

Both sides

29 Refitting is a reversal of removal.

Front direction indicator

30 The direction indicator bulbs are accessed by bending back the front section of the wheelarch liner. In order to access the liner fasteners, turn the steering wheel to the full lock position, on the right-, or left-hand side as applicable.

31 Unscrew the centre pin, prise out the plastic expansion rivets, and pull back the front section of the wheelarch liner **(see illustration 6.3)**.

32 Disconnect the wiring plug, then rotate the bulbholder anti-clockwise and pull it from the rear of the headlight **(see illustration)**.

33 Pull the capless bulb from the holder.

34 Press the new bulb gently into the holder, then insert the holder into the headlight, and turn it clockwise to the stop.

35 Reconnect the wiring plug.

36 Press the wheelarch liner back into place, insert the plastic expansion rivets, then press-in the centre pins to secure them.

Side repeater

37 Remove the side repeater light assembly as described in Section 8.

38 Rotate the bulbholder anti-clockwise and pull it from the lens, pull the capless bulb from the holder **(see illustration)**.

39 Refitting is a reverse of the removal procedure.

Front foglight

40 Undo the fasteners and and pull back the front, lower section of the front wheel arch liner. To improve access, raise the front of the vehicle, support it securely on axle stands (see *Jacking and vehicle support*). Remove the relevant front roadwheel.

41 Depress the tab and disconnect the wiring plug from the bulb/holder assembly.

42 Rotate the bulbholder anti-clockwise and pull it from the foglight. Note that the bulb is integral with the holder **(see illustration)**.

43 Refitting is a reversal of removal. If necessary, adjust the aim of the light by rotating the adjusting screw on the underside of the unit **(see illustration)**.

Rear light cluster

44 Open the boot, unscrew the centre pins, lever out the plastic expansion rivets, then remove the boot rear trim panel, and the panel from the relevant side **(see illustrations 8.12a, 8.12b and 8.12c)**. Disconnect any wiring plugs as the panels are withdrawn.

45 Rotate the relevant bulbholder anti-clockwise and pull it from the light cluster **(see illustration)**.

46 Pull the capless bulb from the holder **(see illustration)**.

47 Refitting is a reversal of removal.

High-level brake light

48 The high-level brake light is illuminated by non-replaceable LEDs.

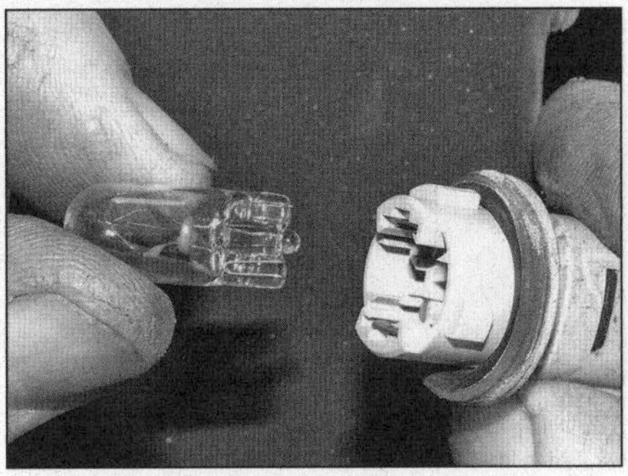
6.38 Pull the capless side repeater bulb from the holder

6.42 The fog light bulb is integral with the holder

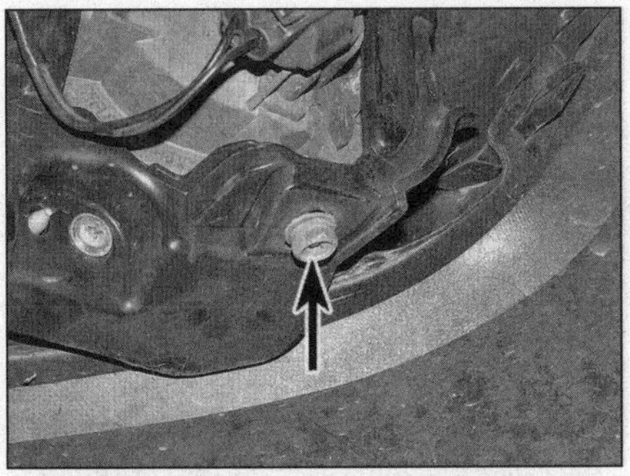
6.43 Foglight aim adjusting screw

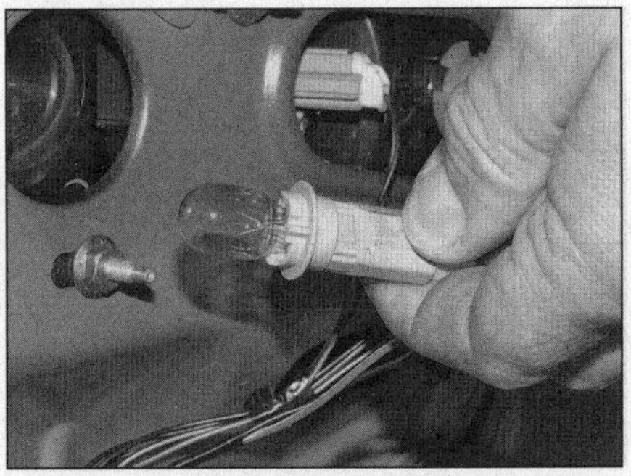
6.45 Rotate the relevant bulbholder anti-clockwise

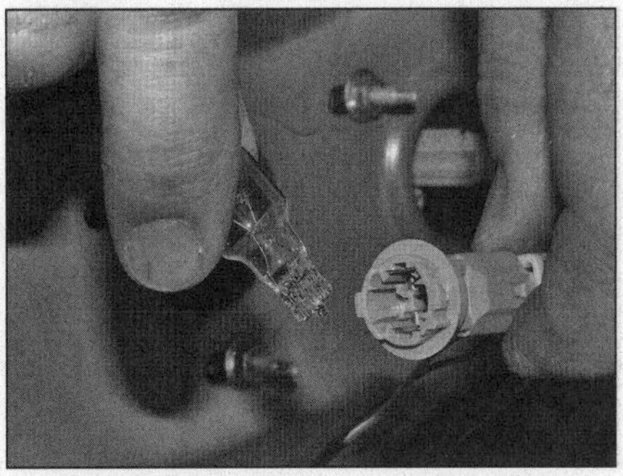
6.46 Pull the bulb from the holder

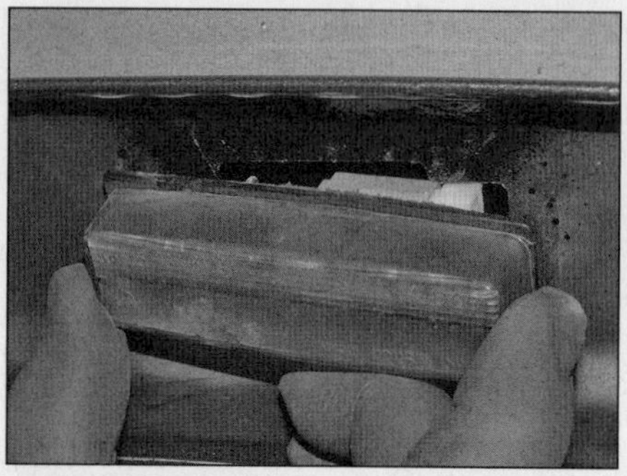
6.49 Push the lens to the left, then pull the right-hand end from place

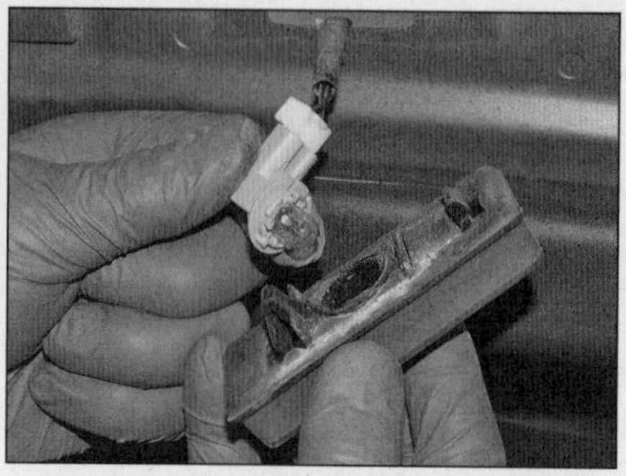
6.50 Rotate the bulbholder anti-clockwise and pull the capless bulb from place

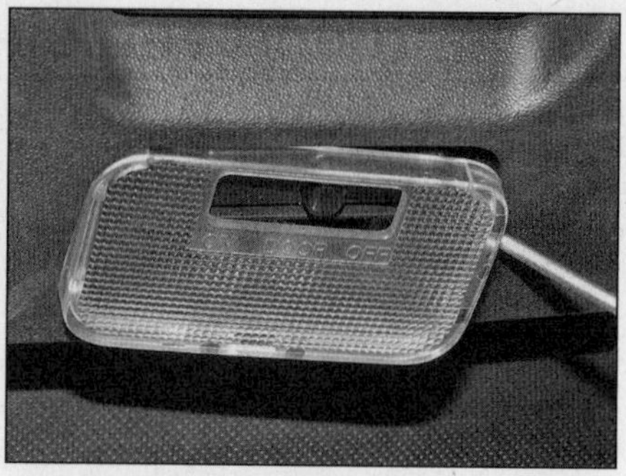
7.2 Gently prise the lens from the header trim

7.3 Prise out the festoon bulb from the contacts

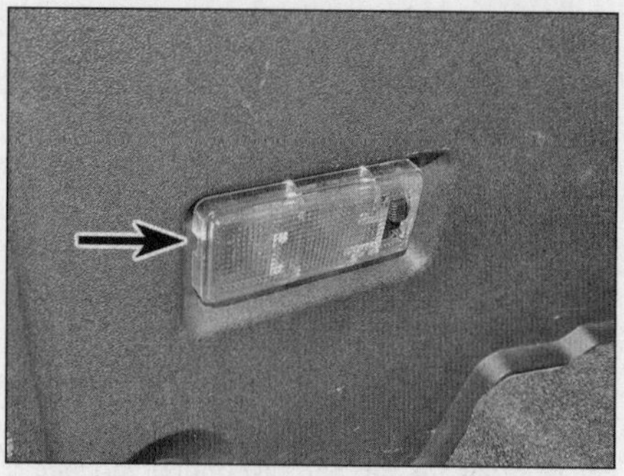
7.5 Using the slot provided, prise the light unit from the trim

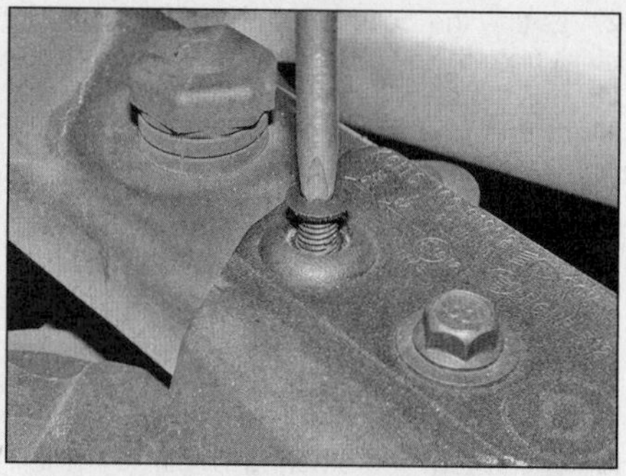
8.2 Unscrew the centre pin and prise out the expansion rivet

Number plate light

49 Carefully push the light unit to the left, and remove it **(see illustration)**.

50 Rotate the bulbholder anti-clockwise and remove it from the light unit **(see illustration)**. Pull the capless bulb from the holder.

51 Refitting is a reversal of removal.

7 Bulbs (interior lights) – renewal

General

1 Refer to Section 6, paragraph 1.

Courtesy lights

2 Carefully prise the lens from place **(see illustration)**.

3 Pull the festoon bulb from the contacts **(see illustration)**.

4 Refitting is a reversal of removal.

Luggage compartment light

5 Using a wooden or plastic spatula, carefully prise out the side edge of the interior light and remove it **(see illustration)**.

6 Pull the festoon bulb from the contacts.

7 Refitting is a reversal of removal.

8 Exterior light units – removal and refitting

Headlight

1 Remove the front bumper as described in Chapter 11, Section 6.

2 Unscrew the centre pin, and prise out the plastic expansion rivet at the top of the headlight **(see illustration)**.

3 The headlight is now secured by 4 bolts around its circumference **(see illustrations)**. Undo the bolts and pull the headlight forwards a little. Note that it's only necessary to slacken the lower mounting bolt.

4 Disconnect the headlight wiring plugs and remove the headlight.

5 Refitting is a direct reversal of the removal procedure. Lightly tighten the retaining screws and check the alignment of the headlight with the bumper and bonnet. Once the light unit is correctly positioned, securely tighten the retaining screws and check the headlight beam alignment using the information given in Section 9.

Front indicator side repeater

6 Using finger pressure, push the side repeater lens gently rearwards. Pull out the front edge of the lens and withdraw it from the wing **(see illustration)**. Disconnect the wiring plug as the unit is withdrawn.

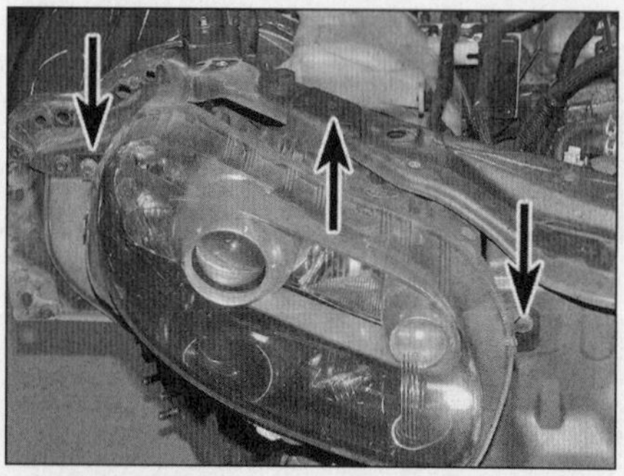
8.3a The headlight is secured by one bolt at the top, one each side...

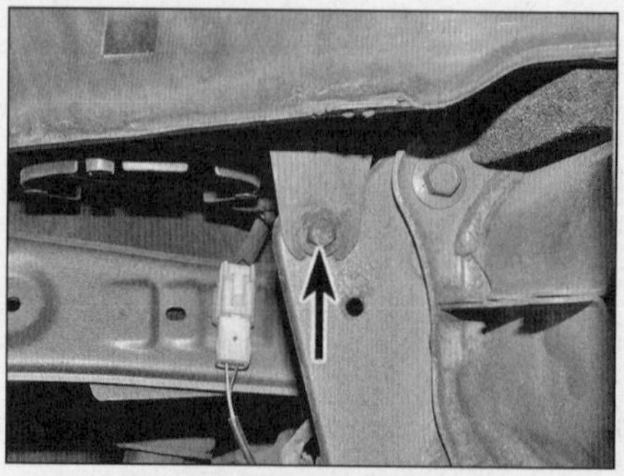
8.3b... and one underneath

8.6 Push the side repeater rearwards to compress the clip, then pull out the front edge

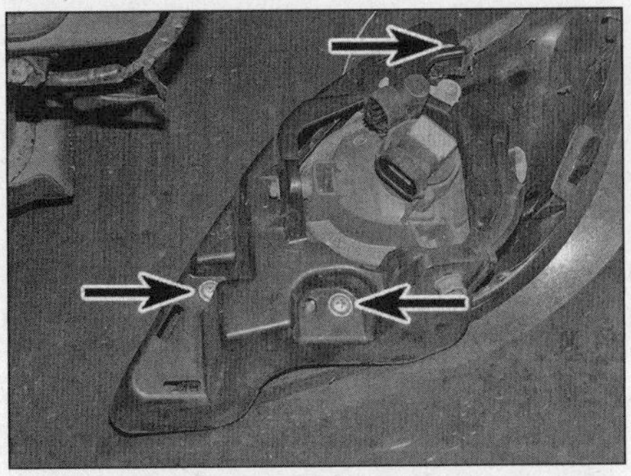
8.10 Front foglight mounting bolts

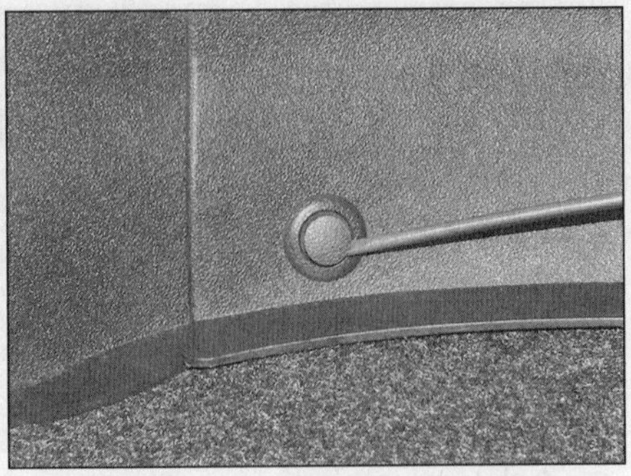
8.12a Prise up the centre pins, and lever out the expansion rivets

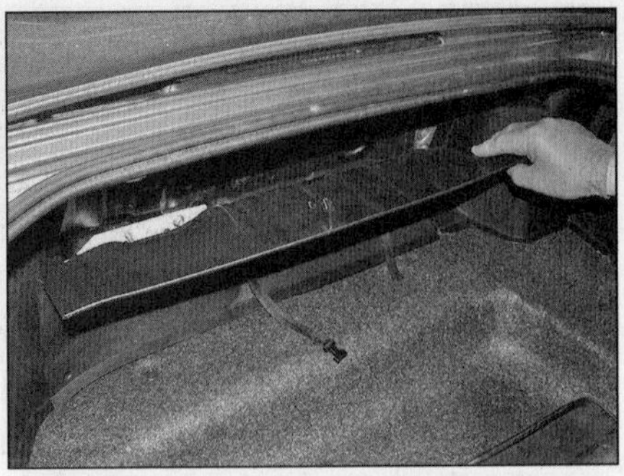
8.12b Remove the panel behind the seats...

8.12c... and the panel(s) in front of the rear lights

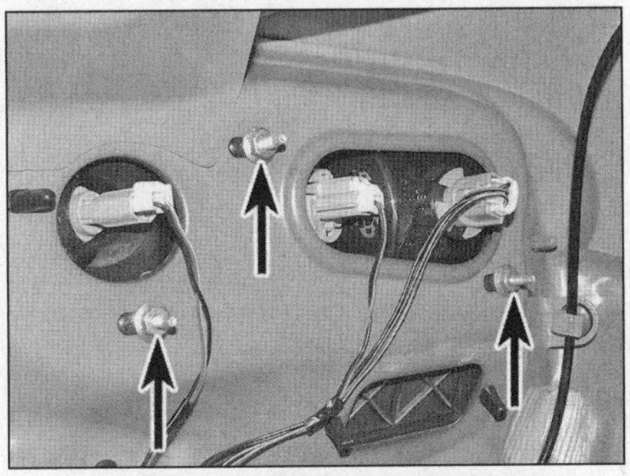
8.13a Rear light retaining nuts

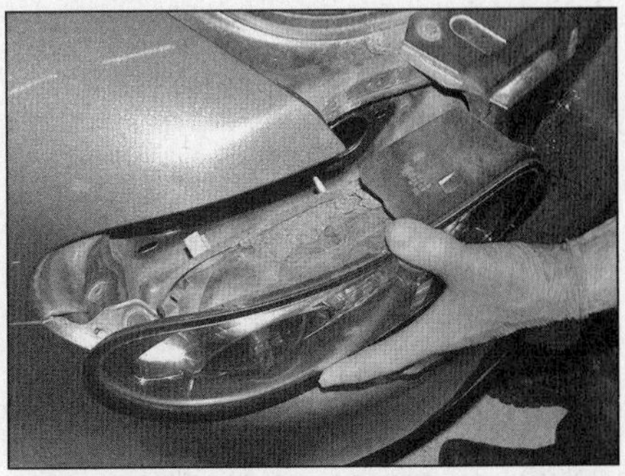
8.13b Pull the rear light cluster rearwards

7 Refitting is a reverse of the removal procedure.

Front foglight

8 Remove the front bumper as described in Chapter 11 Section 6.
9 Disconnect the fog light wiring plug.
10 Undo the mounting bolts, and remove the foglight **(see illustration)**.
11 Refitting is a reversal of removal. If required, the foglight aim can be adjusted by rotating the adjuster screw **(see illustration 06.42)**.

Rear light cluster

12 Working in the luggage compartment, prise up the centre pins, lever out the expansion rivets and pull away the trim panels in front of the rear light unit(s) **(see illustrations)**.
13 Undo the 3 retaining nuts and manoeuvre the light cluster rearwards **(see illustrations)**. Disconnect the wiring plugs as the light unit is withdrawn.
14 Refitting is a reversal of removal.

High-level brake light

Soft-top convertible models

15 Undo the fasteners and remove the panel behind the rear seats **(see illustration 8.12b)**.
16 Disconnect the high-level brake light wiring plug.
17 Squeeze together the sides of the clips then ease the high-level brake light upwards from place **(see illustrations)**.

Retractable hardtop models

18 Operate the controls and fully open the deck panel.
19 Partially peel back the seal cover **(see illustration)**. Note that the cover will probably be damaged during the procedure – a new one may be required.
20 Disconnect the wiring plug, then undo the 3 nuts and gently ease the high-level brake light out of the deck panel.

9 Headlight beam alignment – general information

1 Accurate adjustment of the headlight beam is only possible using optical beam setting equipment and this work should therefore be carried out by a Mazda dealer or suitably-equipped workshop.
2 For reference, the headlights can be

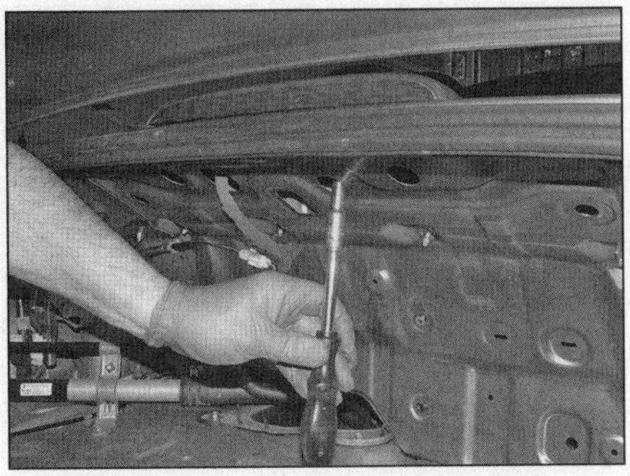
8.17a Push a small diameter socket...

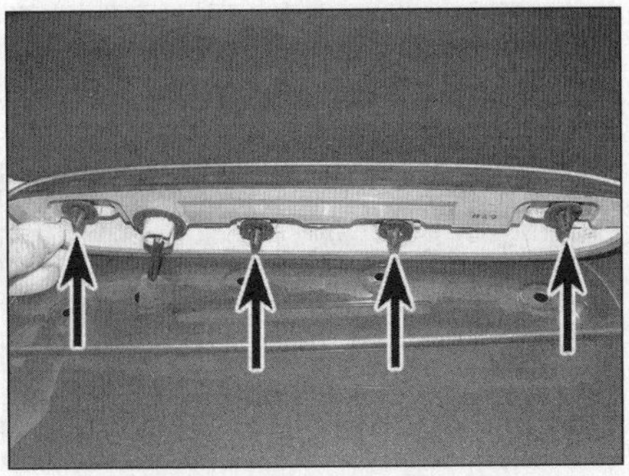
8.17b... over the ends of the clips to release them

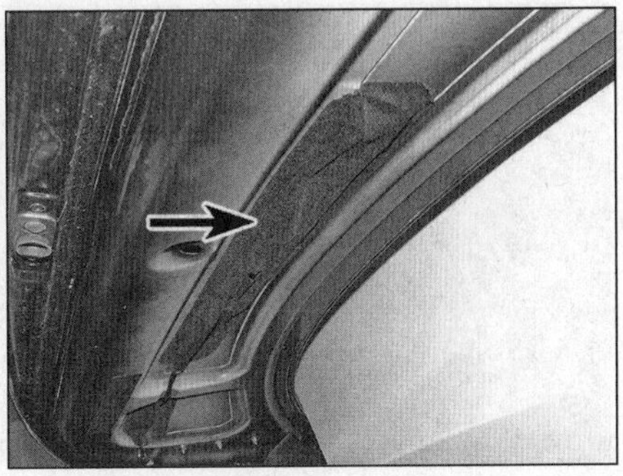
8.19 Peel back the seal cover

9.2a Vertical adjustment screw

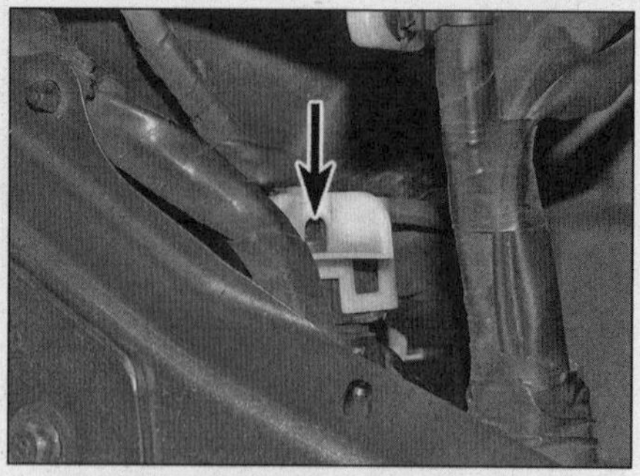
9.2b Horizontal adjustment screw

adjusted by rotating the adjuster screws with a cross-head screwdriver **(see illustrations)**.

3 All models have an electrically-operated headlight beam adjustment system which is controlled through the switch in the facia. Ensure that the switch is set to position 0 before adjusting the headlight aim.

10 Gas discharge lights (Xenon) control modules and sensors – removal and refitting

Warning: Due to the high-voltages involved, prior to starting work on any Xenon headlight system components, disconnect the battery as described in Chapter 5A Section 4, then allow at least 5 minutes for any residual energy to dissipate.

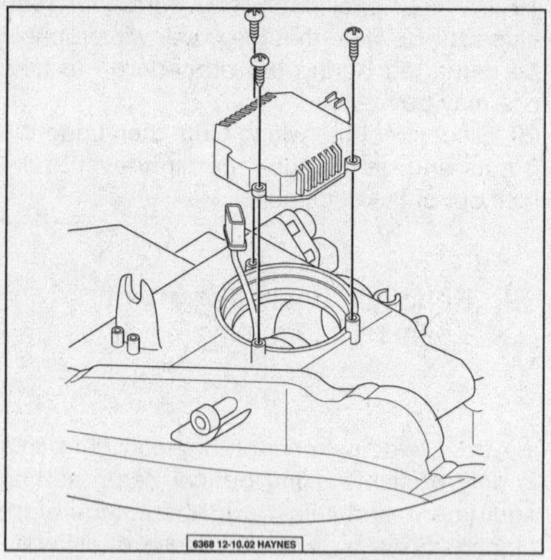

10.2 Undo the screws and detach the module from the base of the headlight

Gas discharge bulb (Xenon) control module

1 Remove the headlight as described in Section 8.

2 Undo the 3 retaining screws and detach the control module from the base of the headlight **(see illustration)**. Undo the screw and disconnect the wiring plug as the module is withdrawn.

3 Refitting is a reversal of removal.

Auto leveling control module

4 Remove the passengers glovebox as described in Chapter 11 Section 26.

5 Disconnect the control module wiring plug.

6 Undo the retaining bolt and remove the control module.

7 Refitting is a reversal of removal.

Ride height sensors

8 Raise the front or rear of the vehicle (as applicable), and support it securely on axle stands (see *Jacking and vehicle support*).

9 Disconnect the wiring plug from the sensor.

10 If removing the front sensor, undo the bolts securing the sensor arm bracket to the lower arm, and the sensor mounting bracket bolts.

11 If removing the rear sensor, undo the nut securing the sensor arm to the bracket, then undo the bolt securing the sensor mounting bracket.

12 Refitting is a reversal of removal.

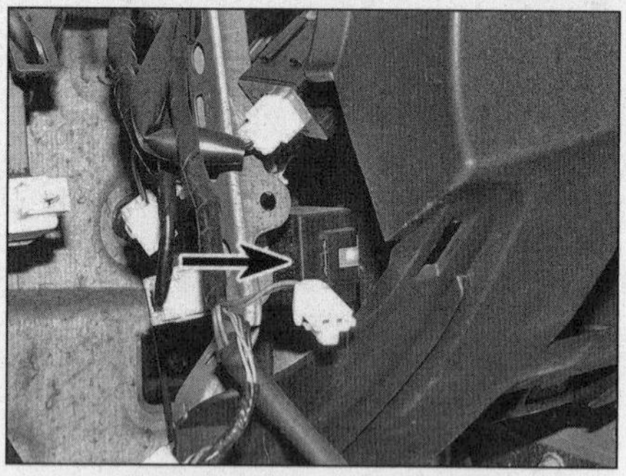
11.1 Flasher control module (steering column removed for clarity)

11 Flasher control module – removal and refitting

1 The flasher control module is located on the front side of the facia at the drivers end. Access is limited, but it is just possible to reach up behind the facia to access the module. The module is located just to the left of the bonnet release lever **(see illustration)**.

2 Disconnect the wiring plug, undo the retaining screw, and detach the flasher module from the panel.

3 Refitting is a reversal or removal.

12 Instrument cluster – removal and refitting

Note: *If a new instrument cluster is to be fitted, the configuration procedure must be completed* ***before*** *and after renewal, using Mazda diagnostic equipment. Entrust this task to a Mazda dealer or suitably equipped specialist.*

Removal

1 Disconnect the battery negative lead as described in Chapter 5A Section 4.

2 Remove the drivers side lower facia panel as described in Chapter 11 Section 28.

3 Remove the steering column shrouds as described in Chapter 11 Section 26.

4 Using a trim removal tool, carefully prise the instrument cluster hood upwards from the facia **(see illustration)**. Disconnect any wiring plugs as the hood is withdrawn.

5 The instrument cluster is retained by 3 screws – 2 longer ones in each corner and one shorter screw at the top **(see illustrations)**.

12.4 Gently prise the hood upwards to release the clips

12.5a Instrument cluster lower mounting screws...

12.5b... and upper mounting screw

13.3 Horn retaining bolts

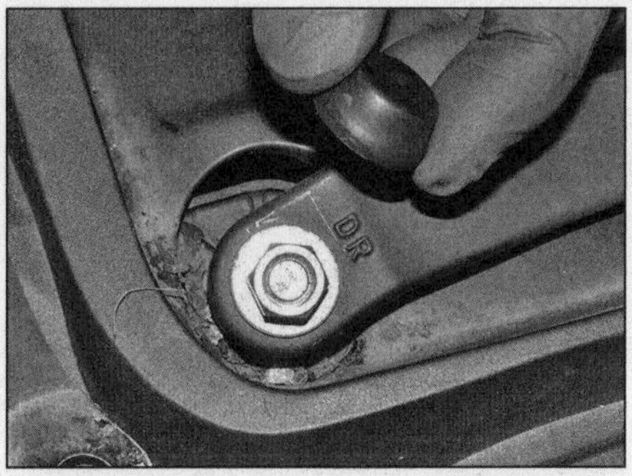

14.3 Prise off the cover, undo the spindle nut

14.5 The centre of the blade should be 20 mm above the windscreen trim

Undo the screws, pull the lower edge of the cluster rearwards and disconnect the wiring plug. Manoeuvre the cluster over the top of the steering wheel.

Caution: The instrument cluster must be stored with the display side facing upwards, otherwise grease may leak into the display.

Refitting

6 Refitting is the reverse of removal, making sure the instrument panel wiring is correctly reconnected and securely held in position by any retaining clips. On completion reconnect the battery (see Chapter 5A Section 4) and check the operation of the panel warning lights to ensure that they are functioning correctly.

13 Horn(s) – removal and refitting

1 Raise the front of the vehicle and support it securely on axle stands (see *Jacking and vehicle support*).

2 Undo the fasteners and remove the front section of the engine undershield. The horns are located behind the front bumper.

3 Undo the retaining bolt and remove the horn, disconnecting the wiring connector as it becomes accessible **(see illustration)**.

4 Refitting is the reverse of removal.

14 Wiper arm – removal and refitting

Removal

1 Operate the wiper motor, then switch it off so that the wiper arms return to the 'at rest' position. Open the bonnet

2 Stick a piece of masking tape on the windscreen alongside the edge of the wiper blade to use as an alignment aid on refitting.

3 Prise off the wiper arm spindle nut cover(s) then slacken and remove the spindle nut(s). Lift the blade off the glass and pull the wiper arm off its spindle. If necessary the arm can be levered off the spindle using a suitable flat-bladed screwdriver or suitable puller **(see illustration)**.

Refitting

4 Ensure that the wiper arm and spindle splines are clean and dry then refit the arm to the spindle, aligning the wiper blade with the tape fitted on removal. Refit the spindle nut, tightening securely, and clip the nut cover back in position.

5 If the position of the front wiper arms has been lost, set the arms so the centre of the blade end is approximately 20 mm above the edge of the windscreen trim **(see illustration)**.

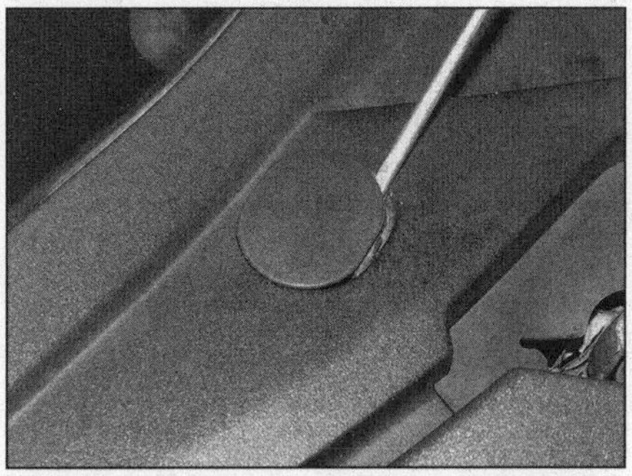

15.2 Prise up the cover and undo the screw at each end

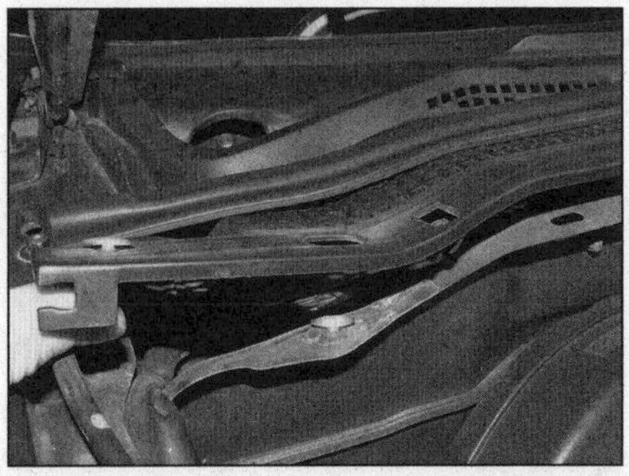

15.4 Pull up the front edge, then slide the cowl grille down from the windscreen

15 Windscreen wiper motor and linkage – removal and refitting

Removal

1 Remove the wiper arms as described in Section 14.

2 Prise up the covers, then undo the screw at each end of the cowl grille **(see illustration)**.

3 Carefully prise up the rubber weatherstrip **(see illustration)**.

4 Pull up the front edge of the cowl grille, then slide it down from the lower edge of the windscreen **(see illustration)**.

5 Disconnect the wiring plug and unclip it, then undo the two bolts/one nut and manoeuvre the motor and linkage assembly from place **(see illustration)**.

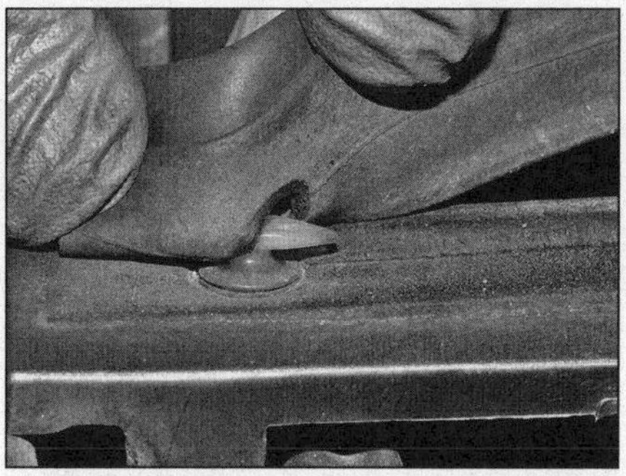

15.3 Pull the weatherstrip from the clips

15.5 Undo the bolts/nut then remove the motor and linkage assembly

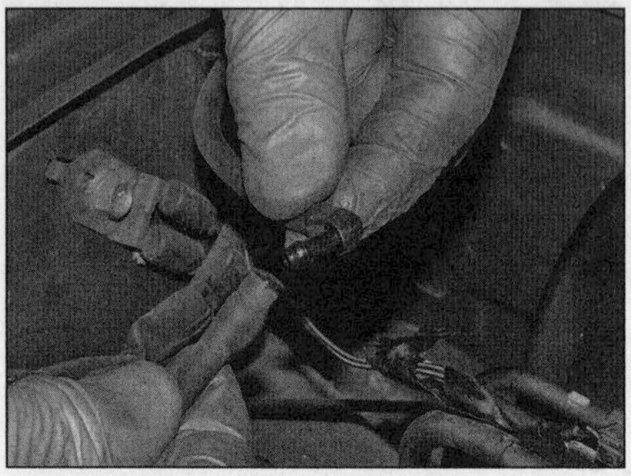

16.3 Trace the hose back and disconnect it

16.4 Washer reservoir retaining nut and bolt

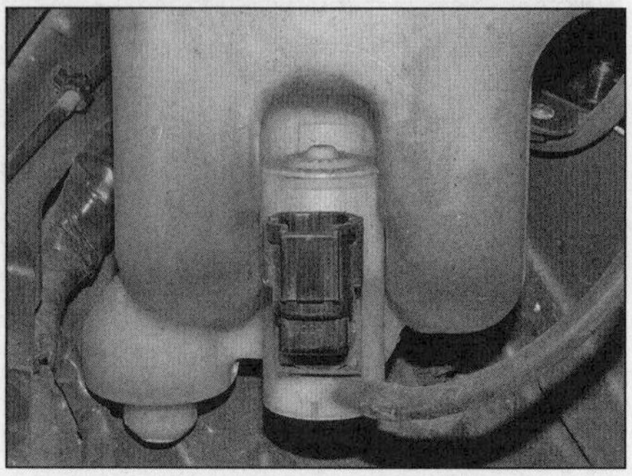

16.8 Pull the washer pump from the grommet

6 Use a screwdriver to prise the linkage rod from the motor arm.
7 Undo the mounting bolts and manoeuvre the motor from position.

Refitting

8 Refitting is the reverse of removal.

16 Windscreen washer system components – removal and refitting

Washer system reservoir

1 The windscreen washer reservoir is located on the right-hand side of the engine compartment.
2 Syphon out the contents of the reservoir or be prepared for fluid spillage.
3 Disconnect the hose from the pump at the connector **(see illustration)**.
4 Undo the reservoir retaining but and bolt **(see illustration)**.
5 Manoeuvre the reservoir from position, and disconnect the wiring connector(s) from the reservoir level switch (where fitted) and pump, then note their fitted locations, and disconnect the various hoses from the reservoir.
6 Refitting is a reversal of removal. Ensure the locating lugs on the base of the reservoir engage correctly with the corresponding holes in the inner wing. Refill the reservoir and check for leakage.

Windscreen washer pump

7 Remove the fluid reservoir as previously described in this Section.
8 Carefully pull the pump from the grommet in the side of the reservoir **(see illustration)**.
9 Refitting is the reverse of removal, using a new sealing grommet if the original one shows signs of damage or deterioration. Refill the reservoir and check the pump grommet for leaks.

Windscreen washer jets

10 Open the bonnet and remove the cowl grille as described in Section 15.
11 Disconnect the hose from the base of the washer jet.
12 Squeeze together the clip each side of the jet and manoeuvre it out the top of the bonnet **(see illustration)**.
13 On refitting, push the jet back into position in the bonnet, and securely connect the jet to the hose. If necessary insert a needle into the jet nozzle and adjust the aim.

17 Audio unit and amplifier – removal and refitting

Note: *The following procedure is for the unit fitted to the project vehicle. Removal and refitting procedures of other units may differ slightly.*

Audio unit

Removal

1 Disconnect the battery negative lead as described in Chapter 5A, Section 4.
2 Remove the facia centre panel as described in Chapter 11 Section 28.
3 Remove the four retaining screws **(see illustration)** and remove the audio unit from its mounting bracket.

Refitting

4 Refitting is a reversal of removal.

Amplifier

Removal

5 Remove the Back trim as described in Chapter 11 Section 26.
6 Lift the insulation cover, undo the retaining bolts and manoeuvre the amplifier from the drivers side of the seat back crossmember **(see illustration)**. Disconnect the wiring plugs as the unit is withdrawn.

Refitting

7 Refitting is a reversal of removal.

18 Loudspeakers – removal and refitting

Door main loudspeaker

1 Remove the door inner trim panel as described in Chapter 11, Section 11.

16.12 Squeeze together the clips and push the washer jet from the bonnet

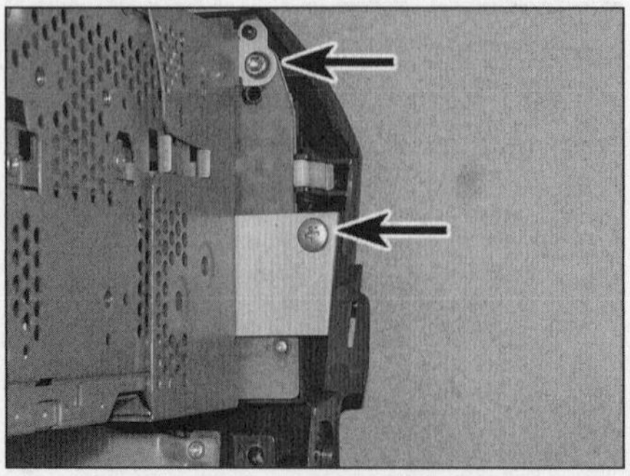

17.3 Undo the two screws each side

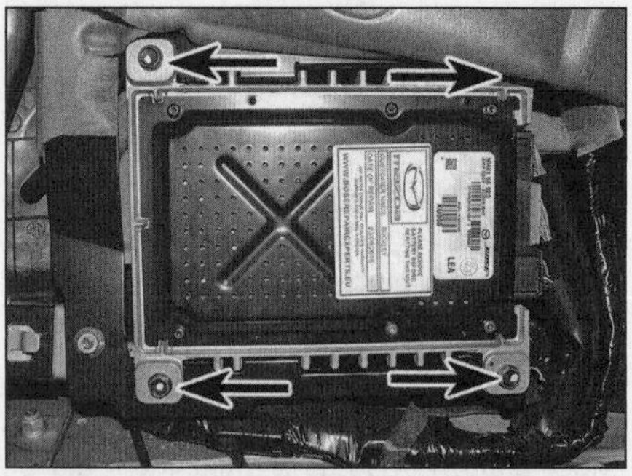

17.6 Amplifier retaining bolts

2 Undo the retaining screws and remove the speaker **(see illustration)**. Disconnect the wiring plug as the speaker is withdrawn.
3 Refitting is the reverse of removal.

Door upper loudspeaker

4 Remove the door inner trim panel as described in Chapter 11, Section 11.
5 Undo the retaining screws and detach the speaker from the door trim **(see illustration)**.
6 Refitting is a reversal of removal.

Facia speaker

7 Using a blunt trim removal tool, carefully prise up and remove the speaker grille, then remove the speaker retaining screws. Unplug the electrical connector as the speaker is withdrawn **(see illustration)**.
8 Refitting is the reverse of removal.

Rear speakers

9 Remove the Back trim as described in Chapter 11 Section 26.
10 Disconnect the wiring plugs, undo the retaining screws and remove the speakers **(see illustration)**.
11 Refitting is a reversal of removal.

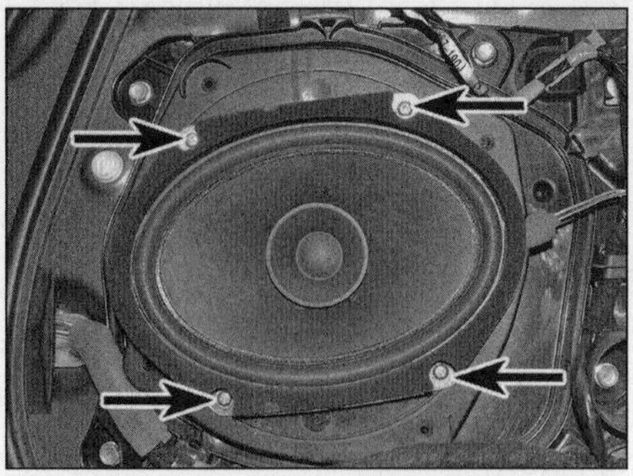

18.2 Speaker retaining screws

18.5 Upper speaker retaining screws

18.7 Carefully prise up the speaker grille

18.10 Undo the screws and remove the rear speakers

19 Radio aerial – removal and refitting

1 Open the boot and disconnect the aerial wiring plug **(see illustration)**. Note: The aerial may be tested if desired, by checking continuity at the aerial wiring plug end. The aerial should have full continuity (no resistance).
2 Place masking tape around the aerial base to protect the paint.
3 On models with a manual aerial, unscrew and remove the mast **(see illustration)**.
4 On all models, unscrew and remove the aerial base **(see illustration)**.
5 To remove the aerial assembly, remove the boot side trim on the side with the aerial. Disconnect the aerial wiring plug(s) and bolt or nut, then lift out the aerial assembly.
6 Refitting is the reverse of removal.

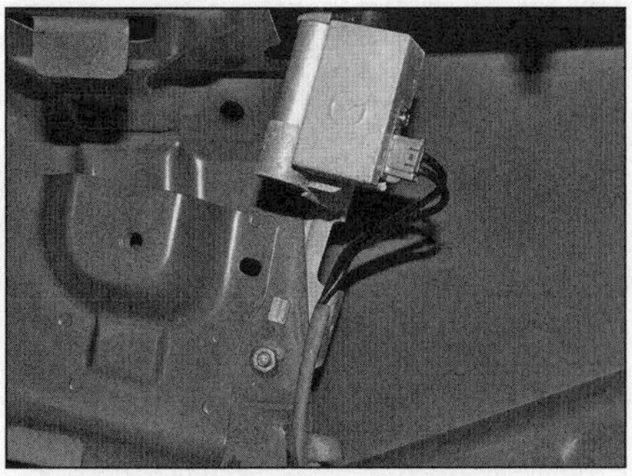

19.1 Aerial wiring plugs and retaining nut

19.3 Unscrew the mast from the base

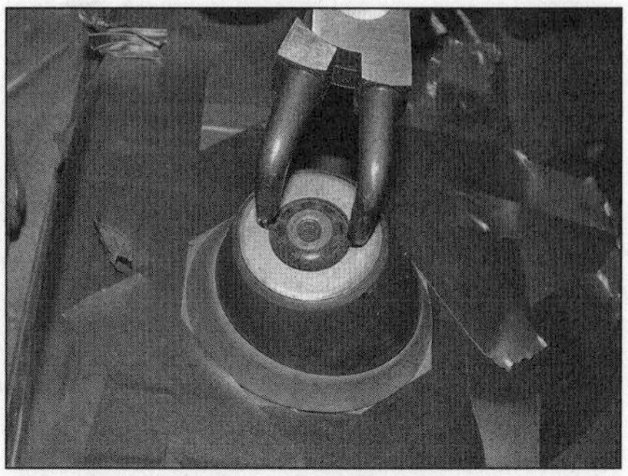

19.4 Use a pair of circlip pliers (or similar) to unscrew the aerial base

20 Anti-theft alarm system – general information

1 The MX5 models are equipped with a sophisticated anti-theft alarm and immobiliser system. Should a fault develop, the system's self-diagnosis facility should be interrogated using dedicated test equipment. Consult your Mazda dealer or suitably-equipped specialist.

21 Airbag system – general information and precautions

1 The models covered by this manual may be equipped with a driver's airbag mounted in the centre of the steering wheel, a passenger's airbag located behind the facia and side airbags located in the seat backrests. The airbag system comprises of the airbag unit(s) (complete with gas generators), impact sensors, the control unit and a warning light in the instrument panel.
2 The airbag system is triggered in the event of a heavy frontal or side impact above a predetermined force; depending on the point of impact. The airbag(s) is inflated within milliseconds and forms a safety cushion between the cabin occupants and the cabin interior, and therefore greatly reduces the risk of injury. The airbag then deflates almost immediately.
3 Every time the ignition is switched on, the airbag control unit performs a self-test. The self-test takes approximately 2 to 6 seconds and during this time the airbag warning light on the facia is illuminated. After the self-test

has been completed the warning light should go out. If the warning light fails to come on, remains illuminated after the initial period, or comes on at any time when the vehicle is being driven, there is a fault in the airbag system. The vehicle should be taken to a Mazda dealer for examination at the earliest possible opportunity.

Warning: Before carrying out any operations on the airbag system, disconnect the battery negative terminal, and wait for at least 1 minute. This will allow the capacitors in the system to discharge. When operations are complete, make sure no one is inside the vehicle when the battery is reconnected.

Warning: Note that the airbag(s) must not be subjected to temperatures in excess of 90°C. When the airbag is removed, ensure that it is stored the correct way up to prevent possible inflation (padded surface uppermost).

Warning: Do not allow any solvents or cleaning agents to contact the airbag assemblies. They must be cleaned using only a damp cloth.

Warning: The airbags and control unit are both sensitive to impact. If either is dropped or damaged they should be renewed.

Warning: Disconnect the airbag control unit wiring plug prior to using arc-welding equipment on the vehicle.

22.2a Prise out the cover each side...

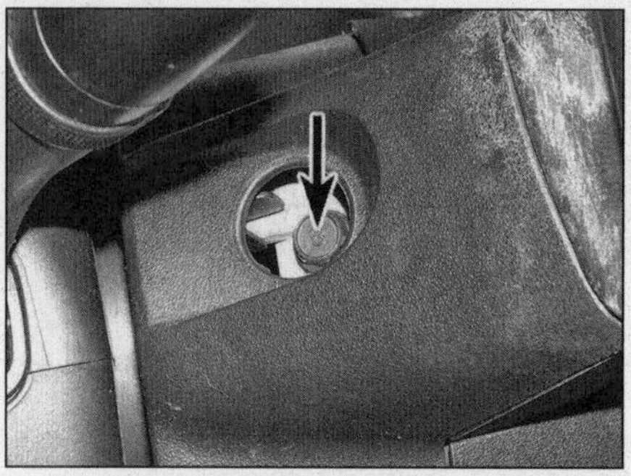

22.2b... and undo the airbag retaining bolt each side of the steering wheel boss

22 Airbag system components – removal and refitting

Note: *Refer to the warnings in Section 21 before carrying out the following operations.*

1 Disconnect the battery negative terminal (see Chapter 5A, Section 4), then continue as described under the relevant heading.

Driver's airbag

2 With the wheel in the straight-ahead position, prise out the plastic cover each side (where fitted), then undo the airbag retaining bolts **(see illustrations)**.

3 Carefully lift the airbag assembly away from the steering wheel. Note their fitted positions and disconnect the wiring plug(s) from the airbag unit **(see illustration)**. Note that the airbag must not be knocked or dropped and should be stored the correct way up with its padded surface uppermost.

4 On refitting reconnect the wiring connector(s) and seat the airbag unit in the steering wheel, making sure the wire does not become trapped. Tighten the bolts to the specified torque. Reconnect the battery as described in Chapter 5A, Section 4.

Passenger airbag

5 Remove the passenger's glovebox as described in Chapter 11, Section 26.

6 Remove the cap from the underside of the airbag **(see illustration)**.

Note: *Mazda insist that the cap cannot be re-used. A new one must be fitted on reassembly.*

7 Release the locking catch(es), and disconnect the airbag wiring plug(s) **(see illustration)**.

8 Undo the four nuts, and three screws securing the airbag and brackets **(see illustrations)**. Note the earth lead under the mounting bracket nut.

9 Slide the airbag module upwards to release the lock tabs, then rearwards, and downwards.

10 Refitting is a reversal of removal. Tighten the airbag retaining nuts/bolts to the specified torque, and reconnect the battery negative terminal.

Side airbags

11 The side airbags are located within the seat backrests. In order to remove the airbags, the seat upholstery must be completely

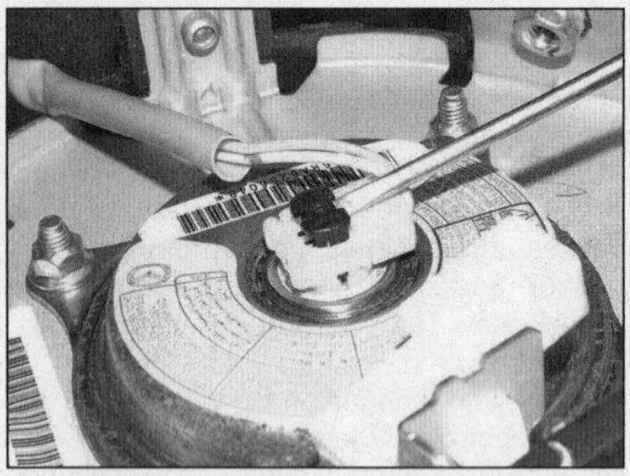

22.3 Prise up the locking clip and disconnect the airbag wiring plug

22.6 Prise the cap down from the mounting studs

22.7 Prise out the black locking catch slightly

22.8a Undo the airbag/bracket screws/ nuts...

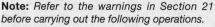

22.8b... including the screw at the top of the bracket

22.14 Rotary contact unit retaining screws

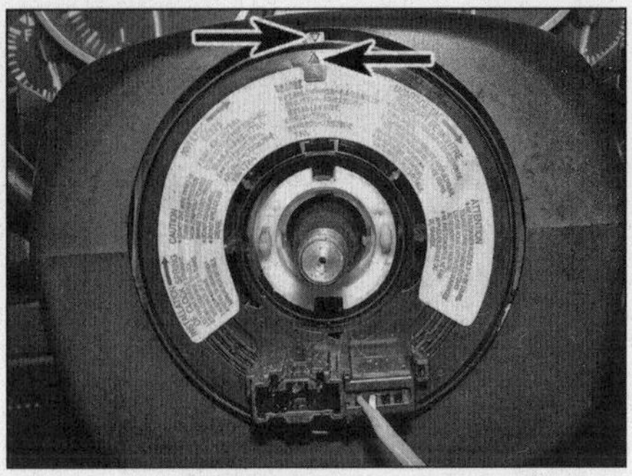

22.15 Align the marks

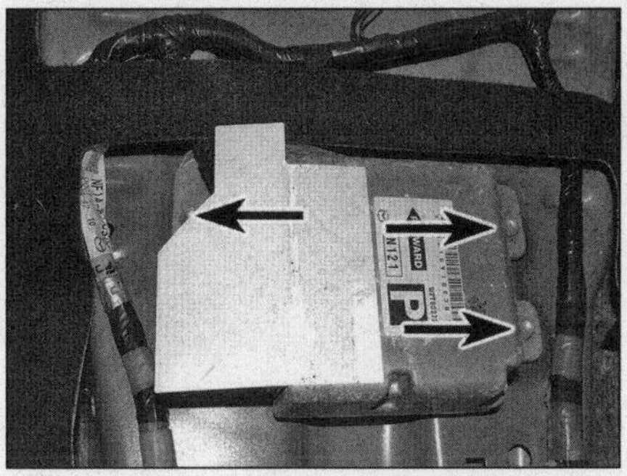

22.17 Air bag control unit retaining bolts (facia removed for clarity)

removed. This is a task best entrusted to a dealer or upholstery specialist, and is beyond the scope of this manual.

Rotary contact assembly

12 Remove the steering wheel as described in Chapter 10, Section 14.

13 Remove the steering column shrouds as described in Chapter 11 Section 26.

14 Undo the 3 screws and remove the rotary contact unit **(see illustration)**.

15 Refitting is the reverse of removal. If the contact unit has been rotated with the wheel removed, centralise it by rotating its centre fully clockwise until it stops. From this position, rotate the centre back through 2.75 complete rotations in an anti-clockwise direction until the marks align **(see illustration)**.

Control unit

16 Remove the console panel as described in Chapter 11 Section 28.

17 Disconnect the wiring plug from the control unit, then undo the three retaining bolts and manoeuvre it from place **(see illustration)**.

18 Refitting is a reversal of removal. Tighten the retaining bolts to their specified torque.

Note: *If a new control unit has been fitted, open completion, turn the ignition on for at least 20 seconds to allow the self-configuration to complete.*

Impact sensors

Front sensor

19 Remove the front bumper as described in Chapter 11 Section 6.

20 Undo the fasteners and remove the fresh air duct.

21 Undo the bolt and remove the cover over the sensor **(see illustration)**.

22 Disconnect the wiring plug, undo the two bolts and remove the sensor **(see illustration)**.

23 Refitting is a reversal of removal. Tighten the sensor retaining bolts to the specified torque.

Side sensors

24 Remove the tyre house trim as described in Chapter 11 Section 26.

25 Disconnect the wiring plug, unto the two retaining bolts and remove the sensor **(see illustration)**.

26 Refitting is a reversal of removal.

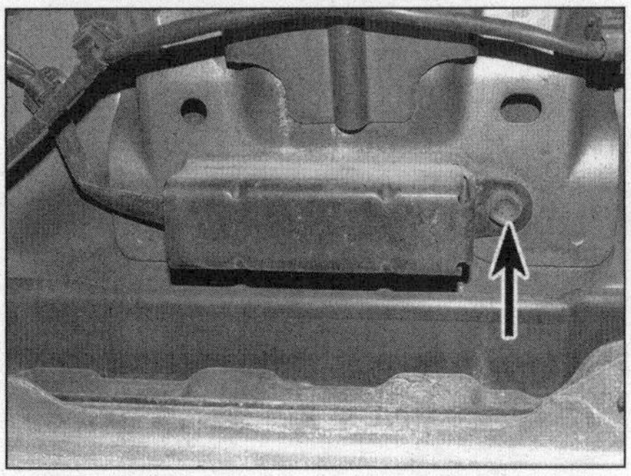

22.21 Undo the bolt and remove the cover

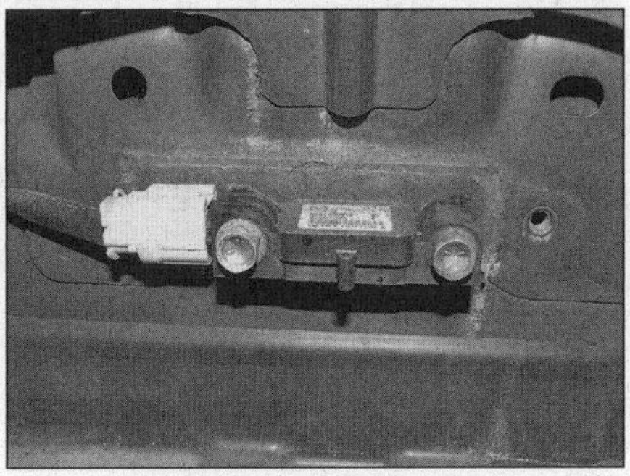

22.22 Front impact sensor

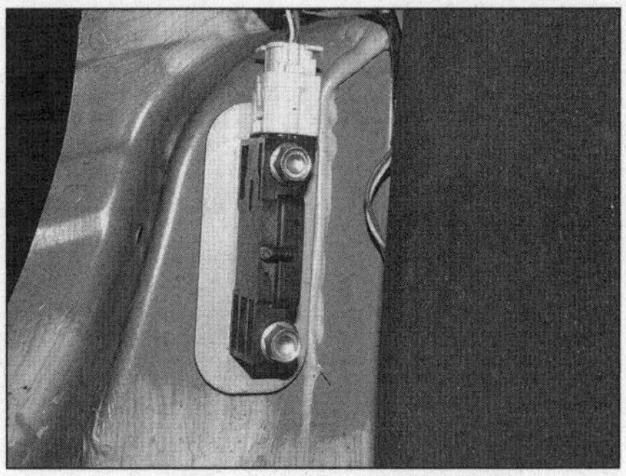

22.25 Side impact sensor

FUSE AND RELAY BOX IN ENGINE COMPARTMENT

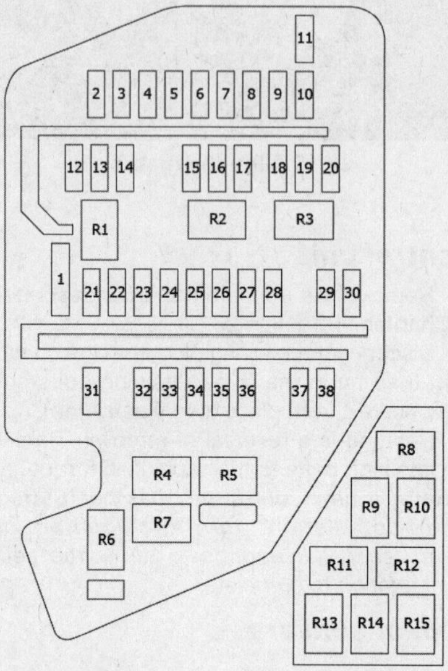

FUSE/RELAY	VALUE	DESCRIPTION
F1	120 A	Generator Fuse and relay box in engine compartment, fuses 27, 31, 32, 35, 36
F2	15 A	Daylight running system (DRL)
F3	15 A	Horn
F4	10 A	Brake lights
F5	15 A	Main relay Powertrain control unit (PCM) Throttle control motor relay
F6	-	Fuel pump control unit Fuel pump relay
F7	10 A	Not used
F8	20 A	Direction indicators hazard warning lights flasher
F9	20 A	Power windows
F10	40 A	Ignition switch, ignition relay
F11	-	Not used
F12	10 A	Injectors
F13	10 A	Canister purge solenoid EGR valve Variable air inlet or Canister purge solenoid EGR valve Variable air inlet Tumble generator valve Oil control valve
F14	10 A	Throttle control motor relay Powertrain control unit (PCM) Mass airflow meter
F15	15 A	Left headlight, dipped beam
F16	15 A	Right headlight, dipped beam
F17	15 A	Headlights, main beam
F18	20 A	Power windows
F19	15 A	Ignition relay or Fuel pump relay Powertrain control unit (PCM)

F20	20 A	Windscreen wash/wipe system
F21	30 A	ABS
F22	15 A	Front fog lights
F23	7.5 A	No information is available
F24	30 A	Convertible roof opening
F25	30 A	Convertible roof closing
F26	7.5 A	Air conditioning or not used
F27	20 A	Starter relay Starter
F28	15 A	Tail lights Parking lights Number plate lights Illumination
F29	40 A	ABS
F30	30 A	No information is available
F31	30 A	Cooling fan motor Cooling fan relay No. 1 Cooling fan relay No. 2 Or Cooling fan motor Cooling fan relay No. 1 Cooling fan relay No. 2 Cooling fan relay No. 3
F32	7.5 A	Cooling fan motor Cooling fan relay No. 1 Cooling fan relay No. 2 Cooling fan relay No. 3 Or Cooling fan motor Cooling fan relay No. 1 Cooling fan relay No. 2
F33	20 A	Rear windscreen defroster
F34	20 A	No information is available
F35	15 A	DLC Powertrain control unit (PCM)
F36	15 A	Ignition switch Starter relay
F37	-	Not used
F38	40 A	Air conditioning or not used
R1	-	Main relay
R2	-	Headlight relay
R3	-	Ignition relay
R4	-	Starter relay
R5	-	Throttle control motor relay
R6	-	Blower relay
R7	-	Fuel pump relay
R8	-	Front fog light relay
R9	-	Air-conditioning relay
R10	-	TNS relay
R11	-	Rear windscreen defroster relay
R12	-	Horn relay
R13	-	Cooling fan relay No. 3
R14	-	Cooling fan relay No. 2
R15	-	Cooling fan relay No. 1

Fuses and relays (continued)

FUSE BOX IN PASSENGER COMPARTMENT

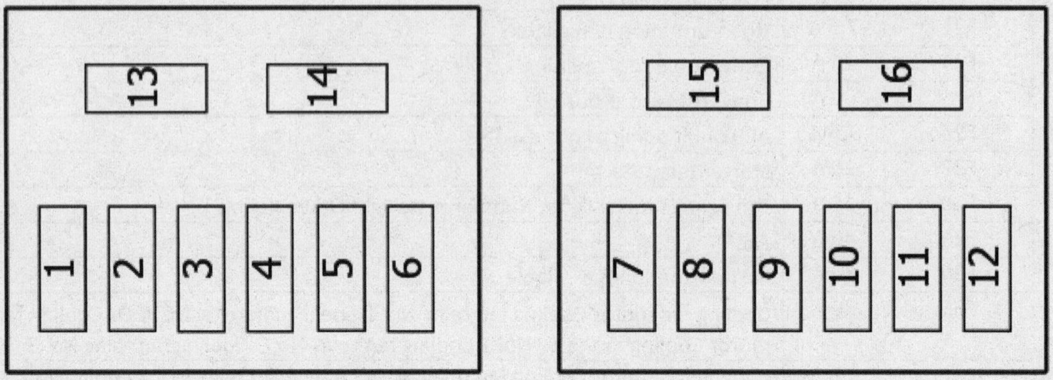

FUSE/RELAY	VALUE	DESCRIPTION
F1	7.5 A	Audio system Electric mirror control
F2	15 A	Additional socket
F3	15 A	Instrument cluster
F4	20 A	Seat heater
F5	7.5 A	Illumination
F6	7.5 A	Air conditioning or not used
F7	7.5 A	No information is available
F8	20 A	Audio system
F9	20 A	Central locking Luggage compartment opening
F10	7.5 A	No information is available
F11	-	Not used
F12	-	Not used
F13	7.5 A	Engine control system
F14	-	Not used
F15	-	Not used
F16	-	Not used

Fuses and relays (continued)

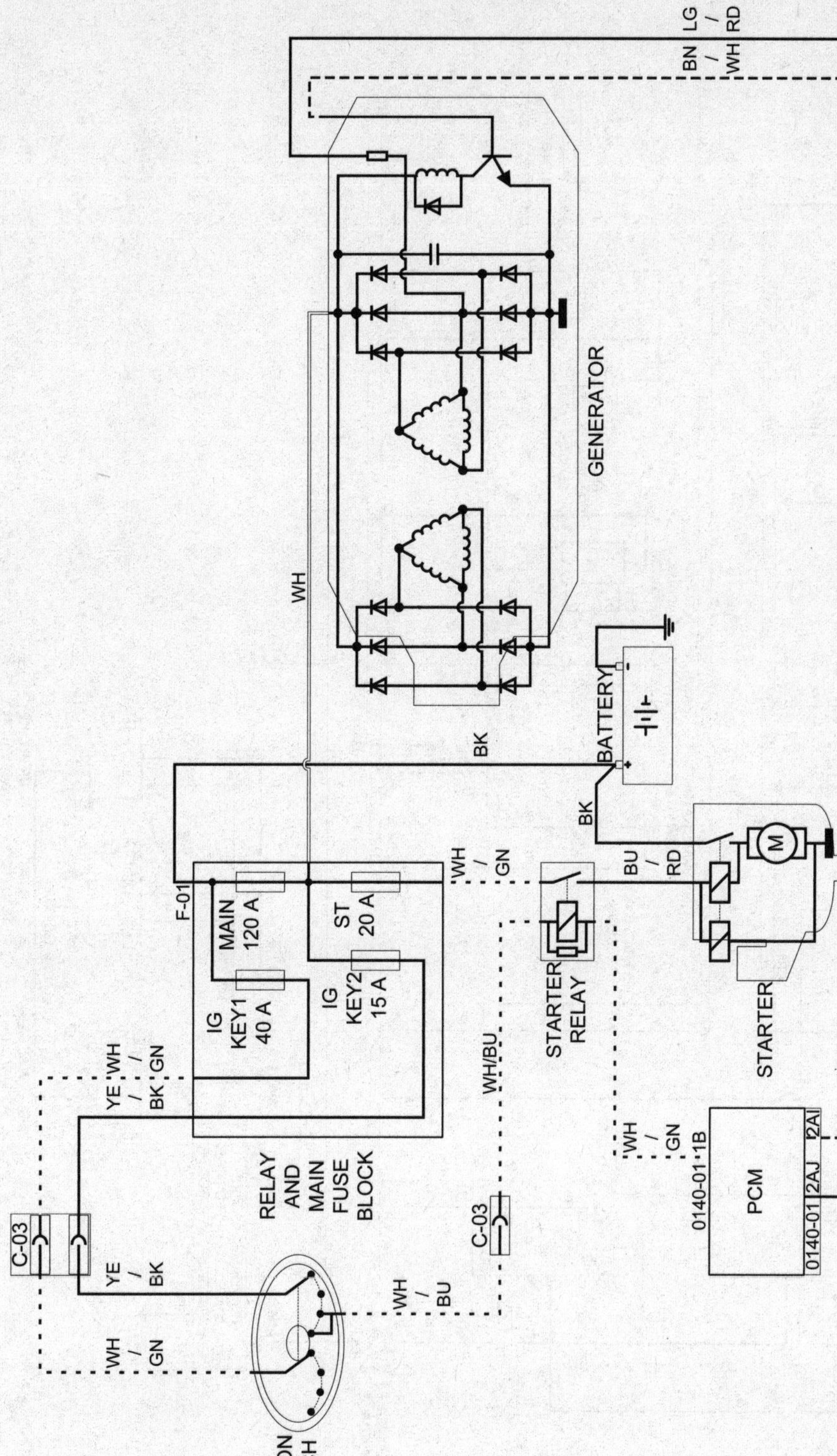

Starting and charging

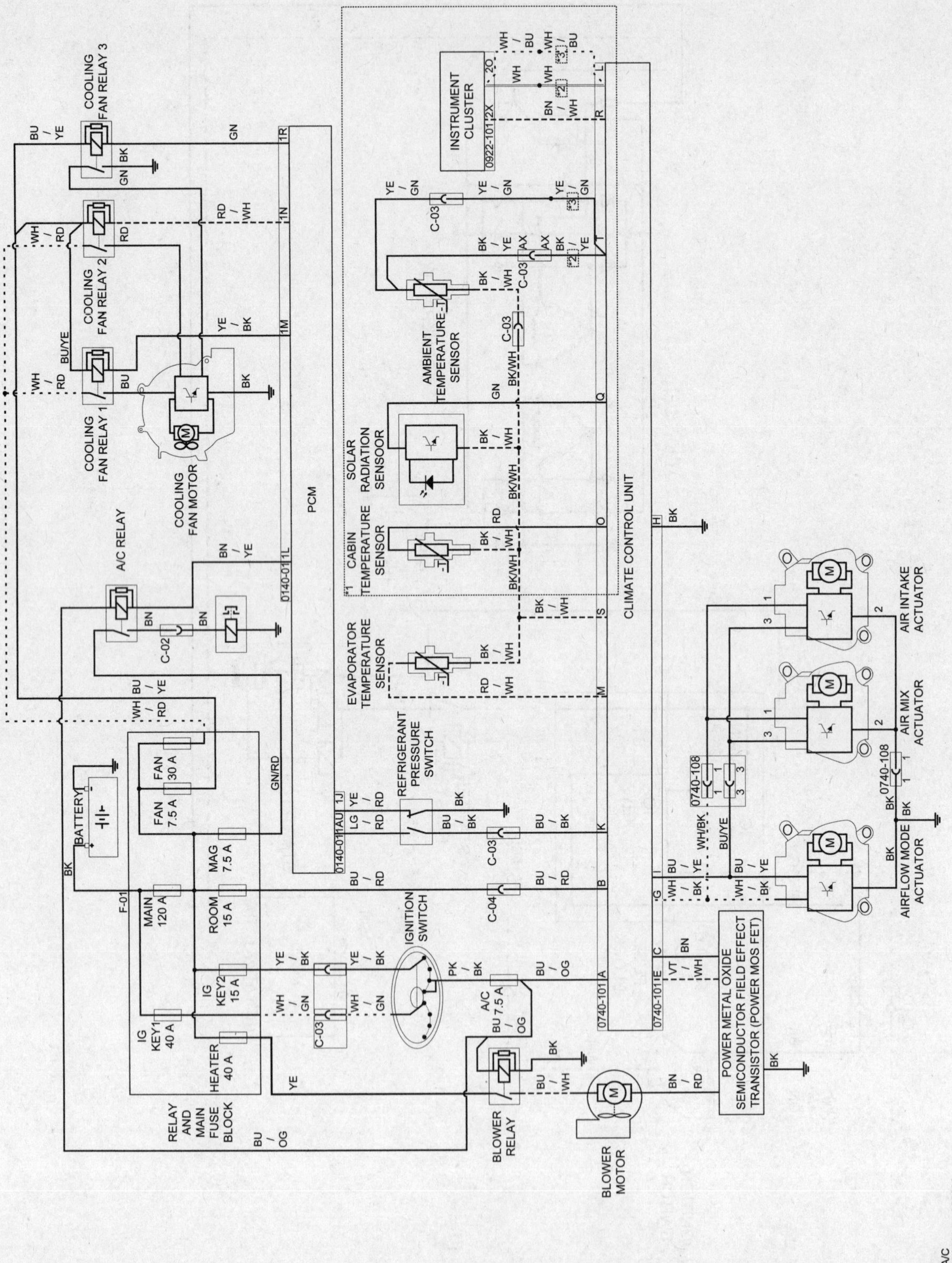

*1 With auto A/C
*2 From VIN 100001 to 200000
*3 From VIN 200001

Heating and air conditioning

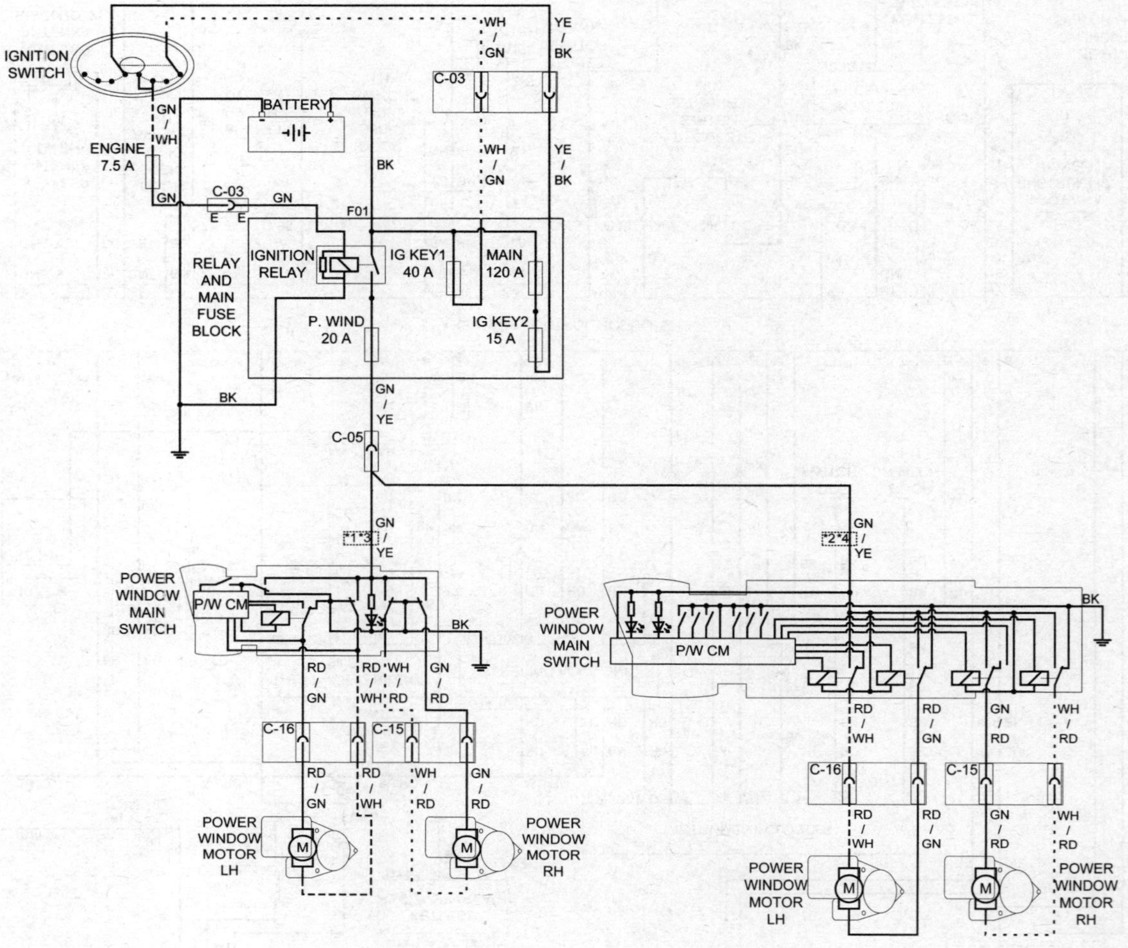

*1 Without power retractable hardtop
*2 With power retractable hardtop
*3 From VIN 100001 to 200000
*4 From VIN 200001

Power windows

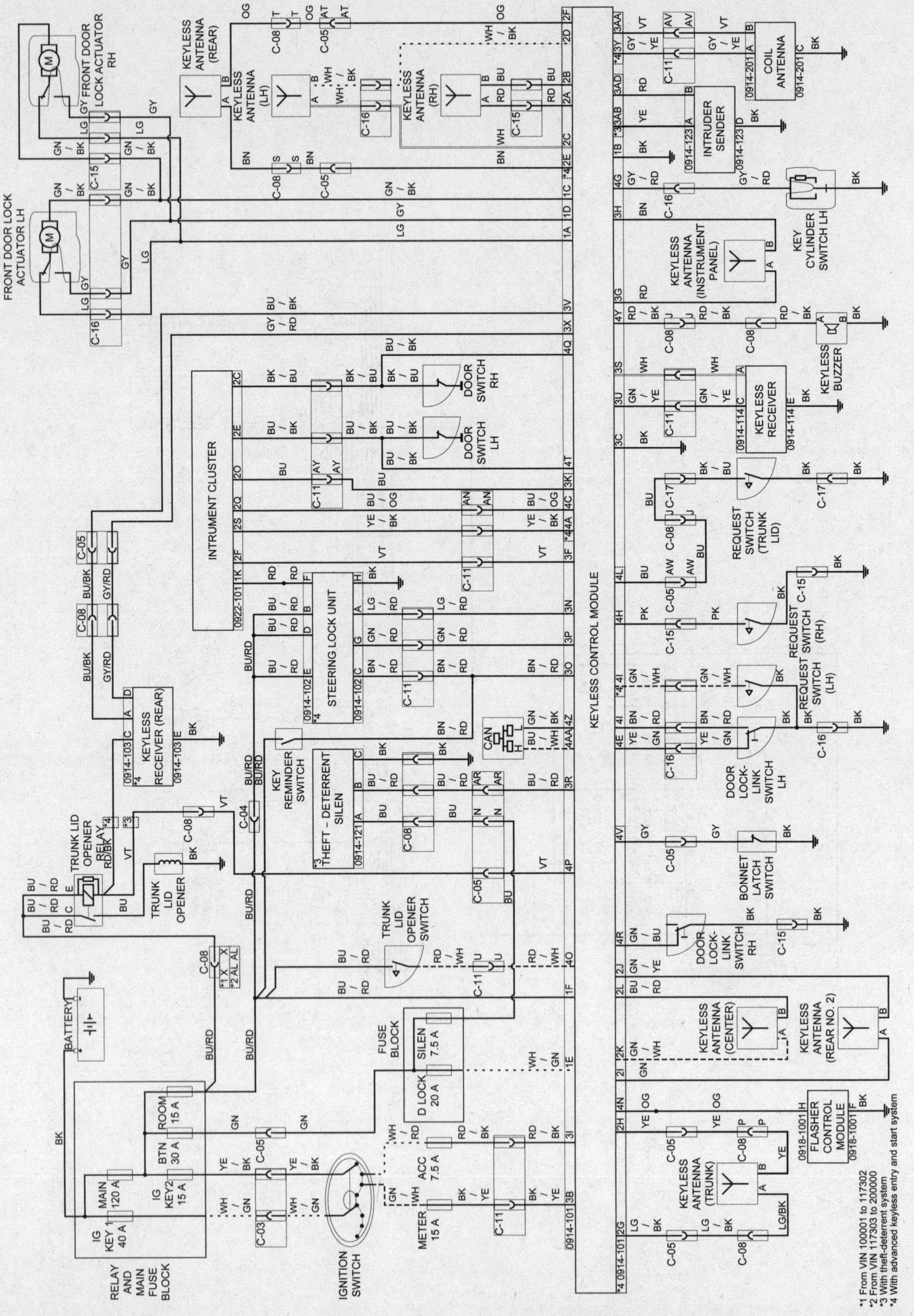

*1 From VIN 100001 to 117302
*2 From VIN 117303 to 200000
*3 With theft-deterrent system
*4 With advanced keyless entry and start system

Central locking – from VIN 100001 to 200000

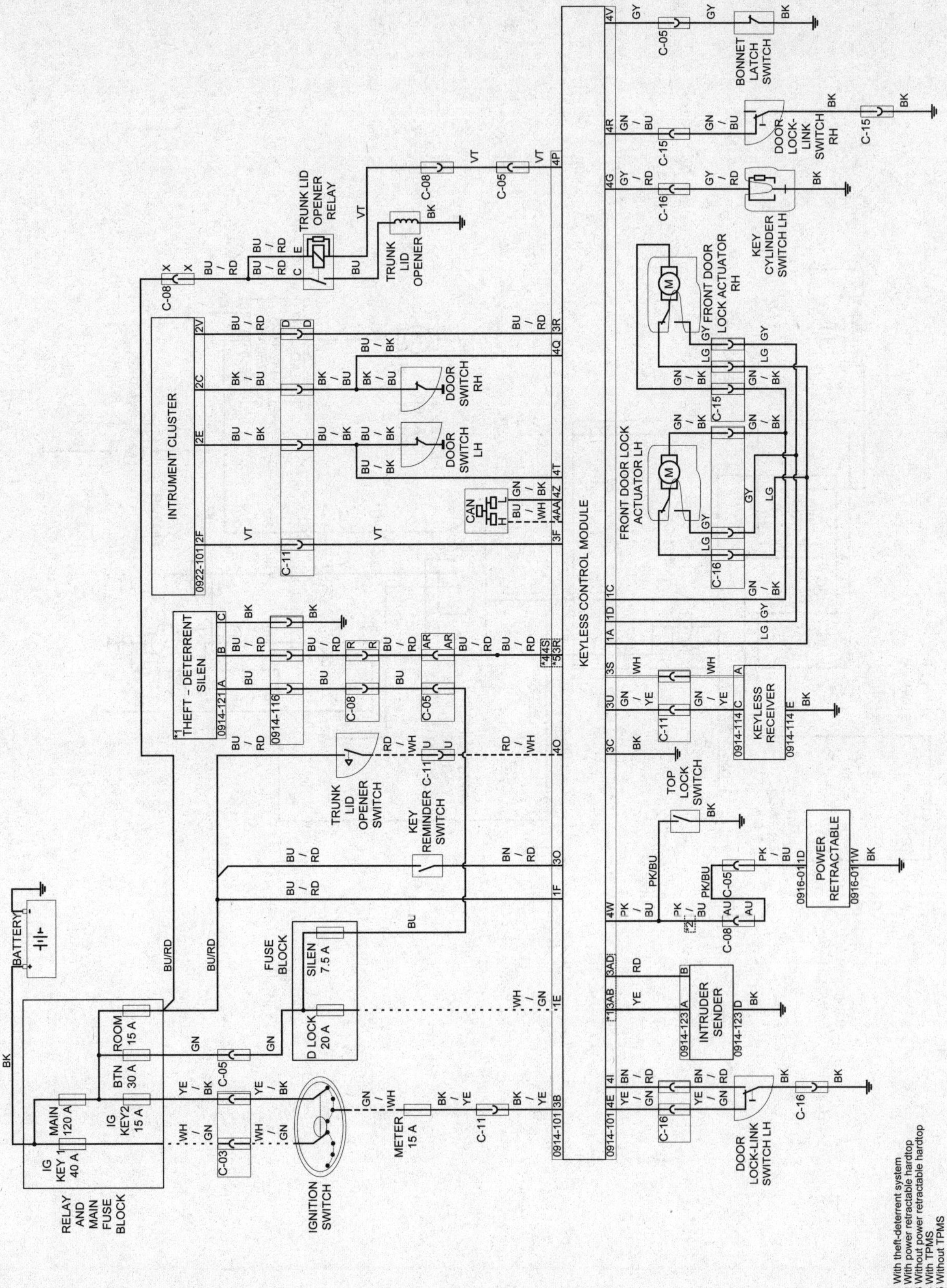

*1 With theft-deterrent system
*2 With power retractable hardtop
*3 Without power retractable hardtop
*4 With TPMS
*5 Without TPMS

Central locking – from VIN 200001

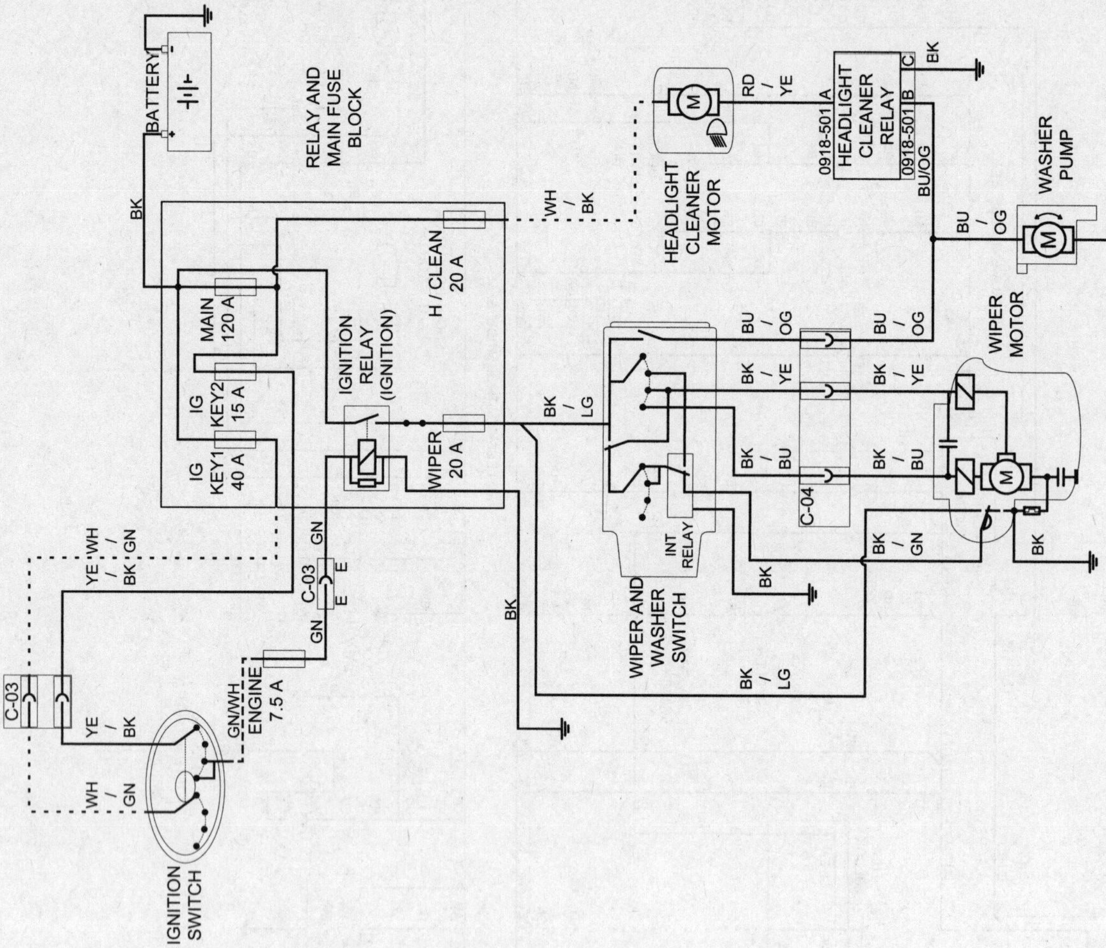

Washer and wipers

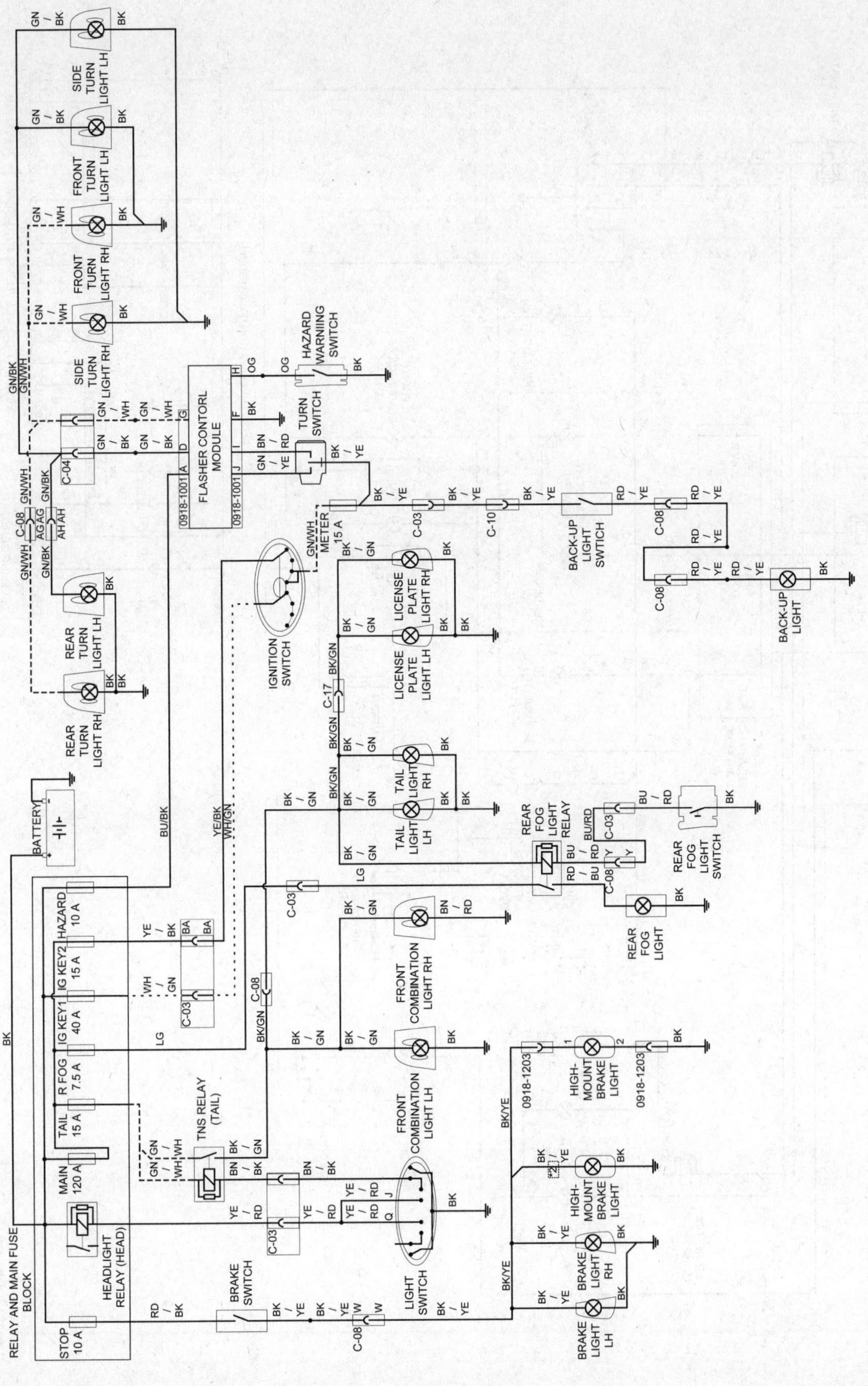

*1 With power retractable hardtop
*2 Without power retractable hardtop

Exterior lighting

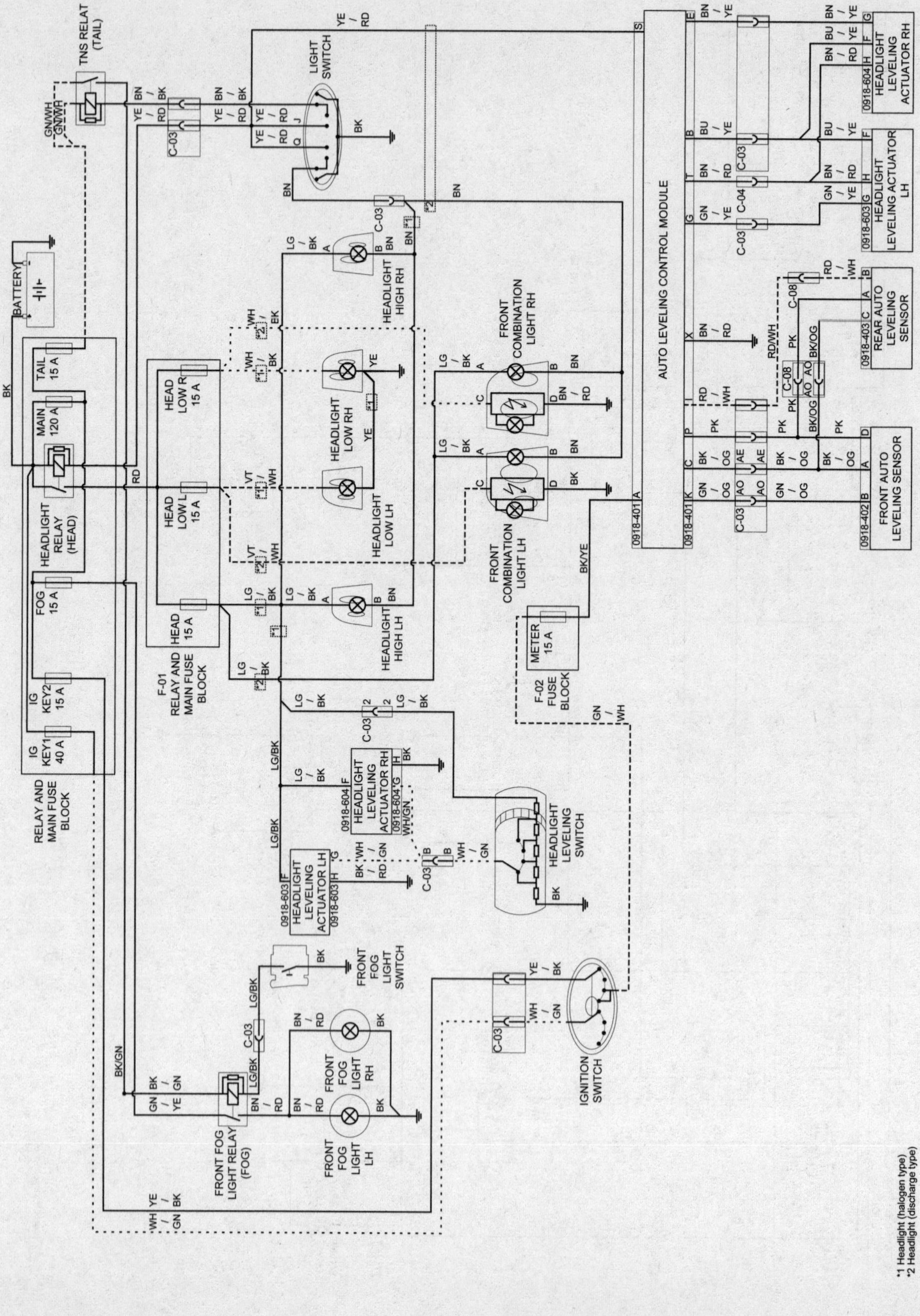

*1 Headlight (halogen type)
*2 Headlight (discharge type)

Headlights and fog lights

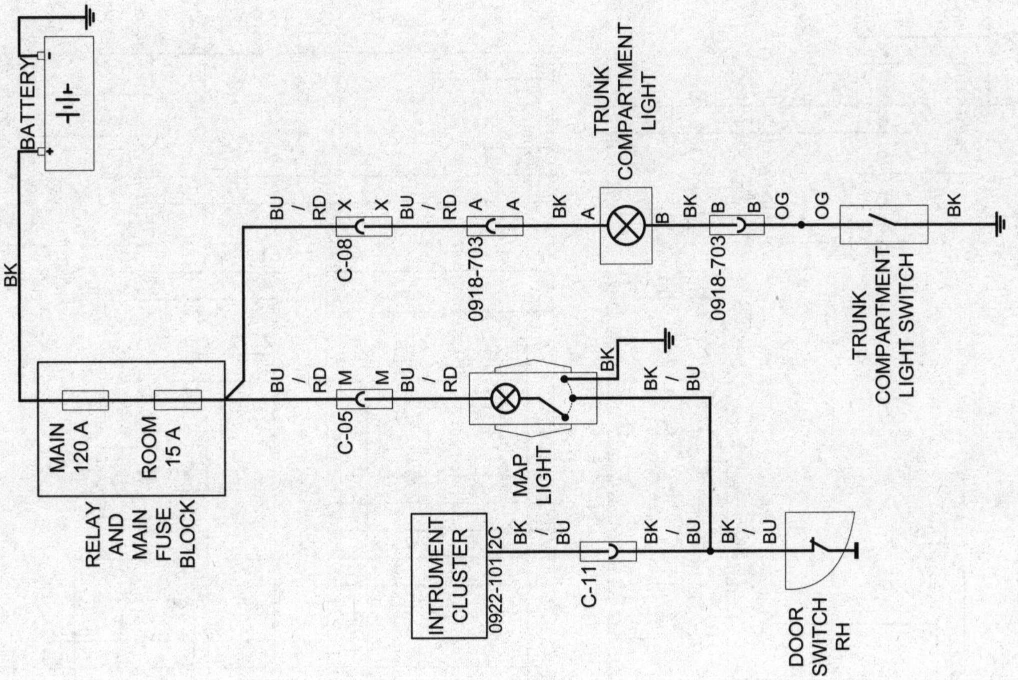

Interior lighting

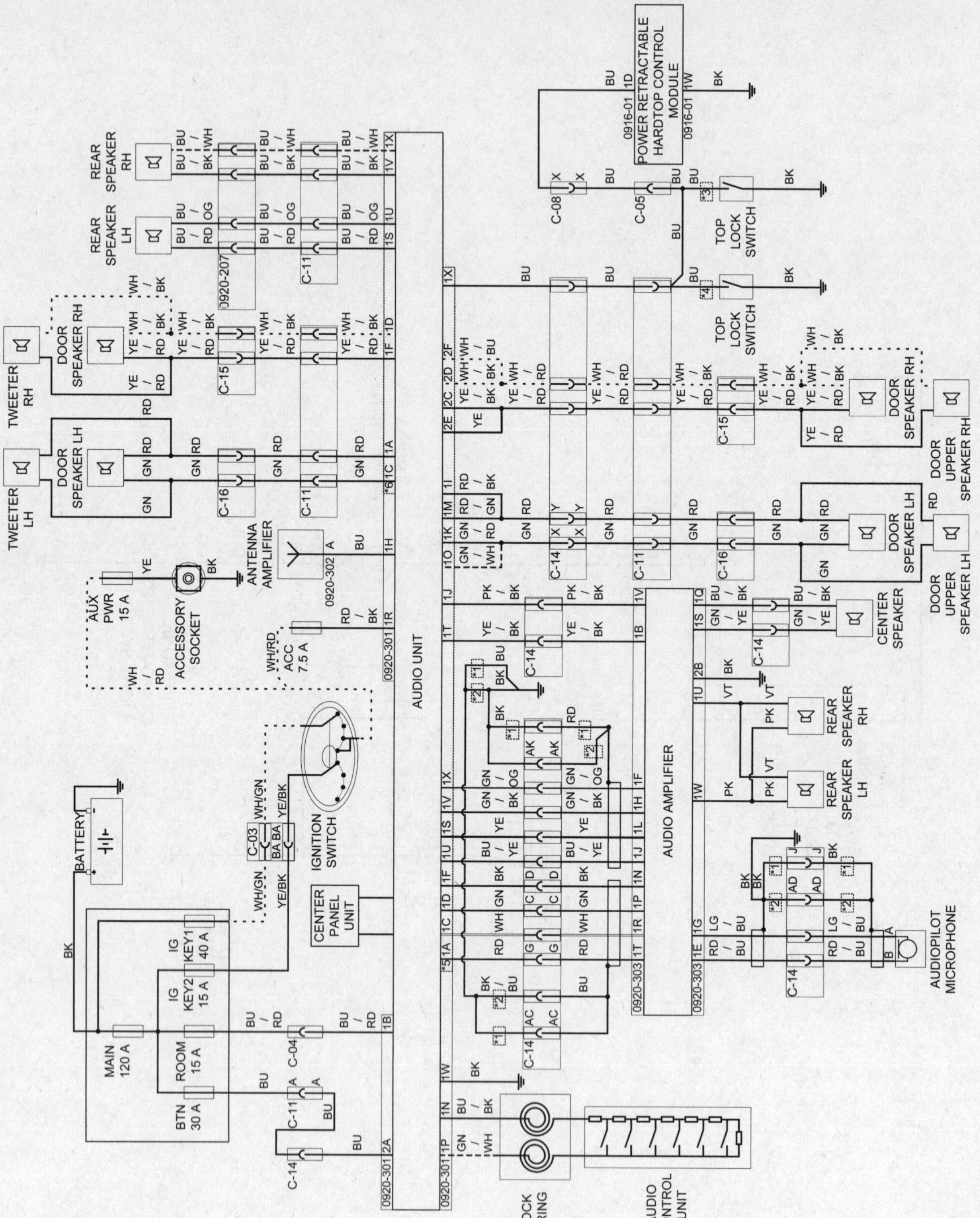

*1 From VIN 100001 to 117302
*2 From VIN 117303 to 200000
*3 With power retractable hardtop
*4 Without power retractable hardtop
*5 With Bose audio
*6 Without Bose audio

Sound system

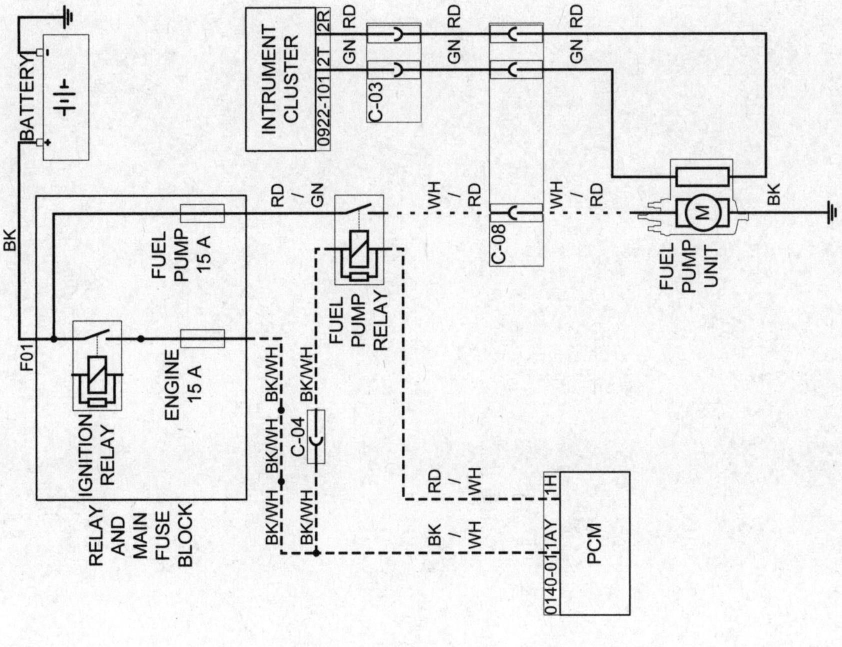
BATTERY
BK
F01
RELAY AND MAIN FUSE BLOCK
IGNITION RELAY
ENGINE 15 A
FUEL PUMP 15 A
RD / GN
BK/WH
C-04
FUEL PUMP RELAY
INTRUMENT CLUSTER
0922-101
2T
2R
GN
RD
C-03
WH / RD
C-08
FUEL PUMP UNIT
M
RD / WH
BK / WH
PCM
0140-011
1AY
1H

Fuel pump

Dimensions

Note: *All figures are approximate, and may vary according to model. Refer to manufacturer's data for exact figures.*

Overall length	4020 mm
Overall width	1720 mm
Overall height:	
Soft-top	1245 mm
Hardtop	1255 mm
Wheelbase	2330 mm

Fuel economy

Although depreciation is still the biggest part of the cost of motoring for most car owners, the cost of fuel is more immediately noticeable. These pages give some tips on how to get the best fuel economy.

Working it out

Manufacturer's figures

Car manufacturers are required by law to provide fuel consumption information on all new vehicles sold. These 'official' figures are obtained by simulating various driving conditions on a rolling road or a test track. Real life conditions are different, so the fuel consumption actually achieved may not bear much resemblance to the quoted figures.

How to calculate it

Many cars now have trip computers which will display fuel consumption, both instantaneous and average. Refer to the owner's handbook for details of how to use these.

To calculate consumption yourself (and maybe to check that the trip computer is accurate), proceed as follows.

1. Fill up with fuel and note the mileage, or zero the trip recorder.
2. Drive as usual until you need to fill up again.
3. Note the amount of fuel required to refill the tank, and the mileage covered since the previous fill-up.
4. Divide the mileage by the amount of fuel used to obtain the consumption figure.

For example:

Mileage at first fill-up (a) = 27,903
Mileage at second fill-up (b) = 28,346
Mileage covered (b - a) = 443
Fuel required at second fill-up = 48.6 litres

The half-completed changeover to metric units in the UK means that we buy our fuel in litres, measure distances in miles and talk about fuel consumption in miles per gallon. There are two ways round this: the first is to convert the litres to gallons before doing the calculation (by dividing by 4.546, or see Table 1). So in the example:

48.6 litres ÷ 4.546 = 10.69 gallons
443 miles ÷ 10.69 gallons = 41.4 mpg

The second way is to calculate the consumption in miles per litre, then multiply that figure by 4.546 (or see Table 2).

So in the example, fuel consumption is:

443 miles ÷ 48.6 litres = 9.1 mpl
9.1 mpl x 4.546 = 41.4 mpg

The rest of Europe expresses fuel consumption in litres of fuel required to travel 100 km (l/100 km). For interest, the conversions are given in Table 3. In practice it doesn't matter what units you use, provided you know what your normal consumption is and can spot if it's getting better or worse.

Table 1: conversion of litres to Imperial gallons

litres	1	2	3	4	5	10	20	30	40	50	60	70
gallons	0.22	0.44	0.66	0.88	1.10	2.24	4.49	6.73	8.98	11.22	13.47	15.71

Table 2: conversion of miles per litre to miles per gallon

miles per litre	5	6	7	8	9	10	11	12	13	14
miles per gallon	23	27	32	36	41	46	50	55	59	64

Table 3: conversion of litres per 100 km to miles per gallon

litres per 100 km	4	4.5	5	5.5	6	6.5	7	8	9	10
miles per gallon	71	63	56	51	47	43	40	35	31	28

Maintenance

A well-maintained car uses less fuel and creates less pollution. In particular:

Filters

Change air and fuel filters at the specified intervals.

Oil

Use a good quality oil of the lowest viscosity specified by the vehicle manufacturer (see *Lubricants and fluids*). Check the level often and be careful not to overfill.

Spark plugs

When applicable, renew at the specified intervals.

Tyres

Check tyre pressures regularly. Under-inflated tyres have an increased rolling resistance. It is generally safe to use the higher pressures specified for full load conditions even when not fully laden, but keep an eye on the centre band of tread for signs of wear due to over-inflation.

When buying new tyres, consider the 'fuel saving' models which most manufacturers include in their ranges.

Driving style

Acceleration

Acceleration uses more fuel than driving at a steady speed. The best technique with modern cars is to accelerate reasonably briskly to the desired speed, changing up through the gears as soon as possible without making the engine labour.

Air conditioning

Air conditioning absorbs quite a bit of energy from the engine – typically 3 kW (4 hp) or so. The effect on fuel consumption is at its worst in slow traffic. Switch it off when not required.

Anticipation

Drive smoothly and try to read the traffic flow so as to avoid unnecessary acceleration and braking.

Automatic transmission

When accelerating in an automatic, avoid depressing the throttle so far as to make the transmission hold onto lower gears at higher speeds. Don't use the 'Sport' setting, if applicable.

When stationary with the engine running, select 'N' or 'P'. When moving, keep your left foot away from the brake.

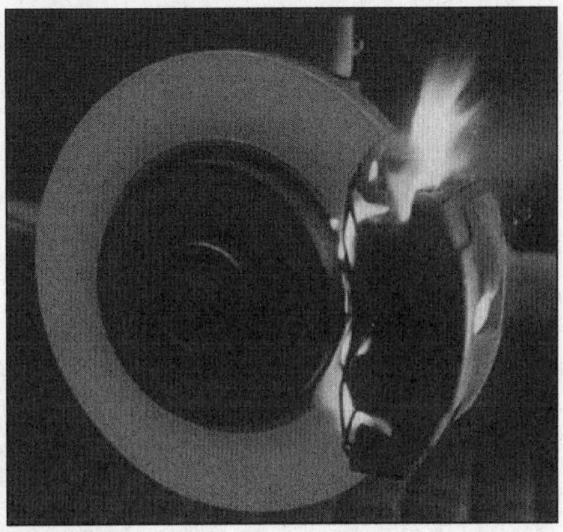

Braking

Braking converts the car's energy of motion into heat – essentially, it is wasted. Obviously some braking is always going to be necessary, but with good anticipation it is surprising how much can be avoided, especially on routes that you know well.

Carshare

Consider sharing lifts to work or to the shops. Even once a week will make a difference.

Electrical loads

Electricity is 'fuel' too; the alternator which charges the battery does so by converting some of the engine's energy of motion into electrical energy. The more electrical accessories are in use, the greater the load on the alternator. Switch off big consumers like the heated rear window when not required.

Freewheeling

Freewheeling (coasting) in neutral with the engine switched off is dangerous. The effort required to operate power-assisted brakes and steering increases when the engine is not running, with a potential lack of control in emergency situations.

In any case, modern fuel injection systems automatically cut off the engine's fuel supply on the overrun (moving and in gear, but with the accelerator pedal released).

Gadgets

Bolt-on devices claiming to save fuel have been around for nearly as long as the motor car itself. Those which worked were rapidly adopted as standard equipment by the vehicle manufacturers. Others worked only in certain situations, or saved fuel only at the expense of unacceptable effects on performance, driveability or the life of engine components.

The most effective fuel saving gadget is the driver's right foot.

Journey planning

Combine (eg) a trip to the supermarket with a visit to the recycling centre and the DIY store, rather than making separate journeys.

When possible choose a travelling time outside rush hours.

Load

The more heavily a car is laden, the greater the energy required to accelerate it to a given speed. Remove heavy items which you don't need to carry.

One load which is often overlooked is the contents of the fuel tank. A tankful of fuel (55 litres / 12 gallons) weighs 45 kg (100 lb) or so. Just half filling it may be worthwhile.

Lost?

At the risk of stating the obvious, if you're going somewhere new, have details of the route to hand. There's not much point in achieving record mpg if you also go miles out of your way.

Parking

If possible, carry out any reversing or turning manoeuvres when you arrive at a parking space so that you can drive straight out when you leave. Manoeuvering when the engine is cold uses a lot more fuel.

Driving around looking for free on-street parking may cost more in fuel than buying a car park ticket.

Premium fuel

Most major oil companies (and some supermarkets) have premium grades of fuel which are several pence a litre dearer than the standard grades. Reports vary, but the consensus seems to be that if these fuels improve economy at all, they do not do so by enough to justify their extra cost.

Roof rack

When loading a roof rack, try to produce a wedge shape with the narrow end at the front. Any cover should be securely fastened – if it flaps it's creating turbulence and absorbing energy.

Remove roof racks and boxes when not in use – they increase air resistance and can create a surprising amount of noise.

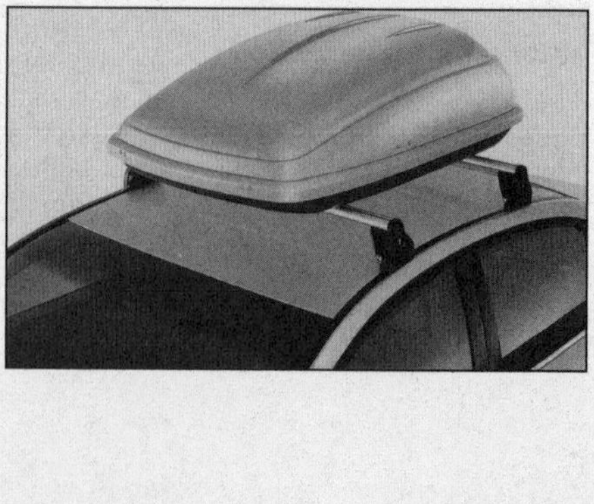

Short journeys

The engine is at its least efficient, and wear is highest, during the first few miles after a cold start. Consider walking, cycling or using public transport.

Speed

The engine is at its most efficient when running at a steady speed and load at the rpm where it develops maximum torque. (You can find this figure in the car's handbook.) For most cars this corresponds to between 55 and 65 mph in top gear.

Above the optimum cruising speed, fuel consumption starts to rise quite sharply. A car travelling at 80 mph will typically be using 30% more fuel than at 60 mph.

Supermarket fuel

It may be cheap but is it any good? In the UK all supermarket fuel must meet the relevant British Standard. The major oil companies will say that their branded fuels have better additive packages which may stop carbon and other deposits building up. A reasonable compromise might be to use one tank of branded fuel to three or four from the supermarket.

Switch off when stationary

Switch off the engine if you look like being stationary for more than 30 seconds or so. This is good for the environment as well as for your pocket. Be aware though that frequent restarts are hard on the battery and the starter motor.

Windows

Driving with the windows open increases air turbulence around the vehicle. Closing the windows promotes smooth airflow and

reduced resistance. The faster you go, the more significant this is.

And finally . . .

Driving techniques associated with good fuel economy tend to involve moderate acceleration and low top speeds. Be considerate to the needs of other road users who may need to make brisker progress; even if you do not agree with them this is not an excuse to be obstructive.

Safety must always take precedence over economy, whether it is a question of accelerating hard to complete an overtaking manoeuvre, killing your speed when confronted with a potential hazard or switching the lights on when it starts to get dark.

Conversion factors

Length (distance)

Inches (in)	x 25.4	= Millimetres (mm)	x 0.0394	=	Inches (in)
Feet (ft)	x 0.305	= Metres (m)	x 3.281	=	Feet (ft)
Miles	x 1.609	= Kilometres (km)	x 0.621	=	Miles

Volume (capacity)

Cubic inches (cu in; in³)	x 16.387	= Cubic centimetres (cc; cm³)	x 0.061	=	Cubic inches (cu in; in³)
Imperial pints (Imp pt)	x 0.568	= Litres (l)	x 1.76	=	Imperial pints (Imp pt)
Imperial quarts (Imp qt)	x 1.137	= Litres (l)	x 0.88	=	Imperial quarts (Imp qt)
Imperial quarts (Imp qt)	x 1.201	= US quarts (US qt)	x 0.833	=	Imperial quarts (Imp qt)
US quarts (US qt)	x 0.946	= Litres (l)	x 1.057	=	US quarts (US qt)
Imperial gallons (Imp gal)	x 4.546	= Litres (l)	x 0.22	=	Imperial gallons (Imp gal)
Imperial gallons (Imp gal)	x 1.201	= US gallons (US gal)	x 0.833	=	Imperial gallons (Imp gal)
US gallons (US gal)	x 3.785	= Litres (l)	x 0.264	=	US gallons (US gal)

Mass (weight)

Ounces (oz)	x 28.35	= Grams (g)	x 0.035	=	Ounces (oz)
Pounds (lb)	x 0.454	= Kilograms (kg)	x 2.205	=	Pounds (lb)

Force

Ounces-force (ozf; oz)	x 0.278	= Newtons (N)	x 3.6	=	Ounces-force (ozf; oz)
Pounds-force (lbf; lb)	x 4.448	= Newtons (N)	x 0.225	=	Pounds-force (lbf; lb)
Newtons (N)	x 0.1	= Kilograms-force (kgf; kg)	x 9.81	=	Newtons (N)

Pressure

Pounds-force per square inch (psi; lbf/in²; lb/in²)	x 0.070	= Kilograms-force per square centimetre (kgf/cm²; kg/cm²)	x 14.223	=	Pounds-force per square inch (psi; lbf/in²; lb/in²)
Pounds-force per square inch (psi; lbf/in²; lb/in²)	x 0.068	= Atmospheres (atm)	x 14.696	=	Pounds-force per square inch (psi; lbf/in²; lb/in²)
Pounds-force per square inch (psi; lbf/in²; lb/in²)	x 0.069	= Bars	x 14.5	=	Pounds-force per square inch (psi; lbf/in²; lb/in²)
Pounds-force per square inch (psi; lbf/in²; lb/in²)	x 6.895	= Kilopascals (kPa)	x 0.145	=	Pounds-force per square inch (psi; lbf/in²; lb/in²)
Kilopascals (kPa)	x 0.01	= Kilograms-force per square centimetre (kgf/cm²; kg/cm²)	x 98.1	=	Kilopascals (kPa)
Millibar (mbar)	x 100	= Pascals (Pa)	x 0.01	=	Millibar (mbar)
Millibar (mbar)	x 0.0145	= Pounds-force per square inch (psi; lbf/in²; lb/in²)	x 68.947	=	Millibar (mbar)
Millibar (mbar)	x 0.75	= Millimetres of mercury (mmHg)	x 1.333	=	Millibar (mbar)
Millibar (mbar)	x 0.401	= Inches of water (inH_2O)	x 2.491	=	Millibar (mbar)
Millimetres of mercury (mmHg)	x 0.535	= Inches of water (inH_2O)	x 1.868	=	Millimetres of mercury (mmHg)
Inches of water (inH_2O)	x 0.036	= Pounds-force per square inch (psi; lbf/in²; lb/in²)	x 27.68	=	Inches of water (inH_2O)

Torque (moment of force)

Pounds-force inches (lbf in; lb in)	x 1.152	= Kilograms-force centimetre (kgf cm; kg cm)	x 0.868	=	Pounds-force inches (lbf in; lb in)
Pounds-force inches (lbf in; lb in)	x 0.113	= Newton metres (Nm)	x 8.85	=	Pounds-force inches (lbf in; lb in)
Pounds-force inches (lbf in; lb in)	x 0.083	= Pounds-force feet (lbf ft; lb ft)	x 12	=	Pounds-force inches (lbf in; lb in)
Pounds-force feet (lbf ft; lb ft)	x 0.138	= Kilograms-force metres (kgf m; kg m)	x 7.233	=	Pounds-force feet (lbf ft; lb ft)
Pounds-force feet (lbf ft; lb ft)	x 1.356	= Newton metres (Nm)	x 0.738	=	Pounds-force feet (lbf ft; lb ft)
Newton metres (Nm)	x 0.102	= Kilograms-force metres (kgf m; kg m)	x 9.804	=	Newton metres (Nm)

Power

Horsepower (hp)	x 745.7	= Watts (W)	x 0.0013	=	Horsepower (hp)

Velocity (speed)

Miles per hour (miles/hr; mph)	x 1.609	= Kilometres per hour (km/hr; kph)	x 0.621	=	Miles per hour (miles/hr; mph)

Fuel consumption*

Miles per gallon, Imperial (mpg)	x 0.354	= Kilometres per litre (km/l)	x 2.825	=	Miles per gallon, Imperial (mpg)
Miles per gallon, US (mpg)	x 0.425	= Kilometres per litre (km/l)	x 2.352	=	Miles per gallon, US (mpg)

Temperature

Degrees Fahrenheit = (°C x 1.8) + 32

Degrees Celsius (Degrees Centigrade; °C) = (°F - 32) x 0.56

** It is common practice to convert from miles per gallon (mpg) to litres/100 kilometres (l/100km), where mpg x l/100 km = 282*

Spare parts are available from many sources, including maker's appointed garages, accessory shops, and motor factors. To be sure of obtaining the correct parts, it will sometimes be necessary to quote the vehicle identification number. If possible, it can also be useful to take the old parts along for positive identification. Items such as starter motors and alternators may be available under a service exchange scheme – any parts returned should be clean.

Our advice regarding spare parts is as follows.

Officially appointed garages

This is the best source of parts which are peculiar to your car, and which are not otherwise generally available (eg, badges, interior trim, certain body panels, etc). It is also the only place at which you should buy parts if the car is still under warranty.

Accessory shops

These are very good places to buy materials and components needed for the maintenance of your car (oil, air and fuel filters, light bulbs, drivebelts, greases, brake pads, touch-up paint, etc). Components of this nature sold by a reputable shop are usually of the same standard as those used by the car manufacturer.

Besides components, these shops also sell tools and general accessories, usually have convenient opening hours, charge lower prices, and can often be found close to home. Some accessory shops have parts counters where components needed for almost any repair job can be purchased or ordered.

Motor factors

Good factors will stock all the more important components which wear out comparatively quickly, and can sometimes supply individual components needed for the overhaul of a larger assembly (eg, brake seals and hydraulic parts, bearing shells, pistons, valves). They may also handle work such as cylinder block reboring, crankshaft regrinding, etc.

Engine reconditioners

These specialise in engine overhaul and can also supply components. It is recommended that the establishment is a member of the Federation of Engine Re-Manufacturers, or a similar society.

Tyre and exhaust specialists

These outlets may be independent, or members of a local or national chain. They frequently offer competitive prices when compared with a main dealer or local garage, but it will pay to obtain several quotes before making a decision. When researching prices, also ask what extras may be added – for instance fitting a new valve, balancing the wheel and tyre disposal all both commonly charged on top of the price of a new tyre.

Other sources

Beware of parts or materials obtained from market stalls, car boot sales, on-line auctions or similar outlets. Such items are not invariably sub-standard, but there is little chance of compensation if they do prove unsatisfactory. In the case of safety-critical components such as brake pads, there is the risk not only of financial loss, but also of an accident causing injury or death.

Second-hand components or assemblies obtained from a car breaker can be a good buy in some circumstances, but this sort of purchase is best made by the experienced DIY mechanic.

Vehicle identification

Modifications are a continuing and unpublicised process in vehicle manufacture, quite apart from major model changes. Spare parts manuals and lists are compiled upon a numerical basis, the individual vehicle identification numbers being essential to correct identification of the component concerned.

When ordering spare parts, always give as much information as possible. Quote the vehicle type and year, vehicle identification number (VIN), and engine number, as appropriate.

The vehicle identification number (VIN) is stamped into the engine compartment bulkhead **(see illustration)**.

A model plate is also located in the drivers door aperture **(see illustration)**. The model plate also gives vehicle loading details, engine type, and various trim and colour codes.

The engine number is stamped on the right-hand side of the cylinder block.

The VIN number

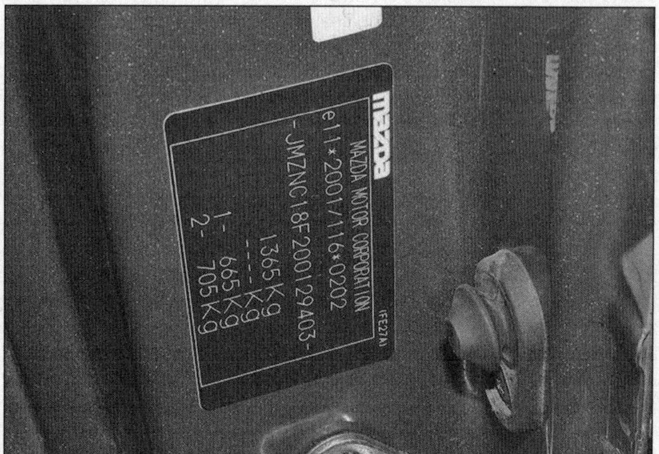

Model plate

Whenever servicing, repair or overhaul work is carried out on the car or its components, observe the following procedures and instructions. This will assist in carrying out the operation efficiently and to a professional standard of workmanship.

Joint mating faces and gaskets

When separating components at their mating faces, never insert screwdrivers or similar implements into the joint between the faces in order to prise them apart. This can cause severe damage which results in oil leaks, coolant leaks, etc upon reassembly. Separation is usually achieved by tapping along the joint with a soft-faced hammer in order to break the seal. However, note that this method may not be suitable where dowels are used for component location.

Where a gasket is used between the mating faces of two components, a new one must be fitted on reassembly; fit it dry unless otherwise stated in the repair procedure. Make sure that the mating faces are clean and dry, with all traces of old gasket removed. When cleaning a joint face, use a tool which is unlikely to score or damage the face, and remove any burrs or nicks with an oilstone or fine file.

Make sure that tapped holes are cleaned with a pipe cleaner, and keep them free of jointing compound, if this is being used, unless specifically instructed otherwise.

Ensure that all orifices, channels or pipes are clear, and blow through them, preferably using compressed air.

Oil seals

Oil seals can be removed by levering them out with a wide flat-bladed screwdriver or similar implement. Alternatively, a number of self-tapping screws may be screwed into the seal, and these used as a purchase for pliers or some similar device in order to pull the seal free.

Whenever an oil seal is removed from its working location, either individually or as part of an assembly, it should be renewed.

The very fine sealing lip of the seal is easily damaged, and will not seal if the surface it contacts is not completely clean and free from scratches, nicks or grooves. If the original sealing surface of the component cannot be restored, and the manufacturer has not made provision for slight relocation of the seal relative to the sealing surface, the component should be renewed.

Protect the lips of the seal from any surface which may damage them in the course of fitting. Use tape or a conical sleeve where possible. Where indicated, lubricate the seal lips with oil before fitting and, on dual-lipped seals, fill the space between the lips with grease.

Unless otherwise stated, oil seals must be fitted with their sealing lips toward the lubricant to be sealed.

Use a tubular drift or block of wood of the appropriate size to install the seal and, if the seal housing is shouldered, drive the seal down to the shoulder. If the seal housing is unshouldered, the seal should be fitted with its face flush with the housing top face (unless otherwise instructed).

Screw threads and fastenings

Seized nuts, bolts and screws are quite a common occurrence where corrosion has set in, and the use of penetrating oil or releasing fluid will often overcome this problem if the offending item is soaked for a while before attempting to release it. The use of an impact driver may also provide a means of releasing such stubborn fastening devices, when used in conjunction with the appropriate screwdriver bit or socket. If none of these methods works, it may be necessary to resort to the careful application of heat, or the use of a hacksaw or nut splitter device. Before resorting to extreme methods, check that you are not dealing with a left-hand thread!

Studs are usually removed by locking two nuts together on the threaded part, and then using a spanner on the lower nut to unscrew the stud. Studs or bolts which have broken off below the surface of the component in which they are mounted can sometimes be removed using a stud extractor.

Always ensure that a blind tapped hole is completely free from oil, grease, water or other fluid before installing the bolt or stud. Failure to do this could cause the housing to crack due to the hydraulic action of the bolt or stud as it is screwed in.

For some screw fastenings, notably cylinder head bolts or nuts, torque wrench settings are no longer specified for the latter stages of tightening, "angle-tightening" being called up instead. Typically, a fairly low torque wrench setting will be applied to the bolts/nuts in the correct sequence, followed by one or more stages of tightening through specified angles.

When checking or retightening a nut or bolt to a specified torque setting, slacken the nut or bolt by a quarter of a turn, and then retighten to the specified setting. However, this should not be attempted where angular tightening has been used.

Locknuts, locktabs and washers

Any fastening which will rotate against a component or housing during tightening should always have a washer between it and the relevant component or housing.

Spring or split washers should always be renewed when they are used to lock a critical component such as a big-end bearing retaining bolt or nut. Locktabs which are folded over to retain a nut or bolt should always be renewed.

Self-locking nuts can be re-used in non-critical areas, providing resistance can be felt when the locking portion passes over the bolt or stud thread. However, it should be noted that self-locking stiffnuts tend to lose their effectiveness after long periods of use, and should then be renewed as a matter of course.

Split pins must always be replaced with new ones of the correct size for the hole.

When thread-locking compound is found on the threads of a fastener which is to be re-used, it should be cleaned off with a wire brush and solvent, and fresh compound applied on reassembly.

Special tools

Some repair procedures in this manual entail the use of special tools such as a press, two or three-legged pullers, spring compressors, etc. Wherever possible, suitable readily-available alternatives to the manufacturer's special tools are described, and are shown in use. In some instances, where no alternative is possible, it has been necessary to resort to the use of a manufacturer's tool, and this has been done for reasons of safety as well as the efficient completion of the repair operation. Unless you are highly-skilled and have a thorough understanding of the procedures described, never attempt to bypass the use of any special tool when the procedure described specifies its use. Not only is there a very great risk of personal injury, but expensive damage could be caused to the components involved.

Environmental considerations

When disposing of used engine oil, brake fluid, antifreeze, etc, give due consideration to any detrimental environmental effects. Do not, for instance, pour any of the above liquids down drains into the general sewage system, or onto the ground to soak away, as this is likely to pollute your local environment. Many local council refuse tips provide a facility for waste oil disposal, as do some garages. You can find your nearest disposal point by calling the Environment Agency on 03708 506 506 or by visiting www.oilbankline.org.uk.

OIL CARE®

Note: It is illegal and anti-social to dump oil down the drain. To find the location of your local oil recycling bank, call 03708 506 506 or visit www.oilbankline.org.uk.

Jacking and vehicle support

The jack supplied by Mazda should only be used for raising the roadwheels in an emergency. When carrying out any other kind of work, raise the vehicle using a heavy-duty hydraulic (or 'trolley') jack, and always supplement the jack with axle stands positioned under the vehicle jacking points. If the roadwheels do not have to be removed, consider using wheel ramps – if wished, these can be placed under the wheels once the vehicle has been raised using a hydraulic jack, and the vehicle lowered onto the ramps so that it is resting on its wheels.

Only ever jack the vehicle up on a solid, level surface. If there is even a slight slope, take great care that the vehicle cannot move as the wheels are lifted off the ground. Jacking up on an uneven or gravelled surface is not recommended, as the weight of the vehicle will not be evenly distributed, and the jack may slip as the vehicle is raised.

As far as possible, do not leave the vehicle unattended once it has been raised, particularly if children are playing nearby.

Before jacking up the front of the car, ensure that the handbrake is firmly applied. When jacking up the rear of the car, place wooden chocks in front of the front wheels, and engage first gear.

When using a hydraulic jack or axle stands, always position the jack head or axle stand head under the relevant jacking points. These are situated directly underneath the vehicle jack location holes in the sill. Note that the vehicle may also be lifted using a hydraulic 'trolley' jack under the rear final drive casing, and the front crossmember **(see illustrations)**.

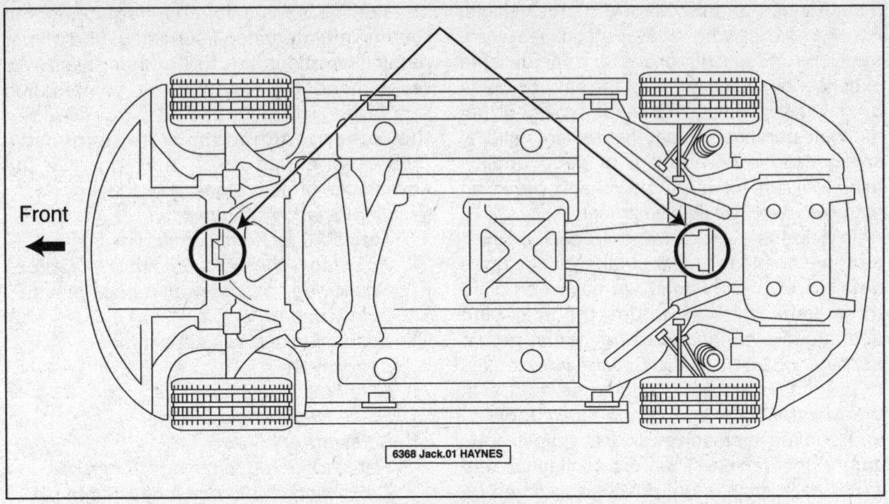

A workshop (trolley) jack can be placed under the front crossmember or final drive unit

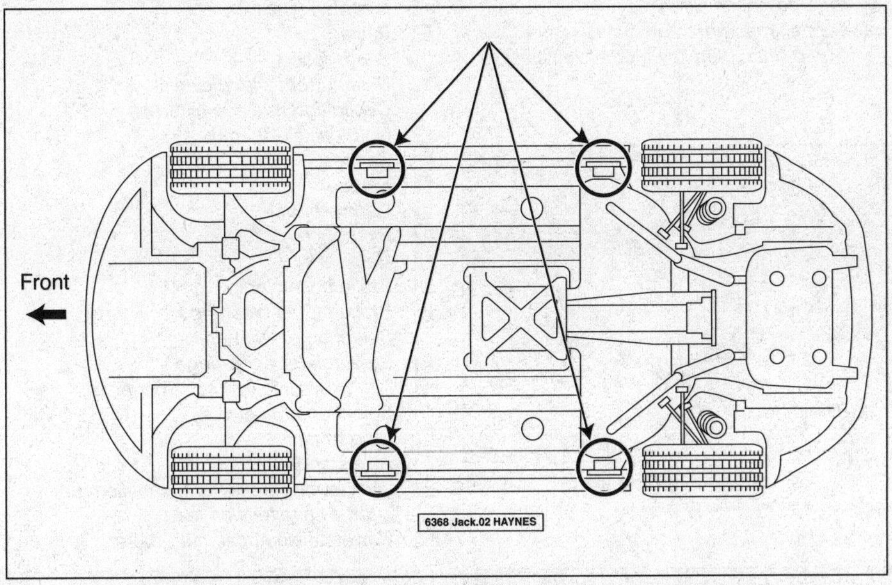

Jacking points under the sills each side (vehicle supplied jack)

Ensure that the jack head is correctly engaged before attempting to raise the vehicle.

Never work under, around, or near a raised vehicle, unless it is adequately supported in at least two places.

When jacking or supporting the vehicle at these points, always use a block of wood between the jack head or axle stand, and the vehicle body. It is also considered good practice to use a large block of wood when supporting under other areas, to spread the load over a wider area, and reduce the risk of damage to the underside of the car (it also helps to prevent the underbody coating from being damaged by the jack or axle stand). Do not jack the vehicle under any other part of the sill, engine sump, floor pan, subframe, or directly under any of the steering or suspension components.

Warning: Never work under, around, or near a raised vehicle, unless it is adequately supported on stands. Do not rely on a jack alone, as even a hydraulic jack could fail under load. Makeshift methods should not be used to lift and support the car during servicing work.

Introduction

A selection of good tools is a fundamental requirement for anyone contemplating the maintenance and repair of a motor vehicle. For the owner who does not possess any, their purchase will prove a considerable expense, offsetting some of the savings made by doing-it-yourself. However, provided that the tools purchased meet the relevant national safety standards and are of good quality, they will last for many years and prove an extremely worthwhile investment.

To help the average owner to decide which tools are needed to carry out the various tasks detailed in this manual, we have compiled three lists of tools under the following headings: *Maintenance and minor repair, Repair and overhaul*, and *Special*. Newcomers to practical mechanics should start off with the *Maintenance and minor repair* tool kit, and confine themselves to the simpler jobs around the vehicle. Then, as confidence and experience grow, more difficult tasks can be undertaken, with extra tools being purchased as, and when, they are needed. In this way, a *Maintenance and minor repair* tool kit can be built up into a *Repair and overhaul* tool kit over a considerable period of time, without any major cash outlays. The experienced do-it-yourselfer will have a tool kit good enough for most repair and overhaul procedures, and will add tools from the *Special* category when it is felt that the expense is justified by the amount of use to which these tools will be put.

Maintenance and minor repair tool kit

The tools given in this list should be considered as a minimum requirement if routine maintenance, servicing and minor repair operations are to be undertaken. We recommend the purchase of combination spanners (ring one end, open-ended the other); although more expensive than open-ended ones, they do give the advantages of both types of spanner.

☐ *Combination spanners:*
Metric - 8 to 19 mm inclusive
☐ *Adjustable spanner - 35 mm jaw (approx.)*
☐ *Spark plug spanner (with rubber insert) - petrol models*
☐ *Spark plug gap adjustment tool - petrol models*
☐ *Set of feeler gauges*
☐ *Brake bleed nipple spanner*
☐ *Screwdrivers:*
Flat blade - 100 mm long x 6 mm dia
Cross blade - 100 mm long x 6 mm dia
Torx - various sizes (not all vehicles)
☐ *Combination pliers*
☐ *Hacksaw (junior)*
☐ *Tyre pump*
☐ *Tyre pressure gauge*
☐ *Oil can*
☐ *Oil filter removal tool (if applicable)*
☐ *Fine emery cloth*
☐ *Wire brush (small)*
☐ *Funnel (medium size)*
☐ *Sump drain plug key (not all vehicles)*

Repair and overhaul tool kit

These tools are virtually essential for anyone undertaking any major repairs to a motor vehicle, and are additional to those given in the *Maintenance and minor repair* list. Included in this list is a comprehensive set of sockets. Although these are expensive, they will be found invaluable as they are so versatile - particularly if various drives are included in the set. We recommend the half-inch square-drive type, as this can be used with most proprietary torque wrenches.

The tools in this list will sometimes need to be supplemented by tools from the *Special* list:

☐ *Sockets to cover range in previous list (including Torx sockets)*
☐ *Reversible ratchet drive (for use with sockets)*
☐ *Extension piece, 250 mm (for use with sockets)*
☐ *Universal joint (for use with sockets)*
☐ *Flexible handle or sliding T "breaker bar" (for use with sockets)*
☐ *Torque wrench (for use with sockets)*
☐ *Self-locking grips*
☐ *Ball pein hammer*
☐ *Soft-faced mallet (plastic or rubber)*
☐ *Screwdrivers:*
Flat blade - long & sturdy, short (chubby), and narrow (electrician's) types
Cross blade – long & sturdy, and short (chubby) types
☐ *Pliers:*
Long-nosed
Side cutters (electrician's)
Circlip (internal and external)
☐ *Cold chisel - 25 mm*
☐ *Scriber*
☐ *Scraper*
☐ *Centre-punch*
☐ *Pin punch*
☐ *Hacksaw*
☐ *Brake hose clamp*
☐ *Brake/clutch bleeding kit*
☐ *Selection of twist drills*
☐ *Steel rule/straight-edge*
☐ *Allen keys (inc. splined/Torx type)*
☐ *Selection of files*
☐ *Wire brush*
☐ *Axle stands*
☐ *Jack (strong trolley or hydraulic type)*
☐ *Light with extension lead*
☐ *Universal electrical multi-meter*

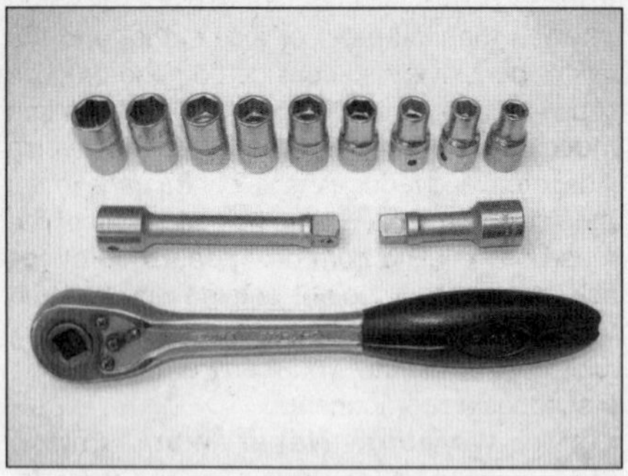

Sockets and reversible ratchet drive

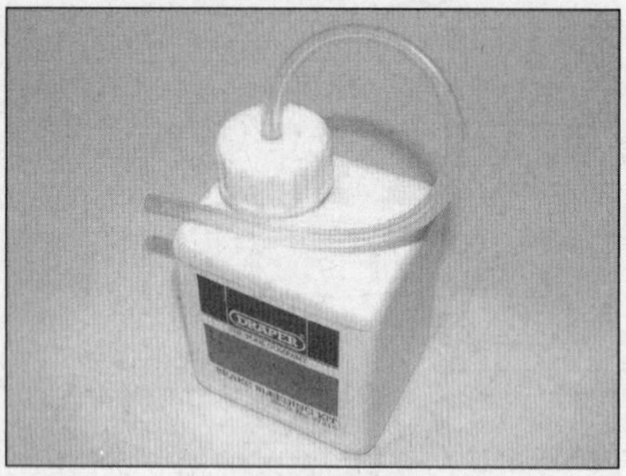

Brake bleeding kit

Torx key, socket and bit

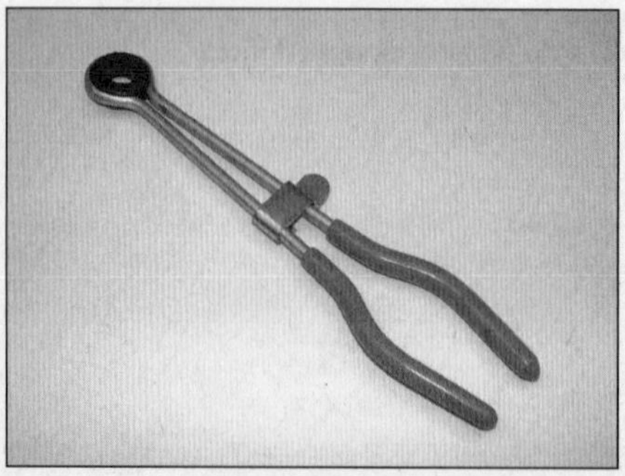

Hose clamp

Angular-tightening gauge

Special tools

The tools in this list are those which are not used regularly, are expensive to buy, or which need to be used in accordance with their manufacturers' instructions. Unless relatively difficult mechanical jobs are undertaken frequently, it will not be economic to buy many of these tools. Where this is the case, you could consider clubbing together with friends (or joining a motorists' club) to make a joint purchase, or borrowing the tools against a deposit from a local garage or tool hire specialist.

The following list contains only those tools and instruments freely available to the public, and not those special tools produced by the vehicle manufacturer specifically for its dealer network. You will find occasional references to these manufacturers' special tools in the text of this manual. Generally, an alternative method of doing the job without the vehicle manufacturers' special tool is given. However, sometimes there is no alternative to using them. Where this is the case and the relevant tool cannot be bought or borrowed, you will have to entrust the work to a dealer.

- ☐ *Angular-tightening gauge*
- ☐ *Valve spring compressor*
- ☐ *Valve grinding tool*
- ☐ *Piston ring compressor*
- ☐ *Piston ring removal/installation tool*
- ☐ *Cylinder bore hone*
- ☐ *Balljoint separator*
- ☐ *Coil spring compressors (where applicable)*
- ☐ *Two/three-legged hub and bearing puller*
- ☐ *Impact screwdriver*
- ☐ *Micrometer and/or vernier calipers*
- ☐ *Dial gauge*
- ☐ *Tachometer*
- ☐ *Fault code reader*
- ☐ *Cylinder compression gauge*
- ☐ *Hand-operated vacuum pump and gauge*
- ☐ *Clutch plate alignment set*
- ☐ *Brake shoe steady spring cup removal tool*
- ☐ *Bush and bearing removal/installation set*
- ☐ *Stud extractors*
- ☐ *Tap and die set*
- ☐ *Lifting tackle*

Buying tools

Reputable motor accessory shops and superstores often offer excellent quality tools at discount prices, so it pays to shop around.

Remember, you don't have to buy the most expensive items on the shelf, but it is always advisable to steer clear of the very cheap tools. Beware of 'bargains' offered on market stalls, on-line or at car boot sales. There are plenty of good tools around at reasonable prices, but always aim to purchase items which meet the relevant national safety standards. If in doubt, ask the proprietor or manager of the shop for advice before making a purchase.

Care and maintenance of tools

Having purchased a reasonable tool kit, it is necessary to keep the tools in a clean and serviceable condition. After use, always wipe off any dirt, grease and metal particles using a clean, dry cloth, before putting the tools away. Never leave them lying around after they have been used. A simple tool rack on the garage or workshop wall for items such as screwdrivers and pliers is a good idea. Store all normal spanners and sockets in a metal box. Any measuring instruments, gauges, meters, etc, must be carefully stored where they cannot be damaged or become rusty.

Take a little care when tools are used. Hammer heads inevitably become marked, and screwdrivers lose the keen edge on their blades from time to time. A little timely attention with emery cloth or a file will soon restore items like this to a good finish.

Working facilities

Not to be forgotten when discussing tools is the workshop itself. If anything more than routine maintenance is to be carried out, a suitable working area becomes essential.

It is appreciated that many an owner-mechanic is forced by circumstances to remove an engine or similar item without the benefit of a garage or workshop. Having done this, any repairs should always be done under the cover of a roof.

Wherever possible, any dismantling should be done on a clean, flat workbench or table at a suitable working height.

Any workbench needs a vice; one with a jaw opening of 100 mm is suitable for most jobs. As mentioned previously, some clean dry storage space is also required for tools, as well as for any lubricants, cleaning fluids, touch-up paints etc, which become necessary.

Another item which may be required, and which has a much more general usage, is an electric drill with a chuck capacity of at least 8 mm. This, together with a good range of twist drills, is virtually essential for fitting accessories.

Last, but not least, always keep a supply of old newspapers and clean, lint-free rags available, and try to keep any working area as clean as possible.

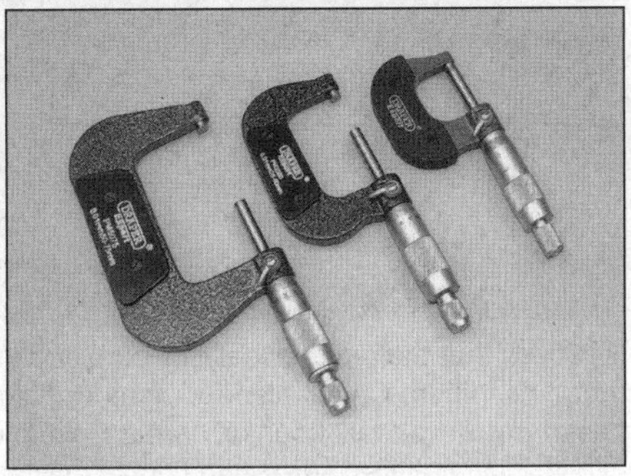

Micrometers

Dial test indicator ("dial gauge")

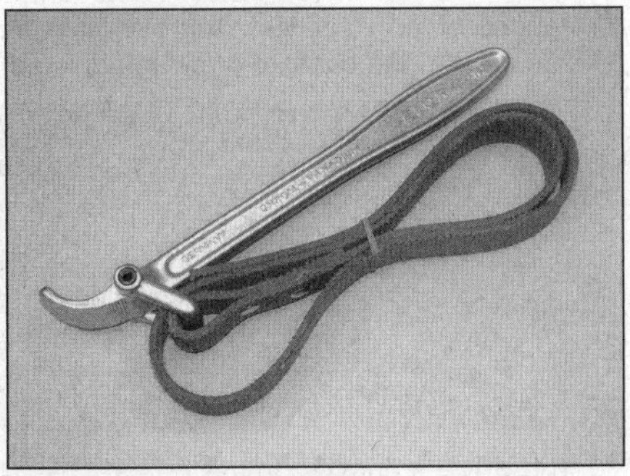

Oil filter removal tool (strap wrench type)

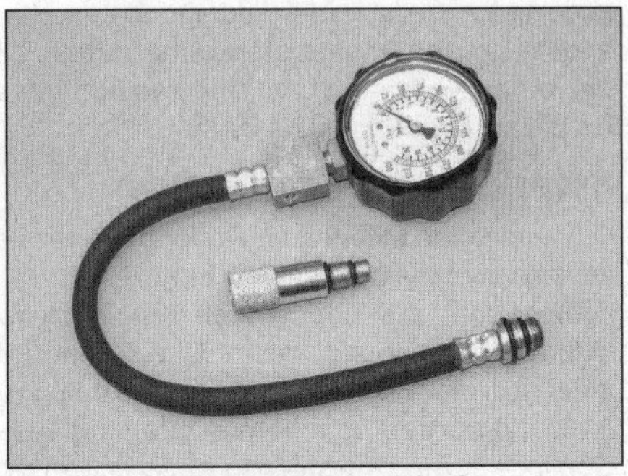

Compression tester

Bearing puller

This is a guide to getting your vehicle through the MOT test. Obviously it will not be possible to examine the vehicle to the same standard as the professional MOT tester. However, working through the following checks will enable you to identify any problem areas before submitting the vehicle for the test.

It has only been possible to summarise the test requirements here, based on the regulations in force at the time of printing. Test standards are becoming increasingly stringent, although there are some exemptions for older vehicles.

An assistant will be needed to help carry out some of these checks.

The checks have been sub-divided into four categories, as follows:

1 Checks carried out **FROM THE DRIVER'S SEAT**

2 Checks carried out **WITH THE VEHICLE ON THE GROUND**

3 Checks carried out **WITH THE VEHICLE RAISED AND THE WHEELS FREE TO TURN**

4 Checks carried out on **YOUR VEHICLE'S EXHAUST EMISSION SYSTEM**

1 Checks carried out FROM THE DRIVER'S SEAT

Handbrake (parking brake)

☐ Test the operation of the handbrake. Excessive travel (too many clicks) indicates incorrect brake or cable adjustment.

☐ Check that the handbrake cannot be released by tapping the lever sideways. Check the security of the lever mountings.

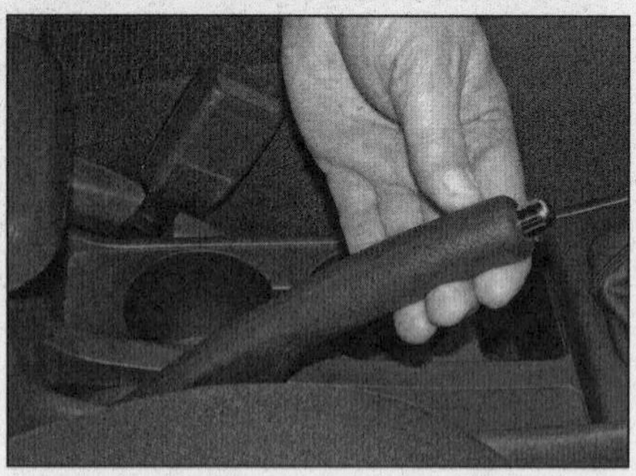

☐ If the parking brake is foot-operated, check that the pedal is secure and without excessive travel, and that the release mechanism operates correctly.

☐ Where applicable, test the operation of the electronic handbrake. The brake should engage and disengage without excessive delay. If the warning light does not extinguish when the brake is disengaged, this could indicate a fault which will need further investigation.

Footbrake

☐ Depress the brake pedal and check that it does not creep down to the floor, indicating a master cylinder fault. Release the pedal, wait a few seconds, then depress it again. If the pedal travels nearly to the floor before firm resistance is felt, brake adjustment or repair is necessary. If the pedal feels spongy, there is air in the hydraulic system which must be removed by bleeding.

☐ Check that the brake pedal is secure and in good condition. Check also for signs of fluid leaks on the pedal, floor or carpets, which would indicate failed seals in the brake master cylinder.

☐ Check the servo unit (when applicable) by operating the brake pedal several times, then keeping the pedal depressed and starting the engine. As the engine starts, the pedal will move down slightly. If not, the vacuum hose or the servo itself may be faulty.

Steering wheel and column

☐ Examine the steering wheel for fractures or looseness of the hub, spokes or rim.

☐ Move the steering wheel from side to side and then up and down. Check that the steering wheel is not loose on the column, indicating wear or a loose retaining nut. Continue moving the steering wheel as before, but also turn it slightly from left to right.

☐ Check that the steering wheel is not loose on the column, and that there is no abnormal movement of the steering wheel, indicating wear in the column support bearings or couplings.

☐ Check that the ignition lock (where fitted) engages and disengages correctly.

☐ Steering column adjustment mechanisms (where fitted) must be able to lock the column securely in place with no play evident.

Windscreen, mirrors and sunvisor

☐ The windscreen must be free of cracks or other significant damage within the driver's field of view. (Small stone chips are acceptable.) Rear view mirrors must be secure, intact, and capable of being adjusted.

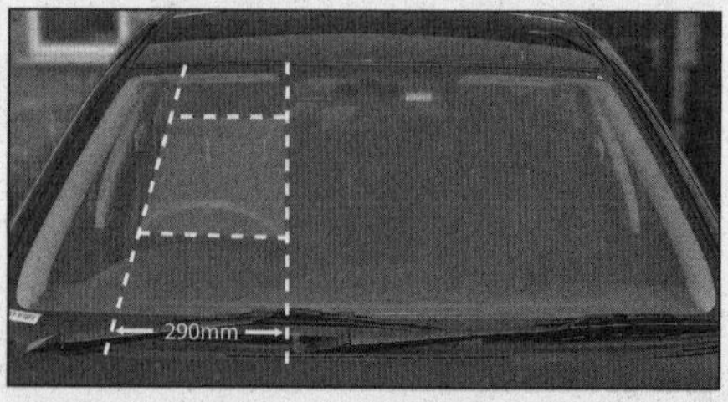

☐ The driver's sunvisor must be capable of being stored in the "up" position.

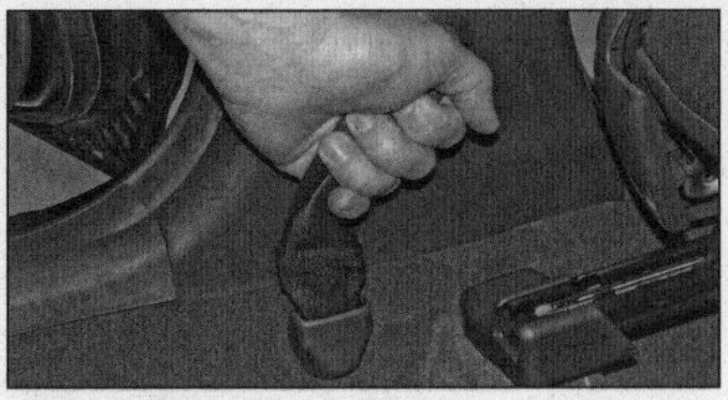

Seat belts and seats

Note: *The following checks are applicable to all seat belts, front and rear.*

☐ Examine the webbing of all the belts (including rear belts if fitted) for cuts, serious fraying or deterioration. Fasten and unfasten each belt to check the buckles. If applicable, check the retracting mechanism. Check the security of all seat belt mountings accessible from inside the vehicle, ensuring any height adjustable mountings lock securely in place.

☐ Seat belts with pre-tensioners, once activated, have a "flag" or similar showing on the seat belt stalk. This, in itself, is not a reason for test failure.

☐ The front seats themselves must be securely attached and the backrests must lock in the upright position.

Doors

☐ Both front doors must be able to be opened and closed from outside and inside, and must latch securely when closed.

Bonnet and boot/tailgate

☐ The bonnet and boot/tailgate must latch securely when closed.

2 Checks carried out WITH THE VEHICLE ON THE GROUND

Vehicle identification

☐ Number plates must be in good condition, secure and legible, with letters and numbers correctly spaced – spacing at (A) should be 33 mm and at (B) 11 mm. At the front, digits must be black on a white background and at the rear black on a yellow background. Other background designs (such as honeycomb) are not permitted.

☐ The VIN plate and/or homologation plate must be permanently displayed and legible.

Electrical equipment

☐ Switch on the ignition and check the operation of the horn.

☐ Check the windscreen washers and wipers, examining the wiper blades; renew damaged or perished blades. Also check the operation of the stop-lights.

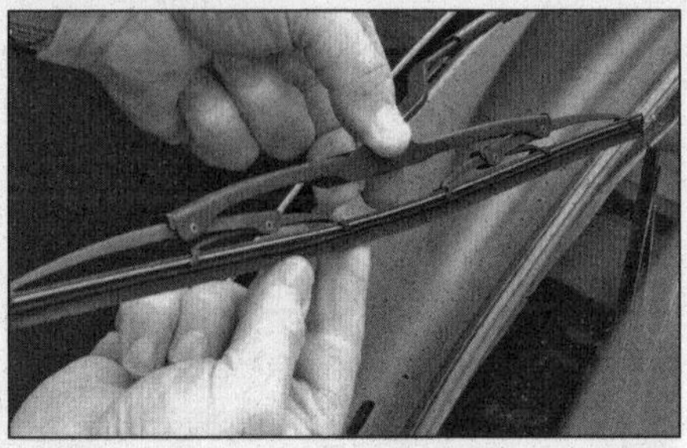

☐ Check the operation of the sidelights and number plate lights. The lenses and reflectors must be secure, clean and undamaged.

☐ Check the operation and alignment of the headlights. The headlight reflectors must not be tarnished and the lenses must be undamaged.

☐ Switch on the ignition and check the operation of the direction indicators (including the instrument panel tell-tale) and the hazard warning lights. Operation of the sidelights and stop-lights must not affect the indicators - if it does, the cause is usually a bad earth at the rear light cluster. Indicators should flash at a rate of between 60 and 120 times per minute – faster or slower than this could indicate a fault with the flasher unit or a bad earth at one of the light units.

☐ Check the operation of the rear foglight(s), including the warning light on the instrument panel or in the switch.

☐ The warning lights must illuminate in accordance with the manufacturer's design. For most vehicles, the ABS and other warning lights should illuminate when the ignition is switched on, and (if the system is operating properly) extinguish after a few seconds. Refer to the owner's handbook.

Footbrake

☐ Examine the master cylinder, brake pipes and servo unit for leaks, loose mountings, corrosion or other damage. If ABS is fitted, this unit should also be examined for signs of leaks or corrosion.

☐ The fluid reservoir must be secure and the fluid level must be between the upper (**A**) and lower (**B**) markings.

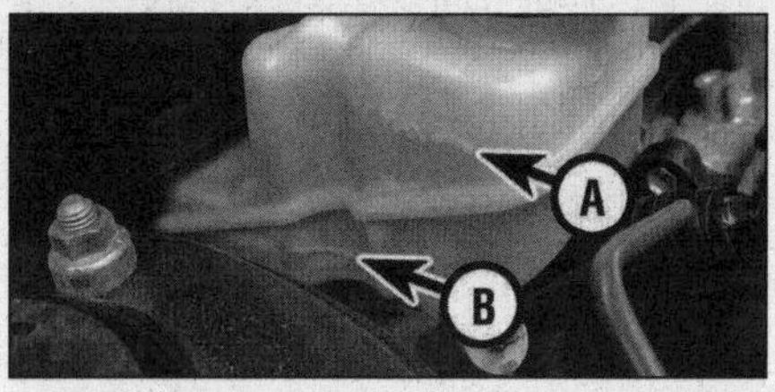

☐ Inspect both front brake flexible hoses for cracks or deterioration of the rubber. Turn the steering from lock to lock, and ensure that the hoses do not contact the wheel, tyre, or any part of the steering or suspension mechanism. With the brake pedal firmly depressed, check the hoses for bulges or leaks under pressure.

Steering and suspension

☐ Have your assistant turn the steering wheel from side to side slightly, up to the point where the steering gear just begins to transmit this movement to the roadwheels. Check for excessive free play between the steering wheel and the steering gear, indicating wear or insecurity of the steering column joints, the column-to-steering gear coupling, or the steering gear itself.

☐ Have your assistant turn the steering wheel more vigorously in each direction, so that the roadwheels just begin to turn. As this is done, examine all the steering joints, linkages, fittings and attachments. Renew any component that shows signs of wear or damage. On vehicles with power steering, check the security and condition of the steering pump, drivebelt and hoses.

☐ Check that the vehicle is standing level, and at approximately the correct ride height.

Shock absorbers

☐ Depress each corner of the vehicle in turn, then release it. The vehicle should rise and then settle in its normal position. If the vehicle continues to rise and fall, the shock absorber is defective. A shock absorber which has seized will also cause the vehicle to fail.

Exhaust system

☐Start the engine. With your assistant holding a rag over the tailpipe, check the entire system for leaks. Repair or renew leaking sections.

3 Checks carried out **WITH THE VEHICLE RAISED AND THE WHEELS FREE TO TURN**

Jack up the front and rear of the vehicle, and securely support it on axle stands. Position the stands clear of the suspension assemblies. Ensure that the wheels are clear of the ground and that the steering can be turned from lock to lock.

Steering mechanism

☐Have your assistant turn the steering from lock to lock. Check that the steering turns smoothly, and that no part of the steering mechanism, including a wheel or tyre, fouls any brake hose or pipe or any part of the body structure.

☐ Examine the steering rack rubber gaiters for damage or insecurity of the retaining clips. If power steering is fitted, check for signs of damage or leakage of the fluid hoses, pipes or connections. Also check for excessive stiffness or binding of the steering, a missing split pin or locking device, or severe corrosion of the body structure within 30 cm of any steering component attachment point.

Front and rear suspension and wheel bearings

☐Starting at the front right-hand side, grasp the roadwheel at the 3 o'clock and 9 o'clock positions and rock gently but firmly. Check for free play or insecurity at the wheel bearings, suspension balljoints, or suspension mount-ings, pivots and attachments.

☐Now grasp the wheel at the 12 o'clock and 6 o'clock positions and repeat the previous inspection. Spin the wheel, and check for roughness or tightness of the front wheel bearing.

☐If excess free play is suspected at a component pivot point, this can be confirmed by using a large screwdriver or similar tool and levering between the mounting and the component attachment. This will confirm whether the wear is in the pivot bush, its retaining bolt, or in the mounting itself (the bolt holes can often become elongated).

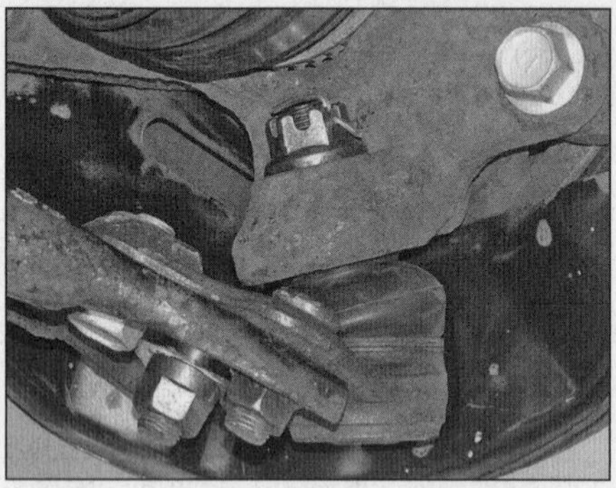

☐Carry out all the above checks at the other front wheel, and then at both rear wheels.

Springs and shock absorbers

☐Examine the suspension struts (when applicable) for serious fluid leakage, corrosion, or damage to the casing. Also check the security of the mounting points.

☐If coil springs are fitted, check that the spring ends locate in their seats, and that the spring is not corroded, cracked or broken.

☐If leaf springs are fitted, check that all leaves are intact, that the axle is securely attached to each spring, and that there is no deterioration of the spring eye mountings, bushes, and shackles.

☐The same general checks apply to vehicles fitted with other suspension types, such as torsion bars, hydraulic displacer units, etc. Ensure that all mountings and attachments are secure, that there are no signs of excessive wear, corrosion or damage, and (on hydraulic types) that there are no fluid leaks or damaged pipes.

☐Inspect the shock absorbers for signs of serious fluid leakage. Check for wear of the mounting bushes or attachments, or damage to the body of the unit.

Driveshafts (fwd vehicles only)

☐Rotate each front wheel in turn and inspect the constant velocity joint gaiters for splits or damage. Also check that each driveshaft is straight and undamaged.

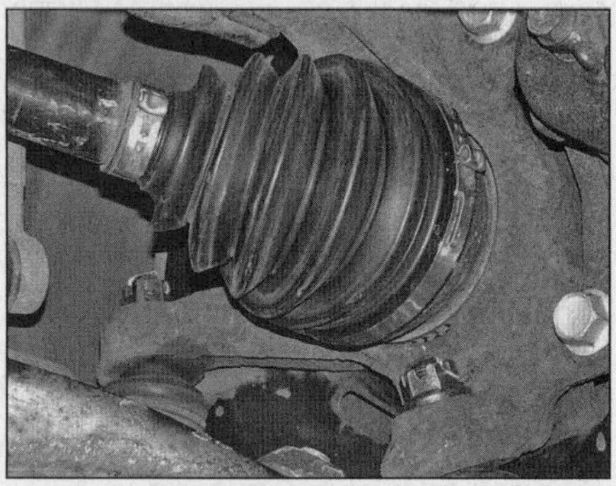

Braking system

☐If possible without dismantling, check brake pad wear and disc condition. Ensure that the friction lining material has not worn excessively, (A) and that the discs are not fractured, pitted, scored or badly worn (B).

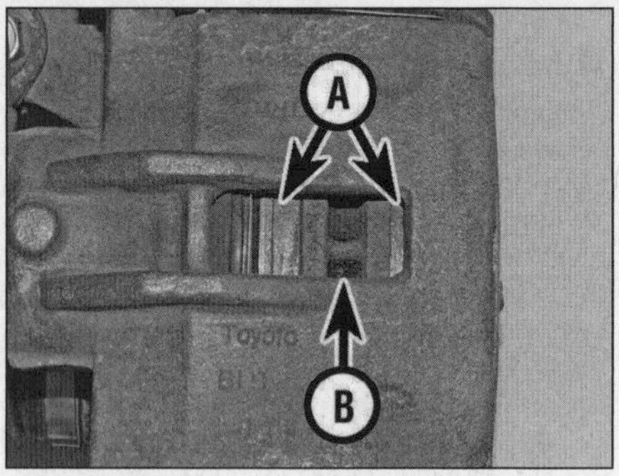

☐Examine all the rigid brake pipes underneath the vehicle, and the flexible hose(s) at the rear. Look for corrosion, chafing or insecurity of the pipes, and for signs of bulging under pressure, chafing, splits or deterioration of the flexible hoses.

☐Look for signs of fluid leaks at the brake calipers or on the brake backplates. Repair or renew leaking components.

☐Slowly spin each wheel, while your assistant depresses and releases the footbrake. Ensure that each brake is operating and does not bind when the pedal is released.

☐Examine the handbrake mechanism, checking for frayed or broken cables, excessive corrosion, or wear or insecurity of the linkage. Check that the mechanism works on each relevant wheel, and releases fully, without binding.
☐It is not possible to test brake efficiency without special equipment, but a road test can be carried out later to check that the vehicle pulls up in a straight line.

Fuel and exhaust systems

☐Inspect the fuel tank (including the filler cap), fuel pipes, hoses and unions. All components must be secure and free from leaks. Locking fuel caps must lock securely and the key must be provided for the MOT test.
☐Examine the exhaust system over its entire length, checking for any damaged, broken or missing mountings, security of the retaining clamps and rust or corrosion.

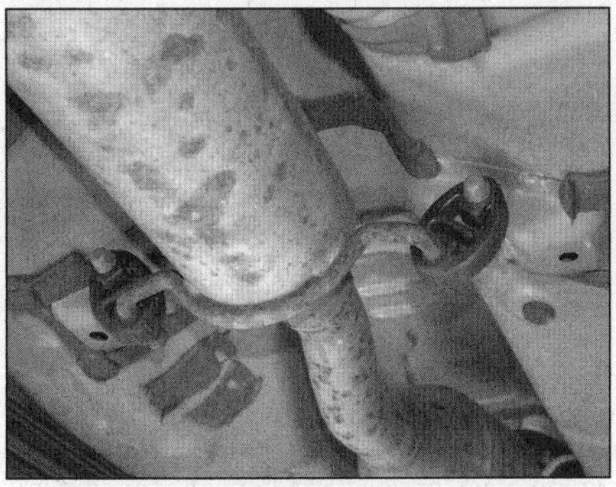

Wheels and tyres

☐Examine the sidewalls and tread area of each tyre in turn. Check for cuts, tears, lumps, bulges, separation of the tread, and exposure of the ply or cord due to wear or damage. Check that the tyre bead is correctly seated on the wheel rim, that the valve is sound and properly seated, and that the wheel is not distorted or damaged.

☐Check that the tyres are of the correct size for the vehicle, that they are of the same size and type on each axle, and that the pressures are correct.

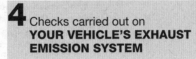

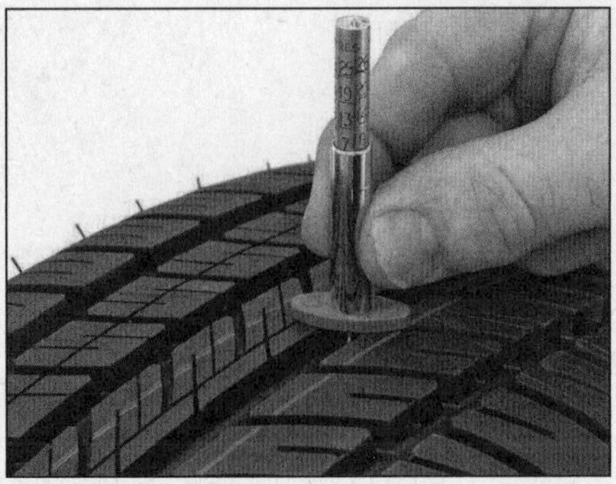

☐Check the tyre tread depth. The legal minimum at the time of writing is 1.6 mm over the central three-quarters of the tread width. Abnormal tread wear may indicate incorrect front wheel alignment or wear in steering or suspension components.
☐If the spare wheel is fitted externally or in a separate carrier beneath the vehicle, check that mountings are secure and free of excessive corrosion.

Body corrosion

☐Check the condition of the entire vehicle structure for signs of corrosion in load-bearing areas. (These include chassis box sections, side sills, cross-members, pillars, and all suspension, steering, braking system and seat belt mountings and anchorages.) Any corrosion which has seriously reduced the thickness of a load-bearing area (or is within 30 cm of safety-related components such as steering or suspension) is likely to cause the vehicle to fail. In this case professional repairs are likely to be needed.
☐Damage or corrosion which causes sharp or otherwise dangerous edges to be exposed will also cause the vehicle to fail.

Towbars

☐Check the condition of mounting points (both beneath the vehicle and within boot/ hatchback areas) for signs of corrosion, ensuring that all fixings are secure and not worn or damaged. There must be no excessive play in detachable tow ball arms or quick-release mechanisms.

4 Checks carried out on **YOUR VEHICLE'S EXHAUST EMISSION SYSTEM**

Petrol models

☐The engine should be warmed up, and running well (ignition system in good order, air filter element clean, etc).
☐Before testing, run the engine at around 2500 rpm for 20 seconds. Let the engine drop to idle, and watch for smoke from the exhaust. If the idle speed is too high, or if dense blue or black smoke emerges for more than 5 seconds, the vehicle will fail. Typically, blue smoke signifies oil burning (engine wear); black smoke means unburnt fuel (dirty air cleaner element, or other fuel system fault).
☐An exhaust gas analyser for measuring carbon monoxide (CO) and hydrocarbons (HC) is now needed. If one cannot be hired or borrowed, have a local garage perform the check.

CO emissions (mixture)

☐The MOT tester has access to the CO limits for all vehicles. The CO level is measured at idle speed, and at 'fast idle' (2500 to 3000 rpm). The following limits are given as a general guide:

At idle speed – Less than 0.5% CO
At 'fast idle' – Less than 0.3% CO
Lambda reading – 0.97 to 1.03

☐If the CO level is too high, this may point to poor maintenance, a fuel injection system problem, faulty lambda (oxygen) sensor or catalytic converter. Try an injector cleaning treatment, and check the vehicle's ECU for fault codes.

HC emissions

☐The MOT tester has access to HC limits for all vehicles. The HC level is measured at 'fast idle' (2500 to 3000 rpm). The following limits are given as a general guide:

At 'fast idle' – Less then 200 ppm

☐Excessive HC emissions are typically caused by oil being burnt (worn engine), or by a blocked crankcase ventilation system ('breather'). If the engine oil is old and thin, an oil change may help. If the engine is running badly, check the vehicle's ECU for fault codes.

Diesel models

☐The only emission test for diesel engines is measuring exhaust smoke density, using a calibrated smoke meter. The test involves accelerating the engine at least 3 times to its maximum unloaded speed.

Note: *On engines with a timing belt, it is VITAL that the belt is in good condition before the test is carried out.*

☐With the engine warmed up, it is first purged by running at around 2500 rpm for 20 seconds. A governor check is then carried out, by slowly accelerating the engine to its maximum speed. After this, the smoke meter is connected, and the engine is accelerated quickly to maximum speed three times. If the smoke density is less than the limits given below, the vehicle will pass:

Non-turbo vehicles: 2.5m-1
Turbocharged vehicles: 3.0m-1

☐If excess smoke is produced, try fitting a new air cleaner element, or using an injector cleaning treatment. If the engine is running badly, where applicable, check the vehicle's ECU for fault codes. Also check the vehicle's EGR system, where applicable. At high mileages, the injectors may require professional attention.

Engine

- ☐ Engine fails to rotate when attempting to start
- ☐ Engine rotates, but will not start
- ☐ Engine difficult to start when cold
- ☐ Engine difficult to start when hot
- ☐ Starter motor noisy or excessively-rough in engagement
- ☐ Engine starts, but stops immediately
- ☐ Engine idles erratically
- ☐ Engine misfires at idle speed
- ☐ Engine misfires throughout the driving speed range
- ☐ Engine hesitates on acceleration
- ☐ Engine stalls
- ☐ Engine lacks power
- ☐ Engine backfires
- ☐ Oil pressure warning light illuminated with engine running
- ☐ Engine runs-on after switching off
- ☐ Engine noises

Cooling system

- ☐ Overheating
- ☐ Overcooling
- ☐ External coolant leakage
- ☐ Internal coolant leakage
- ☐ Corrosion

Fuel and exhaust systems

- ☐ Excessive fuel consumption
- ☐ Fuel leakage and/or fuel odour
- ☐ Excessive noise or fumes from exhaust system

Clutch

- ☐ Pedal travels to floor – no pressure or very little resistance
- ☐ Clutch fails to disengage (unable to select gears)
- ☐ Clutch slips (engine speed increases, with no increase in vehicle speed)
- ☐ Judder as clutch is engaged
- ☐ Noise when depressing or releasing clutch pedal

Manual transmission

- ☐ Noisy in neutral with engine running
- ☐ Noisy in one particular gear
- ☐ Difficulty engaging gears
- ☐ Jumps out of gear
- ☐ Vibration
- ☐ Lubricant leaks

Differential and propshaft

- ☐ Vibration when accelerating or decelerating
- ☐ Low-pitched whining; increasing with roadspeed

Driveshafts

- ☐ Vibration when accelerating or decelerating

Braking system

- ☐ Vehicle pulls to one side under braking
- ☐ Noise (grinding or high-pitched squeal) when brakes applied
- ☐ Excessive brake pedal travel
- ☐ Brake pedal feels spongy when depressed
- ☐ Excessive brake pedal effort required to stop vehicle
- ☐ Judder felt through brake pedal or steering wheel when braking
- ☐ Brakes binding
- ☐ Rear wheels locking under normal braking

Suspension and steering

- ☐ Vehicle pulls to one side
- ☐ Wheel wobble and vibration
- ☐ Excessive pitching and/or rolling around corners, or during braking
- ☐ Wandering or general instability
- ☐ Excessively-stiff steering
- ☐ Excessive play in steering
- ☐ Lack of power assistance
- ☐ Tyre wear excessive

Electrical system

- ☐ Battery will not hold a charge for more than a few days
- ☐ Ignition/no-charge warning light remains illuminated with engine running
- ☐ Ignition/no-charge warning light fails to come on
- ☐ Lights inoperative
- ☐ Instrument readings inaccurate or erratic
- ☐ Horn inoperative, or unsatisfactory in operation
- ☐ Windscreen wipers inoperative, or unsatisfactory in operation
- ☐ Windscreen washers inoperative, or unsatisfactory in operation
- ☐ Electric windows inoperative, or unsatisfactory in operation
- ☐ Window glass fails to move
- ☐ Central locking system inoperative, or unsatisfactory in operation

Introduction

The vehicle owner who does his or her own maintenance according to the recommended service schedules should not have to use this section of the manual very often. Modern component reliability is such that, provided those items subject to wear or deterioration are inspected or renewed at the specified intervals, sudden failure is comparatively rare. Faults do not usually just happen as a result of sudden failure, but develop over a period of time. Major mechanical failures in particular are usually preceded by characteristic symptoms over hundreds or even thousands of miles. Those components which do occasionally fail without warning are often small and easily carried in the vehicle.

With any fault finding, the first step is to decide where to begin investigations. Sometimes this is obvious, but on other occasions, a little detective work will be necessary. The owner who makes half a dozen haphazard adjustments or replacements may be successful in curing a fault (or its symptoms), but will be none the wiser if the fault recurs, and ultimately may have spent more time and money than was necessary. A calm and logical approach will be found to be more satisfactory in the long run. Always take into account any warning signs or abnormalities that may have been noticed in the period preceding the fault – power loss, high or low gauge readings, unusual smells, etc – and remember that failure of components such as fuses or spark plugs may only be pointers to some underlying fault.

The pages which follow provide an easy-reference guide to the more common problems which may occur during the operation of the vehicle. These problems and their possible causes are grouped under headings denoting various components or systems, such as Engine, Cooling system, etc. The Chapter and/or Section which deals with the problem is also shown in brackets. Whatever the fault, certain basic principles apply. These are as follows:

Verify the fault. This is simply a matter of being sure that you know what the symptoms are before starting work. This is particularly important if you are investigating a fault for someone else, who may not have described it very accurately.

Don't overlook the obvious. For example, if the vehicle won't start, is there fuel in the tank? (Don't take anyone else's word on this particular point, and don't trust the fuel gauge either). If an electrical fault is indicated, look for loose or broken wires before digging out the test gear.

Cure the disease, not the symptom. Substituting a flat battery with a fully-charged one will get you off the hard shoulder, but if the underlying cause is not attended to, the new battery will go the same way. Similarly, changing oil-fouled spark plugs for a new set will get you moving again, but remember that the reason for the fouling (if it wasn't simply an incorrect grade of plug) will have to be established and corrected.

Don't take anything for granted. Particularly, don't forget that a 'new' component may itself be defective (especially if it's been rattling around in the boot for months), and don't leave components out of a fault diagnosis sequence just because they are new or recently-fitted. When you do finally diagnose a difficult fault, you'll probably realise that all the evidence was there from the start.

Consider what work, if any, has recently been carried out. Many faults arise through careless or hurried work. For instance, if any work has been performed under the bonnet, could some of the wiring have been dislodged or incorrectly routed, or a hose trapped? Have all the fasteners been properly tightened? Were new, genuine parts and new gaskets used? There is often a certain amount of detective work to be done in this case, as an apparently-unrelated task can have far-reaching consequences.

Engine

Engine fails to rotate when attempting to start

- ☐ Battery terminal connections loose or corroded (see *Weekly checks*)
- ☐ Battery discharged or faulty (Chapter 5A Section 3)
- ☐ Broken, loose or disconnected wiring in the starting circuit (Chapter 5A Section 9)
- ☐ Defective starter solenoid or ignition switch (Chapter 5A Section 9 or Chapter 12 Section 5)
- ☐ Defective starter motor (Chapter 5A Section 10)
- ☐ Starter pinion or flywheel ring gear teeth loose or broken (Chapter 5A Section 10 or Chapter 2A Section 13)
- ☐ Engine earth strap broken or disconnected (Chapter 12 Section 2)
- ☐ Engine suffering 'hydraulic lock' (eg, from water ingested after traversing flooded roads, or from a serious internal coolant leak) – consult a Mazda dealer for advice

Engine rotates, but will not start

- ☐ Fuel tank empty
- ☐ Battery discharged (engine rotates slowly) (Chapter 5A Section 3)
- ☐ Battery terminal connections loose or corroded (see *Weekly checks*)
- ☐ Ignition components damp or damaged (Chapter 1 or 5B)
- ☐ Immobiliser fault, or 'uncoded' ignition key being used (Chapter 12 or Roadside Repairs)
- ☐ Crankshaft sensor fault (Chapter 4A Section 11)
- ☐ Broken, loose or disconnected wiring in the ignition circuit (Chapter 1 or 5B)
- ☐ Worn, faulty or incorrectly-gapped spark plugs (Chapter 1 Section 16)
- ☐ Fuel injection system fault (Chapter 4A)
- ☐ Major mechanical failure (eg, timing belt/chain snapped) (Chapter 2A)

Engine difficult to start when cold

- ☐ Battery discharged (Chapter 5A Section 3)
- ☐ Battery terminal connections loose or corroded (see *Weekly checks*)
- ☐ Worn, faulty or incorrectly-gapped spark plugs (Chapter 1 Section 16)
- ☐ Other ignition system fault (Chapter 1 or 5B)
- ☐ Fuel injection system fault (Chapter 4A)
- ☐ Wrong grade of engine oil used (*Weekly checks*, Chapter 1)
- ☐ Low cylinder compression (Chapter 2A Section 2)

Engine difficult to start when hot

- ☐ Air filter element dirty or clogged (Chapter 1 Section 20)
- ☐ Fuel injection system fault (Chapter 4A)
- ☐ Low cylinder compression (Chapter 2A Section 2)

Starter motor noisy or excessively-rough in engagement

- ☐ Starter pinion or flywheel ring gear teeth loose or broken (Chapter 5A Section 10 or Chapter 2A Section 13)
- ☐ Starter motor mounting bolts loose or missing (Chapter 5A Section 10)
- ☐ Starter motor internal components worn or damaged (Chapter 5A Section 10)

Engine starts, but stops immediately

- ☐ Loose or faulty electrical connections in the ignition circuit (Chapter 1 or 5B)
- ☐ Vacuum leak at the throttle body or inlet manifold (Chapter 4A)
- ☐ Blocked injectors/fuel injection system fault (Chapter 4A)

Engine idles erratically

- ☐ Air filter element clogged (Chapter 1 Section 20)
- ☐ Vacuum leak at the throttle body, inlet manifold or associated hoses (Chapter 4A)
- ☐ Worn, faulty or incorrectly-gapped spark plugs (Chapter 1 Section 16)
- ☐ Valve clearances incorrect (Chapter 1 Section 25)
- ☐ Uneven or low cylinder compression (Chapter 2A Section 2)
- ☐ Camshaft lobes worn (Chapter 2A Section 8)
- ☐ Timing chain incorrectly fitted (Chapter 2A Section 6)
- ☐ Blocked injectors/fuel injection system fault (Chapter 4A)

Engine misfires at idle speed

- ☐ Worn, faulty or incorrectly-gapped spark plugs (Chapter 1 Section 16)
- ☐ Vacuum leak at the throttle body, inlet manifold or associated hoses (Chapter 4A)
- ☐ Blocked injectors/fuel injection system fault (Chapter 4A)
- ☐ Uneven or low cylinder compression (Chapter 2A Section 2)
- ☐ Disconnected, leaking, or perished crankcase ventilation hoses (Chapter 4B Section 2)

Engine misfires throughout the driving speed range

- ☐ Fuel pump faulty, or delivery pressure low (Chapter 4A Section 8)
- ☐ Fuel tank vent blocked, or fuel pipes restricted (Chapter 4A Section 4)
- ☐ Vacuum leak at the throttle body, inlet manifold or associated hoses (Chapter 4A)
- ☐ Worn, faulty or incorrectly-gapped spark plugs (Chapter 1 Section 16)
- ☐ Faulty ignition coil (Chapter 5B Section 3)
- ☐ Uneven or low cylinder compression (Chapter 2A Section 2)
- ☐ Blocked injector/fuel injection system fault (Chapter 4A)
- ☐ Blocked catalytic converter (Chapter 4A Section 13)
- ☐ Engine overheating (Chapter 3)

Engine hesitates on acceleration

- ☐ Worn, faulty or incorrectly-gapped spark plugs (Chapter 1 Section 16)
- ☐ Vacuum leak at the throttle body, inlet manifold or associated hoses (Chapter 4A)
- ☐ Blocked injectors/fuel injection system fault (Chapter 4A)

Engine stalls

- ☐ Vacuum leak at the throttle body, inlet manifold or associated hoses (Chapter 4A)
- ☐ Fuel filter choked (Chapter 4A Section 8)
- ☐ Fuel pump faulty, or delivery pressure low (Chapter 4A Section 8)
- ☐ Fuel tank vent blocked, or fuel pipes restricted (Chapter 4A Section 4)
- ☐ Blocked injectors/fuel injection system fault (Chapter 4A)

Engine lacks power

- ☐ Air filter element blocked (Chapter 1 Section 20)
- ☐ Fuel filter choked (Chapter 4A Section 8)
- ☐ Fuel pipes blocked or restricted (Chapter 4A)
- ☐ Valve clearances incorrect (Chapter 1 Section 25)
- ☐ Worn, faulty or incorrectly-gapped spark plugs (Chapter 1 Section 16)
- ☐ Engine overheating (Chapter 3)
- ☐ Vacuum leak at the throttle body, inlet manifold or associated hoses (Chapter 4A)
- ☐ Blocked injectors/fuel injection system fault (Chapter 4A)
- ☐ Timing chain incorrectly fitted (Chapter 2A Section 6)
- ☐ Fuel pump faulty, or delivery pressure low (Chapter 4A Section 8)
- ☐ Uneven or low cylinder compression (Chapter 2A Section 2)
- ☐ Blocked catalytic converter (Chapter 4A Section 13)
- ☐ Brakes binding (Chapter 1 or 9)
- ☐ Clutch slipping (Chapter 6 Section 2)

Engine (continued)

Engine backfires

- ☐ Timing chain incorrectly fitted (Chapter 2A Section 6)
- ☐ Vacuum leak at the throttle body, inlet manifold or associated hoses (Chapter 4A)
- ☐ Blocked injectors/fuel injection system fault (Chapter 4A)
- ☐ Blocked catalytic converter (Chapter 4A Section 13)
- ☐ Ignition coil unit faulty (Chapter 5B Section 3)

Oil pressure warning light illuminated with engine running

- ☐ Low oil level, or incorrect oil grade (see *Weekly checks*)
- ☐ Faulty oil pressure sensor, or wiring damaged (Chapter 2A Section 15)
- ☐ Worn engine bearings and/or oil pump (Chapter 2A)
- ☐ High engine operating temperature (Chapter 3)
- ☐ Oil pump pressure relief valve defective (Chapter 2A Section 11)
- ☐ Oil pump pick-up strainer clogged (Chapter 2A Section 11)

Engine runs-on after switching off

- ☐ Excessive carbon build-up in engine (Chapter 2B Section 7)
- ☐ High engine operating temperature (Chapter 3)
- ☐ Fuel injection system fault (Chapter 4A Section 9)

Engine noises

Pre-ignition (pinking) or knocking during acceleration or under load

- ☐ Ignition system fault (Chapter 5B)
- ☐ Incorrect grade of spark plug (Chapter 1 Section 16)
- ☐ Knock sensor faulty (Chapter 5B Section 4)
- ☐ Vacuum leak at the throttle body, inlet manifold or associated hoses (Chapter 4A)
- ☐ Excessive carbon build-up in engine (Chapter 2B Section 7)
- ☐ Blocked injector/fuel injection system fault (Chapter 4A)

Whistling or wheezing noises

- ☐ Leaking inlet manifold or throttle body gasket (Chapter 4A)
- ☐ Leaking exhaust manifold gasket or pipe-to-manifold joint (Chapter 4A)
- ☐ Leaking vacuum hose (Chapter 4A or 9)
- ☐ Blowing cylinder head gasket (Chapter 2A Section 9)
- ☐ Partially blocked or leaking crankcase ventilation system (Chapter 4B Section 2)

Tapping or rattling noises

- ☐ Valve clearances incorrect (Chapter 1 Section 25)
- ☐ Worn valve gear or camshaft (Chapter 2A Section 8)
- ☐ Ancillary component fault (coolant pump, alternator, etc)
- ☐ (Chapter 3, Chapter 5A, etc)

Knocking or thumping noises

- ☐ Worn big-end bearings (regular heavy knocking, perhaps less under load) (Chapter 2B Section 2)
- ☐ Worn main bearings (rumbling and knocking, perhaps worsening under load) (Chapter 2B Section 2)
- ☐ Piston slap – most noticeable when cold, caused by piston/bore wear (Chapter 2B Section 2)
- ☐ Ancillary component fault (coolant pump, alternator, etc) (Chapter 3, Chapter 5A, etc)
- ☐ Engine mountings worn or defective (Chapter 2A Section 14)
- ☐ Front suspension or steering components worn (Chapter 10)

Cooling system

Overheating

- ☐ Insufficient coolant in system (see *Weekly checks*)
- ☐ Thermostat faulty (Chapter 3 Section 4)
- ☐ Radiator core blocked, or grille restricted (Chapter 3 Section 3)
- ☐ Cooling fan faulty (Chapter 3 Section 5)
- ☐ Inaccurate coolant temperature sensor (Chapter 3 Section 6)
- ☐ Airlock in cooling system (Chapter 1 Section 19)
- ☐ Expansion tank pressure cap faulty (Chapter 3 Section 1)
- ☐ Engine management system fault (Chapter 4A Section 9)

Overcooling

- ☐ Thermostat faulty (Chapter 3 Section 4)
- ☐ Inaccurate coolant temperature sensor (Chapter 3 Section 6)
- ☐ Cooling fan faulty (Chapter 3 Section 5)
- ☐ Engine management system fault (Chapter 4A)

External coolant leakage

- ☐ Deteriorated or damaged hoses or hose clips (Chapter 3 Section 2)
- ☐ Radiator core or heater matrix leaking (Chapter 3)
- ☐ Expansion tank pressure cap faulty (Chapter 1 Section 19)
- ☐ Coolant pump internal seal leaking (Chapter 3 Section 7)
- ☐ Coolant pump gasket leaking (Chapter 3 Section 7)
- ☐ Boiling due to overheating (Chapter 3)
- ☐ Cylinder block core plug leaking (Chapter 2B Section 2)

Internal coolant leakage

- ☐ Leaking cylinder head gasket (Chapter 2A Section 9)
- ☐ Cracked cylinder head or cylinder block (Chapter 2B Section 7)

Corrosion

- ☐ Infrequent draining and flushing (Chapter 1 Section 19)
- ☐ Incorrect coolant mixture or inappropriate coolant type (see *Weekly checks*)

Fuel and exhaust systems

Excessive fuel consumption

- ☐ Air filter element dirty or clogged (Chapter 1 Section 20)
- ☐ Fuel injection system fault (Chapter 4A Section 9)
- ☐ Crankcase ventilation system blocked (Chapter 4B Section 2)
- ☐ Tyres under-inflated (see *Weekly checks*)
- ☐ Brakes binding (Chapter 1 or 9)
- ☐ Fuel leak, causing apparent high consumption (Chapter 1 or 4A)

Fuel leakage and/or fuel odour

- ☐ Damaged or corroded fuel tank, pipes or connections (Chapter 4A Section 4)
- ☐ Evaporative emissions system fault – petrol models (Chapter 4B Section 2)

Excessive noise or fumes from exhaust system

- ☐ Leaking exhaust system or manifold joints (Chapter 1 or 4A)
- ☐ Leaking, corroded or damaged silencers or pipe (Chapter 1 or 4A)
- ☐ Broken mountings causing body or suspension contact (Chapter 1 Section 12)

Clutch

Pedal travels to floor – no pressure or very little resistance

- ☐ Air in hydraulic system/faulty master or slave cylinder (Chapter 6)
- ☐ Faulty hydraulic release system (Chapter 6 Section 4)
- ☐ Clutch pedal return spring detached or brokenBroken clutch release bearing or fork (Chapter 6 Section 3)
- ☐ Broken diaphragm spring in clutch pressure plate (Chapter 6 Section 2)

Clutch fails to disengage (unable to select gears)

- ☐ Air in hydraulic system/faulty master or slave cylinder (Chapter 6)
- ☐ Faulty hydraulic release system (Chapter 6 Section 4)
- ☐ Clutch disc sticking on transmission input shaft splines (Chapter 6 Section 2)
- ☐ Clutch disc sticking to flywheel or pressure plate (Chapter 6 Section 2)
- ☐ Faulty pressure plate assembly (Chapter 6 Section 2)
- ☐ Clutch release mechanism worn or incorrectly assembled (Chapter 6 Section 3)

Clutch slips (engine speed increases, with no increase in vehicle speed)

- ☐ Faulty hydraulic release system (Chapter 6 Section 5)
- ☐ Clutch disc linings excessively worn (Chapter 6 Section 2)
- ☐ Clutch disc linings contaminated with oil or grease (Chapter 6 Section 2)
- ☐ Faulty pressure plate or weak diaphragm spring (Chapter 6 Section 2)

Judder as clutch is engaged

- ☐ Clutch disc linings contaminated with oil or grease (Chapter 6 Section 2)
- ☐ Clutch disc linings excessively worn (Chapter 6 Section 2)
- ☐ Faulty or distorted pressure plate or diaphragm spring (Chapter 6 Section 2)
- ☐ Worn or loose engine or transmission mountings (Chapter 2A Section 14 or Chapter 7 Section 6)
- ☐ Clutch disc hub or transmission input shaft splines worn (Chapter 6 Section 2)

Noise when depressing or releasing clutch pedal

- ☐ Worn clutch release bearing (Chapter 6 Section 3)
- ☐ Worn or dry clutch pedal bushesWorn or dry clutch master cylinder piston (Chapter 6 Section 5)
- ☐ Faulty pressure plate assembly (Chapter 6 Section 2)
- ☐ Pressure plate diaphragm spring broken (Chapter 6 Section 2)
- ☐ Broken clutch disc cushioning springs (Chapter 6 Section 2)

Manual transmission

Noisy in neutral with engine running

- ☐ Lack of oil (Chapter 1 Section 22)
- ☐ Input shaft bearings worn (noise apparent with clutch pedal released, but not when depressed) (Chapter 7)*
- ☐ Clutch release bearing worn (noise apparent with clutch pedal depressed, possibly less when released) (Chapter 6)

Noisy in one particular gear

- ☐ Worn, damaged or chipped gear teeth (Chapter 7)*

Difficulty engaging gears

- ☐ Clutch fault (Chapter 6)
- ☐ Lack of oil (Chapter 1 Section 22)
- ☐ Worn synchroniser units (Chapter 7)*

Jumps out of gear

- ☐ Worn synchroniser units (Chapter 7)*
- ☐ Worn selector forks (Chapter 7)*

Vibration

- ☐ Lack of oil (Chapter 1 Section 22)
- ☐ Worn bearings (Chapter 7)*

Lubricant leaks

- ☐ Leaking driveshaft or selector shaft oil seal (Chapter 7)
- ☐ Leaking housing joint (Chapter 7)*
- ☐ Leaking input shaft oil seal (Chapter 7)

** Although the corrective action necessary to remedy the symptoms described is beyond the scope of the home mechanic, the above information should be helpful in isolating the cause of the condition, so that the owner can communicate clearly with a professional mechanic.*

Differential and propshaft

Vibration when accelerating or decelerating

- ☐ Worn universal joint (Chapter 8 Section 7)
- ☐ Bent or distorted propeller shaft (Chapter 8 Section 6)

Low-pitched whining; increasing with roadspeed

- ☐ Worn differential (Chapter 8 Section 2)

Driveshafts

Vibration when accelerating or decelerating

- ☐ Worn inner constant velocity joint (Chapter 8 Section 5)
- ☐ Bent or distorted driveshaft (Chapter 8 Section 4)

Braking system

Vehicle pulls to one side under braking

Note: *Before assuming that a brake problem exists, make sure that the tyres are in good condition and correctly inflated, that the front wheel alignment is correct, and that the vehicle is not loaded with weight in an unequal manner. Apart from checking the condition of all pipe and hose connections, any faults occurring on the anti-lock braking system should be referred to a Mazda dealer for diagnosis.*

- ☐ Worn, defective, damaged or contaminated brake pads on one side (Chapter 1 or 9)
- ☐ Seized or partially-seized brake caliper piston (Chapter 1 or 9)
- ☐ A mixture of brake pad materials fitted between sides (Chapter 1 or 9)
- ☐ Brake caliper mounting bolts loose (Chapter 9)
- ☐ Worn or damaged steering or suspension components (Chapter 1 or 10)

Noise (grinding or high-pitched squeal) when brakes applied

- ☐ Brake pad friction lining material worn down to metal backing (Chapter 1 or 9)
- ☐ Excessive corrosion of brake disc (may be apparent after the vehicle has been standing for some time (Chapter 1 or 9)
- ☐ Foreign object (stone chipping, etc) trapped between brake disc and shield (Chapter 1 or 9)

Excessive brake pedal travel

- ☐ Faulty master cylinder (Chapter 9 Section 10)
- ☐ Brake pedal height incorrect (Chapter 9 Section 11)
- ☐ Air in hydraulic system (Chapter 9 Section 2)
- ☐ Faulty vacuum servo unit (Chapter 9 Section 12)

Brake pedal feels spongy when depressed

- ☐ Air in hydraulic system (Chapter 9 Section 2)
- ☐ Deteriorated flexible rubber brake hoses (Chapter 1 Section 7 or Chapter 9 Section 3)
- ☐ Master cylinder mounting nuts loose (Chapter 9 Section 10)
- ☐ Faulty master cylinder (Chapter 9 Section 10)

Excessive brake pedal effort required to stop vehicle

- ☐ Faulty vacuum servo unit (Chapter 9 Section 12)
- ☐ Disconnected, damaged or insecure brake servo vacuum hose (Chapter 9 Section 13)
- ☐ Primary or secondary hydraulic circuit failure (Chapter 9)
- ☐ Seized brake caliper piston (Chapter 9)
- ☐ Brake pads incorrectly fitted (Chapter 9)
- ☐ Incorrect grade of brake pads fitted (Chapter 9)
- ☐ Brake pad linings contaminated (Chapter 1 or 9)

Judder felt through brake pedal or steering wheel when braking

Note: *Under heavy braking on models equipped with ABS, vibration may be felt through the brake pedal. This is a normal feature of ABS operation, and does not constitute a fault.*

- ☐ Excessive run-out or distortion of discs (Chapter 1 or 9)
- ☐ Brake pad linings worn (Chapter 1 or 9)
- ☐ Brake caliper mounting bolts loose (Chapter 9)
- ☐ Wear in suspension or steering components or mountings (Chapter 1 or 10)
- ☐ Front wheels out of balance (see *Weekly checks*)

Brakes binding

- ☐ Seized brake caliper piston (Chapter 9)
- ☐ Incorrectly-adjusted handbrake mechanism (Chapter 9 Section 14)
- ☐ Faulty master cylinder (Chapter 9 Section 10)

Rear wheels locking under normal braking

- ☐ Rear brake pad linings contaminated or damaged (Chapter 9 Section 5)
- ☐ Rear brake discs warped (Chapter 9 Section 7)

Suspension and steering

Vehicle pulls to one side

Note: *Before diagnosing suspension or steering faults, be sure that the trouble is not due to incorrect tyre pressures, mixtures of tyre types, or binding brakes.*

- ☐ Defective tyre (see *Weekly checks*)
- ☐ Excessive wear in suspension or steering components (Chapter 1 or 10)
- ☐ Incorrect front wheel alignment (Chapter 10 Section 22)
- ☐ Accident damage to steering or suspension components (Chapter 1)

Wheel wobble and vibration

- ☐ Front wheels out of balance (vibration felt mainly through the steering wheel) (see *Weekly checks*)
- ☐ Rear wheels out of balance (vibration felt throughout the vehicle) (see *Weekly checks*)
- ☐ Roadwheels damaged or distorted (see *Weekly checks*)
- ☐ Faulty or damaged tyre (see *Weekly checks*)
- ☐ Worn steering or suspension joints, bushes or components (Chapter 1 or 10)
- ☐ Wheel nuts loose (Chapter 1)

Excessive pitching and/or rolling around corners, or during braking

- ☐ Defective shock absorbers (Chapter 1 or 10)
- ☐ Broken or weak spring and/or suspension component (Chapter 1 or 10)
- ☐ Worn or damaged anti-roll bar or mountings (Chapter 1 or 10)

Wandering or general instability

- ☐ Incorrect front wheel alignment (Chapter 10 Section 22)
- ☐ Worn steering or suspension joints, bushes or components (Chapter 1 or 10)
- ☐ Roadwheels out of balance (see *Weekly checks*)
- ☐ Faulty or damaged tyre (see *Weekly checks*)
- ☐ Wheel nuts loose (Chapter 1)
- ☐ Defective shock absorbers (Chapter 1 or 10)

Excessively-stiff steering

- ☐ Seized steering linkage balljoint or suspension balljoint (Chapter 1 or 10)
- ☐ Incorrect front wheel alignment (Chapter 10 Section 22)
- ☐ Steering rack damaged (Chapter 10 Section 17)
- ☐ Faulty steering pump (Chapter 10 Section 18)

Excessive play in steering

- ☐ Worn steering column/intermediate shaft joints (Chapter 10 Section 15)
- ☐ Worn track rod balljoints (Chapter 1 or 10)
- ☐ Worn steering rack (Chapter 10 Section 17)
- ☐ Worn steering or suspension joints, bushes or components (Chapter 1 or 10)

Lack of power assistance

- ☐ Faulty steering pump (Chapter 10 Section 18)
- ☐ Auxiliary drivebelt worn or incorrect tension (Chapter 1 Section 6)

Tyre wear excessive

Tyres worn on inside or outside edges

- ☐ Tyres under-inflated (wear on both edges) (see *Weekly checks*)
- ☐ Incorrect camber or castor angles (wear on one edge only) (Chapter 10 Section 22)
- ☐ Worn steering or suspension joints, bushes or components (Chapter 1 or 10)
- ☐ Excessively-hard cornering or braking
- ☐ Accident damage

Tyre treads exhibit feathered edges

- ☐ Incorrect toe-setting (Chapter 10 Section 22)

Tyres worn in centre of tread

- ☐ Tyres over-inflated (see *Weekly checks*)

Tyres worn on inside and outside edges

- ☐ Tyres under-inflated (see *Weekly checks*)

Tyres worn unevenly

- ☐ Tyres/wheels out of balance (see *Weekly checks*)
- ☐ Excessive wheel or tyre run-outWorn shock absorbers (Chapter 1 or 10)
- ☐ Faulty tyre (see *Weekly checks*)

Electrical system

Battery will not hold a charge for more than a few days

Note: *For problems associated with the starting system, refer to the faults listed under 'Engine' earlier in this Section.*

- ☐ Battery defective internally (Chapter 5A Section 3)
- ☐ Battery terminal connections loose or corroded (see *Weekly checks*)
- ☐ Auxiliary drivebelt worn or incorrectly adjusted (Chapter 1 Section 6)
- ☐ Alternator not charging at correct output (Chapter 5A Section 5)
- ☐ Alternator or voltage regulator faulty (Chapter 5A Section 7)
- ☐ Short-circuit causing continual battery drain (Chapter 5A or 12)

Ignition/no-charge warning light remains illuminated with engine running

- ☐ Auxiliary drivebelt broken, worn, or incorrectly adjusted (Chapter 1 Section 6)
- ☐ Internal fault in alternator or voltage regulator (Chapter 5A Section 7)
- ☐ Broken, disconnected, or loose wiring in charging circuit (Chapter 12 Section 2)

Ignition/no-charge warning light fails to come on

- ☐ Broken, disconnected, or loose wiring in warning light circuit (Chapter 12 Section 2)
- ☐ Alternator faulty (Chapter 5A Section 7)

Lights inoperative

- ☐ Bulb blown (Chapter 12)
- ☐ Corrosion of bulb or bulbholder contacts (Chapter 12)
- ☐ Blown fuse (Chapter 12 Section 4)
- ☐ Faulty relay (Chapter 12 Section 4)
- ☐ Broken, loose, or disconnected wiring (Chapter 12 Section 2)
- ☐ Faulty switch (Chapter 12 Section 5)
- ☐ Faulty flasher control module (Chapter 12 Section 11)

Instrument readings inaccurate or erratic

Fuel or temperature gauges give no reading

- ☐ Faulty level sensor unit (Chapter 4A Section 8 or Chapter 3 Section 6)
- ☐ Wiring open-circuit (Chapter 12 Section 2)
- ☐ Faulty gauge (Chapter 12 Section 12)

Fuel or temperature gauges give continuous maximum reading

- ☐ Faulty level sensor unit (Chapter 4A Section 8 or Chapter 3 Section 6)
- ☐ Wiring short-circuit (Chapter 12 Section 2)
- ☐ Faulty gauge (Chapter 12 Section 12)

Horn inoperative, or unsatisfactory in operation

Horn operates all the time

- ☐ Horn push either earthed or stuck down (Chapter 12)
- ☐ Horn cable-to-horn push earthed (Chapter 12)

Horn fails to operate

- ☐ Blown fuse (Chapter 12 Section 4)
- ☐ Cable or connections loose, broken or disconnected (Chapter 12 Section 2)
- ☐ Faulty horn (Chapter 12 Section 13)

Horn emits intermittent or unsatisfactory sound

- ☐ Cable connections loose (Chapter 12 Section 2)
- ☐ Horn mountings loose (Chapter 12 Section 13)
- ☐ Faulty horn (Chapter 12 Section 13)

Windscreen wipers inoperative, or unsatisfactory in operation

Wipers fail to operate, or operate very slowly

- ☐ Wiper blades stuck to screen, or linkage seized or binding (Chapter 12 Section 15)
- ☐ Blown fuse (Chapter 12 Section 4)
- ☐ Battery discharged (Chapter 5A Section 3)
- ☐ Cable or connections loose, broken or disconnected (Chapter 12 Section 2)
- ☐ Faulty relay (Chapter 12 Section 4)
- ☐ Faulty wiper motor (Chapter 12 Section 15)

Wiper blades sweep over too large or too small an area of the glass

- ☐ Wiper blades incorrectly fitted, or wrong size used (see *Weekly checks*)
- ☐ Wiper arms incorrectly positioned on spindles (Chapter 12 Section 14)
- ☐ Excessive wear of wiper linkage (Chapter 12 Section 15)
- ☐ Wiper motor or linkage mountings loose or insecure (Chapter 12 Section 15)

Wiper blades fail to clean the glass effectively

- ☐ Wiper blade rubbers dirty, worn or perished (see *Weekly checks*)
- ☐ Wiper blades incorrectly fitted, or wrong size used (see *Weekly checks*)
- ☐ Wiper arm tension springs broken, or arm pivots seized (Chapter 12 Section 14)
- ☐ Insufficient windscreen washer additive to adequately remove road film (see *Weekly checks*)

Electrical system (continued)

Windscreen washers inoperative, or unsatisfactory in operation

One or more washer jets inoperative

- ☐ Blocked washer jetDisconnected, kinked or restricted fluid hose (Chapter 12 Section 16)
- ☐ Insufficient fluid in washer reservoir (see *Weekly checks*)

Washer pump fails to operate

- ☐ Broken or disconnected wiring or connections (Chapter 12 Section 2)
- ☐ Blown fuse (Chapter 12 Section 4)
- ☐ Faulty washer switch (Chapter 12 Section 5)
- ☐ Faulty washer pump (Chapter 12 Section 16)

Washer pump runs for some time before fluid is emitted from jets

- ☐ Faulty one-way valve in fluid supply hose (Chapter 12 Section 16)

Electric windows inoperative, or unsatisfactory in operation

Window glass will only move in one direction

- ☐ Faulty switch (Chapter 12 Section 5)

Window glass slow to move

- ☐ Battery discharged (Chapter 5A Section 3)
- ☐ Regulator seized or damaged, or in need of lubrication (Chapter 11 Section 14)
- ☐ Door internal components or trim fouling regulator (Chapter 11 Section 14)
- ☐ Faulty motor (Chapter 11 Section 14)

Window glass fails to move

- ☐ Blown fuse (Chapter 12 Section 4)
- ☐ Faulty relay (Chapter 12 Section 4)
- ☐ Broken or disconnected wiring or connections (Chapter 12 Section 2)
- ☐ Faulty motor (Chapter 11 Section 14)

Central locking system inoperative, or unsatisfactory in operation

Complete system failure

- ☐ Remote handset battery discharged, where applicable (Chapter 1 Section 24)
- ☐ Blown fuse (Chapter 12 Section 4)
- ☐ Faulty relay (Chapter 12 Section 4)
- ☐ Broken or disconnected wiring or connections (Chapter 12 Section 2)
- ☐ Faulty motor (Chapter 11 Section 12)

Latch locks but will not unlock, or unlocks but will not lock

- ☐ Remote handset battery discharged, where applicable (Chapter 1 Section 24)
- ☐ Faulty master switch (Chapter 12 Section 5)
- ☐ Broken or disconnected latch operating rods or levers (Chapter 11 Section 12)
- ☐ Faulty relay (Chapter 12 Section 4)
- ☐ Faulty motor (Chapter 11 Section 12)

One solenoid/motor fails to operate

- ☐ Broken or disconnected wiring or connections (Chapter 12 Section 2)
- ☐ Faulty operating assembly (Chapter 11 Section 17)
- ☐ Broken, binding or disconnected latch operating rods or levers (Chapter 11 Section 12)
- ☐ Fault in door latch (Chapter 11 Section 12)

A

ABS (Anti-lock brake system) A system, usually electronically controlled, that senses incipient wheel lockup during braking and relieves hydraulic pressure at wheels that are about to skid.

Air bag An inflatable bag hidden in the steering wheel (driver's side) or the dash or glovebox (passenger side). In a head-on collision, the bags inflate, preventing the driver and front passenger from being thrown forward into the steering wheel or windscreen.

Air cleaner A metal or plastic housing, containing a filter element, which removes dust and dirt from the air being drawn into the engine.

Air filter element The actual filter in an air cleaner system, usually manufactured from pleated paper and requiring renewal at regular intervals.

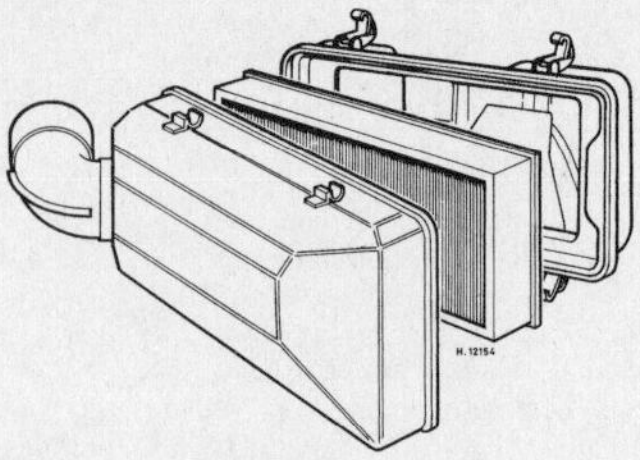

Air filter

Allen key A hexagonal wrench which fits into a recessed hexagonal hole.

Alligator clip A long-nosed spring-loaded metal clip with meshing teeth. Used to make temporary electrical connections.

Alternator A component in the electrical system which converts mechanical energy from a drivebelt into electrical energy to charge the battery and to operate the starting system, ignition system and electrical accessories.

Ampere (amp) A unit of measurement for the flow of electric current. One amp is the amount of current produced by one volt acting through a resistance of one ohm.

Anaerobic sealer A substance used to prevent bolts and screws from loosening. Anaerobic means that it does not require oxygen for activation. The Loctite brand is widely used.

Antifreeze A substance (usually ethylene glycol) mixed with water, and added to a vehicle's cooling system, to prevent freezing of the coolant in winter. Antifreeze also contains chemicals to inhibit corrosion and the formation of rust and other deposits that would tend to clog the radiator and coolant passages and reduce cooling efficiency.

Anti-seize compound A coating that reduces the risk of seizing on fasteners that are subjected to high temperatures, such as exhaust manifold bolts and nuts.

Asbestos A natural fibrous mineral with great heat resistance, commonly used in the composition of brake friction materials. Asbestos is a health hazard and the dust created by brake systems should never be inhaled or ingested.

Axle A shaft on which a wheel revolves, or which revolves with a wheel. Also, a solid beam that connects the two wheels at one end of the vehicle. An axle which also transmits power to the wheels is known as a live axle.

Axleshaft A single rotating shaft, on either side of the differential, which delivers power from the final drive assembly to the drive wheels. Also called a driveshaft or a halfshaft.

B

Ball bearing An anti-friction bearing consisting of a hardened inner and outer race with hardened steel balls between two races.

Bearing The curved surface on a shaft or in a bore, or the part assembled into either, that permits relative motion between them with minimum wear and friction.

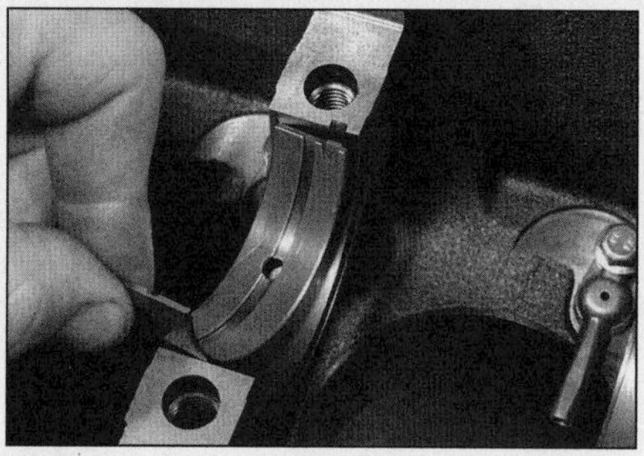

Bearing

Big-end bearing The bearing in the end of the connecting rod that's attached to the crankshaft.

Bleed nipple A valve on a brake wheel cylinder, caliper or other hydraulic component that is opened to purge the hydraulic system of air. Also called a bleed screw.

Brake bleeding Procedure for removing air from lines of a hydraulic brake system.

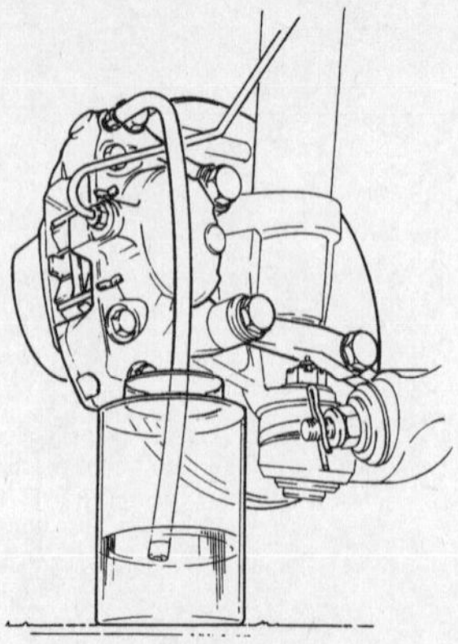

Brake bleeding

Brake disc The component of a disc brake that rotates with the wheels.

Brake drum The component of a drum brake that rotates with the wheels.

Brake linings The friction material which contacts the brake disc or drum to retard the vehicle's speed. The linings are bonded or riveted to the brake pads or shoes.

Brake pads The replaceable friction pads that pinch the brake disc when the brakes are applied. Brake pads consist of a friction material bonded or riveted to a rigid backing plate.

Brake shoe The crescent-shaped carrier to which the brake linings are mounted and which forces the lining against the rotating drum during braking.

Braking systems For more information on braking systems, consult the *Haynes Automotive Brake Manual*.

Breaker bar A long socket wrench handle providing greater leverage.

Bulkhead The insulated partition between the engine and the passenger compartment.

C

Caliper The non-rotating part of a disc-brake assembly that straddles the disc and carries the brake pads. The caliper also contains the hydraulic components that cause the pads to pinch the disc when the brakes are applied. A caliper is also a measuring tool that can be set to measure inside or outside dimensions of an object.

Camshaft A rotating shaft on which a series of cam lobes operate the valve mechanisms. The camshaft may be driven by gears, by sprockets and chain or by sprockets and a belt.

Canister A container in an evaporative emission control system; contains activated charcoal granules to trap vapours from the fuel system.

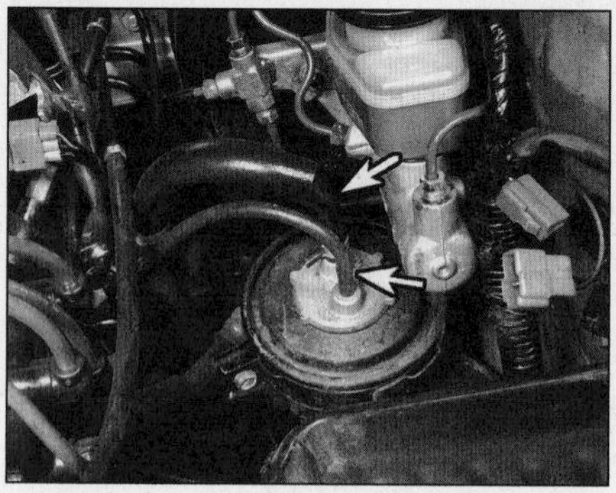

Canister

Carburettor A device which mixes fuel with air in the proper proportions to provide a desired power output from a spark ignition internal combustion engine.

Castellated Resembling the parapets along the top of a castle wall. For example, a castellated balljoint stud nut.

Castor In wheel alignment, the backward or forward tilt of the steering axis. Castor is positive when the steering axis is inclined rearward at the top.

Catalytic converter A silencer-like device in the exhaust system which converts certain pollutants in the exhaust gases into less harmful substances.

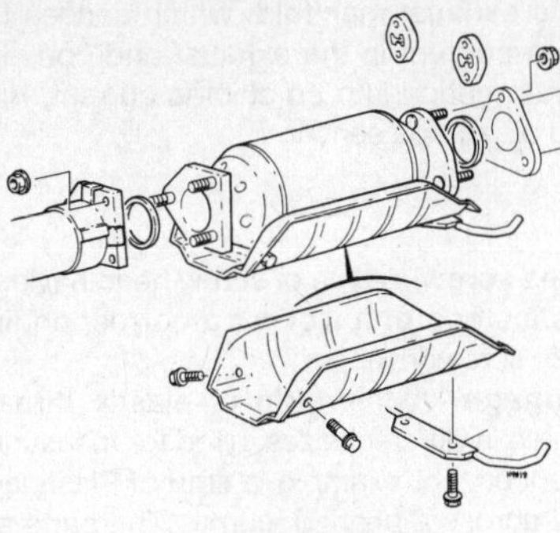

Catalytic converter

Circlip A ring-shaped clip used to prevent endwise movement of cylindrical parts and shafts. An internal circlip is installed in a groove in a housing; an external circlip fits into a groove on the outside of a cylindrical piece such as a shaft.

Clearance The amount of space between two parts. For example, between a piston and a cylinder, between a bearing and a journal, etc.

Coil spring A spiral of elastic steel found in various sizes throughout a vehicle, for example as a springing medium in the suspension and in the valve train.

Compression Reduction in volume, and increase in pressure and temperature, of a gas, caused by squeezing it into a smaller space.

Compression ratio The relationship between cylinder volume when the piston is at top dead centre and cylinder volume when the piston is at bottom dead centre.

Constant velocity (CV) joint A type of universal joint that cancels out vibrations caused by driving power being transmitted through an angle.

Core plug A disc or cup-shaped metal device inserted in a hole in a casting through which core was removed when the casting was formed. Also known as a freeze plug or expansion plug.

Crankcase The lower part of the engine block in which the crankshaft rotates.

Crankshaft The main rotating member, or shaft, running the length of the crankcase, with offset "throws" to which the connecting rods are attached.

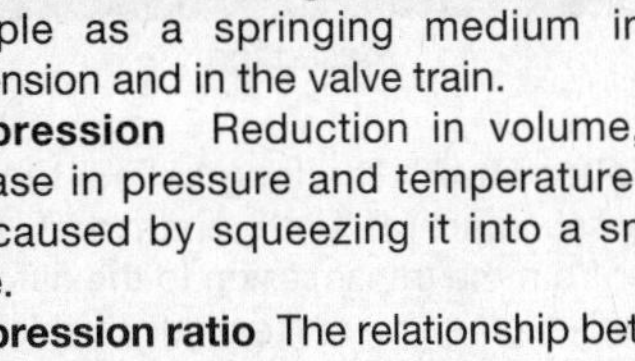

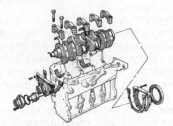

Crankshaft assembly

Crocodile clip See Alligator clip

D

Diagnostic code Code numbers obtained by accessing the diagnostic mode of an engine management computer. This code can be used to determine the area in the system where a malfunction may be located.

Disc brake A brake design incorporating a rotating disc onto which brake pads are squeezed. The resulting friction converts the energy of a moving vehicle into heat.

Double-overhead cam (DOHC) An engine that uses two overhead camshafts, usually one for the intake valves and one for the exhaust valves.

Drivebelt(s) The belt(s) used to drive accessories such as the alternator, water pump, power steering pump, air conditioning compressor, etc. off the crankshaft pulley.

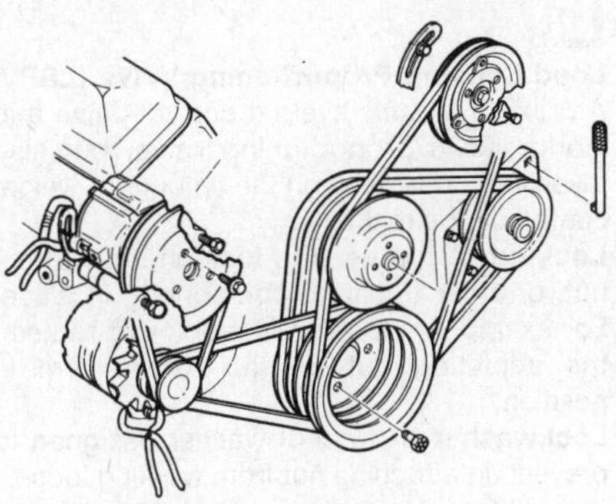

Accessory drivebelts

Driveshaft Any shaft used to transmit motion. Commonly used when referring to the axleshafts on a front wheel drive vehicle.

Drum brake A type of brake using a drum-shaped metal cylinder attached to the inner surface of the wheel. When the brake pedal is pressed, curved brake shoes with friction linings press against the inside of the drum to slow or stop the vehicle.

E

EGR valve A valve used to introduce exhaust gases into the intake air stream.

Electronic control unit (ECU) A computer which controls (for instance) ignition and fuel injection systems, or an anti-lock braking system. For more information refer to the *Haynes Automotive Electrical and Electronic Systems Manual.*

Electronic Fuel Injection (EFI) A computer controlled fuel system that distributes fuel through an injector located in each intake port of the engine.

Emergency brake A braking system, independent of the main hydraulic system, that can be used to slow or stop the vehicle if the primary brakes fail, or to hold the vehicle stationary even though the brake pedal isn't depressed. It usually consists of a hand lever that actuates either front or rear brakes mechanically through a series of cables and linkages. Also known as a handbrake or parking brake.

Endfloat The amount of lengthwise movement between two parts. As applied to a crankshaft, the distance that the crankshaft can move forward and back in the cylinder block.

Engine management system (EMS) A computer controlled system which manages the fuel injection and the ignition systems in an integrated fashion.

Exhaust manifold A part with several passages through which exhaust gases leave the engine combustion chambers and enter the exhaust pipe.

F

Fan clutch A viscous (fluid) drive coupling device which permits variable engine fan speeds in relation to engine speeds.

Feeler blade A thin strip or blade of hardened steel, ground to an exact thickness, used to check or measure clearances between parts.

Feeler blade

Firing order The order in which the engine cylinders fire, or deliver their power strokes, beginning with the number one cylinder.

Flywheel A heavy spinning wheel in which energy is absorbed and stored by means of momentum. On cars, the flywheel is attached to the crankshaft to smooth out firing impulses.

Free play The amount of travel before any action takes place. The "looseness" in a linkage, or an assembly of parts, between the initial application of force and actual movement. For example, the distance the brake pedal moves before the pistons in the master cylinder are actuated.

Fuse An electrical device which protects a circuit against accidental overload. The typical fuse contains a soft piece of metal which is calibrated to melt at a predetermined current flow (expressed as amps) and break the circuit.

Fusible link A circuit protection device consisting of a conductor surrounded by heat-resistant insulation. The conductor is smaller than the wire it protects, so it acts as the weakest link in the circuit. Unlike a blown fuse, a failed fusible link must frequently be cut from the wire for replacement.

G

Gap The distance the spark must travel in jumping from the centre electrode to the side electrode in a spark plug. Also refers to the spacing between the points in a contact breaker assembly in a conventional points-type ignition, or to the distance between the reluctor or rotor and the pickup coil in an electronic ignition.

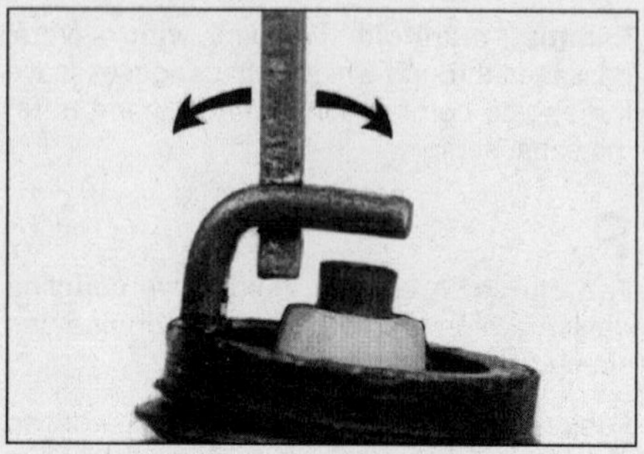

Adjusting spark plug gap

Gasket Any thin, soft material - usually cork, cardboard, asbestos or soft metal - installed between two metal surfaces to ensure a good seal. For instance, the cylinder head gasket seals the joint between the block and the cylinder head.

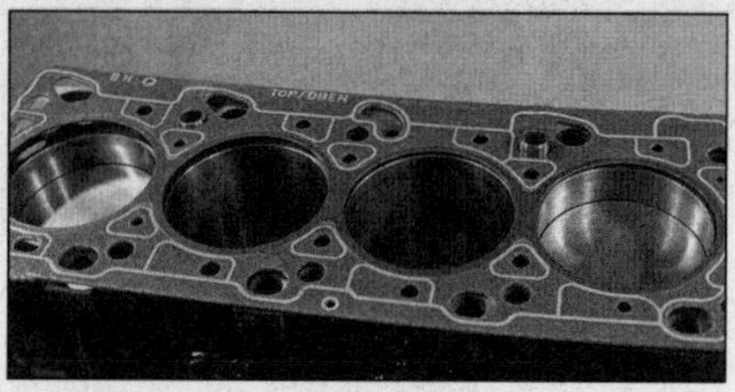

Gasket

Gauge An instrument panel display used to monitor engine conditions. A gauge with a movable pointer on a dial or a fixed scale is an analogue gauge. A gauge with a numerical readout is called a digital gauge.

H

Halfshaft A rotating shaft that transmits power from the final drive unit to a drive wheel, usually when referring to a live rear axle.

Harmonic balancer A device designed to reduce torsion or twisting vibration in the crankshaft. May be incorporated in the crankshaft pulley. Also known as a vibration damper.

Hone An abrasive tool for correcting small irregularities or differences in diameter in an engine cylinder, brake cylinder, etc.

Hydraulic tappet A tappet that utilises hydraulic pressure from the engine's lubrication system to maintain zero clearance (constant contact with both camshaft and valve stem). Automatically adjusts to variation in valve stem length. Hydraulic tappets also reduce valve noise.

I

Ignition timing The moment at which the spark plug fires, usually expressed in the number of crankshaft degrees before the piston reaches the top of its stroke.

Inlet manifold A tube or housing with passages through which flows the air-fuel mixture (carburettor vehicles and vehicles with throttle body injection) or air only (port fuel-injected vehicles) to the port openings in the cylinder head.

J

Jump start Starting the engine of a vehicle with a discharged or weak battery by attaching jump leads from the weak battery to a charged or helper battery.

L

Load Sensing Proportioning Valve (LSPV) A brake hydraulic system control valve that works like a proportioning valve, but also takes into consideration the amount of weight carried by the rear axle.

Locknut A nut used to lock an adjustment nut, or other threaded component, in place. For example, a locknut is employed to keep the adjusting nut on the rocker arm in position.

Lockwasher A form of washer designed to prevent an attaching nut from working loose.

M

MacPherson strut A type of front suspension system devised by Earle MacPherson at Ford of England. In its original form, a simple lateral link with the anti-roll bar creates the lower control arm. A long strut - an integral coil spring and shock absorber - is mounted between the body and the steering knuckle. Many modern so-called MacPherson strut systems use a conventional lower A-arm and don't rely on the anti-roll bar for location.

Multimeter An electrical test instrument with the capability to measure voltage, current and resistance.

N

NOx Oxides of Nitrogen. A common toxic pollutant emitted by petrol and diesel engines at higher temperatures.

O

Ohm The unit of electrical resistance. One volt applied to a resistance of one ohm will produce a current of one amp.

Ohmmeter An instrument for measuring electrical resistance.

O-ring A type of sealing ring made of a special rubber-like material; in use, the O-ring is compressed into a groove to provide the sealing action.

Overhead cam (ohc) engine An engine with the camshaft(s) located on top of the cylinder head(s).

Overhead valve (ohv) engine An engine with the valves located in the cylinder head, but with the camshaft located in the engine block.

Oxygen sensor A device installed in the engine exhaust manifold, which senses the oxygen content in the exhaust and converts this information into an electric current. Also called a Lambda sensor.

P

Phillips screw A type of screw head having a cross instead of a slot for a corresponding type of screwdriver.

Plastigage A thin strip of plastic thread, available in different sizes, used for measuring clearances. For example, a strip of Plastigage is laid across a bearing journal. The parts are assembled and dismantled; the width of the crushed strip indicates the clearance between journal and bearing.

Plastigage

Propeller shaft The long hollow tube with universal joints at both ends that carries power from the transmission to the differential on front-engined rear wheel drive vehicles.

Proportioning valve A hydraulic control valve which limits the amount of pressure to the rear brakes during panic stops to prevent wheel lock-up.

R

Rack-and-pinion steering A steering system with a pinion gear on the end of the steering shaft that mates with a rack (think of a geared wheel opened up and laid flat). When the steering wheel is turned, the pinion turns, moving the rack to the left or right. This movement is transmitted through the track rods to the steering arms at the wheels.

Radiator A liquid-to-air heat transfer device designed to reduce the temperature of the coolant in an internal combustion engine cooling system.

Refrigerant Any substance used as a heat transfer agent in an air-conditioning system. R-12 has been the principle refrigerant for many years; recently, however, manufacturers have begun using R-134a, a non-CFC substance that is considered less harmful to the ozone in the upper atmosphere.

Rocker arm A lever arm that rocks on a shaft or pivots on a stud. In an overhead valve engine, the rocker arm converts the upward movement of the pushrod into a downward movement to open a valve.

Rotor In a distributor, the rotating device inside the cap that connects the centre electrode and the outer terminals as it turns, distributing the high voltage from the coil secondary winding to the proper spark plug. Also, that part of an alternator which rotates inside the stator. Also, the rotating assembly of a turbocharger, including the compressor wheel, shaft and turbine wheel.
Runout The amount of wobble (in-and-out movement) of a gear or wheel as it's rotated. The amount a shaft rotates "out-of-true." The out-of-round condition of a rotating part.

S

Sealant A liquid or paste used to prevent leakage at a joint. Sometimes used in conjunction with a gasket.
Sealed beam lamp An older headlight design which integrates the reflector, lens and filaments into a hermetically-sealed one-piece unit. When a filament burns out or the lens cracks, the entire unit is simply replaced.
Serpentine drivebelt A single, long, wide accessory drivebelt that's used on some newer vehicles to drive all the accessories, instead of a series of smaller, shorter belts. Serpentine drivebelts are usually tensioned by an automatic tensioner.

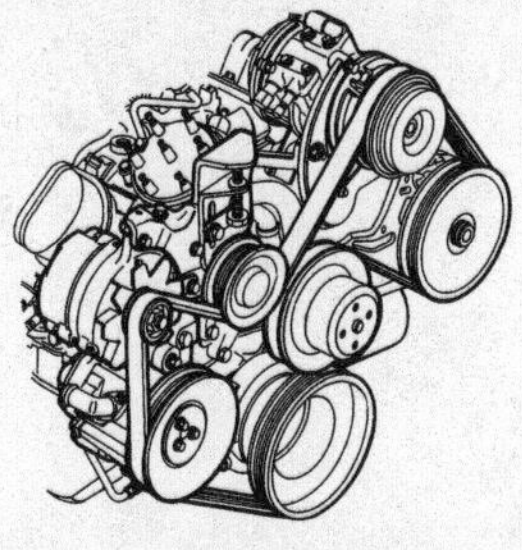

Serpentine drivebelt

Shim Thin spacer, commonly used to adjust the clearance or relative positions between two parts. For example, shims inserted into or under bucket tappets control valve clearances. Clearance is adjusted by changing the thickness of the shim.
Slide hammer A special puller that screws into or hooks onto a component such as a shaft or bearing; a heavy sliding handle on the shaft bottoms against the end of the shaft to knock the component free.
Sprocket A tooth or projection on the periphery of a wheel, shaped to engage with a chain or drivebelt. Commonly used to refer to the sprocket wheel itself.
Starter inhibitor switch On vehicles with an automatic transmission, a switch that prevents starting if the vehicle is not in Neutral or Park.
Strut See MacPherson strut.

T

Tappet A cylindrical component which transmits motion from the cam to the valve stem, either directly or via a pushrod and rocker arm. Also called a cam follower.
Thermostat A heat-controlled valve that regulates the flow of coolant between the cylinder block and the radiator, so maintaining optimum engine operating temperature. A thermostat is also used in some air cleaners in which the temperature is regulated.
Thrust bearing The bearing in the clutch assembly that is moved in to the release levers by clutch pedal action to disengage the clutch. Also referred to as a release bearing.
Timing belt A toothed belt which drives the camshaft. Serious engine damage may result if it breaks in service.
Timing chain A chain which drives the camshaft.
Toe-in The amount the front wheels are closer together at the front than at the rear. On rear wheel drive vehicles, a slight amount of toe-in is usually specified to keep the front wheels running parallel on the road by offsetting other forces that tend to spread the wheels apart.
Toe-out The amount the front wheels are closer together at the rear than at the front. On front wheel drive vehicles, a slight amount of toe-out is usually specified.
Tools For full information on choosing and using tools, refer to the *Haynes Automotive Tools Manual.*
Tracer A stripe of a second colour applied to a wire insulator to distinguish that wire from another one with the same colour insulator.
Tune-up A process of accurate and careful adjustments and parts replacement to obtain the best possible engine performance.
Turbocharger A centrifugal device, driven by exhaust gases, that pressurises the intake air. Normally used to increase the power output from a given engine displacement, but can also be used primarily to reduce exhaust emissions (as on VW's "Umwelt" Diesel engine).

U

Universal joint or U-joint A double-pivoted connection for transmitting power from a driving to a driven shaft through an angle. A U-joint consists of two Y-shaped yokes and a cross-shaped member called the spider.

V

Valve A device through which the flow of liquid, gas, vacuum, or loose material in bulk may be started, stopped, or regulated by a movable part that opens, shuts, or partially obstructs one or more ports or passageways. A valve is also the movable part of such a device.
Valve clearance The clearance between the valve tip (the end of the valve stem) and the rocker arm or tappet. The valve clearance is measured when the valve is closed.
Vernier caliper A precision measuring instrument that measures inside and outside dimensions. Not quite as accurate as a micrometer, but more convenient.
Viscosity The thickness of a liquid or its resistance to flow.
Volt A unit for expressing electrical "pressure" in a circuit. One volt that will produce a current of one ampere through a resistance of one ohm.

W

Welding Various processes used to join metal items by heating the areas to be joined to a molten state and fusing them together. For more information refer to the *Haynes Automotive Welding Manual.*
Wiring diagram A drawing portraying the components and wires in a vehicle's electrical system, using standardised symbols. For more information refer to the *Haynes Automotive Electrical and Electronic Systems Manual.*

Note: *References throughout this index are in the form* "**Chapter number**" • "**Page number**". *So, for example, 2C•15 refers to page 15 of Chapter 2C.*

Note: *References throughout this index are in the form* "**Chapter number**" • "**Page number**"*. So, for example, 2C•15 refers to page 15 of Chapter 2C.*

E

F

G

H

I

Note: *References throughout this index are in the form* **"Chapter number" • "Page number"**. *So, for example, 2C•15 refers to page 15 of Chapter 2C.*

J

K

L

M

O

P

R

Note: *References throughout this index are in the form* "**Chapter number**" • "**Page number**". *So, for example, 2C•15 refers to page 15 of Chapter 2C.*

S

T

V

W